POETRY
for Students

Advisors

Jayne M. Burton is a teacher of English, a member of the Delta Kappa Gamma International Society for Key Women Educators, and currently a master's degree candidate in the Interdisciplinary Study of Curriculum and Instruction and English at Angelo State University.

Mary Beth Maggio teaches seventh grade language arts in Schaumburg, Illinois.

Tom Shilts is the youth librarian at the Okemos branch of Capital Area District Library in Okemos, Michigan. He holds an MSLS degree from Clarion University of Pennsylvania and an MA in U.S. History from the University of North Dakota.

Amy Spade Silverman has taught at independent schools in California, Texas, Michigan, and New York. She holds a bachelor of arts degree from the University of Michigan and a master of fine arts degree from the University of Houston. She is a member of the National Council of Teachers of English and Teachers and Writers. She is an exam reader for Advanced Placement Literature and Composition. She is also a poet, published in *North American Review*, *Nimrod*, and *Michigan Quarterly Review*, among others.

Mary Turner holds a BS in Secondary Education from East Texas State University and a Master of Education from Western Kentucky University. She teaches English 7 and AP English 12 literature and composition at SBEC in Southaven, Mississippi.

Brian Woerner teaches English at Troy High School in Troy, Ohio. He is also a Program Associate of the Ohio Writing Project at Miami University.

POETRY
for Students

Presenting Analysis, Context, and Criticism on Commonly Studied Poetry

VOLUME 40

Sara Constantakis, Project Editor

Foreword by David J. Kelly

GALE
CENGAGE Learning

Detroit • New York • San Francisco • New Haven, Conn • Waterville, Maine • London

Poetry for Students, Volume 40

Project Editor: Sara Constantakis

Rights Acquisition and Management: Sheila Spencer

Composition: Evi Abou-El-Seoud

Manufacturing: Rhonda Dover

Imaging: John Watkins

Product Design: Pamela A. E. Galbreath, Jennifer Wahi

Content Conversion: Katrina Coach

Product Manager: Meggin Condino

© 2012 Gale, Cengage Learning

ALL RIGHTS RESERVED. No part of this work covered by the copyright herein may be reproduced, transmitted, stored, or used in any form or by any means graphic, electronic, or mechanical, including but not limited to photocopying, recording, scanning, digitizing, taping, Web distribution, information networks, or information storage and retrieval systems, except as permitted under Section 107 or 108 of the 1976 United States Copyright Act, without the prior written permission of the publisher.

Since this page cannot legibly accommodate all copyright notices, the acknowledgments constitute an extension of the copyright notice.

For product information and technology assistance, contact us at
Gale Customer Support, 1-800-877-4253.
For permission to use material from this text or product,
submit all requests online at **www.cengage.com/permissions.**
Further permissions questions can be emailed to
permissionrequest@cengage.com

While every effort has been made to ensure the reliability of the information presented in this publication, Gale, a part of Cengage Learning, does not guarantee the accuracy of the data contained herein. Gale accepts no payment for listing; and inclusion in the publication of any organization, agency, institution, publication, service, or individual does not imply endorsement of the editors or publisher. Errors brought to the attention of the publisher and verified to the satisfaction of the publisher will be corrected in future editions.

Gale
27500 Drake Rd.
Farmington Hills, MI, 48331-3535

ISBN-13: 978-1-4144-6707-8
ISBN-10: 1-4144-6707-9

ISSN 1094-7019

This title is also available as an e-book.
ISBN-13: 978-1-4144-7391-8
ISBN-10: 1-4144-7391-5
Contact your Gale, a part of Cengage Learning sales representative for ordering information.

Printed in Mexico
1 2 3 4 5 6 7 16 15 14 13 12

Table of Contents

ADVISORS ii

JUST A FEW LINES ON A PAGE ix
(by David J. Kelly)

INTRODUCTION xi

LITERARY CHRONOLOGY xv

ACKNOWLEDGMENTS xvii

CONTRIBUTORS xix

ANOTHER FEELING
(by Ruth Stone) 1
   Author Biography 2
   Poem Text 3
   Poem Summary 3
   Themes 4
   Style 7
   Historical Context 8
   Critical Overview 9
   Criticism 10
   Sources 16
   Further Reading 17
   Suggested Search Terms 17

CIVILIAN AND SOLDIER
(by Wole Soyinka) 18
   Author Biography 19
   Poem Summary 19

Table of Contents

Themes 21	Style 94
Style 22	Historical Context 94
Historical Context 23	Critical Overview. 96
Critical Overview. 25	Criticism. 97
Criticism. 26	Sources 107
Sources 32	Further Reading 108
Further Reading 32	Suggested Search Terms 108
Suggested Search Terms 32	

DEFINING THE GRATEFUL GESTURE

THE JOURNEY

(by Yvonne Sapia) 33

(by Mary Oliver). 109

Author Biography 34	Author Biography 109
Poem Text 34	Poem Summary 110
Poem Summary 35	Themes 112
Themes 35	Style 114
Style 37	Historical Context 115
Historical Context 39	Critical Overview. 117
Critical Overview. 40	Criticism. 117
Criticism. 40	Sources 122
Sources 46	Further Reading 122
Further Reading 47	Suggested Search Terms 123
Suggested Search Terms 47	

FOR THE YOUNG WHO WANT TO

LEGAL ALIEN

(by Marge Piercy) 48

(by Pat Mora) 124

Author Biography 49	Author Biography 124
Poem Text 49	Poem Text 125
Poem Summary 50	Poem Summary 125
Themes 51	Themes 127
Style 54	Style 129
Historical Context 55	Historical Context 129
Critical Overview. 57	Critical Overview. 131
Criticism. 57	Criticism. 132
Sources 68	Sources 140
Further Reading 69	Further Reading 141
Suggested Search Terms 69	Suggested Search Terms 141

I AM LEARNING TO ABANDON THE WORLD

LONDON

(by Linda Pastan) 70

(by William Blake) 142

Author Biography 71	Author Biography 143
Poem Summary 71	Poem Summary 143
Themes 72	Themes 144
Style 74	Style 147
Historical Context 75	Historical Context 147
Critical Overview. 77	Critical Overview. 150
Criticism. 78	Criticism. 150
Sources 87	Sources 157
Further Reading 88	Further Reading 157
Suggested Search Terms 88	Suggested Search Terms 157

IN JUST

LOVELIEST OF TREES, THE CHERRY NOW

(by e. e. cummings) 89

(by Alfred Edward Housman) 158

Author Biography 89	Author Biography 158
Poem Summary 90	Poem Text 159
Themes 92	Poem Summary 160
	Themes 161

Style	164
Historical Context	165
Critical Overview.	167
Criticism.	167
Sources	176
Further Reading	177
Suggested Search Terms	177

THE MOON AT THE FORTIFIED PASS

(by Li Po)	178
Author Biography	179
Poem Text	180
Poem Summary	180
Themes	181
Style	184
Historical Context	185
Critical Overview.	188
Criticism.	189
Sources	194
Further Reading	194
Suggested Search Terms	195

THE MOTHER

(by Gwendolyn Brooks)	196
Author Biography	197
Poem Text	197
Poem Summary	198
Themes	199
Style	201
Historical Context	202
Critical Overview.	205
Criticism.	205
Sources	215
Further Reading	215
Suggested Search Terms	216

NIGHT JOURNEY

(by Theodore Roethke)	217
Author Biography	218
Poem Summary	219
Themes	219
Style	222
Historical Context	223
Critical Overview.	225
Criticism.	226
Sources	233
Further Reading	233
Suggested Search Terms	233

SPRING AND FALL: TO A YOUNG GIRL

(by Gerard Manley Hopkins)	234
Author Biography	235
Poem Text	235
Poem Summary	236
Themes	237
Style	237
Historical Context	239
Critical Overview.	241
Criticism.	242
Sources	252
Further Reading	252
Suggested Search Terms	253

WE WEAR THE MASK

(by Paul Laurence Dunbar)	254
Author Biography	255
Poem Text	256
Poem Summary	256
Themes	257
Style	259
Historical Context	260
Critical Overview.	262
Criticism.	263
Sources	274
Further Reading	275
Suggested Search Terms	275

WHO UNDERSTANDS ME BUT ME

(by Jimmy Santiago Baca)	276
Author Biography	277
Poem Text	277
Poem Summary	278
Themes	279
Style	282
Historical Context	283
Critical Overview.	285
Criticism.	286
Sources	290
Further Reading	290
Suggested Search Terms	291

GLOSSARY OF LITERARY TERMS. . . .	293
CUMULATIVE AUTHOR/TITLE INDEX.	315
CUMULATIVE NATIONALITY/ETHNICITY INDEX.	327
SUBJECT/THEME INDEX	337
CUMULATIVE INDEX OF FIRST LINES.	345
CUMULATIVE INDEX OF LAST LINES.	353

Just a Few Lines on a Page

I have often thought that poets have the easiest job in the world. A poem, after all, is just a few lines on a page, usually not even extending margin to margin—how long would that take to write, about five minutes? Maybe ten at the most, if you wanted it to rhyme or have a repeating meter. Why, I could start in the morning and produce a book of poetry by dinnertime. But we all know that it isn't that easy. Anyone can come up with enough words, but the poet's job is about writing the *right* ones. The right words will change lives, making people see the world somewhat differently than they saw it just a few minutes earlier. The right words can make a reader who relies on the dictionary for meanings take a greater responsibility for his or her own personal understanding. A poem that is put on the page correctly can bear any amount of analysis, probing, defining, explaining, and interrogating, and something about it will still feel new the next time you read it.

It would be fine with me if I could talk about poetry without using the word "magical," because that word is overused these days to imply "a really good time," often with a certain sweetness about it, and a lot of poetry is neither of these. But if you stop and think about magic—whether it brings to mind sorcery, witchcraft, or bunnies pulled from top hats—it always seems to involve stretching reality to produce a result greater than the sum of its parts and pulling unexpected results out of thin air. This book provides ample cases where a few simple words conjure up whole worlds. We do not actually travel to different times and different cultures, but the poems get into our minds, they find what little we know about the places they are talking about, and then they make that little bit blossom into a bouquet of someone else's life. Poets make us think we are following simple, specific events, but then they leave ideas in our heads that cannot be found on the printed page. Abracadabra.

Sometimes when you finish a poem it doesn't feel as if it has left any supernatural effect on you, like it did not have any more to say beyond the actual words that it used. This happens to everybody, but most often to inexperienced readers: regardless of what is often said about young people's infinite capacity to be amazed, you have to understand what usually does happen, and what could have happened instead, if you are going to be moved by what someone has accomplished. In those cases in which you finish a poem with a "So what?" attitude, the information provided in *Poetry for Students* comes in handy. Readers can feel assured that the poems included here actually are potent magic, not just because a few (or a hundred or ten thousand) professors of literature say they are: they're significant because they can withstand close inspection and still amaze the very same people who have just finished taking them apart and seeing how they work. Turn them inside out, and they will still be able to come alive, again and again. *Poetry for Students* gives readers of any age good practice in feeling the ways poems relate to both the reality of the time and place the poet lived in and the reality of our emotions. Practice is just another word for being a student. The information given here helps you understand the way to read poetry; what to look for, what to expect.

With all of this in mind, I really don't think I would actually like to have a poet's job at all. There are too many skills involved, including precision, honesty, taste, courage, linguistics, passion, compassion, and the ability to keep all sorts of people entertained at once. And that is just what they do with one hand, while the other hand pulls some sort of trick that most of us will never fully understand. I can't even pack all that I need for a weekend into one suitcase, so what would be my chances of stuffing so much life into a few lines? With all that *Poetry for Students* tells us about each poem, I am impressed that any poet can finish three or four poems a year. Read the inside stories of these poems, and you won't be able to approach any poem in the same way you did before.

David J. Kelly
College of Lake County

Introduction

Purpose of the Book

The purpose of *Poetry for Students* (*PfS*) is to provide readers with a guide to understanding, enjoying, and studying poems by giving them easy access to information about the work. Part of Gale's "For Students" Literature line, *PfS* is specifically designed to meet the curricular needs of high school and undergraduate college students and their teachers, as well as the interests of general readers and researchers considering specific poems. While each volume contains entries on "classic" poems frequently studied in classrooms, there are also entries containing hard-to-find information on contemporary poems, including works by multicultural, international, and women poets.

The information covered in each entry includes an introduction to the poem and the poem's author; the actual poem text (if possible); a poem summary, to help readers unravel and understand the meaning of the poem; analysis of important themes in the poem; and an explanation of important literary techniques and movements as they are demonstrated in the poem.

In addition to this material, which helps the readers analyze the poem itself, students are also provided with important information on the literary and historical background informing each work. This includes a historical context essay, a box comparing the time or place the poem was written to modern Western culture, a critical overview essay, and excerpts from critical essays on the poem. A unique feature of *PfS* is a specially commissioned critical essay on each poem, targeted toward the student reader.

To further help today's student in studying and enjoying each poem, information on audio recordings and other media adaptations is provided (if available), as well as reading suggestions for works of fiction and nonfiction on similar themes and topics. Classroom aids include ideas for research papers and lists of critical and reference sources that provide additional material on the poem.

Selection Criteria

The titles for each volume of *PfS* are selected by surveying numerous sources on notable literary works and analyzing course curricula for various schools, school districts, and states. Some of the sources surveyed include: high school and undergraduate literature anthologies and textbooks; lists of award-winners, and recommended titles, including the Young Adult Library Services Association (YALSA) list of best books for young adults.

Input solicited from our expert advisory board—consisting of educators and librarians—guides us to maintain a mix of "classic" and contemporary literary works, a mix of challenging and engaging works (including genre titles that are commonly studied) appropriate for different age levels, and a mix of international, multicultural and women authors. These advisors also consult on each volume's entry list, advising on which titles are most studied, most appropriate, and meet the broadest interests across secondary (grades 7–12) curricula and undergraduate literature studies.

How Each Entry Is Organized

Each entry, or chapter, in *PfS* focuses on one poem. Each entry heading lists the full name of the poem, the author's name, and the date of the poem's publication. The following elements are contained in each entry:

Introduction: a brief overview of the poem which provides information about its first appearance, its literary standing, any controversies surrounding the work, and major conflicts or themes within the work.

Author Biography: this section includes basic facts about the poet's life, and focuses on events and times in the author's life that inspired the poem in question.

Poem Text: when permission has been granted, the poem is reprinted, allowing for quick reference when reading the explication of the following section.

Poem Summary: a description of the major events in the poem. Summaries are broken down with subheads that indicate the lines being discussed.

Themes: a thorough overview of how the major topics, themes, and issues are addressed within the poem. Each theme discussed appears in a separate subhead.

Style: this section addresses important style elements of the poem, such as form, meter, and rhyme scheme; important literary devices used, such as imagery, foreshadowing, and symbolism; and, if applicable, genres to which the work might have belonged, such as Gothicism or Romanticism. Literary terms are explained within the entry, but can also be found in the Glossary.

Historical Context: this section outlines the social, political, and cultural climate in which the author lived and the poem was created. This section may include descriptions of related historical events, pertinent aspects of daily life in the culture, and the artistic and literary sensibilities of the time in which the work was written. If the poem is a historical work, information regarding the time in which the poem is set is also included. Each section is broken down with helpful subheads.

Critical Overview: this section provides background on the critical reputation of the poem, including bannings or any other public controversies surrounding the work. For older works, this section includes a history of how the poem was first received and how perceptions of it may have changed over the years; for more recent poems, direct quotes from early reviews may also be included.

Criticism: an essay commissioned by *PfS* which specifically deals with the poem and is written specifically for the student audience, as well as excerpts from previously published criticism on the work (if available).

Sources: an alphabetical list of critical material quoted in the entry, with full bibliographical information.

Further Reading: an alphabetical list of other critical sources which may prove useful for the student. Includes full bibliographical information and a brief annotation.

Suggested Search Terms: a list of search terms and phrases to jumpstart students' further information seeking. Terms include not just titles and author names but also terms and topics related to the historical and literary context of the works.

In addition, each entry contains the following highlighted sections, set apart from the main text as sidebars:

Media Adaptations: if available, a list of audio recordings as well as any film or television adaptations of the poem, including source information.

Topics for Further Study: a list of potential study questions or research topics dealing with the poem. This section includes questions related to other disciplines the student may be studying, such as American history, world history, science, math, government, business, geography, economics, psychology, etc.

Compare & Contrast: an "at-a-glance" comparison of the cultural and historical differences between the author's time and culture and late twentieth century or early twenty-first century Western culture. This box includes pertinent parallels between the major scientific, political, and cultural movements of the time or place the poem was written, the time or place the poem was set (if a historical work), and modern Western culture. Works written after 1990 may not have this box.

What Do I Read Next?: a list of works that might give a reader points of entry into a classic work (e.g., YA or multicultural titles) and/or complement the featured poem or serve as a contrast to it. This includes works by the same author and others, works from various genres, YA works, and works from various cultures and eras.

Other Features

PfS includes "Just a Few Lines on a Page," a foreword by David J. Kelly, an adjunct professor of English, College of Lake County, Illinois. This essay provides a straightforward, unpretentious explanation of why poetry should be marveled at and how *PfS* can help teachers show students how to enrich their own reading experiences.

A Cumulative Author/Title Index lists the authors and titles covered in each volume of the *PfS* series.

A Cumulative Nationality/Ethnicity Index breaks down the authors and titles covered in each volume of the *PfS* series by nationality and ethnicity.

A Subject/Theme Index, specific to each volume, provides easy reference for users who may be studying a particular subject or theme rather than a single work. Significant subjects from events to broad themes are included.

A Cumulative Index of First Lines (beginning in Vol. 10) provides easy reference for users who may be familiar with the first line of a poem but may not remember the actual title.

A Cumulative Index of Last Lines (beginning in Vol. 10) provides easy reference for users who may be familiar with the last line of a poem but may not remember the actual title.

Each entry may include illustrations, including photo of the author and other graphics related to the poem.

Citing Poetry for Students

When writing papers, students who quote directly from any volume of *PfS* may use the following general forms. These examples are based on MLA style; teachers may request that students adhere to a different style, so the following examples may be adapted as needed.

When citing text from *PfS* that is not attributed to a particular author (i.e., the Themes, Style, Historical Context sections, etc.), the following format should be used in the bibliography section:

"Angle of Geese." *Poetry for Students*. Ed. Marie Napierkowski and Mary Ruby. Vol. 2. Detroit: Gale, 1998. 8–9.

When quoting the specially commissioned essay from *PfS* (usually the first piece under the "Criticism" subhead), the following format should be used:

Velie, Alan. Critical Essay on "Angle of Geese." *Poetry for Students*. Ed. Marie Napierkowski and Mary Ruby. Vol. 2. Detroit: Gale, 1998. 7–10.

When quoting a journal or newspaper essay that is reprinted in a volume of *PfS,* the following form may be used:

Luscher, Robert M. "An Emersonian Context of Dickinson's 'The Soul Selects Her Own Society'." *ESQ: A Journal of American Renaissance* 30.2 (1984): 111–16. Excerpted and reprinted in *Poetry for Students*. Ed. Marie Napierkowski and Mary Ruby. Vol. 1. Detroit: Gale, 1998. 266–69.

When quoting material reprinted from a book that appears in a volume of *PfS,* the following form may be used:

Mootry, Maria K. "'Tell It Slant': Disguise and Discovery as Revisionist Poetic Discourse in 'The Bean Eaters'." *A Life Distilled: Gwendolyn Brooks, Her Poetry and Fiction*. Ed. Maria K. Mootry and Gary Smith. Urbana: University of Illinois Press, 1987. 177–80, 191. Excerpted and reprinted in *Poetry for Students*. Ed. Marie Napierkowski and Mary Ruby. Vol. 2. Detroit: Gale, 1998. 22–24.

We Welcome Your Suggestions

The editorial staff of *Poetry for Students* welcomes your comments and ideas. Readers who wish to suggest poems to appear in future volumes, or who have other suggestions, are cordially invited to contact the editor. You may contact the editor via E-mail at: **ForStudentsEditors@cengage.com.** Or write to the editor at:

Editor, *Poetry for Students*
Gale
27500 Drake Road
Farmington Hills, MI 48331-3535

Literary Chronology

701: Li Po is born in China.

750: Li Po's "The Moon at the Fortified Pass" is written.

762: Li Po dies of drowning in China.

1757: William Blake is born on November 18 in London, England.

1794: William Blake's "London" is published in *Songs of Innocence and of Experience*.

1827: William Blake dies on of unknown causes on August 12 in London, England.

1844: Gerard Manley Hopkins is born on July 28 near London, England.

1859: A. E. Housman is born on March 26 in Worcestershire, England.

1872: Paul Laurence Dunbar is born on June 27 in Dayton, Ohio.

1889: Gerard Manley Hopkins dies of typhoid fever on June 8 in Dublin, Ireland.

1894: e. e. cummings is born on October 14 in Cambridge, Massachusetts.

1895: Paul Laurence Dunbar's "We Wear the Mask" is published in *Majors and Minors*.

1896: A. E. Housman's "Loveliest of Trees, the Cherry Now" is published in *A Shropshire Lad*.

1906: Paul Laurence Dunbar dies of tuberculosis on February 9 in Dayton, Ohio.

1908: Theodore Roethke is born on May 25 in Saginaw, Michigan.

1915: Ruth Stone is born on June 8 in Roanoke, Virginia.

1917: Gwendolyn Brooks is born on June 7 in Topeka, Kansas.

1918: Gerard Manley Hopkins's "Spring and Fall: To a Young Girl" is published in *Poems*.

1920: e. e. cummings's poem "in Just" is published in *Tulips and Chimneys*.

1932: Linda Pastan is born on May 27 in New York City.

1934: Wole Soyinka is born on July 13 in Abekuta, Western Nigeria.

1935: Mary Oliver is born on September 10 in Maple Heights, Ohio.

1936: A. E. Housman dies of heart trouble on April 30 in Cambridge, England.

1936: Marge Piercy is born on March 31 in Detroit, Michigan.

1941: Theodore Roethke's "Night Journey" is published *Open House*.

1942: Pat Mora is born on January 19 in El Paso, Texas.

1945: Gwendolyn Brooks' "The Mother" is published in *A Street in Bronzeville*.

1946: Yvonne Sapia is born on April 10 in New York, New York.

1950: Gwendolyn Brooks wins the Pulitzer Prize for Poetry for *Annie Allen*.

1952: Jimmy Santiago Baca is born on January 2 in Santa Fe, New Mexico.

1962: e. e. cummings dies of a cerebral brain hemorrhage on September 3 in North Conway, New Hampshire.

1963: Theodore Roethke dies of a coronary occlusion on August 1 on Bainbridge Island, Washington.

1967: Wole Soyinka's "Civilian and Soldier" is published in *Idanre and Other Poems*.

1980: Marge Piercy's "For the Young Who Want To" is published in *The Moon is Always Female*.

1980: Pat Mora's "Legal Alien" is published in *Hispanics in the United States: An Anthology of the United States*.

1981: Linda Pastan's "I am Learning to Abandon the World" is published in *Poetry* magazine.

1982: Linda Pastan's "I am Learning to Abandon the World" is published *PM/AM: New and Selected Poems*.

1984: Mary Oliver is awarded the Pulitzer Prize for Poetry for *American Primitive*.

1984: Pat Mora's "Legal Alien" is published in *Chants*.

1986: Mary Oliver's "The Journey's Tale" is published in *Dream Work*.

1986: Wole Soyinka is awarded the Nobel Prize in Literature.

1987: Yvonne Sapia's "Defining the Grateful Gesture" is published in the *Americas Review*.

1990: Jimmy Santiago Baca's "Who Understands Me But Me" is published in *Immigrants in Our Own Land and Selected Early Poems*.

2000: Gwendolyn Brooks dies of cancer on December 3 in Chicago, Illinois.

2004: Ruth Stone's "Another Feeling" is published in *In the Dark*.

Acknowledgements

The editors wish to thank the copyright holders of the excerpted criticism included in this volume and the permissions managers of many book and magazine publishing companies for assisting us in securing reproduction rights. We are also grateful to the staffs of the Detroit Public Library, the Library of Congress, the University of Detroit Mercy Library, Wayne State University Purdy/Kresge Library Complex, and the University of Michigan Libraries for making their resources available to us. Following is a list of the copyright holders who have granted us permission to reproduce material in this volume of PfS. Every effort has been made to trace copyright, but if omissions have been made, please let us know.

COPYRIGHTED EXCERPTS IN *PfS*, VOLUME 40, WERE REPRODUCED FROM THE FOLLOWING PERIODICALS:

African American Review, summer, 2007 for "Intimate Intercessions in the Poetry of Paul Laurence Dunbar" by Joanne Gabbin. Copyright © 2007 by Joanne Gabbin. Reproduced by permission of the author.—*African American Review*, summer, 2007 for "Paul Laurence Dunbar's Performances and the Epistolary Dialect Poem" by Nadia Nurhussein. Copyright © 2007 Nadia Nurhussein. Reproduced by permission of the author.—*American Poetry Review*, May/June, 2006 for "Ruth Stone: A Gift from the Universe" by Rosanne Wasserman. Copyright © 2006 by Rosanne Wasserman. Reproduced by permission of the author.—*ANQ*, winter, 1998. Copyright © 1998 by Taylor & Francis Group. Reprinted by permission of the publisher (Taylor & Francis Group, http://www.informaworld.com).—*Bucknell Review*, May, 1955. Copyright © 1955 by Associated University Press. Reproduced by permission.—*CLA Journal*, March, 1987. Copyright © 1987 by The College Language Association. Used by permission of The College Language Association.—*Hollins Critic*, February, 1989. Copyright © 1989 by *The Hollins Critic*. Reproduced by permission.—*Human Rights Review*, October/December, 2000. Copyright © 2000 by Springer Publishing Company. Reproduced by permission.—*Kliatt Young Adult Paperback Book Guide*, spring, 1980. Copyright © 1980 by *Kliatt Young Adult Paperback Book Guide*. Reproduced by permission.—*MELUS*, fall, 1983. Copyright © 1983 by MELUS: Society for the Study of the Multi-Ethnic Literature of the United States. Reproduced by permission.—*MELUS*, spring, 1996. Copyright © 1996 by MELUS: Society for the Study of the Multi-Ethnic Literature of the United States. Reproduced by permission.—*MELUS*, summer, 2003. Copyright © 2003 by MELUS: Society for the Study of the Multi-Ethnic Literature of the United States. Reproduced by permission.—*Mosaic*, winter, 1980. Copyright © *Mosaic* 2010. Acknowledgment of previous publication is herewith made.—*Nation*, August 30, 1986. Copyright © 1986 by *The Nation*. Reproduced by permission.—*Northwest Review*, 1983. Copyright © 1983 by *Northwest Review*. Reproduced by

Acknowledgements

permission.—***Publications of the Missouri Philological Association***, 1985. Copyright © 1985 by Publications of the Missouri Philological Association. Reproduced by permission.—***Victorian Newsletter***, fall, 1995. Copyright © 1995 by *The Victorian Newsletter*. Reproduced by permission of *The Victorian Newsletter* and the author.—***Victorian Poetry***, v. 14, winter, 1976 for "The Poetry of Insight: Persona and Point of View in Housman" by B. J. Leggett. Copyright © 1976 by B. J. Leggett. Reproduced by permission of the author.—***Victorian Poetry***, winter, 2005 for "'Goldengrove Unleaving': Hopkins' 'Spring and Fall,' Christina Rossetti's 'Mirrors of Life and Death,' and the Politics of Inclusion" by Jude V. Nixon. Copyright © 2005 by Jude V. Nixon. Reproduced by permission of the author.—***Washingtonian***, May, 1996 for "Word Perfect: For Linda Pastan, Revision is the Purest Form of Love" by Linda Pastan and Ken Adelman. Copyright © 1996 by Linda Pastan.—***World Literature Today***, March/April, 2006. Copyright © 2006 by *World Literature Today*. Reproduced by permission of the publisher.—***Writer***, October, 1992 for "Yesterday's Noise: The Poetry of Childhood Memory" by Linda Pastan. Copyright © 1992 by Linda Pastan. Reproduced by permission of the author.

COPYRIGHTED EXCERPTS IN *PfS*, VOLUME 40, WERE REPRODUCED FROM THE FOLLOWING BOOKS:

Ayscough, Florence. From ***Fir-Flower Tablets***. Houghton Mifflin, 1921.—Baca, Jimmy Santiago. From ***Immigrants in Our Own Land & Selected Early Poems***. New Directions Books, 1990. Copyright © 1990 by Jimmy Santiago Baca. Reprinted by permission of New Directions Publishing Corp.—Brooks, Gwendolyn. From ***Selected Poems by Gwendolyn Brooks***. Harper & Row, 1963. Copyright © Gwendolyn Brooks. Reprinted by consent of Brooks Permissions.—Dunbar, Paul Laurence. From ***The Complete Poems of Paul Laurence Dunbar***. Dodd, Mead, 1940.—Hopkins, Gerard Manley. From ***Poems***. Humphrey Milford, 1918.—Housman, A. E. From ***The Poems of A. E. Housman***. Clarendon Press, 1997. —Kennedy, Richard S. From ***E. E. Cummings Revisited***. Twayne Publishers, 1994. Copyright © 1993 by Gale, a part of Cengage Learning, Inc. Reproduced by permission. www.cengage.com/permissions—Mora, Pat. From ***Chants***. Arte Público Press, 1985. Copyright © 1985 by Arte Público Press. Reproduced by permission.—Moramarco, Fred; Sullivan, William. From ***Containing Multitudes: Poetry in the United States since 1950***. Twayne, 1998. Copyright © 1998 Gale, a part of Cengage Learning, Inc. Reproduced by permission. www.cengage.com/permissions—Pagliaro, Harold. From ***Selfhood and Redemption in Blake's "Songs"***. Pennsylvania State University Press, 1987. Copyright © 1987 by The Pennsylvania State University Press. Reproduced by permission of The Pennsylvania State University Press.—Piercy, Marge. From ***Circles on the Water: Selected Poems of Marge Piercy***. Alfred A. Knopf, 1982. Copyright © 1980 by Marge Piercy and Middlemarsh, Inc. Reproduced by permission of Alfred A. Knopf, a division of Random House, Inc. and the Wallace Literary Agency, Inc.—Li Po, "The Moon at the Fortified Pass." From ***The Chinese Translations: The Works of Witter Bynner***. Witter Bynner Foundation, 1978, p. 112. Copyright © 1978 by Witter Bynner Foundation. All rights reserved. Reproduced by permission.—Sapia, Yvonne. From ***The Americas Review***. 1987. Copyright © 1987 by Yvonne Sapia. Reproduced by permission of the publisher.—Stone, Ruth. From ***In the Dark***. Copper Canyon Press, 2004. Copyright © 2004 by Copper Canyon Press. Reproduced by permission.—Vanderbilt, Kermit. From ***A Literary History of the American West***. Western Literature Association, 1987. Copyright © 1987 by The Western Literature Association. Reproduced by permission.

Contributors

Susan K. Andersen: Andersen holds a Ph.D. in English literature. Entry on "We Wear the Mask." Original essay on "We Wear the Mask."

Bryan Aubrey: Andersen holds a Ph.D. in English literature. Entry on "London." Original essay on "London."

Kristy Blackmon: Blackmon is a published writer from Dallas, Texas. Entry on "The Journey." Original essay on "The Journey."

Rita M. Brown: Brown is an English professor. Entry on "I Am Learning to Abandon the World." Original essay on "I Am Learning to Abandon the World."

Catherine Dominic: Dominic is a novelist and a freelance writer and editor. Entries on "The Mother" and "For the Young Who Want To." Original essays on "Defining the Grateful Gesture," "The Mother," and "For the Young Who Want To."

Charlotte M. Freeman: Freeman is a writer, editor, and former academic living in small-town Montana. Entry on "The Moon at the Fortified Pass." Original essay on "The Moon at the Fortified Pass."

Michael Allen Holmes: Holmes is a writer and editor. Entries on "Another Feeling" and "Who Understands Me But Me." Original essays on "Another Feeling" and "Who Understands Me But Me."

David Kelly: Kelly is an instructor of creative writing and literature. Entry on "Civilian and Soldier." Original essay on "Civilian and Soldier."

Michael J. O'Neal: O'Neal holds a Ph.D. in English. Entries on "Defining the Grateful Gesture," "Night Journey," and "Spring and Fall: To a Young Girl." Original essays on on "Defining the Grateful Gesture," "Night Journey," and "Spring and Fall: To a Young Girl."

April Dawn Paris: Paris is a freelance writer who has an extensive background working with literature and educational materials. Entries on "in Just" and "Legal Alien." Original essays on "in Just" and "Legal Alien."

Bradley A. Skeen: Skeen is a classicist. Entry on "Loveliest of Trees, the Cherry Now." Original essay on "Loveliest of Trees, the Cherry Now."

Another Feeling

RUTH STONE

2004

After publishing verse collections with such quiet humility over the last forty years of the twentieth century that her admirers rarely failed to mention how underappreciated she was, American poet Ruth Stone finally received honors considered among poetry's highest in the twenty-first century—the 2000 National Book Critics Circle Award, the 2002 National Book Award, and the 2002 Wallace Stevens Award.

Stone's poetry is unique; she defies classification into any school, movement, or style. In recent collections, she favors free verse but often uses a loose or sporadic rhyme and meter, giving her work a subtle musical vitality. While she is not shy about expressing a woman's perspective on all realms of life, from the sensual to the intellectual, her work is not political and only indirectly feminist. Her wide-ranging interests in the biological and physical sciences are evident in poems such as the sociological "From the Arboretum" and the mind-bending "The Latest Hotel Guest Walks over Particles That Revolve in Seven Other Dimensions Controlling Latticed Space."

Stone's work has been shaped by a tragic event that dramatically altered her life just before her first collection was published: her husband, the father of her three daughters, committed suicide. Many of Stone's poems resound with desolate grief and lonesomeness that not even the passing decades could resolve, and death in general is a

Ruth Stone (AP Images)

common theme in her work. Her poem "Another Feeling," from the collection *In the Dark* (2004), published as she approached ninety years of age, is a poignant lament for a fateful action that proved unfortunate for an innocent animal.

AUTHOR BIOGRAPHY

Born Ruth Perkins, Stone was born on June 8, 1915, in Roanoke, Virginia, in the house of her grandparents, where she was raised among relatives with interests such as poetry and painting. While the infant Stone was nursing, her mother read aloud the works of the Victorian-era British poet laureate Alfred Tennyson. Inspired by her grandparents' large library, Stone began reading at age three. She remained in Roanoke through the first grade, when she moved to Indianapolis, Indiana, to stay with her father's parents. Also staying there was her Aunt Harriet, with whom Stone delighted in playing verse-writing and comic-drawing games. Her father was a drummer whose practice at home planted an affection for rhythms in Stone's mind. He was fond of humorous stories, and he would sometimes bring home a box of chocolates and read aloud. Meanwhile, with a state senator for a grandfather, Stone was present at high-society tea parties and learned to act like a lady—something she would later have to learn to forget.

Growing up, Stone read about meteors and studied the stars, eventually encountering in a library a photograph of a galaxy that she found mind-blowing. She read about physics, botany, and anything else founded in the real world, sometimes bringing encyclopedia volumes to bed. Although school bored her, she consumed literature voraciously, including much of the English canon, Russian works in translation, and everything by Mark Twain. Meanwhile, she began accumulating a private collection of her own poetry, which she shared rarely but to significant praise, such as when she won a citywide contest in grade school.

Soon after high school, Stone married her first husband, John, but later, while attending the University of Illinois, she met Walter Stone, who would become her second husband and the father of her three girls. She considered Walter, a fellow writer, to be a genius, and she took pride in helping him polish his prose. Walter joined the U.S. Navy during World War II. During that time, Stone's work included a stint under the literary and dramatic editor of the *Indianapolis Star*. After the war, the couple lived in Cambridge, Massachusetts, and started their family, then moved to Illinois, following Walter's job as a professor. Walter had been sending out Stone's poetry, and around this time her verse was published in magazines, including *Accent*, the *Kenyon Review*, and *Poetry*, which presented her with the Bess Hokin Prize in 1953.

Just before her first collection *In an Iridescent Time* was published in 1959, Stone's life changed tragically. During a family trip to England, Walter Stone committed suicide. Left with little money and three girls to raise, Stone found the isolated life at their Vermont farmhouse unsustainable and by necessity became a wandering academic. In the 1960s, she taught at Radcliffe, Wellesley, and Brandeis Universities, and through the 1970s she would relocated to a new college nearly every year. Though Stone refrained from using her own poetry in her classes, many of her students became devoted admirers of her work and in their glowing critical assessments also praised her soul-stirring sincerity as a teacher.

Through the end of the twentieth century, her collections, including *Second-Hand Coat: Poems New and Selected* (1987), earned critical praise and quiet but deep admiration within the poetry world—despite Stone's utter indifference to publicity—with acclaim blossoming as her body of work grew. She won the National Book Critics Circle Award for *Ordinary Words* (1999) and the National Book Award for *In the Next Galaxy* (2002). "Another Feeling" is found in *In the Dark* (2004). Even in her nineties, peacefully secluded away in the Green Mountains of Vermont, Stone published yet another volume, *What Love Comes To: New and Selected Poems* (2008).

POEM TEXT

```
Once you saw a drove of young pigs
crossing the highway. One of them
pulling his body by the front feet,
the hind legs dragging flat.
Without thinking,                               5
you called the Humane Society.
They came with a net and went for him.
They were matter of fact, uniformed;
there were two of them,
their truck ominous, with a cage.              10
He was hiding in the weeds. It was then
you saw his eyes. He understood.
He was trembling.
After they took him, you began to suffer regret.
Years later, you remember his misfit body     15
scrambling to reach the others.
Even at this moment, your heart
is going too fast; your hands sweat.
```

POEM SUMMARY

The text used for this summary is from *In the Dark*, Copper Canyon Press, 2004, p. 5. Versions of the poem can be found on the following Web pages: http://www.poetryoutloud.org/poems/poem.html?id=171088, http://www.poetryfoundation.org/poem/171088, and http://www.americanlifeinpoetry.org/columns/004.html.

Lines 1–4
The first line of "Another Feeling" addresses the reader in the second person to relate an incident from the past. While this *you* can have several possible identities, for the sake of discussion, it might be helpful to think of this *you* as simply "the person." In the poem, the person is said to have witnessed a group of young pigs crossing a major road. The person especially notices one pig that is dragging his rear legs along the ground, his front legs doing all the work. This pig is likely trailing behind the others, perhaps at a distance. Such a pig would be especially vulnerable to being hit by a car or captured by a predator.

Lines 5–10
Line 5 begins a new sentence and indicates that what follows is done instinctively, without reflection over what the precise consequences would be. The phrasing suggests an action that is performed with good intentions but that turns out not to be the wisest or most beneficial act under the circumstances. When the person calls what seems to be the appropriate animal control organization—the Humane Society, a group whose name connotes compassionate treatment of all, specifically the ethical treatment of animals—the term is laced with startling irony. The reader may reasonably infer that something relatively inhumane is about to occur.

Line 7 describes, with an abruptness that reflects a sense of intrusion and a flow of events that the person can no longer control, how the agents of the Humane Society appear and seek to capture the lame pig. Their number is yet unspecified, making their presence faceless and even corporate and sinister. These agents operate as corporate agents may be expected to: performing the function of their job as explicitly defined by the company for which they work, without question or emotional consideration. The agents' uniforms signify their distance from the empathetic perspective that a disinterested bystander—such as the person who called them—would have in such a situation. In line 9, the person comes around to noting that there are only two agents. Line 10 leaves little doubt about the person's mounting sense of the misfortune being brought by these agents, describing their vehicle as foreshadowing doom, a prison for the animals they collect.

Lines 11–14
Line 11 shifts the attention back to the unfortunate pig, who by now is concealing himself in the grasses at the side of the road. The last three

words of line 11 heighten the significance of the moment communicated in line 12. From the person's vantage point, the pig's eyes are visible, and in them the person sees that the pig understands. How the pig understands is not specified, but the poem implicitly expresses the person's conviction that the pig at least understands the essence of the situation. The following line locates the person's sense of the pig's understanding in its physical state, observed as succinctly as possible: a sparse three-word sentence noting the fearful shaking of the pig's body.

Line 14 jumps forward in time—forgoing any description of the actual catching of the pig, possible communication between the person and the agents, and the driving away of the truck—to situate the reader beyond the pig's removal by the Humane Society. At that point, following the disturbing experience of watching the pig's capture, the person begins to feel remorse for the role played in causing that act to occur. If the reader has not already inferred the pig's ultimate fate, by this point in the poem—the point at which the central narrative concludes—the reader likely considers that fate: when an animal is physically incapable of ensuring its own survival and cannot be rehabilitated—or its perceived value does not justify an investment in rehabilitation—killing the animal, as if to preclude future suffering, is sometimes seen as the "humane" thing to do.

Lines 15–18

Line 15 brings the reader years beyond the narrated incident. Present-tense verbs, used now for the first time, mark the substantial shift in perspective. The person recalls the deformed body of the pig and how he needed to heighten his exertions simply to keep pace with his fellow pigs. The phrase that opens line 17 further narrows the poem's temporal setting to the immediate present, seeming to introduce a sense instilled or response brought out by the pig's capture that has lingered to this very day. The response in question is a visceral one: the person's heart is beating faster than it ought to, and the person's hands are sweating. The person's empathetic understanding of that pig's terror of death remains so strong that, upon recall of the memory, the pig's foreboding tremors in effect become the person's own.

THEMES

Empathy

In the foreground of "Another Feeling" is the compassion that the person feels for the pig. Sympathy, in the sense of emotional alliance with another, is what originally inspires the person to call the Humane Society, as the pig seems to be injured and in need of care and medical assistance. But the agents who arrive demonstrate an utter lack of sympathy. Their behavior is strictly functional and businesslike; from their perspective, the pig is little more than a defective commodity. As the reality of the role being played by these agents sinks in, the person's compassion for the pig evolves. While the words *sympathy* and *empathy* have similar connotations and are sometimes interchangeable, it may be useful to differentiate them here by regarding sympathy as an emotional alliance in which one is inspired to care *for* another, while empathy is an emotional connection in which one vicariously experiences whatever is felt *by* another. Feeling sorry for the pig—sympathy—was what inspired the original phone call to the Humane Society, but once the agents are there, the person comes to empathetically understand the terror felt by the pig in the presence of the agents.

There remains considerable debate regarding the extent to which animals think and feel emotions in the ways that human beings do. In Stone's poem, while the pig—considered a relatively intelligent animal—arguably may or may not be able to understand on an intellectual level what is happening to him, he can surely viscerally understand that the agents are focusing their cold, predatory attention on him. Furthermore, the mind of such a mammal, whose primitive origins lie in the forest, may interpret the sights of the mesh pattern of the net and the crossbars of the cage as inherently dangerous, like interlocking thorns and brambles too thick to escape through. (Stone, whose poems demonstrate her expansive interest in all branches of science, would perhaps not discourage such evolutionary speculation.) Even a wild animal may see something relevant to its own survival in the sight of a struggling fly caught in the crisscrossing web of a spider. In other words, one need not be able to prove that an animal can think rationally in order to demonstrate that, when faced with a chilling creature many times bigger than itself bearing a web-like contraption, the animal may be instilled

TOPICS FOR FURTHER STUDY

- Think of an episode in your past that caused you to suddenly or gradually gain empathy for an animal. (An episode in which you gained empathy for another person would work as well.) Record the incident in a poem, which you may choose to write in the second person, as in "Another Feeling," or in the first person (using "I") or third person (using "he" or "she") instead.

- Contact a local branch of the Humane Society and ask whether a representative would be willing to read this poem and be interviewed for a response. Ask questions about what the Humane Society protocol would be in such a situation, why this is or is not fair to animals, whether the person agrees with this protocol personally, whether the person thinks the Humane Society is depicted in an unfair light in "Another Feeling," and other questions you devise. Then write a journalistic piece in an informal, online style—that is, not necessarily free of bias—with a title such as "Humane Society Responds to Vicious Poem" or "Humane Society Admits Flaws in Rescue Protocol," citing your source anonymously if he or she prefers. With your teacher's approval, post your article online.

- Read the introduction and pick two poems from *Poetry for Young People: Animal Poems* (2004), which contains thirty-three classic poems about animals by prominent authors, including William Blake's famous work "The Tyger." Write a paper comparing "Another Feeling" with the two poems you chose, discussing such features as the roles of the animals, the narrative perspectives, poetic style, and whether the audience includes children, adults, or both.

- Pretend you work for an online news organization and have been assigned to write a review of the Web site of People for the Ethical Treatment of Animals (PETA). Analyze the presentation of the site, the accessibility of materials, and the informative value or usefulness of the content. Point out what casual Web surfers might particularly enjoy about the site, and find ways that the site encourages involvement in supporting animal rights. You should explore all corners of the site to be sure to comment on everything that merits recognition. Conclude your review by giving the site a grade or rating, and post the review in a blog or similar format.

---

with a definitive mortal fear—the fear of its own impending death.

The lack of interaction between the onlooking person and the Humane Society agents heightens the reader's sense of the distance between the two parties, in terms of both their perspective on the pig and their emotional relationship to each other. The person experiences an empathetic connection with the pig, while the agents clearly do not. They would surely call the pig an *it*, not a *he*. Accordingly, while the person perceives an ailing fellow creature in need of assistance, the agents see a disabled beast that, according to their organization's rules, one presumes, is designated for extermination. The person's empathy toward the pig proves so strong that, years later, the memory of the pig's situation evokes not just an emotional response but a visceral, physical one. As if feeling the threat of death, the person's body shows signs of an instinctive fight-or-flight response. Through the use of second-person narration, this empathy becomes the reader's empathy.

Ethics

Implicit in Stone's poem is an open-ended discussion on ethics, especially the ethical treatment of animals. The person initially calls the Humane Society out of an instinctive ethical obligation: an

The poem begins with baby pigs loose on a road. (Totajla | Shutterstock.com)

animal is hurt, so assistance should be summoned. No conscious thought is required for the person to carry out this internalized ideal course of action. But the end result is the opposite of what was intended; the pig is not tended to but whisked away, never to be seen again. A less thoughtful person might yet have been left with a clean conscience after this turn of events; such a person could self-deceptively conclude, "Well, I don't know what will happen to the pig, but I did the right thing." However, the person in the poem, along with the reader, likely understands the pig's fate precisely when the pig is seen to understand his fate. The fear reflected in the pig's eyes is recognized as accurate: he is right to fear death. Thus, an act that seemed ethically sound, calling the society, proved disastrous, and the person or reader cannot possibly conclude that the right thing was done. The person's ethical system may be revised, then, to prioritize an animal's freedom to live and die as nature decrees over human intervention in animal affairs.

Belief in the ethical treatment of animals depends upon a recognition of the legitimate emotional states experienced by animals. In the twenty-first century, after numerous anecdotal and scientific explorations into animal consciousness—many inspired and carried out by animal rights activists—few would still argue that animals feel nothing that merits the humanistic label of *emotion*. However, animals can vocalize but not verbalize their emotional states (excluding a few carefully trained animals), allowing people with other priorities to dismiss the relevance of animals' feelings. The average American's relative indifference to the feelings of common animals is evidenced by popular support for conventional industrial agriculture despite the demonstrably inhumane conditions in which animals are typically raised. Other cultures throughout history have shown varying levels of sympathy toward the animals fated to become their sustenance. For example, in certain Native American settings, the killing of a wild animal for food would be followed by a prayer of gratitude to the animal's spirit. One factor in certain cultures' declining to engage in animal husbandry (that is, raising domestic animals, generally for food), instead favoring hunting/gathering and plant-based agriculture, may have been an implicit ethical objection to the idea of restricting animals' bodies and thus their spirits. Interestingly, Stone's poem does not specify whether the pigs in question are wild pigs or perhaps locally-owned pigs left to roam free. As such, freed from any definition of circumstances, the lame pig is allowed an independent existence in the present, perhaps enhancing the perceived validity of its life in the reader's eyes.

Regret

While the bulk of the poem focuses on the moments before the pig's abduction, near the poem's close, regret is pinpointed as the dominant emotion lingering afterward, likely the one referred to in the title as "another feeling." Line 14 marks the transition from the past narrative to the present moment, making the last word of that line the poem's pivotal word. Stone does not elaborate on the depth of the regret; she does not even say exactly what was regretted, though the reader surely realizes that it was the fateful phone call. She only describes how the regret is manifested in the memory-driven state of sympathetic alarm, in the quickened pulse and overheating body. Some might perceive regret, akin to shame, as a negative emotion that serves little function—an emotional attachment to the past that only weakens one's ability to deal with the present. By the end of this poem, the pig is long gone—even his healthy fellows have probably met their fates—but the person is still seized, upon remembering the pig, by a visceral regret. This perhaps suggests that the person has yet to resolve that regret; the person surely will never make the same mistake again but may yet feel a need to atone for what was an unintentional but wrong and even lethal action.

STYLE

Second-Person Narration

Stone presents the circumstances in "Another Feeling" through a second-person point of view (that is, using *you*), which is an interesting angle because the poem relates an incident that happened in the past. The poem thus assigns the reader the role of protagonist in that incident, which heightens the reader's sense of sympathy for the pig. As it is related in the past tense, the episode becomes a memory implanted in the reader, and since memories come and go, the reader may feel fairly hypnotized into visualizing the episode as having been personally experienced. In turn, the immediacy of the last four lines strikes the reader all the more acutely, and the most-open readers may even find themselves experiencing the very symptoms described, as if on command.

Considered another way, the poem can be read as Stone addressing herself. The context of the poem within the collection *In the Dark* supports this view. "Another Feeling" is the third poem in the collection, following "Accepting" and "Another Day." In the first poem, written in the first person (using *I*), Stone gives the reader a physical and psychological portrait of herself, as if to provide a foundational persona for the poems that follow. She describes how being half-blind leaves the daylight only ever dusky at best. Her aged body lounges passively; she recalls moving about freely and unsuspectingly receiving gifts from others' hands. The image conveyed is one of a skilled poet in her waning years, so limited by her flesh that her practiced mind instinctively passes the time by remembering expansively all that has come before. The title can refer both to her past acceptance of the gifts she was given and an acceptance of her present reality, limited by her body but rich in remembrances. The second poem, "Another Day," switches to the second person, describing the buzz provided by morning coffee—or perhaps by the sense of achievement of simply having survived for one more day. The sunset is followed by a disoriented darkness, but at least light shining on the skin can be perceived, forming a sort of luminous cocoon. Thus, although the narrative perspective has been switched, this aged persona with failing sight seems a continuation of that established in the first poem. The poet seems to be scrutinizing herself and her feelings at such a deep level that she becomes once removed from herself; she is viewing herself as another person, one she can address as *you*. "Another Feeling," then seems to continue this introspection. Among her passing memories and feelings, the poet feels the regret stirred by this distant episode and thinks it is worth recording.

A third possible explanation for the second-person point of view is that Stone was actually addressing a specific other person in writing the poem. She sometimes addresses her deceased husband in her poetry, especially in relation to stirred memories of their shared lives. Her verse addressed to him gives the sense that writing poetry helped Stone reconcile herself with his absence. However, in "Another Feeling," the switch to present tense in the closing lines makes it seem unlikely that Stone has described an episode that her husband experienced. Still, the poem may yet reflect an experience of a friend of Stone's—perhaps a friend who related the incident to Stone and indeed found her pulse quickened in remembering. In any case, the second-person narration has two effects: it singles out the reader as the main actor in the story, and it makes the story universal because that *you* could be anyone.

Free Verse

"Another Feeling" is free verse, using no meter or rhyme structure. Stone has not shied away from playing with form in past collections, but the poems of *In the Dark* seem to be controlled by their ideas, rather than by their form. This poem does have a loose structure of quatrains (sets of four lines), with an added couplet (set of two lines). The first quatrain describes the scenario. The couplet follows in lines 5 and 6, isolating the fateful act of calling the Humane Society. Lines 7–10, which form a second quatrain, present the agents. Lines 11–14, a third quatrain, portray the fearful pig and close the incident by noting the person's emotional response. Lines 15–18, the final quatrain, bring the reader to the present and describe the visceral response.

In this poem, Stone makes use of enjambment, a poetic technique in which the phrasing of one line runs into the next without any punctuation or natural break in the structure of the sentence. The first two lines separate the nouns at the end of the lines from their associated verbs in a way that emphasizes the pure existence of the pigs. That is, the group of pigs and then the lame pig are each first summoned into existence and then, only after the delay of the line's end, depicted in action. At the end of line 11, the enjambment intensifies the moment when the pig's eyes are seen. At the end of line 15, the separation of noun and verb mirrors that from the poem's opening, again isolating the noun representing the lame pig. Perhaps the most significant enjambment occurs at the end of line 17, where again a noun is separated from its verb. In this case, the noun is the protagonist/reader's heart, allowing a moment in which the reader's consciousness of his or her own heart is likely to intensify. Whether or not the pulse is quickened, then, the reader's acquired sympathy for the pig may literally be heartfelt.

HISTORICAL CONTEXT

In an essay "On Ruth Stone," Leslie Fiedler notes that assigning any historical context to the Stone's work is problematic because she "has never been a member of any school or clique or gaggle of mutual admirers. Nor has she subscribed to any of the fashionable modes that category-loving critics are so eager to tout." Although she has been publishing poetry since the early 1950s, her poetry has not veered in different directions in response to major societal events or the literary tides of the eras. Rather, as Fiedler writes, Stone is

> one of the few contemporaries whom it is possible to think of simply as a 'poet': one of a distinguished company going back to Chaucer or Sappho, who slough off all qualifying modifiers, belonging not to an age but the ages.

Nonetheless, it may be useful to consider alongside Stone the other most notable women poets of her generation, especially Elizabeth Bishop, Gwendolyn Brooks, and Muriel Rukeyser.

Bishop (1911–1979), in both her life and her poetry, shares certain traits with Stone: she was known for leading a private life, she used a feminine viewpoint in her verse without foregrounding her womanhood, and she managed to establish objective emotional distance in her work while nonetheless giving her poems a striking intimacy. Her work is seen as connecting modernist concerns, such as the recognition of a valid aesthetic (a sense of art, beauty, or taste) in the scientific perspective on reality, with postmodern concerns, such as the fragmentation and deconstruction of narrative consciousness.

Rukeyser (1913–1980), raised in a wealthy Jewish family in New York, differed from Stone in her political activism, which she first expressed through civil rights efforts while she was in college. She published her first collection of poetry at age twenty-three. Although favoring complex rhyme and meter in her youth, she later found greater freedom of expression in bypassing explicit structure; her sense of liberation was recognized by

The subject of the poem sadly remembers what happened to the piglet years later. (Voronin76 / Shutterstock.com)

feminists and antiwar activists alike. Like Stone, Rukeyser sometimes draws on a scientific perspective.

Brooks (1917–2000), one of the preeminent African American poets of the twentieth century, won the 1950 Pulitzer Prize for Poetry for her collection *Annie Allen*. Where Stone is largely a personal poet, with her verse derived from her unique perspective on and from within herself, Brooks is known for her exceptional poetic development of fictional characters, ones living in an imaginary city called Bronzeville. She is also recognized for placing the everyday speech of her characters into poems that use a traditional rhyme and meter. While Stone and these poets, along with others of their generation, worked independently from each other, the collective consideration of their work gives an illuminating composite portrait of the last sixty-five years of the twentieth century.

CRITICAL OVERVIEW

Reviewers had highly positive reflections on Stone's 2004 collection *In the Dark*. Mary Kaiser, in *World Literature Today*, considering the volume's theme of Stone's progressing blindness, admires the poet's ability to "make art out of even the most tragic of circumstances... without losing an even deeper passion for life in every moment, no matter how terrible." Kaiser concludes, "Her engagement is stark and unflinching, but ultimately, in the courage and skill with which she faces life, the achievement is triumphant." In *Booklist*, Donna Seaman asserts: "Wry animal parables, spare and intense dramas, gorgeous nature lyrics, and bracing metaphysical musings constitute a clarion collection by a National Book Award–winning, and profoundly rewarding, poet." In *Library Journal*, E. M. Kaufmann suggests that "this late work lacks some of the sharp edge and linguistic energy of the earlier poems"—perhaps reflective of Stone's advanced age—but affirms that "there is a kind of gorgeous ease" in much of the collection.

In his essay "Experiencing Otherness: Ruth Stone's Art of Inference," Roger Gilbert notes that both self-reflection and empathy are hallmarks of Stone's work:

> In addition to being one of our finest poets of the self—or, to be precise, of her own warmly specific self—Stone has also shown herself to be unusually devoted to otherness in all its varied forms.

Her poems compassionately explore and illuminate the existential states of not only other people and even animals but inanimate objects as well. In Stone's "Comments of the Mild," for example, from *Second-Hand Coat*, an anthropomorphized cabinet, an awkwardly constructed assembly-line product, is pitied and given a voice, with which it can only meekly confirm its identity as furniture. "Another Feeling" is a more recent example of a poem characterized by empathy for a typically unconsidered other. Gilbert proposes that by virtue of her invariably profound poetic insight, Stone's name evokes "the fabled philosopher's stone, whose mere presence enables revelations to occur." In "Definitions of Love: Ruth Stone's Feminist *Caritas*," Sandra M. Gilbert invokes the names of two of America's most hallowed poets—Emily Dickinson, whom above all others Stone is often compared to, and Walt Whitman—in elaborating on the "imaginative empathy" that rings throughout her work:

Often Dickinsonian in its terseness and inventiveness, her poetry is also Whitmanesque in the elasticity of sympathies, in its willingness to accept the catalog of differences—the second-hand coats, the trailer parks and the tract houses, the lovers, the children and grandchildren—that this artist encounters on open roads and back roads as she buses around our country.

In general, nearly every critic who approaches Stone's work attempts to describe exactly why her poetry is so wonderful—and nearly every formulation offers a perspective slightly different from all others. In awarding her the Wallace Stevens Prize from the Academy of American Poets in 2002, the poet Galway Kinnell (as quoted on the National Public Radio program *All Things Considered*) remarked, "Ruth Stone's poems startle us over and over with their shapeliness, their humor, their youthfulness, the moral gulps they prompt, their fierce exactness of language and memory." In "Mapping Ruth Stone's Life and Art," Wendy Barker remarks, "Perhaps... part of the fascination of Stone's poetry has to do with the counterpoint between a lyrical, ladylike gentility and a sharp, blunt, even bawdy ability to see into the hard core of experience." In his essay "Ruth Stone's Intricate Simplicities," Gilbert celebrates the powerful connections readers so easily form with her verse: "Stone is one of the most accessible poets alive, and her poems provide a kind of immediate pleasure, both on the page and in her incomparable readings, that one seldom finds in contemporary poetry."

CRITICISM

Michael Allen Holmes

Holmes is a writer and editor. In the following essay, he reflects on what "Another Feeling" reveals about the functioning of memory.

A very high value is placed on memory capacity in modern American society. Through schooling, tests almost universally require the memorization of vocabulary words, facts, names, years, or other pieces of information, even when content and issues are being subjectively discussed. In the real world, while different professions exact different demands, the ability to memorize is critical in nearly every field: engineers must know countless mathematical formulas and processes, trial lawyers must be able to recall legal nuances at a moment's notice, doctors must have an instinctive awareness of which symptoms suggest which diseases, and politicians must adequately remember names, faces, conversations, and meetings or risk confusing issues and alienating supporters. Other professions demand less of factual memory but more of kinesthetic, or muscle, memory. Athletes and dancers who undergo years of training are effectively teaching their bodies to remember exactly which muscles to engage and with what force at any given moment in their realm of action, while also building those muscles so as to function ideally. Much the same can be said of carpenters, construction workers, automotive mechanics, and other professions requiring physical strength and precision. In literature, nonfiction writers can use recording devices but must often rely on their memories of interactions and incidents in reporting them to readers. Fiction writers may benefit most by storing the details of daily existence in their subconscious, so that meaningful details spontaneously arise in their mind as they create a reality of their own; they must then be so attuned to the reality they create that nothing within ends up contradictory. Poets are perhaps allowed the most disconnection from memory, in that poems can easily be inspired by a present reality or passing thoughts that can then be instantly discarded from the mind. Thus, the poet, in particular, may manage to subsist in a Zen-like eternal present, unrestricted by demands on memory, fully conscious of the surrounding reality moment by moment. Ruth Stone gives the impression of having matured into such a poet—and "Another Feeling," from *In the Dark* (2004), seems to reveal much about how such a person's memory, freed of artificial constraints, naturally and beneficially functions.

Stone's comments in interviews suggest that she has had a unique relationship with her mind and memory throughout her life. Her mother planted fields' worth of the poetry of Lord Alfred Tennyson in her infant mind while she was nursing—verse, some of which she came to recite, that she feels certainly made imprints on the patterning of language in her brain. In turn, her musician father's regular practice of drumming at home gave her years of exposure to different rhythms, meanwhile heightening her mind's attention to the present. And with creative impulse overflowing in her grandfather's house—a grandmother who wrote novels and painted hundreds of pictures on an easel in the kitchen, great-aunts who wrote poetry, an uncle who wrote, a mother and a sister who painted—

WHAT DO I READ NEXT?

- Stone's *In the Next Galaxy* (2002) is the work that preceded *In the Dark* and for which Stone won the National Book Award. In this volume, she uses many everyday experiences to portray the cosmic depths of the individual self.

- Stone's *In an Iridescent Time* (1959), her first published collection, reveals the origins of her poetry in a life far removed from the one left in the wake of her husband's death. The poems tend more toward the lyrical, drawing on metric forms and showing sophisticated artistry.

- Stone's concise, declarative style and raw emotional power often earn her comparisons to Emily Dickinson. The collection *Final Harvest* (1962), compiled by Thomas H. Johnson, includes 576 of Dickinson's nearly 1,800 known poems, presented as originally written.

- The poet Sylvia Plath's destiny proved somewhat the opposite of Stone's: after having two children with fellow writer Ted Hughes, the couple separated, and Plath committed suicide. Her posthumous collection *Ariel* (1965) presents a powerful voice communicating the existential and emotional trials faced by a woman in contemporary society.

- Unlike Stone, Denise Levertov was openly political in much of her poetry, such as the anti-Vietnam War verse found in *The Freeing of the Dust* (1975). Her nonfiction work *The Poet in the World* (1973) presents her politicized point of view on the role of the poet in society.

- *The Heinemann Book of African Women's Poetry* (1995), featuring authors from eighteen African countries, including Senegal, Egypt, and Zimbabwe, presents an array of perspectives on the often-tragic situations of women throughout the continent.

- Stone's youngest daughter, Abigail, is a writer whose novel *Recipes from the Dump* (1995) draws on her own family's life, focusing on the day-to-day life of a single mother of three living in small-town Vermont.

- *Hoofbeats, Claws, and Rippled Fins: Creature Poems* (2002), a book of poetry for younger readers edited by Lee Bennett Hopkins and illustrated with intricate woodcuts by Stephen Alcorn, includes fourteen poems exploring the lives and identities of various animals.

---

the young Stone, who began writing poetry at age six and never really stopped, came to permanently inhabit that state of playful creativity that is the special realm of artists and children.

This connection to her artistic side evidently left Stone quite disconnected from her rational side. Although she read extensively, she was bored in school, and as she told Sandra Gilbert in a 1973 interview,

> I was always in a fog. I just don't know about my brain. It seems as though I'm always facing something that I don't understand. I seem to have to take things in through my pores somehow.

In other words, her default method of understanding the world was not rational or logical but rather felt and intuitive. Stone perhaps connected this way of understanding the world with her own relative immaturity, telling Gilbert,

> I was really very, very slow growing up, as you can see. Not at all mature. A total baby.... I don't think I started growing up till I was about thirty. Maybe not till I was fifty. I remained so childish.

Part of her childishness was a lack of concern for the future—or perhaps more accurately, a reluctance to try to dictate her own fate. Gilbert asked her about a poem indicating that she has never had a plan in life, and Stone confirmed, "No plan, that's the way it's always been, all my life. No, I have no plan." Such seeming

> ANY PERSON LACKING THE POETIC IMPULSE WOULD HAVE LIKELY BEEN HAPPY TO TRY TO FORGET IT EVER HAPPENED, BUT HERE STONE NOT ONLY VIVIDLY RECALLS BOTH HER OWN ROLE AND THE PIG'S TERROR BUT FURTHERMORE RECORDS THEM IN VERSE, METAPHORICALLY ETCHING THE INCIDENT IN STONE."

indifference toward the future—which is something of a Buddhist precept—carries the benefits of dissipating both expectations and disappointments; if one expects nothing, one is never disappointed, and much emotional turmoil is avoided. This is not to suggest that Stone successfully evaded emotional upset in her life. Her first marriage quickly dissolved into a disagreeable situation, which left her intently trying to forget her reality on a daily basis. She told Gilbert,

> I used to wake up every day and have *forgotten* all the terrible traumas of the day before, of living with a creature who was so alien, who assaulted me in some strange way and I had no defenses. But every day I'd forget all the happenings of the day before and start out again.

Thus, she came to live her life "without a plan, without any remembrance, without any anger, without anything. Just as though everything was new."

The happiness of Stone's life with her second husband, Walter Stone, and eventually their three children allowed her peace of mind and peace of self. But her husband's sudden death some twenty years into their marriage turned her life upside-down, and her relationship with her mind became all the more convoluted. His absence was so difficult to bear that, as she told Gilbert, "I couldn't live anywhere except in some sort of dreamlike state in which it seemed as though he had never left me." His death had altered her entire world, and the truth of the past invariably intruded on her consciousness. The grief would last for decades and be channeled into dozens of poems written with her husband in mind. Only gradually would she regain her ability to permanently root her consciousness in the present—but once she did so, her ability was stronger than ever, a fact attested to by the relevance and acclaim of her poetry.

As one might expect given her creativity and relationship with memory, Stone has described her poetic process as being a spontaneous one. Much as she did not plan her life, she would not really plan a poem but rather, as she told Robert Bradley in a 1990 interview, "would feel a poem coming way off... feel it physically." And the poem would arise, she said, "sometimes like it had already made itself up in my head. Apparently my mind, for some reason or another, was like some sort of machine. It would just make me up poems all the time." Regarding this process, Stone remarked—foreshadowing the title of her 2004 collection—that a poem needs to emerge because

> it's in the dark in there. Your mind, as it works, is constantly reviewing things. Language goes on electrically, or whatever it does in there; it's a dark process, a kind of auxiliary involuntary nervous system. When you write, bring out language and experience, you're bringing out consolidated moments.

In more technical terms, the instinctive construction of a poem might be interpreted as a function of stored memory being subconsciously analyzed by the brain to derive value or understanding from the memory. Stone continued,

> Although it feels substantial and real, present experience is thin compared to when you speak of it later, after it goes into the mind and comes out again with all of its connection to memory, to the rhythms of the body, and to the history of language and the rhythms of speech.

One might conclude that in the best poetry, such as Stone's, a reality is filtered through the author's consciousness and recorded in a way that enhances that reality, adding layers of perception and significance.

"Another Feeling" may be considered an illustrative example of the beneficial functioning of poetic memory. While the sense of the poem can be interpreted in various ways, it most strongly reads as though Stone is recalling a memory of her own and recording the incident as if speaking to herself. One might assume the poem fairly formulated itself in her head, and she simply wrote it down without any overarching design. But why would this particular incident beg itself to be written down as a poem? Clearly the incident was an unpleasant one. Any person lacking the poetic impulse would have likely been happy to try to forget it ever happened, but here Stone not only vividly recalls both her own role and the pig's terror but furthermore records them in verse, metaphorically etching the incident in stone. Now the pig's fate can never be entirely forgotten. Unrecorded—and probably forgotten by the indifferent Humane Society agents—the memory would have eventually died along with the owner. Instead, Stone has put herself through a minor emotional wringer by reliving the incident, perhaps judging herself essentially responsible for the killing of the animal, and she even experiences physical distress as a result. But then, this is precisely the role she has adopted for herself as a poet: to live and experience, and relive and reexperience, to the fullest all that her life has to offer, and to present her perceptions and revelations in a form designed to inspire the reader not just rationally but intuitively, in a felt way. Stone surely succeeds in communicating this particular experience in such a way that the reader, too, feels the visceral distress of empathetic terror inspired by that disadvantaged, defenseless, mortally fearful pig. A pig may only be a pig, but mortal fear is mortal fear in any creature, and Stone—connected to her emotional, intuitive side—cannot help but share that fear in looking into the creature's eyes.

Considered as relating an actual experience of Stone's, "Another Feeling" can be seen to function on three different levels, two related to memory and one related to the author's role as poet. First, the poem serves as a confession. While some people manage to function adequately by sweeping any moral shortcomings under the rugs in their mind, Stone is too self-aware to practice such self-deception, and confessing to this particular sin benefits her conscience more. Second, the poem serves as memorial. The sin, indeed, might have simply been forgotten, but then the pig, too, would have been lost to history. Now, with its unjust death recorded in a book of poetry that will survive somewhere in the world far into the future, the pig has in a way been immortalized. Third, the poem serves as cautionary tale. In reliving the memory, Stone's agitated body has communicated to her the significance of the episode; surely she has learned to be more careful with the lives of other creatures—not just humans but animals as well. To calm her agitation, then, Stone wrote the poem, and no conscientious reader of "Another Feeling" will fail to think twice before trying to manage an animal's fate.

Source: Michael Allen Holmes, Critical Essay on "Another Feeling," in *Poetry for Students*, Gale, Cengage Learning, 2012.

Mary Kaiser

In the following review, Kaiser muses that Stone's failing eyesight became a metaphor for consciousness in the collection In the Dark, *which includes "Another Feeling."*

Great artists turn crippling disabilities into opportunity; a narrowed scope results in discoveries that might never have occurred if the means were easier. Matisse produced astonishing paper cutouts when he was confined to bed and unable to hold a brush, and Manet painted some of his masterpieces, still-life studies of flowers, while immobilized by a gangrenous leg. In her recent collection *In the Dark*, eighty-nine-year-old National Book Award-winning poet Ruth Stone takes the progressive loss of her eyesight as the occasion for extraordinary poems in which vision—and its limits—become a metaphor for consciousness as it untangles the world.

The narrative arc of the collection follows the stages of the poet's condition, from "half-blind," as she terms it in the opening poem, to complete blindness—or as the devastating line in "Trying to Write" has it, "Blind as a bat, says my doom." Between these two poles, of course, we find our human condition, and so the short lyrics in the collection range through a myriad of ways of experiencing—all mediated by the theme of partial vision.

Beneath a surface that's often disarmingly childlike and musical, Stone's poems conceal a surrealist's ironic perception that things are never what they seem. In this way, Stone negotiates a poetic persona as layered as Emily Dickinson's, which meets the reader's expectation of innocent femininity; and then, when our guard is down, the voice deepens its register with a menacing edge. In "The Sadness of Lies," for example, the poet begins demurely enough with a scene of wine-drinking on a patio, then veers into something quite different: "I wonder if I have Spanish blood, I say. / Perhaps I am Indian. What pterodactyl mothered / my scaled hair? I lift a wineglass to my lips." There's always a hint of brutality in Stone's suburban landscapes, a suggestion that we have bulldozed over a natural vitality that won't stay down forever, though we refuse to see the layers of passionate living that preceded and will follow our own.

In addition to asserting powerfully her own isolating experience, Stone refuses to disengage her poetry from the lives of those around her. She remains intensely empathetic toward people; the stakes for love and intimacy are still very high. And unlike W. B. Yeats or Philip Larkin, who observe the embraces of the young with a tinge of envy, Stone has nothing but good humor, watching people from a window in "In the Arts," for example, and noting: "In plain view of the gallery and well-dressed / lady volunteers, an almost naked couple / are getting it on in the center of the vista." In the final line, the shift into Generation X vocabulary with "getting it on" works beautifully as a strategy in which the poem's speaker can ally herself with the lovers and against the "well-dressed" middle-aged observers.

Ruth Stone is a poet who demonstrates how to make art out of even the most tragic of circumstances—blindness, old age, her husband's suicide, the suffering around her on the streets of American cities—without losing an even deeper passion for life in every moment, no matter how terrible. Her engagement is stark and unflinching, but ultimately, in the courage and skill with which she faces life, the achievement is triumphant.

Source: Mary Kaiser, Review of *In the Dark*, in *World Literature Today*, Vol. 80, No. 2, March/April 2006, pp. 58–59.

Rosanne Wasserman
In the following excerpt, Wasserman discusses the comedic and playful nature present in some of Stone's works in contrast to the darkness in others.

... Stone's wildness to speak for the world is vast, homey, surreal, and hilarious—as if Walt Whitman were wed to Lewis Carroll, Edward Lear, Magritte. Her vocable universe reminds me of the great medieval Persian books of miniatures, such as *The Shah Nameh of Shah Tahmasp* (published by the Metropolitan-Museum of Art as *A King's Book of Kings*), where the landscapes are full of faces: rocks are alive, trees are alive, little spirits peer from every detail, grotesque and funny faces in the terrain. Stone's world is like this, but it's not an aristocrat's pristine archaic wilderness; it's the shabby and littered suburb we inhabit with her, or the impoverished rural community, the backcountry behind the suburb, suddenly transformed into a place where everything is potentially alive. Ruth listens to these voices and reports them back to us. Nothing is lost, on her watch.

> THE SENSIBILITY THAT ACHES TO ENLIVEN EVERYTHING, LIVING OR DEAD, CONTAINS A POWERFUL INTELLECTUAL CURIOSITY, FIFTY YEARS OF EXCRUCIATING EXPERIENCE, AND THE STRONG, BITTER FLAVOR OF HER WIT."

In these comedies, Stone reports from the field, a migrant poet touring academies, but as her wanderings continue, so her ventriloquism extends beyond the animal, vegetable, and mineral kingdoms. She personifies even a pun, a misunderstanding, what Ron Padgett once called "everyday oops," in a talk that traced its poetic trajectory through the New York School. Stone based the following poem from *Topography* entirely on a misheard question from the child beside her while she was driving down to view a piece of property in Vermont; instead of the child's question, "Seat Belt Fastened?" which became the title, she heard "Old Bill Pheasant":

> Old Bill wandered in my waking dream,
> A river dream; when I saw him come
> I was riding by with my gas tank high
> Down to Otter Creek from my just-right home.
> And he stuck his head in the window and said,
> "It's sleazy and greasy but it's in your head.
> Tell me woman, do you carry a comb?"
> ...
> Now tell me when we're passing, and tell me when we gain.
> And laugh, little children, while our gas tank's high.
> "Give thanks for desire," was all he said.
> "It'll either clear up or snow or rain."
> So we tweaked his beard and we punched his head.
> Is your seat belt fastened? Do you sleep in your bed?
> If you're stuck in the river can you shift to red?
> If you're coming are you going?
> If you're living are you dead?
>
> And we drove him away where the otters play,
> Where it's twice on Sunday in the regular way,
> Where they say what they know and they know what they say,
> And the good time's coming on yesterday.

Supremely nostalgic, the poem's actual nostos, its homecoming, occurs beside the impossible one—"the good time's coming on yesterday."

Stone's keynote is often more desperation than anxiety, leading her to employ not the heroic stoicism of the ironist but an outright exhibition of her plight—closer in tone to Emily Dickinson's outcry, "Twice have I stood a beggar / Before the throne of God!... Burglar—Banker! Father! / I am poor once more!" But Stone's abjection is less imperative, if not less self-conscious; in "The Excuse" from *Topography*, she writes:

> It is so difficult to look at the deprived, or smell their decay.
> But now I am among them. I, too, am a leper, a warning.
> I hold out my crippled fingers; my voice flatters Everyone who comes this way. In the weeds of mourning,
> Groaning and gnashing, I display
> Myself in malodorous comic wrappings and tatters,
> In the excess of passion, in the need to be worn away.

Necessity is the inventor of the mother. Her children, from whom she learns to say something when she is in need, are her teachers: her need, duty, and art form are to express anguish so that it may be healed.

As part of this playful and painful ventriloquism, Stone also often genders the inanimate, as in *Second-Hand Coat*'s "When the Furnace Goes on in a California Tract House," where a salt and pepper shaker enact feminine and masculine roles; the salt is female: "'It's degrading,' she confides, 'the way they pinch me.'" Stone may project sexual romances into the street: "A Love Like Ours" in *Simplicity* involves a crack in the macadam and the seed of a linden tree. She will speak for the Hubble Telescope in "The Sad Voice of the Hubble" and for the planet in "The Mothers," both also from *Simplicity*, and for the solar system in "What They Don't Tell Us About" (*In the Dark*). It seems that the universe is so full of voices precisely because Walter's death has silenced his beloved voice. Stone has to throw her voice everywhere, into everything, practicing her magical verbal ability until it can bring him back to life. Every word can conjure his resurrection, as it symbolizes yet another object that she can infuse with empathetic animation. Shay's *Achilles in Vietnam* recognizes a similar effect in combat soldiers whose friends are killed in action; the survivors go berserk, and every vengeful kill serves to remind them of their lost companions, and so to reanimate the dead, if only in memory. Thus blood can make ghosts speak. In contrast, Stone's goal is not to revenge violence by replicating it, but to undo murder: she pours not blood but language on the ground, and everything that speaks invokes the words he should have said.

The magic of resurrection is not by any means a simple spell or spiel. Whole religions get based on it. In *Cheap*, Stone's autobiographical poem "The Tree" offers a very direct equation between Walter and Christ, our ultimate cultural resurrectible. The very next poem, "Becoming You," moves into even more ancient equations: Stone writes, "Now, I shall grow / Until I encompass you," and her closing metaphor is digestion. Poem 8 of *Widow's Muse* tackles this Christian-pagan theme head-on:

> If she wants to have a second coming,
> she's going to have to raise it
> on her own.

In poem 14 of *Widow's Muse*, the inanimate world mourns with her: "even her stockings, even her shoes / wept for him." But in poem 44, he is resurrected like a vegetation god and consumed: she writes that the widow "feels a need to dig in the garden; / to eat, in the summer, the large / male flowers of the squash, / the ones that will not bear fruit."

> This symbolic cannibalism
> is a negative resurrection,
> a logical illogic.

As we might expect from the preceding lines, Stone often feels and speaks for the vegetables she eats: from the eggplant she questions in "Vegetables II" (*Cheap*), "You are so smooth and cool and purple, / ... Which of us will it be?"; to the screaming carrots in *Widow's Muse*.

By the end of the long poem series of *Widow's Muse*, Stone's elusive muse is everywhere and everything: language itself, not the sounds alone, but whatever the words can stand for, wherever they stand, the matter of the universe, matched at every point by the antimatter of the beloved's silence and absence. Small wonder if Stone's "nailed and mailed" Scheherezade in *Simplicity* cheats at solitaire: "Scheherezade has forgotten the executioner. / But she is still walking barefoot over the spikes of words." In "So Be It" from *Ordinary Words*, she tracks a surreal meditation on speech, birth, and writing: a string of words first spoken, then written with ink from Chattanooga. The name invokes a Native American chief, born, like the ink, by pushing down a long tube until he emerged, "holding his belly / by a bloody string he / screamed, "I am me," /

and became a cursive / mark on a notepad"—then Stone examines the notepad's origins. She concludes with an insight nearly Zen; like the muse, the very act of writing is endlessly transformative:

> ... For there
> is nothing that is nothing,
> but always becoming
> something; flinging itself;
> leaping from level to level.

Yet even after achieving such cosmic perspectives, Stone doesn't forget to listen. The poem "Incarnation," from *In the Next Galaxy*, shows a woman standing in her kitchen listening to a bird: not surprisingly, "It is the voice of her dead husband, / only now he has wings and sings / to another female sitting on a nest." I can hear John Keats ("Ode to the West Wind"'s "Be thou me, impetuous one!") and Wallace Stevens (as his birds in "The Poems of Our Climate" quote Keats: "Bethou, bethou, bethou me in my glade") behind her wistful lines here: Walter's not bethou-ing Ruth anymore, but at least he's still out there bethou-ing. Stone willingly, if ironically, shares this particular earthly and winged reincarnation of her lost man with the denizens of her rural cosmos, as she shared him with her daughters decades ago, on that morning of "Love's Relative." The same collection returns overtly to this trope with "To Try Again," where, with voices of sword-grass, water, larch trees, milkweed, and monarch butterfly larvae sounding off around her, she hears something vaster than the wind: "'Look,' the void says, 'What meaning? Be thou me.'"

Some of Stone's funnier poetic voicings and animations may resemble the talking appliances of poet Thomas Disch's cartoon creations in *The Brave Little Toaster*, but her work also recalls Pablo Neruda's great "Elemental Odes," Rainer Marie Rilke's "Duino Elegies," Blake's "Songs of Experience" (especially in her poem "The Tree"), and Lewis Carroll's Alice (the source of her poem "The Principle of Mirrors"). The sensibility that aches to enliven everything, living or dead, contains a powerful intellectual curiosity, fifty years of excruciating experience, and the strong, bitter flavor of her wit. Just after the death of his friend in 1966, John Ashbery wrote of Frank O'Hara,

> that the act of creation and the finished creation are the same, that art is human willpower deploying every means at its disposal to break through to a truer state than the present one. The work of art is in the form of a heroic question: can art do this? Is this really happening? But the fact that the question is at last being asked is itself an affirmation of our power to act on the vagueness.

Stone's art acts on the ultimate vagueness of death, loss, and mourning, and breaks through with us to a truer state. Alone on her cold mountain or surrounded by the music of the universe singing though her voice, she glimpses a world where "Everything shimmers and glitters and shakes with unbearable longing, / The dancers who cannot sleep, and the sleepers who cannot dance" ("Metamorphosis," *Topography*); to the "Floaters" crossing the field of her failing vision from *In the Dark*, when "a slowed perception of the battered brain / strips back like leaves to unexpected glittering." "Our lives and our art," she tells Seiferle, "You know I always feel it's a gift from the universe." She has returned that gift with this remarkable body of poems, these voices that she has woven all around the absence of one dear body. There are some writers with whom an intense life, with its full share of disaster and transcendence, can be lived out, lived through, lived in. Ruth Stone is, most distinctly, that kind of poet.

Source: Rosanne Wasserman, "Ruth Stone: A Gift from the Universe," in *American Poetry Review*, Vol. 35, No. 3, May/June 2006, pp. 49–54.

SOURCES

Barker, Wendy, "Mapping Ruth Stone's Life and Art," in *The House Is Made of Poetry: The Art of Ruth Stone*, edited by Wendy Barker and Sandra M. Gilbert, Southern Illinois University Press, 1996, pp. 33–45.

Barnstone, Aliki, and Willis Barnstone, *A Book of Women Poets from Antiquity to Now*, Schocken Books, 1980, pp. 497, 499, 505–506.

Bradley, Robert, "An Interview with Ruth Stone: 1990," in *The House Is Made of Poetry: The Art of Ruth Stone*, edited by Wendy Barker and Sandra M. Gilbert, Southern Illinois University Press, 1996, pp. 67–77.

Fiedler, Leslie, "On Ruth Stone," in *The House Is Made of Poetry: The Art of Ruth Stone*, edited by Wendy Barker and Sandra M. Gilbert, Southern Illinois University Press, 1996, pp. 3–4.

Gilbert, Roger, "Experiencing Otherness: Ruth Stone's Art of Inference," in *The House Is Made of Poetry: The Art of Ruth Stone*, edited by Wendy Barker and Sandra M. Gilbert, Southern Illinois University Press, 1996, pp. 140–50.

———, "Ruth Stone's Intricate Simplicities," in *Iowa Review*, Vol. 26, No. 3, Fall 1996, pp. 179–93.

Gilbert, Sandra M., "An Interview with Ruth Stone: 1973," in *The House Is Made of Poetry: The Art of Ruth Stone*, edited by Wendy Barker and Sandra M. Gilbert, Southern Illinois University Press, 1996, pp. 52–66.

———, "Definitions of Love: Ruth Stone's Feminist *Caritas*," in *The House Is Made of Poetry: The Art of Ruth Stone*, edited by Wendy Barker and Sandra M. Gilbert, Southern Illinois University Press, 1996, pp. 194–203.

Kaiser, Mary, Review of *In the Dark*, in *World Literature Today*, Vol. 80, No. 2, March/April 2006, pp. 58–59.

Kaufmann, E. M., Review of *In the Dark*, in *Library Journal*, Vol. 129, No. 13, August 2004, p. 87.

"Muriel Rukeyser," in *Poetry Foundation*, http://www.poetryfoundation.org/bio/muriel-rukeyser (accessed May 5, 2011).

"Poet Ruth Stone Reads Her Poetry and Discusses Winning the National Book Award," in *Weekend Edition*, National Public Radio, November 24, 2002.

Rees-Jones, Deryn, "Objecting to the Subject: Science, Femininity, and Poetic Process in the Work of Elizabeth Bishop and Lavinia Greenlaw," in *Kicking Daffodils: Twentieth-Century Women Poets*, edited by Vicki Bertram, Edinburgh University Press, 1997, pp. 267–69.

"Ruth Stone Discusses Her Poetry and Life," in *All Things Considered*, National Public Radio, July 19, 2004.

Seaman, Donna, Review of *In the Dark*, in *Booklist*, Vol. 101, No. 2, September 15, 2004, p. 196.

Stone, Ruth, "Another Feeling," in *In the Dark*, Copper Canyon Press, 2004, p. 5.

Wasserman, Rosanne, "Ruth Stone: A Gift from the Universe," in *American Poetry Review*, Vol. 35, No. 3, May/June 2006, pp. 49–54.

FURTHER READING

Rankine, Claudia, and Juliana Spahr, eds., *American Women Poets in the 21st Century: Where Lyric Meets Language*, Wesleyan University Press, 2002.

This volume, edited by two contemporary poets, presents samplings of work by ten poets writing at the turn of the century, accompanied by poetic statements, critical analysis, and biographical information. It focuses on trends in modern lyrical poetry.

Roberts, Alvin, *Coping with Blindness: Personal Tales of Blindness Rehabilitation*, Southern Illinois University Press, 1998.

Roberts, who is blind himself, presents anecdotes of people learning to live with blindness. He thought these stories might serve to reassure people who are losing their vision (as Stone did in her later years) and show that blind people's lives are still filled with humor and joy.

Scott, Diana, ed., *Bread and Roses: An Anthology of Nineteenth- and Twentieth-Century Poetry by Women Writers*, Virago, 1982.

Scott's volume provides samplings of verse by women from 1820 onward, including such renowned authors as Emily Bronte and Elizabeth Barrett Browning, with section introductions charting the trajectory of poetry by women over the years.

Steinbeck, John, *Of Mice and Men*, Penguin, 1993.

This 1937 novella by one of America's most famous authors culminates in a man's ethical quandary about whether or not to compassionately kill his friend.

SUGGESTED SEARCH TERMS

Ruth Stone AND Another Feeling

Ruth Stone AND In the Dark

Ruth Stone AND poetry AND prize

women poets AND 21st century AND America

feminism AND Ruth Stone

Emily Dickinson AND Ruth Stone

Ruth Stone AND Marcia OR Phoebe OR Abigail

Civilian and Soldier

WOLE SOYINKA

1967

Wole Soyinka's poem "Civilian and Soldier" was written as a response to the rising violence in his native Nigeria in late 1966, a situation that soon led to a three-year-long civil war. In the poem, Soyinka presents a civilian who has recently been shot to death, speaking as a ghost to the man who shot him. He is not angry at the soldier, but he is certain that the soldier does not understand the cause of his own actions, or why he is spreading destruction across the land. He imagines the day that the soldier will be killed in combat, and thinks that then, finally, it will be time to teach him a lesson about life.

Soyinka is one of the greatest writers Nigeria has ever produced. He publishes poetry infrequently, having made his reputation as a dramatist. His plays have been produced in theaters around the world. In 1986, he was the first black African to be awarded the Nobel Prize for Literature.

The collection in which this poem appeared, *Idanre and Other Poems*, was published just as the Nigerian civil war began in 1967. Soyinka, who has always advocated political involvement in his plays and in his teaching, was arrested during the war and imprisoned for twenty-two months, though no charges were ever brought against him. In addition to being recognized for his writing, he is internationally acclaimed for his efforts to bring attention to the struggles of African nations, and for bringing Yoruba literary traditions to an international audience.

Wole Soyinka (AP Images)

AUTHOR BIOGRAPHY

Soyinka, whose full name is Akinwande Olewole Soyinka, was born on July 13, 1934, in Ake Abeokuta, in western Nigeria. His father was a teacher, following family tradition, at the British school in Ake. Despite living under colonial rule, the village Soyinka grew up in was deeply entrenched in the tradition of the Yoruba civilization that had been established for centuries before the British came to Africa.

After attending elementary school in Ake, Soyinka went to secondary school at the Government College in Ibadan, Nigeria's third-largest city, which increased his sense of the tension between old-world customs and the Western ways that were brought to Africa by the English. He transferred to the University of Ibadan, which he attended from 1952 to 1954. While there, he was an active writer, editing the student magazine. He then attended the University of Leeds in England, expanding his skill as a writer, eventually earning a doctorate in 1973. Returning to the University of Ibadan to teach, he was awarded a Rockefeller Foundation research fellowship in 1960, which he used to study African drama. In 1964, Soyinka was a founder of the Orisun Theater in Ibadan, intending it to be an outlet for political ideas.

Soyinka was arrested in 1965 and accused of holding a radio announcer at gunpoint and forcing him to broadcast bogus results of the recent elections. An outcry from writers around the world put pressure on the government, and after three months he was released for lack of evidence. The book that contains "Civilian and Soldier," *Idanre and Other Poems*, was published shortly before his second arrest in 1967. After the start of the Nigerian civil war, he was taken into custody when he returned from a trip to England and accused of trying to buy jets to aid rebel fighters. He was held, mostly in solitary confinement, for two years.

After the war's end, Soyinka wrote about his experiences in prison in *The Man Died*. He published plays, memoirs, and essays, and his fame as an international literary figure grew. He headed the Department of Dramatic Arts at the University of Ife, promoting political writing, and was a visiting professor at Yale University. In 1986, he was awarded the Nobel Prize for Literature. In the time since, he has published frequently, taught at various institutions, and directed productions of his plays at theaters around the globe. He remains a voice for people struggling against repressive governments throughout the world.

POEM SUMMARY

The text used for this summary is from *The Poetry of Our World: An International Anthology of Contemporary Poetry*, HarperCollins, 2002, p. 372. A version of the poem can be found on the following Web page: http://famouspoetsandpoems.com/poets/wole_soyinka/poems/22482.

Lines 1–6

The civilian who is narrating this poem sets the stage by talking about his recent death. In line 1, he has already died, killed by the bullets of the soldier he is addressing. After being shot full of lead bullets, his ghost rose up from where his body fell. In line 3, Soyinka refers to the appearance of the ghost as something that aggravates the soldier's fright, implying that, even when faced with unarmed enemies, the soldier is already afraid.

Beginning in line 3, the speaker shows that he is just as mystified and unsettled by the appearance of his ghost as the soldier must be. His surprise takes a philosophical turn as he points out that he is a physical entity aligning himself with common reality instead of the supernatural realm so often associated with ghosts. This focus on the common, mundane world is continued in line 5. He does not think of death, even his own, as being anything too special, but as a natural event that is bound to happen to everybody at some time.

The poem's first section ends with the narrator describing the other thing that bothers him. The first thing he does not like is that he is alive, in apparition form; the second is that he has not been able to escape from the war by dying. He refers to the cause that has driven this soldier to massacre innocent people as a an argument, indicating that, from the perspective of the deceased, all fighting, even if it might seem to have serious causes and consequences, is based on petty motives.

The second section of the poem begins in the middle of line 6. The first half of the line completes the narrator's thought about wars, or quarrels, being things limited to the physical world, and he breaks the line in half as the focus shifts from the general situation to a description of the soldier's reaction. The second half of line 6 implies a visible sense of awe in the soldier, who stands and stares as if in wonderment.

Lines 7–16

Line 7 begins with a reference to the two moments that have already been described in the poem, the speaker's death and his subsequent resurrection as a ghost. Calling both, each of which would only take a second in real time, an "eternity" helps to show the emotional significance of the two back-to-back events.

The soldier's quiet silence is given an expanded explanation in line 8. Although line 6 implied that the act of killing may have frozen the soldier in his tracks, the speaker explains here that it is part of his military training to walk quietly among the dead, to make sure that any possible survivors are located and taken away. In line 10, Soyinka uses a common expression in military actions that is used to describe the policy of making sure that all life in an attacked area is destroyed and incapable of growing back. The civilian speaks of how those who have been killed might be viewed as neither positive nor negative, but their very neutrality is not quite certain, either. The soldier cannot trust them not to take up arms against him in retaliation for what he has done to their town.

From line 10 to line 16, the speaker puts emphasis on the innocence of the civilians who have been attacked by armed military men. The massacre is referred to as a festival, as if it were a happy celebration for the soldiers, conveying a sense of delight in the way they sprayed lead bullets around those who could not fight back. The speaker, sensing hesitation in the soldier who eventually killed him, says that he could see, at the last moment of his life, when death was almost upon him, the confusion that the soldier felt. At the very moment before he was killed, he understood that the soldier was not entirely comfortable with his role as a killer, which would explain why the poem starts with the soldier appearing to be haunted by his knowledge of the dead civilian.

Line 16, like line 6, is split in two, in the same way that the speaker of the poem says that his soul is split between the land of the living and the land of the dead. The second half of line 16 announces the speaker's hope for what is to come, when this whole violent episode is in the past.

Lines 17–24

In the last section of the poem, the speaker talks about being a ghost, an apparition, still on the earth after some unspecified length of time. His desire is to meet the soldier again in the future, after the soldier has died. At that time, he will attack the soldier in same way that the soldier attacked him. But while the soldier attacked with lead bullets, which are his instrument of spreading death, the civilian intends to attack the soldier with symbols of life. He lists food and wine, and implies sexuality with breasts, which would be so ample, so evocative of life, that he describes them as being in groups. On that future day, when the tables are turned and the soldier is faced with the kind of life-affirming objects that are foreign to him, his every certainty about the meaning of life will be disabled. His mission as a soldier, which is to spread death, will be countered when he sees a new way of viewing the world.

Though the civilian talks of wanting to confuse the soldier, he does not do so maliciously. In the poem's last phrase, he calls the man who murdered him "friend." As he did earlier, in line 16, when he showed sympathy for the soldier's situation, Soyinka acknowledges that both the soldier and the civilian are victims of a larger social and political system that controls their activities, even though neither one of them understands what it is all about.

THEMES

War

There is no specific information given in "Civilian and Soldier" about what war is being fought. Readers who are not familiar with Soyinka's background only know that this poem takes place in a war situation because one character is referred to as a soldier and the other is called a civilian: without these designations, the situation in the poem would be just an act of murder, not a government-sanctioned conflict.

The causes of war are many. They often deal with defense of a country's pride, its heritage, or its very existence. The threats that move a country to the battlefield are frequently abstract and theoretical: they might be actual attacks, but the threats are often anticipated attacks, so that the response is an attempt to prevent things before they occur. The waging of war, on the other hand, is immediate and concrete. Wars are waged so that people will be safe, but, as wars occur, people die.

Soldiers are trained to accept the abstract planning of their superiors. In this poem, Soyinka shows the civilian who has been killed by the impersonal process of war as he plans to give the soldier who killed him a lesson in humanity. At the beginning of the poem, the only true, tangible thing to the soldier is the bullets that he uses to kill, but by the end, the civilian hopes to put him in touch with things that affirm life's richness.

Afterlife

This poem begins moments after its narrator, the civilian, has died. He compares his post-death self, his apparition, to the ideals that the soldier is fighting for. Both are things that are not of this world. The soldier has a plan to destroy as much of life as he can, and the civilian clearly sees how this is like the afterlife that faces him. It is this idea about the end of life that brings their two stories together: the civilian has lost his life, but the soldier's "scorched earth" policy, if it is successful, will create a world as barren and uninhabitable as the civilian's dead body.

In line 18, the civilian talks about seeing the soldier as an apparition some day in the future. The soldier is in his afterlife here, putting him in the same situation as the civilian. In this afterlife that they share, the situation will be reversed: while the soldier shot the civilian with lead in the common reality that we all know, in the afterlife the civilian will be able to shoot the soldier with life-affirming food and wine and companionship.

Victimization

It is clear that the unarmed civilian is a victim of the soldier in this poem, shot down, as countless other civilians have been, for no apparent reason. He does not view himself as being victimized by the soldier, however. He sees the soldier as a victim of the same corrosive social system that killed him.

In lines 14 and 15, he does talk about the soldier aiming a weapon at him and pulling its trigger, but the weapon he wants to shoot at the soldier is life. In the earlier lines, he talks about being shot and about the soldier's fright: the two are clearly connected, but the connection is not made clear in the poem. It is not a connection that the civilian chooses to dwell on.

What he does dwell on is what he and the soldier have in common. They are both in this horrific situation, with the soldier coping with his "quarrel" and the civilian coping with his own "quandary," each to the best of his ability. By the end of the poem, they are both dead. The fact that the civilian does not resent the soldier for making a victim of him becomes clearest in the way that he plans to greet the soldier in the afterlife. He does not plot a terrible revenge, but instead plans ways to show him the importance of life. He calls the soldier "friend," showing readers that he has no hard feelings toward his fellow human.

Uncertainty

This poem ends with a question. In life, the soldier has had the power to take the civilian's life, but, as Soyinka implies in the last line, it is very unlikely that he knows why he is exercising that power. The soldier is confused throughout the poem. In line 3, he is shown to be afraid, even though he is the one with the weapon. He is portrayed as a tool of his training in lines 8 and 9, where his behavior is attributed to the things he was told to do, not to his own judgment. His confusion is mentioned directly in line 14. When he is dead, the poem tells us, the soldier will be even more confused than he was before.

In contrast, when he is killed, the civilian comes to an understanding about the ways of the world. He speaks of looking at the gun that was about to kill him and understanding not only the man holding the gun, but the motivation that is driving all of the soldiers. This understanding gives him such a

TOPICS FOR FURTHER STUDY

- Do research on the Internet on news coverage of the Nigerian civil war of 1966 and the Libyan civil war of 2011. Prepare a slide show or a PowerPoint presentation that compares how the international community responded to the slaughter of Igbo peoples in Nigeria with how it responded to the civil war in Libya. As part of your presentation, draw conclusions about what the world should learn from dealing with each crisis.

- Soyinka incorporates his Yoruba background into his literary works. Do some research into the background of the ethnic group you come from, and write a poem about a contemporary topic that shows that group's perspective, along with an explanation of how the ethnic influences are evident.

- In this poem, Soyinka offers a very basic list of things that he would expose the soldier to if he wanted to remind him of life: meat, bread, wine, and breasts. Create a more extensive list of things that would make a person who had died reconsider life. Work in small groups to narrow your collective lists down to three or four items, presenting arguments for the effectiveness of each. Post your lists to your blog or Web page and invite discussion on the list.

- Choose a section from Soyinka's acclaimed autobiography *Ake*, in which he describes his childhood in a small town in western Nigeria, and adapt it to a short film. Write a script that you think captures the point he is making in the excerpt. If you wish, film the scene and post it to YouTube or your Web page and invite fellow students to review it.

- Stephen Crane's 1895 novel *The Red Badge of Courage* is often considered a classic of young-adult literature about the American Civil War. Read Crane's book and choose one scene in it that would benefit from having the apparition of a dead character, like the one in "Civilian and Soldier." Rewrite Crane's scene with your apparition talking to the living characters.

---

calm sense of acceptance, a perception that the soldier cannot know. In the end he tries to share his knowledge of life and death with the person who attacked him.

STYLE

Oxymoron

An oxymoron is a word or a group of words that is self-contradicting. Soyinka uses this technique in the poem to point out the contradictions inherent in the situation of waging war. His oxymoron is in the phrase "both eternities." Rationally, this expression makes no sense, because eternity is all-encompassing, so there could not be more than one. Readers understand, however, that he is using this expression to challenge them and to make them think how the moment of the civilian's death and the moment after his death could each be considered an eternity.

The point of this poem is that the actions taken during war time violate rational thought, and the use of an oxymoron helps to make that point more clear.

Imagery

Poets often use images to convey ideas, rather than speaking about abstractions that their readers will only understand on a cerebral level. An image is something that can be experienced with the senses. At the end of "Civilian and Soldier," Soyinka includes a sequence of images, from meat and bread to a gourd of wine to breasts in a "bunch," to imply life. Readers know that these things are being used for their imagistic properties,

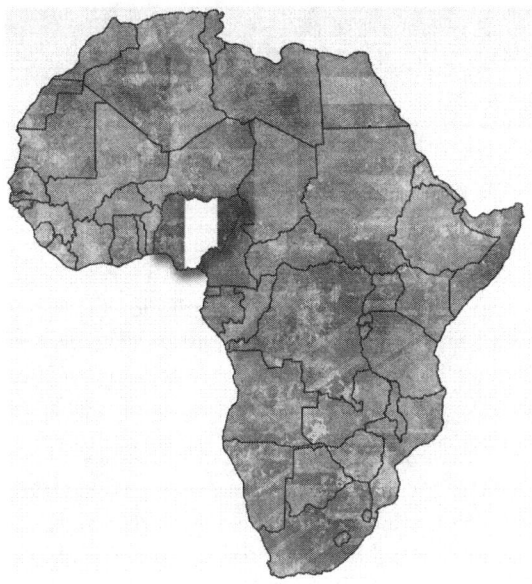

Soyinka wrote about the problems in Nigeria, his native country. (Michal Baranski | Shutterstock.com)

rather than to explain something that might really occur, because the civilian explains that he will use them to "shoot" the apparition of the man who killed him. Shooting a supernatural being with things that imply life is a way of saying that he will attack death with life.

Metonymy

Closely related to imagery is Soyinka's use of metonymy, which is the poetic practice of substituting one word or term for another word that is associated with it. In lines 1 and 13 he refers to the deadly bullets that fly during a war. He does not use the word "bullet," however, but instead uses "lead." Readers understand what he is talking about because it is commonly known that bullets are made from lead. Writing it this way, though, reinforces the poem's connection between the soldiers and the heavy gray sphere of physical reality. The reader's past associations with lead are related to the dull colorlessness of soldiers who indiscriminately kill unarmed civilians.

HISTORICAL CONTEXT

Pre-colonial Nigeria

The land that Soyinka is from and is closely associated with has been inhabited for thousands of years. There is evidence of human life in the area dating back to the Stone Age, 12,000 BCE. Over time, civilizations developed, though most of these were not recorded, owing to the lack of a writing system. One particularly widespread culture in the area is the Yoruba, which have existed since the fourth century BCE. This culture survived over the millennia, down to Soyinka's boyhood. The modern kingdoms of Nigeria that are known now, including the Kanem-Borno, Ife and Oyo, and Igbo, came into existence around 1000 CE.

In the eighteenth century, Europeans established a robust slave trade with Africans in cities along the Atlantic Ocean. Little was known about the people in the interior, though, until relatively late. It was not until 1788 that the African Association was formed in England to subsidize an expedition up the Niger River, giving Europeans their first major opportunity to study the people of the area. With the door open to exploration, missionaries began moving into the area to convert the people to their beliefs. The first wave of these came in 1804, when an Islamic revolution spread across the northern part of the area, while England quit buying slaves from the region. A huge Muslim population was established in the region. That was countered by a concerted push by Christian missionaries, who began in 1842 and for the next half-century continued to establish mission centers throughout the land. The European missionaries built schools and involved themselves in local politics, creating a strong Western presence in the area. The growing European presence led to the formation of the Royal Niger Company in 1886, to establish trade and facilitate treaties with England.

In 1893, to safeguard British interests, the British declared political dominance over the Yoruba kingdoms. The name Nigeria, after the river Niger, was officially adopted in 1897. In the subsequent years, more provinces to the north and south were annexed to the country by the British.

The British held Nigeria until the late 1950s. By then, intolerance for European intervention into the affairs of indigenous people had reached its height, spurred by the diminishment of Britain's power after World War II, as well as the newfound sense of international awareness that developed across the world because of the war. The eastern and western sections of Nigeria were given the right to political self-rule in 1957, and

COMPARE & CONTRAST

- **1960s:** To prevent Biafra, the eastern region of the country, from seceding and forming a separate country, the Nigerian government throws the country into a civil war.

  Today: Nigeria still faces ethnic unrest as disputes are fought over revenues from oil extracted in the delta at the base of the Niger River.

- **1960s:** The British colonial system disintegrates after World War II, starting with Indian independence in 1947. Nigeria declares independence in 1960, one of many African nations becoming independent in the 1960s.

  Today: Great Britain holds a few small island territories, but the process of breaking up the British Empire is considered complete with the 1997 transfer of Hong Kong back to the People's Republic of China.

- **1960s:** The world becomes aware of the humanitarian crisis in Biafra as the Nigerian government cuts off supplies to force a compromise in the civil war. Catholic Charities is a main conduit for collecting donations.

  Today: International satellite communications and social networks such as Facebook and Twitter make people in Europe and the Americas more immediately aware of humanitarian crises abroad. Organizations like Save Darfur establish information networks to publicize what is happening and to collect funds.

- **1960s:** Readers in Western countries are generally familiar with poets from Europe and North America. For a writer like Soyinka to capture an international audience is rare.

  Today: An emphasis on multicultural literature that began in the 1980s and 1990s continues to make new generations of readers familiar with works by African and Asian writers.

---

the northern area earned political independence two years later. Independence from Britain was formalized in October 1960.

Nigerian Civil War

Having been formed of different political entities that were forced together by the British colonial power, the various factions that made up Nigeria did not fit together well. After the country gained its independence, it was left with no clear national identity. Major ethnic groups became important political forces in the country's three regions. The north was dominated by the Hasuo/Fulani, the west by the Yoruba, and the east by the Igbo. The first government formed by the new republic was overthrown by a coup in January 1966. This coup put into power several Igbo ministers. That, along with the fact that there was no coup violence in Benin or the Enugu areas of the country, which had Igbo premiers, raised suspicions that the coup was perpetrated by the Igbo.

A few months later, in May, there was a countercoup, along with general violence against the Igbo people living in the northern part of the country, where they were a minority. In September and October 1966, the country saw massive killings of people of Igbo descent, to which this poem clearly refers, since it is published in a section called "October '66" in *Idanre and Other Poems*.

The land in the east had recently been found to be rich in petroleum, and the Igbo people seceded from Nigeria to form a separate country, Biafra. The other two areas refused to accept the secession, and the Nigerian civil war ensued. From 1967, the year that this poem was published, to 1970, the independent country of Biafra tried to stave off attempts to bring it back into the Nigerian nation, insisting that claims about reunion

In stanza 2, the narrator references a gun pointing at his head. (Olga Popova | Shutterstock.com)

from the other states were just veiled excuses to eradicate the Igbo people from the face of the Earth.

In the end, the military forces of Biafra proved too weak to stand against their Nigerian counterparts. Supplies were cut, causing massive starvation. While the suffering in Biafra was publicized throughout the world, other countries failed to send military support. A truce was announced in 1970, and massive government efforts toward reunion were successful, as retaliations from both sides of the conflict against their former enemies were few.

CRITICAL OVERVIEW

Soyinka is best known as a dramatist and essayist. His poetry was not very well known until the 1967 publication of *Idanre and Other Poems*, which included "Civilian and Soldier." This book brought him international recognition as a major poet, and "Civilian and Soldier" is considered one of the best poems in the book. Roderick Wilson, an African critic, stated as much in the conclusion of his essay "Complexity and Confusion in Soyinka's Shorter Poems." "It is a body of work very varied in scope and uneven in achievement, but the best of these poems"—a category in which Wilson adamantly places "Civilian and Soldier"—"dramatically enact their meanings." He notes a relationship between Soyinka's poems and his plays, with both showing "their common basis of complex awareness."

Critics sometimes have problems with the density of Soyinka's word choices. While some view this as just a minor complaint or as not being true at all, most critics see Soyinka's difficult language as a necessity. In "Poetics and the Mythic Imagination" in *Perspectives on Wole Soyinka: Freedom and Complexity*, Stanley Macebuh captures the trouble people have with reading the poet's works when he states that the "language in Soyinka is difficult, harsh, sometimes tortured; his syntax is often archaic, his verbal structures sometimes impenetrable." Like most critics, Macebuh determines that this condition was "nearly inevitable." Many writers over the years have struggled to explain why this is so, but most end up with some variation of Macebuh's observation that Soyinka's problem comes from trying to present the African worldview by writing in English, which makes the poet responsible "not merely [for] articulating African concepts but [for] making them intelligible also to those whose world view has been conditioned by the vision implicit in European languages."

In 1996 Soyinka was awarded the Nobel Prize in Literature. The rationale behind this choice, as stated by the Nobel committee, was that "in a wide cultural perspective and with poetic overtones [he] fashions the drama of existence." The committee thus gave recognition to both his poetic skills and his dramatic vision.

CRITICISM

David Kelly

Kelly is an instructor in creative writing and literature. In the following essay, he examines the use of contradictions in thought and language that Soyinka uses in "Civilian and Soldier" to highlight the irrational nature of war.

It is not unusual for writers to characterize war as insanity. Few books that have discussed war, from *The Iliad* to *Goodbye to All That, Going After Cacciato, Slaughterhouse Five*, and so many more, have been able to avoid the subject. Often, a sense of craziness is used, as it is in the film *Dr. Strangelove*, to contrast the strict order of military organizations. The idea that war leaves behind it a rift in the sensible order of the universe is understandable, because there really is little point in waging war other than to terrorize one's enemy and rend the social fabric.

But along with realistic pieces about the aftereffects of war, there are a fair share of pieces that postulate that it is the very nature of war to contradict sanity. One example of this is Wole Soyinka's poem "Civilian and Soldier." Written in a time of social chaos, when Nigeria was teetering on the edge of the social breakdown that would lead, a few months later, to civil war, the poem dispenses with any political theorizing about justice, vengeance, security, or national identity. It focuses instead on the ways that a war mentality can push two otherwise similar people into becoming representatives of life and death.

The driving force for Soyinka's poem is opposition. The poet uses opposing concepts, words, and psychological states to mirror the violent opposition that is at the heart of all war. Starting with the poem's title, he presents a situation that he later characterizes as a "quandary." Usually, such an unstable situation would be understood to be temporary, but this poem shows clearly how, during war, a quandary can become the norm and can end up being an accepted way of life.

At the core of Soyinka's method of controlled oppositions in this poem is the use of contradictions. The first line establishes this idea with the speaker's apparition rising after he has been felled by bullets. Pairs of opposites, some exact and some implied, occur in practically every line of the poem: these include the civilian who "served" in the second line, the multiple eternities of the seventh line, the "lead festival" which links a killing spree to an outburst of spontaneous joy, and the way that a violent shooting death is said to have gently "twitched" its unarmed victim.

These word choices fit the charge, often made, that Soyinka is a "complex" writer; however, his complexity does not come from a use of unfamiliar, obscure words, but from his reliance on the reader's ability to sniff out multiple meanings of words. The words that contradict each other on one level actually make coherent sense together if the reader is willing to go beyond each word's obvious first sense and find a secondary or tertiary meaning in which the concepts fall into place.

A clear example of his language control is in the poem's last section, in which the speaker imagines running into his killer at some time in the distant future. Both of them are dead in this scenario, which gives the slain civilian the opportunity to turn the tables: since the soldier was trained to distribute death, the speaker imagines it a fitting revenge to expose him to the things of life. In the poem's lexicon of contradiction, though, exposing him becomes "shooting" him, an action that is not expected from the civilian. It is even expected to be a fair, clean shooting, to contrast it with the way soldiers have been trained to treat civilians. The ultimate contradiction here is, of course, that shooting civilians with bullets kills them, while shooting a soldier with images of life makes him live. The soldier's lead bullets provide a hard, concrete image, with no explanation necessary for how they can kill a person, but the images that represent life—wine, bread, breasts—are so abstract that no one could

WHAT DO I READ NEXT?

- The 1958 novel *Things Fall Apart* is considered a masterpiece of modern Nigeria. The story that Igbo author Chinua Achebe tells highlights the way life was in the country before it was colonized by the British in the early 1900s and shows how colonialism changed their world.

- Soyinka is usually associated with his African heritage, but this poem has much in common with British author Thomas Hardy's classic 1902 poem "The Man He Killed," which takes place in the Boer War (1899–1902) and also features a speaker wondering why war sets human beings against one another. It is included in almost every anthology of Hardy's poetry.

- "Civilian and Soldier" is preceded in Soyinka's 1967 book *Idanre and Other Poems* by a poem called "Massacre, October '66," which is more descriptive of the same brutish military action against civilians that is described in "Civilian and Soldier."

- Soyinka's memoir *The Man Died: The Prison Notes of Wole Soyinka*, about his arrest in 1967 and his twenty-two-month imprisonment, is widely considered a modern classic about the political strife of an emerging country.

- In 2000, David Roberts published *Kosovo War Poetry*, a book of poems for young adults about the Kosovo War, another civil war fought between ethnic groups, this time in the Balkan peninsula, formerly Yugoslavia, between people who had been forced to live together after World War I. Roberts's poem "There Will Be No Peace" has a much simpler structure than Soyinka's, but the spirit of both poems is similar.

- French author André Malraux's 1933 novel *Man's Fate*, regarding an incident in the Chinese Revolution, is viewed as one of the great books of the twentieth century. Among other things, it gives readers a sense of how revolutions start and, like Soyinka's poem, it shows the horrors that soldiers can perpetrate on people who had recently been their neighbors.

---

possibly imagine how they could be shot. They are theory, just as life is in this poem, while death is very, very real.

Even when Soyinka is not using images that contrast with one another, the logic that flows through his language leaves openings, forcing readers to stretch their imaginations. The soldier following his mission is presented as having a quarrel with the world; the wounded civilians who cannot be left behind are depicted as having "dubious neutrality"; living is the deceased civilian's trade; murder is impartial. The strongest of these slightly off-kilter phrasings has already been mentioned, the quandary that civilians must cope with when a war situation suddenly engulfs them.

In ordinary discourse, a quandary poses a choice, while death is a one-way proposition. Here, though, as established in the opening lines, death is just a beginning. Rather than being finished, the dead civilian is rising in the first line. His quandary emerges from what he is to do after death, and the answer he reaches is to bide his time, to force life on the soldier in equal measure to that with which the soldier has handed him death.

Soyinka is known for taking an active role in presenting the world with Yoruba thought, which may well be the inspiration for the poem's conceit of the dead interacting with the living. The division between the two realms is not as clear-cut in the Yoruba frame of mind as it is to Westerners. Westerners are used to thinking of a person who talks and interacts with dead people as an extraordinary person with supernatural powers, but such a view is generally put forth in a patronizing

The Yoruba and Igbo fought for control of Nigeria. (Wessel du Plooy | Shutterstock.com)

way; more often than not, a person who claims there is no difference between the living and the dead would be subject to some sort of psychological evaluation to determine what is wrong with them. Folk tradition, however, is very comfortable with seeing the line between the two as open and flexible. The earth is not just for the living in Yoruba culture.

It is even more significant, though, that the poem is doing to readers just what the civilian is planning to do someday to the soldier: it is assaulting their sense of order, forcing them to acknowledge life in places, war zones, where they would otherwise be inclined to see only death. Readers who expect the poems they read to talk to them with a one-way flow of information will come away from "Civilian and Soldier" feeling disappointed. Those readers who are not interested in doing the intellectual work that will take them to understanding, are treating the poem as a dead thing. Of course a poem full of contradictions will confound such readers. But Soyinka's language is too full of self-worth to lie down in the dirt. Like the apparition narrating it, his poem rises up, much to its audience's surprise.

Source: David Kelly, Critical Essay on "Civilian and Soldier," in *Poetry for Students*, Gale, Cengage Learning, 2012.

Elizabeth Heger Boyle

In the following review of The Burden of Memory, the Muse of Forgiveness, *Boyle investigates the importance of symbolism in Soyinka's work, his perception of the relationship between different African groups, and Soyinka's attitude toward South Africa's Truth and Reconciliation Commission.*

Can symbolic gestures organized around notions of human rights have any real impact on power relations in the global system? Specifically, did the South African Truth and Reconciliation Commission (the "Truth Commission") serve any useful function or did it simply placate the "have nots" in South African society? These are some of the core issues in Wole Soyinka's most recent book, *The Burden of Memory, the Muse of Forgiveness*. Soyinka suggests that memory can foster a shared future for divergent cultures and bring globally dispersed black races together. But some memories are better than

> FOR SOYINKA, THE STORY OF THE SOSSO-BALA PROVIDES A GLIMPSE INTO THE POSSIBILITIES OF GLOBAL HARMONY AND HUMANIZED VISION, DESPITE A HISTORY OF BLOODSHED, EXPLOITATION AND DESPAIR."

others according to Soyinka, and the Truth Commission failed both in creating an honest memory of South African history and in providing reparations that would permit the country to enjoy a shared future.

Recent theoretical development in the social sciences provide a backdrop to Soyinka's ideas. Like Soyinka, sociological institutionalists imagine that the international system of sovereign states and ideas of international law are constructed out of a common and universalistic world cultural frame, in other words, a sense of natural law. Unlike Soyinka, institutionalists would emphasize that truth commissions (as well as legal systems in general) are created to reflect these higher Platonic ideals. From the institutionalist perspective, the South African Truth and Reconciliation Commission's failure to right individual wrongs is not surprising nor does it signify failure for the overall project. The Truth Commission linked the voices of victims to the ideals of the international system. Although the victims received minimal immediate compensation for their suffering, their voices have become part of the universal principles that shape action in the international system and serve as a source of identity for individuals and nation-states. In a very profound way, the victims who appeared before the Truth Commission may have empowered other would-be victims.

The Burden of Memory, the Muse of Forgiveness grapples with many themes, from the effectiveness of the South African Truth and Reconciliation Commission to the proper topics of African poetry. The chapters in the book are derived from three lectures that Soyinka gave at the W. E. B. Du Bois Institute at Harvard University. Soyinka's brilliance is particularly evident in the book when he discusses literature. Soyinka won a Nobel Prize for Literature in 1986, and his vivid description and contextual explanations of "Negritude" poetry is inspiring. In the last two chapters of the book, "L. S. Senghor and Negritude—J'accuse, mais, je pardonne" and "Negritude and the Gods of Equity," Soyinka suggests that Negritude poetry can provide a shared space where Africans around the world come together spiritually, understand their shared history, and fashion a shared future.

Soyinka's thoughts on the importance of symbols in international society frame this article. Within this frame, I discuss his ideas on shared identities among black races and the relationship of modern individuals to history. I then discuss his perspective on the South African Truth and Reconciliation Commission, developing the contrast with sociological institutionalism.

MEMORY AND UNITY THROUGH SYMBOLS

The power of memory is beautifully illustrated in the final pages of *The Burden of Memory, the Muse of Forgiveness* in which Soyinka relates an African legend. In 1230, in pre-enslavement, pre-islamic Africa, a war was fought between Soundiata Keita and Soumare Kante, the king of Soso. In a famous battle, Soumare is defeated by Soundiata. As one of the spoils of war, Soundiata attains a little musical instrument called the Sosso-Bala. Legend says that the Sosso-Bala was inspired by genies and endowed with supernatural power. Soundiata entrusted the instrument to his personal poet/storyteller, Bala Fasseke Kouyate. For nearly eight hundred years, the family of Bala Fasseke has held the Sosso-Bala in trust for the descendents of Soundiata Keita. During those eight centuries, the instrument never left the family of Bala Fasseke until very recently, when it was taken to France as part of the ninetieth birthday celebration of the French/Senegalese poet and politician, Léopold Sédar Senghor. The Sosso-Bala had inspired much of Senghor's poetry, and the rare presence of the Sosso-Bala was to provide the climax of a three-day celebration. Soyinka describes the crowd waiting in great anticipation. But the crowning moment was anti-climatic: a musician carried the instrument—a lightweight xylophone made of unpolished wood laid over an array of irregular sized gourds—in under his armpit. The sound was nothing extraordinary, just a crisp, aged tonality.

Soyinka writes:

> Yet there, right before us, lay eight centuries of history, poetry, of pride, inspiration, and sacred heritage. A simple, unassuming xylophone that was, however, born out of conflict, of a bloody

struggle for power and the travails of nation-building, yet innocuous in its appearance, at once an embodiment of history, yet insulated from it.... (p. 191)

As the musician began to play the instrument, the voice of a female storyteller and a choir created a harmony that enfolded the entire gathering in a "mantle of humanity" that "excluded none, neither the colonizers nor the colonized, neither the slavers nor the enslaved, the disdainers or the disdained" (p. 193).

For Soyinka, the story of the Sosso-Bala provides a glimpse into the possibilities of global harmony and humanized vision, despite a history of bloodshed, exploitation and despair. And Soyinka knows about despair—and hope. Exiled from his native Nigeria by the Sani Abacha regime, he campaigned to keep international pressure on efforts to restore democracy there. With Abacha's unexpected death earlier this year, Soyinka was able to return to his home country.

NEGRITUDE POETRY AND AFRICAN IDENTITY

In the chapter devoted to Senghor, Soyinka describes the tensions which brought African-Francophone and African-American poets together but which also set them apart. In both the United States and the French colonies, Africans have the status of "citizens." Despite the equality of status, equality in fact among Africans and Europeans has never been achieved under either system because of discrimination. Nevertheless, the French and American systems contrast with the British system, where no such pretense of equal status was ever entertained. Thus, despite language differences, the similar political structure of the U.S. and France created a shared sense of identity for African poets in those countries.

On the other hand, the history of African-Francophones and African-Americans is very different, and that difference influences the nature of their forward-looking strategies. Soyinka contrasts Martin Luther King with Senghor to illustrate this point. While both King and Senghor advocated nonviolent means of change, King was a self-described extremist who felled his adversaries by adopting the moral high ground on precisely those fields—law and religion—that his adversaries held dear. Soyinka is less sympathetic to Senghor's strategy of forgiveness, which he sees as playing into the French elite condescension toward Africans:

> [Senghor is] Father Confessor who seizes the poetic privilege of presuming the confession of his sinners, treats their mea culpas as already intoned, then grants them absolution. (P. 113)

Ultimately, Soyinka grasps the common ground between King and Senghor—the desire to create a bridge to other cultures and a "tool for the retrieval of dispersed black races anywhere in the world," and this goal is the theme of his third and final chapter. The shared history uncovered in the process of creating this bridge is like the Sosso-Bala: although it includes imperfections and is occasionally mundane, it nevertheless offers an important source of identity and understanding.

RECONCILIATION IN SOUTH AFRICA?

Given Soyinka's insight into the symbolic importance of the mundane Sosso-Bala, his failure to recognize the symbolic importance of the South African Truth and Reconciliation Commission in the first chapter of the book is surprising. The Truth Commission emerged out of the complex negotiations between political parties in South Africa in the early 1990s. It rested on an historical foundation that limited its design and abilities. The two broad purposes of the Truth Commission were to acknowledge and deal with past human rights abuses and to bring closure to the past.

Soyinka highlights three fundamental concerns with the Truth Commission. First, self-confessed criminals were not remorseful. Soyinka and others have noted that some victims were re-traumatized by perpetrators who disclosed their conduct coldly, with arrogance, and without apology. This behavior is sobering and disturbing; but it does not indicate a failure of the entire project. In fact, the stories of the cold-hearted confessions have spread around the globe, illuminating yet again the illegitimacy of the former regime. Indeed, if the ability to evoke remorse was the basis for determining justice, very few modern criminal justice systems would measure up. The value of the Truth Commission lay in its ability to create a sacred space where South Africans in particular, and the international community in general, could express their shared revulsion for those who perpetuated the former exclusionary regime. In other words, the Truth Commission's value should be measured in whether it successfully delegitimated the conduct of the criminals, not whether it reformed them.

Soyinka's second concern is that the Truth Commission is unlikely to have any deterrent effect on other despotic regimes in Africa because it was not sufficiently punitive. That is indisputable, but once again, it does not undermine the overall value of the Truth Commission. Soyinka himself points out that the 1979 bloody coup in Ghana, in which six military officers were publicly executed (as baying students yelled, "Kill! Kill! Blood! Blood! More blood!") was similarly unsuccessful as a deterrent. Those who exercise power with impunity do not identify with fallen regimes—whether the latter regimes are felled in bloody coups or chastised in formal legal proceedings. Again, the important goal of the South African Truth and Reconciliation Commission was to showcase the humanity of the new regime (in a manner consistent with the strategies of Martin Luther King) and to pointedly exclude those who did not share the same vision. The power of its symbolism was concretely demonstrated within South Africa when ANC's rivals, especially the Inkatha Freedom Party, felt compelled to participate in its proceedings. If corrupt leaders refuse to be moved, they solidify their status as outcasts in the international community, a status that has real consequences in terms of international censure.

Soyinka's final concern—that truth was not accompanied by reparation in South Africa—is the most compelling. Here he returns to his tendency to view the world in broad terms and to appreciate the importance of symbols in creating change. He links reparations in South Africa to African mobilization for reparations generally. In the period since Soyinka's speeches were delivered, the request for reparations has been somewhat successful. For example, a bill currently pending in the U.S. Congress would make U.S. support to the International Monetary Fund contingent on limited loan forgiveness to "heavily indebted poor countries" (H.R. 1305, Debt Forgiveness Act of 1999). While there is still much to be done in this regard, the reparations movement does have a voice in the international system and demonstrates how symbols that draw distinctions between justice and injustice can have real consequences.

THE ROLE OF SYMBOLS IN GLOBAL SOCIETY

The implicit goal of the South African Truth and Reconciliation Commission was to define the future of South African society in terms of general human rights principles. Because the Truth Commission was more a reflection than an instrument of these principles, it was from the beginning unlikely to have great direct influence on social conditions in Africa. This "decoupling" between symbol (international discourse) and action (the actual implementation of policy) in South Africa and elsewhere has generated much controversy and consternation. The essence of decoupling is supporting an ideal but failing to carry out the ideal in day-to-day business and activities. Why does decoupling occur and to what extent does it undermine the overall international project of promoting human rights?

There are at least two explanations for why symbol and action were decoupled in the case of the South African Truth and Reconciliation Commission. First, conflicts that can be evaded at the discursive level must be dealt with concretely when a bureaucracy (such as the Truth Commission) tries to implement an ideal. For example, the members of the Truth Commission felt they had to remain impassive even during the cold-hearted recitations of wrongs alluded to earlier, because if they appeared biased the National Party would withdraw its support from the proceedings. Concrete conflicts, such as these, force a decoupling between the perfect ideal of what the Truth Commission ought to have done and what in fact it reasonably could do. Further, the ambiguity of its goals also increased the likelihood that the Truth Commission would have difficulty linking symbol and action. While very concrete and measurable requests must be rejected outright or adopted—they leave little room for purely ceremonial adoption—moral requests or outcomes that are difficult to assess are more likely to receive formal support but be informally ignored. Because the existence of the Truth Commission was highly negotiated, more specificity in its goals was never a realistic option.

This "decoupling" between symbol and action on the Truth Commission is reasonably taken by Soyinka and others to indicate the ineffectiveness of the Commission. But there is reason to be more optimistic. Despite the practical constraints and limitations of the local reality, the South African Truth and Reconciliation Commission illuminated and empowered perspectives that had been silenced under apartheid. The Truth Commission, while itself derived from the principle of human rights, also fed back into the international system to increase the legitimacy of the human rights message and to make that principle accessible to more individuals. Other truth commissions established after South Africa's can learn concrete lessons from the South African experience while enjoying greater legitimacy (and hence power to make changes) because they follow a model pre-established in South Africa and other countries.

The South African Truth and Reconciliation Commission is part of symbolic rites of passage that make it impossible for South Africa to return to the apartheid system. Such actions at the national level reinforce the legitimacy of the human rights ideals promoted by the international system. Soyinka is correct to be skeptical, in part because the international system that fuels truth commissions and similar reforms is hegemonic and Western in its orientation. Nevertheless, the international system puts real weight behind symbolic action, and in that way empowers an extraordinary range of formerly powerful, but also formerly powerless, individuals. Like the Sosso-Bala, in Soyinka's story truth commissions, in South Africa and elsewhere, have the potential to be profound, but even when mundane, provide a source of identity and shared understanding around the world.

Source: Elizabeth Heger Boyle, "Gesture without Motion? Poetry and Politics in Africa," in *Human Rights Review*, Vol. 2, No. 1, October/December 2000, pp. 134–39.

SOURCES

Falola, Toyin, *The History of Nigeria*, Greenwood Press, 1999, pp. xv-xvi, 15–40.

———, and Matthew M. Heaton, *A History of Nigeria*, Cambridge University Press, 2008, pp. 159, 175–80.

Macebuh, Stanley, "Poetics and the Mythic Imagination," in *Perspectives on Wole Soyinka: Freedom and Complexity*, edited by Biodun Jeyifo, University Press of Mississippi, 2001, p. 31.

Msiska, Mpalive-Hangson, *Wole Soyinka*, Northcote House, 1998, pp. 1–3.

Ojaide, Tanure, *The Poetry of Wole Soyinka*, Malthouse Press, 1994, pp. 5–7, 57–58.

Soyinka, Wole, "Civilian and Soldier," in *The Poetry of Our World: An International Anthology of Contemporary Poetry*, edited by Jeffery Paine, HarperCollins, 2002, p. 372.

Wilson, Roderick, "Complexity and Confusion in Soyinka's Shorter Poems," in *Critical Perspectives on Wole Soyinka*, edited by James Gibbs, Three Continents Press, 1980, p. 168.

"Wole Soyinka—Biography," in *Nobelprize.org*, http://nobelprize.org/nobel_prizes/literature/laureates/1986/soyinka.html (accessed July 1, 2011).

FURTHER READING

Irele, F. Abiola, "The Achievement of Wole Soyinka," in *Philosophia Africana*, Vol. 2, No. 1, March 2008, pp. 5–19.

Abiola's essay gives an overview of Soyinka's career, focusing on the artistic criteria of language and form.

Jeyifo, Biodun, ed., *Conversations with Wole Soyinka*, University Press of Mississippi, 2001.

Starting with a televised panel discussion between Soyinka, Chinua Achebe, and Kofi Awoonor in 1973, and continuing chronologically to a news interview in 1998, this book shows Soyinka in his own words, thinking and talking and explaining his life.

———, *Wole Soyinka: Politics, Poetics, and Postcolonialism*, Cambridge University Press, 2004.

Biodun's study focuses on the radical politics that have marked Soyinka's writings throughout his career, showing a level of intensity that literary analyses sometimes fail to appreciate.

Msiska, Mpalive-Hangson, *Postcolonial Identity in Wole Soyinka*, Rodopi, 2007.

This study is interesting for the way that it uses one particular aspect, postcolonialism, to tie together Soyinka's work in drama, poetry, fiction, and, of course, biography.

Soyinka, Wole, "Nobel Lecture 1986: This Past Must Address Its Present," in *Wole Soyinka: An Appraisal*, edited by Adewale Maja-Pearce, Heinemann Books, 1994, pp. 1–22.

Readers of Soyinka's Nobel Prize speech can see how his values have remained unchanged through the years. At the height of his career as a writer, the focus is kept on the voiceless victims that he has always sought to represent.

Uzokwe, Alfred Obiora, *Surviving in Biafra: The Story of the Nigerian Civil War*, Writers Advantage, 2003.

Rather than a scholarly history of the conflict, Uzokwe presents his personal experiences as a child who survived in the war zone. His perspective gives readers more of a feeling for what it was like there than most historical documents tend to do.

SUGGESTED SEARCH TERMS

Wole Soyinka

Wole Soyinka AND Civilian and Soldier

Wole Soyinka AND Yoruba

Wole Soyinka AND *Idanre*

Wole Soyinka AND Nobel Prize

Nigeria AND October 1966

Biafra

Nigerian civil war

Nigeria AND genocide

Nigeria AND poetry

War AND apparition

Defining the Grateful Gesture

YVONNE SAPIA

1987

"Defining the Grateful Gesture" is a poem by American author Yvonne Sapia. It was first published in the *Americas Review* in 1987. This poem and other poems by Sapia reflect her experiences as the daughter of Puerto Rican immigrant parents. Sapia has been regarded as an important voice in both contemporary immigrant literature and literature by women of color, and her work is widely included in anthologies of literature that reflect these interests.

In "Defining the Grateful Gesture," she comments on the hard work of her parents and the role of food in the family. Food is a precious resource, something that is in short supply for some people. The poet's mother insists that she and her siblings express gratitude for the food they have, but, as the poem suggests, youngsters often fail to understand the wisdom of their parents. Ultimately, the poem is about the tension between immigrant parents and their assimilating children.

Sapia is not only an award-winning poet but also a novelist and teacher. She is the author of a novel and a poetry collection, both titled *Valentino's Hair*, and for more than three decades she has been a professor of English at Florida's Lake City Community College, now called Florida Gateway College, where she also serves as poet in residence.

AUTHOR BIOGRAPHY

Sapia was born on April 10, 1946, in New York, New York. Her father, Facundo Pedro, worked as a barber. Her mother, Antonia, worked as a homemaker. In the 1920s, the family moved from Puerto Rico to the United States, where Facundo acquired some wealth but lost it in the stock market crash of 1929. Sapia attended Miami-Dade Community College in Florida, earning an associate's degree in 1967. She completed a bachelor's degree at Florida Atlantic University in 1970. Early in her career she was a journalist, working as a reporter for the *Village Post* in Miami from 1971 to 1973. She then worked as an editorial assistant at the University of Florida while completing her master of fine arts degree in creative writing in 1976. That year, she took a position teaching English at Lake City Community College in Lake City, Florida, and she has remained on the faculty there ever since. (The college changed its name to Florida Gateway College in 2008.) In the years that followed, she was able to study for her doctorate, earning the degree from Florida State University in 1990.

In 1983, Sapia published her first collection of poems, *The Fertile Crescent*. In 1987, "Defining the Grateful Gesture" appeared in the *Americas Review*, and in that year, Sapia published a second collection, *Valentino's Hair*. In 1991, she published a novel with the same title, *Valentino's Hair*. Both are based on a story her father told her about an occasion when he had cut the hair of silent-film heartthrob Rudolph Valentino shortly before the actor's death, then kept the hair clippings as a talisman, or charm.

Sapia has served as a fellow in the state of Florida's Division of Cultural Affairs and the Florida Fine Arts Council and a fellow for the National Endowment for the Arts. *The Fertile Crescent* won the Poetry Chapbook Award from Florida State University in 1983. She was a Walt Whitman Award finalist in 1985 and 1986, and the collection *Valentino's Hair* won the Samuel French Morse Poetry Prize from Northwestern University Press in 1987. The novel *Valentino's Hair* won the Nilon Award for excellence in minority fiction and was cited as a best book of 1991 by *Publishers Weekly*. Through the years she has contributed poems, articles, and reviews to such publications as *Pacific Review*, *Apalachee Quarterly*, *Panhandler*, *Partisan Review*, *Prairie Schooner*, *Southern Review*, and *Americas Review*. Beginning in 1994, she became a contributing editor of *Kalliope* and a member of the board of directors of Anhinga Press.

POEM TEXT

```
According to our mother,
when she was a child
what was placed before her
for dinner was not a feast,
but she would eat it                              5
to gain back the strength
taken from her by long hot days
of working in her mother's house
and helping her father make
candy in the family kitchen.                      10
No idle passenger
Traveling through life was she.

And that's why she resolved
to tell stories about
the appreciation for satisfied hunger.            15
When we would sit down
for our evening meal
of arroz con pollo
or frijoles negros con plátanos
she would expect us                               20
to be reverent to the sources
of our undeserved nourishment
and to strike a thankful pose
before each lift of the fork
or swirl of the spoon.                            25

For the dishes she prepared,
we were ungrateful,
she would say, and repeat
her archetypal tale about the Pérez
brothers who stumbled over themselves             30
with health in her girlhood town
of Ponce, looking like ripe mangoes,
their cheeks rosed despite poverty.

My mother would then tell us about the day
she saw Mrs. Pérez searching                      35
the neighborhood garbage,
picking out with a missionary's care
the edible potato peels, the plantain skins,
the shafts of old celery to take
home to her muchachos                             40
who required more food
than she could afford.

Although my brothers and I
never quite mastered the ritual
of obedience our mother craved,                   45
and as supplicants failed
to feed her with our worthiness,
we'd sit like solemn loaves of bread,
sighing over the white plates
with a sense of realization, or relief,           50
guilty about possessing appetite.
```

POEM SUMMARY

The text used for this summary is from *The Woman That I Am: The Literature and Culture of Contemporary Women of Color*, edited by D. Soyini Madison, St. Martin's Press, 1997, pp. 135–36.

Stanza 1

The poem consists of four stanzas of irregular length. In the first stanza, the poet makes clear that she is in a sense speaking both for herself and her siblings by referring to *our* mother (not "my" mother). The mother had told the children that when she was a child, dinner was not a feast but rather something she ate to recoup her energy and strength after spending long days in the heat working in her (the poet's) grandmother's house and helping her father make candy at the table in the kitchen. She concludes the stanza by stating that her mother was not idle as she traveled through life.

Stanza 2

In the second stanza, the poet notes that her mother would often tell stories about food and eating. The poet and her siblings would sit down for their evening meal, often consisting of such dishes as arroz con pollo (chicken cooked with rice, onions, tomatoes, and garlic) or frijoles negros con plátanos (black beans with plantains). The mother would then expect that the children show reverence for their nourishment, which, the mother said, they did not deserve. The children were expected to adopt a pose indicating that they were thankful for the food and that they were to do so with each fork- or spoonful.

Stanza 3

In the third stanza, the poet admits that she and her siblings were not very grateful for the food their mother prepared. This lack of gratitude would prompt the mother to tell once again a tale about the Pérez brothers from her childhood home, Ponce (the second-largest city in Puerto Rico). The Pérez brothers looked healthy and had rosy cheeks, despite the family's poverty.

Stanza 4

The fourth stanza continues the story of the Pérez family. The poet's mother would recount the time when she saw Mrs. Pérez going through neighborhood garbage looking for bits of food that she could serve to her *muchachos* (boys or young men), including such discarded items as potato peelings, the skins of plantains, and stalks of old celery. The mother would make clear that Mrs. Pérez could not afford to feed her boys the amount of food they needed. The poet and her siblings, however, were apparently unmoved by this story, for she says that they never were able to comply with their mother's wishes that they show reverence for the food before them. The children would simply sit and sigh over their plates, realizing that they felt both relief and guilt about having an appetite for their food.

THEMES

Hispanic American Culture

"Defining the Grateful Gesture" clearly reflects Hispanic American culture, although no reader would recognize this throughout the first stanza. In the second stanza, however, the poet makes reference to dishes common in the Hispanic community, including arroz con pollo (a chicken dish) and frijoles negros (black beans) with plátanos, or plantains (a fruit similar to a banana but firmer and with a lower sugar content). Plantains are a staple in the diet of people from the Caribbean and other Spanish-speaking cultures (as well as in some African nations). The poet also makes reference to her mother's story about the Pérez family in Ponce, a city in southern Puerto Rico, where the mother had apparently lived before coming to the United States. These details support the poem's depiction of Hispanic American culture.

Immigrant Life

Closely related to the theme of Hispanic American culture is that of immigrant life. "Defining the Grateful Gesture" does not explicitly comment on the life of immigrants to the United States, but the theme is implicit in the poem's subject matter. The poem sets up a contrast between life in the United States and life in Puerto Rico, the homeland of the poet's parents and grandparents. The poem emphasizes how hard the poet's mother and grandparents had to work and how eating was seen as a way of regaining strength after work. The references to the Pérez brothers and Mrs. Pérez in Ponce, Puerto Rico, underline the poverty that many people would have experienced on the island. In contrast, the United States appears to be more of a land of plenty. The poet's mother is able to

TOPICS FOR FURTHER STUDY

- Sapia makes reference to specific foods common in Hispanic communities. Find a cookbook of Hispanic foods or perhaps a collection of online recipes. You might begin with *A Taste of Latino Cultures: Un Toque de Sabor Latino: A Bilingual, Educational Cookbook* by George Kunzel and published by Libraries Unlimited in 2005. Post these recipes on your social-networking site and invite your classmates to comment on whether they have ever sampled similar foods and whether they liked them. If you are adventurous, you might even arrange to cook one or more of these foods for your classmates.

- Conduct Internet and traditional research on Puerto Rico's relationship with the United States. How did the United States acquire Puerto Rico as a territory? What status does Puerto Rico, and Puerto Ricans, have in the U.S. system of government? Are Puerto Ricans U.S. citizens? Why has Puerto Rico not been admitted to the United States as a state in the same way that the territories of Hawaii and Alaska were? In what sense are people who move from Puerto Rico to the U.S. mainland "immigrants"? A good place to start your research might be "Puerto Rican Immigrants: A Resource Guide for Teachers and Students" published at Fitchburg State University and available online (http://www.fitchburgstate.edu/tah/documents/PuertoRicans.pdf). Summarize your findings in an interactive time line with links to information about the history of Puerto Rico and its relationship with the United States.

- The immigrant experience of Puerto Ricans in the United States is unique because Puerto Ricans are technically U.S. citizens, yet they have sometimes been divided from the mainland by language and culture. Conduct research on the Puerto Rican immigrant experience in the United States. You might start with two books by Juan Flores: *Divided Arrival: Narratives of the Puerto Rican Migration, 1920–1950* (published by Markus Wiener in 2003) and *Divided Borders: Essays on Puerto Rican Identity* (published by Arte Publico Press, 1992). Share your findings in an oral report to your classmates. Enhance your report with a PowerPoint presentation of images of Puerto Rican communities in the United States.

- As a point of comparison, locate a nonfiction book titled *A Country Called Amreeka: Arab Roots, American Stories* by Alia Malek (published by Free Press in 2009). The book chronicles the immigrant experience of Arab Muslims in the United States during the period after the September 11, 2001, terrorist attacks. Having sampled the book, write a script in which you imagine a Puerto Rican immigrant and an Arab Muslim immigrant sharing their experiences in the United States with each other. With the help of a classmate, perform your script for your class or post it to YouTube or your Web page. Invite your teacher and classmates to review your short play.

- Gary Soto is a prominent Hispanic author of young-adult fiction, much of it set in California. His collection of short stories, *Baseball in April and Other Stories*, was published in 2000 by Houghton Mifflin Harcourt. Read one or more stories in the collection—such as "Broken Chain"—and write an essay in which you compare and contrast the Hispanic immigrant experience as reflected in the story you chose and in "Defining the Grateful Gesture."

---

place before her children good, hearty foods, but the children, who did not know the poverty of their parents' childhood, lack appreciation for the food. They are unable to summon the gratitude their mother would like them to feel. Perhaps this theme is Sapia's comment on how

The poem is about the role of the kitchen in the family of the narrator. (Monkey Business Images / Shutterstock.com)

the immigrant experience changes people; parents remember the hardships of life before coming to the United States (as represented by Mrs. Pérez scouring for scraps of food), but their children, accustomed to life in the new country, can sometimes fail to appreciate what they have.

Mother-Child Relationships

A third theme, mother-child relationships, is closely connected to the themes of Hispanic American culture and immigrant life. The poem invites the reader to picture the situation: An immigrant mother is in her kitchen, preparing food for her children. She remembers the poverty of her childhood, as well as the poverty experienced by other people in Puerto Rico. She wants her children to exhibit gratitude for the plenty she is able to put before them, but the children are unable to see the world in the same terms. They take the food placed before them for granted. The reader can almost imagine the children rolling their eyes in annoyance, as if to say, "Here she goes again, telling the same old stories about her childhood and her own mother and the people she knew in Puerto Rico." In their view, these stories have no relevance to their lives. Like children everywhere, they go through a period in which they reject the values of their parents. However, the mere fact that Sapia wrote the poem indicates that with the passage of time, she has gained a perspective more in line with her mother's. Only now does she seem to realize that her mother was right, and she indicates this by memorializing her mother through the act of writing the poem.

STYLE

Free Verse

"Defining the Grateful Gesture" is written in free verse, meaning that the poem does not make use of conventional rhyme schemes or metrical devices. Typically, poets who employ free verse still impose on the poetry a sense of the line, and "Defining the Grateful Gesture" is composed of lines that are relatively short. Most contain no more than three stressed syllables, although a few of the lines contain four and even five stressed syllables. The use of free verse in this poem gives it a conversational tone. The poet is telling a story based on recollection and therefore does not want to be bound by traditional forms and metrical devices, which would give the poem a formality that would not be in keeping with her message.

Narrative Poetry

"Defining the Grateful Gesture" is an example of a narrative poem, that is, a poem that tells a story or narrates a sequence of events. Narrative poetry stands in contrast to lyric poetry, which is usually more in the nature of an outpouring of an emotional response to something such as love or the natural world. Narrative poems traditionally have been lengthy, almost novel-like. Good examples include the ancient epics *The Iliad* and *The Odyssey* by Homer. Many narrative poems have been constructed around historical events or around legends such as the legends of King Arthur. This poem, however, is structured around events that took place in the home. The emphasis is not on a particular event but rather on a pattern of repeated events, all revolving around a mother's efforts to persuade her children to express gratitude for the food placed before them and to recognize that people in Puerto Rico might not enjoy the plenty that American life holds. Thus, the poem tells a story, but the story is an amalgamation of numerous, repeated events of a similar nature that took place over time, as indicated by the repeated use of the word "would."

Literal Language

Poetry is most often associated with figurative language, including such figures of speech as similes and metaphors, as well as with patterns of sound created by meter and such devices as alliteration, rhyme, assonance, and consonance. "Defining the Grateful Gesture," however, is made up primarily of literal language, that is, language that emphasizes the denotation of words rather than their connotations. Consider, for example, the first ten lines of the poem. In these lines, the author literally comments on her mother, her mother's childhood, the dinners that were placed before her mother, her days working with her own mother in the home, and her time helping her father make candy in the family kitchen. These lines make no use of poetic devices; they are a literal, factual rendering of events. Only with lines 11 and 12 does the reader encounter language that is slightly more figurative when the mother is compared to a passenger traveling through life. This emphasis on literal language continues through the poem as the poet tells her story. Two noteworthy instances of figurative language are used when the poet compares the faces of the Pérez brothers to ripe mangoes and when she compares herself and her siblings to solemn loaves of bread. Figurative language is also used to give the poem a kind of religious atmosphere, but the poem does not emphasize figurative language. The language is more denotative, perhaps fitting with the author's purpose of narrating a story whose lesson becomes apparent through the details of the events rather than through the author's having filtered and embellished them through the more typical language of poetry.

Tone

Related to the stylistic issues of narrative and literal language is tone. Tone is the sometimes indefinable sense the reader has about the author's attitude to what is being said; sometimes, in dramatic poems (poems spoken by a "character" the author has created), the tone is a reflection of the character's attitude rather than the author's. A poet, for example, can adopt a wistful tone or a tone of indignation, exhilaration, sorrow, regret, anticipation, and numerous other emotions. Some poems adopt a highly formal tone that distances the reader, while others adopt a more intimate, perhaps even playful tone as a way of connecting with the reader in a more direct way.

While different readers might respond to "Defining the Grateful Gesture" in different ways, one way of describing the tone of this poem is that it is matter of fact. It is almost as though the poet expresses no attitude toward the events she is narrating. The language of the poem is very literal; few of the poet's word choices seem designed to guide the reader to an appreciation of a particular tone of voice. Some readers might even characterize the tone of this poem as listless, slightly languid, or lethargic. It is not a poem that arouses the passions or that creates a particular aesthetic response, but again the adoption of this kind of tone is likely part of the author's strategy.

The narrated events speak for themselves. The characters in the poem, particularly the children, experience no epiphany, no moment of realization or insight. They sit, inert, like loaves of bread, as they listen to their mother, who demands that they respond to their meal in a certain way but whose demands meet with no success. Only much later, as the poet reflects on the events of her childhood, is she able to see their significance and perhaps see matters from her mother's point of view. By presenting the reader with the events as she experienced them in childhood, without comment or embellishment and in a largely neutral tone, the poet is able to allow the reader to arrive at an appropriate conclusion about her relationship with her mother and her relationship with the Hispanic community of which she is a part.

HISTORICAL CONTEXT

"Defining the Grateful Gesture" makes no reference to specific historical events. It was published, however, in the context of a time when Hispanic Americans, and particularly Hispanic American women, were becoming more visible in the public sphere. For example, in September 1983, President Ronald Reagan appointed Katherine Devalos Ortega to the position of treasurer of the United States. (This position is to be distinguished from the secretary of the Treasury, a cabinet-level position.) Traditionally, the U.S. treasurer has handled the receipt and disbursement of federal funds, but in recent years the treasurer's duties have included oversight of the Bureau of Engraving and Printing and of the U.S. Mint. Ortega served under Reagan and his successor, George H. W. Bush, until 1989; she went on to become the first female bank president in the state of California. Latina women have continued to hold the position of treasurer. Catalina Vasquez Villalpando served under President George H. W. Bush; Rosario Marin, a native of Mexico, served under President George W. Bush, to be succeeded by Anna Escobedo Cabral. Under President Barack Obama, Rosa Gumataotao Rios has served as U.S. treasurer.

The early 1980s also witnessed significant advances for women of all ethnicities. A key event occurred on June 18, 1983, when astronaut Sally Ride became the first American woman to travel into space, and just two years earlier, on September 21, 1981, the U.S. Senate unanimously confirmed Reagan's nomination of Sandra Day O'Connor as the nation's first female Supreme Court justice. Further, just a year later, in 1984, Democratic presidential candidate Walter Mondale selected Geraldine Ferraro as his vice presidential running mate, the first woman to appear on the presidential ticket of a major political party. In Great Britain, Margaret Thatcher achieved worldwide prominence as the nation's first female prime minister, serving from 1979 to 1990.

In connection with Ortega's appointment as U.S. treasurer in 1983, President Reagan proclaimed National Hispanic Heritage Month, which runs from September 15 to October 15. In 1968, President Lyndon Johnson had proclaimed National Hispanic Heritage Week, but Reagan expanded the observance, which celebrates the history and contributions of Americans whose ancestors immigrated to the United States from Spain, Central America, South America, and the Caribbean. Reagan's proclamation later became law on August 17, 1988. The dates for National Hispanic Heritage Month are significant, for they encompass several historically important dates. September 15 is celebrated as Independence Day in Costa Rica, El Salvador, Guatemala, Nicaragua, and Honduras, while Mexico celebrates its independence on September 16 and Chile on September 18. Additionally, Dia de la Raza ("Race Day") corresponds with the celebration of Columbus Day on October 12; this holiday is designed to call attention to the varied ethnic makeup of the Americas.

In 2011, the issue of illegal immigration to the United States, principally by people from Mexico and Central America, remains widely debated. The issue was on the front burner of public discussion in the 1980s as well. Reagan wanted to control illegal immigration, but at the same time he wanted to face the reality that millions of illegal immigrants lived in the United States, and the likelihood that even a small percentage of them would be sent back to their native countries was equally small. The result was the passage of the Immigration Reform and Control Act of 1986. One purpose of the law was to curtail illegal immigration by requiring employers to verify the eligibility of employees to work in the United States. It was expected that this requirement would affect large numbers of agricultural workers, particularly migrant farm workers. Another, more controversial provision of the law was to give illegal aliens the opportunity to apply for amnesty and remain in the United States legally. Those who wanted to seek amnesty had until May 4, 1988, to apply. As a result of the law, nearly three million illegal immigrants—again, a large percentage of them from Mexico and Central America—were granted amnesty in the United States.

COMPARE & CONTRAST

- **1980s:** The United States begins to climb out of a steep recession, with high unemployment and high inflation that persisted throughout much of the 1970s and continue into the early 1980s. Causing the recession in part are high and escalating energy prices.

   Today: The United States is once again mired in recession, with high unemployment and signs of impending inflation. The recession began in 2008 with a sharp decline in the stock market and the bursting of a housing "bubble" during which many Americans see the value of their homes decline precipitously.

- **1980s:** A significant segment of the Puerto Rican immigrant population—about 986,000 people—lives in New York City. Florida ranks fifth among U.S. states with about 95,000 Puerto Rican immigrants.

   Today: Although New York continues to be home to the largest number of Puerto Rican immigrants to the U.S. mainland, Florida moves into second place. As of the early 2000s, estimates are that about 3.8 million people of Puerto Rican descent live on the U.S. mainland.

- **1980s:** President Ronald Reagan proclaims a National Hispanic Heritage Month.

   Today: The theme for National Hispanic Heritage Month in 2010 is "Heritage, Diversity, Integrity and Honor: The Renewed Hope of America."

- **1980s:** Singers José Feliciano and Roy Brown are two among many popular musicians of Puerto Rican descent.

   Today: As of mid-2011, the winner of the singing competition on the popular television program *American Idol* is Scotty McCreery, a country-western singer of partial Puerto Rican descent. Actress/singer Jennifer Lopez is also of Puerto Rican ancestry.

CRITICAL OVERVIEW

Although her work has garnered praise, Sapia is not a major American poet, so her work has not been widely reviewed, particularly in major publications. However, a good example of the reactions of critics to her work can be found in a review of her poetry collection, *Valentino's Hair*, by M. Gillan and published in *Choice*. Gillan is effusive, writing that the poems are written "in a voice vibrant and singular." Gillan also refers to Sapia's "strong, musical language" and says that "the family poems are powerful and ... memorable." The review concludes by writing that "the poems are rich with intense detail and refreshing in their originality."

Sapia's novel, *Valentino's Hair*, actually attracted more attention from reviewers. Janet Ingraham, writing in *Library Journal*, calls the novel "passionate and compact" and then "elegant and strange yet accessible." A *Publishers Weekly* contributor, in a review of *Valentino's Hair*, reports that Sapia "burrows inside the skin of her characters, making them believable." *Publishers Weekly* admired the book so much that it named it one of its "Best Books of 1991."

CRITICISM

Michael J. O'Neal

O'Neal holds a Ph.D. in English. In the following essay, he examines the religious connotations of "Defining the Grateful Gesture."

In chapter 16 of the Gospel of Luke (verses 19–31), Jesus narrates the parable of Dives and Lazarus, a parable that does not appear in the other three gospels. (As a side note, some biblical scholars argue that the story is not a parable but rather a narration of an actual event, but for our

In stanza 4, the narrator describes how the neighbor got ingredients for meals from other people's garbage. (Sam72 | Shutterstock.com)

purposes, the distinction is not important.) Dives seems to be the *name* of a rich man, but in fact, in Hebrew, the word *dives* means "rich man." Lazarus, on the other hand is a poor beggar. (One more side note: This Lazarus is not to be confused with the Lazarus whom Jesus raises from the dead in Chapter 11 of the Gospel of John.) In the parable, Dives sits at his table, dressed in purple—traditionally the color of royalty and wealth—and enjoying the good things of life. Each day he feasts magnificently. Outside is Lazarus, who is covered in sores and lives on the crumbs that fall from the rich man's table. The parable goes on to explain that both men die. Lazarus is sent to Abraham's embrace, or heaven. The rich man, who ignored Lazarus, is sent to Hades, where he suffers the torments of hell. The parable is a call to repentance and illustrates God's wish that those with plenty share with those in need. It calls to mind the famous biblical quotation, found in the Gospel of Matthew (Chapter 19) and the Gospel of Mark (Chapter 10), to the effect that it is easier for a camel to pass through the eye of a needle than for a rich man to enter the kingdom of heaven.

"Defining the Grateful Gesture" does not explicitly retell the parable of the rich man and Lazarus, but in Catholic Hispanic culture, and among Christians generally, the parable is part of a cultural inheritance, the belief that riches can have a corrupting effect on people. It comes as little surprise, then, that Sapia would draw on the contrast between rich and poor in her poem. "The poor" are represented by the Pérez family in Ponce, Puerto Rico, the girlhood hometown of the poet's mother. Pérez, a common Hispanic surname, has an interesting history. The name actually appears in the Bible and is derived from the name Peter, referring to Christ's apostle, the "Rock," on whom Christ founded the Christian church. In effect, Peter was the first pope. The name Pérez spread widely, entering Spain from Morocco during the Middle Ages. It then spread throughout Europe and is thus related to numerous given names such as Peter, Pieter, Peers, and Pierre, and to such surnames as Petre, Petres, Peters, and Peterson. Thus, by selecting the name Pérez, Sapia sees the family in Puerto Rico as a kind of biblical "everyman," a representative of people everywhere and perhaps of the millions

WHAT DO I READ NEXT?

- Judith Ortiz Cofer is the author of *An Island Like You: Stories of the Barrio* (1995). The stories for young adults chronicle the lives of Puerto Rican teenagers in New Jersey as they come of age and develop a sense of cultural and personal identity.

- Barbara Garland Polikoff is the author of *Why Does the Coquí Sing?*, published by Holiday House in 2004 for a young-adult audience. The novel is about "reverse migration," that is, about Puerto Ricans who move back to the island from the mainland—in this case, from Chicago. When a young girl returns with her family to Puerto Rico, she is reluctant, and she feels like an outsider. Over time, though, she begins to appreciate her new homeland.

- Readers interested in nonfiction accounts of life in America as a Puerto Rican immigrant will enjoy the autobiographical essays in *A Puerto Rican in New York, and Other Sketches* by Jesus Colon, originally published in 1961 but available in a more recent edition published by International Publishers in 1982.

- Julia Alvarez is the author of *How the Garcia Girls Lost Their Accents*, published by Algonquin Books of Chapel Hill in 1991. The sequence of tales, narrated in reverse from adulthood to childhood, tells the story of four sisters who settled in New York City after their family had fled the Dominican Republic. The focus is on their rebellion against their immigrant parents.

- Yvonne Sapia's "Grandmother, a Caribbean Indian, Described by My Father" is a poem available in *Unsettling America: An Anthology of Contemporary Multicultural Poetry*, edited by Maria M. Gillan and Jennifer Gillan and published by Penguin Books in 1994.

- Lori M. Carlson is the editor of a 1994 collection, *American Eyes: New Asian-American Short Stories for Young Adults*, published by Fawcett Juniper. This volume is a collection of short stories about young Asian Americans, focusing on their home life. The characters wrestle with their different cultures and wonder how and where they fit in.

- Readers interested in a nonfiction account of the Puerto Rican immigrant experience written for young adults might start with *The Puerto Rican Americans* by Jerome J. Aliotta and Sandra Stotsky and published by Chelsea House in 1995.

- *Red Hot Salsa: Bilingual Poems on Being Young and Latino in the United States* is a collection of poems for young adults assembled by Lori Marie Carlson and published by Henry Holt in 2005. The collection includes a variety of Latino poets whose work illustrates the difficulties of having one foot in each of two cultures and languages. The poems celebrate love, food, family, and achievement.

- *Strange Objects*, by Australian writer Gary Crew, is a historical novel published in 1990. It depicts a very different type of immigrant experience, that of the earliest white settlers of Australia and their encounters with the aboriginal people of the continent.

---

of poorer people who can be found throughout the world.

The family depicted in the poem, including the poet herself, her siblings, and her mother, are not explicitly rich. The poem does suggest, however, that they are comfortable. Emphasis is placed on the hard work in the old country, but that hard, exhausting work was of another time, another place. Now the mother is able to serve rich, nourishing foods to her children on white plates—a detail that suggests that the plates are likely china and not coarse stoneware. The children, however,

> THROUGH ITS USE OF THESE SUBTLE REFERENCES, 'DEFINING THE GRATEFUL GESTURE' NARRATES A TYPE OF RELIGIOUS EXPERIENCE, OR AT LEAST AN EXPERIENCE WITH STRONG RELIGIOUS CONNOTATIONS."

do not appreciate the food, at least not to the extent that the mother would prefer. The mother repeatedly has to tell the children about the hardships of the old country and remind them of Mrs. Pérez, who had to rummage for scraps of food she could give to her boys, just as Lazarus had to survive from the crumbs that fell from the rich man's table. The mother wants the children to be grateful, as the poem's title indicates, and she wants them to make "gestures" that indicate their gratitude. The children, however, perhaps like Dives of the parable, cannot bring themselves to accede to their mother's wishes.

The language of the poem reinforces its religious connotations. The children are expected to be reverent. Mrs. Pérez is said to pick through garbage, looking for scraps of food with a level of care described as that of a missionary. The poet refers to mealtime as a ritual, as though mealtime were a religious observance, and she describes herself and her siblings as supplicants, a word often used in religious contexts (along with a variant spelling, suppliants) to refer to those who pray, especially those who ask forgiveness from God. Even such details as their solemnity (a word commonly used to mean something like "serious" but originally used to describe a formal observance or religious rite) and their feeling of guilt suggest a religious reaction to the meal and to their mother's stories. The reference to the loaves of bread echoes the biblical parable of the loaves and the fishes, recounted in all four of the gospels of the New Testament (the books of Matthew, Mark, Luke, and John). The essence of the parable is that Christ was miraculously able to feed a multitude with just a handful of loaves of bread and fishes, suggesting that plenty comes from the hand and mercy of God.

Through its use of these subtle references, "Defining the Grateful Gesture" narrates a type of religious experience, or at least an experience with strong religious connotations. In the culture from which Sapia drew her values and beliefs, a meal is not just a process of "chowing down," and a true meal does not come from the nearest pizza parlor or fast-food joint. A meal is something that is lovingly prepared in the home. It reflects the values and traditions of a person's heritage, as suggested by references to Hispanic dishes. It links a person with his or her family and culture, and with his or her ancestors. It comes from the kitchen, but ultimately it comes from a higher power. It demands thankfulness, usually expressed by a blessing, or "grace," a prayer to God. Dives in the person of the children do not understand this, perhaps because they have been pulled up from their cultural roots, perhaps because they are just kids who never knew the poverty of Lazarus in the person of Mrs. Pérez. They are unable to "define the grateful gesture." They cannot obey. They fail. They just sit. They feel guilty. They cannot appreciate satisfied hunger, perhaps because they have never known the kind of hunger that forces one to search for scraps.

The adult poet, however, is compelled to look back on the experience and the urgings of her mother. In memorializing them in the poem, she accepts her mother's point of view. In this way, "Defining the Grateful Gesture" transcends the limits of a particular culture or ethnicity and describes an experience of growth and realization that people the world over can share.

Source: Michael J. O'Neal, Critical Essay on "Defining the Grateful Gesture," in *Poetry for Students*, Gale, Cengage Learning, 2012.

Catherine Dominic

Dominic is a novelist and a freelance writer and editor. In the following essay, she explores the way Sapia treats the Catholic notions of sin and guilt in her poem "Defining the Grateful Gesture."

Some critics have offered an overview of certain religious elements in Sapia's "Defining the Grateful Gesture," focusing on the language of ritual in the poem. The poem alludes to religion in other significant ways as well. Although "Defining the Grateful Gesture" makes no references to Roman Catholicism specifically, Sapia uses language that strongly suggests aspects of that religion. Sapia specifically emphasizes the Roman Catholic concept of sin. In particular, the sinning

In the last stanza, the children are compared to loaves of bread in the kitchen. (aarrows | Shutterstock.com)

of the children becomes in many ways a focal point in the poem, as important as the ritual of mealtime, as significant as the contrast between the abundance of the narrator's table and the scarcity at her mother's. The poem consequently takes on an almost unrelieved tone of sadness and shame, as the narrator recalls her mother's attitude toward her children and their participation in the family meal.

Recent estimates suggest that approximately 85 percent of Puerto Ricans are Roman Catholic, and the nation has a history in which the Church has been inextricably intertwined with the politics and culture of Puerto Rico since the fifteenth century. Historically, emigrating Puerto Ricans have taken with them to their new homes a cultural background infused with Catholicism. Sapia's own parents immigrated to New York City in the 1920s. In "Defining the Grateful Gesture," Sapia, herself a Catholic, describes a mother who recalls the poverty of her past and reflects upon it in a decidedly Catholic manner when placing food in front of her own children.

In the poem's first stanza, the poet recounts her mother's stories about her own childhood. A meal, however small, was gratefully consumed after a day of hard work. The mother's constantly busy youth and the help she provided to her family is the focus of the opening stanza. It is because of such experiences in the mother's youth, the poet explains, that the mother now tells her children stories about how appreciative she was of being able to have her hunger satisfied by even a meager meal. The poet describes how such stories were related during the mealtimes.

The mother in the poem, presumably intended to represent Sapia's own mother, demands of her children reverence for the food placed before them. In this language, and in that to follow, the overlay of Catholicism coloring the poem becomes apparent. The deeply spiritual respect with which the children are intended to regard their meal is coupled with the fact that the children are

> IN PARTICULAR, THE SINNING OF THE CHILDREN BECOMES IN MANY WAYS A FOCAL POINT IN THE POEM, AS IMPORTANT AS THE RITUAL OF MEALTIME, AS SIGNIFICANT AS THE CONTRAST BETWEEN THE ABUNDANCE OF THE NARRATOR'S TABLE AND THE SCARCITY AT HER MOTHER'S."

perceived by their mother as undeserving; they have not earned their right to be nourished in the same way that their mother did as a child. An attitude of thankfulness is demanded of the children. This reverence and thankfulness insisted upon by the mother in the poem suggest an attitude of Catholic gratitude for one's blessings, in this case, the meal the children are about to eat. What is perhaps most striking about this stanza, however, is the fact that the children's need to eat, their requirement for nourishment, is regarded as unearned. This notion of unworthiness can be directly tied to the Catholic notion of sin.

According to Catholic beliefs surrounding the idea of original sin, a child is born having inherited the effects of Adam's disobedience to God in the Garden of Eden. Many Catholics believe, and Catholic tradition holds, that an infant who has not been baptized is damned because of the "stain" of original sin. (Baptism is a Catholic sacrament whereby an individual is accepted into the Church community.) Strict Catholics believe that although baptism saves an individual's soul from the fate of damnation, the soul is still tainted by this sin. Catholics additionally believe in the notion of sin as a choice to use the free will God bestowed to act in an immoral manner. Such choices are commonly repented by Catholics through the act of confessing sins to a priest, who offers absolution. The prevalence of the notion of sin in Catholic religious practices, the regular acknowledging and atoning for sin, and the reminder at daily or weekly masses of the sinful and therefore unworthy nature of every individual, has led some critics of the Church to characterize the Catholic religion as overly focused on sin and on the consequent emotions of guilt and shame.

Such ideas of unworthiness and guilt pervade Sapia's poem. To return to the second stanza, what stands out is not that the children are deemed unworthy because they lacked the proper attitude of thankfulness for their meal, but rather that they are inherently undeserving of being nourished. Thankful or not, undeserving or not, they are fed their portion of rice, chicken, beans, and plantains, but the text implies that they remain, in some sense, unworthy.

Sapia to comments in the third stanza on how her mother perceived her children to lack a sense of gratefulness for the meal she has prepared. The mother recalls for the children's benefit a family in Puerto Rico, who, although poor and deprived, were rosy-cheeked (suggesting their thriving, healthy nature). The implication here is that what the mother offers her own children is an overabundance of food, an almost gluttonous amount unnecessary for good health. The Perez brothers, she reminds her offspring, could survive on what little food they could scrounge and still managed to thrive.

Repeatedly, the mother in the poem appears to express her resentment toward her children's needs and instills in the children the sense that they are unworthy of receiving what they are being given. The sentiment in some ways reflects a prayer recited during a Catholic Mass just prior to communion (the sacrament in which wafers of bread, believed to have been transformed into the body of Jesus Christ, are distributed to the congregation): "Lord, I am not worthy to receive you, but only say the word and I shall be healed." (As of 2006, the wording of this prayer was changed by Catholic bishops to read "Lord, I am not worthy that you should enter under my roof, but only say the word and I shall be healed.")

The idea that children's needs are disproportionate to their worth as well as to a parent's ability to provide for them is reinforced in the fourth stanza of the poem. Once again, the mother tells her children of the Perez family. Mrs. Perez picks food from the garbage of others, with the careful deliberateness that Sapia likens to that of a missionary. (A missionary is an individual who is sent as a representative of a particular religion to other parts of the world to spread that religion while bringing humanitarian aid to poor countries.) With the reference to the missionary underscoring the religious underpinnings of the poem, Sapia describes the way the Perez children ungratefully needed more sustenance than what the mother was able to afford.

In the final stanza, the notion of unworthiness is repeated, as Sapia notes the way she and her brothers were unable to strike the proper tone of obedient reverence at the table. She describes her failure, and that of her siblings, to cast themselves as humble beggars. Further, Sapia laments her and her brothers' inability as children to sustain their mother with a sense of their own worth. In the poem's last line, Sapia acknowledges specifically the sense of guilt with which the children were overwhelmed, simply for having an appetite.

The ways in which the children are perceived as sinners in the poem is expressed by Sapia with some bitterness. She acknowledges that she and her siblings felt guilty for the simple act of being hungry. They are regarded as inherently unworthy, as ungrateful, as failing to cultivate the proper posture of humble thankfulness. Just as the children's unworthiness for what they are about to receive at the table calls to mind the precommunion prayer, the children's array of perceived transgressions is reminiscent of the Penitential Rite said during a Catholic Mass. In asking for God's forgiveness, the congregation states, "I have sinned through my own fault, in my thoughts and in my words, in what I have done and in what I have failed to do." Through action (being hungry) and inaction (not presenting themselves as sufficiently grateful and humble), the children mark themselves as unworthy and therefore, shameful. In this way, although Sapia does not use the word "sin" in the poem, the Catholic notion of sinfulness repeatedly surfaces in the poem and emphasizes the poet's negative reactions to mealtimes shared with her family.

The fact that the poem is structured around the gathering of a family at the table for sustenance calls to mind the culmination of a Catholic Mass in its similarity to the sacrament of communion. All elements of a Catholic Mass lead toward communion, or as it is also called, the Eucharistic celebration. The congregation is led in prayer, readings from the Bible, and song toward preparing their souls to receive the bread that they believe has been transformed into Jesus Christ's body. This preparation centers on the acknowledgment of sinfulness and the request for forgiveness from God and from the community. Similarly, the children in Sapia's poem are guided by stories—from their mother's past rather than from the Bible—toward recognizing their own unworthiness. In an effort to prove to their mother their gratefulness, the children sit solemnly over their plates, feeling the sense of guilt that inevitably arises when one is repeatedly reminded of one's worthlessness. Although they are sinners, they are allowed to eat, just as the congregation is allowed to receive communion once their sins are acknowledged and lamented, and forgiveness is sought. The ritual will repeat itself for the children at the next meal, and for Catholics at the next Mass.

Sapia's attitude toward her mother, and toward the sense of sin the children in the poem are encouraged to develop, comes across as bitter and somber. While the children's appetites may be assuaged, the children are reminded that they should feel guilty both about being hungry and about having eaten. The mother's stories do not inspire a sense of family unity; there is no laughter or camaraderie around this table. The poet and her brothers are taught only about their failures. In the end, "Defining the Grateful Gesture" reads as a poem of sorrow in which joy is as notably absent as the children's father.

Source: Catherine Dominic, Critical Essay on "Defining the Grateful Gesture," in *Poetry for Students*, Gale, Cengage Learning, 2012.

SOURCES

"About National Hispanic Heritage Month," in *National Hispanic Heritage Month*, http://hispanicheritagemonth.gov/about/ (accessed May 16, 2011).

"Best Books of 1991," in *Publishers Weekly*, November 1, 1991, p. 22.

Gillan, M., Review of *Valentino's Hair*, in *Choice*, May 1988, pp. 1405–406.

"Immigration Reform and Control Act of 1986," in *Economic Research Service*, U.S. Department of Agriculture, http://www.ers.usda.gov/publications/ah719/ah719f.pdf (accessed May 16, 2011).

Ingraham, Janet, Review of *Valentino's Hair*, in *Library Journal*, November 1, 1991, p. 133.

"Introductory Rites," in *Order of Mass: Basic Texts for the Roman Catholic Eucharist*, http://catholic-resources.org/ChurchDocs/Mass.htm (accessed June 21, 2011).

"Original Sin," in *The Catholic Encyclopedia*, http://www.newadvent.org/cathen/12291b.htm (accessed June 21, 2011).

"Porto Rico," in *The Catholic Encyclopedia*, http://www.newadvent.org/cathen/12291b.htm (accessed June 21, 2011).

"The Puerto Rican Community: From Neighbors to Citizens," in *National Puerto Rican Coalition*, http://www.bateylink.org/community (accessed May 13, 2011).

"Puerto Rican Population," in *StateMaster.com*, http://www.statemaster.com/graph/peo_pue_ric_pop_1980-people-puerto-rican-population-1980 (accessed May 13, 2011).

"Puerto Rico," in *CIA: World Factbook*, http://www.cia.gov/library/publications/the-world-factbook/geos/rq.html (accessed June 21, 2011).

"A Reagan Legacy: Amnesty for Illegal Immigrants," in *All Things Considered*, National Public Radio, http://www.npr.org/templates/story/story.php?storyId=128303672 (accessed May 16, 2011).

Review of *Valentino's Hair*, in *Publishers Weekly*, September 27, 1991, p. 52.

Rodgers, Ann, "Liturgy Changes for U.S. Catholics," in *Pittsburgh Post-Gazette*, June 16, 2006, http://www.post-gazette.com/pg/06167/698798-84.stm (accessed June 21, 2011).

"Sin," in *The Catholic Encyclopedia*, http://www.newadvent.org/cathen/14004b.htm (accessed June 21, 2011).

Sapia, Yvonne, "Defining the Grateful Gesture," in *The Woman That I Am: The Literature and Culture of Contemporary Women of Color*, edited by D. Soyini Madison, St. Martin's Press, 1994, pp. 135-36.

"Yvonne Sapia," in *Glencoe Publishing*, http://www.glencoe.com/sites/common_assets/literature/authorsearch-hs/center.php?fileName=G 9-12_AS_Sapia_AL.xml (accessed May 16, 2011).

FURTHER READING

Augenbraum, Harold, and Margarite Fernandez Olmos, eds., *The Latino Reader: An American Literary Tradition from 1542 to the Present*, Mariner Books, 1997.

> This anthology collects works documenting the Latino experience in America dating all the way back to 1527. It includes primarily literary works and also primary sources such as historical accounts, memoirs, letters, and essays.

Batchelor, Bob, and Scott F. Stoddart, *The 1980s*, Greenwood, 2006.

> This volume is part of Greenwood's "American Popular Culture through History" series. Readers who are interested in the popular culture of the decade in which Sapia wrote her poem will find in this volume discussion of the decade's advertising, architecture, entertainment, fashion, food, leisure activities, travel, and the arts.

Bode, Janet, *New Kids in Town*, Scholastic, 1989.

> This volume is a collection of interviews with teenagers who immigrated to the United States. It records the excitement and fear felt by the members of the culturally diverse people she interviews. The teens explain the circumstances of their move to the United States and contrast their life before they came with their life afterward. They chronicle their efforts to adapt to American culture while retaining their own culture.

"Celebrate America's Diversity: Holidays, Festivals and Historical Events Celebrated and Recognized by African Americans, American Indians, Asian/Pacific Islanders and Latinos," in *American Library Association*, ALA Graphics, 1993.

> This pamphlet was written as a resource guide for teachers. Other readers will find in it useful information about historical events, festivals, and holidays of numerous ethnic groups, including Latinos.

Mendoza, Sylvia, *The Book of Latina Women: 150 Vidas of Passion, Strength, and Success*, Adams Media Corporation, 2004.

> This volume is for readers interested in the contributions of Latina women. It includes sketches of Latina women from all periods of history and all walks of life, including science, history, art, politics, and entertainment.

Noble, Judith, and Jaime Lacasa, *The Hispanic Way: Aspects of Behavior, Attitudes and Customs in the Spanish-Speaking World*, Passport Books, 1990.

> This relatively brief volume, written primarily for students, is intended as a kind of reference guide to the common and divergent traits of the Hispanic world. It touches on such matters as bullfighting, dating, holidays, work. and includes a chapter about meals and food.

SUGGESTED SEARCH TERMS

free verse

Hispanic authors

Hispanic culture

Hispanic culture AND Yvonne Sapia

immigration

Latina poets

Latina poets AND Yvonne Sapia

Puerto Rican immigrants

Puerto Rico

women poets

Yvonne Sapia

Yvonne Sapia AND Defining the Grateful Gesture

For the Young Who Want To

MARGE PIERCY

1980

Prolific novelist and poet Marge Piercy repeatedly explores the themes of usefulness, purpose, and dedication in her work. In her 1980 poem "For the Young Who Want To," Piercy returns to these themes. In this short poem, Piercy examines the nature of the talent and passion an artist possesses. She contemplates the way such motivation, and the skill with which it is pursued, are evaluated by outsiders, including the world of critics and other artists, as well as the more intimate circle of the writer's friends and family. Throughout the course of the poem, Piercy's tone approaches bitterness. Her scorn for the critics of the artist is revealed through her language and imagery. Piercy is equally derisive in her attitude toward writers who seek master's degrees and who attend writing workshops as avenues toward proving their worth as an artist, for Piercy contends that such educational resources can do little to improve upon an artist's talent. Piercy then emphasizes the qualities of a true writer and praises those who work hard at writing despite the lack of appreciation for or acknowledgment of their talent or value. Aside from the six-stanza structure of the poem, the work does not employ other standard formal features and may therefore be regarded as a free verse poem.

"For the Young Who Want To" was published in 1980 in the journal *Mother Jones*, and in the poetry collection *The Moon Is Always Female*. It was later reprinted in another Piercy collection,

Marge Piercy (AP Images)

Circles on the Water: Selected Poems of Marge Piercy, in 1982.

AUTHOR BIOGRAPHY

A native of Detroit, Michigan, Piercy was born on March 31, 1936, to working-class parents Robert Douglas Piercy and Bert Bernice Bunnin Piercy. After attending public schools in Detroit, Piercy was accepted at the University of Michigan in Ann Arbor. Having overcome an often troubled adolescence, Piercy studied creative writing and won the University of Michgan's prestigious literary award, the Hopwood, in 1956 and 1957, for submissions in both the fiction and poetry categories. In 1957, Piercy graduated with a bachelor's degree, and earned a master's degree from Northwestern University a year later.

Also in 1958, Piercy married Michel Schiff, and the couple moved to France for a short time. The marriage ended in divorce in 1959. Piercy then worked a variety of jobs and became actively involved in the civil rights movement. In the early 1960s, she wrote several novels that she was unable to get published. Piercy married Robert Shapiro in 1962, and she and her husband became active in the opposition to the Vietnam War. Piercy continued to pursue her writing at this time. Her focused efforts came to fruition in 1968 when her first volume of poetry, *Breaking Camp*, was published; it was followed one year later by her first novel, *Going Down Fast*.

After moving to Cape Cod with her husband in 1971, Piercy continued to write poetry and fiction. *To Be of Use*, a poetry collection published in 1973, reflected Piercy's interest in contemporary social issues. In the late 1970s, Piercy's activist nature was put to use in the women's rights movement, and her writing continued to reflect her political interests.

In 1980, she and Shapiro divorced. That same year, Piercy published the poetry collection *The Moon Is Always Female*, which contained the poem "For the Young Who Want To." Piercy's poetry collections, as she explained in the introduction to the 1982 *Circles on the Water*, are arranged "in a particular order to work as a whole as well as individually." Piercy married her third husband, Ira Wood, in 1982. As of 2011, the couple resided in Wellfleet, Massachusetts. Piercy and Wood collaborated on a number of projects, including the 1998 novel *Storm Tide*. The couple also established a small literary press, Leapfrog Press, in 1997. Piercy's poetry collection, *Hunger Moon: New and Selected Poems, 1980–2010*, was published in 2011.

Piercy has won a number of literary prizes for her poetry and fiction and received a National Endowment for the Arts award in 1978.

POEM TEXT

Talent is what they say
you have after the novel
is published and favorably
reviewed. Beforehand what
you have is a tedious   5
delusion, a hobby like knitting.

Work is what you have done
after the play is produced
and the audience claps.
Before that friends keep asking   10
when you are planning to go
out and get a job.

Genius is what they know you
had after the third volume

of remarkable poems. Earlier
they accuse you of withdrawing,
ask why you don't have a baby,
call you a bum.   15

The reason people want M.F.A.'s,
take workshops with fancy names   20
when all you can really
learn is a few techniques,
typing instructions and
somebody else's mannerisms

is that every artist lacks   25
a license to hang on the wall
like your optician, your vet
proving you may be a clumsy sadist
whose fillings fall into the stew
but you're certified a dentist.   30

The real writer is one
who really writes. Talent
is an invention like phlogiston
after the fact of fire.
Work is its own cure. You have to   35
like it better than being loved.

MEDIA ADAPTATIONS

- Although Piercy's poem "For the Young Who Want To" has no available media adaptations, Piercy has recorded other poems on the audio CD *Louder, We Can't Hear You Yet: The Political Poems of Marge Piercy*, published in 2004 by Leapfrog Press.

POEM SUMMARY

The text used for this summary is from *The Moon Is Always Female*, Alfred A. Knopf, 1988, pp. 84–85. Versions of the poem can be found at the following Web pages: http://www.poetryfoundation.org/poem/176837 and http://www.margepiercy.com/sampling/poems-from-moon-female.htm.

Stanza 1

"For the Young Who Want To" is broken into six stanzas. A stanza is a unit that divides the lines of poetry into a thematically related grouping in the same way that paragraphs divide prose. In the first stanza, Piercy explores the notion of talent. The term is viewed from two points in time: before a writer has been published and received positive reviews, and after. Piercy maintains in this stanza that, prior to publication and to the receiving of critical praise, a writer's talent is not recognized as such. Rather, whatever it is that a writer possesses before such events is regarded as a tiresome daydream, or something trivial that the writer does to occupy his or her time. Piercy establishes in this stanza the structure that much of the rest of the poem will follow. A concept is identified and then defined from two perspectives, a point in time prior to the achievement of what people typically regard as success, and a point in time after. She also establishes the tone of the poem as darkly humorous; there is a bitterness to her irony that is conveyed through her imagery and language.

Stanza 2

In the second stanza, Piercy discusses the notion of productive work. While she focuses on novel writing in the first stanza, in this stanza, she targets the playwright and maintains that it is only after a successful production of a play, after the clapping of the audience is heard, that the activities of a playwright are viewed as work. Prior to the production of the play and its being well received and appreciated by an audience, a playwright at work is regarded by his or her friends simply as unemployed. Again, Piercy's tone emphasizes the irony of these perspectives. She encourages the reader to contemplate the way a writer's activities are perceived by non-artists.

Stanza 3

Piercy continues to explore an artist's activities through the dual perspective she has established in the first two stanzas. Here, she examines the nature of creative genius. Only after a poet has published her third volume of exemplary poems, Piercy contends, is the poet's genius recognized and praised. Prior to this achievement, the poet's life choices are criticized by those around her, those who wonder why she does not yet have a baby, or a job. A poet is only regarded as successful, Piercy suggests, after the publication of a number of volumes of well-received poetry. In the absence of such achievement, everything that the poet is not accomplishing is emphasized, such as the fact that she has not pursued what many regard as the more traditional paths of becoming a mother, or following a career path with more tangible measures of success than those available to the poet.

Stanza 4

In the next two stanzas, Piercy shifts the structure of the poem. Instead of exploring the "before" and "after" of a particular concept, she opens the fourth stanza with a statement about the way writers justify pursuing a master of fine arts degree, yet she does not provide the reasons until the next stanza. She continues the fourth stanza by stressing how little can be gained from master's programs and writing workshops. All that can be gained, she emphasizes, is a limited number of skills, and some instruction on how to physically present your work on the page. Significantly, the last item in Piercy's list of things to be learned in such writing programs is the one for which she seems to hold the most contempt, specifically, the particular writing style of someone else. Piercy suggests that writing programs and workshops teach the writer how to write like someone else; the writer is schooled out of his or her own true voice.

Stanza 5

In this stanza, Piercy returns to the reasons why people seek advance degrees and take writing workshops in the first place. She observes that what artists lack are the obvious signifiers of education and training and skill that other professionals have and suggests that writers participate in degreed programs and workshops in order to arm themselves with such documentation in the face of the criticism (outlined in the first three stanzas) with which their writing methods are often met. Doctors and veterinarians and dentists have degrees and licenses that speak at least to the fact that they have received some sort of preparation, even if they do not possess the skill to correspond with the license. Piercy offers the example of a dentist who may fumble through his tasks, inflict pain on his patients in the process, and ineptly repair fillings, but who nevertheless possesses the type of professional certification that eludes the artist.

Stanza 6

In the final stanza, Piercy turns to her definition of a true writer. She states simply that a writer writes, and that act is what makes him or her a writer. The published novel of the first stanza, the produced play of the second, the three acclaimed volumes of poetry in the third stanza, the master of fine arts degrees and the workshops of the fourth stanza, and the unattainable certification implied by the fifth stanza, are all irrelevant to the real writer, who simply writes because she must write. Piercy emphasizes the way that perceived talent is a concept created in the aftermath of a writer's activity, a label ascribed after measures established by the outside world have already been achieved. Working, writing, Piercy stresses, are all a writer can do, and to continue pursuing this path, one must enjoy the work more than anything else, including being praised, rewarded, or appreciated as an artist.

THEMES

Art and Society

In "For the Young Who Want To," Piercy explores the relationship between the artist and society, including the society of one's peers as a writer and the society of one's close circle of family and friends. She focuses in particular on the way society regards the working artist, and the judgment leveled by society against the artist who has not attained the achievements designated as markers of success. Piercy finds these designations arbitrary, and not representative of the talent, dedication, skill, or work ethic of the artist.

In Piercy's poem, the notions of success identified by society are extremely challenging for writers to achieve. It is not enough for a novelist to be published; he or she must receive the praise of critics as well. For the playwright, a produced play does not connote success; it must be applauded by a delighted audience. For the poet, the publication of three volumes of poetry chock full of poems that can be fully commended by the critics is the measure of success. Without such achievements, according to Piercy, the artist is regarded by society, by friends and family and critics, as without value. Not only is the artist's worth as a productive member of his or her society questioned; but artists who have not vaulted toward publication and the subsequent popular and critical success are held in contempt by society as being delusional. They appear to be dabbling in their writing as if it were a frivolous hobby and are regarded as being unemployed and purposeless. The world sees them as having withdrawn from society, as having failed to settle

TOPICS FOR FURTHER STUDY

- Piercy's poem "For the Young Who Want To" has distinct similarities to her more famous poem "To Be of Use." Both poems advocate a certain message, defend or praise a certain group of people, and express a sense of duty or calling. Compare the two poems and, in an essay, discuss the similarities and differences in theme, style, language, imagery, and structure. Cite examples from the poems to aid in your comparison.

- "For the Young Who Want To" serves as a message from an experienced writer to aspiring writers. Consider your own experiences or dreams for the future and write a poem that similarly encourages its readers. Think about ways in which you can incorporate images or metaphors to emphasize your message. Consider the obstacles or objections a person might encounter on the path you are describing in your poem. Carefully contemplate your word choice and work at revising your poem until you have refined it to its essential core. Share your poem with the class orally or by posting it on a Web page or blog site that you have created.

- Piercy's poetry often focuses on women and women's issues. Many of the poets featured in *These Are Not Sweet Girls: Poetry by Latin American Women* take a similar approach to their work. Peruse the poetry in this collection, published by White Pine Press in 1994, and identify one of the female Latin American poets whose work speaks to you on some level. Write a critique of one of her poems, or research her life and write a biographical essay. If you choose to critique the poem, be sure to examine both the content of the poem, in terms of themes and images used, for example, and the formal elements of the poem, such as its stanzaic structure, its sense of rhythm, its rhyme scheme or lack thereof. If you write a biographical essay, be sure to cite all print and Web sources you used to compile your essay.

- Piercy is known for her activism, in particular for her feminist writings. Research the history of the feminist movement, using such sources as Jacqueline Laks Gorman's 2011 young-adult work *The Modern Feminist Movement: Sisters under the Skin, 1961–1979*, published by Chelsea House, and the 2001 young-adult book *The Riot Grrrl Movement: Feminism of a New Generation*, written by Cherie Turner and published by Rosen. What were some of the key issues of the early- to middle years of the feminist movement? How did the focus of the movement shift over the years? Write a research paper in which you explore and discuss this history. Cite all Web and print sources, using Gorman's and Turner's works as starting points.

- *19 Varieties of Gazelle: Poems of the Middle East* is a collection of poems targeting a young-adult audience and written by Arab American poet Naomi Shihab Nye. Published by Greenwillow Books in 2002, the collection explores the Middle East, Arab American experiences, and themes of family, war, faith, and daily life. Gather a small group and assign each person two or three poems to read. Orally or in an online blog, discuss each of the poems. Compare the way the poet explores various themes in the works you have selected. Share with the group the images the poet used, and exchange views on personal reactions to the poems. Can you detect similarities in structure and style among the works? If you opt to discuss the poems orally rather than online, record your group discussions so that your teacher has a record of your work.

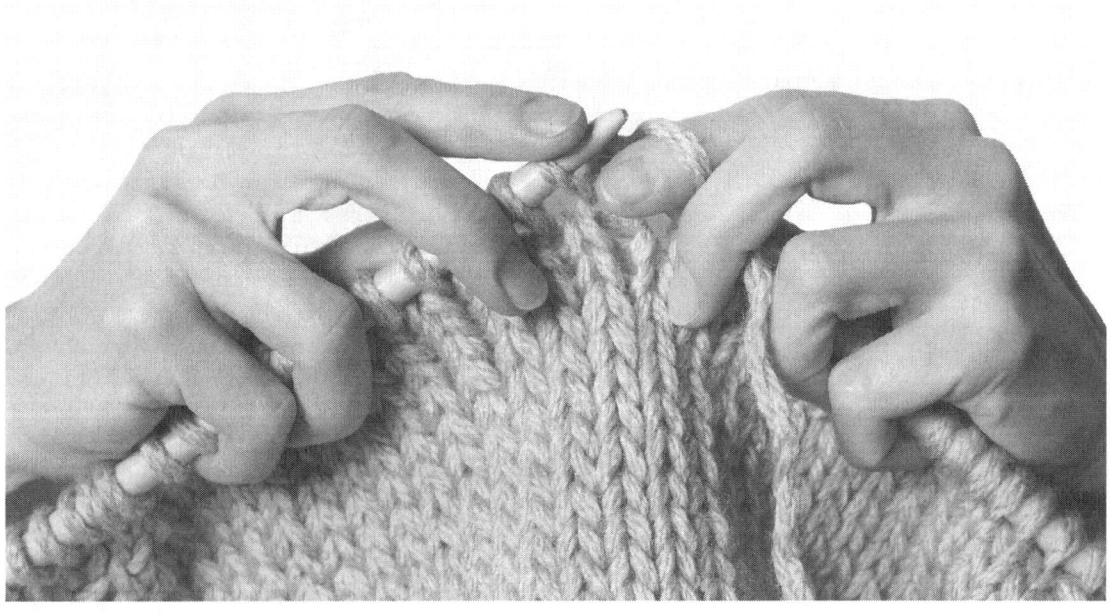

In stanza 1, the narrator compares knitting and writing. (drohn | Shutterstock.com)

down and have families and lead productive lives.

Piercy's depiction of society's perceptions of the artist is a bleak one. According to Piercy, the literary artist is treated with contempt, pity, or revulsion until published and applauded, at which point the same artist is regarded as a true talent, a genius. This shift in perception strikes Piercy as incredibly unfair, and ruthlessly arbitrary. Piercy's advice to artists, to the young, aspiring writers she addresses in the poem's title, is to disregard the constructs for artistic success outlined by society. In fact, in the last line of the poem, Piercy suggests that the artist must disregard society as a whole, or must at least forgo the love such a collective entity can offer. One's work as an artist must be more important than one's need for validation by society, peers, or family.

Education

Just as Piercy wryly criticizes the critics of artists, she also admonishes artists themselves, particularly those who seek validation through writing programs and workshops. In the first three stanzas of the poem, Piercy builds a case to help the reader understand an artist's frustrations and engenders in the reader the sympathy with the artist who feels compelled to seek some sort of official validation of his or her artistic pursuits. Yet from master's of fine arts programs and from writer's workshops, the writer can learn little that is valuable, Piercy suggests. As the poem progresses, Piercy transfers her focus from the societal expectations placed upon artists to the artists' attempts to justify and validate their art as a legitimate career choice. Yet Piercy maintains that a few guidelines, formatting instructions, and someone else's stylistic conventions are the only things a writer will receive from such educational programs.

In fact, in this last item in Piercy's list, one senses a strong warning to writers about workshops and writing programs. The poet hints at the danger writers face in submerging themselves in their efforts to seek official stamps of approval for their artistic endeavors. Piercy warns that writers may lose their own style and voice as they mirror the style of another writer in order to suit the conventions of the writing program. Not only is there little for a writer to gain by straining after such educational credentials, Piercy suggests, but there is also potential for a great loss. Piercy points out that master of fine art degrees and writing program completion certificates are just as subjective as any other degree, diploma, license, or certificate. Just as the proper certification does not guarantee that one's dentist will be capable, gentle, and efficient, educational degrees and writing workshop certificates do not ensure that a writer will be able to craft a prize-winning or best-selling work. The act of writing, Piercy emphasizes, is a writer's best education.

STYLE

Free Verse Poetry

Piercy structures her poem "For the Young Who Want To" as a free verse poem. In writing free verse poetry, the poet eschews regular metrical structure as well as rhyme patterns. Meter is a pattern of unaccented and accented syllables in a line of poetry. Piercy's poem does not include examples of end rhyme (where the sounds or words at the end of lines rhyme) nor does it include internal rhyme (where sounds or words within a line of verse rhyme). Although this poem is free from the structure provided by meter and rhyme, Piercy does incorporate stanzaic structure in her poem. A stanza is a unit of poetry that divides the lines of verse thematically, functioning in the poem in the same manner as a paragraph does in a work of prose.

"For the Young Who Want To" contains six stanzas of six lines each. By structuring the work in this fashion, Piercy provides the reader with tightly connected units of verse that can be digested individually as the reader makes his or her way through the poem. Each six-line stanza focuses on a single idea. The first, for example, explores the temporal aspects of the notion of talent. Before publication, an author is considered a delusional dabbler in the field of literature. After publication and critical acclaim, the talent the writer has always possessed, as Piercy suggests, is now acknowledged for what it is. This temporal focus on talent, work, and creative genius is employed in the first three stanzas of the poem. The last three stanzas focus on the motivation of the writer to seek degrees, certification—the approval of an educational institution. Most important, however, is the focus in the final stanza on the motivation of a writer to write. Although the final three stanzas possess a similar thematic focus, Piercy saves her most emphatic statements and the thematic thrust of the poem for this final stanza.

Language: Imagery and Irony

The language Piercy uses in "For the Young Who Want To" is straightforward, uncomplicated, and literal. The poet employs little figurative language in the poem, giving the work a matter-of-fact tone. Figurative language is language that is infused with symbols, exaggerations, or metaphorical comparisons; it is the type of language commonly associated with poetic expression. Although Piercy does include some comparisons in the poem, they are often used ironically, and are intended to contrast two ideas. Broadly defined, irony is the identification of the discongruity between what is, and what seems, between reality and appearances. For example, as a writer, one may become labeled as talented after one has published a well-reviewed novel, but prior to that experience what a writer possesses, as Piercy describes in the poem's first stanza, is not skill but rather an unrealistic notion, or something considered to be an entertaining, leisurely diversion such as knitting. Piercy's language is ironic, for, as a writer, she recognizes that although a writer's work may be regarded as a waste of time by some people before the work is published, the same work is regarded as evidence of the writer's talent after publication. Piercy draws attention to the fact that the work is perceived differently after critics have lauded the work as a success.

As the poem progresses, it becomes increasingly clear that Piercy's language and comparisons are meant to emphasize her derisive view of commonly held opinions about writers who have not achieved conventional measures of success. Another ironic image, like that of the novelist who has taken up writing as a hobby in the same way someone decides to start knitting, is that of a dentist, certified to practice in his field, but who is nonetheless unskilled, as evidenced by the fact that he hurts his patients and that he implants fillings that later fall out in one's dinner. Labels attributed to a writer in a post hoc fashion (after the fact) are meaningless, Piercy stresses in the final stanza. This emphasis is made through the comparison of talent to a substance known as phlogiston, and by Piercy's subsequent labeling of this notion as a contrivance. Prior to the discovery of oxygen and its role in combustion, phlogiston was believed to be a chemical substance

COMPARE & CONTRAST

- **1980s:** American poetry is characterized by a variety of styles and modes. Free verse poetry has been in vogue since the 1950s and 1960s, when poets such as Jack Kerouac and Allen Ginsberg revolutionized American poetry through exploration of non-traditional modes of expression. Poets such as Marge Piercy and Maya Angelou are popular free verse poets. New formalist poets such as Dana Gioia and Timothy Steele write poetry with traditional formal structures; New formalism is regarded as a reaction against free verse poetry.

   Today: Twenty-first century American poetry is marked by as much variety as that of the last decades of the twentieth century. Poetry written both in free verse and in traditional modes abounds. Poets such as Peter Meinke are known for using traditional forms, such as the sonnet, to discuss modern themes. Others, such as Daisy Fried and Christopher Bursk write lighter poems infused with humor. Poets such as Billy Collins and Denise Duhamel are considered accessible, whereas Reginald Shepherd and Larry Levis are described as more intellectual and challenging.

- **1980s:** The women's rights movement stagnates as the ratification process for the Equal Rights Amendment (ERA) loses momentum. The ERA is not ratified by the thirty-eight states necessary for it to become law by the 1982 deadline set for ratification. The proposed amendment must be reintroduced with each Congressional session to stay alive.

   Today: In 2011, Democratic Senator Robert Menendez of New Jersey and Democratic Representative Carolyn Maloney of New York reintroduce the ERA to the Senate and the House of Representatives, respectively, in the 112th (2011–2012) session of Congress. Democratic Representative Tammy Baldwin of Wisconsin introduces a House Resolution designed to remove the ERA ratification deadline and to make the amendment law when three additional states ratify it.

- **1980s:** Marge Piercy, in her poem "For the Young Who Want To," draws attention to a debate that rages among writers concerning the necessity or perceived value of obtaining a master of fine arts degree to one's career as a writer. These programs have grown increasingly popular since the 1930s.

   Today: The debate regarding the impact of master of fine arts degree programs on the world of literature is as charged as ever. Mark McGurl, in the *Los Angeles Review of Books*, debates the issue hotly with Elif Batuman, of the *London Review of Books,* who in 2010 wrote a scathing response to McGurl's 2009 book on the history of postwar creative writing and the role of creative writing programs in American literature. While McGurl describes and defends this type of education, Batuman derides such programs, finding that works produced by writers with master of fine arts degrees are characterized by "oversophistication combined with an air of autodidacticism."

---

released through combustion; its existence has since been disproved. The fact that something burned was evidence that it contained phlogiston, according to this theory. Piercy likens talent to phlogiston, and publication to the act of combustion. An author's talent is proved by the fact that he or she was published. This notion, she points out through the course of the poem, is nonsense.

HISTORICAL CONTEXT

American Poetry in the Late 1970s and Early 1980s

Poetry in America during the early portion of Piercy's career was characterized by a number of poetic movements. Free verse poetry, particularly that of the experimental nature, remained in fashion, having exploded in popular culture in

In stanza 5, the narrator comments that artists lack a visible credential, like a diploma on the wall. (Kurhan / Shutterstock.com)

the 1950s and 1960s with the work of such poets as Jack Kerouac and Allen Ginsberg, and as a reaction against more traditional, structured, academic poetry. During this time, many poets continued the experimentation begun in the work of such Beat movement poems (as Kerouac, Ginsberg, and others, including Gary Snyder and Lawrence Ferlinghetti) and experimented with sound, language, and structure, developing abstract methods for expressing meaning. As Claudine Rankine and Lisa Sewell explain in *American Poets in the 21st Century: The New Poetics*, poetic trends of the 1960s and 1970s continue to be noticed today. Such trends include "the postconfessional mainstream voice-centered lyric of introspection and revelation," along with multicultural and feminist poetry concerned with self-identity.

During the 1970s and 1980s, American poets found numerous outlets for their work. As Christopher Beach states in *The Cambridge Introduction to Twentieth-Century American Poetry*, "The number of published poets continued to grow, bolstered by a burgeoning network of journals, presses, and academic creative writing programs." New poetic movements also came into being during this time period. The avant-garde language poetry movement focused on the linguistic and formal features of the poem and explored the apparent disconnectedness between language and what it is intended to signify. Another movement gaining popularity during this time period was the new formalist movement. New formalism in many ways was a reaction against the experimental nature of the free verse poetry of the 1960s and 1970s, and poets writing in this mode favored traditional poetic metrical structures and rhyme schemes.

The Women's Rights Movement in the Late 1970s and Early 1980s

At the heart of the women's rights movement was, and is, the struggle for constitutional protection for women against gender-based discrimination. After years of political efforts by groups such as the National Women's Party, the Equal

Rights Amendment was proposed by the U. S. Senate and House of Representatives in 1972. However, before the Constitution can be amended, thirty-eight states must ratify a proposed amendment. Despite advocacy efforts by the National Organization for Women, the 1979 deadline for ratification by thirty-eight states expired. Congress granted an extension, until 1982, but by that time, only thirty-five states had ratified the proposed amendment. Momentum toward ratification slowed by 1980, with the injection of conservatism in American politics marked by the election of Republican President Ronald Reagan in 1980.

In 1982, the Equal Rights Amendment was reintroduced in Congress and continues to be reintroduced before every session of Congress. Nancy Whittier observes in *Feminist Generations: The Persistence of the Radical Women's Movement* that "the 1980s contained massive opposition and setbacks to feminism that drove longtime activists out of social movement organization and into more individual forms of agitation. 'Feminism' became a dirty word in many circles." In exploring the ways the feminist movement shifted during this time period, Whittier cites the way national organizations evolved. Former radical activists became involved in providing services for women (such as aid for battered women, rape treatment and counseling, job-training programs) rather than pursuing political and legal changes. "Veterans of the 1970s movement faced unpleasant dilemmas," Whittier states, "whether to participate in organizations that they viewed as insufficiently radical in analysis or structure but that addressed issues with which they were concerned, and how to respond to the institutionalization of radical feminist organizations."

CRITICAL OVERVIEW

Piercy's poetry collections, such as the *The Moon Is Always Female* (1980) and *Circles on the Water* (1982), both of which contain the poem "For the Young Who Want To," are often regarded within the context of her political activism in general and her feminism in particular. Critics such as Susan Neunzig Cahill, in *Wise Women: Over Two Thousand Years of Spiritual Writing by Women*, notes that Piercy's poetry, such as that found in *The Moon Is Always Female*, is often focused on "themes of women's spirituality, especially a reverence for the body of mother earth."

Similarly, Mary Ellen Snodgrass, in the *Encyclopedia of Feminist Literature*, states that in *The Moon Is Always Female* Piercy "voices outrage at low wages and limited citizenship for women." This observation regarding Piercy's work is echoed in other assessments, such as the introduction to her science fiction novels contained in *The Science Fiction Handbook* by M. Keith Booker and Anne-Marie Thomas. These critics comment that her poems in such collections as *The Moon Is Always Female* and *Circles on the Water* criticize "the marginalization and victimization of women by the patriarchal structures of mainstream American society."

Cecelia Tichi, in *Embodiment of a Nation: Human Form in American Places*, likewise acknowledges Piercy's feminist approach to her work but also discusses critical views of that work. In identifying Piercy's creative influences, Tichi asserts that Piercy "identifies Walt Whitman as a major influence." Tichi comments that some critics have faulted Piercy for pursuing her political agenda in a manner that mars her work with an "inattention to craft," while others have applauded Piercy's use of "direct statement" in her poetry.

Piercy's work has also been analyzed in terms of the overarching structure of her poetry collections as whole units in and of themselves. Felicia Mitchell, for example, in the *Dictionary of Literary Biography*, Volume 120, *American Poets since World War II, Third Series*, maintains that "structure and sequencing are important elements in Piercy's collections." Even in collections such as *Circles on the Water*, a collection that draws from a number of earlier collections, Mitchell contends that "the integrity is maintained even as poems are presented as excerpts from specific collections."

CRITICISM

Catherine Dominic

Dominic is a novelist and a freelance writer and editor. In the following essay, she explores the way "For the Young Who Want To" exemplifies Piercy's sense of activism, as well as her sense of duty as a writer to be useful.

Critics repeatedly draw attention to the feminist aspects of Piercy's work. In both fiction and poetry, she depicts the struggles women face and

WHAT DO I READ NEXT?

- Piercy's latest collection, *Hunger Moon: New and Selected Poems, 1980–2010*, was published in 2011 by Knopf. The collection traces the arc of Piercy's more mature poetry and expresses her still-political nature and explores personal themes, such as the death of the poet's mother.

- Originally published in 1976, Piercy's much-studied *Woman on the Edge of Time* is at once a psychological novel, a science fiction novel, and a utopian novel. In it, a woman declared insane and admitted to a mental hospital travels through time to a future world in which society is based on gender equality and fairness in all things. The work has been reprinted a number of times and is available in a 2000 edition published by Women's Press.

- Edited by Nguyen Thi Minh Ha, Nguyen Thi Thanh Binh, and Lady Borton, *The Defiant Muse: Vietnamese Feminist Poems from Antiquity to Present* collects over one hundred poems by female Vietnamese poets concerned with women's lives and issues in a bilingual volume. The collection includes a selection of poetry from new, twenty-first century Vietnamese poets, and was published by The Feminist Press at CUNY in 2007.

- In the young-adult novel *The Firefly Letters: A Suffragette's Journey to Cuba*, Cuban American poet and novelist Margarita Engle tells the true story of Fredrika Bremer, a Swedish suffragist (a suffragist is a person advocating the right to vote among a particular group of people, in this case, women) who travels through Cuba with her translator, Cecilia, a teenage slave from the Congo. Engle tells the women's stories in poetry. The poetic narrative, or novel in verse, was published by Henry Holt in 2010.

- Mark McGurl's *The Program Era: Postwar Fiction and the Rise of Creative Writing* is a history and defense of the role of master of fine arts programs in the development of American literature. In his study, McGurl offers explorations of the works of numerous postwar writers. The volume was published by Harvard University Press in 2009.

- *Word: On Being a [Woman] Writer*, edited by Jocelyn Burrell, is an anthology of essays by women of various nationalities and ethnic backgrounds about the challenges and experiences of being a female writer. Topics range from notions of self-identity to the political backlash many writers in war-torn countries have experienced. The anthology was published in 2004 by The Feminist Press at CUNY.

---

the way they rise above them, and portrays visions of a more equitable future. In *Woman on the Edge of Time*, for example, Piercy offers a utopic vision of a future in which gender distinctions have been virtually eliminated. Her work is often spiritual in nature and embraces the concept of an "earth goddess," as Maureen Langdon Shaiman points out in the 2002 *Contemporary American Women Poets: An A-to-Z Guide*, a notion that highlights Piercy's feminist sensibilities. Although many of Piercy's individual poems often receive critical attention, "For the Young Who Want To" is not such a poem. The work does, however, express Piercy's feminism to some degree. Its larger message is also one of advocacy for a group often discriminated against, according to Piercy, in the court of public opinion: unpublished writers. The poem's title emphasizes that the poem to follow is a message, intended for an audience perhaps naïve in the ways of the publishing world. Yet Piercy addresses not just young people, but aspiring artists in general. Through her straightforward language, and through her sometimes sarcastic, sometimes

" **IN DEFENSE OF WRITERS, PIERCY CLAIMS THAT SUCCESS IS ARBITRARY, AND THAT A WRITER IS COMPELLED TO WRITE. THE POEM, TINGED WITH ANGER AND INFUSED WITH IRONIC LANGUAGE, IS A REBUTTAL TO ALL THE COMMENTS WRITERS RECEIVE THROUGHOUT THEIR CAREERS IN WHICH THE VALUE OF THEIR WORK IS QUESTIONED."

---

derisive or even strident tone, Piercy takes a stand against unfair criticism and demands that writers be recognized for their talent by their friends, family, and peers at all stages in their career, pre- and post-publication.

In discussing Piercy's work, John Rodden states in *Performing the Literary Interview: How Writers Craft Their Public Selves* that Piercy's poetry is "rooted in the oral tradition, a spoken art that is written to be performed and heard. This also reflects Piercy's activist politics." The statement aptly describes Piercy's simple yet urgent language as well as her activist aims in "For the Young Who Want To." The tone of the poem conveys her activist spirit. The group she is championing, writers, is discriminated against in the unfairly negative way they are perceived by others. In the introduction to the 1982 collection *Circles on the Water*, Piercy describes her response to the opinions of others about her writing: "I am not a poet who writes primarily for the approval or attention of other poets." This ambivalence regarding the opinions of one's peers finds its way into "For the Young Who Want To" as well. In defense of writers, Piercy claims that success is arbitrary, and that a writer is compelled to write. The poem, tinged with anger and infused with ironic language, is a rebuttal to all the comments writers receive throughout their careers in which the value of their work is questioned. The concept of one's sense of value or worth is a vital one to Piercy's poetry; explorations of the topic repeatedly recur. In one of Piercy's best-known poems, "To Be of Use," published in the 1973 volume by the same name, Piercy declaims her views on usefulness, and praises people who work hard at things they believe in, things that come to them naturally and call to them urgently, and emphasizes the importance to the larger world of people fulfilling their inherent sense of purpose. In her Introduction to *Circles on the Water*, Piercy insists on the sense of usefulness that infuses her poetry by describing her desire that her poetry "work for others." She feels a sense of responsibility to speak for others, to speak, she states, "for a constituency, living and dead," so that she may "give utterance to energy, experience, insight, words flowing from many lives." This sense of responsibility is hinted at in the closing stanza of "For the Young Who Want To." The poem, less studied than some of Piercy's more prominent works, is imbued with the poet's activist stance, her attitudes about the opinions of critics, and her deeply held beliefs regarding personal responsibility and worth.

As the poem opens, Piercy describes the way one's talent as a writer is acknowledged after one has published a novel that has received positive reviews. To an aspiring writer, to those young people to whom the poem is addressed, this may come as a surprise, for in the mind of the inexperienced writer, getting a novel published at all is contemplated as the mark by which the world knows success has been achieved. Piercy knows differently and is aware of the importance of critical acclaim to one's professional standing. Her tone drips with sarcasm when she states that before a writer publishes that well-reviewed novel, his or her efforts are regard as delusional, or worse, trivial. As any aspiring writer knows, to have the craft that one pursues doggedly, despite the absence of any guarantee of critical or financial success, relegated by others to the category of hobby is maddening and hurtful.

Piercy continues to use her ironic tone to demonstrate the pain caused by people who belittle and demean the work of the writer. A playwright's measure of success, as Piercy describes it from the perspective of society, is not just the penning of the play, but having it produced and enjoyed by an audience. The playwright, working steadily day after day toward this goal, is often derided by his or her friends, as Piercy depicts in her poem. The playwright is regarded as lazy, or as indulging in a silly fantasy, and is urged repeatedly to seek real employment. What these images hint at, the image of the playwright hunched over a keyboard, working without reward, with his or her friends suggesting to their deluded companion, in a well-meaning way, that he or she go get a job, is the pain endured by the writer who feels misunderstood and undervalued.

In the third stanza, this pain becomes even more apparent. The standard for success that a poet must achieve, according to this stanza, is publishing the third collection of praiseworthy poems. Then, one is considered a poetic genius. The poet who diligently toils at her craft but has not overcome these professional hurdles is accused by those around her of having withdrawn from society or reality. She is asked why she has not yet had a child and is described in terms of her worthlessness as a contributing member of society. Piercy's feminism is revealed here, for while a male poet may be asked, "When are you going to settle down and start a family?" only a female poet can be confronted with "Why haven't you had a baby?" While the implications of the question may appear on the surface to be similar, for a woman to be asked such a question cuts to the heart of society's conflicting and often harsh views regarding women who pursue a career rather than a family. In this stanza, with this example, the negative attitudes that many possess about the "unsuccessful" writer are now colored by Piercy in an increasingly political context. Readers familiar with Piercy's feminism and political activism will recognize her questioning of the inequities inherent in American culture. While Piercy has elsewhere examined the cultural inequities based not only on racial and gender stereotypes, here she applies her cultural analysis to the critical climate in which the writer lives and works. Piercy responds viscerally to individuals being held to unfair standards or being treated in an unnecessarily judgmental manner. The feminist elements of this stanza remind readers that stereotypes and biases are unfortunately applied to many groups and must be investigated and dismantled whether the individuals under attack are women, members of a racial minority, or writers.

In the next two stanzas, Piercy turns the operating perspective of the poem from that of the outsider, the non-writer and their views of writers, to that of the writer himself or herself. Given the fact that their worth, their value to society, is questioned in the ways outlined in the first three stanzas of the poem, it is no wonder that writers seek validation in the form of degrees and certification, Piercy demonstrates. While the writer's motivation is immediately understandable, based on the evidence Piercy has presented, the validity of such approaches is now questioned.

Here, Piercy's sense of derision is emphasized once again. She scoffs at the notion that anything truly valuable can be ascertained through master of fine arts degree programs or writers' workshops. Although she does not deny that some techniques may be learned, she qualifies this in her way of phrasing the sentiment when she states that the only things that one can actually learn are a few skills, along with instructions for typing one's work. She points to an inherent danger in these programs as well by noting that a writer may absorb or mimic someone else's writing style. Unspoken is the fear that a writer might lose his or her own voice. Piercy's sentiment expressed in the Introduction to *Circles on the Water* is echoed in this stanza. "I am not a poet who writes primarily for the approval or attention of other poets," she states. A poet in a writing program is essentially what the poet Piercy has insisted she is not, a poet writing to gain approval from other poets. In the penultimate stanza, Piercy makes plain through comparison that a degreed poet is neither more nor less likely to be good at what he or she does than a dentist. Although Piercy does not elaborate on this comparison, following it through to its logical conclusions, one may surmise that, according to Piercy, a novelist with an master of fine arts degree, for example, may write sloppy prose in the same way that the dentist she depicts in the poem, one with all the proper certification, may inflict pain and fill cavities with fillings that fall out. A novelist without the master of fine arts degree may write prose just as sloppy as the degree-possessing novelist, Piercy implies, but it is not the having or the not having of the degree that makes the difference.

The poem's final stanza exemplifies Piercy's notion of usefulness and value. A true writer, Piercy states, actually writes, regardless of whether or not his or her talent has been applauded. In her statement regarding the way work may be viewed as a cure, Piercy emphasizes the notion of the writer's responsibility. The statement initially may be seen as a prescription from Piercy, the experienced writer, to the young writers, the aspiring writers reading her work. The work of writing insulates a writer from the criticism he or she may receive from friends and family. Work diligently, she seems to be saying, and the satisfaction of doing what you are compelled to do will protect you (act as a cure) from the pain inflicted by those who tell you that you are crazy, that writing is nothing more than a hobby, that you should get a job, that you should have a baby, that you should contribute to society. By describing work as a cure, though, Piercy reiterates the statements she makes in the *Circles on the Water* introduction. The work of writing may be regarded as something that restores people, that provides the writer with the opportunity, and the duty, to speak up, speak out, to, like Piercy, "speak for a constituency, living and dead," to "give utterance to energy, experience, insight, words flowing from many lives." Piercy goes on, "I have always desired that my poems work for others." She emphasizes that "poetry with a conscious rather than an unconscious politics" has often been considered "impermissible or impure." Yet if one is unsatisfied with the way things are, as a writer one has the responsibility to work toward a cure. In the final stanza of "For the Young Who Want To," then, Piercy emphasizes this sense of responsibility, and directs the readers of the poem as aspiring writers to seek a way to be of use, to be or provide cures for the ills they see in the world around them.

Source: Catherine Dominic, Critical Essay on "For the Young Who Want To," in *Poetry for Students*, Gale, Cengage Learning, 2012.

Fred Moramarco and William Sullivan

In the following excerpt, Moramarco and Sullivan provide an overview of the central themes and preoccupations in Piercy's poetry.

> I am an instrument in the shape of a woman trying to translate pulsations into images for the relief of the body and the reconstruction of the mind. —Adrienne Rich

Although many of the central poets of the modernist movement were women, including Amy Lowell, Gertrude Stein, H. D., and Marianne Moore, for many male writers, the idea of a "women's poetry" in the late 1950s and early 1960s still conjured visions of genteel lyricism by what were then called "poetesses," such as Sara Teasdale, Josephine Preston Peabody, or Edna St. Vincent Millay. Some of it was skillfully crafted and memorably expressed, but it did not seem to embody the realities of many women's situation in life. Not until poets like Muriel Rukeyser, Adrienne Rich, Sylvia Plath, Anne Sexton, Audre Lorde, and Marge Piercy and, more recently, emergent writers like Sharon Olds, Olga Broumas, Louise Glück, and Marilyn Hacker became established did the phrase "women's poetry" come to imply resistance to the social limitations placed on women's lives.

Rukeyser, Brooks, Rich, and Plath opened new worlds for a whole generation of women

> PIERCY'S POETRY IS UNEVEN, OFTEN RAW AND UNFILTERED BY A CONCERN FOR FORMALIST CONSTRAINTS."

who became empowered to speak what had previously been unspeakable. The dissatisfactions of motherhood, the stifling conformity of suburban housewifery, the dominance of male intellectuality, the dismissal of female perceptions of reality, the objectification of women's bodies, the social tolerance of rape and sexual harassment of all kinds, the politics of abortion, the blatant economic inequality of the sexes, and many other subjects previously ignored or actively repressed began to be dealt with openly and in depth. Ironically, "women's poetry" became in some ways the opposite of what it had previously been. No longer genteel and lyrical, it began to carry a political edge. Much of this poetry was controversial and rejected, especially by male critics, who often viewed it as self-indulgent and artless. But as its body began to gather heft and momentum throughout the sixties, seventies, and eighties, it could no longer be ignored as a dominant force in contemporary poetry.

Women were demonstrating that gender is an important component of poetic value, although many writers, both men and women, continued to resist that idea. Elizabeth Bishop, for example, refused to be anthologized in any women-only poetry anthology because she believed that the art of poetry transcends gender. And although Diane Wakoski clearly writes a "woman-centered" poetry that focuses especially on relationships between men and women, she believes that any gender adjective that precedes the word *poet* diminishes it. But to say that gender is a component of poetic value is not to argue that it is the only component. Writing is related to life experience, and the experiences of men and women in our society are significantly different in many respects: childbearing, childrearing, domestic responsibilities, military experience (until recently), and economic opportunities are just a few differences that create the foundation for a poetry influenced by gender.

Some women take the gender issue a step further and talk about a "female poetics" that informs the women's poetry of note in our time. In her important revisionist history of women's poetry in America, Alicia Suskin Ostriker writes about "an assertive desire for intimacy" that she believes characterizes this poetics: "As the poet refuses to distance herself from her emotion, so she prevents us [as readers] from distancing ourselves." For Ostriker and for other feminist writers like Adrienne Rich, Suzanne Juhasz, and Audre Lorde, a woman-centered poetry has emerged that has as its project the definition of a "female self" unmitigated by the assumptions and cultural priorities of male writers. This poetry intends to transform literary culture as well as the social culture it both grows out of and affects. Consequently, much of the women's poetry of our time is involved in revising traditional myths, whether explicitly, as in Anne Sexton's *Transformations*, or implicitly, as in Marge Piercy's reconstruction of male-female relationships. In addition, Adrienne Rich sees "a passion for survival" as one of the great themes of women's poetry today and finds it ironic "that male critics have focused on our suicidal poets, and on their 'self'-destructiveness rather than their capacity for hard work and for staying alive as long as they did." Combining a desire for intimacy with the shaping of a new female identity based on revising the myths of the past and transforming the realities of the present has produced an intensely personal poetry that is also pointedly political. In fact, the distinctive contribution of contemporary women's poetry is that the personal and political are identified with each other and conjoined.

In addition to the women mentioned above, many other writers have been instrumental in creating this new kind of "woman-centered" poetry that departs from the constricted sensibility often associated (usually by men) with feminine norms. These include Sonia Sanchez, Gloria Anzaldúa, Paula Gunn Allen, Wendy Rose, and others who are creating what Adrienne Rich calls "a whole new poetry beginning here." Those women who also broadened the context of writing in the United States by underscoring their ethnic and cultural heritages will be explored more fully in chapter 7. Here we will look at how the assertion of gender reshaped American poetry in the seventies and eighties....

Born to a working-class family in Detroit, Marge Piercy now lives on two acres in Wellfleet, Massachusetts, and both her midwestern urban roots and her New England village present are important factors in her poetry. A prolific writer, she has published more than a dozen collections of poetry as well as many works of fiction, including *Woman on the Edge of Time* (1976), an important feminist work that influenced a generation of women and encouraged their involvement in the women's movement. Piercy also edited an anthology of American women's poetry in 1987 called *Early Ripening*, in which she argues that women's poetry in late twentieth-century America is characterized by a fused rather than "dissociated" sensibility—emotion and intellect working together rather than at war with each other. Women's poetry in our time, according to Piercy, tends also to be a poetry of "re-invention" that is often confrontational vis à vis traditional social institutions and structures. There is in much of the work included in *Early Ripening* "a remaking, a renewing, a renaming, a re-experiencing, and then recasting."

This understanding of contemporary women's poetry permeates nearly all of Piercy's own work. Though that work is diverse and reflects different stages of her life, it is important to her that poetry be *useful*, particularly to other women who will recognize themselves in various aspects of her life journey. Several kinds of poem make up the bulk of Piercy's canon. First there are feminist-oriented poems on topics like rape, abortion, abused women, and working-class women that tend to speak directly to other women with the idea of enrolling them in the "we" of the poem. Second, there are poems of social criticism that deal with issues other than those exclusively concerned with women: automation, technology, war, inhumanity, indifference to suffering, and many others that constitute the "cancers" of modern life that need to be exposed and rooted out. Third, there are poems about Piercy's Detroit working-class childhood, especially family poems about her troubled relationship with her mother and father. Fourth, there are love poems, especially apparent in the later work, either celebrating the renewal of love or lamenting its demise. A persistent theme that crosses the boundaries of several of these subjects is the need for transformation, particularly the transformation of relationships between men and women.

Piercy's best work through 1980 is collected in *Circles on the Water: Selected Poems* (1982). Most of these poems were written in the sixties and seventies phase of the contemporary feminist movement and are predominantly political in orientation and militant in tone, although they also deal with the status of male/female relationships in the period. In "Doing it differently," Piercy makes a dramatic attempt to alter the status quo. She wants to reconstruct male-female relationships and move them out of the wasteland that many have inhabited. Although the poem is preachy, it is also affecting, and very much a document of its time. The lovers in the poem are "bagged in habit," but the woman feels they have the power to choose their destiny and not simply accept the conventions handed down to them. The woman appears vulnerable as she crawls into the man "as a bee crawls into a lily," but while the woman is always vulnerable, the man is vulnerable only when he is making love. The narrator asks if men and women can ever be free of the roles of dominance and submission. Sounding surprisingly apolitical, Piercy evokes the image of a rose as a symbol of male-female union.

> I am a body beautiful only when fitted with yours.
> Otherwise, it walks, it lifts packages, it spades.
> It is functional or sick, tired or sturdy. It serves.
> Together we are the rose, full, red as the inside
> of the womb and head of the penis,
> blossoming as we encircle, we make that symmetrical fragrant emblem,
> then separate into discrete workday selves.

Can this rosy picture actually become the norm? Can there be a "new man and woman" committed to this kind of beautiful union? The woman in the poem feels powerless to make it happen because her inferiority is encased in the language, laws, institutions, and traditions of society. To create this kind of equal union, men need to take positive steps toward change:

> We are equal only if you open too on your heavy hinges
> and let your love come freely, freely, where it will never be safe,
> where you can never possess.
> (*Circles*)

In the books published since *Circles on the Water*, Piercy's poetry is even less politically programmatic, more complex. *Stone, Paper, Knife* (1983), *My Mother's Body* (1986), and *Available Light* (1988) contain some of her strongest work. The central elements of these books are an insistence on dealing with the specifics of her experience; a willingness to see both men and women as individual, real people rather than as stereotypical role models; an introspective sense of self-discovery; and an attempt to understand the roots of the anger that permeates so much of her life and work. For like Audre Lorde and Adrienne Rich, Piercy values anger as a spur for her muse and almost fears its dissipation. In a poem called "How divine is forgiving?" from *Available Light*, she sees forgiveness as a weakness—a recognition of our imperfections rather than a large, magnanimous gesture:

> We forgive because we too have done
> the same to others easy as a mudslide;
> or because anger is a fire that must be fed
> and we are too tired to rise and haul a log.
> (*Circles*)

My Mother's Body, written shortly after her mother's death, locates the source of that anger very specifically:

> The anger turned inward, the anger
> turned inward, where
> could it go except to make pain?
> It flowed into me with her milk.
> (*Circles*)

Rummaging through her mother's things after her death, she finds artifacts that connect her to her mother's experience. Piercy, a middle-class woman, a successful writer, looks back at her mother's working-class life with a feminist eye, venting what she believes were her mother's repressed feelings of anger. She notices that her mother, like so many women of her generation, used "ugly" things for everyday and kept her beautiful things locked in storage. They were never used because "no day of hers was ever good enough" to use them, and so they become an emblem of the repressed beauty and creativity of the women of her mother's generation.

In the lovely title poem of this collection, mother and daughter become interchangeable:

> My mother is my mirror and I am hers.
> What do we see?
> (*Circles*)

Looking back from the vantage point of a mature and seasoned life, the narrator realizes that the two women are less mother and daughter than twin sisters who happen to live in different times. Her feelings of youthful rebellion and resentment give way to mature self-recognition as the narrator takes on her mother's anger as her own:

> I will not be the bride you can dress,
> the obedient dutiful daughter you would chew,
> a dog's leather bone to sharpen your teeth.
> You strike me sometimes just to hear the sound.
> Loneliness turns your fingers into hooks
> barbed and drawing blood with their caress.

> My twin, my sister, my lost love,
> I carry you in me like an embryo
> as once you carried me.
> (*Circles*)

My Mother's Body is also notable for its sequence of love poems called "Chuppah," after the canopy used in Jewish wedding ceremonies. These poems were written for Piercy's marriage to writer Ira Wood, and she includes two poems by Wood in the sequence.

Available Light continues in this vein of self-discovery and retrospection. More than any of her books it chronicles the transformation of a "bad girl" from the inner city into a successful woman and widely respected writer. The poem "Joy Road and Livernois," though clearly feminist in its depiction of the lot of working-class women, is also a very personal poem about Piercy's Detroit upbringing and the grim fate of some of her girlfriends, dead from accidents or drug overdoses, dying of cancer, or trapped in a mental institution. Offering short biographical sketches of each of these women—Pat, Evie, Peggy, Theresa, Gladys—in the vein of Edgar Lee Masters's *Spoon River Anthology*—Piercy emerges as a survivor of a world nearly impossible to transcend.

In a poem called "I see the sign and tremble," inspired by a "Self Storage" sign glimpsed from the highway advertising a company offering storage lockers, Piercy creates a metaphor for the evolution of her poetry. She thinks of her poems as places where she has stored her various "selves" at different parts of her life. The poem itself is a catalog of Piercy's various identities, from "the gang girl running over the tarred / roofs sticky under her sneakers" through "the New York femme fatale dancing through a maze of mirrors" to "the woman alone / in the Midwest of a rented room sent into exile."

Available Light is also a very sensuous book, containing some of Piercy's best love poems, rich in the physicality of an opulent sexuality yet also tempered by the actual ups and downs of a long-term relationship. She chronicled the end of one love affair and the beginning of another in *Stone, Paper, Knife*, and here she writes about both the abundance of a happily married sex life as well as the bumpy road to reconciliation after horrendous arguments:

> Eat, drink, I am your daily bread
> and you are mine made every morning fresh
> In the oven of the bed we rise and bake
> yeasty, dark, full of raisins and seeds
> You have come back from your hike

> up the sandblasted mountains of ego
> and I have crawled out from my squat
> in the wind caves of sulk
> (*Circles*)

Finally, a poignant poem, "Burial by Salt," is an important landmark in Piercy's work, representing her attempt to let go of her anger about her father's distant silence and lack of personal support. The iciness of the father-daughter relationship is captured in two lines that underscore the tragedy of too many American families:

> To you I made no promises. You asked none.
> Forty-nine years we spoke of nothing real
> (*Circles*)

Although desperate for her father's love, Piercy never felt it. The two have between them, as Piercy sees it, only "history / not love," and as she scatters his ashes to the wind (as she did with her mother's ashes, recorded in an earlier poem, "What remains"), she tries finally to come to terms with that limitation.

Her poetry published in the 1990's, *Mars and Her Children* (1992) and *What Are Big Girls Made Of?* (1997) carry on her lifetime concerns, showing a growing awareness of the "precarious balance" between the social and natural worlds. A poem like "The ark of consequence," which organizes the sections of the former volume according to the colors of the rainbow, deals with ecological issues (the consequences of an oil spill). The title poem of that book, "For Mars and her children returning in March," laments the threat humanity poses to the humpback whale. Animal rights issues surface as well in the latter book. "Death of a doe on Chequesset Neck" projects the narrator into the pain of a dying animal, and "Crow babies" sees the society of crows as superior to our own.

Piercy's poetry is uneven, often raw and unfiltered by a concern for formalist constraints. One critic even describes her poetry as seeming "for the most part to have been poured out and then cut up into lines." That assessment does capture something of the "I must get all of this down" quality of Piercy's work. Yet despite the unedited feel of many of the poems, they also contain what Marianne Moore called "a place for the genuine."

Source: Fred Moramarco and William Sullivan, "'A Whole New Poetry Beginning Here': The Assertion of Gender," in *Containing Multitudes: Poetry in the United States since 1950*, Twayne, 1998, pp. 163–94.

Edith J. Wynne

In the following essay, Wynne discusses emotional and psychological motifs associated with the imagery of Piercy's poetry.

Under the title, *Circles on the Water*, Marge Piercy published, in 1982, a collection of more than one hundred and fifty poems selected from seven of her previously published volumes. In the introduction to *Circles on the Water*, Piercy remarks,

> One of the oldest habits of our species, poetry is powerful in aligning the psyche. A poem can momentarily integrate the different kinds of knowing of our different and often warring levels of brain, from the reptilian part that recognizes rhythms and responds to them up through the mammalian centers of the emotions, from symbolic knowing as in dreams to analytical thinking, through rhythms and sound and imagery as well as overt meaning. A poem can momentarily heal not only the alienation of thought and feeling Eliot discussed, but can fuse the different kinds of knowing and for at least some instants weld mind back into body seamlessly.

Piercy's allusion to T. S. Eliot in her discussion of what poetry can do to integrate our ways of knowing is significant. While Piercy gives some attention to the relatively new psychological theory of opposing brain hemisphere functions, she also recalls the old debate between the functions of logic and emotion in the metaphysical poets, a group with which Piercy has some commonality in her imagistic techniques. Piercy's collected poems contain a startling array of images which, in their variety and number, in their apparently haphazard distribution, in their wide-ranging sensuousness, and in their seemingly antithetical juxtaposition of thought and feeling, create that kind of *discordia concors* so often associated with the metaphysical tradition. On the surface, Piercy's poems might aptly be described by Samuel Johnson's observation on the poet, Cowley:

> The most heterogeneous ideas are yoked by violence together; nature and art are ransacked for illustrations, comparisons, and allusions; their learning instructs, and their subtilty surprises.

Yet, Piercy's poetry does more than merely surprise and instruct. Eliot and other theorists have made commonplace the critical edict that the metaphysicals were able to express experience both emotionally and intellectually at the same instance. Piercy contends that, in her poems, the richness of thought and feeling possessed by all human beings informs her choice of

> "PIERCY SPEAKS DIRECTLY TO HER READERS IN HER OWN VOICE ALTHOUGH SHE REMINDS US THAT THE EXPERIENCES SHE RECOUNTS ARE NOT ALWAYS HER OWN, NOR ARE THE POEMS CONFESSIONAL."

images and brings a kind of unity out of chaos for us:

> That the poems may give voice to something in the experience of a life has been my intention. To find ourselves spoken for in art gives dignity to our pain, our anger, our lust, our losses.... We have few rituals that function for us in the ordinary chaos of our lives.

Piercy speaks directly to her readers in her own voice although she reminds us that the experiences she recounts are not always her own, nor are the poems confessional. She states that when she is writing she is not aware of any distinction between her own and other people's experiences, but that she is "often pushing the experience beyond realism." In this sense, Piercy creates a vortex of images which are often paradoxical but "reader-friendly." As Cleanth Brooks noted in his discussion of the language of paradox,

> The poet must work by analogies, but the metaphors do not lie in the same plane or fit neatly edge to edge. There is continual tilting of the planes; necessary overlappings, discrepancies, contradiction. Even the most direct and simple poet is forced into paradoxes far more often than we think, if we are sufficiently alive to what he is doing.

Piercy is such a direct and simple poet as Brooks describes, particularly in diction, tone, and form. She writes, she tells us, as a social animal and intends her poems not for other poets, but to be "of use" to the reader; she says, "I am not a poet who writes primarily for the approval or attention of other poets.... Poetry is too important to keep to ourselves." She admits to occasional didacticism and to conscious feminist politics; she believes that her poems "coax, lecture, lull, seduce, exhort, denounce." Her poetry reminds us in several ways of the metaphysical tradition but stripped of the intellectual pyrotechnics of that tradition.

Piercy's use of imagery is one of the major assets of her poetic technique. The title of the volume *Circles on the Water* provides a descriptive metaphor for the recurrent, intertwined, echoic use of images so characteristic of her work. A few of her poems are built upon a single, extended metaphor; among these are "A work of artifice" in which a bonsai tree is compared throughout the poem to the stunted growth of a stereotyped female, and "The best defense is offensive" in which the actions of a turkey vulture are equated with a useful political stance. Much more typical of her work, however, is a lyrical, almost free-flowing series of images, built upon emotional and psychological associations rather than upon logical paradox or metaphysical conceit. Like circles on water created when a pool's surface tension is disturbed, her images form concentric, ever-widening patterns linked only by the energy and force of the precipitating experience. Usually, we are made fully aware of the initial event, for Piercy often begins with a narrative and maintains a strong sense of time and place. The force and energy of the image patterns is, therefore, one of the most exciting and unique qualities of the poems, but a quality not easily analyzed.

One of the poems which most clearly and dramatically displays the image-by-association artistry through which Piercy constructs an organic whole is "Sign," written in 1967 and included in her first published volume, *Breaking Camp*. As in the majority of her poems, Piercy provides a dramatic narrative structure; an event in the present precipitates contemplation. In "Sign," this event is quite commonplace—the poet discovers an emblem of aging:

> The first white hair coils in my hand,
> more wire than down.
> Out of the bathroom mirror it glittered at me.
> I plucked it, feeling thirty creep in my joints,
> and found it silver. It does not melt.

This brief opening stanza contains four images which are interwoven throughout the remainder of the poem in a carefully orchestrated, psychological point counter-point. The hair itself is the focal object, but one made up of several different sense impressions. The hair has color (white, then silver), texture (more "wire" than "down"), and substance (unlike quicksilver, it does not "melt" at body warmth). Furthermore, the hair is seen in a mirror, glitters, and is "plucked." Then, the poet feels thirty "creep" in her joints.

These visual, tactile, and kinaesthetic impressions of the hair are repeated in the next stanza, but within a completely different time and place:

> My twentieth birthday lean as glass
> spring vacation I stayed in the college town
> twangling misery's electric banjo offkey.
> I wanted to inject love right into the veins
> of my thigh and wake up visible:
> to vibrate color
> like the minerals in stones under black light.
> My best friend went home without loaning me money.
> Hunger was all of the time the taste of my mouth.

This shift to past time is perfectly natural; finding a white hair at thirty precipitates a realistic and commonplace reaction; the subject remembers her twentieth birthday. What is not so commonplace is the subtle, almost incremental, repetition of images from the first stanza, given new meaning in this different context. The mirror in which she first sees the hair is now transformed into her body, for she is "lean as glass." She spends time "twanging" an electric banjo "offkey," as in the first stanza she "plucked" the offending wire-like hair. Both actions call up misery, an emotion. At twenty, she twangs "misery's" banjo; at thirty, she experiences the misery of awareness of aging. The hair is, in its natural state, white or silver, almost colorless; at twenty, she had wanted to "vibrate color," but as minerals do, under "black" light. In both stanzas, the parts of the body receive attention. At twenty, she wished to inject love directly into "veins" and "thigh." At thirty, age is felt creeping into her "joints." Finally, in the second stanza, a new sense impression is added to the catalogue of recurrent images; "hunger" and "taste" provide a gustatory dimension which will be repeated in the third stanza, as the poet returns to present time:

> Now I am ripened and sag a little from my spine.
> More than most I have been the same ragged self
> in all colors of luck dripping and dry,
> yet love has nested in me and gradually eaten
> those sense organs I used to feel with.
> I have eaten my hunger soft and my ghost grows
>   stronger.

The love which the subject wished to inject into thigh and vein in her twentieth year, when she was lean, constantly hungry, and eager for an awakening to visible self, has now "nested" in her and gradually "eaten" her sense organs. The aging process of which she has become dramatically aware causes her spine to sag, as a parallel to the creeping of age into her joints in stanza one. The hunger of her college vacation now consumes itself, but her "ghost" grows stronger although she is the "same ragged self" with "all colors of luck" within her. The word "ghost" appears intentionally ambiguous, open to several interpretations, all of which may best be treated after examination of the final stanza which brings together again the colors, textures, and motions of the opening lines:

> Gradually, I am turning to chalk,
> to humus, to pages and pages of paper,
> to fine silver wire like something a violin
> could be strung with, or somebody garroted,
> or current run through: silver truly,
> this hair, shiny and purposeful as forceps
> if I knew how to use it.

Once again, the color motif returns to become central to the message. Chalk and paper are white or colorless, as is the found hair. Humus is dark, as is black light, and as are youthful tresses. With these colors, attention to the ambiguity of aging is further disclosed. Darkness (or blackness) is both life-giving and death-dealing. Black light brings up colors in minerals; humus is fertile loam; dark hair is abundantly youthful growth. On the other hand, humus is soil, black soil, the earth to which we return in death. Black light is an artificial means which uncovers natural mineral beauty hidden to the naked eye, just as death perhaps transforms the soul (or "ghost"), or as a mirror brings attention to the sign of aging. White is played upon equally paradoxically. Now the subject becomes white chalk and colorless paper, inert, yet potentially productive. The coarse white hair of the opening stanza has become "fine silver wire" strung into a violin, in sharp contrast to the wire strung into an offkey electric banjo in her twentieth year. Paradoxically, however, this same fine silver wire is associated with death by garroting or by electrocution. Finally, the hair shines as purposefully and usefully as forceps, instruments commonly associated with birth rather than death. The poet ultimately perceives in the silver wire-hair a power as ambiguous as the images employed to re-tell the experience. Life or death, creativity or repression, growth or stagnation—the meaning lies not within the discovered object itself, the emblem of aging, but within the human spirit. The ghost which grows stronger within the poet may be death or life; the outcome depends upon the qualifying clause, "If I knew how to use it."

This intensive study of the images in "Sign" demonstrates the intricate networking and intertwining of seemingly disparate elements which is one of the great strengths of Piercy's poetic vision. While not every poem in her canon is so full of leit-motifs as is "Sign," patterns of psychological association appear in many other places in her work. A brief glance at three other pieces can identify the pattern. In "Erasure" from the volume *Hard Loving*, the poet's subject is the loss of a lover. Images of light, vision, and a mouse graphically convey the emotional impact of the experience. The poet moves from "blood turned grey," to a burning out of the "glittering synapses of the brain," to "stars fading in the galaxy," and on to a picture of the imaginary animal figures of the constellations that "would photograph more like a blurry mouse." Falling out of love she then defines as a "correcting vision" which nevertheless damages the optic nerve. The final lines of the poem powerfully unite all these loosely connected images:

> To find you have loved a coward and a fool
> is to give up the lion, the dragon, the sunburst
> and take away your hands covered with small festering bites
> and let the mouse go in a grey blur
> into the baseboard.

A further example of Piercy's technique is found in the poem "Some collisions bring luck" which is from her third volume, *To Be of Use*. A chance meeting with a lover during the month of October provides the poem's speaker with momentary relief from the state of mind with which she opens the narrative:

> I had grown invisible as a city sparrow.
> My breasts had turned into watches.
> Even my dreams were of function and meeting.

The chance encounter is reported in the ten lines of the next stanza. The setting is a "pumpkin afternoon"; the lover is "bright rind carved into a knowing grin." The couple run upstairs, and at the lover's sexual touch, the poet "flew open." Soon, "orange and indigo feathers" break through her skin and she rolls in the lover's "coarse rag-doll hair." She sucks the lover "like a ripe apricot down to the pit." The images circle around the visions and colors of fall, orange and apricot, like the hair of a Raggedy-Ann doll. Once again, the concluding lines of the stanza switch from objects to emotions:

> Sitting crosslegged on the bed we chattered
> basting our lives together with ragged stitches.

In the closing stanza, the stitches do not hold, yet the warmth of the chance encounter in the October afternoon replaces the mechanical self expressed in the opening lines:

Of course it all came apart
but my arms glow with the fizz of that cider sun.
My dreams are of mating leopards and bronze waves.
We coalesced in the false chemistry of words
rather than truly touching
yet I burn cool glinting in the sun
and my energy sings like a teakettle all day long.

One final example from the volume *The Twelve-Spoked Wheel Flashing*, a poem entitled "The window of a woman burning" will underscore what Piercy accomplishes with her rich imagery. The poem opens with what appears to be the realistic description of a woman caught up in a fire, her hair a "cone of orange snakes," as she writhes in flames. Quickly, however, the burning woman is differentiated from other martyrs; she is neither a Joan at the stake nor a crucified madonna or saint. She is, instead, "the demon of a fountain of energy," energy which flows from her brain, from her fiery hair:

> flickering lights from the furnace in the solar
> plexus, lush scents from the reptilian brain,
> river that winds up the hypothalamus
> with its fibroids of pleasure and pain
> twisted and braided like a rope,
> firing the lanterns of the forebrain
> till they glow blood red.

The next stanza emphasizes the strong firewoman's dance, in "beauty that crouches / inside like a cougar in the belly / not in the eyes of others measuring." This transformed woman leaps through a green forest. In the final stanza, she becomes "the icon of woman sexual," who is "with the cauldrons of her energies / burning red, burning green." From the opening images of death by fire and sacrifice to the concluding image of red and green as life and growth in the sexual cycle, Piercy bombards the senses with quick, agile turns of impression that somehow hold together. What Marge Piercy accomplishes with her circling, concentric, seemingly disparate images is exciting, fresh, and flexible poetry as demanding of the reader as any metaphysical performance by Donne. With Piercy, as with Donne, we are always in touch with the human elements, body and mind, flesh and spirit. Piercy's purposeful and powerful use of images is perhaps most clearly stated in her own words. Introducing a series of poems based upon the Tarot deck, she says:

> We must break through the old roles to encounter our own meanings in the symbols we experience in dreams, in songs, in vision, in meditation.... What we use we must remake. Then only are we not playing with dead dreams but seeing ourselves more clearly, and more clearly becoming.

Piercy is, then, constructing a poetic vehicle through which old ways of seeing, old ways of knowing, are wrenched out of old contexts to be given new meaning. True to the feminist movement which she claims changed her life, she intends to break with linear, patriarchal patterns in favor of circles, moons, emotions superior to logic. These form a dialectic which teaches us, as she says in her recent poem "Digging in":

> You are learning to live in circles
> as well as straight lines

Source: Edith J. Wynne, "Imagery of Association in the Poetry of Marge Piercy," in *Publications of the Missouri Philological Association*, Vol. 10, 1985, pp. 57–63.

SOURCES

Batuman, Elif, "Get a Real Degree," in *London Review of Books*, Vol. 32, No. 18, September 23, 2010, pp. 3–8, http://www.lrb.co.uk/v32/n18/elif-batuman/get-a-real-degree (accessed July 5, 2011).

Beach, Christopher, Introduction and "The New Criticism and Poetic Formalism," in *The Cambridge Introduction to Twentieth-Century Poetry*, Cambridge University Press, 2003, pp. 1-6, 137–53.

Booker, M. Keith, and Anne-Marie Thomas, "Marge Piercy," in *The Science Fiction Handbook*, Wiley-Blackwell, 2009, pp. 167–69.

Cahill, Susan Neunzig, "Marge Piercy," in *Wise Women: Over Two Thousand Years of Spiritual Writing by Women*, W. W. Norton, 1996, pp. 252–54.

"The ERA in Congress: 112th Session (2011-2012)," in *The Equal Rights Amendment*, http://www.equalrightsamendment.org (accessed July 5, 2011).

Francis, Roberta W., "The History behind the Equal Rights Amendment," in *The Equal Rights Amendment*, http://www.equalrightsamendment.org/era.htm (accessed July 5, 2011).

Lawson, Anton E., "The Nature of Scientific Theories: The 'Discovery' of Oxygen," in *Teaching Inquiry Science in Middle and Secondary Schools*, Sage, 2010, pp. 25–29.

McGurl, Mark, "The MFA Octopus: Four Questions about Creative Writing," in *Los Angeles Review of Books*, May 11, 2011, http://lareviewofbooks.org/post/5389807479/the-mfa-octopus-four-questions-about-creative-writing (accessed July 5, 2011).

Mitchell, Felicia, "Marge Piercy," in *Dictionary of Literary Biography*, Volume 120, *American Poets since World War II, Third Series*, Gale Research, 1992, pp. 248–53.

Ochester, Ed, ed., Introduction to *American Poetry Now: Pitt Poetry Series Anthology*, University of Pittsburgh Press, 2007, pp. xix–xxviii.

Piercy, Marge, "For the Young Who Want To," in *The Moon Is Always Female*, Alfred A. Knopf, 1988, pp. 85–86.

———, Introduction to *Circles on the Water: Selected Poems of Marge Piercy*, Alfred A. Knopf, 1982, pp. xi–xv.

Rankine, Claudia, and Lisa Sewell, eds., Introduction to *American Poets in the 21st Century: The New Poetics*, Wesleyan University Press, 2007, pp. 1–15.

Rodden, John, "'Bitter' Poet-Prophet: Marge Piercy," in *Performing the Literary Interview: How Writers Craft Their Public Selves*, University of Nebraska Press, 2001, pp. 67–96.

Shaiman, Maureen Langdon, "Marge Piercy," in *Contemporary American Women Poets: An A-to-Z Guide*, edited by Catherine Cucinella, Greenwood Press, 2002, pp. 278–83.

Snodgrass, Mary Ellen, "Marge Piercy," in *Encyclopedia of Feminist Literature*, Facts on File, 2006, pp. 423–24.

Tichi, Cecelia, "America's Moon: 'A Dream of the Future's Face,'" in *Embodiment of a Nation: Human Form in American Places*, Harvard University Press, 2001, pp. 126–72.

Whittier, Nancy, "Feminists in the 'Postfeminist' Age: The Women's Movement in the 1980s," in *Feminist Generations: The Persistence of the Radical Women's Movement*, Temple University Press, 1995, pp. 191–224.

Piercy, Marge, *Sleeping with Cats: A Memoir*, William Morrow, 2002.

> Piercy's memoir describes the tragedies of her past, such as the abortion she performed on herself at the age of seventeen, the trajectories of her various romantic relationships and three marriages, her global travels, her political activism, and her writing career.

———, and Ira Wood, *So You Want to Write: How to Master the Craft of Writing Fiction and Memoir*, 2nd ed., Leapfrog Press, 2005.

> In this updated and revised edition of the 2001 volume, Piercy and Wood offer a series of essays on the writing process.

Stansell, Christine, *The Feminist Promise: 1792 to the Present*, Modern Library, 2010.

> Stansell offers a detailed historical account of feminist history, tracing it back to Mary Wollstonecraft's 1792 publication of the tract "A Vindication of the Rights of Woman," and highlighting the contributions of numerous leaders in the movement over years. She additionally links the modern feminist movement to the issue of global human rights.

FURTHER READING

Dowdy, Michael, *American Political Poetry in the 21st Century*, Palgrave Macmillan, 2007.

> Dowdy's study offers an analysis of contemporary political poetry that includes a focus on the work of hip-hop artists, mainstream poets, and writers of various ethnic pasts and nationalities, providing the historical context within which their work may be understood. Students of Piercy's poetry have the opportunity to see the way activist poetry has evolved into the twenty-first century.

SUGGESTED SEARCH TERMS

Marge Piercy AND The Moon Is Always Female

Marge Piercy AND free verse poetry

Marge Piercy AND political activism

Marge Piercy AND feminism

Marge Piercy AND biography

Marge Piercy AND awards

Marge Piercy AND fiction

Marge Piercy AND memoir

Marge Piercy AND Leapfrog Press

Marge Piercy AND Jewish poets

For the Young Who Want To

For the Young Who Want To AND Marge Piercy

I Am Learning to Abandon the World

LINDA PASTAN

1981

Linda Pastan's "I Am Learning to Abandon the World" is a poem about the slow and inevitable approach of death as the narrator's years advance. For Pastan, the act of writing is her means of bearing up under an unavoidable fate; it is writing that gives meaning to her life. In an interview with Lisa Granik in *Truthtellers of the Times: Interviews with Contemporary Women Poets*, Pastan characterizes her identity as a writer and the function of writing in her life: "There is great joy in being a writer. The discoveries you make about the world and about yourself give the greatest pleasure. The real pain is when I can't write." "I Am Learning to Abandon the World" expresses how Pastan uses poetry as a defense against death, or at least the effect of approaching death, in a necessarily losing battle.

"I Am Learning to Abandon the World" was first published in *Poetry* magazine in September 1981; the next year, it was included in Pastan's anthology *PM/AM: New and Selected Poems*. The poem uses Pastan's main themes of nature and death. It is also firmly anchored within her secular identity. The domesticity of her poems is at war with her feminist leanings.

Although Pastan has not received any major poetry awards, she is one of the most prominent living American poets, the kind of writer who is always seriously considered for the post of poet laureate of the United States, a post she has already held in her home state of Maryland.

AUTHOR BIOGRAPHY

Pastan was born on May 27, 1932, in the Bronx, New York, to Jacob and Bess Olenik. Her parents were the children of Jewish immigrants from Eastern Europe. Like many children of immigrants, they took advantage of new educational opportunities in America, and Jacob Olenik became a physician. The family became completely secularized. Linda, for instance, never entered a synagogue until she was an adult and attended a friend's wedding. Her parents hoped that she would also become a doctor, or in any case follow some profession (which was not that common for women at the time), and accordingly sent her to Fiedelston prep school and to Radcliffe College. In 1954, her senior year, she married Ira Pastan, then a medical student. Although she obtained the qualifications to work as a librarian and earned a master's degree in English literature at Brandeis University, as her husband's career developed, Pastan rebelled against the expectations of her parents and devoted herself to homemaking and raising her three children.

After a rather spectacular public premier as a poet, winning *Mademoiselle*'s Dylan Thomas Award for poetry (not to be confused with the later Dylan Thomas Award based in Great Britain) and receiving a nationally prominent publication in 1955, Pastan stopped writing poetry for fourteen years. By 1970, Ira Pastan became chief of the Laboratory of Molecular Biology at the National Cancer Institute, a position he still holds and where he has become a leading researcher in immunotoxin therapy (destroying cancer cells by using their natural biology to absorb poisons). He is also a member of the National Academy of Sciences. Since her husband works in Washington, DC, Pastan lives in a semi-rural area of Maryland.

By the late 1960s, her children were sufficiently grown up to allow Pastan to return to writing poetry. Her poems quickly found prominent publication, thanks to her previous fame. She also began to work as an editor, educator, and lecturer. Pastan follows a disciplined schedule of writing every morning, and she publishes about twenty-five poems a year. Her work has been collected in more than a dozen anthologies, and Pastan has won numerous awards, including the Bess Hokin Award from *Poetry* magazine and the Virginia Faulkner award from the *Prairie Schooner*. Her book *PM/AM*, which contains "I Am Learning to Abandon the World," was nominated for a National Book Award. In 1991, she served as the poet laureate of Maryland, and in 1992, she became a judge for the poetry section of the National Book Award. *The Five Stages of Grief* (1978) is well thought of and is sometimes considered her most important work.

POEM SUMMARY

The text used for this summary is from *PM/AM: New and Selected Poems*, W. W. Norton, 1982, pp. 17–18. A version of the poem can be found on the following Web page: http://www.poetryfoundation.org/poetrymagazine/poem/24167.

In general, the speaker, or *I*, in a poem should be understood as a narrator who is not necessarily the same as the poet himself or herself. In Pastan's work, though, these two personas often come closer than in most poets, so the speaker in this poem may be identified, cautiously, as Pastan herself. In the first two lines, the narrator sets up a contrast that is also is a unity. She is going to be separated from the world one way or another. The question is whether separation will be brought about by the poet herself or by the unavoidable process of the world. Whether the narrator or the world does the abandoning, the result is the same—the death of the narrator—so what is the difference? In part, the difference is the continuing subject of the rest of the poem, but clearly it is also a matter of agency, or the power to act. Suffering something is worse than doing something. If the narrator chooses to give up a thing, then it is not lost.

The next sentence (lines 3–5) reveals what the narrator has given up, namely the moon and snow. Both have been abandoned to white. The moon and snow are both white in color (except when the moon is near the horizon or snow is soiled), but yielding them up to white—as if the color were a person—is a strange idea. White is the color of death: the color of corpses and winding sheets, the color of ghosts and fairies. The moon and snow are given up to death because they belong to death. And since the narrator has voluntarily given them up by closing the window blinds, she simply does not see them any longer and so they are no loss to her. The moon here is also contrasted with the sun, introduced as a symbol of life that is by no means given up yet at the end of the poem. This pairing has another peculiar meaning for Pastan. She once noted that a critic complained that she wrote of the moon too much, so she made a conscious decision to write of the sun instead, and here is the very moment of transition between them.

In contrast to her act of giving things up, the narrator's father and friends have been taken from her, having died, before she was ready to give them up, so for them she must count the loss.

In lines 8 and 9, the narrator reveals more that she has given up. These things are very strange indeed: music and the landscape, merged into one entity. She has given up melody and the beautiful variety of a line of hills and is left without music and without scenery. She may be talking about poetry itself. Certainly Pastan has never used traditional poetic forms, the forms that are directly comparable to music, in any important way. The same is true of most poets of her generation. It is hard to see, though, how meter—the pattern of stressed syllables in a poem—has been given up to death. Perhaps she means, as some critics think, that the breakdown of meter is a sign of the English poetic tradition waning over time and reaching an end. In any case, the poet again does not feel the loss of what she has voluntarily set aside.

In lines 10–12, the narrator sleeps, and she takes sleep as a rehearsal for death. Sleep is something that moves through her body, taking it over piece by piece, moving from below to the heart, just as death will some day. Whether to sleep or death, the poet says she gives up her own body. Again, she cannot lose something she gives up on her own. When she speaks of giving up her body, she must also be speaking of love and even of physical love. These things are the opposite of death and constantly struggle against death, so the poet is referring to that opposition. But she is giving up the struggle, which in the end is unequal and whose outcome is inevitable, so that the loss of love and the loss of life will not be something imposed on her.

So far, however, sleep is only practicing for death. It comes to an end each morning with the renewal of domestic pleasures and the beauty of nature, both favorite themes of Pastan's.

Next, in lines 15–18, the narrator gives the most important image of the poem: the sun rising and shining its light on a tree outside her window. This is the outward scene and action of the poem; the narrator emphasizes the suddenness of the transition. An onlooker to the scene would see this revelation and the poet sitting in bed, as if seeing a few frames of film. Everything else takes place inside the poet. The tree had been a shadow, a shade, a thing of death, but the sun catches its topmost branch and moves downward, revealing leaf and twig as the tree comes to life, or comes back to life. The progression is the mirror image of the spread of sleep over the poet's body the previous night. Life has the power to resist death after all—for a time.

In the last sentence of the poem (lines 19–21), the narrator takes back her body, which she is not quite ready to relinquish yet. The sun, which stands for life against death, now spills over into her room and fawns on her like a dog happy with the joy of living. It also seems to make love to her, a warm golden act that strikes back against the cold whiteness of death.

THEMES

Death

In her interview with Granik, Pastan reported that when she "was about twelve, she became obsessed with death, even though no one she knew had died." As she does so often, it seems, Pastan is creating a tension between her history and her identity, a conflict that often seems to underlie her creativity. Pastan also told Granik that she was an only child. In fact, however, she had an older brother who died as a child. Perhaps she indeed did not know him, in the sense of being too young to have memories of the time before his death, but his death was nevertheless profoundly influential on her life.

As Pastan told Stan Rubin in "'Whatever Is at Hand': A Conversation with Linda Pastan," her father pressured her to become a surgeon, or in any case a professional (admittedly not the most usual life for a woman in the late 1940s and 1950s), in part as compensation for the career he had imagined for his son. Her father shifted part of Pastan's dead brother's identity onto her. Pastan rebelled at this and eagerly became a housewife instead. At the same time, though, she felt unhappy in her decision, not because she was dissatisfied with her family but because she could not quiet the other voice that called her to a different life. It is hardly surprising that eventually she let that voice speak as a poet, or that death looms largest in her poetry. This may relate to the description of her own narrative voice she also supplied to

TOPICS FOR FURTHER STUDY

- It is a melancholy fact that young adults sometimes die. Anne Grinyer, in *Cancer in Young Adults: Through Parent's Eyes* (2002), throws light on the experience through documents written by the parents of young-adult cancer patients, offering access to their inner thoughts in this tragic time. Write a poem based on the experiences of one such parent.

- In Japan, Shinto is a traditional religion that shares with many forms of American Judaism an emphasis on the observance of traditional ritual rather than belief alone. Research Shinto and its beliefs about the dead. Stuart Picken's 2002 *Historical Dictionary of Shinto* is a good place to start. Using the abundant photographic resources on the Internet depicting Shinto shrines and rituals, present your findings in a PowerPoint presentation to your class.

- Find an old photo from a family album and write a poem expressing the feelings it evokes in you. Post the photograph and the poem on your Web page or online blog site to share with your classmates. Expand the project by finding a dozen or more photographs and use a computer program to create a slide show that matches the photos to the lines of the poem and set the presentation to music.

- Use a search engine to track the term *atheist* on blog sites. How is the term used, and with what connotations in blogs by atheists and by the religious? Is there a continuity between the self-representation of atheists and writings about atheists by religious believers? Present your finding in a brief presentation to your class or essay for your teacher.

- Laurie Brown's *When Dinosaurs Die* (1998) helps young people deal with the death of friends or family without recourse to religious comfort. Write a short story in which you imagine Pastan explaining the death of her own father to her young daughter, using Brown's book as a guide.

Rubin: "I've always thought that the poetic 'I' is more like a fraternal than an identical twin." It was in some sense the changes that death brought about in her family that made her a poet, or, at least, the poet that she is.

Like many of Pastan's poems, "I Am Learning to Abandon the World" is principally about death. Indeed, the title is a description of preparing for death. Everyone she knows is dead or dying (it is a universal condition), and she is dying herself by stages. Each night she dies a little bit; in the morning she is revived but is closer to death than before. This is symbolized by the tree she sees outside her window. In myth—from the Norse *Eddas* to the Greek philosopher Plato to the Jewish mystical tradition of the Kabbalah—the tree stands for the bridge between life and death.

Nature

One of the most frequent observations of Pastan's work, whether or not it is perceived as a fault, is how often trees appear in it. The poet readily admits this and attributes it to her source material in her everyday experience. Pastan told Rubin:

> I think that any poet can write about absolutely anything. My subjects aren't deliberately chosen, they just happen to be what my life is full of. It's full of children, and we live in the woods so it's full of trees. Whatever is at hand I write about.

Indeed, "I Am Learning to Abandon the World" contains one of her most prominent trees. The poem is organized around an image of the poet watching a tree revealed by the light of dawn falling upon it. As the tree is lit up from top to bottom, it is said to reclaim its parts—twigs and leaves—from the shadows. The image supports the other reclamations of the poem:

The theme of the poem is the mourning of the dead. (Ashley Whitworth | Shutterstock.com)

the reclamation of the self from sleep and that of the self from the world that is death.

STYLE

Imagism

Properly speaking, imagism was a short-lived but influential trend in English poetry during the first years of World War I (1914–1918). Influenced by the Japanese poetry form of haiku and by ancient Greek lyric poetry (especially the work of the poet Sappho), Ezra Pound and a small group prominent poets (including H. D., known by her initials, and T. S. Eliot) produced work that described simple, almost photographic scenes in brief passages of lavish, even extravagant language. Although the imagists quickly moved on to new styles and projects, their work was heavily influential on the American poet William Carlos Williams and later, the Beat poets. Imagism in particular helped to popularize the breakdown of traditional poetic form in modern verse.

Pastan's poetry cannot be described as imagist in the strictest sense, but she acknowledges the important influence of Eliot on her work, and she has many points of contact with imagism. One of the most widespread critical opinions of Pastan's work is that her poems describe images, as if she were talking about a photograph or painting. As Pastan told Rubin in their interview: "In terms of starting a poem, or getting into a poem, it's usually a specific visual image that I need." Her work differs from that of the imagists, though, in the prosaic language she uses to describe an image. Some readers find the plainness of Pastan's language a fault, but for her it is a virtue since, like her whole poetic art, it grows out of her everyday experience.

The image in "I Am Learning to Abandon the World" is very clear. The poet is sitting up in bed, drinking coffee, and looking out the window at a tree, just after dawn. In fact, she sees the first sunlight fall on the tree with the line between light and darkness sweeping down to reveal its leaves and twigs. The image is not truly photographic but is more like a brief video loop. The characteristic birdsong of dawn is heard on the soundtrack.

Allusion

An allusion is, in general, a reference to another work, in this case a reference to another text that the poet has read. It is not an exact quotation, but something that recalls the text she has in mind and puts it in the mind of the reader. It is a conversation, then, between the reader and two authors, one present on the page, the other present only in memory. *You remember our old friend, don't you?* the poet asks. *What he says makes what I'm saying more meaningful.*

There is only one important allusion in "I Am Learning to Abandon the World," in the second to last line, but it is quite dramatic. In this line, the poet imagines the sunlight falling on her as if it were a dog nuzzling her, laying its head on her lap, in fact. The sexual meaning of the passage is quite clear, as Gerda S. Norvig notes in *Jewish American Women Writers: A Bio-Bibliographical and Critical Sourcebook*. This image also recalls another line, from Shakespeare's *Hamlet*. In act 1, scene 2, Hamlet asks his fiancée, Ophelia, "Lady, shall I lie in your lap?" (line 112). In part because she believes he has lost his sanity, she thinks he is making a sexual proposition there in public. But Hamlet explains in his next line that he is speaking in a literal fashion, "I mean, my head upon your lap?" (line 114), as he sits on the floor next to her. Surely Pastan intends her reader's memory to be jogged when reading her line, and to turn towards Shakespeare's. But that is only the beginning of what is going here. Pastan uses the second, explanatory line, not the misunderstood first line, as a sexual metaphor. She is suggesting that matters in *Hamlet* are not quite what they seem. Pastan seems to be reading Hamlet's first line as a Freudian slip (the speaking of an unconscious desire by accident), revealing what he might like to do if all of the circumstances of life did not make it impossible. Pastan uses Shakespeare's work to make clear the meaning of her poem, and at the same time she uses her poem to make Shakespeare's meaning clear. This grants to her work a greater nobility and significance it could not otherwise aspire to: not because she is name-dropping Shakespeare, but because the use of allusion engages the reader's mind and attention in a different way.

HISTORICAL CONTEXT

Second-Wave Feminism

In the late nineteenth and early twentieth centuries, the women's suffrage—or "suffragette"—movement won the right to vote for women. Today, that movement is considered part of first-wave feminism. After the passing of the Nineteenth Amendment to the Constitution in 1920, the issue of women's rights took a back seat to the crises of the Great Depression and World War II. In the 1950s, though, the newfound security and prosperity of American society caused many women to rethink their place in society. Although many women had either served in support roles in the armed forces or become industrial workers to free men for combat service during the war, there was an expectation in the 1950s that middle-class women would find fulfillment in devoting themselves to home and family and not enter the work force. This was a false image of women's roles in the American past, created in part to answer cold war hostilities with an enemy that was portrayed as opposed to family life.

Betty Friedan's 1963 book *The Feminine Mystique* acted as a lightning rod to spark second-wave feminism, which focused on gaining for women lives more similar to men's in being based on work outside the home, on terms of equality with men. Friedan argued that women were expected to create an idealized suburban household, with their sense of self subjected to the care of their husbands and children. Women's magazines and advertising created what Friedan called the feminine mystique, the idea that women had a special gift for domesticity, and that any woman who tried to establish a career outside of the house was doomed to become bitter and neurotic. The solution, in Friedan's view, was for women—including married women—to enter the world of work outside the home alongside men and create their own self-actualized and independent identity.

Pastan strongly identified with the plight of women described by Friedan. In a 1976 interview with Rubin published in *The Post-Confessionals: Conversations with American Poets of the Eighties*, she said that after she had completed her master's degree in English at Brandeis University, she stopped writing for fourteen years and devoted herself to her family:

COMPARE & CONTRAST

- **1980s:** Thanks to the feminist revolution of the 1960s and 1970s, women increasingly attend colleges and universities, take advanced degrees, and pursue professional careers.

    Today: Women outnumber men in American universities and are approaching parity with men in the professions.

- **1980s:** American atheists are generally closeted out of fear of social disapproval, and the public face of atheism is the rather strident and combative Madalyn Murray O'Hair.

    Today: American atheists are a rapidly expanding group buoyed up by their acceptance of science and reason and represented by prominent public intellectuals such as Daniel Dennett, the philosopher, and Christopher Hitchens, the author and journalist.

- **1980s:** End-of-life decisions for incapacitated patients are generally made by physicians and family members, with a bias toward sustaining life even for patients in a persistent vegetative state.

    Today: Living wills, advance directives, and other means to give individuals control over their own lives and their care at the end of life, are becoming increasingly common as part of estate planning.

I was very young when I married and started having children, and it didn't seem to me possible for me to do the sort of job I felt was expected of me as a woman and to give myself a really serious commitment to writing. I was, after all, a product of the fifties.

Once Pastan did begin to publish poetry in the late 1960s, she immediately fell afoul of feminist critics who attacked her work for its immersion in domesticity. Pastan appears highly conflicted about her roles as housewife/mother and poet. Pastan's parents certainly did not see their daughter's role as limited to being a suburban homemaker. They sent her to Fiedelston, an exclusive prep school in the Bronx, New York, and on to Radcliffe College, the sister school to Harvard (at the time, major universities were still segregated by sex). Pastan's father was a medical doctor and encouraged her to become a surgeon. Even after her marriage, Pastan earned a master's degree in library science (before her degree in English), so she was well prepared to establish her own career. By her account, Pastan rebelled against these expectations and sought out a more conventional way of life. When her husband accepted a position at the Yale medical school in 1958, she was unable to enroll part time in a Ph.D. program at Yale, so she devoted herself fully to taking care of her children. She describes her choice to not write for fourteen years as both a "decision" and a "nondecision," as if the prevailing culture of the 1950s forced it upon her.

Perplexingly, she complains of her education at Radcliffe in the interview with Rubin: "The not nice thing was that I didn't get a chance to do any writing myself." In fact, though, during her senior year she won the prestigious Dylan Thomas Award for poetry against a competitive field that included the noted poet Sylvia Plath. Perhaps such statements process the intense guilt she feels over the years she did not write. It was finally Pastan's domestic arrangements that granted her the leisure to practice writing poetry increasingly as her children grew up. She could devote hours to poetry every day because she did not have to work as a librarian to support herself. By the 1980s, Pastan had become one of the most prominent and honored American poets, so it seems her career after all fulfilled the postmodern ideal of having both family and career.

One of the themes of second-wave feminism was the struggle of women to gain reproductive control of their bodies, as well as the mere physical control of their own bodies in terms of secure rights to divorce and to form relationships outside

The narrators accepts the nightfall with her heart, mind, and body. (Dalibor Sevaljevic | Shutterstock.com)

patriarchal control. Although this self-determination is not the only or the most important meaning of the poem, the images of the speaker giving up her body at night (line 11) and reclaiming it at dawn (line 19) may well relate to these feminist concerns.

CRITICAL OVERVIEW

In *Jewish American Women Writers: A Bio-Bibliographical and Critical Sourcebook*, Norvig summarizes the state of criticism on Pastan's poetry. With few exceptions, she says that "published discussion of Pastan's work has been limited to either dust-jacket blurbs by fellow poets, newspaper reviews of her individual books, or poetry-journal essays in which Pastan is one of several writers being critiqued." Most often Pastan's poetry is found to be limited in scope, largely concerned with the affairs of her household and everyday life. Pastan's language is seen to be equally pared down. Although critics acknowledge her depth of feeling, she seems helpless to meet the daily difficulties she describes. Her strong imagery is most often ignored, while many critics read her poems as a straightforward representation of her true character.

Pastan (as represented in her interviews with Rubin and Granik) is especially attuned to feminist criticism of her work, since she feels she had to go through the feminist struggle of the 1950s and 1960s in her own life. Many of her poems revolve around Pastan's own experience of domesticity as a wife and mother. One of the most common themes in her work is the life of the Greek heroine Penelope, whose daily weaving and nightly unweaving of her father-in-law's burial shroud perfectly represents feminine domestic labor. The feminist criticism is that Pastan's work excessively praises and values women's domestic labor, even though Pastan sees her own work as merely making use of the substance of her own life. Pastan sees Penelope's weaving and Odysseus's wandering as representing feminine and masculine poles, between which the poet's own identity oscillates. Norvig's essay, brief as it is, is currently the most sustained critical treatment of Pastan's poetry. She acknowledges the familiar and domestic character of Pastan's verse but finds in it a Stoic moral voice and an ambivalence that underlies her essential stance to the world. She is drawn toward a larger unknown world but turns away from it and back to her domestic anchor. Norvig sees this also as a tension between the romantic (which values nature as a source of inspiration) and the postmodern (which rejects objective systems of meaning). Increasingly, the themes that Pastan uses are the nature of poetic composition itself, the boundary between life and death, and finally the emergence of both narrative (in relations to both Greek and Biblical myth) and traditional verse forms.

Norvig is also the only critic to offer commentary on "I Am Learning to Abandon the World" specifically. Another major theme Norvig sees in Pastan's work is the erotic, expressed in various symbols including the warm penetrating power of sunlight in many poems. Norvig illustrates this theme, noting that

> the same image, domesticated, retains its sexual suggestiveness at the close of 'I Am Learning to Abandon the World,' where a dog-like sun comforts the speaker for her losses as it lays its warm muzzle on [her] lap.

In her analysis of this image, Norvig suggests:

> One might think that depressive poems like this... would prove inhospitable ground for images of such sensual intimacy. But in the economy of Pastan's ambivalent universe, the opposite is true: Melancholia or abject resignation seems actually to depend upon a strong undertow of erotic sensibility.

More recently, Fred Chappell, in *A Way of Happening*, an extended comparison of Pastan's verse with that of A. R. Ammons, reads the natural images familiar in Pastan's poetry as "emblematic and charged with transcendental meaning. She retreats from setting down the meanings she might prefer;... she leaves it to the reader to address his own possibilities for belief." Most often, Chappell insists, Pastan's symbols evoke in the reader the unwelcome visitor death.

CRITICISM

Rita M. Brown

Brown is an English professor. In the following essay, she examines the philosophical character of Linda Pastan's "I Am Learning to Abandon the World."

Linda Pastan is not a religious poet, though death, her main subject matter (especially in "I Am Learning to Abandon the World"), might seem to call for religious treatment. But religion is palliative to death: its promise of comfort in an afterlife is meant to soften the sting of death. Pastan prefers to face death squarely without that aid. Pastan comes from a Jewish background, but there is very little of Jewish tradition in her poetry. Some poems deal with the Eden mythology from the Book of Genesis, but noticeably fewer than make use of classical mythology. Both traditions seem for Pastan to be interesting sources of tradition and of literary inspiration, a language of reference in which she can work. For the more fundamental meaning of her poems, Pastan turns sometimes to Stoicism, an ancient philosophy that helps to guide people through the difficulties of life without recourse to any personal gods, elaborating her own secular background.

In her quest to find the key to Pastan's individual poetic voice, Gerda S. Norvig, in her comprehensive article on the poet found in *Jewish American Women Writers: A Bio-Bibliographical and Critical Sourcebook*, suggests that many critics "will cite as fundamental the stoic moral vision her poems so often project." Although Stoicism, an ancient Greek system of philosophy, addressed every conceivable area of human learning and knowledge, the school is appreciated today, and was even in the Roman Empire, for its moral dimension. Stoicism was founded in the third century BCE by Zeno of Citium and his students Cleanthes and Chrysippus, but it is known chiefly through the writings of two Stoics who lived about four centuries later, the Roman emperor Marcus Aurelius and his teacher Epictetus. These later works deal almost exclusively with moral philosophy. Although the whole range of Stoic thought cannot possibly be described here, it is necessary to explain the larger framework of Stoic morals as a background to understand the Stoic elements in "I Am Learning to Abandon the World."

The most basic aim of Stoicism was to end human suffering and thereby increase human happiness. Human suffering, the Stoics believed, is caused by a misunderstanding. People think that they have a right to enjoy the good things of life: a right to children, to a good job, to fulfilling work, to success, to power, to long life. But for the Stoic, human beings do not have a right to those things. The world can give them or take them away, and humans have no say in the matter. People have no way to control or decide about whether or not they get fired from their jobs,

WHAT DO I READ NEXT?

- *Carnival Evening: New and Selected Poems 1968–1998* (1999) is the most extensive collection of Pastan's poetry, drawn from her previous anthologies.

- *The Norton Anthology of Modern and Contemporary Poetry* (2003), edited by Jahan Ramazani, Richard Ellmann, and Robert O'Clair, is a large collection with some analysis by Pastan's contemporaries that provides a context for appreciating and understanding her poetry.

- *Counties of Central Maryland* (1998), written by Elaine Bunting and Patricia D'Amario and illustrated by Marcy Dunn Ramsey, is a guide for young adults to the area mentioned in the title, where Pastan lives. It includes the ecology and natural history of the area.

- Buddhism is a religious philosophy that is primarily concerned with the avoidance of human suffering without the promised consolation of a blessed afterlife. Diana Winston's *Wide Awake: A Buddhist Guide for Teens* (2003) offers an introduction to Buddhism aimed at young adults.

- *The Hunger Song* is a 1983 anthology of poetry by Kim Chernin, a Jewish feminist poet whose work is comparable to Pastan's.

- David Biale's 2010 work *Not in the Heavens: The Tradition of Jewish Secular Thought* provides a history of secularism within the Jewish community based on the biography of its leading exponents.

- Christina Rossetti, sister of the pre-Raphaelite painter Dante Gabriel Rossetti, wrote a large body of poetry for young adults that address the subject of death, including "Life and Death," "Sweet Death," "A Death of a First Born," and "After Death." Her complete works have been collected and published many times, including the 2001 Penguin edition of *The Complete Poems*, edited by Rebecca W. Crump and Betty S. Flowers.

- It is an old custom in Japanese for the dying, if they are able, to a write death poem reflecting their feelings a short time before their demise. Some of these poems were translated by Yoel Hoffmann and published in the 1986 collection *Japanese Death Poems Written by Zen Monks and Haiku Poets on the Verge of Death*.

---

whether or not they lose their houses, not even whether or not their child dies in an accident or how long they themselves will live. No one decides what will happen to him or herself. People can only decide how they will react to what happens to them. When people lose something, such as a job, they think to themselves, *I had a right to that, and now I am suffering since I lost it*. The Stoic way to view the situation is to realize that these things did not come with a promise that they would be kept forever. When something that a person did not own to start with is taken away, it is not the loss that causes suffering but the not wanting to let it go.

Epictetus in his *Enchiridion*, or *Manual*, says that "what disturbs men's minds is not events but their judgments on event.... Death is nothing dreadful.... No, the only dreadful thing about it is men's judgment that it is dreadful." The Stoic believes that everything that is in the world belongs to the world and no individual has any claim on a particular piece of property or condition. If the Stoic lacks something, or if he loses something that he does not think is his, the lack will not cause him to suffer. Epictetus also states:

> Never say of anything, "I lost it," but say, "I gave it back." Has your child died? It was given back. Has your wife died? She was given back. Has your estate been taken from you? Was not this also given back?

Whatever human beings have does not belong to them, so when Stoics lose something, they think

> FOR PASTAN, DEATH IS INEVITABLE, BUT IT MAKES ALL THE DIFFERENCE WHETHER IT IS SOMETHING THAT HAPPENS TO HER OR SOMETHING SHE CHOOSES FOR HERSELF."

themselves no worse off than is a traveler who leaves a hotel room. Beyond this, however, a Stoic can win a greater victory by doing more than merely recognizing the temporary nature of possessions and goods. This is achieved by rejecting utterly the kinds of temporary possessions that other people long for, not accepting them to begin with, and by living a life of renunciation free of everything that is not under personal control. For the Stoics, the ultimate renunciation was suicide, if one suddenly found the circumstances of life unbearable (for example, if one found oneself enslaved, a real possibility in the Greek world). Constantly having that option left one free to react even to the most impossible situations. Even this had a positive value for the Stoics. If one's life seemed completely out of control, the possibility of taking action to leave it actually restored a sense of control.

This kind of Stoic moral teaching is very closely related to Pastan's views expressed in "I Am Learning to Abandon the World." For Pastan, death is inevitable, but it makes all the difference whether it is something that happens to her or something she chooses for herself. If she no longer cares whether she lives or dies, then she will not suffer anything when she dies. She is clearly experiencing grief over the death of her father and other people she loved, but rather than suffer under the impact of these deaths, she is giving them back to the world that gave them to her for a time. Death is not a loss if she consents to it, as one consents to return a loan. This is what she means by abandoning the world before the world abandons her. To live by such principles is difficult and she claims only to be learning how. Even so, by the end of the poem she finds the simple joys that are still in her possession to be sufficient to make her life worth living as she learns to moderate her grief. Although the title of the poem might suggest its speaker is contemplating suicide, it seems clear that merely adopting the Stoic perspective makes such a drastic step unnecessary. Pastan has argued against suicide on quite un-Stoic grounds (making it clear she does not adopt the philosophy wholesale), telling interviewer Granik in *Truthtellers of the Times: Interviews with Contemporary Women Poets*, "I think suicide is immoral, primarily because the people you leave behind never recover."

A remarkable fact about "I Am Learning to Abandon the World" is that Pastan never makes the slightest suggestion that her grief over the deaths of those she loves and fear about her own death might be assuaged by religious hope of an afterlife. In fact, as Norvig observes, Pastan's poems exist in a "referential universe... without a theodicy," that is, without any sign of divine justice, and therefore without god. It seems Pastan cannot seriously consider the possibility of a god. And, indeed, it is abundantly clear from many of her poems, as well as from her biography, that despite her Jewish cultural identity, Pastan is a person who has no religion. She can best be described as a secular Jew, a term applied to many Jews whose parents came to the United States as immigrants, who received a secular education and for whom religious belief simply plays no more role in their lives. Pastan described her religious background to Stan Rubin in "'Whatever Is at Hand': A Conversation with Linda Pastan": "I didn't have any kind of strict Jewish upbringing of any sort. My only real connections were a generation removed—with my grandparents. My parents had both rebelled from that kind of thing so that I had never even been inside a synagogue until I was grown and went to somebody's wedding." This kind of transition is especially easy in the Jewish community, where practice has always had more cultural significance than belief and where the impact of the Holocaust makes ideas of divine justice particularly hard to accept. Indeed, some synagogues are self-avowedly atheist, belonging to the Society for Humanistic Judaism. The same shift from belief can be seen in European Christianity, where only a small proportion of the Christian population attend church services outside of Easter, Christmas, and a few other special occasions. The situation appears quite different in the United States, where religious feeling is more widespread and where public discourse is dominated by the large minority movement of Protestant fundamentalists. Fundamentalism began in the 1890s in response to the perceived infiltration of liberal theology into mainline Protestant sects, and has become increasingly important since World War I. The explicitly atheist philosophy of America's cold war communist adversaries also tended to reinforce public religiosity in the 1950s. In this religious climate, atheism is largely vilified.

This had not always been the case. In earlier decades, even the most prominent Americans, such as Benjamin Franklin, Thomas Jefferson, and Abraham Lincoln, could be public atheists without fear of disapproval, even in the sensitive world of politics. By 1964, the outspoken atheist Madalyn Murray O'Hair had become, in the title of Jane's Howard's article in *Life* magazine, "The Most Hated Woman in America" because of her lawsuit *Murray vs. Curlett*, in which the Supreme Court recognized that the Constitution forbids the government to force people to pray. This is, in fact, one of the religious liberties necessary for a free society, as the founders realized in writing the First Amendment to the Constitution. But the prevailing public view of the time was that the decision was somehow a blow against religious liberty. Even in 2006, polling data (analyzed by Penny Edgell, Joseph Gerteis, and Douglas Hartmann in the *American Sociological Review*) showed that atheists were the most widely hated minority group in America. Part of the problem is that atheists are often not understood on their own terms but stereotyped in the image of everything that religious believers find objectionable.

This public prejudice against atheists partly explains why Pastan simply ignores religion and religious belief, rather than undermining it from an explicitly atheistic perspective in a poem like "I Am Learning to Abandon the World." On the other hand, religious belief is so far removed from her consciousness that the possibility of religious solace in the face of death is simply not a consideration. Taking examples closest to hand to "I Am Learning to Abandon the World," in the introductory "Instructions to the Reader" in *PM/AM*, Pastan ridicules belief in biblical inerrancy by pointing out that it requires belief in unicorns. In "A Short History of Judaic Thought in the Twentieth Century," she attacks Jewish purity law from the Hebrew Bible and later Rabbinic literature as barbaric, citing the example that Jews are not allowed to touch someone they know is dying. She asks who is not dying that she might be allowed to touch them? Perhaps this poem grows out of the observation that in the modern world, almost everyone will attend the hospital deathbed of a parent or even of a child, a circumstance that makes the religious prohibition seem inhuman. Still, Pastan neither self-identifies nor is identified by critics as an atheist or an atheist poet because of a complex balance between not wishing to invite controversy, while at the same time considering the controversy to be a kind of antique best left in the attic.

Source: Rita M. Brown, Critical Essay on "I Am Learning to Abandon the World," in *Poetry for Students*, Gale, Cengage Learning, 2012.

Ken Adelman

In the following interview, Pastan and Adelman discuss Pastan's process for writing poetry.

Above her desk, poet Linda Pastan has posted a quote from Tennessee Williams: "The only honor you can confer upon a writer is a good morning's work."

> To me all poetry is, in a sense, political. Evil acts generally grow out of a failure of imagination, and poetry, by exercising the imagination as if it were a muscle, can ultimately help influence decisions made out in the real world.

Pastan is one of the lucky poets for whom many good mornings' work have yielded tangible honors, including nine published books, the Dylan Thomas Award, the Di Castagnola Award, a Pushcart Prize, and a recent four-year stint as Maryland's poet laureate. The *Gettysburg Review* said of her latest book, *An Early Afterlife*, that it "reaffirms her place among the finest contemporary poets in America."

Born in New York City, Pastan began submitting poems to the *New Yorker* at the age of 12. (The magazine did not publish its first Pastan poem until almost 30 years later.) She graduated from Radcliffe and later received a master's degree in English literature from Brandeis.

After a ten-year break to raise her three children, she resumed writing. Her poems soon began appearing in the *Atlantic Monthly*, the *New Yorker*, the *New Republic*, the *Paris Review*, and the *Georgia Review*. She has read her works at Harvard, Yale, Princeton, the Folger Shakespeare Library, the Library of Congress, and other institutions.

Pastan lives with her husband, Ira, head of the Laboratory of Molecular Biology at the National Cancer Institute. They have three grown children: Stephen, a nephrologist with Emory Medical

> "DON'T BE AFRAID. DON'T THINK ABOUT WHAT THE POEM 'MEANS.' READ IT FOR THE JOY OF LANGUAGE AND FOR THE WAY IT MOVES YOU."

School in Atlanta; Peter, a chef who owns two restaurants, Obelisk and Pizzeria Paradiso, in downtown DC; and Rachel, who writes fiction in Madison, Wisconsin.

It was in the study of her Potomac home, filled with books and with a vista of the surrounding forest, that we discussed what she's learned.

[Ken Adelman:] What does one do as poet laureate of Maryland?

[*Linda Pastan*:] Six years ago, someone in the governor's office approached me about becoming poet laureate and asked if I'd be willing to write poems for state occasions. "Absolutely not," I replied. "You'll have to find somebody else." Then she asked what I would be willing to do if I took the post. I said I'd be happy to read poems and talk about poetry to people around Maryland who usually had no contact with poetry or poets. I'd like to help those who think they don't know anything about poetry, and are therefore afraid of it, learn that there isn't that much to "know."

Not much to know about poetry?

No. Poetry is not a matter of knowledge but of emotional experience. It's there to be enjoyed, to be used for celebration and for consolation. I find that people ask me if they can use a certain poem of mine for a funeral or a wedding. They sense they need poetry in their lives, especially on these important occasions, but they don't always know how to find it.

So, as poet laureate, I traveled around the state a lot, to a prison, an old-age home, hospitals, schools, talking to people about poetry and reading some of my own poems aloud to them.

Do you read your poems differently than other people do?

Yes. Every writer has a unique way of viewing his or her own work, and that comes out in the way she reads it aloud. I go to many public readings by poets I like, mainly to hear their voices. Then, when I read their poems to myself, I can still hear that voice in my head.

Should a reader care what you intended to put in a poem?

Only to some degree. All readers bring to each poem their own experiences and emotions and interpret and enjoy the poem in their own ways. Personally, I am interested in knowing a writer's specific intent, but only later and more professionally—that is, from a craft point of view.

Suppose I can find different meaning in your poem than you intended?

That does happen, and it's all right with me, at least up to a point. I mean, if you come to an opposite conclusion—if I were praising something you thought I was denigrating—that would upset me. I certainly don't want to be completely misconstrued.

But if you find meanings in one of my poems that I hadn't realized were there, that would be fine. I've often learned about my own work from hearing other peoples' interpretations of it. There can be things that perhaps I knew in my subconscious that I hadn't realized I knew and that someone else helped me to see.

For instance, the title poem of my first book, *A Perfect Circle of Sun*, has a layer of meaning I hadn't consciously intended. In that poem I described the experience of looking at the world through a skylight. In fact, the poem is called "Skylight." Some critic wrote that the poem was really about looking at the world through the lens of poetry. Once I read that I thought, "Yes. That really is one of the things the poem is about." I must have known it on some level but hadn't known I knew it. And that's good. Because though writing poetry certainly doesn't bring you fame or fortune, it can bring you—as William Stafford, a poet I very much loved and admired, pointed out— a way of discovering things you didn't know you knew. And so the act of writing a poem can become an act of exploration and discovery.

Why did you choose poetry over fiction?

It seems to me that most writers have an impulse to expand or to condense language and experience, and in general the first path leads to fiction, the other to poetry. Of course there are some poets like Walt Whitman who are very expansive and some fiction writers who write small, jewel-like stories. And a few writers, like Thomas Hardy or, in our time, Margaret Atwood, can do both well. But my impulse to condense is very strong.

What drove you into poetry?

I've always written, at least I have from the time I was 12 or 13. As an only child, books were my main companions, and writing became my way of talking to the characters in those books and to the authors of those poems. But I stopped writing after I got married and started having children. That was in the '50s, and I didn't think, then, that I could be the right kind of wife and mother and keep pursuing something as important to me as poetry always has been. I think now that I was wrong. And a young woman probably wouldn't make that mistake today. Anyway, when I returned to writing, almost ten years later, I did try a novel, but I soon found I wasn't interested in the plot or the characters. I was interested in the descriptive passages, and particularly in the metaphoric language. And my novel kept getting shorter and shorter, becoming almost a short story. Before long I realized that what it really wanted was to become a poem.

Your poems deal with nature and art.

Whatever is in my life seems to end up in my poems. I do go to a lot of museums and galleries, and some of my poems are about what I see there. And living here in the middle of the woods, I watch the leaves changing and the snow falling, and I write about that too. But I don't consider myself primarily a nature poet. I use the natural world for metaphoric material rather than trying to simply describe it.

Do you need a burst of creativity to write a poem?

No; there aren't that many bursts. If I waited to be inspired, I'd write maybe one or two poems a year.

But I make myself sit at my desk each morning, whether I feel like it or not, and when I get bored enough, I always start writing something. Inspiration, I find, can be coaxed. And if things get really desperate, I do allow myself to read other people's poems, and that may get me started, may trigger my own imagination.

It's always the getting started that's so hard. I often wish I were a novelist so I could work on one thing for three or four years at a time, but a poet has to keep starting from scratch, over and over again. I finish one or two poems a month, if I'm lucky.

Do you revise a lot?

Oh yes. One of my poems, "The Myth of Perfectibility," even deals with revision as a subject. In it I try to say that a poet must be in love with revision in order to write. The original ideas and metaphors may take only a few hours to get on paper. Then the revision may take a couple of months, years even. I go through maybe 100 revisions for nearly every poem.

Do you finally say, "That's it. I've had it!"

Sure, I say that. But I don't necessarily stick to it. Between a poem's publication in a magazine and later in a book, I often make changes. Then when I put together a collection of selected poems from various books, as I'm doing again now, I may change a few more things, particularly titles. It's called fear of closure, I guess.

In my latest book I have a poem called "Vermilion." It's about the painter Pierre Bonnard, who would never feel that his paintings were finished. He'd even walk into museums where his pictures were hanging and take a paintbrush to them there. In my poem I try to show how life, as well as art, entails constant revision. The poem ends: "As if revision were the purest form of love," and I think it is.

What's your advice to a young poet?

Read, read, read! Revise, revise, revise!

What's the purpose of poetry?

For the writer it's an act of discovery and of letting out, and onto the page, what's deep within. It doesn't cure the pain of feelings but it expresses it through intense language, and if the poet gets it right, it can help the reader to see the world in new ways. To me all poetry is, in a sense, political. Evil acts generally grow out of a failure of imagination, and poetry, by exercising the imagination as if it were a muscle, can ultimately help influence decisions made out in the real world.

Is judging poetry subjective?

To some degree, yes. It is usually clear when poetry is really bad, but it is harder to agree on what's really good.

After time, though, a few poets are still read and most are forgotten.

I guess so. But many are forgotten because of accident or bad luck. The great poems handed down to us usually are great, but I bet there are a lot of wonderful poems we've never had the chance to see or hear.

How do you deal with rejection?

Quite well, actually. That's probably because I started writing poems seriously when I was in my thirties and isolated from any writing community. I didn't know even one other writer. So for me, sending out my poems and getting them back was exciting. I liked the action. A note from an editor, even a form rejection slip, made me feel as if something more were happening in my life than just changing diapers.

In any case, all poets get rejected, even the most famous and honored. I tell young poets one trick I've learned. For each group of poems you send out, have an envelope ready on your desk to resubmit those poems. Then, when they come back, don't leave them sitting around on your desk; send them right back out into the world.

Do you learn from other poets?

I certainly try to. In fact I can't read poems anymore simply for pleasure, the way I read fiction. I always feel I have to try to learn something.

What have you learned?

Different things from different poets. From William Stafford I learned to trust myself, to start quietly and be willing to stay quiet within the poem. From Charles Simic I learned to try strange and daring metaphors. From Ann Sexton and Sylvia Plath, I learned that no subject matter was really off limits. That lesson was very liberating, especially when I first began writing poems again.

Is your poetry autobiographical?

Some of it is, but only up to a point. I think of the "I" in my poems as my fraternal, not identical twin. And though I may use my own children's names, for instances, I am inventing some of what I have them do or say. I am after emotional truth, not literal fact.

How should an amateur begin to read poetry?

Don't be afraid. Don't think about what the poem "means." Read it for the joy of language and for the way it moves you. Later you can go back and read it again and perhaps find new things in it you didn't notice right away. Too many people have had poetry ruined for them in school by bad teachers. Read a poem for pleasure, and if it's a really good poem, it will draw you back again and again.

How does a poet make a living?

A poet doesn't make a living. Most poets I know teach, since that leaves them some time at least for their own writing. But poets have supported themselves many ways—for instance, Wallace Stevens was an insurance executive, and William Carlos Williams was a doctor.

What have you learned from writing poetry?

I've learned more about myself than I would have known otherwise, since writing is such an introspective act. To do it well, you must examine your deepest feelings honestly and somehow articulate them on the page.

I've also learned that my family is the most important thing to me and will always come first. If one of my kids was in a play and I was invited to something that might help my career, I'd always go to the play. When my daughter gets a short story published, I'm much more excited than when I get a poem published.

I've learned to tolerate some loneliness living out here in the woods. I'd probably be happier living in town where things are more lively, but I've learned that I have to accept some isolation to gain the space to think and to write. I've learned that an artist and a scientist can have a good life together.

Lessons of life?

Commit yourself to your work and to your family and friends. Try to actually enjoy the too-brief time we all have here.

Source: Ken Adelman, "Word Perfect: For Linda Pastan, Revision Is the Purest Form of Love," in *Washingtonian*, Vol. 31, No. 8, May 1996, pp. 29–31.

Linda Pastan

In the following essay, Pastan reflects on the poems of childhood and the effect they might have on student writers.

> How sweet the past is, no matter
> how wrong, or how sad.
> How sweet is yesterday's noise.
> —Charles Wright, "The Southern Cross"

I wrote an essay ten years ago called "Memory As Muse," and looking back at it today I am struck by the fact that in the poems I write about childhood now the mood has changed from one of a rather happy nostalgia ("Memory as Muse") to a more realistic, or at least a gloomier, assessment of my own childhood and how it affects me as a writer ("Yesterday's Noise"). Let me illustrate with a poem called 'An Old Song,' from my most recent book.

An Old Song

> How loyal our childhood demons are,
> growing old with us in the same house

> PERHAPS IT IS THE VERY WAY OUR CHILDHOODS CHANGE IN WHAT I CALLED 'THE FRACTURED LIGHT OF MEMORY' THAT MAKE THEM SUCH AN INEXHAUSTIBLE SOURCE OF POETRY."

like servants who season the meat
with bitterness, like jailers
who rattle the keys
that lock us in or lock us out.

Though we go on with our lives,
though the years pile up
like snow against the door,
still our demons stare at us
from the depths of mirrors
or from the new faces across a table.

And no matter what voice they choose,
what language they speak,
the message is always the same.
They ask "Why can't you do
anything right?"
They say "We just don't love you anymore."

As A. S. Byatt said about herself in an interview: "I was no good at being a child." My mother told me that even as a baby I would lie screaming in the crib, clearly terrified of the dust motes that could be seen circling in the sun, as if they were a cloud of insects that were about to swarm and bite me. By the time I was five or six, I had a series of facial tics so virulent that I still can't do the mouth exercises my dentist recommends for fear I won't be able to stop doing them. I'm afraid they'll take hold like the compulsive habits of childhood that led my second-grade teacher to send me from the room until I could, as she put it, control my own face. There was the isolating year (sixth grade) of being the one child nobody would play with, the appointed victim, and there was the even more isolating year (fourth grade) of being, alas, one of the victimizers. There was my shadowy room at bedtime, at the end of a dark hallway, and, until some worried psychologist intervened, no night light allowed.

I thought about calling my last book Only Child because something about that condition seemed to define not only me, but possibly writers in general who sit at their desks, necessarily alone, for much of the time. In some ways, of course, it defines all of us, born alone, dying alone, alone in our skins no matter how close we seem to be to others. I tried to capture my particular loneliness as a child, my difficulty in making friends, my search for approval, in what I thought would be the title poem of that book:

Only Child

Sister to no one,
I watched
the children next door
quarrel and make up
in a code
I never learned to break.

Go Play!
my mother told me.
Play! said the aunts,
their heads all nodding
on their stems,
a family of rampant
flowers
and I a single shoot.
At night I dreamed
I was a twin
the way my two hands,
my eyes,
my feet were twinned.
I married young.

In the fractured light
of memory—that place
of blinding sun or shade,
I stand waiting
on the concrete stoop
for my own children
to find me.

At a reading I gave before a group of Maryland PEN women last year, someone who had clearly not read beyond the tables of contents of my books introduced me as a writer of light verse. I remember thinking in a panic that I hardly had a single light poem to read to those expectant faces, waiting to be amused. Did I have such an unhappy life, then—wife, mother, grandmother, with woods to walk in, books to read, good friends, even a supportive editor?

I am, in fact, a more or less happy adult, suffering, thank God, from no more than the usual griefs age brings. But I think my poems are colored not only by a possibly somber genetic temperament, but also by my failure at childhood, even when I am not writing about childhood per se. And more and more, as I grow older, those memories themselves insist upon inserting themselves into my work. Perhaps it is the very way our childhoods change in what I called "the fractured light of memory" that make them such an inexhaustible source of poetry. For me, it is like the inexhaustible subject of the seasons that can be seen in the changeable light of the sun, or the versatile light of the imagination, as benign or malevolent or indifferent, depending upon a particular poet's vision at a particular moment.

I want to reflect a little then on those poems we fish up from the depths of our childhoods. And for any teachers reading this, I want to suggest that assigning poems to student writers that grow out of their childhoods can produce unusually good results, opening up those frozen ponds with what Kafka called the axe of poetry.

Baudelaire says that "genius is childhood recalled at will." I had a 19-year-old student once who was not a genius but who complained that he couldn't write about anything except his childhood. Unfortunately, his memory was short, and as a result, all of his poems were set in junior high school. He had taken my course, he told me, in order to find new subjects. I admit that at first glance junior high doesn't seem the most fertile territory for poems to grow in. On the other hand, insecurity, awakening sexuality, fear of failure— many of the great subjects do exist there. It occurred to me that when I was 19, what I usually wrote about were old age and death. Only in my middle years did I start looking back into my own past for the subjects of poems. This started me wondering about the poetry of memory in general. Did other poets, unlike my young student, come to this subject relatively late, as I had? As I looked rather casually and unscientifically through the books on my shelves, it did seem to me that when poets in their twenties and thirties wrote about children, it was usually their own children that concerned them, but when they were in their late forties or fifties or sixties, the children they wrote about tended to be themselves.

Donald Justice, in an interview with the *Missouri Review*, gave as good an explanation of this as anyone. He said, "In the poems I have been thinking of and writing the last few years, I have grown aware that childhood is a subject somehow available to me all over again. The perspective of time and distance alter substance somewhat, and so it is possible to think freshly of things that were once familiar and ordinary, as if they had become strange again. I don't know whether this is true of everybody's experience, but at a certain point childhood seems mythical once more. It did to start with, and it does suddenly again."

There are, first of all, what I call "Poems of the Happy Childhood," Donald Justice's own poem "The Poet At Seven" among them. But for poets less skilled than Justice, there is a danger to such poems, for they can stray across the unmarked but mined border into sentimentality and become dishonest, wishful sort of recollections. When they are working well, however, these "Poems of the Happy Childhood" reflect the Wordsworthian idea that we are born "trailing clouds of glory" and that as we grow older we are progressively despiritualized. Even earlier than Wordsworth, in the mid-17th century, Henry Vaughan anticipated these ideas in his poem, "The Retreat."

I mention Wordsworth and Vaughan because in looking back over the centuries at the work of earlier poets, I find more rarely than I expected poems that deal with childhood at all. Their poems are the exceptions, as are Shakespeare's *30th Sonnet* and Tennyson's "Tears, Idle Tears." Perhaps it wasn't until after Freud that people started to delve routinely into their own pasts. But nostalgia per se was not so rare, and in a book called *The Uses Of Nostalgia: Studies in Pastoral Poetry*, the English critic Laurence Lerner comes up with an interesting theory. After examining pastoral poetry from classical antiquity on, he concludes that pastoral poems express the longing of the poets to return to a childhood arcadia, and that in fact what they longed to return to was childhood itself. He then takes his theory a step further and postulates that the reason poets longed for childhood is simply that they had lost it. He writes, "The list is varied of those who learned to sing of what they loved by losing it.... Is that what singing is? Is nostalgia the basis not only of pastoral but of other art too?" Or as Bob Hass puts it in his poem "Meditation at Lagunitas," "All the new thinking is about loss. / In this it resembles all the old thinking."

But though there are some left who think of childhood as a lost arcadia, for the most part Freud changed all of that.

We have in more recent times the idea of poetry as a revelation of the self to the self, or as Marge Perloff put it when describing the poems of Seamus Heaney, "Poetry as a dig."

The sort of poems this kind of digging often provides are almost the opposite of "Poems of the Happy Childhood," and they reflect a viewpoint that is closer to the childhood poems I seem to be writing lately. In fact, a poem like "Autobiographia

Literaria" by Frank O'Hara actually consoles the adult by making him remember, albeit with irony in O'Hara's case, how much more unpleasant it was to be a child. If the poetry of memory can console, it can also expiate. In his well-known poem, "Those Winter Sundays," Robert Hayden not only recreates the past but reexamines his behavior there and finds it wanting. The poem itself becomes an apology for his behavior as a boy, and the act of writing becomes an act of repentance.

If you can't expiate the past, however, you can always revise it—and in various, and occasionally unorthodox, ways. Donald Justice in the poem "childhood" runs a list of footnotes opposite his poem, explaining and clarifying. Mark Strand in "The Untelling" reenters the childhood scene as an adult and warns the participants of what is to occur in the future.

Probably the most ambitious thing a poem of childhood memory can accomplish is the Proustian task of somehow freeing us from time itself. Proust is perfectly happy to use random, seemingly unimportant memory sensations as long as they have the power to transport him backwards. When he tastes his madeleine, moments of the past come rushing back, and he is transported to a plane of being on which a kind of immortality is granted. We can grasp for a moment what we can never normally get hold of—a bit of time in its pure state. It is not just that this somehow lasts forever, the way we hope the printed word will last, but that it can free us from the fear of death. To quote Proust: "A minute emancipated from the temporal order had recreated in us for its apprehension the man emancipated from the temporal order." Proust accomplished his journey to the past via the sense of taste, but any sense or combination of senses will do. In my poem "PM/AM," I used the sense of hearing in the first stanza and a combination of sight and touch in the second. Here is the second:

> AM
> The child gets up
> on the wrong side of the bed.
> There are splinters
> of cold light on the floor,
> and when she frowns
> the frown freezes on her face
> as her mother has warned her it would.
> When she puts her elbows roughly
> on the table her father says:
> you got up on the wrong side of the bed;
> and there is suddenly
> a cold river
> of spilled milk.

> These gestures are merely formal,
> small stitches in the tapestry
> of a childhood she will remember
> as nearly happy. Outside
> the snow begins again,
> ordinary weather
> blurring the landscape
> between that time and this,
> as she swings her cold legs
> over the side of the bed.

But did I really say: "A childhood she will remember as nearly happy"? Whom are you to believe, the poet who wrote that poem years ago or the poet who wrote "An Old Song"? As you see, the past can be reinterpreted, the past can be revised, and the past can also be invented. Sometimes, in fact, one invents memories without even meaning to. In a poem of mine called "The One-Way Mirror Back," I acknowledge this by admitting: "What I remember hardly happened; what they say happened I hardly remember." Or as Bill Matthews put it in his poem "Our Strange and Lovable Weather"—

> ...any place lies about its weather, just as we lie about our childhoods, and for the same reason: we can't say surely what we've undergone and need to know, and need to know.

This "need to know" runs very deep and is one of the things that fuels the poems we write about our childhoods.

But the simplest, the most basic thing such poems provide are the memories themselves, the memories for their own sakes. Here is the third stanza of Charles Simic's poem "Ballad": "Screen-door screeching in the wind / Mother hobble-gobble baking apples / Wooden spoons dancing, ah the idyllic life of wooden spoons / I need a table to spread these memories on." The poem itself, then, can become such a table, a table to simply spread our memories on.

Looking back at some of my own memories, I sometimes think I was never a child at all, but a lonely woman camouflaged in a child's body. I am probably more childlike now. At least I hope so.

Source: Linda Pastan, "Yesterday's Noise: The Poetry of Childhood Memory," in *Writer*, Vol. 105, No. 10, October 1992, pp. 15–18.

SOURCES

Chappell, Fred, *A Way of Happening: Observations of Contemporary Poetry*, Picador, 1998, pp. 72–77.

Edgell, Penny, Joseph Gerteis, and Douglas Hartmann, "Atheists as 'Other': Moral Boundaries and Cultural

Membership in American Society," in *American Sociological Review*, Vol. 71, 2006, pp. 211–34.

Epictetus, *The Manual, or Enchiridion*, in *The Discourses of Epictetus*, translated by P. E. Matheson, Heritage, 1968, pp. 275–92.

Friedan, Betty, *The Feminine Mystique*, Norton, 1963.

Granik, Lisa, "Linda Pastan," in *Truthtellers of the Times: Interviews with Contemporary Women Poets*, edited by Janet Palmer Mullaney, University of Michigan Press, 1998, pp. 82–88.

Howard, Jane, "The Most Hated Woman in America," in *Life*, June 19, 1964, pp. 91–92, 94.

Norvig, Gerda S., "Linda Pastan," in *Jewish American Women Writers: A Bio-Bibliographical and Critical Sourcebook*, edited by Ann R. Shapiro, Greenwood, 1994, pp. 288–97.

Pastan, Linda, "I Am Learning to Abandon the World," in *PM/AM: New and Selected Poems*, W. W. Norton, 1982, pp. 17–18.

———, "Instructions to the Reader," in *PM/AM: New and Selected Poems*, W. W. Norton, 1982, p. 1.

———, "On 'The World as Meditation' by Wallace Stevens," in *Touchstones: American Poets on a Favorite Poem*, edited by Robert Pack and Jay Parini, Middlebury College Press, 1996, pp. 184–85.

———, "A Short History of Judaic Thought in the Twentieth Century," in *PM/AM: New and Selected Poems*, W. W. Norton, 1982, p. 70.

Rubin, Stan Sanvel, "'Whatever Is at Hand': A Conversation with Linda Pastan," in *The Post-Confessionals: Conversations with American Poets of the Eighties*, edited by Earl G. Ingersoll, Judith Kitchen, and Stan Sanvel Rubin, Fairleigh Dickinson University Press, 1989, pp. 135–49.

Shakespeare, William, "Hamlet," in *The Riverside Shakespeare*, Houghton Mifflin, 1974, pp. 1135–97.

FURTHER READING

Pastan, Linda, *Traveling Light: Poems*, W. W. Norton, 2011.
    This anthology is drawn from Pastan's most recent published poems.

Pastan, Rachel, *Lady of the Snakes*, Mariner, 2009.
    During the last few years, Pastan's daughter Rachel has acted as her mother's first reader and trusted editor. This is her own first novel.

Plath, Sylvia, *The Bell Jar*, Faber & Faber, 1963.
    The novelist and poet Plath was a contemporary of Pastan; she lost the 1955 Dylan Thomas award to Pastan. Plath represents something like the road not taken for Pastan. Plath continued her literary career during her marriage to the poet Ted Hughes. This novel's main character descends into suicidal depression and suicide. Shortly after its publication, Plath in fact killed herself.

Seid, Judith, *God-Optional Judaism: Alternatives for Cultural Jews Who Love Their History, Heritage and Community*, Citadel, 2001.
    This book presents a case of a redefinition of the Jewish community as a secular, rather than a religious, identity in the postmodern world.

SUGGESTED SEARCH TERMS

Linda Pastan

I Am Learning to Abandon the World AND Linda Pastan

post-confessional poetry

imagism

Tree of Life

I mean, my head upon your lap?

secular Judaism

Linda Pastan AND death

Linda Pastan AND trees

Linda Pastan AND imagism

Linda Pastan AND post-confessional poetry

in Just

E. E. CUMMINGS

1920

"in Just" was originally published in the *Dial* in 1920, along with several other poems by e. e. cummings. The poem was later included in the author's 1923 collection *Tulips and Chimneys*. The poem can easily be found in various online sources. It also appears in a number of print sources such as the 1994 Liveright volume, *E. E. Cummings: Complete Poems 1904–1962*.

"in Just" is the first of three poems in *Tulips and Chimneys* to fall under the title "Chansons Innocentes," which means "songs of innocence" and it concentrates on the joys of childhood and spring. Like many other modern poems, "in Just" is written in free verse. It shows the author's flair for using unusual typography to make artistic statements. "in Just" is one of cummings's most beloved poems and offers a glimpse into his own childhood.

AUTHOR BIOGRAPHY

e. e. cummings was born Edward Estlin Cummings on October 14, 1894, in Cambridge, Massachusetts. His father was a Harvard professor of sociology and political science who became a Unitarian minister when his son was six. cummings began writing and painting at a young age, and he continued these passions throughout his life.

e. e. cummings *(The Library of Congress)*

From 1911 to 1916, cummings attended Harvard University, where he was introduced to the work of Ezra Pound and other modern poets. His poetry was featured in the Harvard Poet Society's publication *Eight Harvard Poets* in 1916. He joined the French ambulance service the next year to assist the Allies in World War I. The French were suspicious of cummings and other foreign volunteers, and cummings was detained after he and his friend William Taylor Brown wrote letters that were considered incriminating. His first book, *The Enormous Room*, was published in 1922 and describes his experiences in France.

cummings was released by the French in 1918, and drafted into the United States Army shortly thereafter. In this same year, cummings traveled to New York, where he developed a romantic relationship with Elaine Thayer, the wife of his friend and patron Scofield Thayer, who was the editor of the *Dial*. Thayer apparently approved of the relationship between his wife and cummings.

After leaving the army, cummings continued his affair with Elaine Thayer, and she gave birth to their daughter, Nancy, in 1919. cummings and Thayer remained friends, and his poetry appeared in the *Dial* in 1919 and 1920. *Tulips and Chimneys*, his first volume of poetry, was published in 1923. The Thayers divorced in 1924, and cummings swiftly married Elaine and formally adopted his daughter. This marriage was short-lived. Elaine left cummings for another man in 1925 and took Nancy with her. Nancy did not even know that she was cummings's daughter until 1948.

cummings spent the 1920s and 1930s traveling between Paris and New York, where he focused on painting and writing. In 1925, the same year Elaine divorced him, cummings began a tumultuous relationship with the model Anne Barton. They married, but Anne divorced him in 1932.

cummings traveled to Russia in 1931 and "saw first hand the secret police in action," according to Christopher Sawyer-Lauçanno in *E. E. Cummings: A Biography*. Originally supportive of the Bolshevik Revolution, cummings became wary of the political changes in Russia. He detailed his point of view in the 1933 publication *Eimi*. The reviews were poor, and many of his friends "were disturbed by what they perceived as Cummings's right-wing turn," according to Sawyer-Lauçanno.

In 1932, cummings met Marion Moorehouse, the woman with whom he would spend the rest of his life. He had difficulty finding publishers in the 1930s, and often published his own work. For example, one volume of poems, *No Thanks*, was dedicated to the various publishers who refused his work. Over the decades, cummings wrote a ballet, two plays, fiction, poetry, and essays. He was awarded his second Guggenheim fellowship in 1951, and later served as a Harvard lecturer. cummings's poetry became more widely accepted in the 1950s and 1960s. He died of a cerebral hemorrhage on September 2, 1962, in North Conway, New Hampshire.

POEM SUMMARY

The text used for this summary is from *E. E. Cummings: Complete Poems, 1904–1962*, Liveright, 1994, p. 27. Versions of the poem can be found on the following Web pages: http://www.poetryfoundation.org/poem/176657 and http://www.poets.org/viewmedia.php/prmMID/15398.

MEDIA ADAPTATIONS

- *The Voice of the Poet: e. e. cummings* is an audio recording of cummings reading many of his better-known poems, including "in Just." Released by Random House Audio Voices in 2005, the CD also includes a literary commentary presented by J. D. McClatchy.

---

cummings's beloved poem "in Just" is a free verse poem that illustrates the "slippery typographical stepping-stones" described by early critic Harriet Monroe in her review "Flare and Blare" reprinted in *E. E. Cummings: The Critical Reception*. As he does in most of his work, cummings deliberately implements incorrect grammatical constructions and makes up compound words for artistic emphasis in "in Just." He does not implement traditional meter in the poem, and the rhythm is irregular. The erratic spacing between certain words varies for dramatic effect and takes the place of missing punctuation. The poem is composed of five stanzas that are made up of four lines each, called quatrains. Single lines that resemble refrains follow the first four stanzas. These single lines differ from traditional refrains because they do no repeat the same words. The lack of a repeated metrical or rhyme pattern as well as the odd typography differentiate the format of this poem from traditional quatrains and refrains.

The first quatrain of the poem emphasizes the setting. The first line is the title, which is true of most of cummings's poems. The name of the season is the first word of the second line, but a hyphen connects it to the last word of the first line, making the name of the season the second half of a compound word. There are extra spaces between the season and the rest of the line to indicate its significance. The narrator takes the point of view of a child in the poem and develops a playful tone. He describes the season of spring with wonder and awe and invents an adjective that is split between the second and third lines of the poem to create a broken rhyme.

The main character of the poem, the balloonman, is introduced in the third line. He cannot walk, so the children have to come to him. The balloonman is actually based on memories from the poet's past. cummings's sister is quoted in Sawyer-Lauçanno's *E. E. Cummings: A Biography* as saying: "The first and most exciting sign that spring had really come was the balloon man."

How the sound of the balloonman travels is described in the first single or separated line. The first word has extra spaces between it and the other words on the line to demonstrate visually that the sound travels a long way. Rather than using the common phrase "far and wide," cummings ends the line with a word that keeps the playful, childish tone of the piece.

The second quatrain describes how the children react when they hear the whistle of the balloonman. The names of the two boys in this stanza are run together to create a single word. As Norma Pollack points out in the article "Poems of Cummings Set to Music," "joining the names of the children not only conjures a vision of innocence and play but contributes momentum as well." It conveys the sense of the children running toward the balloonman. The boys are playing typical childhood games. They immediately abandon these childhood pastimes to follow the sound of the balloonman. The stanza ends with the season, which is described again in the following refrain.

The second single line portrays the wonders of the spring and how delightful its wet weather can be for children. cummings makes up a compound word to illustrate the childish pleasure found by jumping in puddles.

This description of spring with its childish wonders is followed by another quatrain that explores the balloonman and the effect of his whistle. The balloonman is described using a colloquial term in this quatrain, an adjective that simply means he is strange. We also discover that he is not a young man. This description is followed by a repeat of the first refrain. In this stanza, however, there is extra space between "and" and the words around it. Here, a pair of girls hear the sound. Again, the names are written as a single word to signify movement. The girls, however, do not run to the balloonman like the boys do. They dance toward the sound.

The following separate line describes what the girls are doing before they hear the whistle. Like the boys, the girls cease their playing to follow the sound of the balloonman.

The next stanza is a quatrain like the other stanzas, but each line is made up of single words that announce it is spring. The final line is "the." This simple article is spaced over to the right of the other line, which visually separates it from the rest of the poem. "The" acts as an introduction. The next line is a refrain that consists of a single compound word. This adjective is spaced further over to the right from "the," creating an image of movement in the typography that reflects the action of the girls' games.

The complete description of the balloonman suggests that he is a satyr, a mythical creature that is half man and half goat. Many critics, such as Albert C. Labriola, believe that the balloonman of this poem represents the Greek god Pan because of his age, goat-feet, and whistle. *The Oxford Companion to Classical Literature* defines Pan as the "Greek god of shepherds and of flocks, for whose fertility he is responsible." He is also credited with inventing the pan flute or syrinx from whistling reeds. Given the nature of satyrs, the balloonman might indicate the sexual awakening of the children as they hear his whistle.

The final stanza of the poem is another quatrain. The first line begins with the balloonman, but this time the word balloonman is written "balloonMan." The change in capitalization emphasizes the word "man" to remind readers that he is an adult. The narrator wants to make clear the distinction between the balloonMan and the children. There are extra spaces between the balloonMan and the word that ends the line. The following three lines repeat the first refrain. Each line is a single word. The poem ends with the balloonman's sound going out, which implies that more children will hear him.

THEMES

Innocence

Themes of innocence and childhood are common in cummings's work. In the volume *Tulips and Chimneys*, "in Just" appears under the title *Chansons Innocentes*, which means "songs of innocence." The children in the poem, as well as the narrator, are caught up in the wonders of spring. All exhibit joyful innocence. According to *Webster's Online Dictionary*, innocence can come from lack of knowledge or from inexperience. The narrator uses vivid compound words

TOPICS FOR FURTHER STUDY

- Read *Paint Me Like I Am*, the young-adult collection of poems by teenage poets working with WritersCorp. Choose a poem and compare it with "in Just." Compare the styles and themes of the two poems. How are they alike? How are they different? How do you think cummings would react to the teenager's poem? Create a single-act play in which the two poets meet and discuss their styles and experiences. Perform the play with a classmate and record it. Post the play on your social networking site or YouTube.

- Research the changes in technology that occurred in the United States after World War I using both print and online resources. Focus on the effects of technology in communication and art. For example, radios changed music and entertainment. How did artists and writers respond to the advances in technology? Create a video or multimedia presentation of the changes that occurred in the 1920s and 1930s. Show this information within a time line of cummings's art and poetry and how he was affected by them.

- Read the book *Talking with Mother Earth/Hablando con Madre Tierra: Poems/Poemas* by Jorge Arqueta, which explores nature and childhood. Write your own poem based on your experiences with nature. Make a Web page for your poem and place links throughout it that help explain the meaning. These may be pictures, art, links to other poems, etc.

- Explore the art of Pablo Picasso and cummings from the 1920s. cummings was a great admirer of Picasso. Research their relationship, and create a Web page for each of them. Comment on specific pieces of art, reporting specifically on their style and the emotions and stories they are meant to convey.

to describe spring. These adjectives highlight the differing viewpoints of children and adults when it comes to the wet weather. While adults see the mud and the puddles as obstacles to be avoided, children typically enjoy playing in both. For the moment, the narrator and the children mentioned are lost in the excitement of spring, and their joyful exuberance is mirrored in the typography, imagery, and rhythm of the poem. The children and the narrator have not yet learned to avoid mud and stay out of puddles. For them, the entire world is as cummings describes it.

The children in the poem are playing common childhood games before the balloonman whistles. These pastimes are abandoned when the children hear the sound of the balloonman. With true innocence, the children simply trust that it is safe to follow the sound. They show no signs of fear or caution. In fact, they come running and dancing to the sound. As the only adult to appear in the poem, the balloonMan stands in stark contrast to the children and the narrator. The speaker describes the balloonman, but the readers are never told how he views the changing season. He is an adult and a satyr, however, which makes it safe to assume that he does not share the same innocence as the children around him.

Nature

Nature is a theme that cummings frequently explores in his poetry. Spring is the perfect season to enjoy nature, and "in Just" celebrates nature in all of its glory, beginning with the first line. According to the poet and the narrator, the season needs no introduction. The words do not exist to describe the season adequately, so the narrator is forced to invent adjectives to describe it. In the view of the narrator, the world is a playground of wonders that nature provides with the changing season. In spring, the weather becomes warmer and the days grow longer. Nature gives the children mud and puddles to delight them, and the additional daylight allows the both boys and girls more time to play their outdoor games.

The character of the balloonman also reflects the theme of nature. He is described as both human and animal, and acts as a bridge between humanity and nature. As part animal, the balloonman is representative of nature. He is also a man. Therefore, as a satyr, he is in a unique position to

A balloon man features prominently in the poem.
(Steven Sum / Shutterstock.com)

bridge the gap between nature and humanity and help the children reach the next phase of life.

Change

Spring is a season that is frequently associated with change. The transition from winter to spring brings with it sunshine, warmth, and rain. It is a time of transformation and rebirth, a season in which snow melts, plants bloom, and the weather is mild and enjoyable. Like any other season, however, spring is temporary and will quickly fade into summer. cummings sets the poem "in Just" during this season of change for two reasons. The nation was beginning to experience large-scale social change when the poem was first published in 1920, and "in Just" is a poem that reflects this change. It also highlights the natural transition between the seasons of life.

The whistle of the balloonman comes with the advent of spring, and it is a signal of the change to come. The children enjoy the season and their pastimes, but they all leave behind their games to follow the sound of the balloonman. They do not return to their childish activities after they hear the sound. Their encounter with the balloonman represents the beginning of their transition to adulthood.

STYLE

Free Verse
"in Just" is a free verse poem, as are most of cummings's poems. Free verse is a term for a poem that is not organized into a traditional format such as a sonnet. Most English free verse poems have an iambic flow (consisting of an unstressed syllable followed by a stressed syllable) because English is a naturally iambic language, as noted in the definition of *iamb* in *Representative Poetry Online*. In "Introduction to Meter," Timothy Steele confirms that iambic meters are more common, "because iambic rhythm suits English speech more naturally and flexibly than other rhythms." Free verse was a popular poetic style in the early twentieth century as artists chose to reject the restrains of traditional forms. A free verse poem, however, may develop a pattern in its rhyme or meter, but "in Just" has neither. The poem is broken into five different stanzas that slightly resemble traditional quatrains and refrains, which are four-line stanzas followed by single lines.

Typography
cummings employed creative typography in much of his poetry. Typography is the art of determining how a text will appear once it is printed. A 2007 art exhibit at the University of Delaware, *Avant-garde Typography in Literature*, featured some of Cummings's poetry and reminds us that he was an artist who used typography to "paint a picture." The poem "in Just" is a classic example of how unconventional typography can create visual cues that increase reader understanding without punctuation. The poet uses spacing to signal pauses, create distance, and develop motion. Typography can also give a distinct visual pattern that imitates the action of the poem. The fourth quatrain, for example, is made up mostly of single words that resemble the hopping motion of the girls playing "hop-scotch," as Robert Mayo points out in "Chansons Innocentes (I)."

Broken Rhyme
Broken rhyme breaks up words between lines of poetry. Traditionally, this technique is used for the sake of the rhyme pattern. cummings used this device extensively to emphasize meaning rather than rhyme. This technique appears twice in "in Just." A hyphen appears between the last word of the first line and the first word of the second line, placing emphasis on the word "spring." "Mud-luscious" is divided between the second and third line of the poem. The word "luscious" matches the consonance of the words "little" and "lame" that appear on the same line.

Cubist Poetry
As a painter, cummings was familiar with Picasso and cubism, making cubist poetry a natural transition. Cubist poetry breaks down the basic elements of writing and uses them to create something different. The poem "in Just" uses unconventional syntax, punctuation, and capitalization. For example, "balloonman" is not capitalized throughout the poem, and it is a single word constructed from two separate words. The names of the children are not capitalized, and there are no spaces between them. Rather than solely relying on punctuation, cummings uses spacing and typography to indicate pauses and breaks.

HISTORICAL CONTEXT

The Lost Generation
The coinage of the term "Lost Generation" is typically attributed to Gertrude Stein. Ernest Hemingway also used the expression in his novel *The Sun Also Rises*. Generally, the Lost Generation refers to a group of American artists and writers who were profoundly affected by the events of World War I. The end of the war saw many changes in American culture, and members of the Lost Generation tried to make sense of the world around them through art and literature.

Called "the war to end all wars," World War I saw the rise of modern warfare. Advances in technology led to inventions such as tanks, landmines, and submarines that made mass death and destruction possible from a distance. Many members of the Lost Generation were involved in the war and never recovered from the horrors they witnessed. They grew disillusioned and rejected

COMPARE & CONTRAST

- **1920s:** The effects of World War I linger into the 1920s because of the devastation it caused throughout Europe. Advances in technology are responsible for the considerable loss of life in World War I, and the Lost Generation explores their feelings of disillusionment as a result of the physical and emotional devastation wrought by the war.

  Today: International conflicts and wars are ongoing, but new smart-bomb technology makes it easier for militaries to locate the enemy and take out military targets without necessarily killing civilians. The continuing conflicts and the aftereffects of 9/11 cause many American writers such as Charles Bernstein and Khaled Hosseini to express the changes they observe in society.

- **1920s:** Modern art evolves in the 1920s. Artists such as Picasso drift away from traditional painting techniques, embracing cubism with its broken or abstract representations. Cubism is reflected in the literature of the time, particularly in cummings's work.

  Today: Artists still use cubist techniques, but modern art continues to grow and change. The Museum of Modern Art in New York City, and other museums, showcase all forms of art, including photos, collage, performance art, sketches, and paintings. The rise of social networks and online publishing also changes the methods that writers use to communicate their ideas.

- **1920s:** Technology changes the way Americans live and communicate. More people choose to live in cities and take advantage of modern conveniences such as radios and household appliances. cummings has a profound love of nature and often chooses to live in and write about natural settings.

  Today: Technology continues to advance and provide us with more conveniences such as smartphones and personal computers. People grow more aware of the need to protect nature. Legislation to reduce carbon emissions and preserve natural resources is passed at the state, federal, and international levels, including the Kyoto Protocol in 2005. Additionally, more companies offer "green" products.

---

the Victorian ideals of their parents. Through art and literature, young people voiced their distaste for conformity and war. Writers associated with the Lost Generation include e. e. cummings, Ernest Hemingway, Ezra Pound, F. Scott Fitzgerald, William Faulkner, Gertrude Stein, and T. S. Eliot.

"in Just" was originally published in the *Dial* in 1920. Small literary publications such as the *Dial* helped to establish the careers of many Lost Generation writers who, like cummings, abandoned convention and explored new themes and styles. The theme of change that appears in "in Just" was also explored by many of cummings's peers and contemporaries.

1920s

The 1920s saw the end of World War I along with many changes in American culture and society. There are numerous titles associated with this famous decade such as the Roaring Twenties, the Jazz Age, the New Age; Gary Dean Best calls it the Machine Age in *The Dollar Decade: Mammon and the Machine in 1920s America*, according to reviewer David Goldberg in the *Historian*.

The 1920s were a complex decade. While it is true that many people were disillusioned with society, Gene Smiley explains in his article "The U.S. Economy in the 1920s" that "the American economy exhibited impressive economic growth during the 1920s." Luxuries became more affordable, and

A picture of spring as described in stanza 1 (Stephanie Frey | Shutterstock.com)

the middle class began to grow. This decade saw the introduction of mass production and increased industry. People celebrated life and wealth while defying societal conventions. Flappers cut their hair and dressed provocatively, and speakeasies became popular with the middle class. The Nineteenth Amendment to the U.S. Constitution, which granted women the right to vote, was passed in 1920, the same year that "in Just" was first published, and divorce was becoming more common. The theme of change in cummings's poetry echoes the changing world around him.

Not everyone reacted well to change in society, however, and some people took steps to combat the shift in American culture. The Eighteenth Amendment establishing Prohibition also took effect in 1920. According to "Clash of Cultures in the 1910s and 1920s," many people were alarmed by the changes in morality, particularly by women abandoning their traditional roles in society. Catholic organizations, Protestant organizations, and the Ku Klux Klan actively opposed the new gender roles and worked against what they believed to be a threat to American society.

CRITICAL OVERVIEW

cummings's poetry has always elicited an extreme response from critics. His style has been both praised and reviled from the beginning. Many early critics, such as Harriet Monroe, who gave *Tulips and Chimneys* a positive review in "Flare and Blare," had issues with his typography. She refused to print "in Just" and other poems as written because "Mr. Cummings has an eccentric system of typography which, in our opinion, has nothing to do with the poem, but intrudes itself irritatingly." Other critics praised his creativity. Robert L. Wolf, for example, announces in "E. E. Cummings's Poetry," included in *E. E. Cummings: The Critical Reception*, that the poet's first volume of verse "contains, in its own individual and unprecedented style, as beautiful poems as have been written by any present-day poet in the English language."

In the 1930s and 1940s, cummings had difficulty finding publishers and was forced to publish many poems at his own expense. Besides poetry, he wrote the travel journal

Eimi, plays, and a ballet of *Uncle Tom's Cabin*. After the 1920s, some critics began to feel that cummings showed little growth as a writer and poet. Yvor Winters calls cummings's work "mildly unpleasant and infinitely tedious" in a 1939 review in *American Literature*.

Other critics have defended cummings and claimed that his poems do show growth but that he began as an eccentric, so the change is not drastic or obvious. Rudolph von Abele argues in the 1955 article "'Only to Grow': Change in the Poetry of E. E. Cummings" that "the earlier poems impress one as *trying* to deal concretely with their themes while the later ones *try* to achieve a kind of abstractness."

By the 1960s, interest in cummings's work increased, and reviews were predominantly positive toward the end of his life. There were, and will always be, detractors, however. Even after his death, cummings's unique style continued to divide his critics. Whether critics love or hate cummings's work, there is no denying his influence. As Richard D. Cureton explains in "E. E. Cummings: A Study of the Poetic Use of Deviant Morphology," "Certainly, few poets have done such violence to language with such unerring poetic success."

CRITICISM

April Dawn Paris

Paris is a freelance writer who has an extensive background working with literature and educational materials. In the following essay, she argues that cummings draws from the imagery of the romantic poets to address modern themes in "in Just."

cummings uses the theme of nature along with the symbolism associated with spring to establish the sense of time moving forward and hint at the future in his poem "in Just." Borrowing from the themes of the romantic poets, cummings implements a modern poetic style to address the themes of nature and change. This poem is a snapshot of a season, but the symbols and imagery he uses provide clues about the inevitable changes that the future will bring to the poem's characters. Time and change are unstoppable forces of nature, and while a moment may be beautiful, it cannot last forever. Just as spring transitions into summer, children must grow into adults.

WHAT DO I READ NEXT?

- Chin Yeung Russell's free verse poem *Tofu Quilt* explores her childhood experiences in Hong Kong. This novel-length poem won an honorable mention in the young-adult category from the Asian/Pacific American Awards for Literature (APAAL). Released in 2009, the book is available through the publisher Lee & Low Books.

- *Ezra Pound: Poems and Translations* is a collection of the works by the poet who influenced modern writers such as cummings, Hemingway, and Moore. Published by Library of America in 2003, this volume also includes a brief biography, which provides insight into Pound's life.

- cummings's *i–six nonlectures* is an excellent example of his prose. Created while cummings was serving as a Charles Eliot Norton lecturer at Harvard, these lectures provide insight into his life and creative process. The Harvard University Press released the lectures in 1991.

- Available through Da Capo Press, *New World Coming: The 1920s and the Making of Modern America* explores the setting in which cummings wrote "in Just" and many other poems. This 2004 edition examines the social and economic changes of the decade as well as their impact on art and culture.

- Using the name Nancy Cummings de Fôret, e. e. cummings's daughter, Nancy Andrews, explores her life and her relationship with her father through art, poetry, and prose in *Charon's Daughter: A Passion of Identity* (1977).

- *The Sun Also Rises* was originally published in 1926 and re-released by Scribner in 2006. Hemingway's famous novel is forever linked to the Lost Generation and life after World War I.

cummings's poetic style reflects the modernist movement. His unusual typography, syntax, capitalization, and word use were considered revolutionary, even among his contemporaries.

" THIS POEM IS A SNAPSHOT OF A SEASON, BUT THE SYMBOLS AND IMAGERY HE USES PROVIDE CLUES ABOUT THE INEVITABLE CHANGES THAT THE FUTURE WILL BRING TO THE POEM'S CHARACTERS."

His decision to highlight nature and innocence in his work, however, reflects the tradition of the romantic poets, as Pushpa N. Parekh points out in his article "Nature in the Poetry of E. E. Cummings." Some of the poet's contemporaries found the use of traditional themes and subject matter to be distasteful in a time when many artists chose to delve into darker and more realistic settings. For example, in his article for *American Literature*, Yvor Winters describes cummings's subject matter as immature when compared to that of his contemporaries. The fact that cummings shares the theme of nature with the romantics, however, is not surprising when one considers the time in which he lived.

Romantic poets such as William Blake and Percy Bysshe Shelley lived in the later part of the eighteenth century and the early part of the nineteenth century. This literary period in Europe saw the rise of the Industrial Revolution, when changes in technology created an urban environment and the decline of the natural rural landscape. The evolution of industry combined with the French Revolution (1789–1799) created lasting changes across Europe. The romantic poets pushed aside the conventional forms of their predecessors and turned to nature and beauty to explore the changing world around them.

cummings also lived in a time of societal change. Technology and mass production evolved in the wake of World War I. Gary Dean Best calls the 1920s the "Machine Age," and David Goldberg's *Historian* review of Best's book *The Dollar Decade: Mammon and the Machine in 1920s America* reports that Best finds that "significant developments in the United States were connected in some way to new technology." Like the romantic poets, cummings turned to the theme of nature as mass production, machinery, and war changed the landscape of the United States. In fact, "in Just" and the other "Chansons Innocentes" poems mirror Blake's *Songs of Innocence*, as Albert C. Labriola notes in *Cithera*. cummings may have adapted the themes of the romantic poets; however, he explored these themes by using his own unique and modern style.

Nature, spring, and water are all symbolic in romantic poetry, and they provide similar symbolism in the poem "in Just." On the surface, the poem celebrates the simple joys of childhood, which are based on the poet's own youthful experiences. The tone is playful and the imagery delightful. The symbols cummings chooses, however, serve as reminders that change is imminent and inevitable. Water, for example, is a predominant symbol in "in Just." The narrator's descriptive compound words to describe the joys of the season are related to water. While water is associated with spring in many parts of the world, it is also a symbol of birth, change, growth, and new life in much of Western literature. In this way, water complements the meaning of spring, the season celebrated by the poem.

Spring is a time of new beginnings, growth, life, and change. The narrator finds delight in both spring and water, but the symbolism of each is associated with change. The reader understands, without being told, that the season of spring will bring changes to the lives of the children in the poem. The children, however, are blissfully unaware of what the future holds.

The narrator speaks from the point of view of a child. Indeed, a childish tone is necessary to convey the actions of the poem effectively. The activities of the children make up the landscape of the poem, which is evident in the typography of the final four quatrains. The typography in the second and third quatrains shows the image of running and dancing, while in third and fourth illustrates a hopping pattern. The narrator explains the joy of mud and puddles while the children play games outside. Nature, childhood, and innocence are intertwined throughout "in Just." As Iain Landles reminds us in "An Analysis of Two Poems," "it is only this childhood/innocence which can recognise the 'secrets of nature.'" The narrator and the children who appear in the poem are completely innocent and free from the knowledge and experience that comes with age. They are free to enjoy their outdoor activities and fully appreciate nature and the season of spring. The children and the narrator stand in contrast to the balloonman, who, being an adult, cannot view the world in the same way they do.

The balloonman does not symbolize innocence, but he is closely linked with nature. He appears consistently throughout the poem; but, as an adult, he is not able to join the children in their activities. cummings describes the balloonman as an adult twice. The balloonman is described as not being young in the third quatrain, and the capitalization changes to "balloonMan" in the final quatrain. At first glance, the balloonman may seem out of place in the childish and natural setting. The fact that he is "goat-footed," however, connects him to nature in a way that would not be possible for a human adult. Most critics agree that the balloonman is a satyr or a representation of the Greek god Pan. As a god, he is well acquainted with the cycle of nature, and here he assists the children as they enter into a new season of life.

The balloonman calls the children away from their games with his calling sound, the whistle, and they follow him willingly. The meaning of the sound is debated, but Landles points out that many critics associate the sound with a sexual awakening of the children who hear it. This makes sense because Pan was associated with fertility, and satyrs were considered sexual creatures in mythology. Limiting the meaning of the sound to a single adult characteristic, however, is too simplistic. The sound does more than awaken hormones; it helps guide the boys and girls as they begin their journey to adulthood with all its knowledge and experiences. It introduces them to a new season of life.

The children do not automatically become adults when they hear the balloonman. The poem does, however, hint at the changes the balloonman causes. The children leave their games to follow the sound. In the second quatrain and third single line the children do not simply stop playing; they run and dance away from their games. While the typography and language suggest that they are still children, they are quickly moving away from their innocent outdoor pastimes. The children are altered by the sound of the balloonman, but they remain children for the moment. They embrace change and run toward it with childish glee. cummings captures the moment when their transition to adulthood begins within the images of the poem.

The narrator never explains what the children will find when they reach their destination. The

An image from stanza 5 (Cheryl Casey | Shutterstock.com)

readers only know that the children leave to follow the sound. There are two reasons for this lack of information. First, the narrator does not follow the sound of the balloonman with the other children. Having established that the voice of the narrator is that of a child, it is safe to assume that the narrator lacks both the knowledge and experience to share what happens next. The narrator remains behind in a state of childish innocence.

On another level, cummings does not explore what occurs after the children leave so that his audience can determine this for themselves. For some, the balloonman may seem like a danger to the children because he results in the loss of their childhood and innocence. When considered in the light of nature, however, the balloonman's sound is not nefarious. It simply calls the children to the next season of life, which is unavoidable.

The tone of "in Just" is playful and innocent, but the reader understands that the season described in the poem cannot last forever. Guy Rotella explains in "Nature, Time, and

Transcendence" that "the very fact of time permitting spring's return also makes inevitable its loss (as specific season, especially as specific human season)." Spring cannot last forever because time cannot stand still. The innocence of childhood is a season that, like spring, is over quickly. The change that the children experience, however, is natural. One season is lost, but another replaces it, and spring is not gone forever. Change occurs within the different seasons, but the cycle of nature does not change. Spring will come again, and it will bring the same joys and transformations.

Source: April Dawn Paris, Critical Essay on "in Just," in *Poetry for Students*, Gale, Cengage Learning, 2012.

Richard S. Kennedy

In the following excerpt, Kennedy considers the significance of his career to cummings's original version of Tulips & Chimneys.

Sometime in 1919 Cummings had assembled a hefty manuscript of poems entitled "Tulips & Chimneys," which he gave to his friend Stewart Mitchell, the managing editor of the *Dial*, asking him to help find a publisher. Mitchell tried six publishing houses without success. Cummings then removed some of the poems that an editor might find either unpoetic or obscene, rearranged their order, and tried again in 1922, through John Dos Passos, to find a home for his wayweary volume. This 1922 collection of 152 poems eventually saw publication, but not all at once. Dos Passos managed to persuade Thomas Seltzer to publish a selection of sixty-six of the poems under the title *Tulips and Chimneys* in 1923. (Cummings was furious that Seltzer did not use the ampersand in the title.) Lincoln MacVeagh of the Dial Press made another selection from what was left over and published *XLI Poems* in 1925. What the two editors avoided were the most experimental as well as the most sexually daring of the poems. Cummings was thus reduced to venturing a private publication with the items that remained, to whose company he restored some of the poems he had withdrawn in 1922, and to which he also added a few more pieces he had written when he returned to Paris in 1921. He called the volume *&* (his ampersand at last dignified into a title) and brought it forth early in 1925.

If Cummings' first version, "Tulips & Chimneys," had been put before the public in 1919 it would have established, four years earlier, his place in the twentieth-century revolution in literature. It

> THE ILLOGICAL ADJECTIVE 'EXACT' HAS, BY NOW, BEEN SO OVERUSED BY CUMMINGS THAT IT HAS BECOME A HACKNEYED TERM IN HIS POETIC VOCABULARY."

is now possible to see what such a volume would have been like because George Firmage reconstructed and published the 1922 version in 1976. Since this edition represents the stage of development that Cummings had reached by 1919, we should consider its contents in close detail.

The first portion, "Tulips," contains an immense variety of Cummings' earlier work, including poems that had appeared in the *Harvard Monthly*; poems that he had written for Dean Briggs in classroom assignments; a long Hellenistic "Epithalamion" that he had composed for Scofield Thayer's wedding; a long tribute ("Puella Mea") to Elaine Thayer, Scofield's wife, with whom he had fallen in love; and a Keatsian fantasy inspired by *Aucassin and Nicolette*. This early work, which was divided into the categories "Songs," "Chansons Innocentes" (which contained "in Just-" and "Tumbling-hair"), "Orientale," and "Amores," is, for the most part, a series of free-verse exercises traditional in tone. The only Cummings touch that adds distinction is his manipulation of typography through lowercase and capital letters and his play with spacing. Two of these early poems give evidence that even his classroom exercises disclose a true poetic voice. One is a genuinely singable lyric that begins "when god lets my body be / From each brave eye shall sprout a tree" and ends "and all the while shall my heart be / With the bulge and nuzzle of the sea" (*CP* [*The Complete Poems*]). The other is a ballad-like piece in the medieval manner that begins

> All in green went my love riding
> on a great horse of gold
> into the silver dawn.
> four lean hounds crouched low and smiling
> the merry deer ran before.
> Fleeter be they than dappled dreams
> the swift sweet deer
> the red rare deer.
> Four red roebuck at a white water
> the cruel bugle sang before...

Then comes a more untraditional series of poems grouped under the headings "La Guerre," "Impressions," "Portraits," and "Post Impressions." By their references to both modern music and painting, the categories thus far suggest a mixture of the arts, and one can sense the presence of Debussy, Monet, and Cézanne even in the table of contents. The "Impressions" are, appropriately, descriptive poems, usually with an emphasis on light. The especially delicate "Impression II" uses the metaphor of piano-playing to carry the image of springtime rain before it changes into mist and fog:

> the sky a silver
> dissonance by the correct
> fingers of April
> resolved
>   into a
> clutter of trite jewels
> now like a moth with stumbling
> wings flutters and flops along the
> grass collides with trees and
> houses and finally,
> butts into the river
> (*CP*)

But death still intrudes upon some of these renderings of the diurnal variations of light, as in the opening lines of "Impressions IX":

> The hours rise up putting off stars and it is
> dawn
> into the street of the sky light walks scattering poems
> on earth a candle is
> extinguished the   city
> wakes
> with a song upon her
> mouth having death in her eyes
> and it is dawn
> the world
> goes forth to murder dreams...

Among the "Portraits," along with "bestial Marj," we have several representations of the seamy side of life expressed in the Satyric style: a drunken woman passed out on the sidewalk ("the / nimble / heat"); a street evangelist ("the skinny voice"); a grubby Greek restaurant ("it's just like a coffin's / inside when you die"); a family in an ugly street scene ("i walked the boulevard"); a prostitute in monologue ("raise the shade / will youse dearie"); five men in a Middle Eastern café ("5 / derbies-with-men-in-them smoke Helmar"), and so on. The settings are frequently crowded with repellent detail. This nightclub scene is representative:

> between nose-red gross
> walls   sprawling with tipsy
> tables the abominable
> floor belches smoky
> laughter into the filagree
> frame of a microscopic
> stage whose jouncing curtain, rises
> upon one startling doll...

Yet the metaphorical language here compresses the features and actions of drunks into the description of the scene, and the handling of the punctuation suggests the motion of the curtain—so that an aesthetic complex begins to form. Thus in spite of all the repulsiveness we are getting genuine free-verse poems in this section. Moreover, Buffalo Bill and Picasso appear as a couple of bright spots among the "Portraits."

Next come the "Post Impressions." As they begin we look at the natural scene again—the sunset, a seascape, cloud cover, and so on—but the forcing of language and the jumbled typography now take us to the far edge of expression. For example, in "Post Impressions II" we are buffeted with the Hephaestian style as adjectives are mismatched with their nouns:

> beyond the brittle towns asleep
> i look where stealing needles of foam
> in the last light
> thread the creeping shores
> as out of dumb strong hands infinite
> the erect deep upon me
> in the last light
>
> pours its eyeless miles
> the chattering sunset ludicrously
> dies,i hear only tidewings
> in the last light
> twitching at the world

Yet sometimes, when it is dealing with an appropriate subject, the style can soothe, as in the poem entitled "SNO," which carries metaphors of cleansing and of gentle, scarcely perceptible sounds of falling snowflakes:

>   a white idea (Listen
> drenches:earth's ugly)mind.
> ,Rinsing with exact death
> the annual brain
>   clotted with loosely voices
> look
> look.   Skilfully
> .fingered by(a parenthesis
> the)pond on whoseswooning edge
> black trees think
> (hear little knives of flower
> stropping sof a.   Thick silence)
> blacktreesthink
> tiny,angels sharpen:themselves
> (on
>   air)
> don't speak
>   A white idea,
> drenching.   earth's brain detaches

clottingsand from a a nnual(ugliness
of)rinsed mind slowly:
from!the:A wending putrescence. a. of, loosely;
voices

Images, space, and oddities of punctuation combine to develop a snowfall breathlessly heard rather than depicted. Color and concept merge in the image of the snow; then the command to "Listen" is suddenly intruded. The space that follows here and elsewhere in the poem allows, each time, for quiet to prevail. The "drenching" of earth makes it a wet snowfall and thus able to do the "Rinsing." Earth is given a "mind" for the "idea" to cleanse, but its brain is only annual and thus comes to death in the natural cycle because it has become "clotted." The snowflakes, "loosely" falling, that bring the cleansing death are now "voices" that we have been asked to listen for. The period and the comma are presumably other pauses for listening. Then we are commanded to "look" and perceive that the earth is touched ("fingered") by a pond, where the snow is melting ("swooning") and where the contrasting black of the trees is another concept. Now new sound metaphors are introduced: snowflakes as flower petals gently sliding over a razorstrop or as angel feathers. Repetition of the command for silence and the metaphor of the "white idea" cleansing the earth now lead to the visual breakup of words and intrusions of punctuation marks to suggest the dissolving of the clotted brain and an image of a muddy stream of melted snow ("A wending putrescence") winding into the pond.

There are troubles in expression however. The illogical adjective "exact" has, by now, been so overused by Cummings that it has become a hackneyed term in his poetic vocabulary. The "(a parenthesis / the)" device is an arbitrary item of logographic teasing. In his experiments with expression Cummings can be careless in his early work.

But among the "Post Impressions" we also have glimpses of the human scene, especially in three prose-poems (forms that Cummings learned from Mallarmé and Rimbaud) about an organ grinder and his monkey, about the rush hour in lower Manhattan, and about McSorley's saloon on the lower East Side. The last is especially notable in its attempt to create a collage of sound. What the poem presents in this vignette is a suggestion of evil as it makes its appearance in a bar-room. But of greatest interest is Cummings' play with words that have rhyme and consonance—*dint, grin, point, glint, squint,* and *wink*—or words that begin or end with similar consonant sounds—*piddle, spittle, topple, dribble, gobble*. In addition there is a collage of onomatopoeic bar-room sounds mixed with snippets of the customers' talk. We might call this work a sound painting. Here is an excerpt from the opening of the piece:

i was sitting in mcsorley's. outside it was
New York and beauti-
fully snowing.
Inside snug and evil. the slobbering
walls filthily push witless
creases of screaming warmth chuck pillows are noise
funnily swallows
swallowing revolvingly pompous a the swallowed
mottle with smooth or

a but of rapidly goes gobs the and of flecks of and a
chatter sobbings
intersect with which distinct disks of graceful oath,
upsoarings the
break on ceiling-flatness
the Bar.tinking luscious jigs dint of ripe silver with
warmlyish
wetflat splurging smells waltz the glush of squirting
taps plus slush
of foam knocked off and a faint piddle-of-drops she
says I ploc spittle
what the lands thaz me kid in no sir hopping sawdust
you kiddo he's a
palping wreaths of badly Yep cigars who jim him
why gluey grins topple
together eyes pout gestures stickily point made glints
squinting who's
a wink bum-nothing and money fuzzily mouths take
big wobbly foot-steps
every goggle cent of it get out ears dribbles soft right
old feller
belch the chap hic summore eh chuckles skulch....
and i was sitting in the din thinking drinking the ale,
which never
lets you grow old blinking at the low ceiling my
being pleasantly was
punctuated by the always retchings of a worthless
lamp....

Source: Richard S. Kennedy, "Tulips, Chimneys, &," in *E. E. Cummings Revisited*, Twayne Publishers, 1994, pp. 53–67.

Robert E. Maurer

In the following essay, Maurer contends that cummings knows the rules of language and breaks them on purpose, to challenge the reader.

[Cummings] has used language with no concession to conventional recognition; he has always wanted his reader to drop all the accoutrements of the grammarian and the rhetorician that he may be wearing as protective clothing and to approach his poems, as it were,

> TO REFER, HOWEVER, TO CUMMINGS' WORDS AS NOUNS AND VERBS IS TO MAKE THINGS SOUND MUCH SIMPLER THAN THEY ARE, FOR THE ONE OUTSTANDING CHARACTERISTIC OF HIS MATURE STYLE IS HIS DISRESPECT FOR THE PART OF SPEECH."

naked and unafraid. The reader should be free of preconceptions about English poetry, unafraid to "reconsider his standards of acceptance."

This is not to say, however, that Cummings does not know rules and tradition. He is instead a prime example of the old adage that an artist must know all the rules before he can break them. Cummings is no primitive, though he sometimes uses words as a child does; he is no Walt Whitman with a barbaric yawp, no untutored child of the prairie working in what is essentially an alien medium.... His first book of poems, *Tulips and Chimneys* (1923), revealed the fact that he had had a classical education, although the poems in it that looked forward to his later writing were much more noteworthy than those which were traditionalist. And although he continues to work in the sonnet—perhaps his most memorable poetry is in this form—he long ago abandoned the language of Rossetti and Keats for one which fits his highly personal insight into experience. At its most highly developed state, in his later books, Cummings' language becomes almost a foreign one, usually possible to figure out for a reader who knows English, it is true; but he will get its full meaning only if he has read a great deal of Cummings and if he "knows the language."

It is unfortunate that most of the critical appraisals of Cummings' poetry were made early, shortly after his first books were published. Since those days—the twenties—were full of literary and artistic ferment, and a new poetic talent was to many people at least as exciting as a new baseball player, it is natural that he should have received a great deal of attention then; it is perhaps also natural that as the first shock caused by his poetry died down into acceptance of what seemed a fixed technique of an established poet, the critics should have turned their eyes elsewhere. Cummings, too, was somewhat out of the mainstream in the thirties. He was not popular with the New Critics because he was too personal and unintellectual; he did not think or write in their groove. Nor was he popular with the critics of the left who demanded their own variety of social consciousness in a writer. His "immorality" was too blunt for the Humanists, and his verse was too uncommunicative for the attackers of the cult of unintelligibility. When his last three volumes of verse came out, no one took the trouble to give Cummings the reappraisal that his poetry needed and deserved; very few people noticed the fundamental change of attitude which manifested itself in his growing reverence and dedication to lasting love; even fewer noted the development in his use of language. Thus in 1955 an essay, "Notes on E. E. Cummings' Language," by Richard P. Blackmur, written in 1930, remains the only extensive treatment of the subject; and too many people think of his language, as they think of the subject matter of his poetry, as if it were all of a piece, which it most emphatically is not. (pp. 80–2)

Many of the things that Mr. Blackmur said are still accurate descriptions of some of the phenomena of Cummings' language; the trouble is that his remarks are incomplete. They do not consider Cummings' later practices of using one part of speech as another, of leaving out words so that the resulting condensation is so dense as to be almost impenetrable, of thoroughly scrambling English word order with the same effect. Mr. Blackmur was instead occupied with such things as Cummings' tough-guy attitude and his romantic egoism, with his overuse of certain favorite words to which he seemed to assign private meanings, and with the question of whether such diction did not make his poetry impenetrable. Mr. Blackmur concluded unequivocally that it did; and, if in 1952 he saw no need for modification of his note [in his *Language As Gesture*], one assumes that he still thinks so. (pp. 82–3)

Although his language, especially in the later books, is intricate and difficult, what [Cummings] asks of his reader is, as always, the frank approach of a child; and it is this attitude which he himself takes to his mother tongue and to its tenets and rules. Of course, such an approach is consistent with that most salient feature of his viewpoint, his glorification of the child (or the "maturely childish" adult); he is, when he fashions language as a child would, merely practicing what he preaches. It is doubtful whether he ever said to himself, "I shall form and use words as if I have not completely mastered the idiom of the English language, although I know its rules"; but this is precisely what, in his first ventures into unusual language, he began to do. He divested himself of the literate adult's prejudices against such things as double negatives, redundant superlatives and comparatives, and non-dictionary words. (p. 83)

[In] *Tulips and Chimneys*, although the greater part of his language is conventional and sometimes even banally "poetic," one finds such unusual usages as *unstrength, purpled, Just-spring, eddieandbill, puddle-wonderful, almostness, greentwittering, quiveringgold, flowerterrible, starlessness, fearruining, timeshaped, sayingly*. Except for *sayingly* and *almostness*, which are among the first examples of his changing one part of speech into another, and *unstrength*, there is nothing very startling about most of these words. The mere printing of two words together, as in *greentwittering*, might be considered more a typographical technique than a linguistic one, although it is apparent that when Cummings combines two words to form one adjective he usually creates a new concept by the juxtaposition of two unlike descriptives: *flowerterrible, timeshaped*. (It is such language as this that Mr. Blackmur objects to; he would say that it is impossible to determine the exact meaning of such words as *flowerterrible* and *timeshaped*, and undoubtedly he is right.) *Tulips and Chimneys* abounds with such words and with phrases that are made up of conventional words in unconventional juxtapositions....

These phrases that (one must agree with Mr. Blackmur) convey a thrill but not a precise impression swarm through the book but are not able to occupy it exclusively. In contrast to them are many images which depend for their power upon the unexpected but which manage to convey an accurate reproduction of the poet's thought, which show, indeed, that the poet *had* a thought and not merely a rush of words. (p. 86)

The language of *Tulips and Chimneys*,... like the imagery, the verse forms, the subject matter, and the thought, is sometimes good, sometimes bad. But the book is so obviously the work of a talented young man who is striking off in new directions, groping for original and yet precise expression, experimenting in public, that it seems uncharitable to dwell too long on its shortcomings. (p. 88)

Cummings' linguistic usages in *Tulips and Chimneys* and in the two books which soon followed it *& [AND]* and *XLI POEMS* [are similar]. These books were published within three years and are fairly much alike (although the typographical distortions that reach extremes in *& [AND]* were barely hinted at in the first book); in style and in subject matter the three books are the work of the same youthful poet. (p. 89)

Although... the early books are punctuated with favorite words (*thrilling, flowers, utter, skillful, groping, crisp, keen, actual, stars*, etc.) almost as copiously as another author would use commas, an awareness of these words is not unrewarding if one wishes to understand Cummings. The words *flower* and *stars* are, as he uses them, not mere substantives representing a thing in nature but are metaphorical shorthand for concepts which Cummings finds admirable: the flowers, for example, representing growth, being, aliveness; the stars standing for the steadfastness of beauty in nature.

Such adjectives as he continually uses..., though they are admittedly overworked in the early books to the point of tiresomeness, are nevertheless indicative of his viewpoint: he admires phenomena that can be described as crisp, keen, actual, gay, young, strong, or strenuous, and dislikes the groping, the dim, the slow, the dull. In reading the early poetry, it is often necessary to know which of Cummings' words are, in Hayakawa's terms, "purr words" and which are "snarl words" in order to get any meaning from the poem. As Cummings progressed, he outgrew his penchant for such expressions as "thy whitest feet crisply are straying"... and grew into his mature style, which is something infinitely more precise, often more concrete, and which relies more on such straight-forward words as nouns and verbs than on piled-up adjectives for its effects.

To refer, however, to Cummings' words as nouns and verbs is to make things sound much simpler than they are, for the one outstanding characteristic of his mature style is his disrespect for the part of speech. It would be more accurate instead to say that he *uses* words as nouns, for instance, which are not normally so; it would be hard to find any one of his later poems which does not utilize a word in a sense other than its usual one. *Yes* is used as a noun to represent all that is positive and therefore admirable, *if* to stand for all that is hesitating, uncertain, incomplete. The style thus becomes spare; the later books contain many poems written in extremely short lines, lines which, utilizing the simplest words, say a great deal. (pp. 89–90)

[By] accepting the fact that the poet may be saying something worthwhile and may be seriously trying to convey both truth and beauty as he sees it, one will try to look through the poet's eyes. To understand Cummings fully, more so than in understanding most other poets, it is necessary for one to have read much of Cummings. To a reader familiar with his techniques such a statement as "yes is a pleasant country" is as penetrable as a deep, clear pool; it might, however, seem more opaque to one reading him for the first time. Such words as *yes* and *if* take on a historical meaning within the body of his poetry, a meaning not divorced from their traditional ones but infinitely larger: *yes*, for instance, conventionally is used in a particular situation; as Cummings uses it, *yes* represents the sum of all the situations in which it might be used. And such a technique as "who younger than / begin / are" is not too complicated to be used by some practitioners of the art of writing for mass consumption, as witness the first line of a very popular song from *South Pacific*: "Younger than springtime, you are." (pp. 90–1)

Babette Deutsch has described Cummings' use of these words as follows [see *CLC*, Vol 3]:

> His later poems make words as abstract as "am," "if," "because," do duty for seemingly more solid nouns. By this very process, however, he restores life to dying concepts. "Am" implies being at its most responsive, "if" generally means the creeping timidity that kills responsiveness, and "because" the logic of the categorizing mind that destroys what it dissects. Here is a new vocabulary, a kind of imageless metaphor.

Why, Miss Deutsch might further have explained, generally means to Cummings a state of uncertainty, a searching for direction from sources outside oneself, an unspontaneous demanding of reasons and causes in the face of life. A person who is a *why* is generally a subject for ridicule, being, like an *if*, a timid creature who thinks, fears, denies, follows, unlike an all-alive *is*. (p. 92)

Right though she is in assigning meanings to Cummings' *am's*, *if's*, and *because's*, Miss Deutsch does not get to the root of the technique used in these words when she describes them as examples of "imageless metaphor." Metaphor has as its base the use of comparison and analogy, of the verisimilitude within dissimilitude that exists between two images, actions, or concepts. Actually, a closer insight into the real nature of these words is found in Mr. Blackmur's study, though, in contrast to Miss Deutsch's commitment to the technique, his definition of the process comes within a general attack on Cummings' language. He says at the end of his essay that all of Cummings' "thought" (the quotes are Mr. Blackmur's) is metonymy, and that the substance of the metonymy is never assigned to anything. "In the end," he concludes, "we have only the thrill of substance." Metonymy is based on reduction rather than comparison: an object associated with a thing is substituted for the thing itself (as *crown* for *king*), or a corporeal object is used to represent an abstract concept or idea (as *heavy thumb* for *dishonesty*). When Mr. Blackmur says that Cummings' metonymy contains only the "thrill of substance," he means that in the case of such a word as *flower*, one of Cummings' favorite metonymical vehicles, the substance—flower—is there but the idea of which it is a reduction is neither present nor ascertainable. If the reader receives a "thrill" from such a word as *flower*, well and good; but Mr. Blackmur asserts that a thrill is all he will receive.

It must be remembered that Mr. Blackmur's essay was written after only the earliest of Cummings' books had appeared; none of them exemplify his mature style—in those days *flower* and *star* were about as far as he had gone in the direction of metonymy. In his use of *why*, however, he has extended not only the uses to which a particular word can be put but also the accepted limits of metonymy: he has taken an abstract word and made it stand for a host of ideas, the negative characteristics mentioned above. Mr. Blackmur's "thrill of substance" is therefore not applicable to Cummings' present use of metonymy, for such words as *why* do not represent a substance and certainly, if they are isolated, convey no thrill. That it is possible for *why* to induce a thrill is seen in the lines quoted above, but the thrill comes not from the "substance" of *why* but from the uniqueness of its use; perhaps also there is a thrill of comprehension which comes when the implication of the metonymy strikes the reader.

Again, if one accepts Mr. Blackmur's argument it is unanswerable; he would say that to derive an implication from a metonymical concept is not enough, that the idea or object which the "substance" represents must be precisely known. However, there must perhaps have been a day when *heavy thumb* was not a universally accepted reduction for dishonesty; the person who created this particular metonymy must have been doing a rather original thing, and his created expression must have had to go through a process of recognition into acceptance before it came to be unquestioned. That Cummings' metonymical usages are unlikely to go through this particular process is immaterial; such metonymies as *why* and *yes* are a little too subtle, too closely based on a poet's private convictions, to find a place in ordinary language. It should not be concluded, however, that their meaning cannot be understood.... (pp. 92–3)

To understand a Cummings metonymy, one can bring his plain common sense to bear first, and, in the case of such expressions as "who younger than / begin / are" or "and should some why completely weep," common sense is often enough to establish a correct meaning. (p. 93)

[His] technique in creating new uses for such words as *if, why, because, which, how, must, same, have,* and *they* on the one hand and *now, am, yes, is, we, give,* and *here* on the other is to accumulate meanings for each of them that total up to the same kind of positive and negative oppositions that are set against each other throughout his work.... (pp. 94–5)

[He] makes each of these words self-subsistent in terms of the context in which they appear, and, by varying the meanings in each usage, makes the words metonymical reductions for a whole set of concepts. In a way he is creating an easy cipher of meaning, penetrable but not completely so at first sight. And is this not also the case of any author who utilizes a few dominant symbols in order to express his special insight into experience, who must make each use of a symbol function in its context and yet adds to its meaning with each repeated use? (Hawthorne's repeated use of light and shadow in his works might be cited as an example of this method.) The success of a metonymous or symbolic system of this sort depends partly upon the degree to which the poet objectifies and clarifies his conception of the world, partly upon the effects of freshness and vitality his language produces; when one comes across such lines as the following there can be no doubt that Cummings is successful in both respects:

> she laughed his joy she cried his grief
> bird by snow and stir by still
> anyone's any was all to her

Using a traditional rhetorical pattern in the second line (*little by little* serves as a model for it), he superimposes a metonymous structure: *bird* and *snow* are reductions of summer and winter; *stir* and *still*, of all manner of activities. The net result of such a line is a new and delightful sense of linguistic invention, precise and vigorous.

To say that Cummings is successful in objectifying his conception of the world and in achieving a freshness and vitality of language is not to diminish the difficulty of many of his poems. Nor is it meant to say that his metonymical usages are not overworked, just as were his favorite adjectives in *Tulips and Chimneys*. What was originally a fresh idea, and what still has great power if used with discrimination—his utilizing abstract words to be the "substance" of a metonymy—can become boring, tiresome, and even meaningless if called upon constantly to carry the whole weight of a poem. Just as the word *flower*, which obviously was a symbol for something, when used in every poem became a mere word, to be accepted and passed over; so a constant succession of *which's* and *who's* and *why's* and *they's* begins to roll off the tongue too quickly for the mind to make the transference from the "substance" to the idea for which it stands; and the force of the metonymy is lost. A poem written almost exclusively in these words loses, too, its beauty and grace; one-syllable abstract words are not particularly melodious, and a poem in which they are not frequently interspersed with words which are more interesting in themselves, or more concrete, is likely to plod along (like Pope's "And ten low words oft creep in one dull line"), one metonymy after another, never skipping or dancing or singing.

However, at the same time that Cummings developed the metonymy to its ultimate use he was growing in another direction: many of his poems became much more, not less, musical than his earlier ones. In the earlier books he had placed his dependence upon the sonnet form.

often upon a grand manner, and sometimes upon free verse; but he very seldom wrote a poem which cried out to be sung, which could be read only with a joyous, pronounced rhythm. Such poems as these occur frequently in the last three books. Cummings has given up being grand and derivative and become simple and himself. If he utilizes old verse forms, they are more likely to be of the nursery rhyme than of the Spenserian stanza. His lines, as has been mentioned, are often short; his meter is usually iambic; his words—when they are not metonymies—are colloquial. As a result, one can read these poems with a sense of the child's pure delight in poetry; Cummings himself has become more maturely childish as he has grown.

The rhythmical poems do utilize the typical abstract word metonymies—it is a rare poem in his later books which does not; even his satires make use of them to some extent—but the metonymies are likely to be placed in the context of concrete words and lively happenings. (pp. 95–6)

[A] progression from the external to the personal, from the outer world of "mostpeople" to the inner world of "us," finds its expression, sometimes quietly, sometimes with childish innocence, sometimes with a dauntless courage, in poem after poem in the volume *1 x 1*.... And, as he begins one of the most beautiful of his sonnets: "one's not half two. It's two are halves of one:"....This whole conception of i-you-we (or my-your-our) becomes one of Cummings' most frequently used metonymies. Its impact, to anyone who knows that "two are halves of one," is immediate.... In the i-you-we metonymy the whole is greater than the sum of its parts, and the metonymy itself becomes a prime example of Cummings' ability to use the simplest words as a shorthand for concepts which represent his own convictions. It is fitting that his most musical poems should be the ones...in celebration of i-you-we; for to Cummings love is still the most joyous of all things. Mature love to him becomes not more sober and settled but more intensely lyrical, less tortured, more a thing for singing and dancing and child-like delight. *We* takes its place along with *yes* and *now* and *is* as the metonymies for all that is best in this "really unreal world." (pp. 98–9)

Source: Robert E. Maurer, "Latter-Day Notes on E. E. Cummings' Language," in *Bucknell Review*, May 1955.

SOURCES

Abrams, M. H., ed., *A Glossary of Literary Terms*, 7th ed., Harcourt Brace College Publishers, 1999, p. 175.

"Avant-garde Typography in Literature," in *Special Collections*, University of Delaware Library, http://www.lib.udel.edu/ud/spec/exhibits/typoglit.htm (accessed June 3, 2011).

"Clash of Cultures in the 1910s and 1920s," in *ehistory*, Ohio State University Department of History, http://ehistory.osu.edu/osu/mmh/clash/NewWoman/oppositionpage1.htm (accessed June 3, 2011).

cummings, e. e., "in Just," in *E. E. Cummings Complete Poems, 1904–1962*, edited by George Firmage, Liveright, 1994, p. 27.

Cureton, Richard D., "E. E. Cummings: A Study of the Poetic Use of Deviant Morphology," in *Poetics Today*, Vol. 1, No. 1–2, Autumn 1979, pp. 213–44.

Goldberg, David J., Review of *The Dollar Decade: Mammon and the Machine in 1920s America*, in *Historian*, Vol. 67, No. 1, March 2005, pp. 103–104.

"Iamb, iambus," in *Representative Poetry Online*, http://rpo.library.utoronto.ca/display_rpo/terminology.cfm#acatalectic (accessed on June 4, 2011).

"Innocence," in *Merriam-Webster Dictionary*, http://www.merriam-webster.com/dictionary/innocence?show=0&t=1310160785 (accessed June, 3, 2011).

Labriola, Albert, C., "Reader-Response Criticism and the Poetry of E. E. Cummings: 'Buffalo Bill's defunct' and 'in Just–,'" in *Cithera*, Vol. 31, May 1992, pp. 40–42.

Landles, Iain, "An Analysis of Two Poems by E. E. Cummings," in *Spring*, No. 10, 2001, pp. 31–43, http://www.gvsu.edu/english/cummings/issue10/Landles10.html (accessed on June 1, 2011).

Mayo, Robert, "Chansons Innocentes (I)," in *English "A" Analyst*, Vol. 2, May 1947, pp. 1–4.

Monroe, Harriet, "Flare and Blare," in *E. E. Cummings: The Critical Reception*, edited by Lloyd N. Dendinger, Burt Franklin, 1981, pp. 30–31; originally published in *Poetry*, January 1924.

"Pan," in *The Oxford Companion to Classical Literature*, 2nd ed., edited by M. C. Howatson, Oxford University Press, 1991, p. 406.

Parekh, Pushpa N., "Nature in the Poetry of E. E. Cummings," in *Spring*, No. 3, 1994, pp. 63–71, http://www.gvsu.edu/english/cummings/issue3/Parekh3.htm (accessed June 4, 2011).

Pollack, Norma, "Poems of Cummings Set to Music," in *Spring*, No. 4, 1995, pp. 121–29, http://www.gvsu.edu/english/cummings/Pollack4.htm (accessed June 1, 2011).

Rotella, Guy, "Nature, Time, and Transcendence in Cummings' Later Poems," in *Critical Essays on E. E. Cummings*, edited by Guy Rotella, G. K. Hall, 1984, p. 285.

Sawyer-Lauçanno, Christopher, *E. E. Cummings: A Biography*, Sourcebooks, 2004, pp. 25, 346–47, 367.

Smiley, Gene, "The U.S. Economy in the 1920s," in *EH.net*, February 1, 2010, http://eh.net/encyclopedia/article/smiley.1920s.final (accessed June 2, 2011).

Steele, Timothy, "Introduction to Meter," in *CSULA Instructional Web Server*, California State University at Los Angeles, http://instructional1.calstatela.edu/tsteele/TSpage5/meter.html (accessed on June 4, 2011).

von Abele, Rudolph, "'Only to Grow': Change in the Poetry of E. E. Cummings," in *PMLA*, Vol. 70, No. 5, December 1955, pp. 913–33.

Winters, Yvor, "E. E. Cummings's Poetry," in *E. E. Cummings: The Critical Reception*, edited by Lloyd N. Dendinger, Burt Franklin, 1981, pp. 209–10; originally published in *American Literature*, May 1939.

Wolf, Robert L., "E. E. Cummings's Poetry," in *E. E. Cummings: The Critical Reception*, edited by Lloyd N. Dendinger, Burt Franklin, 1981, p. 27; originally published in *New York World*, November 18, 1923.

FURTHER READING

cummings, e. e., *The Enormous Room*, edited by George James Firmage, Liveright, 1994.
> This work of prose explores the details of cummings's time in France when he was detained under suspicion of treason. Originally published in 1922, *The Enormous Room* showcases the author's unique writing style and provides a glimpse into his personal life.

Eksteins, Modris, *Rites of Spring: The Great War and the Birth of the Modern Age*, Mariner Books, 2000.
> This nonfiction volume considers the events leading up to World War I, the war itself, and its influence in the following decade.

Fussell, Paul, *The Great War and Modern Memory*, Oxford University Press, 2000.
> Fussell examines World War I in the context of social history and literature. This nonfiction book shares poems, essay, and letters from soldiers to explore the experiences of individuals and the impact that World War I had on their lives.

Karmel, Pepe, *Picasso and the Invention of Cubism*, Yale University Press, 2003.
> This volume examines how cubism developed as an art form in the early twentieth century. Concentrating on the years 1906 to 1913, Karmel explores the effect of cubism on visual language as well as on painting and drawing.

Kennedy, Richard S., *Dreams in the Mirror: A Biography of E. E. Cummings*, Liveright, 1994.
> Kennedy's respected biography of e. e. cummings provides in-depth information about the life of the controversial artist and writer. Along with the enlightening biographical information, this book includes several of cummings's sketches and unpublished poems.

Patea, Viorica, and Paul Scott Derrick, *Modernism Revisited: Transgressing Boundaries and Strategies of Renewal in American Poetry*, Rodopi, 2007.
> This collection of essays examines the modernist movement in America and beyond. The essayists come from both American and European backgrounds, and they provide different points of view about culture, art, and twentieth-century comparative literature.

SUGGESTED SEARCH TERMS

e. e. cummings

In Just-spring

modern poetry

e. e. cummings AND in Just

modern poetry AND e. e. cummings

e. e. cummings AND biography

1920s AND art

Lost Generation

World War I AND Lost Generation

America AND 1920s

The Journey

MARY OLIVER
1986

"The Journey" by Mary Oliver appears in *Dream Work*, Oliver's sixth book of poetry. Typical of Oliver's style, the poem is a free verse lyric with multiple associations with the natural world. Its theme of self-preservation in the context of the chaotic modern world has resonated with readers worldwide, and it has been reprinted and quoted widely. Oliver stays true to her roots in romanticism with her use of everyday language and extensive metaphor to capture the emotional and psychological complexities of the human condition and explore the notion of feeling trapped by obligation and manipulation. Published in 1986, "The Journey" has remained on the lists of favorite poems in blogs, magazines, and books for the last twenty-five years.

AUTHOR BIOGRAPHY

Oliver was born on September 10, 1935, in Maple Heights, Ohio, on the outskirts of Cleveland. As a teenager, she visited the home of deceased poet Edna St. Vincent Millay in Austerlitz in upper New York State, eventually moving to the estate to help sort the work and correspondence Millay left behind and to serve as a companion for Millay's sister, Norma. It was there that she met photographer Molly Malone Cook, and the two entered into a romantic relationship that lasted

Mary Oliver (Getty Images)

over forty years until Cook's death in 2005. Oliver briefly attended both Ohio State University and Vassar College in the mid-1950s but never earned a degree.

In 1963, at the age of twenty-eight, Oliver published her first collection of poetry, *No Voyage, and Other Poems*. A prolific writer, Oliver has since published more than twenty books of poetry and six books of prose, including books on the craft of poetry. Her 1983 poetry collection *American Primitive* won the 1984 Pulitzer Prize for Poetry. *Dream Work*, published in 1986, contains many of her best-loved poems, including "The Journey." She won the 1992 National Book Award for Poetry with *New and Selected Poems* and the 1998 Christopher Award and the L. L. Winship/PEN New England Award for *House of Light*. In addition, Oliver was the recipient of a Guggenheim fellowship and has received honorary doctoral degrees from the Art Institute of Boston, Dartmouth College, and Tufts University.

Oliver has taught workshops and held residencies at numerous colleges and universities. She held the Catharine Osgood Foster Chair for Distinguished Teaching at Bennington College from 1995 to 2000. Intensely private, Oliver reveals the most about herself through her poetry, which combines a love of nature and examination of the self with autobiographical details integrated into her poems. As of 2011, she resided in Provincetown, Massachusetts.

POEM SUMMARY

The text used for this summary is from *Dream Work*, Atlantic Monthly Press, 1986, pp. 38–39. A version of the poem can be found on the following Web page: http://www.english.illinois.edu/maps/poets/m_r/oliver/online_poems.htm.

"The Journey" is a free verse poem with no stanza breaks. Because of the lack of rhyme, meter, or apparent structure, it may seem at first that the poem lacks form. However, free verse poetry does not mean poetry without form. The elements that lend form and structure to the poem are more subtle and require more concentration and exploration to spot, which also means that the form of the poem is open to interpretation much more than other poetic forms, such as the sonnet or villanelle, which have set structures. "The Journey" can be broken up into roughly three parts.

Lines 1–11

The first part of the poem sets the stage for the reader. The first two lines accomplish several important things. Perhaps most noteworthy, in the first line the speaker reveals, by addressing the reader as "you," that the subject of the poem is in fact that reader. The first line also tells the reader that the action is one that was a long time in coming. The first part of the second line starts the theme in the poem of necessary action, and it deepens the reader's curiosity—*what* had to be done?—which pulls the reader further into the poem. The title of the poem tells the reader that it is about a journey, and the first part tells the reader that it started chaotically. The reader gets a sense of terror. This is not a happy beginning to a journey. Perhaps the decision to begin was not even a deliberate one; rather, it was a journey of necessity.

The journey itself is a metaphor, but the text of the poem hides other metaphors. Lines 6 and 7 introduce a trembling house. The personification of the house clues the reader in to the fact that the speaker is not referring to an actual building. The choice of the word "house" is important. It is a building of personal space (as opposed to an

MEDIA ADAPTATIONS

- *At Blackwater Pond: Mary Oliver Reads Mary Oliver* is a 2006 recording of Oliver reading forty of her own poems spanning a twenty-five-year period, from 1985's *Dream Work* to 2010's *New and Selected Poems, Volume Two*.

- In 2010, Oliver followed up *At Blackwater Pond* with *Many Miles: Mary Oliver reads Mary Oliver*, a recording of Oliver reading another thirty-seven of her own poems.

- The Lannan Foundation hosts a podcast (http://www.lannan.org/lf/rc/event/mary-oliver1/) of Oliver reading and discussing her poetry with Joseph Parisi, poetry critic and former editor of *Poetry* magazine.

- *Poetry Sky Watch...Looking Inward...*, composed by Deborah J. Anderson in 2010, is a musical adaptation of Oliver's poetry for a flute quartet.

---

office or a church); however, the speaker does not refer to it as a home. It is merely a frame, a shell inside which day-to-day activity takes place. The house could symbolize an empty life or even an old self that is unstable and shaking. It is not a place of refuge but a place from which to escape.

The speaker mentions unknown, unseen speakers in line 3 who are yelling at the "you" in the poem. This group of people adds to the chaos and terror that serve as the impetus to the journey. In line 10, these voices stop yelling and instead begin to plead. These people are trying different tactics to serve as obstacles to the person undertaking the journey. Their emotional manipulation is what is holding traveler back. In lines 8 and 9, this psychological pressure is portrayed in physical terms as these people try to trip up the traveler, to stop the journey that will lead that person away from them.

Lines 12–22

Line 12 signals the second part of the poem. Often, transitional words such as *but, yet, however*, or *though* indicate a shift in mood or tone. Subtleties such as this are what the reader of free verse poetry should look for in place of formal elements of traditional meters and structures. Line 13 repeats line 2 and acts as a stanza break since it starts the structure cycle all over. The repetition of a transitional word at the beginning of lines 14 and 17 mirrors that of lines 3 and 6. The first segment describes the setting right before the journey began, and this second part describes the start of the journey itself. The house metaphor surfaces again when the reader speaks of the base of the house. In the first segment, the house trembled without a stated cause from the speaker. In the second segment, the speaker blames the wind for the instability of the house. Just as the reader deduced that the house in the first part symbolized the self or life, the reader can use contextual clues in the second part to determine what it is the wind stands for. The wind is trying to knock down the house here. Something is trying to destroy the essence of the person—still directly addressed as "you"—who has begun this journey. The speaker brings up the voices again implicitly in line 17, describing the emotional and psychological impact they have had.

The speaker goes into more detail now than before in the description of the setting, giving the time that the journey began and the conditions the traveler will have to face. At this point, it is clear that the journey is an emotional or psychological journey of self-preservation away from destructive forces in the traveler's life. The speaker tells the reader that the journey was overdue. The conditions were bad, the road littered with debris. The journey will not be an easy one. The language of these lines has a slightly rushed feel. Oliver is writing as a person might think; there is no formality to the language at all. Verbs are missing, and thoughts are left incomplete. It is as if too much time has been wasted already to be overly concerned with articulation. The holes are automatically filled in by the reader, who by now has become the central character in the poem. The reader is the "you," the actor.

Lines 23–36

Another transition word begins the third and last segment, at line 23, just as it did the second segment. This third section describes the setting of the journey after the traveler has managed to break free of the voices, ignore or evade the wind, and prevail over darkness and obstacles. The speaker brings light into the poem for the first time with the introduction of the stars, which banish the clouds. Instead of the chaotic, demanding, destructive voices of others, the speaker says that the only voice that can be heard is that of the reader. The traveler does not feel alone. The tone shifts dramatically in the third section, denoting confidence and strength. The speaker paints a picture of a stronger person striding instead of struggling, focused on the only thing anyone ultimately has any control over: the self. The poem closes with a sense of resolve. The self *will* be preserved.

THEMES

Feminism

Feminist criticism in literature has only been in existence since the 1960s, and in that time, numerous approaches, opinions, theories, and experts have emerged and entered into debate. The overriding theme of feminist literary theory is that there are certain social constructs that are strongly associated with one gender or another and are so ingrained in our culture that they go largely unnoticed. Many things, from large concepts like politics, religion, and economics right down to single words, carry gender bias. Housework, for example, is still largely thought of as "women's work," just as the construction field is associated far more with men. Words such as "dainty" and "delicate" carry female connotations, while "aggressive" or "strong" may seem more associated with males. The topic is far too large to address in any detail here; however, it is important to understand the basic concept in any critical examination of Oliver's work because of her position as a female nature poet. Nature is full of genderless things that our culture tends to imagine as male or female. In addition, poetry throughout the ages has used nature as a metaphor for human characteristics to such an extent that certain phrases, when used in a poetic context, imply gender where feminists believe there should be none. If a poet compares a loved one to a flower, it is almost certain that a majority of readers will assume the loved one is a woman. Oliver's work has inspired heated debates about the place of nature in poetry and whether female poets have any obligation to attempt to change these long-standing associations. In contrast to the history of literature and literary criticism dating back to the time of Aristotle and Plato, feminist theory is still in its infancy. Female poets such as Oliver are subject to intense scrutiny by feminist critics, and this in itself is a topic of debate: should poetry be read with special emphasis paid to implied gender bias, or does that detract from the purpose of the poem and intent of the poet? Feminist literary theory attempts to answer questions such as these.

Nature

Since before the invention of writing, people have looked to nature to provide a reflection of the human soul with which they could interact and identify. Nature mirrors the human experience in nearly any way imaginable. It has its cycles of life just like humans: birth is seen in the characteristics of spring, death in those of winter. Nature even has personality traits like those of humans or life itself. We associate rain with sadness, storms with trouble, and sun with happiness. Poets have always looked to nature as a means of studying what it means to be human and a way to express what they feel to others. Often, elements of nature are personified, that is, given human characteristics, such as the wind in "The Journey," which is pictured as having fingers. Writers often draw comparisons through metaphor, analogy, and other figures of speech in order to illustrate concepts that can be better understood with a familiar point of reference. A caterpillar emerging from a cocoon as a butterfly symbolizes transformation and growth. Leaves falling from a tree bring to mind aging or dying. The examples are endless. By using nature, poets can express their views on spirituality, creation, mortality and the interconnectedness of all living creatures. Oliver has written extensively on the importance of paying attention to the natural world and is open about the fact that she finds much of her inspiration in nature. "The Journey" is not a poem explicitly about nature, but Oliver, like thousands of years of poets before her, uses elements of nature to better express her intended message.

Self-Preservation

Self-preservation is the instinct that propels individuals to protect themselves from pain or death. Though this seems a simple concept, thinkers such as Sigmund Freud and Friedrich Nietzsche have debated the drive behind self-preservation, and the theory has been applied to the study of psychology, society, economics, and politics. Freud associated self-preservation with the ego, or self, and stated that, along with the sex drive, it is what ensures the continuation of life. In subsequent years, however, there has been much debate and discussion on the exact scope of the concept of

TOPICS FOR FURTHER STUDY

- Keep a dream journal for one week. As soon as you can after you wake up, if possible even before you get out of bed, record the details you remember from your dreams. Note any specific images that are particularly vivid or out of place. Also write down any obvious sources of anxiety or joy in your life. Research Sigmund Freud's concepts of condensation and displacement. Do you find any connections between these ideas and your dreams? Make a list of the "dream metaphors" you have discovered and explain why you think certain images represent certain real-life things. Create a poem that includes those dream metaphors.

- Using online and print sources, research the idea of psychological self-preservation and find examples of individuals exhibiting this instinct in magazines, newspapers, and blogs from around the world. In what cultural context is each person situated? What social problems, conflicts, or movements are influencing his or her everyday life? Working in groups, pick examples from several different cultures and create a blog detailing the story of each person. Include images, examples from the subjects' popular culture (such as commercials or advertising campaigns), and summaries of the pertinent social issues, including links to relevant Web sites of government and non-profit groups.

- "For the poet as well as anyone else," Oliver writes in *Blue Pastures*, "each day in the private realm is filled with its mundane details...amusements, trips to the grocery store, to the mall for socks, to the car wash, to the ball game." Poets take inspiration from such details and, through the poem, fill them with special meaning. Think of a recent everyday event in your life, such as doing your homework, driving to class, or eating breakfast. Record every detail of the experience that you can think of. Using these details as a starting point, create a poem that uses the event as a metaphor for an emotional or psychological experience.

- Choose a poem from Carol Ann Duffy's 1997 anthology *I Wouldn't Thank You for a Valentine: Poems for Young Feminists* that uses free verse and has no defined stanza breaks. Analyze the poetic structure using the language of the poem as your guide. With the help of an online literary terms dictionary, note examples of techniques such as alliteration, consonance, assonance, repetition, shifts in tone, and so forth. How does the poet use language to sculpt the poem in place of traditional form? Pick three to five structural elements and write an analysis of them. Include their definitions and an explanation of their use in the poem.

- In today's electronic and technology-centered world, it is easy to overlook the evidence of the natural world around us. Even in the busiest and most industrial of cities, elements of nature can be found. A line of ants on the sidewalk, a pigeon near a restaurant patio, even the sun and moon in the sky are all examples of nature that can be easily seen. Challenge yourself to spend a specific amount of time—from a couple of hours to an entire weekend, if you can—"unplugged" from electronic life. Turn off your phone, step away from your computer, and study the nature in which you live. Write an essay about how successful or unsuccessful your attempt to "return to nature" was. Read about the worldview of Henry David Thoreau, Ralph Waldo Emerson, and other romantic poets and essayists. Do you believe that modern individuals can live in the way these thinkers advocated? Why or why not?

A terrible storm is described in the poem. (Hal_P | Shutterstock.com)

self-preservation, just as there has always been discussion on what exactly constitutes "life." Nietzsche and philosophers from his school of thought believe that the self-preservation instinct is not purely a survival instinct but the result of an individual's desire for power. Many psychologists have stated that self-preservation also includes a need to be loved. From a sociological standpoint, self-preservation is tied to an individual's ability to function within a culture and belong to an identity group. Self-preservation as Freud imagined it, then, has evolved into a concept that includes not only the physical but the psychological. It is this instinct that drives every action and reaction, both conscious and subconscious, on both mental and physical levels. In "The Journey," Oliver uses poetry to examine the concept of self-preservation.

STYLE

Free Verse

Free verse poetry has no set meter (organized pattern of stressed and unstressed syllables) or rhyme scheme. However, this does not mean that it does not have form. Instead, the poet uses other patterns and methods to organize the poem. Often, the poem contains a pattern in spoken sounds (assonance or consonance), visual form (the way the poem looks on the page), or poetic devices (such as metaphor or simile). Poets who write in free verse and are not forced to manipulate their words into a traditional, set form are often able to mirror the cadence and patterns of modern everyday speech and draw the reader in closer to the poem. Free verse is a relatively new form of poetry. It originated in France in the late nineteenth century and was popularized in America in the early twentieth century by poets such as Ezra Pound and T. S. Eliot. "The Journey" has no apparent rhyme or meter; however, the repetition of certain phrases and words lends the poem form and consistency. The line breaks are not arbitrary. Oliver had a deliberate reason for ending each line where she did, usually to emphasize some portion of the poem or to allow the language to flow more freely. Free verse poets put just as much thought into the placement of their words as poets who write in traditional verse, though it might not be apparent to the reader at first glance.

Romanticism

Romanticism emerged in the early nineteenth century as an artistic movement centered on themes of emotion, intuition, and the superiority of nature over industrialization. It was a direct response to the Enlightenment of the late eighteenth and early nineteenth centuries, which focused on reason. Though romanticism appeared and flourished in the early nineteenth century, its basic ideas can still be seen in visual art, music, and literature today, including in the work of Oliver. Romanticism aims to express individual emotion and also connect each individual to a universal and infinite whole, and this belief influenced not only the arts but how people viewed religion, politics, economics, and other philosophies. Romantics believe that nature is truer and more meaningful than human-created constructs, and it is through a connection to nature that the human self can best be understood. In "The Journey," Oliver sprinkles elements of nature throughout the entire poem, and she is known for work that puts an emphasis on nature. The romantic poets turned away from formal, stylized language and instead focused on ordinary colloquial (conversational) language that could be understood easily by everyone. "The Journey," for example, is written as though one person is speaking to another. Oliver even uses contractions, which do not appear in most formal writing. Romanticism is often seen as the precursor to modernism (a twentieth-century philosophy that rejected tradition), and many of the ideals and theories popularized by the romantics greatly influenced modern notions of individualism and self. "The Journey" is a poem about preservation of the individual self and the personal struggle that entails. Oliver's poetry pulls heavily from inspiration found from the natural world around her, and her poetic voice is one of personal expression of emotion, intuition, and perception. This has led many critics to classify her work as romantic.

Metaphor

Metaphor is a figure of speech used in poetry and literature to describe things or ideas by comparing them to other things or ideas. This comparison will emphasize the characteristics the two elements do or do not share. Some metaphors are straightforward. For example, "a heart of gold" compares someone's heart to gold, implying that it is pure and highly valuable. Some metaphors, however, are more difficult to spot, especially in poetry. Poets use things that can be found in everyday life as symbols or metaphors for bigger or more abstract concepts, either to deepen the emotional impact of the poem or as a means of drawing attention to the specific use of language. In "The Journey," Oliver uses a number of metaphors to illustrate her overall theme of asserting independence and courageously moving away from bad situations as a means of self-preservation. Oliver is not really speaking about a house in the sixth line of the poem. The house is a metaphor for the individual. Similarly, when she writes of a road littered with debris, she is not writing of a literal road. The road is a metaphor for the obstacles the individual must move past figuratively. Even the title of the poem is a metaphor, because Oliver is not writing a poem about an actual act of traveling. She is writing about moving from one emotional, mental, or imaginative state to another.

HISTORICAL CONTEXT

Feminism

Although the late nineteenth and early twentieth centuries brought great political gain for women in terms of suffrage (voting rights) and other legal rights, feminism as a cultural movement began in earnest in the 1960s. The publication of Betty Friedan's *The Feminine Mystique* in 1963 shocked the country with its frank and unflinching look at the realities of the oppression felt by the average American woman. For the first time, the vague discontent that wives and mothers often experienced was classified as a social issue rather than a personal one. Friedan stated that the very structure of society forced women into limited roles that often were far from satisfying. By the 1960s, activists were focused more on addressing insidious issues such as discrimination in the workplace and the social structure that discouraged women from deviating away from the traditional roles they had always played. Suddenly, the personal lives of women were up for debate on the political stage. Activists urged women to realize that their societal standing was a direct result of their political power and cultural bias.

COMPARE & CONTRAST

- **1980s:** Feminists such as Gloria Steinem work passionately for equal rights for women in the workplace, including fighting for legislation to end sexual harassment and the practice of paying female workers less than men for the same job.

  Today: Women occupy a firm place in the American workplace, and many companies have female executives. Several women have served as secretary of state of the United States.

- **1980s:** The environmental justice movement is born in the early part of this decade. Local, grassroots groups of citizens fight to protect the land on which they live from exploitation by the government and big business.

  Today: Global warming is a household topic of discussion, and "green" initiatives involve ordinary people in recycling, carbon emissions offsets, and energy conservation.

- **1980s:** Nature poetry is largely romantic in tone, and contemporary literary critical methods, such as deconstruction and new historicism, are not very effective when applied to these poems.

  Today: Ecopoetry and ecocriticism are legitimately recognized literary critical theories in their own right. These approaches seek to apply environmental critical methods to literature in many areas, not just the nature poetry genre.

By the 1980s, many women were struggling with understanding their new places in society. Throughout history, the fate of a woman was quite literally largely decided by the men in her life. For the first time, in the last quarter of the twentieth century, women were free to decide their own fate. An emotional conflict that was essentially societal in its scope arose between many women's desire for a traditional home and family and their desire for political and economic power and equality. "The Journey" beautifully exemplifies this tension felt by a nation of women who, faced with the reality that they could not "have it all," were forced to make difficult decisions and assert their independence against both external and internal forces that were not prepared for such a paradigm shift.

Environmentalism

The environmental damages caused by the Industrial Revolution sparked the real beginning of environmentalism in Europe in the mid to late nineteenth century. In the United States, concerns about urban areas affected by industrial waste and the destruction of natural resources combined to bring conservationists, politicians, and artists together to assert that nature had an inherent right to be protected. In the middle of the nineteenth century, writers such as Emerson and Thoreau advocated a return to rural lifestyles and a respect for the natural world. The movement grew consistently in the early to mid-twentieth century, and conservation and environmental protection began to be legislated. By the 1980s, concern for the environment encompassed issues such as the hazardous results of the widespread use of chemicals, conservation of wilderness, protection of endangered species, and air pollution. Environmentalism was no longer simply a conservationist way of life but a full-fledged political movement. Initiatives such as Earth Day became established traditions, and the environment became a divisive issue. Oliver's entire body of work is reflective of her deep respect for nature and wholehearted belief in society's responsibility to protect natural resources. Her nature poetry has more to do with politics than that of her romantic predecessors such as Thoreau. Regardless of whether or not she intends her poetry to carry political weight, simply the time period in which she is writing high praise, when critic J. P. Lewis, in a review for *Library Journal*, commends her "precision similes and astonishing metaphors."

At times, Oliver has been accused of flatness, especially in her later work. In *Hudson Review*, Dennis Sampson comments that she "risks sentimentality when love of the world almost gives in to emotions not won by the poem." The simplicity of her verse has caused some to criticize the depth of emotional thought behind her work; however, most critics recognize her exploration of the human condition as a calm inquisition into the essential motivations of modern life. "This is a poet whose enduring preoccupation lies with posing apparently simple questions, the answers to which involve contemplation of the deepest mysteries of knowing and being," writes Robert Hosmer in a 1994 article in the *Southern Review*. Her nature poetry is in the traditions of a century earlier. Katherine Soniat, writing for the *Hollins Critic*, says that "in *Dream Work* . . . one discovers a poetry of natural history likened by many to the work of Elizabeth Bishop, Mariannne Moore and D. H. Lawrence."

Most often, however, critics and readers alike note her similarities to the great romantic and transcendental poets. "She is as visionary as Emerson," Ostricker writes, "and is among the few American poets who can describe and transmit ecstasy, while retaining a practical awareness of the world."

Oliver implies that changes takes a long time to come about. (Alexey Stiop | Shutterstock.com)

makes it more politically relevant because the issue has become such a passionately and widely debated topic.

CRITICAL OVERVIEW

Dream Work, Mary Oliver's sixth collection of poetry, continues to showcase her nature poetry to critical acclaim. Oliver's collections have been consistent best sellers, and she is generally considered to be a commercially successful poet. The accessibility of language in her poetry and the universal themes she addresses serve to inspire readers, and some of her most successful poems are widely circulated, reprinted, and incorporated into everything from scientific journal articles to commencement speeches. Alicia Ostricker, in her 1986 review of *Dream Work* for the *Nation*, calls Oliver's verse "intensely lyrical, flute-like, slender and swift." Her lyricism receives

CRITICISM

Kristy Blackmon

Blackmon is a published writer from Dallas, Texas. In the following essay, she explains the ways in which Oliver puts a modern spin on the romantic poetic tradition in her poem "The Journey."

Numerous schools of literary criticism have their own interpretations of Mary Oliver's work. Some critics, such as Janet McNew, take a feminist approach. In her essay "Mary Oliver and the Tradition of Romantic Nature Poetry," McNew writes of the "necessity of woman-identification as a prerequisite to a strong womanly self." Ecocritics analyze Oliver's relationship to and portrayal of nature as a reflection of her views on the environment. In 2008, Dana Phillips, for example, said in her essay "Ecocriticism, Ecopoetics, and a Creed Outworn" that "a nature poet is never a straightforward thing to

WHAT DO I READ NEXT?

- In her 2007 young-adult book *Wildly Romantic: The English Romantic Poets: The Mad, the Bad, and the Dangerous*, Catherine M. Andronik offers an intimate look at the personal lives of the five major poets of the English romantic era—William Wordsworth, Samuel Taylor Coleridge, George Gordon Byron, Percy Bysshe Shelley, and John Keats—and discusses how their views on life and poetry changed the face of literature.

- Mary Oliver won the 1984 Pulitzer Prize for Poetry with her collection *American Primitive*, published in 1983, which celebrates nature, the cycles of life, and the beauty of living things.

- *The Essential Writings of Ralph Waldo Emerson*, published in 2000, organizes Emerson's major works into categories and includes an introduction by Oliver.

- Joy Harjo's *For a Girl Becoming*, published in 2009, is part of the "Sun Tracks: An American Indian" literary series. With illustrations by Mercedes McDonald, the poem follows one girl from birth through adulthood, acknowledging each milestone and personal achievement while reminding the reader of our ever-present connections to nature and the world around us.

- Oliver's *Our World*, published in 2009, is a rare glimpse into the personal life of Oliver. The book intertwines Oliver's prose with photographs taken by her lifelong partner, Molly Malone Cook, providing an intimate view of the world and life that they shared for over forty years.

- *Pumpkin Butterfly: Poems from the Other Side of Nature* by Heidi Mordhorst is a 2010 collection of free verse nature poetry for young-adult readers. The text is accompanied by watercolor illustrations by Jenny Reynish.

- *The West Side of Any Mountain: Place, Space, and Ecopoetry*, written in 2005 by J. Scott Bryson, is a study of contemporary ecopoetry and environmental theory. It emphasizes Yi-Fu Tuan's place-space context and its application to four major contemporary ecopoets, including Oliver.

---

be, since the poet's relationship to nature... is bound to be reflective of and refracted by cultural assumptions." Some critics, such as Martina Antretter, even combine the two. In her essay, "The Surrender of the Body in Mary Oliver and Amy Clampitt's Ecopoetry," published in 2003, Antretter takes the title of ecofeminist. "Ecofeminist literary critics are concerned with discussing the symbolism that links women and nature," she writes. Particular attention is paid to "the oppression of women and the environment."

Oliver, however, accepts none of those labels. While her poetry shows a deep appreciation of nature, it is not environmental in the activist sense, and in a 1992 interview with Steven Ratiner for the *Christian Science Monitor*, she openly stated that she is not part of the feminist movement. Politics have a place in the poetic world, but Oliver maintains that that place is not in her poetry. "I see very good poets defeating their own poems with polemic," she told Ratiner. Taking into consideration the love of the natural world she is most celebrated for, the didactic nature of much of her work, and the search for self and meaning in which she is constantly engaged, a strong claim can be made that if any *-ism* can be applied to Oliver's work, it is a fresh twist on romanticism. "The Journey" carries the hallmarks of traditional romantic poetics but portrays them in a contemporary form and colors them with psychoanalytic tones to produce a modern lyric that is accessible to all readers.

"'THE JOURNEY' CARRIES THE HALLMARKS OF TRADITIONAL ROMANTIC POETICS BUT PORTRAYS THEM IN A CONTEMPORARY FORM AND COLORS THEM WITH PSYCHOANALYTIC TONES TO PRODUCE A MODERN LYRIC THAT IS ACCESSIBLE TO ALL READERS."

Oliver borrowed the title of her collection *Dream Work* from a Freudian psychoanalytic concept about the meaning and purpose of dreams. Freud theorized that dreams are a person's subconscious defense of sleep. The noise and confusion of everyday life, both its anxieties and its joys, do not leave us when we sleep. Instead, the emotion that is left behind—what Freud termed *day residue*—is filtered by the subconscious in a number of ways that reduce its effect on our minds and keep us from waking up. This filtering process is called the *dream work*.

Freud articulated two processes, *condensation* and *displacement*, as the means by which the subconscious transforms the latent (present but not obvious) content of what was actually experienced and is actually felt into the content that is manifest, or recognizable, in the dream. Condensation is the combination of two or more thoughts or emotions into one symbolic thing or situation. Displacement is the substitution of a meaningless object for the true object of an emotion. Thus, in poetic terms, the dream work can be seen as a subconscious creation of metaphor.

Poets are never arbitrary. Every aspect of a poem as a poet presents it to the reader carries intention: the way it looks on the page, the word choices, the title of the poem, the form, and so on. When a poem is presented in a collection, this assumption broadens to cover its placement in the sequence of poems, any illustrations that may accompany it, elements such as epigraphs and, of course, the name of the collection. Taking this knowledge into account when studying poems from Oliver's *Dream Work*, including "The Journey," gives a starting point to any analysis, since Oliver would not have put such a specific concept in the mind of the reader had she not intended it to carry significant meaning. When reading "The Journey," then, a natural first step is to look for the metaphors and surprising elements in the poem, and then ask, what ideas were condensed or displaced to create this?

Right away, Oliver introduces a jarring concept. In the first line, we learn that the speaker in "The Journey" is not the subject of the poem. Instead, Oliver's use of "you" makes the reader the subject. In so doing, Oliver consciously and deliberately bridges the distance between the reader and the speaker. As Judith Barrington puts it in "Nostalgia Trip," a 1995 review of Oliver's *Blue Pastures*, "The reader, instead of replacing the poet in a reenactment of the poet's story, must instead engage with the poet, while the poet stays present." This connection with the reader adds to the psychological weight of "The Journey." The sense of desperation and emotional claustrophobia conveyed hits the reader twice: once in reading the poem as the experience of the poet, and again through a subconscious emotional recall that occurs when the words are processed as a recollection of the reader's own experience. The instinct of self-preservation is active in all individuals. Hand in hand with the dread of death that comes with the human realization of mortality, what Freud called the *life instinct* is the driving force behind conscious and subconscious action. It is a universal experience, and Oliver means to portray it as such. In her 1991 essay "The Poet's Voice," Oliver says, "No poem is about one of us, or some of us, but is about all of us.... Every poem is about my life but also it is about your life, and a hundred thousand lives to come." By engaging the reader directly, Oliver creates an intimacy that does not allow for distance and almost demands an engaged reading.

At the same time, the metaphors present throughout the poem serve to buffer the emotional impact of the psychological meaning in much the same way that the dream work does. Oliver does not need to explicitly name who or what it is that is terrifying "you" through emotional manipulation. She leaves the details up to the reader to supply. All the poem gives is the manifest image, painted with powerful words. The house, the wind, the night—none of it is specific enough to penetrate the illusion of a shared experience between the poet and reader. However, each metaphor becomes a condensation of ideas already present in the subconscious, a ready-made displacement provided by Oliver.

Mark Johnson, in his essay "'Keep Looking': Mary Oliver's Emersonian Project," identifies "this urge to affect the reader [as] a didactic art" as quintessentially romantic in nature. The modern lyric poem as we know it is a direct descendant of romanticism. Its reliance on emotion over reason and its need to place the individual within a universal construct can be traced back to a reaction against the Enlightenment. The colloquial, easily identifiable language and self-searching meditative stance of "The Journey" place it squarely within the romantic tradition. The trait that most aligns Oliver with the great romantic poets is the homage to nature that is found in almost every poem she has written in her long career. Though "The Journey" is not as expressly nature-oriented as the vast majority of her work, there is still a heavy reliance on images drawn from the natural world. Significantly, the nature symbols slowly overtake the metaphors of the human world as the poem progresses and the act of self-preservation is successfully carried out. The "you" that is the subject of the poem starts out trapped in a symbolic emotional construct, but by the end of the poem, this person is walking confidently into the natural world.

"Modernism," Johnson writes, "had a healthy strain of Romanticism...and Oliver is only one of many contemporary poets whose latter-day Romanticism goes misread or unappreciated." The almost overwhelming emphasis on theory that dominated literary criticism in the second half of the twentieth century at times seems to have left critics with such an overabundance of theoretical approaches that comprehensible analysis, not to mention appreciation, of poetry is nearly impossible. This is not to say that all theory is overly convoluted or contrived. On the contrary, the development of literary theory over the last five decades or so has, on the whole, served to help illuminate the sometimes dimly lit corners of the critical process. However, the reader and critic must be careful not to miss the poem for the theory, so to speak. Ecocritic Evie Shockley, in "On the Nature of Ed Roberson's Poetics," classifies Oliver among those poets who recognize that "their ecological model of the culture/nature relation as one of interdependence between two sovereign realms maintains a binary framework." In her article "The Surrender of the Body in Mary Oliver and Amy Clampitt's Ecopoetry," Antretter claims Oliver as "the 'equivoice,' the mythic lost mother who is the central source of femininity and female writing." McNew suggests that Oliver's poetry may "involve resignation to participation in a patriarchal plan that involves a repudiation of what is mythically female and maternal." Somewhere in all of that lies truth and validity about Oliver's work, but perhaps the simpler explanation better serves the student of her poetry. Oliver epitomizes the romantic ideal in the modern age. She has taken traditional romanticism, put it in modern form, endowed it with contemporary understanding of psychology, and, as the modernist poet Ezra Pound would say, made it new.

Source: Kristy Blackmon, Critical Essay on "The Journey," in *Poetry for Students*, Gale, Cengage Learning, 2012.

Katherine Soniat

In the following review, Soniat reveals that the collection is the poetry of natural history, comparable to Marianne Moore, Elizabeth Bishop, and D. H. Lawrence.

In *Dream Work*, Mary Oliver's sixth collection of poetry, one discovers a poetry of natural history likened by many to the work of Elizabeth Bishop, Mariannne Moore and D. H. Lawrence. In many cases, her "natural histories" have both public and private implications. Courage, in both its communal and individual manifestations, is essential in Oliver's aesthetic for a person to remain autonomous in human culture and the natural world. Oliver underscores how one must face that which is not "easy." This single word reappears with increasing ironic complexity. The natural world is emblematic of that stoic confrontation where one admits to the real "like a blind stone/without a pinch of hope" ("Knife"). In contrast to the primal world, Oliver offers a sociopolitical fabric which thrives on the need to save, to control and to know (see "Dogfish"). In this struggle "to know" vast energies are consumed and "run amok," and it is the individual who is ultimately responsible for this misuse of power, as she states in "Shadows":

> Everyone knows the great energies running amok cast
> terrible shadows, that each of the so-called
> senseless acts has a thread looping
> back through the world and into a human heart.

In Oliver's opinion things are easier said than done, and it is this process of doing that concerns much of her poetry; mere "answers" are deceitful for they avoid the contradictory nature of process. One needs "... the earthtalk, / the root-wrangle, the arguments of energy" ("Trilliums"). Oliver encourages one to see that "catastrophe is not the opposite of love" ("Shadows") for events in the natural world have no malevolence behind them. "Plotting," with all the word connotes of evil intentions, is the result of man's volition." As she states in "Shadows": "I mean / water rises without any plot upon / history or even geography."

The grounding of a more holistic consciousness is suggested throughout this collection—a consciousness which includes the spontaneous awareness of one who "can't see / herself apart from the rest of the world / or the world from what she must do" ("The Turtle"). Imagination is the element which allows one that immersion in experience and, also, it allows the knowledge of "otherness" in the world. This perception of "other" acts as a catalyst that both serves to alienate man and to create in him that sense of the unique.

As Oliver says in "Acid," "once in a while / you can creep out of your own life / and become someone else."

This poetry deals with the history of process and survival. This dual motif is made dramatically clear at the end of "Dogfish":

> And look! look! look! I think those little fish
> better wake up and dash themselves away
> from the hopeless future that is
> bulging toward them.
>
> And probably,
> if they don't waste time
> looking for an easier world,
> they can do it.

Source: Katherine Soniat, Review of *Dream Work*, in *Hollins Critic*, Vol. 26, No. 1, February 1989, pp. 10–11.

Alicia Ostriker

In the following review, Ostriker applauds the lyricism of Dream Work *and notes a shift in emphasis from the natural world in Oliver's earlier works to more human-based themes in this collection.*

Where [Donald] Hall's line is classically conversational and descriptive, Mary Oliver's is intensely lyrical, flutelike, slender and swift. Where he gathers detail, she will fling gesture. Her poems ride on vivid phrases: "the click of claws, the smack of lips" outside her tent turns out to be a bear's "shambling tonnage" in "The Chance to Love Everything." In a poem about an oncoming storm emblematic of human disaster, "the wind turns / like a hundred black swans / and the first faint noise / begins." She dreams the memory of past lives in the Amazonian landscape of "The River," a poem of the soul's birth and rebirth:

> Once among the reeds I found
> a boat, as thin and lonely
> as a young tree. Nearby
> the forest sizzled with the afternoon
> rain.

Behind Oliver's New England is Ohio—not the sorry Ohio of James Wright, but a frontier still untouched by cultivation and corruption, where you enter to find "your place / in the family of things," with a real hope of success if you work hard. Woodland and marsh are Oliver's kingdom, animals and plants her kin and alternative selves. There are some dazzling poems of deer, bear, geese, turtle, of trilliums and sunflowers. She is as visionary as Emerson, and is among the few American poets who can describe and transmit ecstasy, while retaining a practical awareness of the world as one of predators and prey, "the rapacious / plucking up the timid / like so many soft jewels."

Quite a number of the poems contain advice that is both right enough and rooted enough to be called (it's an old-fashioned term) wisdom. "Dogfish," the opening poem of *Dream Work*, describes a dogfish with its chin "rough / as a thousand sharpened nails," coming in on the tide:

> And look! look! look! I think those little fish
> better wake up and dash themselves away
> from the hopeless future that is
> bulging toward them.
>
> And probably,
> if they don't waste time
> looking for an easier world,
>
> they can do it.

"One or Two Things" hovers between the mobility of a butterfly and the poet's own immobility, which feels to her like an iron hoof she can't lift from the center of her mind unless she has "an idea." The poem concludes:

> For years and years I struggled
> just to love my life. And then
>
> the butterfly
> rose, weightless, in the wind.
>
> "Don't love your life
> too much," it said,
>
> and vanished
> into the world.

Dream Work, coming after Oliver's 1984 Pulitzer-Prize-winning *American Primitive*, is an advance on her earlier writing in two ways, which are probably connected. Formally, her verse feels increasingly confident, smoother, and thus bolder—the work of someone able to take risks, take corners faster. At the same time she has moved from the natural world and its desires, the "heaven of appetite" that goes on without much intervention or possibility of control, further into the world of historical and personal suffering. In a half dozen or so poems she sketches a past burdened by trauma and breakdown, the temptation to die, the resolution to recover, the actual work of insisting on sanity: "I began to take apart / the deep stitches / of nightmares." In one poem the poet makes herself walk away, though the night is wild, from voices crying "Mend my life!" In another she is building a larger house, a daily labor.

She confronts as well, steadily, what she cannot change. In the climactic piece of *Dream Work*, a meditation on the Holocaust, there are two adjacent pictures linked by a half-refrain. "Oh, you never saw / such a good leafy place" introduces an anecdote about meeting a fawn while walking with her dog; neither fawn nor dog knew "what dogs usually do," so they "did a little dance, / they didn't get serious." Then the line "Oh, you never saw such a garden!" brings a new picture, a Jamesian scene of a hundred kinds of flowers, cool shade, garden furniture and a man peacefully finishing lunch and lifting wine in a glass of "real crystal"—but "It is the face of Mengele." At the end of this poem the people have gone and the doe enters, sniffing the air where her fawn has been: "Then she knew everything." In her own garden of knowledge Mary Oliver moves by instinct, faith and determination. She is among our finest poets, and still growing.

Source: Alicia Ostriker, Review of *Dream Work*, in *Nation*, Vol. 243, No. 5, August 30, 1986, pp. 148–50.

SOURCES

"About Mary Oliver," in *Mary Oliver: Pulitzer Prize and National Book Award Winning Poet*, http://maryoliver.beacon.org/aboutmary/, (accessed May 1, 2011).

Antretter, Martina, "The Surrender of the Body in Mary Oliver and Amy Clampitt's Ecopoetry," in *The EmBodyment of American Culture*, edited by Maureen Devine, Michael Draxlbauer, and Heinz Tschachler, Transaction Publishers, 2003, pp. 175–77.

Barrington, Judith, "Nostalgia Trip," in *Women's Review of Books*, Vol. 13, No. 6, March 1996, p. 10.

Hosmer, Robert, Review of *New and Selected Poems*, in *Southern Review*, Vol. 30, No. 3, Summer 1994, pp. 631–41.

Johnson, Mark, "'Keep Looking': Mary Oliver's Emersonian Project," in *Massachusetts Review*, Vol. 46, No. 1, Spring 2005, pp. 78–84.

Lewis, J. P., Review of *Dream Work*, in *Library Journal*, Vol. 111, No. 10, June 1, 1986, p. 126.

McNew, Janet, "Mary Oliver and the Tradition of Romantic Nature Poetry," in *Contemporary Literature*, Vol. 30, No. 1, Spring 1989, p. 64.

Oliver, Mary, "The Journey," in *Dream Work*, Atlantic Monthly Press, 1986, pp. 38–39.

———, "The Poet's Voice," in *Blue Pastures*, Harcourt Books, 1991, p. 109.

Ostriker, Alicia, "Natural Facts," in *Nation*, August 1986, pp. 148–49.

Phillips, Dana, "Ecocriticism, Ecopoetics, and a Creed Outworn," in *New Formations*, Vol. 64, Spring 2008, p. 40.

Ratiner, Steven, "Poet Mary Oliver: A Solitary Walk," in *Christian Science Monitor*, December 9, 1992, p. 20.

Sampson, Dennis, "Poetry Chronicle," in *Hudson Review*, Vol. 44, No. 2, Summer 1991, p. 333.

Shockley, Evie, "On the Nature of Ed Roberson's Poetics," in *Callaloo*, Vol. 33, No. 3, Summer 2010, p 731.

Soniat, Katherine, Review of *Dream Work*, in *Hollins Critic*, Vol. 26, No. 1, February 1989, pp. 10–11.

FURTHER READING

Bevington, Douglas, *The Rebirth of Environmentalism: Grassroots Activism from the Spotted Owl to the Polar Bear*, Island Press, 2009.
    Bevington explains the development of modern environmental activism in America. Educated as a sociologist, Bevington explores the fringes of the movement and draws parallels to social groups and their contemporary issues.

Felstiner, John, *Can Poetry Save the Earth? A Field Guide to Nature Poems*, Yale University Press, 2010.
    Felstiner examines nature poems from the Psalms to Whitman and Dickinson and explores the ways in which attention to the natural world around us through poetry can help spur our society to environmental action.

Freud, Sigmund, *The Interpretation of Dreams*, Avon, 1980.
    Freud revolutionized the way humans thought about themselves and the psychological experience. In this influential text, first published in 1899, he introduces the concepts of the id, the superego, and the ego. He explains his theory behind dreams and gives the reader a first exposure to dream interpretation and analysis.

Friedan, Betty, *The Feminine Mystique*, Dell, 1964.

> Friedan's groundbreaking work largely considers the impetus behind the second-wave feminist movement of the 1960s through 1980s. Her research into "the problem that has no name" led to the theory that the dissatisfaction felt by American women was a socially constructed rather than personal issue, and it spawned an inquiry into the nature of feminism that changed history.

McKibben, Bill, ed., *American Earth: Environmental Writing since Thoreau*, Library of America, 2008.

> McKibben has collected samples from more than 100 writers from Thoreau to Henry Beston. Conservationist poets, nature poets, and activists are represented here, each with an introduction by McKibben that places the writer in the context of an overarching environmental movement. The volume has an introduction by Al Gore.

Ress, Mary Judith, *Ecofeminism in Latin America*, Orbis Books, 2006.

> Ress explores the development of the ecofeminist movement in Latin America and its relationship to what she calls other feminist "theologies." The book is a comprehensive look at the nature of feminism and the environmental dialogues of Latin America.

SUGGESTED SEARCH TERMS

Mary Oliver

Dream Work AND Mary Oliver

The Journey AND poem

nature poetry

ecopoetry

romanticism

Mary Oliver AND The Journey

Mary Oliver AND nature

ecocriticism

Dream Work AND The Journey

Legal Alien

PAT MORA

1980

"Legal Alien" originally appeared in the 1980 publication *Hispanics in the United States: An Anthology of Creative Literature*. Pat Mora's first collection of poetry *Chants*, which was published in 1984 and includes the poem as well, and was awarded the Southwest Book Award from Border Regional.

"Legal Alien" explores the speaker's attempt to understand her identity while living between two separate cultures that equally reject her. Like most of Mora's work, "Legal Alien" combines English and Spanish to express powerful emotions. The poem reflects the poet's own experiences as a Mexican American, and the two languages serve as a dialogue between the two cultures. Besides its inclusion in *Chants*, the poem is available on many different Web sites such as *Voices from the Gaps* and *southwestcrossroads.org*.

AUTHOR BIOGRAPHY

Mora was born in El Paso, Texas, in 1942, and grew up speaking both Spanish and English at home. Mora's grandparents had fled to the United States during the Mexican Revolution in the early twentieth century, and both of her parents grew up in the United States. As a child, Mora traveled back and forth across the border to visit family. Mora's mother, grandmother, and aunts told her traditional tales from Mexico, which she later incorporated into her children's stories. Her mother always encouraged her to read, and Mora established a lifelong love of literature.

In 1963, Mora graduated from Texas Western College with a bachelor of arts degree, and in 1967 she earned a master's degree from the same school (now the University of Texas at El Paso). She taught at both the secondary and college levels and worked in college administration. Mora married and had three children, but she divorced her husband in 1981. In the late 1970s, Mora began to write poetry for several different venues, but individual books of her poetry were not published until the 1980s. *Chants*, which concludes with "Legal Alien," was her first volume of poetry, and it was released in 1984. Critics immediately noted Mora's ability to blend English and Spanish effectively. After establishing herself as a poet, Mora expanded her career, writing children's books, fiction, poetry for teens, and nonfiction that celebrate Mexican American culture.

Along with her literary success, Mora has worked diligently to champion bilingual literacy and education. She tirelessly promotes El día de los niños/El día de los libros, Children's Day/Book Day, the national day she established to celebrate bilingual families and literature. Libraries across the country recognize the April 30 celebration with an annual book list of recommended reading from the American Library Association, and story times, events, and crafts to promote bilingual reading and culture. Along with promoting bilingual literacy, Mora devotes her time to advancing diversity in American literature and the publishing field. She has received numerous awards for her work including the National Endowment for a Arts Creative Writing fellowship in poetry, a Kellogg National Leadership fellowship, the Luis Leal Award for Distinction in Chicano/Latino Letters, and the Southwest Book Award.

According to her official biography, Mora holds honorary doctorates from North Carolina State University and SUNY-Buffalo, and she worked as a visiting lecturer at the University of New Mexico. She is married to Vern Scarborough, a professor of anthropology, and lives in New Mexico. Besides writing, Mora also speaks publicly about issues that are important to her and her community.

POEM TEXT

> Bi-lingual, Bi-cultural,
> able to slip from "How's life?"
> to "*Me'stan volviendo loca*,"
> able to sit in a paneled office
> drafting memos in smooth English,   5
> able to order in fluent Spanish
> at a Mexican restaurant,
> American but hyphenated,
> viewed by Anglos as perhaps exotic,
> perhaps inferior, definitely different,   10
> viewed by Mexicans as alien,
> (their eyes say, "You may speak
> Spanish but you're not like me")
> an American to Mexicans
> a Mexican to Americans   15
> a handy token
> sliding back and forth
> between the fringes of both worlds
> by smiling
> by masking the discomfort   20
> of being pre-judged
> Bi-laterally.

POEM SUMMARY

The text used for this summary is from *Chants*, Arte Público Press, 1984, p. 52. Versions of the poem can be found on the following Web pages: http://voices.cla.umn.edu/artistpages/mora_pat.php and http://southwestcrossroads.org/record.php?num=869&hl=legal::alien.

"Legal Alien" is a short, free verse poem that is composed of twenty-two lines. The lines of the poem are not divided into stanzas, and it does not follow a pattern with its rhyme or its meter. Unlike traditional poetic forms, the first word in each line of "Legal Alien" is not capitalized. Mora reserves capitalization for proper nouns and to create artistic emphasis. The poem is primarily written in English, but it does include a Spanish phrase. Weaving Spanish into her predominantly English work is distinctive of Mora's poetic style. In "Legal Alien," Mora creates the persona of the speaker to explore very painful feelings and experiences.

Line 1 has only two words. The words in this line repeat the prefix *bi-* in each word to demonstrate consonance within the line. Each word is also capitalized, which emphasizes the importance of these words to the poet. The first line of the poem essentially describes the speaker, establishing her point of view from the beginning. She is an individual caught between two different languages and cultures.

Line 2 and line 3 juxtapose English and Spanish phrases. This reinforces the knowledge that the speaker is bilingual, but it also creates an inner dialogue. At first glance, the phrases seem like common colloquialism; however, the Spanish statement in the third line answers the English question posed in the second. When translated into English, the third line of the poem means: "They are making me crazy." This statement both answers the English question—how the persona is doing—and explains the strain of being bilingual and bicultural.

Lines 4 through 7 provide examples how being bicultural affects the speaker's daily activities. The fourth and fifth lines take place in an office setting. Here, the speaker is expected to speak like an American. The office has wood walls, which conjures the image of a luxurious, professional workspace. In this setting, the speaker does not only speak English; she writes in excellent English.

Lines 6 and 7 take place in a restaurant that serves Mexican food. Here, the speaker moves from a professional environment to a more personal setting. The speaker uses Spanish expertly in this venue. Outside of the workplace, the speaker connects with her Mexican heritage through her language.

Line 8 reiterates the fact that the speaker is, indeed, a citizen of the United States, but it ends with the word "hyphenated." The poem itself contains a number of hyphenated words. The word "hyphenated" combined with the hyphenated words in the poem create a visual description of how the speaker attempts to bridge the two different cultures together within herself.

The next two lines tell the audience how the speaker believes the Anglos, from the American world, see her. The speaker knows that she is seen as not being the same as Anglo Americans. Some people consider themselves superior to the speaker, while others view her as foreign. Those who make assumptions simply based on her family heritage do not accept her as an American, even though she is a citizen and speaks the language.

Lines 11, 12, and 13 shift from the speaker's experience with Anglo Americans to the challenges she faces within the Mexican community. Line 11 ends with the word "alien." This is a play on the English term *illegal alien*, and it brings the readers' minds back to the title of the poem. The speaker is considered an alien and a stranger in the Mexican community. Lines 12 and 13 explain that speaking fluent Spanish and having Mexican ancestry is not enough to be fully accepted. This rejection is not blatantly spoken. The speaker, however, sees the dismissal in the expressions of the Mexican people around her who will not believe that she is like them.

In lines 14 and 15, the speaker uses Mexican and American as the antithesis of each other. Here the speaker explains that the Mexicans will always see her as an American, while the Americans will always see her as Mexican. She cannot find acceptance for her hyphenated identity from either world.

The speaker describes herself as a "token" in line 16. While this noun can be an object of value or a symbol, token also has another meaning. *Merriam-Webster's Dictionary Online* provides the following definition: "a member of a group (as a minority) that is included within a larger group through tokenism; *especially*: a token employee." With this term, the speaker expresses how she believes other people feel about her. She does not feel that she is valued as a person or for her skill sets. Rather, her ancestry allows certain companies and groups to claim that they embrace tolerance and diversity.

Lines 17 and 18 describe how the speaker moves between her two separate cultures. She does not, however, fit completely into either world. Neither Mexican society nor American society will completely accept the speaker because she will always have a dual identity. She lives outside the realm of her peers, and, in a sense, the speaker does not feel like she belongs anywhere or that she can be honest with anyone.

In line 19, the speaker explains that a smile is the only way she is able to navigate between both worlds. In line 20, this smile, however, is defined as a mask that the speaker uses to hide her true feelings. Her smile is both her protection and her disguise. The image of pleasant expression contrasts with the feeling of unpleasantness that the speaker experiences as she attempts to find her identity and struggles along the edge of two cultures. This poem offers a rare glimpse behind the speaker's mask as she confesses her experiences and real feelings.

The final two lines of "Legal Alien" explain the cause of the discomfort that the speaker must go to such great lengths to hide. She knows that she is critiqued by everyone that she meets because of her family background and her citizenship. The last line of the poem consists of a single capitalized word, meaning two-sided, which recalls the capitalization used in the first line of the poem. This signals the importance of the word to the poet. The prefix *bi-* relates back to the description of the speaker in the first line. Here, however, it describes how the speaker's two different cultures judge her. Each world is equally judgmental and intolerant, and the speaker feels like an alien no matter where she goes.

THEMES

Self-Identity

The speaker in "Legal Alien" struggles with her self-identity. She is forced to live, continually, between two different cultures or, as she sees it, two different worlds. The speaker must behave as either an American or as a Mexican when she interacts in each culture, because she is aware that people from each culture have already judged her as an outsider. People surrounding the speaker dismiss her as not fitting in because she is bicultural, which prevents her from connecting to either world. She is competent in both English and Spanish because a mistake will only confirm the idea that she does not belong in either American society or Mexican society. The speaker attempts to embrace both cultures, but she can only participate in one culture at a time.

As someone who experiences prejudice and rejection from different groups, the speaker is forced to put on a happy mask. By hiding her uncomfortable feelings, she hides her self-identity. Behind her mask, the speaker is frustrated, angry, and lonely. These feelings, however, must remain hidden. Her mask is all that protects her from the unspoken hostility from both worlds. As she slips between each world, the speaker makes an effort to understand herself and what it truly means to be a Mexican American.

Cultural Conflict

Conflict between cultures is a common theme in Mexican American literature, and "Legal Alien" explores the cultural conflict that comes with being an American citizen of Mexican descent. According to Elizabeth Mermann-Jozwiak and Nancy Sullivan in *Conversations with Mexican American*

TOPICS FOR FURTHER STUDY

- Read *A Step from Heaven*, An Na's young-adult novel and winner of the 2002 Michael L. Printz Award. It tells the story of Young Ju, a young immigrant from Korea who struggles between her cultural heritage and her life in America. Compare her experiences with the poem "Legal Alien." What advice do you think the speaker of the poem would give Young Ju? Create a social network page or a blog for each character. Have them discuss their struggles and feelings.

- Research the Mexican American/Chicano movement in the United States from the 1960s through the 1990s using both print and online resources. Create a video or multimedia presentation of the time period. Focus on the changes in art and literature as well as society. Include an interactive time line of Mora's life and work within your presentation.

- Read the young-adult collection of poetry *Time You Let Me In: 25 Poets under 25* compiled by Naomi Shihab Nye. Choose a poem in the book to compare or contrast with "Legal Alien." Write a poem of your own that reflects themes from both poems. Post your poem on a Web page or blog site. Feel free to add links, music, or images that illustrate the feelings or ideas of the poem.

- Read the story of Pat Mora's family in *House of Houses*. Research your own family history. Write a creative account of your family using techniques such as epistolary (told through letters) style or magic realism. Present your story and share family photos using PowerPoint or another form of media presentation.

Writers: Languages and Literatures in the Borderlands, Mora explores the "social ramifications of bilingualism and biculturalism." The speaker describes herself as being identified with two cultures repeatedly in the poem. These descriptions express how she feels as someone who is part of two unique cultures that are often hostile to each

Immigration to the United States from Mexico is a theme of the poem. (sprinter81 | Shutterstock.com)

other. The prevalence of hyphenated words throughout the poem visually separates words the same way that the worlds of the speaker remain connected yet separate.

As a Mexican American, the speaker is fluent in both Spanish and English. She respects and follows the customs of each culture, yet she remains on the edge of both worlds. The speaker voices frustration with the way that she feels people from both American society and Mexican society view and treat her. Neither culture will fully accept her, and the speaker lives with the knowledge that she will be critiqued and classified simply because of the combination of her ancestry and her citizenship. Individuals from each culture see her as belonging to the other society. This reaction reveals the social and political discord that exists between Mexican culture and American culture.

Loneliness

"Legal Alien" demonstrates themes of loneliness, alienation, and isolation. The speaker's social circle does not grow because she is bicultural; rather, it shrinks due to the prejudice and judgment of others. She is rejected by people in both cultures, and she does not feel free to be herself with anyone. From the beginning of the poem, the speaker exhibits a tone of frustration that stems from her isolation. The third line of the poem is a Spanish answer to the English question that describes her life: "They are making me crazy." Being judged of two cultures places undue stress on the speaker. Neither her Mexican culture nor her American culture will embrace her, and she remains on the outside, looking in.

Caught between two worlds, the speaker feels that everyone objectifies her. No one accepts the speaker as a bicultural individual, and she is forced to lie about her personal identity. The facial expression that the speaker wears protects her, but it also keeps anyone from getting to know her. She smiles as she wanders through the two different cultures that refuse to admit her. The speaker remains alone as she navigates the edges of both worlds, never able to enter either one as an equal. She sees no way out of her lonely condition because, as long as she is classified as one or the other, no one will accept her for who she is.

STYLE

Free Verse
"Legal Alien" is a free verse poem. Free verse is a term that means a poem is not organized into a traditional format with an established rhyme and meter pattern, such as a sonnet. A free verse poem may develop a unique pattern with its rhyme or meter, but Mora does not use a repetitive rhyme or meter pattern in this poem.

The poem is made up of twenty-two continuous lines, and is not broken into stanzas or refrains. "Legal Alien" is an English poem that incorporates a Spanish phrase for artistic emphasis and to reinforce the central themes of the piece.

Confessional Poetry
Confessional poetry offers a "painful display of private, personal matters," according to the ninth edition of *A Handbook to Literature* by William Harmon and Hugh Holman. In "Legal Alien," the speaker expresses her emotions as someone who feels that she is rejected by both Mexican society and American society. Poetry is an outlet that allows the speaker to be herself in a world that forces her to hide. She removes her disguise for the audience and confesses the struggles that she experiences as a bicultural individual.

Antithesis
Mora uses antithesis to illustrate the conflict between Mexican culture and American culture. Often used as a dialectic device in persuasive writing, antithesis juxtaposes two ideas in a sentence to show how they contrast with each other. Mora plays the terms Mexican and American against each other in line 14 and line 15 to show the conflict between cultures and, hence, the rejection of the speaker's duality.

Persona
The speaker of the poem is a persona. Persona comes from the Latin *dramatis personae*, which is the term for masks that ancient actors wore, according to M. H. Abrams in *A Glossary of Literary Terms: Seventh Edition*. A persona allows a poet to express feelings and ideas separate from the poet. The speaker in "Legal Alien" describes her mask in the poem, which refers back to the Latin term. It also calls into question who is the real person and who is the persona?

HISTORICAL CONTEXT

Mexican American Literature
Jose Antonio Villarreal is considered by many critics to be the founder of Mexican American literature, according to Mermann-Jozwiak and Sullivan in "Stories That Must Be Told." His work, and the work of other writers, including Sandra Cisneros and Richard Vasquez, coincided with the Chicano civil rights movement. The first wave of artists and writers who came in the 1960s and 1970s had a strong impact on Mexican American art and culture, and they focused on political issues. The early movement, however, did not include the voices of many women.

By the 1980s, women became an important voice in the second wave of Mexican American literature. Authors such as Mora explored language, bicultural identity, borders, and feminism. Their political concerns were "more nuanced," according to Frederick Luis Aldama in *Spilling the Beans in Chicanolandia*, and were often depicted in a lighter fashion. Mora and many other Mexican American authors have worked as social activists for cultural preservation and political change. Mora has been influential in promoting bilingual literacy and Mexican American literature.

The 1980s
The 1980s was a difficult decade for the United States and the rest of the world. The early part of the decade saw a global recession due to the energy crisis of 1979, the Latin American debt crisis, and other global economic factors. As a result of the economic crisis, unemployment rose in America. This decade also saw a growth in the influence of conservative economic policies and politicians with the presidencies of Ronald Reagan and George H. W. Bush.

During the 1980s, high levels of unemployment and other factors led to the legal immigration of over one million people to America from Mexico. This is also the estimated number of

COMPARE & CONTRAST

- **1980s:** A global recession leads to high levels of unemployment in the United States. There are also fewer jobs in Mexico due to the Latin American debt crisis, when the country's foreign debt is greater than its earnings. This leads to greater immigration from Mexico to America.

   Today: The international recession beginning in 2008 again affects employment in the United States and other countries. People still immigrate to the United States looking for work and better lives.

- **1980s:** Controversy surrounds the speaking of Spanish in the United States. Not being able to speak English is seen as un-American. Legislation is passed to make English the official language in several states.

   Today: Many organizations embrace bilingualism. There is, however, still resistance to people speaking other languages in public. There is a political movement against English-only policies in the workplace. Unfair policies result in lawsuits and protection for Spanish speakers by the Equal Employment Opportunity Commission.

- **1980s:** A rise in immigration leads to a backlash from people who fear changes in American society. Mexican Americans face prejudice even if they are born in the United States.

   Today: Mexican Americans still face resistance, such as the state immigration law passed in Arizona in 2010, which requires immigrants to carry registration documents at all times. Awareness of Mexican American culture, however, is growing. Mexican American literature is taught in schools, and telenovelas, such as *Ugly Betty*, are adapted for American audiences.

---

individuals deported over the decade. Some Americans feared that people from other nations would take their jobs and discriminated against them. When "Legal Alien" was first published, the experiences of Mexican Americans were still not widely recognized in the United States. In fact, the Commission on Civil Rights did not proclaim that Mexican Americans had been denied equal treatment until 1970, according to Allan Englekirk and Marguerite Marín in *Countries and Their Cultures*.

Chicano Civil Rights Movement

There has been tension between Anglo and Mexican communities since the end of the Mexican-American War in 1848. At that time, certain Mexican territories, along with their Mexican inhabitants, were granted to the United States. Later, the Mexican Revolution in 1910 led to a mass exodus from Mexico, as people attempted to escape the political instability of the country. Mora's grandparents, for example, moved to El Paso in the early part of the century. Additionally, the wealth of America in the 1920s attracted new immigrants from around the world. Many Mexican Americans lived for generations in the United States, yet they faced discrimination, according to Mermann-Jozwiak and Sullivan in "Stories That Must Be Told." Their communities were segregated from Anglo communities, an arrangement that persisted into the second half of the twentieth century.

American awareness of the rights of minority groups in general grew in the 1960s, thanks to the work of political activists. Members of the Chicano civil rights movement confronted the segregation, inequality, and violence that Mexican Americans faced, as Englekirk and Marín explain. For example, César Chávez and others took action to improve equality for

Border station between the United States and Mexico (Jim Parkin | Shutterstock.com)

farm workers and other members of the Mexican American community in the 1960s. College students were a powerful force for promoting the civil rights movement, and Mexican American history became a recognized subject by the late 1960s, largely due to their efforts. The fight against legal discrimination was long. The Voting Rights Act of 1965 was extended to Hispanic Americans in 1975. This act prevented states from voter discrimination tactics, such as literacy tests, and eventually required Spanish-language ballots to be available in certain areas.

On a literary level, artists fought against assimilation through the loss of language and culture. As Mermann-Jozwiak and Sullivan point out in "Stories That Must Be Told," "Many parents buy into the belief that eliminating Spanish is the only way for their children to succeed." As well as championing equal rights, the Chicano civil rights movement increased pride in Mexican heritage and culture. Writers of the first wave of the movement paved the way for Mora and other Mexican American authors.

CRITICAL OVERVIEW

Criticism of Mora and other female Mexican American authors has been complex in literary circles. As María Herrera-Sobek explains in *Chicana Creativity and Criticism: New Frontiers in American Literature*, many people feel that someone outside of the female Mexican American experience is not capable of providing accurate criticism. As a writer, Mora faced rejection from publishers in her early career, but criticism of her published work has been predominantly positive with critics in general.

Beatriz Terrazas reviewed Mora's first volume of poetry, *Chants*, which includes "Legal Alien," in the *Texas Observer*. While she admits that the book's "compression and metaphors will put off some readers," she praises the author's "accessibility."

As Mora successfully transitioned to being the author of children's books, fiction, nonfiction, and essays, critics have recognized her versatility and skill at creatively portraying life on the border. Many critics call her a regional writer because so much of her work focuses on the borderlands where she grew up; however, a biographical sketch in the University of Minnesota *Voices from the Gaps* Web site points out that Mora has expanded her point of view, and speaks about "women's experiences from other parts of the world." Regardless of her genre or topic, Mora's work serves to validate the importance of diversity in American literature.

In an article he wrote for *MELUS*, Patrick D. Murphy points out that Mora is "one of many speaking out against what she labels 'the safety of uniformity.'" Rather than conforming to the standards of different cultures, Mora celebrates embracing one's heritage and being unique. Considering the ongoing political debate over immigration, Mora's work remains relevant as she continues to portray the experiences of people who live on the border of Texas and Mexico.

CRITICISM

April Dawn Paris

Paris is a freelance writer who has an extensive background working with literature and educational materials. In the following essay, she argues that as the speaker in "Legal Alien" confesses her feelings of loneliness and isolation, she validates her audience and gives them hope for the future.

Pat Mora explores the isolation that comes to Mexican Americans and other biculturalindividuals in her poem "Legal Alien." The speaker of the poem walks a virtual tightrope because of her bicultural status. As Elisabeth Mermann-Jozwiak and Nancy Sullivan explain in *Conversations with Mexican American Writers: Languages and Literatures in the Borderlands*, the speaker lives in a world "where competency in Spanish does not give the speaker full access to Mexican culture and where mastering English does not mean acceptance."

The poem begins with the speaker defining herself as bicultural and bilingual; she does not hide who she is. Overall, the poem concentrates on the rejection and cultural conflict that comes with living between two different worlds. "Legal Alien" is a popular poem because so many people are able to identify with the speaker's thoughts and feelings. When asked about the poem "Legal Alien" by Frederick Luis Aldama in *Spilling the Beans in Chicanolandia*, Mora replied, "To be honest, I'm never sure how much an author

WHAT DO I READ NEXT?

- *Girl in Translation* tells the story of a young girl, Kimberly, who moves from China to Brooklyn. Over the course of the book, Kimberly struggles between the different worlds as a scholar, sweatshop worker, American, and Chinese immigrant. Jean Kwok's young-adult novel was published in 2010.

- Mora's *Nepantla: Essays from the Land in the Middle* is a collection of essays that explores life on the border of two different cultures. This book transitions away from poetry, but it explores multiculturalism and the Mexican American experience just as her poetry does. This volume was first published in 1993.

- *The Essential Neruda: Selected Poems* (bilingual edition) is an overview of the Chilean poet's work, which influenced the poetry of Mora and other writers. The 2004 release is a useful introduction to Neruda's poetry.

- Elizabeth Jacob's *Mexican American Literature: The Politics of Identity* was published in 2006. This nonfiction book introduces Mexican American literature to students within its cultural, political, and historical context.

- Alma Luz Villanueva's volume of poetry *Soft Chaos* is an emotional journey. Released in 2009, this book provides beautiful examples of contemporary Mexican American poetry.

- *America* by E. R. Frank is a young-adult novel in which the main character struggles with his personal identity. This 2003 book examines the effects of abuse, neglect, forgiveness, and self-awareness.

knows about what he or she is doing consciously. I like to remain somewhat unaware." In exploring the idea of isolation and rejection, the poet, consciously or not, unites people who live on the borders of different worlds and reminds them that they are not alone. Within this "hyphenated"

"BY EXPLORING THE HUMAN CONDITION THROUGH THE LENS OF PERSONAL EXPERIENCE, THE POET BECOMES A DRIVING FORCE FOR UNITY AND CHANGE."

state, there is hope for the speaker and the future of all individuals who live in the fringes of society.

The first seven lines of "Legal Alien" explore the seemingly positive aspects of being bilingual before the poem identifies the rejection that the speaker experiences from both worlds. The second and third lines establish her ability to speak both English and Spanish fluently. The speaker is able to shift easily from one language to the other, as she demonstrates in these two lines. The English and Spanish phrases she uses are common colloquialisms, but they provide an early clue into the frustration that comes with being bilingual. It is interesting to note that, even early on in the poem, the speaker does not appear personally uncomfortable with her bicultural or bilingual identity. She uses the third person plural in the Spanish phrase, which translates: "they are making me crazy," to explain that other people are the cause of her distress. The conflict between the English language and Spanish language is one that the speaker cannot escape. This linguistic conflict represents an ongoing cultural conflict and reflects the growing controversy involving English and Spanish in the 1980s.

The 1980s saw a growing debate over language and American identity. Four years after the 1984 publication of *Chants*, Florida and other states legally made English their official language. According to Samuel Huntington's "The Challenge to English," speaking English was, and occasionally still is, defined by many citizens as part of being an American. In fact, Huntington explains that there was a great debate surrounding "businesses requiring their employees to speak English, government documents in languages other than English, ballots and election materials in districts with significant non-English-speaking minorities." Rules against speaking Spanish in school or the workplace were common in Mexican American history. In "Legal Alien," speaking English provides the speaker with an upscale office job that would probably not be available to her if she only spoke Spanish. Being bilingual, however, does not make life easy for her.

Mora grew up at a time when many Mexican American families did not encourage bilingualism in their children in an attempt to Americanize them. She was fortunate to be part of a bilingual household, but many children of her time did not grow up speaking both languages. Being bilingual would eventually become a trait that many companies would desire, as positions within international businesses began to thrive in the United States. As Mermann-Jozwiak and Sullivan's interview with author Diane Montejano reveals in "Braiding Languages, Weaving Cultures," "When we grow older, all of a sudden there's a big demand for bilingual this, bilingual that, and you're wondering, 'What happened here?'" While some people associate speaking Spanish with being Mexican, language is not the only thing to define a person's culture.

The speaker switches between speaking fluent Spanish in her personal life and fluent English at work. While speaking Spanish makes her feel personally connected to her heritage, the speaker cannot make linguistic mistakes, even to order a meal at a Mexican restaurant. Being bilingual and bicultural appears advantageous on the surface, but it comes with a cost. The speaker is hyphenated as an American. Her attempts to live in both worlds and speak both languages only limit her in each one.

The speaker is an American citizen who speaks English. She is not in the country illegally. In fact, she probably grew up in the United States. Anglos, however, do not view her as their equal. She may speak English like an American, but she is still not fully accepted into Anglo American society. They may not all see her as inferior, but she is definitely not the same. Denied acceptance by people of her country, the speaker looks for admittance into her cultural heritage.

The speaker uses highly charged language to describe how the Mexican community sees her. In this instance, she chooses to use a word that Americans often associate with immigrants from other countries. The term *alien* was originally defined an individual from a foreign country, but it later developed a darker, more negative connotation. In science fiction circles, it means something from another planet. It can also have

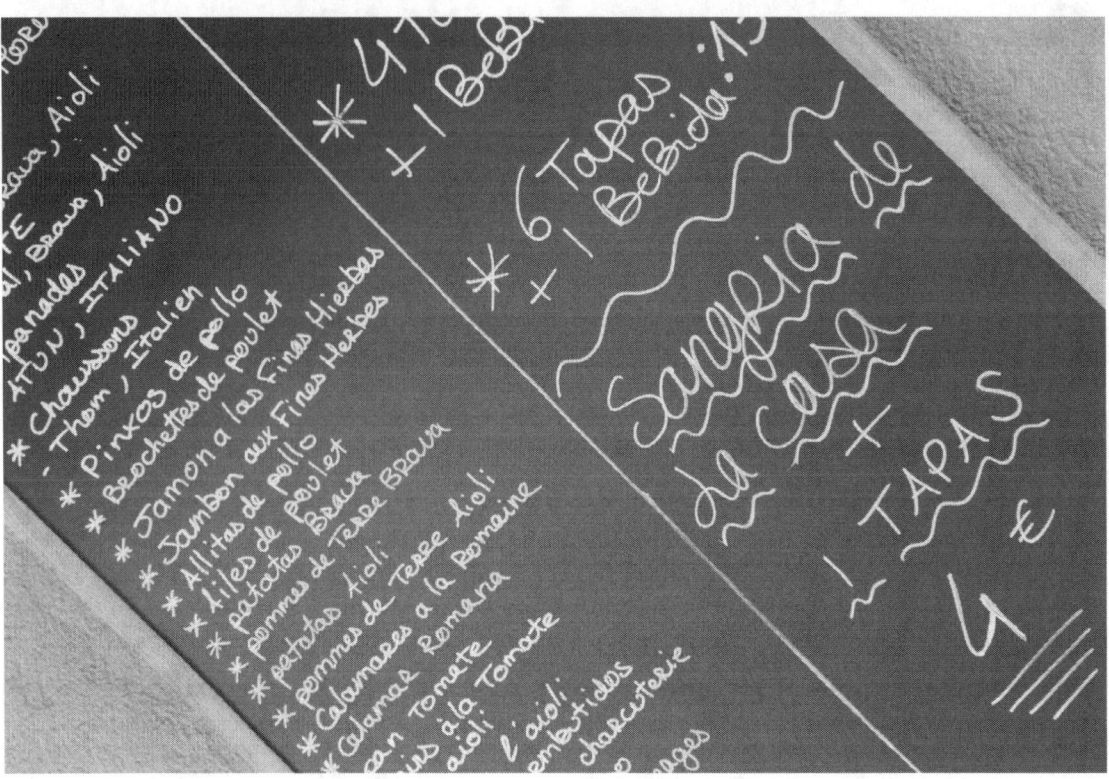

Bilingualism is a theme of the poem. (loflo69 | Shutterstock.com)

a pejorative connotation, which is why the National Association of Hispanic Journalists is currently advocating that the media refrain from using the term *illegal alien* and adopting *undocumented immigrant*. The term alien, even in the 1980s, is one that signals a feeling of separation and distrust. The speaker does not officially belong to Mexican society, even if she can speak the Spanish language fluently. Her isolation is echoed in the sad and frustrated tone of the poem.

The terms Mexican and American are juxtaposed to show the conflict of two cultures. They do, however, agree on one thing: each one believes that the speaker cannot be trusted or fully accepted. Neither world sees the speaker accurately. She is viewed as coming from one world or the other because she is bicultural. In reality, however, each society is part of her. Being bicultural is not what causes her discomfort. Again, it is the world, or worlds, surrounding the speaker that take issue with her bicultural status, not the speaker herself.

Just as the speaker has the ability to transition between languages, she also slides between worlds. It is not surprising, however, to discover that she is relegated to the edges of each world. Having established that both Anglo and Mexican societies view her as a foreigner, she is prevented from fully accessing either culture. Here the speaker's tone becomes bitter. Always a token or visitor in each culture, the speaker must take what the different worlds are willing to offer her.

The speaker confesses that she wears a happy expression to hide her pain and discomfort. The speaker knows that there is nothing that she can do to change the way that other people view her. She is forced to lie, hide her feelings, and act as though the judgment of these worlds does not affect her. The speaker is not given a chance to prove herself to anyone. She bitterly accepts the fact that she is critiqued by the two worlds that equally define her.

Through the speaker's pain and frustration, "Legal Alien" is a poem that validates individuals and brings an end to their feelings of loneliness and isolation. The speaker expresses what many Mexican Americans both experience and feel. These emotions, however, are not limited to the

Mexican American experience. People throughout the world are lonely, misunderstood, and isolated. "Legal Alien" legitimizes the experiences and feelings of the disenfranchised everywhere. The themes of loneliness, cultural conflict, and identity are universal, which explains why readers are still drawn to it. By confessing her Mexican American experiences, the speaker comments with the human condition. Those who identify with her take comfort in the knowledge that they are not alone.

Mora fulfills her goal to "construct wholeness" with "Legal Alien." She defines this goal in her interview in *Spilling the Beans in Chicanolandia*, and she says that "in a way it's an issue that incorporates ethnicity or gender or class, but it also includes the challenge of being human." By exploring the human condition through the lens of personal experience, the poet becomes a driving force for unity and change. The speaker echoes the pain of her audience and, by giving a voice to their experiences and feelings, she gives them hope that things may be different in the future.

Source: April Dawn Paris, Critical Essay on "Legal Alien," in *Poetry for Students*, Gale, Cengage Learning, 2012.

Elisabeth Mermann-Jozwiak and Nancy Sullivan

In the following excerpt, Mermann-Jozwiak and Sullivan converse with Mora on the use of Spanish words in her poetry, the importance of the border to her work, and the issues facing Chicana writers.

...*NS: You use some Spanish words in your work, but not a lot. How would you describe your use of the languages?*

PM: I'm writing to a great extent for an English-speaking audience. I am bilingual, though English-dominant. I'm interested in including Spanish because it's part of my world, it's part of my mind. On the other hand, I am not writing for a primarily Spanish-speaking audience, or I would be writing in Spanish. To use *House of Houses*, I built in humor for the person who is bilingual. There is subversion in the use of Spanish, very consciously.

NS: That's what I was wondering. Do you actually go back and look at your writing again and think, "This is going to work better with a Spanish word"?

PM: Sometimes. And sometimes an editor might say.... For example, my editor at Beacon does not read Spanish, but she gives me free rein.

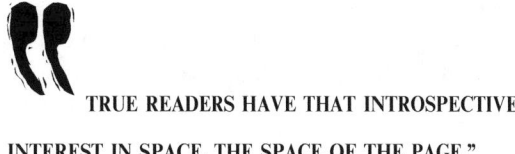

TRUE READERS HAVE THAT INTROSPECTIVE INTEREST IN SPACE, THE SPACE OF THE PAGE."

Her assistant editor at the time was African American, so that was interesting. My editor would read it, then her assistant editor would read it, and sometimes the assistant editor would say, "I can't follow along enough. I need a little more help." So then I might go in and add a word or look at context clues to make sure that, yes, there was going to be double pleasure if you were bilingual, there were going to be times in which you were going to get to savor things in a special way, but that on the other hand if you weren't bilingual you could stay with me, because I want that.

Particularly after I left Texas and moved to the Midwest, I was aware of people who were very interested in the Latina experience but had never even heard Spanish around them, whereas in Texas we would say, "Well, people have heard it, and they could piece things together." But I think in the Midwest I became aware of many people who were very interested, but they wanted to be able to follow along.

Also, the characters influence the language. If the character is primarily Spanish-speaking, I will use more Spanish because I hear her or him that way. In New Mexico you often have someone who is second or third generation—there they would say hispanos—who may spend most of their lives in English. That was sort of a surprise to me but influenced the language in *Aunt Carmen's Book of Practical Saints*. The speaker is a fictional character, but I used that as a guide in creating her.

NS: I noticed a couple of your poems in Borders, *two in particular that are very intimate, one about divorce and one about cancer. There was no Spanish at all. So I was wondering if it's the topic and how close it is to you or how personal it is to you is the reason why there were no Spanish words at all.*

PM: Only a good critic is going to be able to go back and tell me some of those things that I not only don't notice but don't want to notice. But if the question were, "Do I think that the level of intimacy affects the use of Spanish?" my initial reaction would be, "no," because I have written some very intimate poems, I would say, particularly about relatives, that do have a lot of Spanish. In fact the tribute to my father in *Agua Santa* is the only poem I have attempted, a long poem that is totally in Spanish. I did that on purpose because I wanted to do something special in his memory. It was a very tough thing for me to do. A totally new form. I don't think the issue is intimacy, but it might have to do with the nature of the topic.

EMJ: I've got a couple of thematic questions. Much of your writing seems to explore the concept of borders and borderlands. Borders between people, between men and women, between upper and lower classes, Mexican Americans and Euro-Americans. Why is that concept so important to you?

PM: Because I am a border woman. I grew up moving back and forth between these two countries with ease. I always lived in the United States, but when you live on the border, you go to Mexico. It's very hard for people in the middle of the United States to understand. I say in *Nepantla* that I was blessed that I could look at the country of my grandparents all the time, which many Americans cannot do. On the campus at which I went to school and where I worked, you actually look out at these very poor colonias on the other side of the Rio Grande. I've always had that sense that I could have been born on the other side. So borders interest me.

EMJ: And that ties in with what you mentioned earlier, space in general, your interest in space and geography. It's not just the landscapes of the Southwest, especially the desert and its fauna that keeps recurring in your poetry, but also the private spaces of the home. Your poetry contains many spatial metaphors, such as being on the edge, or being in between, "in the door well," I think you say in one poem. How does space figure in your writing?

PM: Consciously I wasn't that aware of the interest except when I began to realize, again when I left the desert, how I would feel every time I returned. Every time I saw that plane begin to land and I would look out at this tremendous space and think how totally I felt at home there. Many of my Midwestern friends would confide to me that they found the desert sometimes even terrifying. I remember one of the brightest women I know who is an academic in Cincinnati said to me that the first time she came to the Southwest she was afraid she would fall off because she was so used to the protection of trees. I do say in *House* that I think geography shapes us; our early geography shapes us in complex ways.

When I taught at UNM this past fall, one of the pleasures was that I got to create a course on a topic of my choice, and the course I created was called "Spirit and Space," in preparation for another book. I do want to do another book of prose, a contemplative book, thinking about the desert as a place of contemplation, both looking at that tradition of the desert fathers or Christ going into the desert, the desert that is often looked at so negatively—the desert of my life, the desert of a relationship, this parched sense, but flipping that a bit and playing with what are the gifts that the desert offers.

And you're right, I'm very interested in internal space, intensely interested in that. I'm very interested in one's internal rooms, issues of the psyche. I'm a big fan of *The Poetics of Space* by Bachelard. It's very important to me. The world of dreams, mental space. I think it comes from being a reader. True readers have that introspective interest in space, the space of the page.

EMJ: Space has also become more politicized and seen in a geopolitical sense, especially the space of the border. I see a lot of that in your poetry, especially for women. In your poem "Sonrisas," for example, the speaker is positioned between two very different rooms, and there is a political message.

PM: Well, the idea of claiming space. Both claiming external space of course I think that is a big issue, certainly a big issue for Chicanas. There's a lot of discomfort sometimes, and I encounter that even with highly successful professionals who are reluctant to claim space, who see it as inappropriate, who will say things to me like, "Well, we've been taught not to do that." But I'm also interested in how we really claim our internal space and that can have everything to do with reproductive questions, but also psychologically. It's very complex because of patriarchy.

NS: Gloria Anzaldua talks a lot about the conflict a border person experiences and the linguistic terrorism associated with it. She portrays a constant conflict within herself, for a number of reasons, but this space issue of "Where do I belong? I don't belong in either place" is very important.

PM: Or the flip, "I belong in both." I think it's in *Nepantla*, that I say, "On a good day, it's double pleasure in a way. I have the advantage of moving back and forth." Then there are situations where, yes, it's plenty difficult. I don't know at this point in my life whether I would say "in conflict." I don't know that I would use that language. I would say that there are "conflicts" involved for all of us, and how we negotiate space. That's really what we're talking about. There are conflicts.

NS: But you don't feel the psychological turmoil Anzaldua discusses with respect to ethnic identity?

PM: I think it has to do with time in life. At this time I'm really interested in how we construct wholeness. I've become very interested in Zen and that whole idea of how we honor the self and how we reflect on the self. In a way it's an issue that incorporates ethnicity or gender or class, but it also includes the challenge of being human.

NS: Anzaldua spends a lot of time on the language issue also.

PM: Well, and these have all been issues for me. I wouldn't ever want to seem Pollyannish about it. These are intense issues for me, obviously, whether I'm talking about writing for children or writing for adults. I deal with them all the time, almost on a daily basis. I'm interested in the political issues. But within the last couple of years I've become very interested also in some philosophical issues. They are related, but they are different approaches to the same thing.

One of the most important quotes in my life, for the last two or three years, has been from Gandhi, "You must be the change you wish to see in the world." I'm very interested in exploring that. But given what I have experienced, given what I have inherited, given the privilege I've had, given the scars I may carry, what is it that I can best do? What is the change that I wish to explore?

NS: Do you think that Chicana writers face different problems than other mainstream writers do in getting published?

PM: Definitely. Oh, definitely. In spite of all these comments about the "Latin Boom," or whatever, all you have to do is look at the numbers. All you have to do is look at the numbers or, for example, as someone very interested in poetry, at the Academy of American Poets. It does not have a single Latino on its letterhead. Not a chancellor, not a member of their honorary board. Why? Well, because they would tell you, there isn't one who's good enough. They might not say it publicly, but believe me, they would say it privately. They would think, "If there were one good enough, we'd have them." And we're talking about probably the most prestigious of the poetry organizations that affect fellowships, awards, everything.

In this state [Texas], the most important children's book award is the Bluebonnet Award, which began in 1979. In the history of that award, I believe, one Mexican American has been on the committee who picks the twenty books that the children will vote on. Nobody seems to notice that! I'm always sitting there thinking, "How can this be?" I always feel: why is it people aren't ashamed? That's my response. And there are a lot of publications that I almost don't let myself look at now because I would get so upset. Instead, I say to myself, "Well, take that same money and give it to National Council of La Raza. Why take that publication if it's just going to drive you crazy?"

So it does remain very, very hard, and in part I have become more and more convinced that until Latinos are part of the entire publishing industry, until that happens, I don't know how much change will take place. That is, until they are bookstore owners, they manage Barnes and Noble, they're the vice-president of Borders, all over, until that happens. Between now and then, I spend a lot of time talking about the kind of actions that I think people can take. I think people can go to the manager of their local bookstore and say, "Why is it we have all these columns of books on African Americans, gay/lesbian, and Native American, and yet look at the population here!"

NS: Teachers can go to their school boards and say, "We need more literature that interests us."

PM: You bet they can! And they can talk to these publishers that wine and dine them, look them right in the eye, I tell them, and ask, "How diverse is your editorial staff?" I say to them, "Ask impertinent questions." That's a tough request. But I get these catalogues from major publishing companies that list the books for fall, the books for spring, and there will be one book by a Latino. And we know what the demographics of this country are. We have a long way to go.

NS: One other question. As a linguist, I'm interested in labels. We talk about this in class. "Chicana," "Mexican American," we talk about students having problems with it. What do you like to be referred to as?

PM: I'm very comfortable if people say "Chicana, Latina, Mexican American." I don't have any trouble with those. "Hispanic" I have a little more problem with. In the introduction to *Nepantla*, I talk a little bit about that. I don't resent it. For example, publishers like the word "Hispanic." There are certain campuses that like the word "Hispanic." The problem with the word is that when we celebrated the Quincentenary in 1992 there was a big discussion because the word connotes European. It connotes, whether we want it to or not, middle class; it connotes pride in European roots, which means, "I am connected to Spain" when in truth most of us are that grand "mestizaje, la mezcla," a mix. To be more proud of the Spanish side than of the indigenous side bothers me a lot. "Latina" is a word that right now seems to be more encompassing, but five years from now it may be another word, and I'm very comfortable with that. I think language is fluid, but I also believe that people have a right to their own self-referents. I'm not the kind that scolds students, and I know there are people who do and say "you should say Chicana." I feel people need to come to their own decision about their identity, but part of our responsibility as academics is to help them see the connotation of these words. People are choosing the words for particular reasons, and students need to be aware of those fine distinctions.

Source: Elisabeth Mermann-Jozwiak and Nancy Sullivan, "Interview with Pat Mora," in *MELUS*, Vol. 28, No. 2, Summer 2003, pp. 139–51.

Patrick D. Murphy

In the following excerpt, Murphy examines Mora's theme of the recovery of heritage.

Pat Mora writes in *Nepantla: Essays from the Land in the Middle* that the United States "has both the opportunity and responsibility to demonstrate to this world of emerging representative governments that nurturing variety is central, not marginal to democracy." The use of the word "nurturing" seems in no way fortuitous, because she recognizes natural and cultural diversity as integral threads of the lifeweb labeled Humanity, which is one thread of a much larger lifeweb labeled Earth. As a result, she calls for emphasizing cultural conservation with the same enthusiasm with which some movements labor for "historical preservation" and "natural conservation." This recognition of the interrelationship of natural and cultural diversity and emphasis on the nurturing practice of cultural conservation

> FOR SOUTHWESTERN LATINOS, ONE SUCH UNTELLING INVOLVES EMBRACING THE INDIAN HERITAGE OF THE MESTIZO/A, IN OPPOSITION TO THE IMPOSITION OF THE 'SPANISH' HERITAGE AS THE PRIMARY CULTURAL DETERMINANT."

are to be found throughout the poetry of *Chants* (1985), *Borders* (1986), and *Communion* (1991), as well as in *Nepantla* (1993), of which she says: "The essays are about my encounters with my world" (*Nepantla*).

Pat Mora is a Chicana who began writing around 1980 and has won awards for both her poetry and her children's books. Born in 1942, she grew up, raised three children, and worked in El Paso before moving in 1989 to Cincinnati, Ohio. She has taught at the high school, community college, and university levels and served in various administrative capacities at the University of Texas at El Paso from 1981 to 1989. Of those years, Mora remarks that "I was fortunate to work on issues of outreach to women and to the local Mexican American population.... For those of us committed to extending the opportunities of the university to our community, it was a frustrating but exciting time to participate in that gradual transformation" (*Nepantla*). "Nepantla" is a Nahuatl word meaning "place in the middle," and Mora makes it clear that she not only recognizes herself as having come from such a physical place, the Tex-Mex borderlands, but also from such a psychic and cultural place as a Mexican-American. Mora seeks in her writing, as well as her life, to conserve the generative tension of the dynamic plurality that is borderland existence. "I am in the middle of my life, and well know," she declares, "not only the pain but also the advantage of observing both sides, albeit with my biases, of moving through two, and, in fact, multiple spaces" (*Nepantla*). One of the dangers of a segment of the natural conservation movement is the recovery or preservation of a small section of a larger bioregion. Tourists can then visit that parcel and experience nostalgia for the rest that was allowed to be destroyed. One can see the same danger evident in urban historical preservation, particularly in historically ethnic areas being crowded out by skyscrapers and highways. As Tey Diana Rebolledo and Eliana S. Rivero observe in the *Introduction to Infinite Divisions*, "since many freeways in large urban areas were built in the barrios, the freeways often run along Chicano residential areas. In addition, they may have also destroyed much of the older sections of the barrios, thus destroying traditions" (32). And in such urban renewals/removals, one often sees that the buildings preserved as representative of a particular cultural heritage are ones that are of interest to tourists and tourism promoters rather than inheritors of the culture.

But Mora is well aware of the danger of token wilderness preserves and Potemkin-village mercados and warns against any idea of recovering the Mexican-American heritage as curio or artifact: "a true [ethic] of conservation includes a commitment to a group's decisions, its development and self-direction" (*Nepantla*). Just as the ecology movement warns that biological diversity is crucial to biotic survival, Mora warns that cultural diversity is crucial to human survival, since it actually helps to maintain diversity in general:

> Pride in cultural identity, in the set of learned and shared language,
> symbols, and meanings, needs to be fostered not because of nostalgia
> or romanticism, but because it is essential to our survival. The oppressive
> homogenization of humanity in our era of international technological and
> economic interdependence endangers us all. (*Nepantla*)

Human diversity can be maintained only when cultural conservation is practiced by the marginalized and subordinated groups who defend and recover their heritages in order to generate their futures. Many of the essays in *Nepantla* focus precisely on the issue of cultural conservation, even as they embody such a practice. Mora rightly emphasizes the conservation of Chicano/a and Latino/a cultures, but does not stop there. She also addresses respect for, and awareness of, other cultures internationally and the differing degrees and kinds of effects that dominant U.S. culture has on subordinated cultures within the U.S. and worldwide.

Mora's first book of poetry, *Chants*, demonstrates some of the ways by which the recovery of heritage dimension of cultural conservation may be realized. Part of such recovery requires the retelling of old tales and the untelling of old interpretations by others of one's culture. For Southwestern Latinos, one such untelling involves embracing the Indian heritage of the mestizo/a, in opposition to the imposition of the "Spanish" heritage as the primary cultural determinant. Mora opens *Chants* with the poem "Bribe." In it she retells the story of the "long ago" practices of "Indian women" to seek inspiration for their weaving arts from "the Land." She then claims those traditional practices as part of her own heritage through ritual imitation: "Like the Indians / I ask the Land to smile on me, to croon / softly, to help me catch her music with words." But it is not only an imitative relationship of artistic practices, weaving and writing, that she claims; she also claims a parallel relationship with the personified "Land" through identifying both the women weavers' practice and hers as efforts to represent the earth's creativity through their artistry. She thus claims and images an inheritance and continuation of a human cultural relationship with the rest of the world in which respect, honor, and humility define human-non-human interaction.

Another part of such recovery of heritage consists of reaffirming the situatedness of culture, the relationship of values, beliefs, practices, and character to place. As Mora notes, "Many Mexican American women from the Southwest are desert women" (*Nepantla*). This is not merely anecdotal, but a delineation of identity and source of pride, as well as a claim about historical residence (see Fast 30). Mora, for example, opens "Desert Women" in *Borders* with the lines, "Desert women know / about survival." Survival must be understood not as a minimal condition of existence but as an achievement against odds and concerted efforts, not by "nature" but by other cultures. Survival is thus not some passive form of endurance, but an ongoing practice of resistance and self-education. "Mi Madre," the third poem of *Chants*, celebrates "the desert" that is a "strong mother," because the skills not only to survive but also to flourish there are part of what defines the culture Mora celebrates. And the use of Spanish here differentiates her own cultural identity of Mexican heritage from the pre-concert heritage of desert Native Americans. Her use of turquoise defines a commonality without conflating the difference between the native and immigrant cultures sharing and struggling over the same terrain through generations of inhabitation (Murphy 39).

Several poems that follow "Mi Madre" elaborate the desert's "strong mother" role. For example, "Lesson 1" and "Lesson 2" emphasize the desert's power to reassure and emotionally heal the speaker. "Lesson 1" consists of three stanzas, with the first focusing on the desert's return to balance after a thunderstorm and the second depicting the speaker's seeking out of the desert when "shaken, powerless" with "sadness." The third stanza imparts the lesson. The speaker, knowing she is the "Mi'ja" of the desert mother, feels free to express her emotions while not surrendering to disempowerment and learns to "cry away the storm, then listen, listen." "Lesson 1" begins with rain pounding the land and the lesson of the poem derives from the desert's rapid recovery from this downpour. "Lesson 2," on the next page, also begins with water, but this time it is rising from the river through the evaporative power of sunlight. Here the desert again speaks a lesson about overcoming sadness, but Mora has added an interesting dimension. In the first lesson, she emphasizes imitating the solidity of the land to weather sadness and the lifestorms causing the emotion. In the second lesson, she emphasizes imitating the fluidity of the water, rising about her river of troubles, strengthened, transformed, and active. Mora moves from the desert mother's instruction to "listen" to her challenge to "dance," recognizing that both solidity and fluidity are processes of a single dynamic system.

A third part of recovery of heritage, particularly for the building of a future, is to critique the oppressive and exclusionary elements of one's heritage: "to question and ponder what values and customs we wish to incorporate into our lives, to continue our individual and our collective evolution" (*Nepantla*). In *Nepantla* Mora critiques, for example, dominant Mexican culture's suppression of indigenous peoples and languages. In *Chants*, she critiques the sexual oppression of women enforced through the virgin/whore dichotomy by depicting the fear of two brides-to-be in "Discovered" and "Dream." In the first poem, the speaker fears that she will be denied a dignified wedding and be ostracized by the community if her loss of virginity is discovered, and also, perhaps, that "her lover" will see her as a "whore" (i.e., a sexually active being, rather than as a wife, a supposedly sexually passive being. This speaker remains firmly subjected to cultural oppression. In the second poem, the bride-to-be has the same fear on her wedding day of public censure, but relishes the sexual awakening she enjoyed the night before and speaks to her groom as someone who understands. Here the speaker breaks free ideologically of cultural restrictions and "Mexican superstitions" and also asserts a relationship of equality with her lover, unlike the speaker of the first poem. Interestingly enough, this speaker seeks assistance from the flowers for her hair—a symbol of nonhuman, uncultured nature to keep her secret through the wedding....

Source: Patrick D. Murphy, "Conserving Natural and Cultural Diversity: The Prose and Poetry of Pat Mora," in *MELUS*, Vol. 21, No. 2, Spring 1996, pp. 59–70.

SOURCES

Abrams, M. H., ed., *A Glossary of Literary Terms: Seventh Edition*, Cornell University, 1999, p. 217.

Aldama, Frederick Luis, "Introducing a Second Wave of Chicano/a Visual/Verbal Artists," in *Spilling the Beans in Chicanolandia*, University of Texas Press, 2006, pp. 1–33.

———, "Pat Mora," in *Spilling the Beans in Chicanolandia*, University of Texas Press, 2006, pp. 153–65.

Englekirk, Allan, and Marguerite Marín, "Mexican Americans," in *Countries and Their Cultures*, http://www.everyculture.com/multi/Le-Pa/Mexican-Americans.html (accessed June 5, 2011).

Harmon, William, ed., *A Handbook to Literature: Ninth Edition*, Prentice Hall, 2003, pp. 113.

Herrera-Sobek, María, *Chicana Creativity and Criticism: New Frontiers in American Literature*, University of New Mexico Press, 1996, p. 2.

Huntington, Samuel, "The Challenge to English, Reprint from Huntington's Who Are We?," in *Social Contract*, Vol. 15, No. 1, Fall 2004, http://www.thesocialcontract.com/artman2/publish/tsc1501/article_1258_printer.shtml (accessed on June 3, 2011).

Larson, Jeanette, "Talking with Pat Mora," in *Book Links*, January 2011, http://www.patmora.com/morafiles/other/booklinks2011.pdf (accessed on June 5, 2011).

Mermann-Jozwiak, Elisabeth, and Nancy Sullivan, "Be the Change You Wish to See in the World," in *Conversations with Mexican American Writers: Languages and Literatures in the Borderlands*, University Press of Mississippi, 2009, pp. 35–44.

———, "Braiding Languages, Weaving Cultures," in *Conversations with Mexican American Writers: Languages and*

Literatures in the Borderlands, University Press of Mississippi, 2009, pp. 21–34.

———, "Stories That Must Be Told," in *Conversations with Mexican American Writers: Languages and Literatures in the Borderlands*, University Press of Mississippi, 2009, pp. vii–xxv.

Mora, Pat, "Legal Alien," in *Chants*, Arte Público Press, 1984, p. 52.

Murphy, Patrick, D., "Conserving Natural and Cultural Diversity: The Prose and Poetry of Pat Mora," in *MELUS*, Vol. 21, No. 1, Spring 1996, pp. 59–69.

"NAHJ Urges News Media to Stop Using Dehumanizing Terms When Covering Immigration," in *National Association of Hispanic Journalists*, http://www.nahj.org/nahjnews/articles/2006/March/immigrationcoverage.shtml (accessed June 15, 2011).

"Pat Mora," in *Voices from the Gaps*, University of Minnesota, May 16, 2000, http://voices.cla.umn.edu/artistpages/mora_pat.php (accessed on June 3, 2011).

"Pat's Awards," in *Pat Mora's Home Page*, http://www.patmora.com/awards.htm (accessed on June 1, 2011).

Terrazas, Beatriz, "Between the Lines," in *Texas Observer*, March 30, 2011, http://www.texasobserver.org/reviews/between-the-lines (accessed on June 2, 2011).

"Token," in *Merriam-Webster Dictionary*, http://www.merriam-webster.com/dictionary/token (accessed on June 4, 2011).

Gonzalez, Norma, *I Am My Language: Discourses of Women and Children in the Borderlands*, University of Arizona Press, 2006.
> This nonfiction book combines research with personal narratives from women on the border. The contents explore the effect of language on culture and social identity of women and children.

Gonzalez, Rita, Howard Fox, and Chon A. Noriega, *Phantom Sightings: Art after the Chicano Movement*, University of California Press, 2008.
> This book shows how Mexican American art evolved during the Chicano movement and through the following decades. Complete with pictures and essays, this nonfiction book explores different types of art, including painting, performance art, and media.

Munoz, Carlos, *Youth, Identity, Power: The Chicano Movement*, Verso, 2007.
> This volume details the Chicano civil rights movement of the 1960s. Told by one of the leaders of the student movement, this history focuses on the influence of student protests on initiating political change.

Saldivar-Hull, Sonia, *Feminism on the Border: Chicana Gender Politics and Literature*, University of California Press, 2000.
> This work examines the work of different feminists authors to trace feminism in Mexican American culture and across the border.

FURTHER READING

Anzaldua, Gloria, *The Gloria Anzaldua Reader*, edited by AnaLouise Keating, Duke University Press Books, 2009.
> This collection of essays, poetry, drawings, prose, and criticism provides an overview of this influential author's work, and it offers insight into the evolution of Mexican American literature.

García, Alma M., ed., *Chicana Feminist Thought: The Basic Historical Writings*, Routledge, 1997.
> García's history examines the rise of the feminist movement after the Chicano movement of the 1960s ignored the rights of women. This collection of essays shows the political fight for gender equality from the 1960s to the 1990s.

SUGGESTED SEARCH TERMS

Pat Mora

Legal Alien AND Chants

Mexican American literature

Pat Mora AND Legal Alien

Chicano literature AND Pat Mora

1980s AND United States

Mexican American history

Mexican American poetry

Chicano civil rights movement

Mexican American literature AND Pat Mora

London

WILLIAM BLAKE

1794

"London" is a poem by William Blake, who was one of the greatest of the English romantic poets. It was first published in 1794 in Blake's *Songs of Innocence and of Experience*, a collection of poems written and illustrated by Blake and also published by him using a method of printing he invented himself. "London" is one of the *Songs of Experience*, which show the suffering that people endure when they lose or forget their former innocent state.

It is one of Blake's best-known and most powerful short poems, offering a keen sense of the indignation Blake felt at the social injustices of his day. Blake lived in London, and the speaker of the poem, who can safely be identified as the poet himself, walks the streets and records impressions of what he sees and hears in the city. It is not a flattering or uplifting picture of England's capital city. Blake thought that people did not have a clear understanding of the way life should be lived, in joy and freedom. He blamed the institutions of church and state for enslaving people's minds with limiting beliefs that led only to emotional and physical suffering.

Widely anthologized, "London" can also be found in *Blake: Poetry and Designs*, edited by Mary Lynn Johnson and John E. Grant and published by W. W. Norton in 1979.

William Blake (Painting by John Linnell)

AUTHOR BIOGRAPHY

Blake was born on November 18, 1757, in London, to James Blake and his wife, Catherine. Blake's father was a hosier. Blake was tutored at home until he was eleven and was then sent to a drawing school, which he attended until 1772. He was then apprenticed to an engraver, Joseph Basire, for seven years. In 1779, he began to study at the Royal Academy of Art and did commercial engravings for Joseph Johnson, a bookseller. Three years later he married Catherine Boucher, the illiterate daughter of a market gardener. They had no children, but by all accounts it was a happy marriage.

Blake had started writing poetry when he was twelve, and in 1783, his *Poetical Sketches* was printed, although no copies were sold. In 1784, he wrote a satire, *An Island in the Moon*, which was never published. In the late 1780s, Blake developed his own method of printing and began to produce his illuminated books, which combine text and design. He also came under the influence of the Swedish mystical philosopher Emanuel Swedenborg. In 1789, Blake wrote and published *Songs of Innocence* and *The Book of Thel*, and the following year his satire *The Marriage of Heaven and Hell* was published.

During the 1790s Blake produced a series of books in which he developed his own mythology. These included *Visions of the Daughters of Albion* (1793), *The First Book of Urizen* (1794), and *The Book of Los* (1795). He also published *Songs of Innocence and of Experience* in 1794, the collection that includes "London." This was also the period in which he produced a series of twelve color prints, including "Nebuchadnezzar" and "Newton" (1795). During this time, Blake worked as a commercial engraver; he was barely known as a poet and little known as a painter. The only exhibition of his work during his lifetime was one he arranged himself, at his brother's shop, in 1809–1810. Very few people went to see it.

In 1800, Blake and his wife moved from London to Felpham, a village on the South Coast, where Blake received commissions from the minor poet William Hayley. In 1803, a drunken soldier accused Blake of making threats against the king. Blake was tried and acquitted in 1804. The previous year he had returned to live in London, where in 1805, he completed his commissioned series of eighty Biblical watercolors.

Blake's major late poems include *Milton: A Poem* (completed in 1804) and *Jerusalem*, which he worked on for many years and published in 1820. Other work from this period includes his watercolor drawings for *The Book of Job* (1810, published 1826). Blake was never well-off, and in 1821, he had to sell his collection of prints to raise some money. In the year of his death he was working on engravings for Dante's *Divine Comedy*. After some months of ill health, Blake died on August 12, 1827, at the age of sixty-nine. A witness reported that just before Blake died he sang songs of what he saw in heaven.

POEM SUMMARY

The text used for this summary is from *Blake: Poetry and Designs*, edited by Mary Lynn Johnson and John E. Grant, W. W. Norton, 1979, p. 53. A version of the poem can be found on the following Web page: http://www.blakearchive. org/exist/ blake/archive/transcription.xq?objectid = songsie. a.illbk.47&term = london& search = yes.

MEDIA ADAPTATIONS

- "London" was set to music by twentieth-century British composer Benjamin Britten in his *Poems and Proverbs of William Blake* (2010). It is available on CD on the Hyperion label.
- American composer William Bolcom included "London" in his *Songs of Innocence and of Experience*, released on CD in 2004 by Naxos American.

Stanza 1
The poem is narrated in the first person by a speaker who walks the streets of London and records his impressions of what he sees. In the first stanza he walks near the River Thames. In the first two lines, he twice refers to London's charters, in connection with both the streets and the river. A charter was a guarantee of liberty, and London had many of them, going back hundreds of years, but lines 3 and 4 make it clear that in the eyes of the speaker, the citizens of London are enjoying neither freedom nor happiness. On the contrary, everyone the speaker encounters is worn down by care.

Stanza 2
The speaker elaborates on what he sees in stanza 2. He hears in the voices of adults and children many cries of distress, including curses. The word "ban" in line 7 means a curse, although it also has another meaning relevant for the poem: a prohibition or a law. In the last line of this stanza, he describes what he thinks causes at least some of this distress: the people are enslaved, not by a physical tyranny but a mental one, connected to the way they are taught to think about and view the world. This is a result of what they are taught by churches and the government. It is the people's beliefs that enslave them, and these beliefs are imposed on them by their rulers.

Stanza 3
In stanza 3, the speaker gets more specific about what he sees and hears. He brings attention to the plight of the young chimney sweepers in the city. Boys as young as four were forced to work as chimney sweepers in the London of Blake's day, and many suffered injuries and deformities as a result of having to squeeze themselves into such small openings. In line 10, the speaker makes it clear that he blames the churches for not speaking up about the situation. The churches themselves are stained black by the soot that comes from the chimneys and the smoke that rises everywhere in the industrialized city.

In lines 11 and 12, the speaker turns his attention from the church to the monarchy, which he believes is equally to blame for the misery Londoners endure. He refers to the distress of a soldier. Blake may here be referring to soldiers discharged from the army and left destitute, having no way of supporting themselves in the city. More generally, it applies to any soldier wounded or killed in the prosecution of a war designed to enrich the monarchy. Line 12 reveals how the bloodshed by the soldiers in what the speaker regards as unjust or unnecessary wars metaphorically stains the walls of the royal palace, just as the soot from the chimneys stained the churches.

Stanza 4
In stanza 4, the speaker adds to the list of the woes suffered by people in London. Not only are church and state to blame, but also the institution of marriage. The sound he hears at midnight are the curses yelled by a young prostitute. Line 15 shows how prostitution leads to disease that can infect newborn babies. Prostitution also affects marriages, sowing disease there also, as line 16 shows. However, the speaker's target here is not to condemn prostitution as such but to bring attention to what he saw as a harmful attitude to sex that prevailed at the time. When natural sexual desire is repressed as something shameful, sex is driven underground, so to speak, and prostitution, with all its attendant ills, flourishes.

THEMES

Social Protest
The poem is a protest against the social conditions that the speaker observes as he walks the streets of London. Although London is the

TOPICS FOR FURTHER STUDY

- Walk the streets of your own town and take note of the people you see and the sounds you hear. Then write a free verse poem based on your impressions. Blake's poem conveys a sense of indignation and anger at the situation he sees. What dominant mood or emotion will your poem convey? Try to reflect those feelings with the words you choose for the poem.

- Consult *Poetry for Young People: William Blake* (2007), edited by John Maynard. Read the introduction to Blake's life, poetry, and ideas, and then pick out two poems, one from the *Songs of Innocence* and the other from the *Songs of Experience*. Give a class presentation in which you read each of these poems aloud and use them to illustrate Blake's idea of the two different states of mind and soul: innocence and experience. Alternately, create a digital presentation in which you use slides to illustrate a comparison of the poems side-by-side.

- Make an audiovisual recording of yourself reading "London" and select some appropriate copyright-free images to illustrate each stanza. Then upload your reading to YouTube or your Web page and invite students to comment on it.

- Bearing in mind what you have learned about Blake's categories of innocence and experience, write an autobiographical essay in which you chart your own course from innocence to experience. In what ways have you been able to maintain an open, receptive mode of being, similar to innocence, and to what extent have you become disillusioned or hardened by what you have experienced as you have grown from childhood into your teenage years? Make references to Blake's poetry in your essay.

reference point, the poet might have made similar protest about another city or about English society generally. As he patrols the streets he becomes like a biblical prophet, pointing out injustice with a kind of controlled fury and indignation. He knows that what is happening is wrong and feels compelled to speak out about it. He believes that everyone in the city, not just certain groups of people, are afflicted by the prevailing malaise.

For the miseries the poet observes, he blames the institutions of church and state, which combine to create a society in which oppression flourishes and is justified by those in authority. The church is to blame because it does not speak out against the evils of child labor, as seen in the plight of the city's boy chimney sweepers. The church, says the speaker, should be ashamed of its silence and inaction by which it allows, even condones, such abuses.

The government is also to blame because it passes repressive laws that restrict the activities of anyone who questions the rightness of the established order or who protests at political corruption. Charters originally marked out people's freedom from tyranny. The Magna Carta signed in 1215, for example, asserted the rights of citizens that the monarch could not take away. But the way poet uses the word "charter'd" suggests that such liberties may not be exactly what they appear. The granting of charters to large commercial interests, for example, as was common at the time, meant that many other people or groups were excluded from such rights. The granting of special liberties to one group denied those same liberties to others. This was the argument mounted by Tom Paine in his *Rights of Man* (1790), which Blake certainly knew.

Wars

The British government's penchant for waging war is another target of the indignant speaker. The poem was written at a time when Britain had become a formidable European power and was establishing its global empire. From the 1780s to the first two decades of the nineteenth century, Britain, in spite of losing the American colonies, solidified and extended its power in Canada and India, began the colonization of Australia, and took possession of other territories around the world by military conquest. Blake had lived through the period of the American War of Independence and had sympathized with the colonists, regarding America as a land where freedom flourished. He disliked the expansionist policies of George III and his government, which he saw as motivated by greed and materialism and

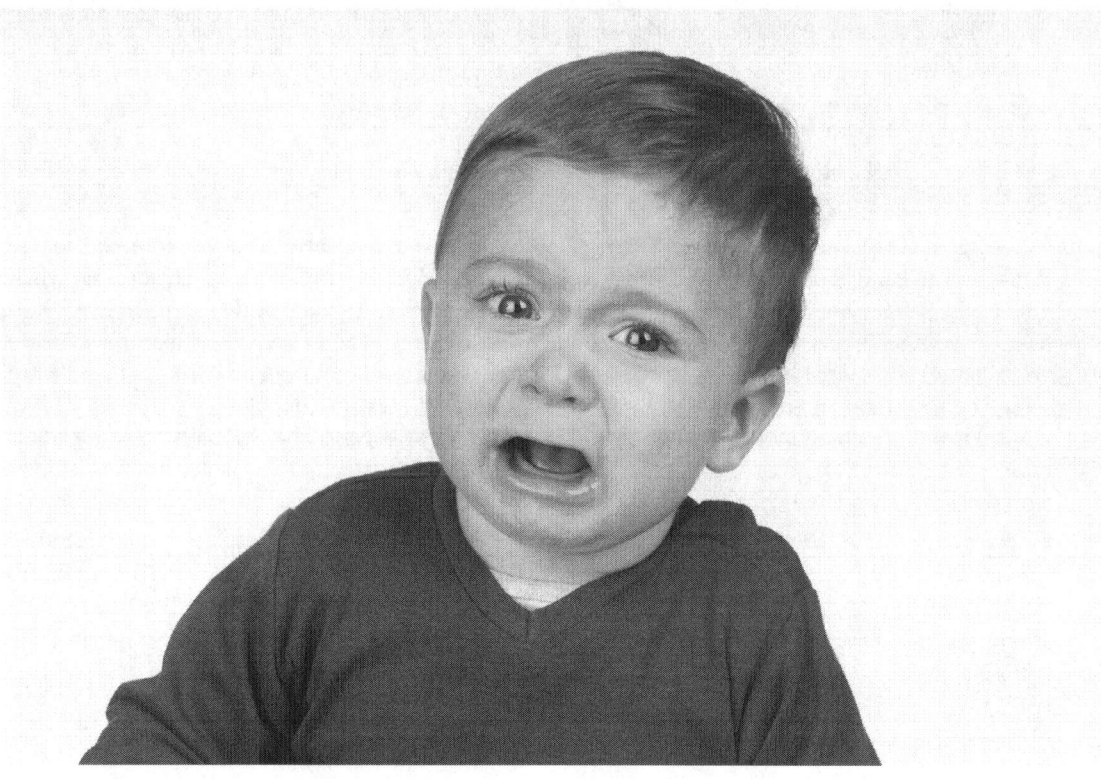

Fear is a recurring theme in the poem. (Gelpi | Shutterstock.com)

which he thought resulted in oppression. In the poem, he blames the monarchy and its allies for the unnecessary suffering of the soldiers, who do the bidding of their masters but after discharge are left on the street to fend for themselves—their sad fate pointing an accusing finger at the entire political system and the injustices it perpetrates.

Religion

The poem emphasizes that the institutions of church and state combine to enslave people not so much by physical force as a kind of mind force. The chains that bind them—invisible yet formidable—are in part self-created by people who allow the church and the state to convince them that they, the authorities, know best. The religious and secular authorities claim that the ideas and beliefs they promote and the laws they pass are wise and prudent, based on God's law and the dictates of human reason. The poet, on the other hand, sees those same beliefs as limited, harmful, and simply wrong. Adherence to them makes people live stunted, restricted lives that are less than fully human.

In this highly compressed poem, Blake conveys this point by making the word "ban" in stanza 2 serve triple duty. Although not a common meaning in today's usage, a ban is, first, a curse, and in this poem, it refers to the curses uttered by any of the unhappy people the poet observes on the streets of London. Second, a ban is a prohibition, something that people are not allowed to do because it is illegal. The poet has in mind a society full of unjust laws that people are compelled to obey. These restrictive laws help to create a mentality, backed up by religious authority, of "thou shalt not."

The third meaning that the word "ban" puts in mind, because it is close to it in sound, is the wedding banns, an announcement of a proposed marriage in a church. This topic aroused Blake's ire because he objected to what he saw as the church's narrow and misguided teachings about sexuality. Blake believed that church teachings did not value sexual love and made people ashamed of having such physical desires, even in marriage. The result of this attitude was repression, loveless marriages, and the diversion of the sexual instinct into secret channels in which it became the subject of a commercial transaction between a man and a prostitute, which, as the poem makes clear, has terrible consequences for society, for marriage, and for children.

STYLE

Meter and Rhyme
The poem is written in iambic tetrameters. An iamb is a poetic foot consisting of two syllables, an unstressed syllable followed by a stressed syllable. It is the most common poetic foot in the English language. A tetrameter consists of four poetic feet.

The poet varies the meter on several occasions to create the effect he wants. In the last line of stanza 1, for example, the first foot is an inverted iamb, known as a trochee, in which a stressed syllable is followed by an unstressed one. This gives particular emphasis to the word "mark," which stands out against the expected metrical rhythm. The trochaic rhythm continues throughout the line. To accomplish this effect, Blake has simply omitted the first syllable of the first foot in order to begin the line with a stressed syllable. The line is one syllable shorter than the others. Blake uses exactly the same technique in the first foot of the last line of stanza 3 and in the first foot of stanza 4, line 13.

Another metrical variation occurs in the last line of stanza 2, in which in the second foot Blake has used a spondee in place of the iamb. A spondee is a foot containing two stressed syllables. This gives particular emphasis to one of the themes of the poem: that people are enslaved because their minds are being controlled. This particular phrase is sharpened even further in its effects by the use of alliteration (the repetition of initial consonants, in this case the two "m" sounds).

The poem is also rhymed. In each stanza, line 1 rhymes with line 3, and line 2 rhymes with line 4. This can be represented as an *abab* rhyme scheme.

Repetition
The poem gains some of its effect by simple repetition of words. The repetition of "charter'd" in lines 1 and 2 prepares the way for the ironic meaning Blake applies to that word in the poem. London may have charters, but its residents are not free. The word "mark" occurs twice, first as verb and second as noun. The most notable repetition is of the word "every." It first occurs in the third line of the first stanza and then three times, in exactly the same place within each line, in lines 5, 6, and 7 of the second stanza. The repetitions produce an effect of rising oratorical intensity. What the poet is observing, he wants to convince his reader, are not isolated incidents but a universal condition. The word "every" appears again in the third stanza, which means it occurs no less than five times in the poem as a whole.

Images
The images in the poem appeal first to the eye, but then switch to the ear. In the first stanza, the speaker notes what he sees—the faces of London's inhabitants that betray their unhappiness. In the remaining stanzas, however, the predominant images are related to the sense of hearing. They are the sounds of the city as the poet hears them. There is not a positive sound among them. They are all sounds of distress: fear, anger, and despair.

Intermingled with these sounds are some startling visual images. The churches blackened by soot seem to be a symbolic image, but in fact the churches of the day in London were indeed blackened by soot and smoke. The palace, on the other hand, is not literally running with blood; the latter image is symbolic. However, the visual images that these compressed phrases conjure up for the reader serve the same purpose: they forcefully drive home the poet's message. The same is true of the final image, which fuses opposites to create a grim picture of what Blake saw as the corrupt institution of marriage. Marriage is usually associated with joy and celebration, but in this image Blake yokes it to a symbol of death. Instead of allowing life to flourish, marriage stifles it. When this is combined with the equally grim image of the baby born already diseased, a situation that should be full of life and hope for the future instead is presented as sick and lifeless.

HISTORICAL CONTEXT

London in the Late 1700s
London during Blake's time was the greatest city in England and one of the world's most important ports. Like most cities, it was full of contrasts, with great wealth and opulence existing alongside abject poverty and squalor. As a denizen of London all his life, Blake knew the city extremely well, and he is a good witness

COMPARE & CONTRAST

- **Late 1700s:** London is the largest city in England with a steadily rising population. By 1760, the population is 740,000 and increases to approximately one million by the end of the century.

  Today: London is the capital city of the United Kingdom and the most populous city in the European Union. In mid-2005, the population, counting only the thirty-two administrative boroughs and the City of London, is 7,517,700. However, the London metropolitan area covers a much wider area, and its population is estimated to be almost fourteen million.

- **Late 1700s:** London is polluted by smoke from the burning of wood and coal fuels. It hangs over the city, and buildings are blackened by soot.

  Today: In 2010, London is reported to be one of the most polluted cities in Europe. The levels of minute particles in the air, caused by vehicle emissions, breach European Union regulations. A report commissioned by the mayor of London concludes that poor air quality causes more than 4,300 deaths in the city every year.

- **Late 1700s:** The British Army finds it difficult to recruit sufficient men during times of war. It recruits through voluntary enlistment, offering a bounty, and also accepts prisoners, pardoning them if they enlist. In addition, two press acts are passed forcing men into service who cannot prove they have a trade or other employment. Men resist the press gangs; some cut off a finger to avoid recruitment; many desert as soon as an opportunity presents itself. In 1793, when Britain goes to war against France, the British Army numbers 13,000 men.

  Today: The British Army is an all-volunteer force that offers an array of benefits to encourage recruitment. In addition to salaries, these include learning a trade while serving, bonuses and bounty payments, subsidized accommodation, free sport facilities, medical and dental care, cut-price rail travel, and a pension scheme, as well as many education benefits. For example, when a soldier leaves the Army, he or she can return to full-time education heavily subsidized by the army through its Enhanced Learning Credits scheme. In 2010, the British Army numbers 98,000 men and women. However, because of budget cuts, that number will decrease in the early 2010s.

---

of what life there was like for many of its inhabitants.

In his draft of the poem "London," preserved in his notebook, Blake used the term "dirty" to describe London's streets and the River Thames. That word did not appear in the final version, but it was no doubt an accurate one. London was in the eighteenth century "a smoky and dirty city," according to David Daiches and John Flower in *Literary Landscapes of the British Isles: A Narrative Atlas*. The authors quote a Swedish visitor to the city who complained that "thick coal smoke" obscured the view of the city on all sides from the top of St. Paul's Cathedral (thus literally blackening the buildings, including the churches, just as Blake describes). As for the dirt, the city did begin to offer street-cleaning services in 1763 to deal with the accumulated filth, but Blake's choice of words suggests that such services left much to be desired.

London was a growing industrial city, and there were at the time no laws regulating child labor. When Blake put the spotlight on the plight of the boy chimney sweepers, there was much to be indignant about. In his biography of

A deserted church *(Meewezen Photography | Shutterstock.com)*

Blake, Peter Ackroyd describes the appalling lives that these young boys were forced to lead. Boys between the ages of four and seven were sold by their parents or taken from the poorhouse and placed in a so-called apprenticeship that was little better than slavery. Ackroyd describes the conditions under which the boys worked:

> There was a great need for their services in London, where the flues were characteristically narrow or twisted so that they easily became constricted. The average size of these vents was something like seven inches square, and the small child was prodded or pushed into the even smaller spaces within; sometimes they were encouraged with poles, or pricked with pins, or scorched with fire to make them climb with more enthusiasm.

Many child chimney sweepers died or were maimed in the course of their work, which began at dawn and ended at midday. After that they were left to roam the streets, hungry and dressed in rags. It was not until well into the 1800s that the British parliament passed a law banning the use of children for climbing chimneys.

In addition to observing the chimney sweeps as he walked the streets, Blake likely came across many discharged soldiers. Their lot was not an easy one. between 1784 and 1785, after the American War of Independence, 160,000 soldiers and sailors were discharged from the British army and navy. Left without employment, many gravitated to London, where they had to survive in any way they could; many became beggars or vagrants or turned to crime.

Blake might most likely knew, and heartily disliked, one method of recruitment used by the army. This was the press system, by which men were forced to join the army. Impressment was used during times of war, when recruitment in sufficient numbers was difficult. Acts of Parliament were passed in 1778 and 1779, for example, during the American War, that permitted the army to recruit from among the poor who had received relief from the local parish under the poor laws. As Sylvia R. Frey points out in "The Common British Soldier in the Late Eighteenth Century: A Profile," this was a way in which the state could control the civilian population:

> Prominent citizens...were aware of growing social problems caused by new economic conditions and complicated by a burgeoning population. The army was seen as the solution to the persistent problem of poverty and disorder exacerbated by the industrial revolution.

CRITICAL OVERVIEW

"London" has consistently attracted the attention of Blake scholars, who have admired its compact form and searing condemnation of social injustice. S. Foster Damon, one of the pioneering scholars of Blake studies, comments in *A Blake Dictionary* that Blake, although he loved London, was also "depressed by its darkness...the pillars of smoke from the mills, and the degradation of its inhabitants: the beggars, the crowds of ragamuffins, the swarms of prostitutes." "London," in Damon's view, is "a record of his depression." E. D. Hirsch, Jr., in *Innocence and Experience: An Introduction to Blake*, describes the poem as one of the "bitterest" of the *Songs of Experience*, a "social satire, directed against social institutions. It implicitly advocates political and social revolution."

During the 1970s, some critics switched the focus of interpretation from the social ills described in the poem to the nature of the speaker himself. D. G. Gillham, in *William Blake*, comments that the speaker is a "lonely wanderer," typical of the kind of speaker found in the *Songs of Experience* generally. Gillham also notes,

> He lives in isolation, but has no freedom to choose to do other than what is required of a social being.... He...cannot reach out to the persons whose cries of distress penetrate his solitude.

Heather Glen, in "Blake's Criticism of Moral Thinking in *Songs of Innocence and of Experience*," approaches the poem from a similar point of view, arguing that the speaker is "obsessive" and indulges in "relentless categorizing." His repetition of certain words reveals that he is "imaginatively bankrupt" and convey "the sense of a harsh, restrictive categorizing which seeks to contain all within its own mould."

E. P. Thompson, however, in the essay "London," one of the most detailed of all readings of the poem, prefers the more traditional view, the emphasis being on what the speaker is denouncing, his "moral realism." Through

> unified images of great power Blake compresses an indictment of the acquisitive ethic, endorsed by the institutions of State, which divides man from man, brings him into mental and moral bondage, destroys the sources of joy, and brings, as its consequence, blindness and death.

The speaker himself exhibits "contemplation and pity" and "grave compassion" in his contemplation of this reality.

More recently, Nicholas Marsh, in *William Blake: The Poems*, sees the poem as a "comprehensive attack on the political and religious establishment." Blake's targets, according to Marsh, include "the economic system...Church hypocrisy... oppression, injustice and suffering...the State... militarism, and...imperialism." In "William Blake's America, 2010," an article that appeared in the *Chronicle of Higher Education*, Mark Edmundson argues that the poem presents a "compressed vision of the state of America now." Describing how Blake condemned the social evils he saw around him, Edmundson sees parallels in today's United States, in which

> great numbers of American children do not get enough to eat. Perhaps they are not starving, but they are hungry.... Meanwhile, rich Americans plunder the nation, taking all they can get and then diving in for more.

CRITICISM

Bryan Aubrey

Aubrey holds a Ph.D. in English. In the following essay, he considers "London" in the context of William Blake's Songs of Innocence and of Experience *as a whole.*

Although William Blake is now regarded as a literary and artistic giant, he was not a well-known figure in his own time. The lower-middle-class artisan who walked the streets of late-eighteenth-century London would not have been much noticed by those he observed. His outward appearance was unremarkable, and he did not lead a very eventful life. However, Blake's inner world was quite different, packed full of visionary spiritual experiences and esoteric philosophical ideas that found expression in his highly original poetry and art.

WHAT DO I READ NEXT?

- Several other poems in Blake's *Songs of Innocence and of Experience* protest the social injustice in London. "The Chimney Sweeper," for example, is a far more explicit attack on the institutions of the church and the monarchy and the plight of the chimney sweepers than that contained in "London." "Holy Thursday" is another attack on the miseries inflicted on children, while "The Garden of Love" amplifies Blake's views on the restrictive sexual morality enforced by the church. These poems can be found in the facsimile edition of *Songs of Innocence and of Experience* published by Tate in 2007.

- Another poem about London is "A Description of the Morning," by the eighteenth-century English satirist Jonathan Swift. It was first published in 1709, nearly a century before Blake's "London." It gives a gritty, realistic rather than romantic, portrait of an early morning in London, as the city comes to life. Swift also mentions a boy chimney sweeper, but his tone is devoid of the biting indignation that characterizes the speaker in Blake's poem. "A Description of the Morning" can be found in *Jonathan Swift: Major Works* (2008), edited by Angus Ross and David Woolley in the Oxford "World's Classics" series.

- Yet another poem about London is William Wordsworth's sonnet "Composed upon Westminster Bridge, September 3, 1802," written less than a decade after Blake's poem. Like Blake, Wordsworth was a romantic poet, but unlike Blake he had no interest in protesting against social injustice. Wordsworth looks out over London from his vantage point on Westminster Bridge and watches the sun rise over the great city. For him, it is a beautiful sight. The poem can be found in many editions of Wordsworth's work, such as *Selected Poems of William Wordsworth*, edited by Mark van Doren (2002).

- Blake had a keen sympathy for the oppressed and the dispossessed, and he would perhaps have understood the anger that pervades "The White City," a poem by Claude McKay written nearly a hundred years after Blake's death. McKay was born in Jamaica and immigrated to the United States, where he became an important figure in the Harlem Renaissance. "The White City" records the anger he feels at a city dominated by white people that excludes him, a black man. The poem can be found in McKay's *Selected Poems* (1999).

- *City Kids: Street and Skyscraper Rhymes* by the well-known American poet X. J. Kennedy, illustrated by Phillipe Beha (2010), are poems that explore and celebrate, with a light touch, life in a vibrant city. The poems show the wide variety of experiences available for children, from the child's point of view.

- *William Blake: The Gates of Paradise* (2006) by Michael Bedard, is a biography of Blake written for a young-adult readership. There are many descriptions of what life in London was like for the less privileged classes during Blake's time, and although Blake's outward life was uneventful, Bedard creates an engaging narrative that reveals Blake's extraordinary creativity and his lifelong devotion to his art. There are many black-and-white illustrations of Blake's work.

At the time Blake wrote "London," he was a man of radical political views, opposed to the established order, although he was not an activist who joined with others to achieve political change. He expressed himself through his art rather than his actions, but underlying Blake's radicalism was far more than a sense of the deep injustices in English society—thousands of his

> BLAKE BELIEVED THAT HUMANS HAD ACCEPTED TOO NARROW A VERSION OF REALITY; THEY HAD CLOSED THEMSELVES OFF FROM THE INFINITE AND HAD TO BE CAJOLED BACK INTO SEEING THINGS THE WAY THEY REALLY ARE."

fellow Englishmen and women shared his feelings about that. Rather, Blake was driven by a personal vision that seems to have sprung from his own spiritual experience, reinforced by what he read in the works of mystical philosophers such as Emanuel Swedenborg and Jacob Boehme.

For Blake, humans were not "fallen" creatures born into a state of original sin, such as the churches taught. They need not go about their lives trying to avoid offending the laws given by a tyrannical God. They should not think of themselves as divided beings, possessing a body (which has bad, sinful desires) and a soul (which is good). They should not have to fight against their natural instincts and desires, trying to conform to what the churches tell them is a good life, which Blake regarded as a miserable travesty of what humans really are. Blake said, again and again and with a passionate, urgent conviction, that human life is something quite different: it flows in the infinite, the eternal; it is joy, delight, and bliss; it is unbounded and unrestricted; it can never be confined, and it does not belong within the restrictive realm of laws and morality.

Blake knew this, so it would seem from his writings and anecdotes about his life told by those who knew him, from his own experience. He seems to have had access, even as a child, to spiritual realms of being. As a boy of eight or ten, walking in Peckham Rye near his home, he looked up and saw a tree filled with angels, their wings covering the boughs of the tree like stars. As a man, he retained this ability to perceive the essence of things, in the sense that he saw the material world as flowing out of the spiritual world, and human life, including the physical body, as a vessel for the divine. In other words, Blake felt that humans are receptacles for divine bliss and joy; this is their essential nature, and not to realize it is to miss the point of life entirely and waste one's existence in a lie.

When in 1790 Blake wrote his exuberant satire, *The Marriage of Heaven and Hell,* in which he celebrates his vision that all life, from the smallest manifestation to the greatest, is holy, it seems as if the energy of the cosmos is flowing through him. He is in the grip of a thrilling new revelation that he absolutely must, and will, convey to others, and he does it through humorous sketches, proverbs in which conventional wisdom is turned upside down, and direct challenges to his readers to see the world differently. Blake believed that humans had accepted too narrow a version of reality; they had closed themselves off from the infinite and had to be cajoled back into seeing things the way they really are.

One model Blake chose to illustrate this more pure form of perception was the child. His *Songs of Innocence*, published in 1789, are illustrations of life as experienced by children. Blake wanted to counter the prevailing church-based view that children are born into original sin and need to have their basically evil natures curbed and broken. In the eighteenth century, infant and child mortality rates were extremely high, and it was better, according to evangelical as well as Methodist church teachings, that a child should have its evil nature thoroughly rectified by a stern moral education than for it to spend eternity in hell. Children should be trained to work hard; idleness was considered a sin, and there were no games at Methodist schools.

Blake saw children quite differently. In *Songs of Innocence*, children do not work, they play, and they are happy. The speakers in these poems, whether children or adults, are representative of a childlike state of innocence. Many of them live in a world in which a spiritual reality underlies all temporal phenomena (in "Night," for example). A compassionate savior God watches over His creation and seeks only to comfort, not to punish ("A Cradle Song" is one example), and the divine is present within the human ("The Divine Image"). The innocent speakers in these poems are playful, open to life, spontaneous, and receptive. They do not burden themselves with guilt; they instead interact joyfully with others. The adults allow the children to play as long as they want ("Nurse's Song").

However, there are also poems in *Songs of Innocence* in which the innocent are exploited. The innocent speakers may not be aware of it, but the reader certainly is ("Holy Thursday" and "The Chimney Sweeper"), and poems such as these anticipate the *Songs of Experience*, which Blake added five years later. The *Songs of Experience* are full of indignation and anger at social injustice and the many ways, both physical and mental, that humans can be enslaved, often with the help of their own passive acceptance of their chains as the way life ought to be and must be. It is not surprising that a man like Blake, who was so acutely attuned to what life might be, raged like a biblical prophet when he observed all the ways in which this divinely human life might be twisted, distorted, reduced, and ruined by those who stood to gain from doing so.

John Milton, the poet whom Blake most admired, once observed that it was the man who had walked in heaven who best understood hell, and that is certainly true of Blake. "London" is a perfect example. As Blake walked the streets of the city he loved, he was simply appalled at the degradation of life that he observed there. The harsh, despairing cries of the oppressed in this poem stand in stark contrast to the happy shouts and laughter of the children who inhabit the *Songs of Innocence*. Something terrible must have happened when the light of innocence slid into the darkness of experience. In innocence, people communicate with each other; in experience, they often talk to themselves or to no one in particular (as in "London") or lose sight of their true nature in negative contemplation or faulty reasoning.

In poem after poem, Blake savagely attacks the kind of thinking, particularly that advanced by the church, that permits such a travesty of the truth to impose an iron grip on so many thousands of his fellow countrymen. "The Human Abstract," for example, shows how the church rationalizes injustice by claiming that without the poor and if everyone was happy, there would be no opportunity to show compassion. Moreover, it is when people are afraid of each other that peace results, because people are too nervous to break the rules imposed on them by their betters.

Of course, in the state of innocence, qualities such as compassion and peace are intrinsic to the human mind and heart; they do not have to be manipulated into existence by heartless church apologists to justify cruelty and deprivation. It was to combating such erroneous beliefs, which were based ultimately on a limited system of principles that failed to perceive the true nature of life, that Blake devoted his entire poetic and artistic career.

Source: Bryan Aubrey, Critical Essay on "London," in *Poetry for Students*, Gale, Cengage Learning, 2012.

Harold Pagliaro

In the following excerpt, Pagliaro examines the flow of the inner state to the outer world in the poem "London."

... The two songs that most intensely represent the powerful overflow of inner state into outer world are "London" and "The Human Abstract." lsqb;The latter is from Blake's *Book of Thel*.] Both have seemed to many readers to say that the destructive work done by humans to their kind can be undone once it is intelligently identified and its unfortunate consequences understood. And yet both poems ultimately imply such complexities of energized psychological and physical damage that one is left wondering whether it can be stopped and its root causes done away with ever. Though for Blake the answer is affirmative, it is by no means simply so. "London" gives us the vision of a speaker who sees and hears by means of human symptoms—facial expressions, cries in the night—their implications for the sufferer and for the world those symptoms disclose. Though his perceptions are extraordinarily intense, they identify the context in which we all live. It is as inappropriate to say about the wanderer through the chartered streets that he perceives selectively as it is to say that Thel does. Both have been moved to respond openly, without psychological deflection of painful impressions, to the destructive forces at work around them. Thel has been prepared for her vision by means of a special past. And the speaker of "London," to judge from his intense and immediate sense of penetration and discovery, has just crossed a threshold of susceptibility to the world around him, having left his customary orientation behind. His routine guard is down, for reasons the poem does not provide. It only affirms that it is so by implying that he observes with a fresh intensity and observes what ordinarily one masks or quickly turns away from or explains factitiously.

Not only are the streets of his London "charter'd"—accounted for in the terms of assigned property and power that deprive many more people than they enrich—so is the flowing

> "NOT ONLY ARE INFANTS, CHIMNEY-SWEEPERS, SOLDIER, MAN, HARLOT CONTROLLED BY DEATH, SO IS LONDON ITSELF, FUTILELY DEFINED BY CHARTER AGAINST CHANGE, AS IF WHAT WERE LEGALLY RENDERED 'IN PERPETUITY' COULD CONTROL MUTABILITY."

Thames, whose movement away from London might otherwise have offered the imagination escape from confinement.

> I wander thro' each charter'd street,
> Near where the charter'd Thames does flow.

The consequences of this implicit demand for control of the whole world, presumably by the few in authority, is recorded in the rest of the poem as the physical and psychological reduction of the many. In fact, the repetition of "every"—"every face," "every cry," "every Infants cry," "every voice," "every ban"—implies the everywhereness of these consequences. And the other early repetition, "mark" or "marks," greatly intensifies their potency. "Weakness" and "woe" have passed into "every face" the speaker meets, the internal affliction having "marked" its human covering with its own significance. This flow of meaning from mind to face continues to the speaker, who "marks" it in the sense that he notices and gives it heed, attention, consideration. The terrible movement is endless.

In Blake's London, the correspondence between inner and outer worlds is suggested in various ways. Chartered streets and river are an expression of the greed of entrepreneurs and others in authority. The weak and woeful state of Londoners comes through their faces. The speaker's sympathetic perceptions become the poem he speaks. In fact, "mind-forging" is an accommodation of inner and outer realities. In this poem of sounds, it accounts for all the notes of distress the speaker hears after he has marked weakness and woe visually. They are the audible consequences of emotional distortion, though of course the mind-forging itself has a basis in the threat of physical power over life and death, the chartered world, with its unjust distribution of good things. Cries of men, cries of infants, cries of chimney-sweeping children, sigh of youthful soldier, curse of youthful harlot, a cacophony of the distraught that culminates in the plagued "Marriage hearse," which is the cry of the speaker himself. Psychological and physical disease have everywhere come together, and in this context the promise of life has become the carriage of death.

The series in some ways implies its own continuity of disease from unfortunate harlot to man and, through marriage, to infant, youth, harlot. No one is untouched and no one can be cured in the painfully lifelike fiction of this system. And beyond the cycle of disease in love and marriage are the intimations of another. Owners order and control the physical world everywhere—river as well as streets—supported by "Church," whose priests permit the utter exploitation of its children, and by "Palace," which calls on soldier's blood to maintain the status quo of chartered things, or, alternatively, which is to be overthrown by the soldiers it exploits after the "apocalyptic omen of mutiny and civil war..." appears in blood on its walls. Everywhere, authority confines the lives of the many and makes use of their flesh, in terminal work or war or prostitution, as if it were the currency of the reduced world.

In the *Songs* and elsewhere, Blake understands that the world, like his London, has been brought to its terrible state by a combination of natural and social causes, which promise death. For as long as fear determines psychological and physical behavior, it multiplies constraint and intensifies humanity's confinement. Not only are Infants, Chimney-sweepers, Soldier, Man, Harlot controlled by death, so is London itself, futilely defined by charter against change, as if what were legally rendered "in perpetuity" could control mutability. And so are those who control the charter, taken in as they are by the greediest illusion of Selfhood, that natural life can be mastered by natural means. Obviously at one level Blake wants to save the victims of this greed. He was a reformer who certainly favored measures for improving the general well being of the socially exploited. But he was not like Hobbes or Godwin, or Coleridge in the days of Pantisocracy, a thinker whose social remedies relied ultimately on natural methods. Blake never dismisses the physical world. Rather he is deeply concerned that its perception by the eyes of fear, which have reduced it to a place of misery, must be understood, for the sake of the liberty from fear such understanding may bring. But the youthful Harlot's curse in the midnight streets of London is a far cry from the Bard's promised "break of day," whatever redemptive value there maybe in it for "London's" speaker.

As if it were a gloss on "London," "The Human Abstract" opens by indicting a destructive social behavior, the general human willingness to provide the grounds for Pity, an ostensible virtue, by allowing people to be poor and therefore pitiable; and it concludes by locating the problem, and by implication its solution, in the "Human Brain." The opening stanza also treats Mercy as it has treated Pity, as a virtue resting on social culpability: "And Mercy no more could be, / If all were as happy as we." The transition to the next stanza is cryptic, suitable to the speaker's movement from outside world to inside mind. But it soon becomes clear that in the first line of the second stanza he is explaining how the injustices he has identified are maintained. He points out that all involved in the unconscious conspiracy to provide the grounds for pity and mercy, and all for whom pity and mercy may be felt—the poor and unhappy—are so afraid of each other that the result is a momentary social stability; "mutual fear brings peace." But this gives way in the minds of those who have the upper hand. Out of self-interest, spurred by cruelty, in whose name the unmasking speaker has them operate, the exploiters cunningly identify and pretend to believe in an otherworldly or holy basis of human affairs and they imply their own proprietary control of this holiness. With expressions of false humility, they induce the exploited, who are already frightened, humbly to accept their own adversity.

> And mutual fear brings peace;
> Till the selfish loves increase.
> Then Cruelty knits a snare,
> And spreads his baits with care.
> He sits down with holy fears,
> And waters the ground with tears:
> Then Humility takes its root
> Underneath his foot.

The personified Cruelty of the exploiters, having succeeded in this first part of his program of human management, extends his control through the growth of Mystery from the root of Humility. That is, he takes advantage of the fear and pliability of the exploited, institutionalizing their low status by getting them to believe their well-being is located in the context of Mystery, which seems to sponsor his authority, though it is his own brainchild. Reduced to unthinking reproductive entities which grow out of each other and no more—"catterpiller" and "butterfly"—they believe themselves nourished by Mystery. But its fruit is a lie, borne by the tree that harbors not life, but death (the Raven).

> Soon spreads the dismal shade
> Of Mystery over his head;
> And the Catterpiller and Fly,
> Feed on the Mystery.
> And it bears the fruit of Deceit,
> Ruddy and sweet to eat;
> And the Raven his nest has made
> In its thickest shade.

Finally, it becomes clear that the most thorough search of the natural world reveals no sign at all of this Tree of Mystery. Its only habitat is the human mind.

> The Gods of the earth and sea,
> Sought thro' Nature to find this Tree
> But their search was all in vain:
> There grows one in the Human Brain

Both "The Human Abstract" and "London" are concerned with two very closely related matters—the mind's constrained predicament and the fact that the manacles that constrain it are "mind-forg'd." In both poems, the speaker reveals his awareness that the manacles have been abstracted from the mind and methodized as institutions. In "London," the institution is chartering, the legalized acquisition of rights (property, authority) by the few against the many. In "The Human Abstract," the institution is (at the first level) religion, the church-sanctified acquisition of authority by the few over the many. But the poems complement each other. Each gives its major emphasis to one of the two matters. "London" stresses humanity's predicament, and "The Human Abstract" stresses the making and the operation of the mind-forged manacles. This division of interests, incidentally, is well supported by the illustrations to the poems.

The speaker's vision in "London" identifies the "limits of opacity"; the world of night he sees there is defined by death ("Marriage hearse"), not life. Yet the very fact that his vision is as close to darkness as it is implies some liberty from Selfhood's control. He sees worldly things for what they are, and he is no longer capable of turning away or accepting the intolerable as tolerable. More important, his vision is shaped so intensely that we as readers may share with him something of his clarified sense for the fullness and continuousness of destruction and pain. By contrast, the speaker of "The Human Abstract" seems to have stepped back from human anguish. From the nature of his immense practical wisdom, we may conclude that he has perceived that anguish sympathetically in the past. But as we encounter him, he is regarding it ironically. Human virtue, he says, is a luxury we make possible by the cruel handling of our fellows. As he moves quickly from human misery to his chief subject, mental operations, the immediacy and intensity of his involvement increase. Like the speaker of "London," he finds death to be the beneficiary of the mind's coercions. What death begins by nourishing—the mind's intermittent willingness to make life an exercise in survival—it ends by controlling, to the disadvantage of both outer life and the life within. Also like the speaker of "London," he understands false vision—sees how it works—and this too is a sign of his increasing power of eternal vision. But he takes a further step by denying a truly visionary correlation between mind and outer world as the basis for the holy Mystery, the archetype of institutional and familial coercion. The responsible agent is the human brain. Taken singly and together, these two poems imply both the mind's (hence the body's) enormous susceptibility to the coercive force of other minds, and the mind's capacity to discover that imposition, which is the beginning of redemptive control.

Of course physical death itself exists in Blake's world. But it is chiefly as a mind-forging threat that death appears in the *Songs*, usually in the form of one of its proxies, or as a means of characterizing the minds and lives death has come to dominate—Marriage hearse, Raven, clothes of death, coffins of black, graves in the Garden of Love, shaken blossoms, the School Boy's nipped buds and so on. The proportions of this usage correlate well with Blake's own view of things. Though he is profoundly interested in mind and world and how the two work on each other, and though he sees the heavy hand of death in both, he himself is not emotionally arrested by the fact of mortality. Even in the management of Thel, who is so arrested, Blake the artist controls her unprotected mind and presents its brief exposure to experience so as to make psychological process, rather than morbidity, the matter of interest. Aware of death's enormous power over life, including his own, no doubt, Blake can see the worst and yet understand the best the imagination is capable of in response to it. He was well able to balance his sense that Los and Enitharmon, our representatives, are "Terrified at Non Existence / For such they deemd the death of the body," with his conviction that "When the mortal disappears in improved knowledge cast away / . . . so shall the Mortal gently fade away / And so become invisible to those who still remain."

Death nevertheless reveals itself in compelling physical ways for Blake. Given the "little curtain of flesh on the bed of our desire," and the "tender curb upon the youthful burning boy," can it be only mind-forging by the "Selfish father of men" that accounts for Earth's being held by a "heavy chain, / That does freeze [her] bones around"? Or is it that the natural world and the people in it are intractably mortal? If Blake entertained this conclusion, he probably did so in the way most do who waver at times about vital matters knowable only in the imagination. Perhaps he had doubts. But he had a strong overriding belief, psychologically grounded, that though the world's coercers "impress on men the fear of death; . . . / Trembling & fear, terror, constriction; abject selfishness," it is possible "to teach Men to despise death & to go on / In fearless majesty annihilating Self." Certainly he could teach himself well enough that about a year before he died he was able to say to Henry Crabb Robinson that he could not "consider death as anything but a removing from one room to another."

But the world most people live in is a terrible place, as "Earth's Answer," "A Little Girl Lost," "The Human Abstract," and "London," no less than The Argument of *The Marriage of Heaven and Hell* or the song of the Bard in *Milton*, make dreadfully clear. Fortunately, certain of the *Songs of Experience* allow us to observe the psychology of self-discovery that begins one's liberation from that world. One of these is the mischievous "Infant Sorrow," from which this chapter takes its title. But others represent the mind so profoundly controlled by manacles that it seems not to have a chance to mediate between its error-filled vision of life and eternity. These apparently transfixed minds seem almost beyond salvation. It is the study of particulars identifying their state that must engage us. We know they can be saved. The interesting intermediate question is, what must they overcome on their journey?

Source: Harold Pagliaro, "Into the Dangerous World," in *Selfhood and Redemption in Blake's "Songs,"* Pennsylvania State University Press, 1987, pp. 35–51.

SOURCES

Ackroyd, Peter, *Blake: A Biography*, Knopf, 1996, p. 124.

Blake, William, "London," in *Blake's Poetry and Designs*, edited by Mary Lynn Johnson and John E. Grant, W. W. Norton, 1979, p. 53.

Curtis, Edward E., *The Organization of the British Army in the American Revolution*, Yale University Press, 1926, http://www.americanrevolution.org/britisharmy3.html (accessed May 23, 2011).

Daiches, David, and John Flower, *Literary Landscapes of the British Isles: A Narrative Atlas*, Paddington Press, 1979, p. 47.

Damon, S. Foster, *A Blake Dictionary: The Ideas and Symbols of William Blake*, Thames and Hudson, 1973, p. 244.

Edmundson, Mark, "William Blake's America, 2010," in *Chronicle of Higher Education*, October 24, 2010, http://chronicle.com/article/William-Blakes-America-2010/125024/ (accessed May 21, 2011).

Fox, Robert, "British Army Could Shrink to Its Smallest Since the Boer War," in *London Evening Standard*, June 7, 2010, http://www.thisislondon.co.uk/standard/article-23842126-british-army-could-shrink-to-its-smallest-size-since-the-boer-war.do (accessed May 24, 2011).

Frey, Sylvia R., "The Common British Soldier in the Late Eighteenth Century: A Profile," in *Societas*, Vol. 5, Spring 1975, p. 119.

Gillham, D. G., *William Blake*, Cambridge University Press, 1973, p. 116.

Glen, Heather, "Blake's Criticism of Moral Thinking in *Songs of Innocence and of Experience*," in *Interpreting Blake*, edited by Michael Phillips, Cambridge University Press, 1978, pp. 57–58.

Hirsch, E. D., Jr., *Innocence and Experience: An Introduction to Blake*, Yale University Press, 1964, p. 94.

Jarrett, Derek, *Britain: 1688–1815*, Longman, 1970, p. 408.

"London Population," in *London Online*, http://www.londononline.co.uk/factfile/population/ (accessed May 23, 2011).

Marriott, John, "The Spatiality of the Poor in Eighteenth-Century London," in *The Streets of London: From the Great Fire to the Great Stink*, edited by Tim Hitchcock and Heather Shore, Rivers Oram Press, 2003, p. 131.

Marsh, Nicholas, *William Blake: The Poems*, Palgrave, 2001, p. 129.

Thompson, E. P., "London," in *Interpreting Blake*, edited by Michael Phillips, Cambridge University Press, 1978, pp. 18, 21–22.

Vidal, John, "London Air Pollution 'Worst in Europe,'" in *Guardian* (London, England), June 25, 2010, http://www.guardian.co.uk/environment/2010/jun/25/london-air-pollution-europe (accessed May 23, 2011).

FURTHER READING

Ackroyd, Peter, *London: The Biography*, Nan A. Talese, 2000.
> This contemporary book offers a lively history of London from prehistory to modern times. Ackroyd represents London as a living thing and writes with the aplomb that he uses in his fiction.

Bayne-Powell, Rosamond, *Eighteenth-Century London Life*, E. P. Dutton, 1938.
> Although published many years ago, this book remains one of the best surveys of life in the London that Blake would have known.

Michael, Jennifer Davis, *Blake and the City*, Associated University Presses, 2006, pp. 67–74.
> Michael examines "London" to show how compassion can emerge when people become aware of the way society is structured. She additionally attempts to bridge the gap between the transcendental and historical interpretations of the poem.

Roberts, Jonathan, *William Blake's Poetry: A Reader's Guide*, Continuum, 2007.
> Understanding Blake is a big task for those new to his work. This concise 124-page introduction is a good place to start. Roberts writes in a fresh and engaging way, and this is a reliable guide to Blake's thought and how to read his poems.

SUGGESTED SEARCH TERMS

William Blake

William Blake AND London

London

Songs of Experience

Songs of Innocence and of Experience

Eighteenth-century London

boy AND chimney sweepers

Blake AND Emanuel Swedenborg

William Blake AND church

Blake AND illuminated books

Songs of Innocence and of Experience AND William Blake

William Blake AND romanticism

Loveliest of Trees, the Cherry Now

A. E. HOUSMAN

1896

Alfred Edward Housman's *A Shropshire Lad* precisely caught the mood of England at the end of the Victorian age. The poem cycle combines a nearly sentimentalized view of youth with a nearly sentimentalized view of death. The second poem in *A Shropshire Lad*, "Loveliest of Trees, the Cherry Now," eloquently expresses the brevity of human life and its fragility compared to the beauty of the natural world. Through a complex tapestry of allusion, the poem calls on the reader to experience that beauty before it is too late, and the chance is missed in death. That call is all the more poignant because the circumstances of Housman's life made it impossible to experience the happiness he desired. Behind his back, Housman was sometimes called a maiden aunt, that is, someone who failed in meeting society's expectations, eschewing the personal satisfaction of making a relationship and substituting service to a more extended family. There is an undeniable kernel of truth in the accusation. Housman compensated for any failure in his private life by throwing himself into his work as a professor, becoming one of the most important classical scholars of modern times. *A Shropshire Lad* is one of the most beloved collections of English poetry.

AUTHOR BIOGRAPHY

Housman was born on March 26, 1859, in Fockbury, Worcestershire, England. His father was a solicitor (a lawyer). His younger brother Laurence

A. E. Housman (Getty Images)

also became a poet and acted as Housman's literary executor. Housman attended Bromsgrove, an English public school, part of the aristocratic educational system that produced the British Empire's intellectual and cultural elite. While at school, Housman won prizes for his poetry, including his "The Death of Socrates." He won a scholarship to St. John's college, Oxford. By chance he became the roommate of Moses Jackson, a popular athlete who rowed for Oxford and went on to a career as a secondary educator in various parts of the British Empire. Housman fell in love with Jackson, a love that formed the emotional ground of Housman's whole life. Jackson, however, had no interest in a homosexual relationship and so could not return Housman's affections. He did befriend Housman, however, later arranging Housman's job in a patent office and making Housman the godfather of one of his children.

Housman failed reading classics at Oxford. While he did much work in philology as an undergraduate that would eventually stand up to peer review publication, he completely neglected other parts of the curriculum, such as history and philosophy, and he failed his final exams. In as much as he left whole sections of his exam books blank, it has been speculated that he simply refused to write on areas of scholarship that did not interest him, or that he suffered some kind of mental breakdown caused by a crisis in his relationship with Jackson. In any case, Housman did not obtain an undergraduate degree, which seemed to end any chance he had of becoming a classical scholar.

After 1879, Housman began working as a clerk in the patent office, however, and devoted all of his free time to the publication of articles in the classics. In particular, he proposed a number of improvements to the text of the Roman poet Propertius. These were so impressive that when he applied for a teaching post at University College London in 1892, he obtained it, despite his lack of formal qualifications. In 1896, Housman published *A Shropshire Lad*, a collection of poetry written in English (Housman also wrote poetry in Latin) that quickly became one of the most beloved works of Victorian literature. (After several publishers rejected him, Housman had to self-publish the work, which contains "Loveliest of Trees, the Cherry Now.") The collection seemed out of place to his colleagues and students, who knew him as a stern, reclusive, and eccentric professor. In 1922, Housman published *Last Poems*, expressly for the purpose of allowing Jackson (who by then was dying of cancer in Canada) to see more of his work. After Housman's death, his brother Laurence published *More Poems* at his direction, and since then a number of his manuscript poems have also been collected and published. Housman's entire poetic oeuvre was finally edited in 1997 by Archie Burnett.

In 1911, Housman became the Kennedy Professor of Latin at Trinity College, Cambridge, a further acknowledgement of his importance as a scholar. His editions of Juvenal and Lucan, and especially Manilius (which was dedicated to Jackson), established Housman as the leading British text critic of his generation. Housman died of heart disease on April 30, 1936, at a nursing home near Cambridge.

POEM TEXT

Lovliest of trees, the cherry now
Is hung with bloom along the bough,
And stands about the woodland ride

Wearing white for Eastertide.
Now, of my threescore years and ten,   5
Twenty will not come again,
And take from seventy springs a score,
It only leaves me fifty more.

And since to look at things in bloom
Fifty springs are little room,   10
About the woodlands I will go
To see the cherry hung with snow.

POEM SUMMARY

The text used for this summary is from *The Poems of A. E. Housman*, edited by Archie Burnett, Clarendon, 1997, pp. 4–5. A version of the poem can be found on the following Web page: http://www.housman-society.co.uk/loveliest-trees.htm.

"Loveliest of Tress, the Cherry Now" is the second poem in Housman's volume *A Shropshire Lad*. It consists of twelve lines divided into three four-line stanzas (quatrains). The poem is spoken in a narrative persona that is ostensibly that of the Shropshire lad (identified as Terrence in later poems in the cycle), but critics have increasingly realized that the detachment of the persona from the events described detracts from any such simple identification. The persona describes himself walking through the countryside overcome by the beauty of nature and then by realization of the shortness of human life, resulting in a new urgency in his desire to enjoy nature while he can.

Stanza 1

The first stanza describes a path through the forest crowded with cherry trees heavy with their white blossoms. The time is Easter or not long after. Easter can fall almost any time in March or April. Since (as will be revealed in the last line), there is snow on the ground in England, the date is likely to be earlier rather than later. Eastertide is a sacred division of the year used in the Church calendar and is the fifty days following Easter. Within liturgical symbolism, white is the color for Easter. Easter, which marks the crucifixion and resurrection of Jesus for Christians, is a symbol of death and regeneration, but it would seem in the context of the poem, and of *A Shropshire Lad* as a whole, that death is the more important reference here.

MEDIA ADAPTATIONS

- "Loveliest of Trees, the Cherry Now" has been set as an art song by several composers. The first to do so was Arthur Somervell in 1904, as the first song of his cycle *A Shropshire Lad*.

- The most popular setting of the poem to music is by George Butterworth, the first of his *Six Songs from "A Shropshire Lad"* (1911). Butterworth set six more of Housman's poems the following year in *Breden Hill and Other Songs*. Butterworth was killed fighting on the Somme in 1916.

- Two recent settings of "Loveliest of Trees, the Cherry Now" to music include the arrangement by Annetta Hamilton Rosser, published in her *An Offering of Song* in 1977, and a 1992 arrangement by John Linton Gardner.

Although it is a personal judgment, for anyone who has seen a thickly planted grove of cherry trees in bloom, it would be hard to argue that it is not indeed the most beautiful of trees. Their loveliness has inspired a longstanding custom of cherry blossom viewing parties in Japan, which has been transplanted to a lesser degree to the United States. Even outside of this literary context, it is obvious that the cherry had a special personal significance for Housman. His boyhood home of Perry Hall had an especially beautiful tree that was something of a local tourist attraction. In the fragments of Housman's diary that survive from the 1890s (the years in which he composed *A Shropshire Lad*), he frequently mentions the blossoming of the cherries in London (usually during the last few days of March and lasting as late as mid-May), and it is known he spoke on the same subject freely to his acquaintances. In the late 1920s, Housman used his influence at Cambridge to have large areas of the campus relandscaped with cherry trees.

Stanza 2

The second stanza proceeds in an entirely different direction, and with an entirely different tone. Although the persona now speaks in the first person, the material is completely abstract and detached. It is in fact the presentation of a mathematical equation in poetical form. The speaker takes the biblically allotted (Psalms 90:10) span of life of three score years and ten (seventy years, since a score stands for twenty in the same way a dozen stands for twelve). From this he subtracts his current age of twenty and concludes that he may expect fifty more years of life. But when he produces the answer, he speaks not of years but of springs, using in the trope of synecdoche (naming the whole by one of its parts). This relates back to the first stanza. The persona is not interested in life, but in the best part of life, symbolized by the beauty of the cherry blossoms that bloom in the spring. This stanza harkens back to a treatment of the same matter Housman had made in prose, in his introductory lecture delivered in 1892 in *Selected Prose*, when he took up his position at University College London. He wrote, "The complexity of the universe is infinite, and the days of a man's life are threescore years and ten." What he is getting at is the disparity between how much a human wishes to learn compared to how short the time is that has been allotted for that task. In the poem, learning has been replaced with living. It may be that for Housman the two things were more closely allied than for most.

Stanza 3

If the first stanza stands as a thesis of beauty, the second the antithesis of mortality, the third stands as a synthesis of the two that draws the poem to its conclusion. Compared to the intensity of the experience of seeing the beauty of the cherry blossoms, fifty springs are too few to fully enjoy the experience, so the persona resolves to devote himself to contemplation. The futility of this task is emphasized in the last line. The white cherry blossoms are now covered with snow (and spring snows are nothing unusual in England), so the birth of beauty that they symbolize is limited by the icy white shroud of death. This sums up the meaning of the poem in a single image. The person must take pleasure in beauty while he can, for the time granted is swiftly coming to an end.

THEMES

Death

Descriptions of the boughs of cherry trees heavy with blossoms and coated with spring snow make up the main physical imagery of "Loveliest of Trees, the Cherry Now." In itself, this image reconciles life and death symbolized in the new growth of the flowers and chill white blanket of the snow. Moreover the speaker laments that he has only a brief human lifetime to appreciate the beauty of the spring blossoms, perhaps fifty more springs before he inevitably succumbs to death. The immediate implication of the poem's imagery is that beauty is rare and fleeting, and one had better take as much as one can before it is too late. This is a common theme in literature, going back to Roman poet Horace with his dictum of *carpe diem* (seize the day), and was a very popular one in the Victorian period. Compare, for example, the painting *Gather Ye Rosebuds While Ye May* (1909) by the pre-Raphaelite artist William Waterhouse, whose image of two girls picking flowers (natural beauty cut-off in death at the same instant it is fully experienced) conveys the same idea.

The meaning of death in the "Loveliest of Trees, the Cherry Now," however, takes on greater significance when the poem is considered as part of the whole cycle of *A Shropshire Lad*. A major theme in this larger work is the untimely death of young men, especially in the wars that sustained the British Empire (for example in the first poem, "From Clee to Heaven the Beacon Burns"). Viewed in this light, "Loveliest of Trees, the Cherry Now" becomes more poignant since, while the twenty-year-old speaker expects to live to see another fifty springs, he might instead have his life cut short while still in his youth. In the minds of many readers after World War I, the millions of parents of the British war dead, this expression of death, and of death coming in youth, expressed in the beautiful image of the snow-laden cherry boughs, became positively funereal. It is a parallel case to *Banks of Green Willow*, a musical composition by George Butterworth (who also set to music "Loveliest of Trees, the Cherry Now" and who himself died at age thirty-one while fighting in Flanders), another bucolic (rural and idyllic) evocation of natural beauty that was reinterpreted after 1918 to serve as a memorial hymn to the war dead. Moreover, "Loveliest of Trees, the Cherry Now" contains this whole complex of imagery within

TOPICS FOR FURTHER STUDY

- As a class reading "Loveliest of Trees, the Cherry Now," before students see the printed poem, have one student look at the text and copy it out by hand (or perhaps just the first stanza, if time is pressing), then give what he has written to the next student to copy and so on until each student has made a copy seeing only the copy produced by his neighbor (this could go on during another class activity). When this is done, give a Xeroxed copy of the last copy to all students and have them compare it to the printed original, noting any errors and conjecturing about how they arose. The teacher or a chosen student could then survey the results and give a general talk on how the text was changed. This provides students with some idea of the problems involved in the text criticism work done by Housman on classical pieces.

- "Loveliest of Trees, the Cherry Now" is a popular subject for videos on Web sites like YouTube. Make your own video in which you read the poem and illustrate with a slide show of appropriate images. If you have musical bent, do the same while singing one of the many musical settings.

- Many parks and botanical gardens in the United States host cherry blossom viewing festivals each spring, in imitation of the Japanese custom. If you can, attend such a viewing for firsthand experience. Search for information about the practice using traditional and online sources, especially searching blogs and photo sharing sites like Flickr. How has this Japanese custom become integrated into American culture? To what extent does it form a nexus with other practices imported from Japan, such as cosplay? To what extent is its social context in the United States different from in Japan? Note that in 2011, cherry blossom festivals in the United States became a nexus for memorialization and fund-raising for the earthquake in Japan, while in Japan the practice was largely curtailed in 2011 so as to not make an ostentatious display in the face of disaster. Lead a class discussion (perhaps using a PowerPoint presentation to display images or video) concerning the role of cherry blossom viewing as a bridge between cultures. Using transliterated search terms such as *sakura* (cherry blossom) or *hanami* (cherry blossom viewing party) will provide many useful Internet sources.

- Housman wrote "Loveliest of Trees, the Cherry Now" in middle age, after he was well established in his career, and the shape of his life had been largely set. Most students using this text, however, will be teenagers with an unknown future before them. How does Housman's perspective seem different from yours? Write a poem on the theme of *carpe diem* (seize the day) from a youthful perspective.

- Many places in the United States hold an annual beauty pageant in which a local high school girl is named as Cherry Blossom Princess or Queen. Such an experience forms the basis of Marjorie Homes's 1982 young-adult novel *Cherry Blossom Princess*. Imagining that you are a contestant in such a pageant, and that each contestant must answer a question explaining her cherry blossom philosophy, reformulate the sentiments expressed in Housman's "Loveliest of Trees, the Cherry Now" as a speech in answer to such a question.

---

itself, though in a very compressed and referential manner. The speaker on the one hand assumes that he can look forward to the biblically allotted life-span of threescore years and ten, or seventy years. But on the other hand, his viewing of the cherry takes place shortly after Easter, which is the commemoration of the execution of Jesus (suggested also by the word

In stanza 1, the speaker is enjoying the cherry blossoms of the spring. (Smileus | Shutterstock.com)

hung, referring to the crucifixion). According to Christian tradition, this occurred when Jesus was thirty-three years old, and so he stands as the archetype of young life cut off at its prime. This juxtaposition of ideal ages, all by itself, makes the speaker's hope of a longer life uncertain at best.

Nature

The Victorian era saw the transformation of Britain from a rural society to an urban one based on industrial production. This resulted in the creation of an idealized view of the past—a past that never actually existed—that is natural, countrified, and medieval, everything that the modern world is not. This sentimental construct is sometimes called Merry England. It was propagated through children's literature such as Beatrix Potter's animal tales, and in the medievalist element of the pre-Raphaelite and arts and crafts movements, as well as the creation of a whole false past of fairy mythology, Christmas Carols, Morris Dancing, and May Day celebrations that were either invented or substantially transformed in the Victorian period. Writers like Thomas Hardy and composers like Ralph Vaughn Williams also invoke this idealized, pastoral, image of Britain. A notable achievement of this movement was the fantasy literature created by J. R. R. Tolkien. In the early 1930s, Tolkien created in his character Tom Bombadil a spirit embodying the Oxfordshire countryside that was fast being swallowed up by urban sprawl, a remembrance of things that were not quite the real past.

Housman's *A Shropshire Lad* has many points of contact with this kind of idealization of the lost natural world of the English countryside. This fictional Shropshire is a land inhabited by peasants tormented by ghosts and an overwhelming sense of loss. To live in London, the modern city, is to be constantly dying. The sense of bleak nostalgia is the strongest feature of Housman's poems, and what made them so quickly successful, as they caught a popular mood. Literature about the beauty of nature was, not surprisingly, in great demand among soldiers fighting in the trenches during World War I. In a letter of April 14, 1934, to his friend Houston Martin, Housman confessed that he chose the name of Shropshire because of the romantic image the name had in his memories of childhood. But the bucolic ideal is something that Housman is inventing, rather than recalling. Housman had never even been to Shropshire before the publication of his famous poetry collection. While the Shropshire hills are a rural countryside of great natural beauty, now protected from development by the British government, Shropshire was also the birthplace of the British iron-working industry in the eighteenth century that sparked the industrial revolution, a pertinent fact that Housman does not seem to have been aware of, or was at least uninterested in.

The second poem in *A Shropshire Lad*, "Loveliest of Trees, the Cherry Now," does not take place in any particular time, or indeed any particular place, but rather narrates with great lyrical beauty the speaker's realization that the meaning of his existence is stored up in the vision of the natural world with cherry trees coming into blossom against the background of the snow-covered earth. The speaker intends to hold onto this vision throughout a long life, but the larger context of the cycle shows this is clearly impossible, as death will soon come, from the needs of the empire, or the breakdown of family and society in irrational passions.

STYLE

Allusion
In a quotation, an author reproduces the exact words of an earlier author. An allusion is a reference to a familiar character, real person, event, or concept, used to make an idea more easily understood. For example, describing someone as a "Romeo" makes an allusion to William Shakespeare's famous young lover in *Romeo and Juliet*. In "Loveliest of Trees, the Cherry Now," Housman quotes threescore years and ten from the King James version of Psalms 90:10, the only biblical text in which that exact order of the words occurs, but he alludes to many more works than that. The conceit of blossoms hanging of the bough in line 2 recalls Shakespeare's *The Tempest*, v.i. 94–96. Lines 3 and 4 echo "The Last Maying" (1885) by Andrew Lang, while the final two lines of Housman's poem recall the fourth poem in Robert Louis Stevenson's *Underwoods* (1887). So while Housman was writing in 1895, he had on the surface of his mind lines of Shakespeare and two recent poems.

Poetics
Housman set out his thoughts on the art of poetry in his lecture *The Name and Nature of Poetry*. For him, poetry was about the effect of the beauty of language on the reader; the meaning of the poem was at best irrelevant and might even distract from the enjoyment of it. He wrote, "Poetry is not the thing said but a way of saying it." Indeed, he had little patience for literary critics trying to find meaning in poems. He expresses greater interest, therefore, in what he calls the "Artifice of Versification," by which he means the "scientific" application of the traditional forms of meter and rhyme to verse. (He clearly could not imagine a poetry of the modern kind which rejected these formal structures.) He discussed the consideration of

> the reason why some lines of different length will combine harmoniously while others can only be so combined by great skill or good luck;...why, of two pairs of rhymes, equally correct and both consisting of the same vowels and consonants, one is richer to the mental ear and the other poorer.

While this might seem to dispose Housman to a nearly mechanical type of composition, turning out lines like shaping wood on a lathe, in describing the composing of the last poem in *A Shropshire Lad*, he wrote:

> Two of the Stanzas...came into my head, just as they are printed, while I was crossing the corner of Hampstead Heath.... A third stanza came with a little coaxing after tea. One more was needed, but it did not come: I had to turn and compose it myself, and that was a laborious business. I wrote it thirteen times, and it was more than a twelvemonth before I got it right.

Housman seems to have gone through much the same process, though perhaps not so protractedly, in "Loveliest of Trees, the Cherry Now," since in the notebook in which it was originally written out, the first and third stanzas are written very fluidly and rapidly without corrections, while the second stanza comes on the following page and shows evidence of a much more difficult composition with many corrections. In any case, it seems that his advice about composition applies only to the "laborious business," and Housman is claiming that the other parts of his work came, as it were, by inspiration, which is, on the face of it, paradoxical. No doubt the same process went on in both cases, but at different mental speeds. The fact that the second stanza is more repetitive and relies so heavily on the biblical threescore and ten formula makes it more of a merely technical problem to solve, in contrast to the freer development of the other two.

"Loveliest of Trees, the Cherry Now" is composed of three four-line stanzas of iambic trimeter, meaning that each line consist of three iambic feet—an unstressed followed by a stressed syllable—or an allowable substitution. Each stanza follows an *AABB* rhyme scheme, meaning that the endings of the first and second lines rhyme, and the endings of the third and fourth lines rhyme. The caesura, or stop, in the middle of the first line is reminiscent of medieval English poetry, and creates a majestic effect, adding to the rather old-fashioned effect of the poem's form and vocabulary. While some of the poems in *A Shropshire Lad* are plagued by dead lines where the irregular meter detracts from the lyric unity of the composition, "Loveliest of Trees, the Cherry Now" is perfect in that respect, accounting, no doubt, for its frequent musical setting.

HISTORICAL CONTEXT

Victorian Classical Scholarship

Classics is the study of literature written in Greek and Latin during and before the period of the Roman Empire (roughly 750 BCE to 750 CE). Victorian British society, particularly the ruling class, whose power was based partly on ancestral aristocratic privilege and partly on wealth generated from the new industrial economy, consciously modeled their own worldwide empire, which stretched from Canada to India, Australia, and Hong Kong, on the Roman Empire. Accordingly, education in the classics, especially in the system of elite public (really private in American terms) schools and at the two great universities of Oxford and Cambridge, became the basis for professional careers in politics, government service, and business.

Housman, the son of a not particularly successful or prominent lawyer, went through this system, going to Bromsgrove school and on scholarship to Oxford. His command of classical languages was exceptional, even in an age when every educated person read at least Latin fluently. As an undergraduate, Housman began to devote himself to text criticism, the most difficult and important part of classical scholarship. Ancient books were written out by hand and copied by hand. Eventually copies were made from other copies through several generations of manuscripts. Errors were made by the scribes every time a copy was made for a variety of reasons, from simple carelessness to the scribe thinking he was making a correction, but was actually making a new mistake through misunderstanding. Textual criticism is the art of examining all the surviving manuscripts of a given text, taking all variants into account, and trying to determine what the author originally meant to say. Housman was a genius at this. Even as a student at Oxford, he did important work on the text of the Roman poet Propertius that advanced scholarly understanding of the text beyond the work of any previous critic. But the Greats curriculum at Oxford (*Litterae Humaniores*) required a broader context in ancient studies, with detailed learning in history, philosophy, and archaeology, areas that held little interest for Housman's monomaniacal personality. Whatever the proximate cause of his failure in his final exams, it was his lack of study in these areas that prevented him from receiving his formal degree.

Nevertheless, his work while at university, and then as a private scholar, marked him out as probably the greatest British classicist of his generation. His talent was eventually rewarded with teaching posts, regardless of the formalities of a degree. Housman's first position at University College London was essentially training bureaucrats who had no professional interest in classics. Once he moved to Cambridge, he was able to take up the more suitable work of training the next generation of classics professors. Housman produced a huge body of scholarship, beginning with work on Horace and Propertius, and eventually making fundamental editions of the Roman Poets Lucan and Juvenal. His greatest work, however, was his edition of the astronomical poet Manilius. Ancient astronomy was an almost unknown field in Housman's time because, inextricably linked in the ancient mind with astrology, it did not seem quite respectable to a generation reared on science and the industrial revolution. Besides his magisterial edition of Manilius, Housman was able to resolve long-standing questions and problems concerning other ancient astronomical writers, as well as to make fundamental contributions to the entries on the technical terms of astronomy in the Greek lexicon being edited at the end of the nineteenth century by Henry Liddell and Robert Scott, still the standard Greek dictionary used today.

COMPARE & CONTRAST

- **1890s:** The study of classics (Greek and Latin literature) is seen as culturally vital to British society, and a university degree is the usual path to careers in government or business.

  Today: The classics, often dismissed as elitist, are marginal in modern British culture, and degrees in classics are generally sought mostly as an introduction to fields of study such as law or English literature, or by a relatively small number of students dedicated to philology.

- **1890s:** Typewriters have little impact on scholarly and literary writing, and manuscripts sent to publishers are still generally written out by hand. (Housman never learned to type and prepared his fair copies in an exquisitely beautiful book hand.) Mechanical means of type compositing, such as linotype, are still new and rare. Printing plates are assembled by hand from font matrices. Because of this, errors can creep into a text at several stages of the printing process, but corrections can only be applied to an individual step: to the manuscript, then again to the plates, and finally to the proofs. Housman, a professional text critic, is agonizingly aware of this and constantly complains in his letters about errors he discovers in printed editions of *A Shropshire Lad*. He is particularly infuriated when he is not given the opportunity to review the printed proofs. For instance, the first American edition is reset by a sloppy type-compositor from a text printed in England and contains a huge number of new errors, especially in the punctuation.

  Today: Texts are written in a word-processing program which is used to directly generate the printed form (although increasingly the reader is presented with an electronic form), so all corrections made by the author and editor are automatically saved and go on to the next stage of production, with no new errors introduced in the transmission process. Nevertheless, many scholarly texts produced today have more textual errors than those produced a generation ago, because the economics of publishing have decreased the number of man-hours devoted to editing.

- **1890s:** Homosexuality, as an emerging concept, is proscribed by British society. Homosexuality is punishable by lengthy prison sentences and by the death penalty until 1861.

  Today: Homosexuals are guaranteed equal rights under British law, including the right to form civil partnerships that are identical to marriage in all but name. Some major British political parties endorse the authorization of same-sex marriage.

In the midst of his dramatic, even spectacular career as a classical scholar, Housman produced a volume of English poetry, *A Shropshire Lad*, seemingly out of nowhere. Even more mysteriously, Housman claimed that his poetry had nothing to do with his classicism. Certainly it does not treat classical material (such as mythology) or imitate classical forms, in the way that the highly classicizing poetry of, for instance, Alfred Tennyson did. It is hardly surprising that Housman would speak about poetry in those strict technical terms. But Housman would not have devoted his life to Latin poetry if it did not mean something to him, and it is this meaning that his verse shares with the texts he edited and taught. The classical influence on *A Shropshire Lad* is not in its technical form, or its language, but in its themes. For instance, Housman's first poetic love was the Latin elegist Propertius, whose third book is largely devoted to love and youth being extinguished by untimely death. A main theme of "Loveliest of Trees, the Cherry Now" is the fleetingness of beauty compared to the brevity of life, so that one must take every opportunity to enjoy pleasure in life while it is possible. This is one of the most familiar ideas from Latin poetry, best known in Horace's dictum *carpe diem* (seize the day) from his *Odes* 1.11 (and picked up in *Odes* 1.9 and *Epode* 13). The melancholy appreciation of the beauty of nature is also drawn from Horace (*Odes* 4.7—the only Horatian poem of which Housman published a translation). One way to understand Housman's *A Shropshire Lad* is picturing Housman thinking Latin thoughts in English.

CRITICAL OVERVIEW

Housman's original notebooks used in the composition of *A Shropshire Lad* and "Loveliest of Trees, the Cherry Now" were preserved (at least in part), on Housman's instructions, by his brother Laurence, together with a collection of unpublished poems. The study of these texts has given insight into the process of Housman's composition that the great classicist could scarcely have dreamed of in his work editing the texts of Propertius and other Latin poets.

Archie Burnett, editor of the standard edition of Housman's poems, presents a critical apparatus showing, not printed variations, as do the apparatuses in most modern poets like Keats or Shelley, but alternative readings in Housman's own manuscript copies of the poem. This allows the interested reader to recreate the growth of the poem in Housman's imagination.

Tom Burns Haber goes even further in *The Making of "A Shropshire Lad": A Manuscript Variorum*. Haber demonstrates that the original composition of the poem took place in the notebook designated by editors as *B*, in which Housman sketched out many of the *Shropshire Lad* poems in the spring of 1895. The first and second stanzas of "Loveliest of Trees, the Cherry Now" were written as a substantially complete poem on page 33 of the notebook. The second stanza was added on the following page, and evolved through three complete drafts before Housman had it to his liking.

Although "Loveliest of Trees, the Cherry Now" is among the most beautiful of Housman's poems and one of his most popular, its brevity and apparent simplicity have meant it is not one of the most intensively studied. The principal interpretation of the poem is given by B. J. Leggett in *The Poetic Art of A. E. Housman*. Leggett is interested in the poetic persona's reevaluation of the world in the light of his realization of his own mortality, one of many parallels he finds between Housman's poem and Robert Frost's "Stopping by Woods on a Snowy Evening." Housman escapes sentimentality through his matter-of-fact presentation of the persona's inner calculus of self-realization. Leggett's discussion was extended by Miriam B. Mandel in the 1988 volume of the *Housman Society Journal*. She suggests that the apparent *carpe diem* theme of the poem undercuts the persona's sluggishness and inaction in the poem itself.

CRITICISM

Bradley A. Skeen

Skeen is a classicist. In the following essay, he considers "Loveliest of Trees, the Cherry Now" in light of Housman's personal life and the restrictions imposed by Victorian culture.

A. E. Housman's brother Laurence was a successful poet, novelist, and dramatist, a liberal activist for pacifism, women's suffrage, and gay rights, and was also named as Housman's literary executor. In 1937 Laurence published *A. E. H.*, a collection of his brother's unpublished poetry and a few letters, prefaced by his own memoir of his deceased brother. In this work he mentions Moses Jackson as the greatest friendship of Housman's life, but makes no mention of any romantic entanglement at any point in his brother's life. A. F. S. Gow, Housman's friend and colleague, follows precisely the same line of silence in his memoir in 1936. This silence was meant to contribute to an image of Housman as a curmudgeonly old professor with less time for marriage and family than philology. It was a silence that Housman himself welcomed for the sake of privacy: well before his death he burned masses of his letters and virtually all of his diaries, so that the prying eyes of scholars could never see them. His will directed Laurence to destroy still more documents, including the greater part of his unpublished verse. Rarely has anyone so carefully planned to control their image in posterity as Housman. In Gow's words Housman had the very Horatian desire "to build himself a monument," but curiously a monument built by destroying most of the available material, like a sculptor revealing an image by chipping away flakes from a block of stone. Of

WHAT DO I READ NEXT?

- Tom Stoppard's 1997 play *The Invention of Love* tells the story of Housman's life, particularly his love for Moses Jackson.
- *The Classical Papers of A. E. Housman*, edited by F. R. D. Goodyear, collects in three volumes, published between 1972 and 2005, all of Housman's scholarly journal articles on Greek and Latin texts.
- *A. E. Housman: A Reassessment*, edited by Alan W. Holden, is a collection of scholarly articles covering every aspect of Housman's intellectual production and reception. The text grew out of a conference celebrating the centenary of *A Shropshire Lad* in 1996 and was published in 2000.
- Emiko Ohnuki-Tiernney traces the background of the Japanese Kamikaze aviators in European romanticism in his 2002 *Kamikaze, Cherry Blossoms, and Nationalisms: The Militarization of Aesthetics in Japanese History*. He finds that the cherry blossom, long a symbol of natural beauty in Japan, was given a new meaning as the symbol of the souls of fallen Japanese soldiers, a symbolic meaning very close to the received reading of Housman's "Loveliest of Trees, the Cherry Now."
- Eliza Scidmore was the first female member of the National Geographic Society, and in the first decades of the twentieth century, she became a popular travel writer. Enchanted by Japanese culture, she promoted the idea of importing Japanese cherry trees to Washington, D.C. and starting a Japanese-style annual cherry blossom festival. As a result of her lobbying, Japan gave the necessary cherry saplings as a gift to the United States in 1912. Her story is told in *Eliza's Cherry Trees*, a 2011 book for young adults, written by Andrea Zimmerman with illustrations by Ju-Hong Chen.
- Housman's magnum opus was his five-volume edition of the *Astronomica* of Manilius. His text is largely the basis of G. P. Goold's 1977 text and translation in the Loeb Classical Library. Manilius is currently the subject of a small publishing boom, with Housman's original text reissued by Cambridge in 2011 and the first English language monograph on Manilius published in 2009, followed by a half-dozen more important volumes in the next few years.

---

course, the monument does not have the same shape as the original block.

This necessary silence supported an image that seemed safe and well-suited to protect Housman's reputation and influence in a society where homosexuality was widely believed to have been a psychological disorder and was a criminal offense. Homosexuality was a new word in English in the 1890s, introduced by Havelock Ellis in his *Sexual Inversion* (1897). This introduced an undertaking of homosexuality as a psychological disease. The British criminal code was amended in 1885 to make male homosexuality a specific crime (female homosexuality did not exist as a legal concept). Both of these changes replaced the older idea of sodomy, which included any sexual act that could not result in procreation. Sodomy had been seen as contrary to nature and hence a sin, rather than a disease. The law likewise changed from considering specific acts to outlawing an orientation.

But Housman was a homosexual and as much was early inferred by critics from various of his poems in *A Shropshire Lad* and elsewhere. And Laurence, to whom Housman made it a point of keeping quiet about his private life, clearly knew it and began to hint at obscurely in *A. E. H.* The last item in that volume is Housman's horoscope, which he may well have had occasion to cast himself for practice in connection

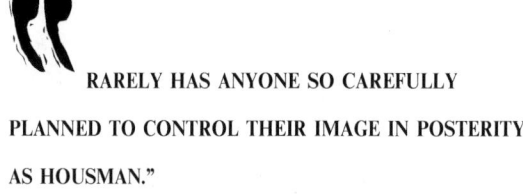

RARELY HAS ANYONE SO CAREFULLY PLANNED TO CONTROL THEIR IMAGE IN POSTERITY AS HOUSMAN."

with his research into ancient astrology. It is appended by a supposed interpretation that is clearly by Laurence. This text, presenting itself as a prediction, again goes through the events of Housman's life as in the memoir that opened the volume, but in a more pointed and satiric way. Under the heading "Friendship, Love and Marriage," it has this to say:

> There is likely to be disappointment in life, and marriage will be long-delayed if it ever takes place. There is a strong inclination for a celibate life ... but some kind of secret and irregular union is more likely than an ordinary marriage.... If the marriage ever took place it would be of an unusual kind; it might be with one who was in some way afflicted or crippled physically, mentally, or morally.

This begins by supplying the implied reaction to the general silence on the subject, but it ends by suggesting that any marriage for Housman would have been highly unusual. In what way is suggested by the last line. Mentally and morally crippled is how the homosexual orientation was conceived of by the medical profession and the public at large throughout Housman's lifetime, and it is his brother's homosexuality to which Laurence is obliquely referring. The only details we know of Housman's love life come from the few scraps of his diary that Housman passed on to his brother, and which Laurence left sealed, together with his own comments on them, to be kept from public view until a quarter century after his own death. These were published in a limited edition of 500 copies in 1976 as *A. E. Housman's "De Amicitia,"* a volume which is still only accessible in a few libraries' rare-book rooms. The diary entries concern only two subjects, one of which is the details of his brief correspondence and infrequent meetings with his old college roommate Moses Jackson after he went overseas to work as an imperial bureaucrat. Laurence explains that Jackson was the great, unrequited love of Housman's life.

Another milestone in the development of the idea of homosexuality in the 1890s was marked by the legal difficulties of the prominent writer Oscar Wilde. Wilde had been publicly accused of sodomy by the Marquis of Queensbury, the father of his lover Arthur Edward Douglas. Wilde sued Queensbury for libel, but lost. This left the crown little choice but to try Wilde for homosexuality, which it did, sending him to jail for two years. The celebrity of the case helped to forge the new homosexual cultural identity and spurred on efforts at gaining civil rights for homosexuals, a movement in which Laurence Housman became a leader, though there was little that he or anyone could do openly in that climate for fear of legal retaliation. Housman also took notice of Wilde's legal difficulties in a poem Laurence published in *A. E. H.* (now known as *Additional Poems* XVIII "Oh! Who Is That Young Sinner"). In this Housman describes the nature of Wilde's punishment consequent to his prison sentence of two years at hard labor, but at the end of each stanza he says Wilde is being punished for the color of his hair. In the second stanza, the color is said to be nameless, recalling Wilde's famous description during the trial of homosexuality as the love that dare not speak its name. Through metaphor, Housman endorses the Victorian medical hypothesis of homosexuality as an innate physical trait, no different from hair or eye color, that cannot, for that very reason, be criminalized.

This medicalized understanding of homosexuality was at war with a more common Victorian understanding of homosexuality as a sinful depravity. Housman addressed this also in *A Shropshire Lad*. "Shot? So quick, so clean an ending?" (XLIV) is an address to a young man who commits suicide because he recognizes that his own nature has betrayed him and turned him into a monster who would have been better off never having been born and who is doomed to corrupt others. What specifically this betrayal consists of is never revealed in the poem. But Laurence found inter-leaved next to the poem in Housman's own copy of the first edition of *A Shropshire Lad*, a newspaper clipping from August 5, 1895, that contained the suicide note left by a young soldier who had killed himself. He confessed that he was a homosexual, saw no possibility of ever having a fulfilling romantic relationship because of the prevailing social conditions, and saw himself as doomed to constantly corrupt other young men in an endless cycle of desire and regret. From Housman's viewpoint the tragedy was made more pathetic in light of the contrast between the medical and popular understandings of homosexuality. More to the current point, there could hardly be a clearer demonstration of the importance of Housman's sexuality for understating the poetry in *A Shropshire Lad*.

In the theme of seizing the day in "Loveliest of Trees, the Cherry Now," the thing that is to be seized is the beauty of the cherry blossoms. This is readily understood as a metaphor for whatever it is that one thinks makes life worth living. But what that is precisely for Housman is never really mentioned, just as the true subject of "Shot? So quick, so clean an ending?" is only spoken around, not named. Some light is thrown, suggesting that this thing is desire, by a poem about Jackson that Housman himself published in *More Poems* in a slightly censored form (compared to the manuscript), "Because I Like You Better" (XXXI). In this poem, Housman approaches Jackson and is rebuffed, and agrees not to pursue him. He attributes Jackson's departure for India and then Canada as a means of putting distance between them. Housman is left essentially dead, with the cold comfort that he followed his beloved's wishes. This shows the result in Housman's life of not seizing the day, not taking the one thing that would make him happiest. It is not a very great stretch that for Housman, the cherry blossoms that he urges the Shropshire lad to take was his love for Jackson. This seems to be confirmed by the remains of Housman's diaries. As mentioned above, half of the few entries that Housman could not bear to destroy concerned even the most trivial mention of Jackson. The other half consists of his noting the date each spring when the cherry trees bloomed. The two categories must indeed have been linked in Housman's psyche.

Source: Bradley A. Skeen, Critical Essay on "Loveliest of Trees, the Cherry Now," in *Poetry for Students*, Gale, Cengage Learning, 2012.

Peter E. Firchow
In the following excerpt, Firchow discusses the significance of Housman's representations of nature in the pastoral settings of A Shropshire Lad.

...Perhaps the most interesting recent development in Housman criticism has been the renewed attempt—in reaction to these disparagements of his authentic regionalism—to link *A Shropshire Lad* with the tradition of pastoral poetry. This argument, put forward by R.

> IT IS SIMPLY TOO CONVOLUTED AND VERBOSE; IT ATTEMPTS TOO OBVIOUSLY TO DELAY, BY MEANS OF ELEMENTARY ARITHMETIC, THE FINAL SUPERIMPOSITION OF THE TWO CHERRY TREES, AND THEREBY TO PRODUCE A MORE INTENSE 'SHOCK.'"

L. Kowalczyk among others, maintains that "the damaging attacks upon Housman as witless and sentimental stem from a misunderstanding of his purpose in creating his Shropshire world"—a world which is actually "an emanation of the classical pastoral world which the poet sees as a dramatic myth for conveying his poetic vision of man as a minute, but tragically honorable, particle in the impersonal universe." B. J. Leggett extends this insight into more modern versions of pastoral: "When Housman, in describing his Shropshire as 'not exactly a real place,' compares it to the Cambridge of *Lycidas*, he provided a key to an understanding of its true function, for the symbolic associations involved in the transfer from Shropshire to London should be regarded as a part of the pastoral tradition to which both *A Shropshire Lad* and *Lycidas* belong. Shropshire is, in effect, the pastoral Arcadia. Like Milton's Cambridge in *Lycidas*, it does not conform to the real land whose place names and geography it adopts, but instead provides the environment for the experience which the poet is able to recount only through the pastoral mask." The Housman of *A Shropshire Lad*, in other words, is not a realistic poet and never intended to be. He is imitating Milton, not Shropshire.

I shall be returning later on in this essay to some of the more specific issues raised by this pastoral school of Housman criticism, but for the moment what needs to be addressed is the central question of Housman's relation to the natural setting of his poems. It is tempting to try to resolve this critical debate simply by proposing that Garrod, Ransom and MacNeice—with their wide poetical and critical experience—are more reliable guides to Housman's Shropshire than Kowalczyk and Leggett. That, however, would be too simple. Another approach which does,

I think, take into account more fairly the complexity of this issue, is to ask why—if Kowalczyk and Leggett are right—readers as obviously sensitive as Garrod, Ransom and MacNeice should ever have reached the conclusions they did about *A Shropshire Lad*? And, once we ask this question, a corollary question immediately presents itself: why is it that no one—or no one at least with any substantial claims to being a sensitive reader of poetry—has ever interpreted *Lycidas* as a realistic poem, or supposed that Milton's primary intention in that poem was to provide a down-to-earth description of Cambridge life in the seventeenth century?

...When A. S. F. Gow first met Housman in 1910 and inquired about where he went for his vacations, the reply he received was "Paris"; and in the twenties Housman became one of the first passengers to use the London-Paris air link, an even more symbolic removal from the earth. A number of the best-known anecdotes about him concern his chill refusal to recognize anyone during his afternoon walks in Cambridge, and Percy Withers, who occasionally accompanied him, tells how he would walk with his eyes fixed to the ground. Indeed Withers observes that "the object of his walks was primarily fresh air and exercise, and these attained I think he minded little about the scenery. His appreciation of natural beauty, as with pictorial art, always seemed to me narrow, unenterprising and frigid—rather that of the scientist" (p. 26). Housman's correspondence corroborates this impression. His letters home to his mother during tours of the continent contain listings, rather than descriptions, of the local flora. Not unjustifiably, therefore, J. W. Beach omits any mention whatever of Housman in his compendious survey of the concept of nature in nineteenth-century English poetry.

"Ploughboys never moved so elegantly," writes Edith Sitwell about Housman's alleged regionalistic realism, "men about to be hanged never expressed their sentiments with such neatness; the brokenhearted groan or they whisper, but they do not confine their outpourings to the brevity of such epigrammatic quatrains as these." This Sitwellian dart, as usual, drives home, though one might argue that it draws too much blood. After all, is there and should there not be such a thing as poetical heightening? Housman's ploughboys are undeniably distant cousins of the shepherds of the pastoral tradition—especially as conceived by Wordsworth—and they therefore have a legitimate right to some of their pastoral airs. True enough: but is this poetical heightening?

> Oh see how thick the goldcup flowers
> Are lying in field and lane
> With dandelions to tell the hours
> That never are told again.
> Oh may I squire you round the meads
> And pick you posies gay?
> —'Twill do no harm to take my arm.
> "You may, young man, you may."
> (poem V)

Aside from the Edward-Learian jingle of the verse and the awkward poetical inverted word order of "posies gay," and aside from the archaic (and hardly rural) "twill," what jars the reader most is the concluding line: "You may, young man, you may." What is this? A courtship 'twixt a swain and his aunt? Cyril Connolly, who patiently made the count, ascertained that the word "lad" occurs sixty-seven times in the sixty-three poems: why then did Housman use "young man" here instead, and do so again in all three remaining stanzas of the poem. "Lad" at least has the sanction of dialectal usage and, to a lesser degree, of pastoral convention, but "young man" introduces a false note of moralistic primness and bourgeois respectability, a note that clashes violently with the supposedly rustic and natural qualities of Housman's Shropshire.

There are other problems of a similar kind in *A Shropshire Lad*. Poem XXXIV, subtitled "The New Mistress," suggests itself as a lengthy "modern" reworking of Lovelace's famous "To Lucasta: Going to the Wars." Here Tommy Atkins goes off to the wars because his old mistress has rejected him, and Tommy wants to be where he is wanted, which he happens to believe is the Queen's army. So far, so good: honor, we are made to understand, among the lower orders in Shropshire during the late Victorian period is not what it was among the aristocracy of an earlier day. This, although self-evident, is not without a certain humorous charm. But Housman is not content to leave it at that. When the army is his theme, or death or love or cricket, he throws discretion to the winds:

> "I will go where I am wanted, for the sergeant does
>   not mind:
> He may be sick to see me but he treats me very kind:
> He gives me beer and breakfast and a ribbon for my
>   cap,
> And I never knew a sweetheart spend her money on
>   a chap."
> (poem XXXIV)

A sergeant who is very kind to a recruit!—is this credible? Surely, even in Shropshire, recruits cannot have been as gullible as this. This is no longer Shropshire, but a martial land of Cockayne. Such a poem, or the preceding one, could have been written only by a man who had never been in the army, had never courted a girl, or, for that matter, had never spoken to a real live country bumpkin.

Nor would an actual yokel, though inhabiting darkest Shropshire, have been capable of the colossal naïveté of poem XXXVI:

> The world is round, so travellers tell,
> And straight though reach the track,
> Trudge on, trudge on, 'twill all be well,
> The way will guide one back.

Even in 1896 and even in Shropshire, flat-earthers were not commonly to be met. Housman's contention that a peasant would rely on "travellers" for reports of the world's roundness, and that such reports would come as a novelty to him, is simply preposterous. A blunder of this sort would never have been committed by someone who really knew the people he was writing about. It would not have been committed by Hardy.

What is surprising is that these howlers have not been much remarked upon, or, if they have, are thought of as mere *Schönheitsfehler*. With rare exceptions such as Jacob Bronowski, who finds Housman's poetry "as wordy and as clumsy as the poems of Swinburne," critics tend to wax ecstatic when commenting on the precision and economy of his poetical style. F. W. Bateson asserts boldly that with *A Shropshire Lad* "Housman in effect turned his back, ostentatiously and offensively, on all that twaddle" being produced by the Rhymers' Club in the nineties. What Housman wrote was, in Bateson's view, "short, precise and the very reverse of slovenly." Surveying the poetical scene in 1930, Charles Williams was moved to proclaim that all poets write badly sometimes, "except Mr. Housman." Homer may nod, it seems, but not Housman.

It would be too tedious to rehearse here all the critical praise that *A Shropshire Lad* has garnered with respect to its style, but it should be noted that this praise is often linked to Housman's alleged concreteness or closeness to the earth. That this connection was made very early is evident from William Archer's essay (1902), where Housman is described as "a vernacular poet, if ever there was one. He employs scarcely a word that is not understood [sic] of the people, and current on their lips." Bateson, writing more than half a century later, makes the same connection by means of a statistical analysis of syllable length in *A Shropshire Lad*. There are in the sixty-three poems of the collection, we learn, no five-syllable words, seven four-syllable words (apart from compounds), and only fifty-three three syllable words. The rest are all words of one or two syllables. J. B. Priestley, in *Figures in Modern Literature*, even registers a mild complaint that Housman sometimes "seems to keep too close to the ground, which is an error." But perhaps the most extended paean to Housman's concreteness is to be found in Cleanth Brooks's careful analysis of poem XL from *Last Poems* (1922), in an article commemorating the centennial of Housman's birth. Since Bateson also refers briefly to this poem in support of his notion of "pictorial emphasis," it may be worthwhile examining a section of it here, in particular the second and third stanzas:

> On russet floors, by water idle,
> The pine lets fall its cone;
> The cuckoo shouts all day at nothing
> In leafy dells alone;
> And traveller's joy beguiles in autumn
> Hearts that have lost their own.
> On acres of the seeded grasses
> The changing burnish heaves;
> Or marshalled under moons of harvest
> Stand still at night the sheaves;
> Or Beeches strip in storms for winter
> And stain the wind with leaves.

In the opening stanza, the poet had asked not to be told of the tune which the enchantress (presumably Nature) plays in autumn, since she and he are "long acquainted / And I know all her ways." This comprehensive knowledge is evidently displayed in the see-saw alternation of the imagery on which most of the poem is built. Russet floors and idle waters suggest peace, but the falling cone strikes a subtly discordant note; the cuckoo's shouting seems cheerful until we learn that it is entirely solipsistic; the traveller's joy (a flower) proffers delight, but only to those who are broken-hearted; and so on. This give-and-take-away-again movement is characteristic of much of Housman's verse, and in small doses it can be quite effective. Effective or not, however, it is rarely particularly concrete or pictorial. What Housman is interested in here is the change in pictures, not in the picture itself. The very notion of Nature as an enchantress, of an allegorical personage playing tricks on man, confirms this suspicion. Compare these "pictures" with the imagery to be found in analogous autumn poems by real nature poets like Edward Thomas or Robert Frost, and the difference becomes apparent. This, for instance, is from a poem by Thomas:

> Lichen, ivy and moss
> Keep evergreen the trees
> That stand half flayed and dying,
> And dead trees on their knees
> In dog's mercury and moss;
> And the bright twitch of the goldfinch drops
> Down there as he flits on thistle-tops.

Here is a scene that has actually been seen (the poet's presence is implicit in the final two lines), and could be reproduced pictorially with a good deal of precision. This is not true of Housman's poem, where even the best images, such as the "changing burnish" of the grass, or the beech leaves that stain the autumn wind, are impressions rather than visualizations. This is not to suggest that Housman's poem is not good. There is unquestionably something moving in this Prosperian farewell to Nature. But it does mean, I think, that such excellence as it possesses derives not from the pictorial emphasis of the imagery.

Moreover, Housman is bidding adieu here to Nature, rather than to nature. Lower-case nature does not come equipped with russet floors. Russet or watery floors (and leafy dells and bowers) are quite appropriate, as we have already noted, in a highly conventional poem like *Lycidas*, but they are not appropriate in a supposedly vernacular, realistic poem. If russet floors are meant to be pictorial—and the emphasis on color suggests that they are—it is pictorial as in picture gallery, not as in nature. The same applies to the pine which lets fall its cone. There is no such thing as "the" pine in nature. There may be a pine or there may be pines, but "the" pine exists only on a plane of Platonic universals. And it is on that plane that Housman's poem abstractly moves.

Even the finest poems in *A Shropshire Lad* are marred by this kind of abstraction—by a quality which D. H. Lawrence might well have called a pastoralism of the mind masking itself as a pastoralism of the body, a quality, moreover, all the more ironic because of Housman's objections to the meddling intellect in poetry. Take poem II, for instance, one of Housman's best known poems, and, according to Louis Untermeyer, arguably the finest lyric in the English language:

> Loveliest of trees, the cherry now
> Is hung with bloom along the bough,
> And stands about the woodland ride
> Wearing white for Eastertide.
> Now, of my threescore years and ten,
> Twenty will not come again,
> And take from seventy springs a score,
> It only leaves me fifty more.
> And since to look at things in bloom
> Fifty springs are little room,
> About the woodland I will go
> To see the cherry hung with snow.

Here it is "the" cherry tree, the typical rather than the individual tree. And here again the focus is on change, rather than on the picture itself: the final image of the cherry tree "hung with snow," though still referring to the bloom of the opening stanza, takes away part of what had been given earlier. The ambiguous "snow" tips the tree away from spring and into winter, from life into death. Moreover, the juxtaposition of an apparently large block of time (fifty years) with the brief period during which cherry trees blossom, seems on the one hand reassuring, but on the other threatening, since implicit in the imagery is the archetypal analogy between man's expected life-span and the passing of the seasons. Besides, the speaker himself at twenty is suggestively like the cherry tree at blossom-time. This is all carefully worked out, and the central stanza, with its reversal, is the hinge-point on which the movement of give-and-take-away is executed. Nevertheless, this skillful construction does not, I think, save the poem as a whole from failure. Partly the failure is due to the characteristic abstraction (as in XL of *Last Poems*) of the natural elements, but more important here is the heavy-handed manner in which the turning movement is carried out in stanza two. It is simply too convoluted and verbose; it attempts too obviously to delay, by means of elementary arithmetic, the final superimposition of the two cherry trees, and thereby to produce a more intense "shock." It is not surprising, therefore, to discover from the evidence of the manuscript of the poem that Housman wrote the first and last stanzas before he wrote the second, which "was evolved with some difficulty."

This clumsiness is apparent elsewhere in *A Shropshire Lad* as well. In the spring-time Poem X ("March"), there occurs a stanza in which

> The boys are up the woods with day
> To fetch the daffodils away,
> And home at noonday from the hills
> They bring no dearth of daffodils.

Why no dearth of daffodils? The answer: because of the alliteration. But what a price to

> "IT WOULD BE MISLEADING TO STATE THAT THE POINT OF VIEW ADOPTED BY THE PERSONA IN 'LOVELIEST OF TREES' IS TYPICAL OF THAT OF THE MAJORITY OF HOUSMAN'S POEMS."

pay for alliteration; here is giving and taking away with a vengeance. And something else: why is it that the boys who started off going to the woods end up by returning from the hills? Boys, to be sure, will be boys, and there is no telling in which direction they will scamper off when given the chance, but here their energetic wanderings seem to be primarily caused by the fact that hills rhymes with daffodils. This being the case, it becomes rather difficult to believe in their substantial existence.

The only genuine area of sympathy, I suspect, between Housman and his literary creations, human and natural, lies in the intellect. The most famous lines from *A Shropshire Lad*, the only ones which have passed wholly into the language, deal with the superiority of matter over mind: "And malt does more than Milton can," says Housman's persona Terence Hearsay, "To justify God's ways to man" (poem LXII). *A Shropshire Lad* is full of this sort of bar-room sententiousness: Housman's fulsome admiration for the active man at arms—or at bat—is not one whit behind that of more "vulgar" poets like Kipling or Newbolt. One is tempted to agree with Pound's jibe that Housman's coarse mental fibre may be deduced from the monotony of his verse forms. "I suspect that Mr. Housman suffers," Pound wrote in 1934, "from a deficient curiosity. Such as he has seems hardly to have led him to consider any verse save that having good heavy swat on every alternate syllable, or at least formed predominantly on the system of tiTum tiTum tiTum, sometimes up to ten syllables...."

Source: Peter E. Firchow, "The Land of Lost Content: Housman's *Shropshire*," in *Mosaic*, Vol. 13, No. 2, Winter 1980, pp. 103–21.

B. J. Leggett
In the following excerpt, Leggett refutes the charge by critics that Housman's poetic philosophy is adolescent and that the persona of the poems does not necessarily represent his philosophy.

One indication of Housman's singular position in the tradition of British poetry at the turn of the century may be seen in his commentators' preoccupation with the nature of his verse. More perhaps than any other poet of his generation Housman has prompted questions of classification and definition in regard to a small body of poetry which does not fit easily into any school or movement. For the critics of the thirties it was primarily a question of classicism versus romanticism.... Yet despite numerous...efforts to articulate the special character of Housman's verse, one must agree with Christopher Ricks's observation that we are still "hard put to say why we like or dislike his poems." It is the very nature of his poetry which remains in question.

Housman, we know from his statements in *The Name and Nature of Poetry*, had little sympathy with the efforts of criticism to label and define what was for him a personal and human response, and there is something to be said for his concern that the tendency of criticism in his time was to confuse the provinces of literature and science. But he was obviously not opposed to the more humanistic branch of literary criticism, typified in the nineteenth century by his favorite critic, Matthew Arnold, and his primary objection to twentieth-century criticism was centered on its attempt to substitute empirical truth for informed opinion and good taste. Housman's cautious position on the limits of the intellect in the appraisal of poetry voiced in *The Name and Nature of Poetry* should serve to remind the commentator how tentative and even capricious his own pronouncements may be, and the tone of tentative inquiry befitting an admirer of Housman and Arnold is the tone I wish to take here....

The theory articulated in *The Name and Nature of Poetry* can provide some help for an approach to Housman's verse if we do not allow it to take us too far. At the very least it can give us some sense of Housman's conception of the tradition out of which he was writing. That is not enough, finally, but it does afford a base from which to proceed. That tradition, as Housman defined it, suggests that we should expect to encounter a poetry of feeling in the manner of the Romantics, although not necessarily in the Romantic style. It suggests further that we should not expect to find anything approaching the formulation of a philosophical world-view or the exposition of ideas, since Housman was convinced that his verse made its appeal not to the intellect but "to something in man which is obscure and latent, something older than the present organisation of his nature."

The opposition between intellect and emotion is central to Housman's own conception of poetry, and in his effort to define the essential nature of poetry he took great pains to show that the intellect is not the seat of aesthetic appreciation. "There is," he says, "a conception of poetry which is not fulfilled by pure language and liquid versification, with the simple and so to speak colourless pleasure which they afford, but involves the presence in them of something which moves and touches in a special and recognizable way...."

I am convinced that Housman's commentators have gone astray in pursuing the philosophy of his poetry, just as Housman believed Wordsworth's admirers were misdirected in concentrating on his philosophy of nature. In both cases we are confronted with a sense of the world which is beyond (or below) the intellect. That is, the poetry does not lend itself readily to philosophical schema or systemization. Further, Housman's poems are not frequently concerned with anything more than dramatizing the moment in which insight occurs. It is a commonplace of Housman criticism that he kept writing the same poem, and that poem most frequently is a means of placing the persona in a situation in which some vague sense of his condition is realized. The structures, the strategies of the poems, moreover, serve most often to convey the shock of recognition, the moment of insight....

One may...note, in examining the best known of Housman's poems, the types of situations in which Housman involves his persona. A celebration of the fifty years that God has saved the Queen serves to remind him of the soldiers buried in foreign fields who shared the work with God, giving him a momentary glimpse of the mortality on which the permanence of the race is founded. A walk through the woods at Eastertide to observe the cherry in bloom produces a sudden intimation of mortality. The lad at two-and-twenty exclaims, of the transience of love, "And oh, 'tis true, 'tis true." A storm on Wenlock Edge, the site of an ancient Roman city, leads to the knowledge that "Then 'twas the Roman, now 'tis I." An athlete dying young, a funeral observed from Bredon Hill, the sounds of the soldiers' tread, the imagined last hour of a murderer who hangs at the stroke of nine—these are the occasions for the innocent's confrontation with the alien world of time and death.

But it is the manner in which Housman conveys to us the significance of the discovery that provides the force of many of his best poems. At times the poem depends on the paradox or irony of "To an Athlete Dying Young" or "1887," so much admired by the New Critics at the expense of the body of his verse. But he may also employ more subtle means in which no daring metaphors or metaphysical conceits are evident. Consider, for example, one of the most straightforward of the poems of *A Shropshire Lad*, "Loveliest of Trees," which has been generally admired. The tone of the poem clearly depends on the point of view of the naive persona, his essential innocence, and even his inability to articulate with any sophistication what he has discovered. His attitude is difficult to characterize, for it is not governed by pessimism or bitterness at his human state; Housman seems interested only in the persona's discovery of his own mortality, and the poem is structured in such a manner as to make that discovery its central element. The poem depends to a great extent on a curious but obscure relationship between the sight of the cherry in bloom at Eastertide and a sense of human limitation. The first stanza concentrates wholly on the description of the cherry, "wearing white for Eastertide," and the second stanza on the persona's realization of his mortality. The causal connection between the two experiences is left unstated. Perhaps it is not capable of discursive statement. The lad's calculation of his threescore years and [ten] is handled in an almost neutral manner, with no betrayal of emotion:

> Now, of my threescore years and ten,
> Twenty will not come again,
> And take from seventy springs a score,
> It only leaves me fifty more.

There is more attention to arithmetic than to feeling here, much in the manner of Frost's "Stopping by Woods on a Snowy Evening," where the persona seems more involved with the owner of the woods and the horse than with the consequences of his experience. But in both cases the effect is the same. The poet escapes the danger of a maudlin treatment of a commonplace experience by the neutrality of tone and the attention to detail. John Ciardi has spoken of the duplicity of Frost's method, and the term is applicable here. In both cases, the force of the poem is greater than the occasion or the accumulation of details would seem to warrant. The opposite effect is sentimentality, a constant threat for poets like Frost and Housman who deal in potentially melodramatic situations.

The understatement of the last stanza provides an instance of Housman's characteristic treatment of the consequences of insight:

> And since to look at things in bloom
> Fifty springs are little room,
> About the woodlands I will go
> To see the cherry hung with snow.

The details of the stanza carry a significance hardly warranted by the commonplace sentiment they express or the bland language in which they are couched, and that is due almost entirely to the feet that they are now weighted by the persona's intuitive sense of his own mortality, introduced in stanza two. "Things in bloom" now suggest something of the vitality of life which has become more precious. The limitations of life are condensed into the almost trite phrase "little room," and the sense of death which now colors all living things is conveyed by the single description of the white blossoms of the cherry, "hung with snow." It is an effect which relies on what is unsaid, comparable to the similar conclusion of Frost's poem, "And miles to go before I sleep," although Frost's line seems almost heavy-handed in comparison. The poem relies also on its progressive structure and on metaphor and allusion, all of which warrant further discussion, but at the moment I should like to pursue the thematics of a poetry of insight, especially as it involves the problems of character and point of view.

It would be misleading to state that the point of view adopted by the persona in "Loveliest of Trees" is typical of that of the majority of Housman's poems. His reaction to the discoveries he makes in poem after poem varies from renewed vitality to melancholy. What remains constant is, however, the degree to which the poems depend for their effect on the character of the persona, his ability to voice afresh sentiments which in the mouth of a more sophisticated speaker would appear trite. Housman avoids the dangers of the trite, the sentimental, by separating himself from his poems through a created character, whereas a poet like Frost pretends actually to be the homely rustic speaker that the poem demands, a role Frost apparently found congenial to his public life as a poet. Housman's poetics are not elaborate enough to allow for Yeats's theory of the mask, but the result of the split between poet and persona produces a similar situation. His solution to the problems of personality and personae which Yeats spent a lifetime working out was simply to create the fiction of the Shropshire lad, substituting for the voice of the learned classical scholar whose reticence was almost legendary that of the rustic innocent.... The persona thus becomes a kind of Yeatsian mask or anti-self, the opposite of all that the poet represents in his private life. The resulting tone, carefully cultivated, controls Housman's verse so pervasively that it has been tempting to blur the distinction between the personalities of poet and speaker. Such a crucial distinction has, of course, been an element of modern criticism for the past forty years, yet Housman criticism gives evidence that the formalist principle of the separation of poet and persona has been more often observed in theory than in practice.

The nature of the persona we may expect to encounter in Housman's verse—initially the innocent confronted with the alien world, later the exile seeking to recapture his lost innocence—has been described in some detail. There is, moreover, the question of the persona's change throughout the sequence of *A Shropshire Lad*—he is certainly not a static character. But that is a related issue which I have attempted to treat elsewhere. I should like to examine here another aspect of the persona, the effect of his presence in the poem as a whole. That is, what does Housman's art gain or lose by his use of the pastoral mask? It is a question which can be answered only by examination of individual poems, for the persona's presence is felt more strongly in some poems than in others. Housman rarely drops the mask, but sometimes it is crucial; at other times it seems only a habit of composition....

Source: B. J. Leggett, "The Poetry of Insight: Persona and Point of View in Housman," in *Victorian Poetry*, Vol. 14, No. 2, Winter 1976, pp. 325–29.

SOURCES

Burnett, Archie, ed., *The Poems of A. E. Housman*, Clarendon, 1997, pp. 4–5.

Ellmann, Richard, *Oscar Wilde*, Alfred A. Knopf, 1988, pp. 435–504.

Gow, A. S. F., *A. E. Houseman: A Sketch, Together with a List of his Writings and Indexes to his Classical Papers*, Macmillan, 1936, pp. 3–57.

Haber, Tom Burns, ed., *The Making of "A Shropshire Lad": A Manuscript Variorum*, University of Washington Press, 1966, pp. 33–36.

Halperin, David M., *One Hundred Years of Homosexuality*, Routledge, 1989, pp. 15–53.

Horace, *The Complete Odes & Epodes, with the Centennial Hymn*, translated by W. G. Shepherd, Penguin, 1983, p. 79.

Housman, A. E., *The Letters of A. E. Housman*, edited by Henry Maas, Harvard University Press, 1971.

———, "Loveliest of Trees, the Cherry Now," in *The Poems of A. E. Housman*, edited by Archie Burnett, Clarendon, 1997, pp. 4–5.

———, *The Name and Nature of Poetry: The Leslie Stephen Lecture Delivered at Cambridge, 9 May 1933*, Cambridge University Press, 1933.

———, *Selected Prose*, edited by John Carter, Cambridge University Press, 1961.

Housman, Laurence, ed., *A. E. H.: Some Poems, Some Letters and a Personal Memoir by His Brother*, Jonathan Cape, 1937.

Hutton, Ronald, *The Rise of Merry England*, Oxford University Press, 1996.

Jebb, Keith, *A. E. Housman*, Siren, 1992, pp. 50–72.

Kowalczyk, R. L., "Horatian Tradition and Pastoral Mode in Housman's *A Shropshire Lad*," in *Victorian Poetry*, Vol. 4, No. 14, 1966, pp. 223–35.

Leggett, B. J., *The Poetic Art of A. E. Housman: Theory and Practice*, University of Nebraska Press, 1978, pp. 47–49, 63–64.

Mandel, Miriam B., "Housman's 'Loveliest of Trees,'" in *Housman Society Journal*, Vol. 14, 1964, pp. 268–84.

Otis, Brooks, "Housman and Horace," in *Pacific Coast Philology*, Vol. 2, 1967, pp. 5–24.

Turner, Frank M., *The Greek Heritage in Victorian Britain*, Yale University Press, 1984.

Vance, Norman, "Horace and the Nineteenth Century," in *Horace Made New*, edited by Charles Martindale and David Hopkins, Cambridge University Press, 1993, pp. 199–216.

FURTHER READING

Bloom, Harold, ed., *Bloom's Major Poets: A. E. Housman*, Infobase, 2003.
  This collection of new and reprinted material provides basic analysis of Housman's poetry by one of the world's preeminent critics.

Brink, C. O., *English Classical Scholarship: Historical Reflections on Bentley, Porson, and Housman*, James Clark, 2010.
  Brink's volume concentrates on Housman's scholarly achievement as an editor of Latin poetry.

Foucault, Michel, *The History of Sexuality*, 3 vols., translated by Robert Hurley, Vintage, 1990.
  This magisterial work has laid the foundation for the modern study of sexuality in human culture, and focuses on the intersection of Greco-Roman and Victorian ideas about sexuality that gave birth to modern attitudes.

Ricks, Christopher, ed., *A. E. Housman: A Collection of Critical Essays*, Prentice Hall, 1968.
  This collection of essays captures an earlier generation's understanding of Housman, and in particular provides assessments of Housman by major twentieth century poets including W. H. Auden, Ezra Pound, and Kingsley Amis.

SUGGESTED SEARCH TERMS

A. E. Houseman

Loveliest of Trees, the Cherry Now AND A. E. Houseman

A Shropshire Lad AND A. E. Houseman

Victorian poetry

classics AND literature

Manilius AND A. E. Houseman

carpe diem

A Shropshire Lad AND Loveliest of Trees, the Cherry Now

textual criticism

Victorian poetry AND A .E. Housman

The Moon at the Fortified Pass

LI PO

750 BC

Li Po (also spelled Li Bai, Li Bo) is one of the great poets of the Chinese canon. Along with Wang Wei and Tu Fu, he is considered one of the three greatest poets of the T'ang Dynasty, the golden age of Chinese poetry. While much of Li Po's biography is shrouded in mythology and is strangely absent from the extensive census records of the Chinese empire, it is generally agreed that he was born in 701 CE, somewhere in the central Asian states outside China's western borders, and that he died in 762 CE.

Li Po was known for drunkenness and spontaneity in his poetry and was particularly famous for his "grass script" poems, which were written in a single rush of inspiration, in a calligraphic style that is flowing and sometimes difficult to read. In this sense "The Moon at the Fortified Pass" is not typical of his work. The 1920 translation is done by Witter Bynner, and the notation indicates that it was written for music. A poem "written for music" or *yüeh-fu*, was a specific type of poem, and one that historically took on themes of war and injustice. Although Bynner renamed his volume *The Jade Mountain*, it is essentially a translation of *Three Hundred T'ang Poems*, a slim volume that was for centuries used as a textbook for Chinese schoolchildren. The original organized the poems by type of poem, ruled and unruled, ancient and modern. Witter Bynner and Kiang Kang-Hu, on whose text the translations are based, rearranged the collection by poet and organized those poets alphabetically.

The Moon at the Fortified Pass

Li Po (© Bettmann | Corbis)

However changed, this translation gives readers a strong sense of what one of the central texts of Chinese poetic history was like, and which poets were included.

A more modern translation of the poem is available. Titled "Frontier-Mountain Moon," it is available in *The Selected Poems of Li Po*, translated by David Hinton, New Directions, 1996, p. 26.

AUTHOR BIOGRAPHY

Li Po was born in 701 CE and much of his biography is swathed in legend and myth, some of it of Li Po's own making. His reputation is that of a wild man, one unwilling to live by convention or rules, a wandering poet who was often drunk, and who, while drunk, spontaneously created some of the most beautiful and lasting poems in the Chinese canon.

Although his exact birthplace is unknown, scholars generally agree that his family came from the Central Asian territories outside of what was then China. Li Po is said to have had a "strange and striking appearance" which could have been a result of his Central Asian heritage—a heritage he claimed to share with the Imperial family, although there is little evidence to support this. There are others who speculate that he might not have been Chinese at all.

In about 724, Li Po left Szechuan, where his family had settled, and travelled east. He married, and he lived in An-lu until the late 730s; after his wife and child died, he began to wander. Li Po is known as the "Banished Immortal," which is a reference both to the idea that great poets are immortal figures, and that Li Po had been banished from their realm on account of his wandering, his drunkenness, and his irresponsible and irreverent behavior. In 742, Li Po obtained a post in the imperial court as a teacher in the Han-lin Academy. Li Po served as a court poet, and his poems were known for pushing the boundaries of what was acceptable, while his indiscreet and erratic behavior made him something of a court jester. Li Po was particularly famous for his drunkenness, a state which was seen as allowing a person's true wild nature to emerge. By 744, Li Po's antics resulted in his being sent away from the capital, and he resumed his wandering ways.

It was during these years that he was befriended by Tu Fu, who looked up to the older poet even as he was building his own reputation as one of the central poets of the T'ang Dynasty. Tu Fu wrote more than a dozen poems about Li Po, and he is responsible for saving many of the older poet's works from destruction. Between 750 and 762, a devastating civil war broke out; census figures of the time show that out of a population of fifty-three million people, thirty-six million were left either dead or homeless. During this time, Li Po continued to wander, and he was incarcerated for a time under a death sentence. His sentence was commuted, he was banished, then pardoned, and in 762, he arrived at the home of his cousin, Yang-ping, one of the great calligraphers of the T'ang Dynasty. Yang-ping copied and saved many of Li Po's poems, and legend has it that in the winter of 762, Li Po died one drunken night in a boat when he reached out to embrace the reflection of the full moon upon the water.

POEM TEXT

> The bright moon lifts from the Mountain of
>   Heaven
> In an infinite haze of cloud and sea,
> And the wind, that has come a thousand miles,
> Beats at the Jade Pass battlements....
> China marches its men down Po-têng Road   5
> While Tartar troops peer across blue waters of
>   the bay...
> And since not one battle famous in history
> Sent all its fighters back again,
> The soldiers turn round, looking toward the
>   border,
> And think of home, with wistful eyes,   10
> And of those tonight in the upper chambers
> Who toss and sigh and cannot rest.

POEM SUMMARY

The text used for this summary is from *The Jade Mountain*, translated by Witter Bynner and Kiang Kang-Hu, Knopf, 1920, pp. 60–61. A version of the poem can be found on the following Web page: http://allpoetry.com/poem/8448275-The_Moon_At_The_Fortified_Pass-by-Li_Po.

Although an exact date for when Li Po wrote "The Moon at the Fortified Pass" is not available, it is a good example of the ways that poets worked with the *yüeh-fu*, or ballad-style poem, during the T'ang dynasty. This poetic form predates the T'ang and is, in fact, one of the oldest forms of Chinese poetry. Unlike the five- and seven-character ruled poems that dominated the Imperial examinations and court poetry, the *yüeh-fu* allowed the poet great flexibility. Many translators have mourned the loss of the music that usually accompanied these poems.

Lines 1–4
The poem opens, as a proper T'ang poem should, with an invocation of place and of nature. Li Po uses as his first images the moon, the mountain, the clouds, the sea, and the wind. These are concrete details of a specific landscape, but they also serve as symbols of immortality. Taoist philosophy states that all mountains are the place where heaven and earth touch, and are thus the location from which the energy of the universe is generated. Li Po takes this one step further by explicitly stating that this is Heaven Mountain itself, the place where the opposite forces of sky and earth meet.

The moon is the central image of all of Li Po's poetry, and he is said to have loved the moon so much that he died trying to embrace its reflection in a moving river. For Li Po, the moon was not only the embodiment of the forces of *yin* (the feminine, passive side of nature) in the universe, it was the embodiment of all that was mysterious and poetic, of poetry and beauty herself. This poem begins with the moon rising bright and clear out of a boundless layer of cloud. The clouds cover all that lies below the mountain: the world of men, the world where wars are started. It is out of this layer of obscurity that the moon rises high into the sky, illuminating the infinite and unchanging forces of the universe, the seat of all creation, the place where the earth and sky meet. The wind, like the soldiers, comes from far away, and is portrayed as a force in opposition to the first man-made item the poem portrays: the fortress.

In these opening lines, Li Po has set the transient actions of men in a landscape of the eternal forces of the universe. The actions of men are small in this world, and like the wind that scours the passageway between the peaks, they too shall soon pass away.

Lines 5–8
In this section of the poem, Li Po introduces humankind, with all its politics and strife, to the eternal landscape of the Taoist worldview he created in the first quatrain. Chinese soldiers march in one direction while enemy troops watch them approach. If the images of the first quatrain are of those eternal forces of the universe that remain unchanged by humans—the moon, the mountain, the sky—then the images in this second quatrain form the other half of a Taoist set of dualisms. The first quatrain concerned the eternal; the second concerns the fleeting lives of humans. While the moon and the Mountain of Heaven will remain, the soldiers marching across the pass will, most likely, not return again. It is a central tenet of the Taoist worldview that the actions of humans are small and inconsequential when compared with the unchanging forces of the universe.

Lines 9–12
While the first two quatrains presented portraits of those forces that are bigger than the individual human, whether they were the universal forces of nature or the manner in which the lives of individual men are subordinate to their social

position and the political forces that govern them, the third quatrain personalizes the situation with its portrait of the soldiers, looking back toward their homes with longing. Just as human beings are less powerful than the forces of the universe, so too are the individual soldiers less powerful than the social and political world in which they live. Just as even the most powerful humans are subordinate to the forces of the Tao, or their fates, so too are the soldiers subordinate to the governments that they serve. These soldiers know, as they march through the narrow gap between heaven and earth, that most of them will not return. In this, they are emblematic of all humans, who must accept at some point that their lives are finite, unlike the heavens and the earth, which will go on eternally. And yet, Li Po brings readers into the pathos of the soldiers' plight. They look back toward home and long for the human comfort of their bed chambers and their wives even as they follow orders and march on toward their doom.

In this, "The Moon at the Fortified Pass" is typical of a *yüeh-fu* poem. Especially during the T'ang dynasty, this poetic form was often used as a way to critique wars and warmongering. While Li Po was often criticized during his lifetime by conservative critics for not writing proper court poetry, in this case, his focus on the lives of lowly soldiers, and on their plight, is a fulfillment of the expectations of a *yüeh-fu* poem. This was a form that Li Po wrote in often, and scholars have speculated that since the formal requirements of a *yüeh-fu* poem were more flexible, it fit his personality and style better than the more formal structures.

THEMES

Symbolism

While "The Moon at the Fortified Pass" is not typical of the majority of Li Po's poetry, in that it espouses not drunkenness, nor spontaneous displays of emotion, nor the life of a wanderer, it does contain references to the moon, the mountains, and the winds, all important symbols that appear throughout Li Po's work. For Chinese poets of the T'ang dynasty, influenced as they were by Taoist and Buddhist thinking, the mountains were, as David Hinton notes in the introduction to *The Selected Poems of Li Po*, "not merely natural, but sacred objects. Quite literally sites where the powers of heaven met those of earth, they were inhabited and energized by those powers." Heaven in Chinese tradition is different from the Western concept of heaven as a place where the monotheistic god lives and where souls go after death. In Chinese thought, particularly in Taoist thinking, heaven and earth are paired concepts, with the one representing everything that is transcendental and the other representing everything material.

And so, mountains, as the place where earth reaches up to touch the heavens, become a site of great power and energy in Chinese theology, a place where men can directly experience the transcendental. That this poem takes place on a pass, a place where men must climb up into the sky to pass through the mountains, is a setting of great significance, as is the fact that we are told explicitly that this is the Mountain of Heaven. The pass has been built up by men with fortifications, and the soldiers are marching to war, marking this as a mountain that has been modified by man, and has in some crucial manner had its generative powers modified. The fortifications and the soldiers are forces of earth, of men's intentions to force their will on one another. While Taoism does not explicitly forbid warfare, its central principle is that people should align themselves with the energy of the universe; that humans should learn to perceive the Tao, or the Way, and to go with it, not to fight against it. The poem is a striking image of how men fail to do this: they build fortifications, they go to war, and they seek to impose their will upon the universe, rather than remaining still and waiting for the universe to impose its will on them.

The other central symbol in this poem, characteristic of Li Po's work, is the moon. The poem opens with an image of the bright moon that illuminates the mountain, the fortifications, and the soldiers. The moon was a powerful symbol in T'ang thinking; it was considered the manifestation of the powers of *yin*, the generative, feminine, mysterious force of the universe. Chinese philosophy divides the world into *yin* and *yang*, forces of opposition without which the universe could not function, and that can exist only and ever in dynamic interdependence with one another. *Yin* is the female force, and is associated with water, earth, nighttime, the cold, the moon, and passivity. *Yang* is the male force, and is associated with fire, the sky, daylight, heat, the sun, and aggression. The name for the

TOPICS FOR FURTHER STUDY

- "The Moon at the Fortified Pass" contains a series of very specific images. Team up with a partner and match each line with an illustration that you feel visually represents that line. Use an online photo program like iPhoto to create a slide show in which there is at least one image for each line. Then using a program like GarageBand, create a podcast of your slide show in which you narrate each slide with the line of poetry it represents. Present your slide show to your class and explain why you chose the images you did.

- Poetry, music, and painting are all integral to the Chinese sense of cultural history. Interview your parents and grandparents about your own ethnic background and the role that stories, poetry, or music play in those cultures. Then build a Web site whose elements include video interviews with your family, visual representations of important artistic works in your own heritage, recordings of traditional performers, and links to research about ethnic organizations working to keep those traditions alive.

- The T'ang Dynasty is famous for the invention of scroll paintings, especially scroll paintings that illustrate journeys through the mountains. Research scroll paintings and pick one to which you feel drawn. Write a history of this genre and an analysis of the painting you chose. Then make a presentation to your class that includes reproductions of the painting. Discuss the impact of scroll paintings on poets of the era, and explain what you found compelling about this particular painting.

- Select another poem by a Chinese poet and write an essay in which you compare it with "The Moon at the Fortified Pass." You might consider a poem by one of other classical poets of the T'ang Dynasty: Tu Fu, Wang Wei, or Po Chüi. Research the aesthetic goals of classical Chinese poetry to show the ways in which the two poems adhere to these goals and diverge from them.

- After the An Lushan rebellion, Li Po was exiled to the far west for two years. Team up with several classmates and write a play in which you dramatize the experience of being exiled. Where is your protagonist when he or she is exiled? Why does the government declare that this person can never return home? What loved ones and possessions does your character leave behind? Your play should have at least three scenes. When it is complete, perform it for your class or record it and post it on YouTube or your Web page.

- Although Lensey Namioka's young-adult novel *An Ocean Apart, a World Away*, takes place centuries later than Li Po's poem, it also concerns a tumultuous period in Chinese history. Read the novel, and then write a paper in which you compare and contrast the political situation in which Xueyan finds herself to the one Li Po portrays in "The Moon at the Fortress Pass." In what ways does Xueyan align herself with the social and political forces that govern her time, and in what way does she struggle against them?

---

moon is *yin-po*; hence, it was considered the heavenly incarnation of *yin* itself. For Li Po, the moon was a source of endless fascination, it appears in over a third of his poems and his legendary death associates him with trying to embrace the moon. That it is the bright moon that rises to illuminate the scene, that it is the force of *yin* that illuminates the warlike movements of men, indicates a gentle criticism of the actions of men and the impulse to go to

The poem is about the protection of the homeland. (Hung Chung Chih | Shutterstock.com)

war. The poem is not concerned with the justice or injustice of the coming battle, but rather with the individual fates of the soldiers, who are after all also men. In submitting to their fates, these men are submitting to the real possibility that they will never return to those at home, to their women who toss restlessly in their bed chambers far away.

Fate

By the eighth century, when Li Po was wandering China and writing poems, Buddhism had arrived from India and had been adapted into its Chinese form known as Ch'an (which later spread to Japan where it was called Zen). Li Po, like the other intellectuals of his time, would have been familiar with the ideas of Ch'an Buddhism; however, he seems to have been more deeply influenced by Taoism. There is some evidence from his biography that he spent time in Taoist monasteries in the mountains, and there is much Taoist imagery in his poems. However, it is important to remember that during the time that he lived, the lines had not yet been completely drawn between belief systems.

The subject of "The Moon at the Fortified Pass" is a line of Chinese soldiers, marching to do battle with an invading army from the north, and the knowledge those men carry that many of them will not be returning from the battlefield. The concept of fate, in any culture, is tied to the notion of death. The ways in which people face the inevitable ending of their lives, whether that death comes at the hand of external forces or is simply the result of the natural processes of aging and death, form the central concept of most religious and philosophical systems.

Taoism is probably the oldest belief system in Chinese philosophy, and it is based on the idea that the world is comprised of dualistic forces that exist in dynamic opposition. The energy generated by the flow of these opposites is what causes the universe to proceed: man/woman, hot/cold, north/south, passive/aggressive, moon/sun. While there is no one term in Taoism that equates to the western notion of fate, one could examine the idea of the Tao as an analogue. The Tao translates as "the Way," and aligning oneself with the Tao becomes the central task of the Taoist. To align oneself with the Tao is to recognize that there are many forces in the universe that can neither be named nor controlled, and it is the task of the proper person to cease struggling. In this sense, the soldiers' march can be seen as an alignment with the Tao, for they are marching along the road (an alternative translation for Tao) that passes between heaven and earth. While they might cast longing glances back toward home, they do not break ranks, and they continue on toward the battlefield from which they realize they might not return. They are illuminated by the moon, the very embodiment of *yin*, the element of passivity and acceptance. While these are not usually qualities one associates with soldiers, who are aggressive by nature, Li Po portrays these soldiers as persons who are subjected to forces beyond their control, and who are acquiescing to the fate that awaits them on the battlefield. In so doing, the soldiers align themselves with the Tao: they follow the Way to the Mountain of Heaven and pass between the earth and the moon. They are perfectly aligned with their fates, and so, become symbolic of how the good Taoist accepts his fate without struggle.

STYLE

Yüeh-fu *or Song Form Poems*

"The Moon at the Fortified Pass" is an example of a Chinese poetic form known as *yüeh-fu*. *Yüeh-fu* were originally written for music, and they retained a loose ballad style that was exempt from the strict rules of most other forms of Chinese poetry. Chinese poetic form in the T'ang dynasty was divided into two major categories: the ancient or unruled poems, which were of undetermined length, and the modern or ruled poems, which were limited to five or seven lines. Since learning to write a proper poem was a crucial part of the Imperial examination system that determined whether one could hold positions in the court bureaucracy, everyone in educated society knew that a good poem was one that followed all the rules and fulfilled the expectations of form and content. Li Po was famous for breaking these rules. His poetry was continually surprising people, which was not considered a positive trait among the more conservative court poets he encountered during his two years serving the Emperor.

Li Po wrote a large number of poems in the *yüeh-fu* form, and "The Moon at the Fortified Pass" falls into a particular subgenre of *yüeh-fu* poetry, poems of war and soldiers. Unlike much of the Greek and Roman poetry about war that forms the foundation of the Western poetic tradition, *yüeh-fu* poems did not glorify battle, nor do they seem to have been used to inspire patriotic feelings among their listeners. On the contrary, *yüeh-fu* poems were part of a long tradition of recording the sufferings and disasters caused by war. This tradition stretches back to the sixth century BCE. By the T'ang Dynasty, *yüeh-fu* poetry had evolved to become the default form for antiwar poetry. The T'ang dynasty was a particularly fertile period for antiwar *yüeh-fu* poems, which were written not only by Li Po, but by Tu Fu, Bai Juyi, and Yuan Zhen as well. Li Po was particularly known for his *yüeh-fu*. As Stephen Owen points out in *The Great Age of Chinese Poetry: The High T'ang*, *yüeh-fu* "make up about one-fifth of Li Po's collection.... During the T'ang, Li Po was best known for his *yüeh-fu* and songs." While "The Moon at the Fortified Pass" depicts the plight of soldiers being sent to war, it is a relatively restrained poem. Many of Li Po's other *yüeh-fu* were famous for their histrionic (over-exaggerated) protagonists, their use of colloquial language, and their depiction of wild drinking matches, during which the poet achieved a state of *wu-wei*, or spontaneous oneness with the world.

Translation

The Chinese language is grammatically different from English in dramatic ways. The Chinese language does not use articles, there are no tenses, no singular or plural, and grammatical relationships must be implied by the contextual relationship of the order in which the characters are organized. Also, characters, while complex, represent words of only a single syllable, the meaning of which is determined by the tone in which it is spoken. Mandarin Chinese, the Chinese spoken in mainland China and Taiwan, has four tones: neutral, rising, falling, and swooping, while Cantonese, the Chinese spoken in Hong Kong and other parts of the far south, can have as many as twelve different tones. Classical Chinese poetry uses the four tones, and tonal patterns, along with the number of characters per line. Some of the most famous Chinese poems can be read in different directions; if one reads left to right the poem has one meaning, while if one reads top to bottom along the columns of characters, the poem has a different meaning. Some poems can also be read front to back, and back to front in a circular fashion.

Since early translators of Chinese poetry like Witter Bynner and Ezra Pound did not speak Chinese, they had to rely on Chinese transliterations. A transliteration is a literal, word-for-word transcription of the original language. Because the meaning of Chinese characters changes depending on their context, this leaves ample room for interpretation on the part of the translator. Also, since the qualities of what is considered poetic varies widely from language to language, and from era to era, many translators sought to make the Chinese poems sound poetic in the manner of the language into which they were translating. This sometimes resulted in poems that bear very little relation to the original.

There are two primary translations of "The Moon at the Fortified Pass" available in English: one translated by Bynner, and one by David Hinton, in *The Selected Poems of Li Po*, published in 1996. Hinton's translation is titled "Frontier-Mountain Moon," and one of the first differences that the reader will notice is that this version is arranged into couplets. Hinton's style, unlike the early-twentieth-century style of Bynner, is sparing in its use of articles, and pays close attention to parallel syllable counts in each couplet, thereby seeking to approximate some of the sound and feeling of the original Chinese. There are differences of vocabulary as well—where Bynner refers to the view as encompassing the clouds and sea in the second line, Hinton translates it as a sea made of clouds, which is a distinctly different concept. The ending of the two poems is also quite distinct. Bynner's version refers to generic sleepers at home who toss and turn, while Hinton makes it specific, referring to an individual woman in a tower, who cries out in her sleep. These differences are emblematic of the interpretive choices that translators are forced to make in any language, but that are amplified by the grammatical differences between English and Chinese.

Translation styles, like all literary styles, evolve over time, and so it is always prudent to consult as many different translations as possible when working with poetry in translation. Many people consider true translation of poetry to be impossible, since each poem carries with it the entire literary tradition of its native tongue, as well as connotations that cannot be accurately carried between languages. However, by consulting multiple translations, one can begin to get a feeling for the choices that each translating poet made, as well as those the original poet intended.

HISTORICAL CONTEXT

The T'ang Dynasty

The T'ang Dynasty lasted from 618 to 907 CE and was a period of reunification of North and South China after several centuries of division and feudal warfare. It was a period during which the Imperial government sought to strengthen its position at home, and this was accomplished by the codification of laws. The T'ang legal code sought to institutionalize the social and political hierarchies upon which the emperor's power rested, and thus, penalties varied depending on the status of the person committing the crime. The consequences were significantly higher for a person of low social status who committed a crime against a person of higher status than vice versa. The legal principles established in the T'ang Dynasty remained central to the Chinese legal system during all the dynasties that succeeded it. The T'ang period also saw an expansion of the Imperial examination system, which was established during the Sui Dynasty to ensure that the thousands of bureaucrats it took to govern the empire were proper Confucians, loyal to the government. During the T'ang period, the examinations were expanded to include the Five Classics, which are major works of Confucian thought. While the examination system still favored sons of the aristocratic elite, it was nonetheless a meritocratic system that allowed some social mobility between classes. It also allowed a rare pathway for talented men from unconnected families to obtain coveted government positions.

Poetry and the Imperial Examinations

Poetry was a crucial element of these imperial examinations, and poems were judged not on their originality of expression or content, but rather on the rigor with which they fulfilled the expectations of that particular form. Not only were poetic forms determined by elements such as

COMPARE & CONTRAST

- **700s:** T'ang Dynasty poets Li Po, Wang Wei, Tu Fu, and Po Chüi expand the boundaries of conventional poetic form. Poets of the T'ang move beyond the dualism of Taoist versus Confucian imagery and ideas by incorporating the increasingly prevalent ideas of Buddhism. The T'ang is considered the golden age of Chinese poetry, and poets from this era will be considered the finest poets of the Chinese canon for centuries to come.

    1920s: Witter Bynner and Kiang Kang-Hu publish *The Jade Mountain*, a translation of *Three Hundred T'ang Poems* in which "The Moon at the Fortified Pass" appears. Chinese poetry begins to make itself known in the West, and the lack of ornament, the reliance on images of the physical world, and the appearance of simplicity appeal to modernist and imagist writers, rendering Chinese poems fascinating to the poets of the day.

    Today: As opportunities for study and cultural exchange expand, Chinese poetry comes to be seen less and less as an exotic area of study. Poets like Gary Snyder, Phillip Whalen, Kenneth Rexroth, Alan Williamson, Jane Hirshfield, and Robert Hass cite the great poets of the T'ang dynasty as serious influences on their own work.

- **700s:** From 755 to 763, the peace of the T'ang dynasty is ripped apart by the An Lushan rebellion. An Lushan's forces brutally sack the capital Chang'an and nearly succeed in overthrowing the central government. Chinese census figures of the time show the terrible toll the rebellion takes: of the fifty-three million citizens of the empire at the war's beginning, thirty-six million are killed, displaced and made homeless.

    1920s: The early decades of the twentieth century are a period of turmoil. With the death of the Empress Dowager, the Qing dynasty comes to an end and a period of instability ensues as China struggles to become a unified modern nation state. Beginning in the late 1920s, Sun Zhongshan's (sometimes transliterated Sun Yatsen) Nationalist party and the Communist party led by Mao Tse-Tung begin what becomes an epic struggle to determine the direction of modern China.

    Today: In the aftermath of Mao's death and calamities like the Cultural Revolution, China's leaders seek to find a middle ground between hard-line communism and democracy. While they open China's economy to outside investment and build thriving export and consumer economies, the Chinese people still lack freedoms of speech and self-determination.

- **700s:** During the T'ang dynasty the Chinese discover gunpowder. Early records describe the use of rolled paper tubes filled with gunpowder and strung together with hemp rope, used on ceremonial occasions to frighten away evil spirits. With the invention of gunpowder, the development of sophisticated fireworks becomes an industry separate from the development of weapons, and fireworks displays are mounted for ceremonial occasions.

    1920s: The Chinese export market in fireworks thrives as fireworks become an established part of public celebration in many parts of the world. Although foreign competitors spring up, including the famous Grucci brothers of New Jersey, authentic Chinese fireworks remain the gold standard until they become unavailable after the revolution of 1948.

    Today: Both the opening and closing ceremonies of the 2008 Olympics in Beijing are accompanied by spectacular fireworks displays to remind the world that the Chinese invented this form of entertainment. Controversy ensues when it is discovered that while actual fireworks over the stadium displayed twenty-nine gigantic footprints walking across the sky, the Chinese broadcasting service, out of concerns for how they would look on live television, cut in fifty-five seconds of computer simulation.

the number of characters per line, the tonal patterns (Chinese is a tonal language, and thus one character might have several meanings depending on the tone in which it is spoken), the use of parallel imagery, and the subsequent restraint from repetitions (for instance, if you have tree in line one, you do not want to have another tree in the poem). Many of the qualities of what defined a good poem were not explicitly set down anywhere, and like any elite, the court poets who judged the examination system and bestowed positions on poets saw the fulfillment of their unspoken expectations as a sign that the poet was one of them, and would uphold the traditions and rules by which poetry was thereby judged. Li Po came from outside the Imperial establishment and never sat for the exams. He came from an indistinct family background, quite likely from one of the Central Asian, non-Chinese populations, and had, by virtue of his talents for writing poetry and for self-promotion, obtained a position for himself at court. In his book *The Great Age of Chinese Poetry*, Stephen Owen notes that Li Po "was a poet who surprised his readers and violated their sense of poetic order and decorum. Poets had always taken pride in writing 'surprising' lines... but such delights occurred within clearly defined boundaries of taste." Owen points out: "Many centuries of literary experience had created these boundaries to preserve the balance and unity of a poem. But Li Po stepped outside... and found that readers loved his effrontery." Despite the strictures of the Imperial examination system, the T'ang was a period of great flowering for Chinese poetry, and poets like Li Po, Wang Wei, Tu Fu, Po Chüi, and Li Shangyin, who expanded the boundaries of acceptable poetic form, are still considered the greatest poets of the Chinese canon.

Buddhism in Chinese Life

Buddhism spread to China from India and Southeast Asia sometime around the beginning of the Common Era, but it was during the T'ang period that Buddhism became integrated into Chinese life, like Daoism and Confucianism before it. Buddhist institutions were allowed to flourish, establishing schools in the cities and providing lodging for travelers in remote areas. The social and political power of the monasteries was the result of their growing economic power. By the T'ang period, monasteries owned large tracts of land and huge numbers of serfs, and while they used their financial resources to establish some industries, they also became sources for moneylending and pawnbroking in many areas of the country.

But it was on the Chinese imagination that Buddhism had its greatest impact during this time. Monks used stories, often illustrated with pictures, to proselytize to the peasants. Among those that have survived to the present day is the story of Mulian, who undertook a perilous journey to the underworld, and survived many hazards, in order to rescue his mother. To this day, Chinese people across the globe put food out on family altars to placate the hungry ghosts that this story describes. By the middle of the T'ang period, several sects of Buddhism had become thoroughly Chinese. The Pure Land sect revered the Buddha Amitabha and his faithful companion, the Goddess of Compassion, Guanyin. The Chan sect also formed during this time. While Pure Land Buddhists believed that entrance to the Pure Land could be obtained by the performance of compassionate acts, the Chan sect rejected all external actions. Chan Buddhists believed that the Buddha nature could be experienced directly and suddenly through a lightning bolt of insight. Chan Buddhism eventually spread to Japan, and then to America where it is more commonly known as Zen Buddhism.

The ideas and beliefs of Buddhism were present and available to the T'ang Dynasty poets, and many of them incorporated Buddhist images and concepts into their poems.

An Lushan Rebellion

While the T'ang was an extended period of reunification, political consolidation, and peace, it was violently torn apart by the An Lushan rebellion in 755 CE, toward the end of Li Po's life. The emperor Xuanzong, like most Chinese emperors of the time, had a large number of wives and concubines by which he fathered thirty sons and twenty-nine daughters. Legend has it that Xuanzong had a favorite concubine named Yang Guifei, who was very beautiful and who shared his love of poetry and music. Xuanzong was an old man, and he fell in love with Yang Guifei. At the same time, a military governor named An Lushan came to the capital. He was one of the many military governors of the time whose background was not ethnically Chinese, and Yang Guifei found him amusing. To please her, Xuanzong bestowed many favors on An Lushan, including allowing him to amass troops along the northern

The Great Wall of China (vincent369 | Shutterstock.com)

and northeastern borders. In 755, An Lushan struck, and civil war broke out. An Lushan's forces took the capital Chang'an and sacked it brutally, and although An Lushan's forces were eventually driven back to the northeast, the central government was in shambles and a period of civil unrest ensued. Chinese census figures of the time show the rebellion's toll, of the fifty-three million citizens of the empire at the war's beginning, thirty-six million were killed, displaced, or made homeless. Although the rebellion ended in 763, the T'ang Dynasty never recovered its prewar stability.

CRITICAL OVERVIEW

Li Po, Tu Fu, and Wang Wei are considered the greatest poets of the greatest period in Chinese poetry. Li Po is one of the central figures in the longest continuous poetic tradition in world literature, a member of a lineage that stretches from 1500 BCE to the present. During this time, poetry has been practiced actively by every member of the educated classes—knowledge of poetic forms and ability to write occasional poetry has always been a central component of Chinese intellectual life. In the west, it was the modernist poets of the early twentieth century who introduced Chinese poetry to readers. Seeking to shake off abstraction and rhetorical formalism, the modernists found a model for their own work in the clarity of image and concrete language that characterizes the Chinese tradition. In the introduction to *The Jade Mountain*, the anthology of Chinese poetry published by Witter Bynner from which this translation of "The Moon at the Fortified Pass" is taken, Bynner points out that

> Whereas western poets will take actualities as points of departure for exaggeration or fantasy, or else as shadows of contrast against dreams of unreality, the great Chinese poets accept the world exactly as they find it in all its terms, and...seldom talk about one thing in terms of another but...make the ultimately exact terms become the beautiful terms.

Originally published in 1920, *The Jade Mountain* was one of the earliest modern anthologies of Chinese poetry for an English audience.

By 1973, Chinese poetry had become sufficiently mainstream that Penguin Classics published *Li Po and Tu Fu* with an extensive introduction by Arthur Cooper. Cooper posits that the two poets represent two deep strains of Chinese thinking, the Taoist and the Confucian. The Confucian strain is represented by all the responsible actions of the daytime citizen, such as going to work, following the rules, and honoring one's parents. The Taoist strain is represented by the liberation of the night time, a time of reflection, or dreams, and in the Chinese tradition, of drunkenness. Li Po is the Taoist while Tu Fu is considered the Confucian poet, and as Cooper notes of Li Po, "his constantly recurring symbol is the reflected light of the moon at night." Cooper goes on to note that over the centuries Li Po has been accused of being an escapist, but that this is not pejorative since

> he has helped provide the healing of escape to his countrymen for twelve centuries; sometimes making them forget their problems in unthinking gaiety, but still more making them feel (by stimulating, as it were, their *peripheral* rather than their *direct* vision) that there is infinitely more in the Universe than what is worrying them, or than they can see directly and understand.

In the later decades of the twentieth century, Americans, including Kenneth Rexroth, Gary Snyder, Robert Hass, and Jane Hirshfield, have all been deeply influenced by Chinese classical poetry. Snyder, in his essay "What Poetry Did in China," notes that "Chinese poetry has had a strong effect on occidental poets tired of heroics and theologies. That this actually elaborate and complex poetic tradition should have made such a contribution to occidental modernism is rather curious." And yet, as one of the poets for whom this was the case, Snyder proceeds to offer this explanation: "it can be understood as having something to do with the twentieth-century thirst for naturalistic secular clarity. Chinese poetry provided the exhilarating realization that such clarity can be accomplished in the mode of poetry."

As western audiences have become more familiar with Chinese poetry, the older translations by writers like Witter Bynner and Kenneth Rexroth, who could not actually read the language but who relied on transliterations, have increasingly come to seem old-fashioned and inaccurate. Newer translations by Americans who read and speak Chinese, like David Hinton and Bill Porter (also known as Red Pine), have naturally come to replace these older versions, although it is to those early translators that we owe a debt of gratitude for bringing these works to the west in the first place.

CRITICISM

Charlotte M. Freeman

Freeman is a writer, editor, and former academic living in small-town Montana. In the following essay, she examines how Li Po's poem "The Moon at the Fortified Pass" demonstrates the central challenge of Taoism: negotiating the relationship between humans and nature, negotiating the relationship between humans and society, and the struggle of the individual to master the emotions.

Li Po is considered one of the central Taoist poets in the Chinese canon. In this, he is often compared to Tu Fu, his contemporary, who is considered the quintessential Confucian poet. Where Tu Fu counsels obedience to hierarchy and the upholding of social norms, Li Po was famous for his drunkenness, his rude remarks, and his advocacy of the spontaneous embrace of the moment. While not one of his drunken poems, "The Moon at the Fortified Pass" shows Li Po working his way through the central challenges each person must navigate to live a proper life according to the Taoist worldview. Taoism posits that the universe is governed by sets of dualisms: heaven and earth, man and woman, hot and cold. These qualities are defined in opposition to one another, but they are also dependent upon one another. None of them can exist in isolation, they can only exist in relationship with and in contrast to the other.

In the Taoist worldview, it is the energy generated by the interplay of these forces that brings the world into existence and keeps the system flowing. The lifetime task of the Taoist practitioner is to align himself or herself with this force. In proper alignment, the individual flows with the energy of the universe; when out of alignment, the individual struggles against it. The Tao is often translated as the Way, and the central image that Taoists use to explain this motivating force is to invoke the flowing nature of the river, or the implacability of the wind. While Taoism is an ancient and complicated belief system, Li Po's poem provides a good introduction to the central challenges the Taoist

WHAT DO I READ NEXT?

- Noted anthologist Tony Barnstone and Chinese poet-scholar Chou Ping have edited *The Anchor Book of Chinese Poetry: From Ancient to Contemporary, The Full 3000-Year Tradition* (2005). This comprehensive volume covers as much of the massive history of Chinese poetry as one is likely to find in English, and it does a masterful job putting the poets and their eras in context.

- American poet Gary Snyder has been deeply influenced by Chinese poetry, and in 1996 he published *Mountains and Rivers without End*, a collection of poetry inspired by a classical work of Chinese scroll art by the same name. Snyder began working on these poems in 1956, and it took him forty years to complete his project of applying Chinese Zen poetics to an American landscape. This collection is an excellent example of how classical Chinese poetry continues as a living influence in contemporary poetry.

- Gene Luen Yang's prizewinning graphic novel for young adults *American Born Chinese* (2008) is the story of Jin Wang, a lonely Taiwanese American boy navigating the challenges of middle school in San Francisco. The novel filters Jin Wang's feelings of being born in the wrong body through the story of the Chinese folk hero the Monkey King and through the figure of Chin-kee, an amalgamation of every ugly Chinese American stereotype. This lively and emotionally affecting book was the first graphic novel nominated for the American Book Award.

- David Hinton is considered the finest contemporary translator of Chinese poetry, and his collection *Mountain Home: The Wilderness Poetry of Ancient China* (2005) is an excellent resource for further exploration how rivers-and-mountain (*shan-sui*) poetry lies at the heart of the Chinese poetic tradition. Rivers and mountains were not considered mere landscape to classical Chinese poets, but were rather thought to be active forces in the universe, whose influence on us is continual. This is an excellent introduction to the ways in which Taoist and Ch'an thought influenced the core poetry of the Chinese canon.

- Although the life of African American botanist George Washington Carver might not seem to have anything in common with the poetry of Li Po, Marilyn Nelson's *Carver, a Life in Poems* (2001) uses many of the qualities of Chinese poetry that so influenced the modernists and Beat poets. These poems are spare, sincere, and rely on the things of the world, not flights of metaphoric fancy, to make their point. Winner of the 2001 *Boston Globe-Horn Book* Award for fiction and poetry, this volume makes an odd, but apt, multicultural read-alike when paired with Li Po.

- Critically acclaimed fantasy novelist Guy Gavriel Kay's *Under Heaven*, published in 2010, features the character Sima Zian, the Banished Immortal, who is based on Li Po. The tale offers a fictionalized retelling of the An Lushan rebellion that combines supernatural elements with the *wuxia* (or martial arts adventure) narrative tradition.

---

faces. These include understanding the proper relationship of the individual to nature, the proper relationship of the individual to society, and the proper manner in which the individual must govern his or her own emotional life.

Li Po opens "The Moon at the Fortified Pass" by invoking both the actual natural world and the metaphoric forces of nature that govern the universe. The first four lines of the poem contain images of the moon, mountain,

"WHILE TAOISM IS AN ANCIENT AND COMPLICATED BELIEF SYSTEM, LI PO'S POEM PROVIDES A GOOD INTRODUCTION TO THE CENTRAL CHALLENGES THE TAOIST FACES."

sea, cloud, and wind, thereby covering all of the forces of nature. The scene is a mountain pass over which the armies of China must travel in order to get to the battlefields along the northwestern border. While nature in Western poetry often appears solely as a metaphor for human emotions, in Chinese poetry, nature remains actual even when, as in this poem, it also carries a metaphoric meaning. In the Taoist worldview, the mountains, which are the place where the earth reaches up to touch the sky, are considered the source of all generative power, the place from whence the waters and winds arise, and also the site of spiritual generation. In order to go to war, the soldiers must pass through this spiritually charged space, the place where the forces of earth rise up to touch the sky. That this particular pass takes them beside the Mountain of Heaven only underscores this point. The pass is illuminated by the moon, which has risen out of the obscurity of the clouds. It is difficult to overstate the importance of the moon as a symbol in Li Po's work. The moon is more than a simple heavenly body in the Taoist cosmology, it is the embodiment and source of the *yin* forces of the universe. *Yin* represents darkness, women, cold, and the qualities of passivity and receptivity that allow the movement of its opposite, *yang*. *Yin* is not negative in the pejorative sense with which Western readers might imagine. Because *yin* and *yang* are inextricably entwined, and because the one cannot exist without the other, they are not seen as binary opposites in the sense of the Western concepts of negative and positive, but rather, are seen as essential qualities without which the world cannot function. For Li Po, the moon was the source of all beauty and mystery. It was the emblem of darkness that nonetheless shines brightly in the night. It was the force from which poetry and song and drinking and conviviality and art all arose. In the poem, the moon rises out of a bank of clouds that stretch below the mountain, obscuring the world of men below. It is an infinite expanse of obscurity, without boundary, and depending on the translation one is using, it either stretches all the way to the sea, with which it seems to meld, or it is itself a sea-like expanse of clouds. In either case, below the brightly illuminated and charged space of the pass between heaven and earth, the rest of the world is hidden by a boundless and amorphous bank of clouds. In beginning the poem here, Li Po is signaling that something extraordinary is going on in this poetic space. He takes readers on a figurative journey into the heart of nature to examine the meaning of life, just as the soldiers, crossing so close to heaven as they march to war, must examine the meaning of the lives many of them are sure to lose.

While the ideal Taoist life was that of the wandering hermit who lived in spontaneous oneness with nature, the cosmology acknowledged that this was hardly possible for the majority of people. Most people were going to have to live in society, and for the majority of them, that meant accommodating themselves to their fates. In "The Moon at the Fortified Pass," the soldiers are portrayed in this manner. This is not a propaganda poem; it does not seek to drum up patriotic or nationalistic support for the war to which these soldiers are marching. Rather, it portrays both the Chinese and the enemy soldiers as being at the mercy of their fates. China sends its men in one direction while the Tartars (or Mongols depending on translation) watch from the opposite direction. There is no reason given for the impending war; the soldiers are fighting because they are soldiers, and they have been given orders, and this is what soldiers do. The poem applies this attitude to both sides. The Chinese are not portrayed as heroes and the Tartars as villains; rather, both sets of soldiers are portrayed as men caught up by forces larger than themselves. The soldiers are examples of Taoist dualism in action. As soldiers (and men), they are by their nature forces of *yang* aggression, and yet they exhibit *yin* as they march passively toward their fates. Soldiers must be aggressive toward the enemy, but passive toward their superior officers and the government they serve. By undertaking their march, the soldiers are in correct alignment with the Tao: they are aligning themselves with forces greater than themselves and are not going against the flow. Historically this is also analogous to the manner

Painting of the Chinese landscape described in the poem (iBird | Shutterstock.com)

in which Taoism coexisted well with Confucianism, since both systems advocated that the individual should recognize his or her role in the social order and should seek to fulfill that role, not to move among classes.

And yet, Li Po's soldiers are not automatons, nor does the poet portray war as a noble pursuit. They are simply men, whose passage so close to the mountain of heaven presages the mortal danger toward which they march. It is in this last section of the poem where Li Po portrays the most difficult struggle that human beings face: the management of inner lives in face of a finite life span. While the soldiers are being forced to confront this in a more dramatic fashion than is required of most people, the fact is, all are doomed to die eventually, and the manner in which the inevitability of fate is accepted or struggled against is the central problem of any philosophic or religious system. Li Po's soldiers continue their march, and they continue it in full knowledge of what awaits them. They are not cosseted in this by the false anger of nationalistic propaganda. They simply march because it is their fate. But they also turn back and look over their shoulders with longing toward their homes. Li Po ends the poem with the image of the wives, left alone in the upstairs bedrooms of the homes the soldiers have left, tossing and turning, unable to sleep. It is a tender image of the difficulty each person faces when attempting to accept fate. Since the world depends on both forces—happy and sad, joy and sorrow, birth and death—the challenge becomes to truly accept the difficult portions of life. In many ways, all people are like the soldiers, fulfilling one tenet of the Tao by accepting a lot in life and marching toward fate, while also being fallible human beings, who look back, longing for home, clinging to the comforts and familiarity of the lives they do not want to lose.

"The Moon at the Fortified Pass" was written to be sung out loud, accompanied by music, most likely in the court of the Emperor who had the power to send men to war. While it is not an explicitly antiwar poem, its tone of melancholy and longing for the comforts of peacetime puts it squarely in the tradition of much *yüeh-fu* poetry, which often offered up gentle social criticism. The Taoist imagery upon which the poem relies would have been readily understandable to any educated Chinese audience of the time, as it represents one of the oldest strains of Chinese cosmological thinking.

Source: Charlotte M. Freeman, Critical Essay on "The Moon at the Fortified Pass," in *Poetry for Students*, Gale, Cengage Learning, 2012.

Florence Ayscough

In the following excerpt, Asycough praises the evocative power of Li's best poems as represented in Fir-Flower Tablets.

Li T'ai-po's poetry is full of dash and surprise. At his best, there is an extraordinary exhilaration in his work; at his worst, he is merely repetitive. Chinese critics have complained that his subjects are all too apt to be trivial, and that his range is narrow. This is quite true; poems of farewell, deserted ladies sighing for their absent lords, officials consumed by home-sickness, [paeans] of praise for wine—in the aggregate there are too many of these. But how fine they often are! "The Lonely Wife," "Poignant Grief During a Sunny Spring," "After Being Separated for a Long Time," such poems are the truth of emotion. Take again his inimitable humour in the two "Drinking Alone in the Moonlight" poems, or "Statement of Resolutions after Being Drunk on a Spring Day." Then there are the poems of hyperbolical description such as "The Perils of the Shu Road," "The Northern Flight," and "The Terraced Road of the Two-Edged Sword Mountains." Mountains seem to be in his very blood. Of the sea, on the other hand, he has no such intimate knowledge; he sees it after, from some height, but always as a thing apart, a distant view. The sea he gazes at; the mountains he treads under foot, their creepers scratch his face, the jutting rocks beside the path bruise his hands. He knows the straight-up, cutting-into-the-sky look of mountain peaks just above him, and feels, almost bodily, the sheer drop into the angry river tearing its way through a narrow gully below, a river he can see only by leaning dangerously far over the cliff upon which he is standing. There is a curious sense of perpendicularity about these mountain rhapsodies. The vision is strained up for miles, and shot suddenly down for hundreds of feet. The tactile effect of them is astounding; they are not to be read, but experienced. And yet I am loth to say that Li Tai-po is at his greatest in description, with poems so full of human passion and longing as "The Lonely Wife," and "Poignant Grief During a Sunny Spring," before me. There is no doubt at all that in Li T'ai-po we have one of the world's greatest lyrists.

Great though he was, it cannot be denied that he had serious weaknesses. One was his tendency to write when the mood was not there, and at these moments he was not ashamed to repeat a fancy conceived before on some other occasion. Much of his style he crystallized into a convention, and brought it out unblushingly whenever he was at a loss for something to say. Sustained effort evidently wearied him. He will begin a poem with the utmost spirit, but his energy is apt to flag and lead to a close so weak as to annoy the reader. His short poems are always admirably built, the endings complete and unexpected; the architectonics of his long poems leave much to be desired. He seems to be ridden by his own emotion, but without the power to draw it up and up to a climax; it bursts upon us in the first line, sustains itself at the same level for a series of lines, and then seems to faint exhausted, reducing the poet to the necessity of stopping as quickly as he can and with as little [jar] as possible. Illustrations of this tendency to a weak ending can be seen in "The Lonely Wife," "The Perils of the Shu Road," and "The Terraced Road of the Two-Edged Sword Mountains," but [that] he could keep his inspiration to the end on occasion, "The Northern Flight" proves.

Finally, there are his poems of battle: "Songs of the Marches," "Battle to the Sought of the City," and "Fighting to the South of the City." Nothing can be said of these except that they are superb. If there is a hint of let-down in the concluding lines of "Fighting to the South of the City," it is due to the frantic Chinese desire to quote from order authors, and this is an excellent example of the chief vice of Chinese poetry, since these two lines are taken from the *Tao Tê Ching*, the sacred book of Taoism; the others, even the long "Songs of the Marches," are admirably sustained.

In Mr. Waley's excellent monograph on Li T'ai-po, appears the following paragraph: "Wang An-Shih (A.D. 1021–1086), the great reformer of the Eleventh Century, [observes]: 'Li Po's style is swift, yet never careless; lively, yet never informal. But his intellectual outlook was low and sordid. In nine poems out of ten he deals with nothing but wine and women.'" A somewhat splenetic criticism truly, but great reformers have seldom either the acumen or the sympathy necessary for the judgment of poetry. Women and wine there are in abundance, but how treated? In no mean or sordid manner certainly. Li T'ai-po was not a didactic poet, and we of the Twentieth Century may well thank fortune for that. Peradventure the Twenty-first will dote again upon the didactic, but we must follow our particular inclination which is, it must be admitted, quite counter to anything of the sort. No low or mean attitude indeed, but a rather restricted one we may, if we please, charge against Li T'ai-po. He was a sensuous realist, representing the world as he saw it, with beauty as his guiding star. Conditions to him were static; he wasted none of his force in speculating on what they should be. A scene or an emotion *was*, and it was his business to reproduce it, not to analyze how it had come about or what would best make its recurrence impossible. (pp. lxxvii–lxxx)

Source: Florence Ayscough, introduction to *Fir-Flower Tablets*, edited and translated by Florence Ayscough and Amy Lowell, Houghton Mifflin, 1921, pp. xix–xcv.

SOURCES

Barboza, David, "Olympics Close with a Bang and a Double-Decker Bus," in *New York Times*, August 25, 2008, http://www.nytimes.com/2008/08/25/world/asia/25iht-25beijing.15596232.html?scp=2&sq=beijing%20olympics%20fireworks&st=cse (accessed July 1, 2011).

Bynner, Witter, and Kiang Kang-Hu, "Introduction," in *The Jade Mountain*, translated by Witter Bynner and Kiang Kang-Hu, Knopf, 1920, pp. xvii.

———, "The Moon at the Fortified Pass," in *The Chinese Translations*, Witter Bynner Foundation, 1978, pp. 112.

Cai, Zong-Qi, *How to Read Chinese Poetry*, Columbia University Press, 2008, pp. 360–61.

Cooper, Arthur, "Introduction," in *Li Po and Tu Fu*, Penguin, 1973, pp. 18–19.

Ebrey, Patricia Buckley, "A Cosmopolitan Empire: The Tang Dynasty 618–907," in *Cambridge Illustrated History of China*, Cambridge University Press, 2010, pp. 108–35.

Hinton, David, "Introduction," in *The Selected Poems of Li Po*, translated by David Hinton, New Directions, 1996, p. xiii.

Owen, Stephen, "Li Po: A New Concept of Genius," in *The Great Age of Chinese Poetry: The High T'ang*, Yale University Press, 1981, pp. 109–46.

Po, Li, "Frontier-Mountain Moon," in *The Selected Poems of Li Po*, translated by David Hinton, New Directions, 1996, p. 6.

———, "The Moon at the Fortified Pass," in *The Jade Mountain*, translated by Witter Bynner, Knopf, 1920, pp. 60–61.

Snyder, Gary, "What Poetry Did in China," in *A Place in Space*, Counterpoint, 1995, p. 91.

Spencer, Richard, "Beijing Olympic 2008 Opening Ceremony Giant Firework Footprints Faked," in *Telegraph* (London, England), August 10, 2008, http://www.telegraph.co.uk/sport/othersports/olympics/2534499/Beijing-Olympic-2008-opening-ceremony-giant-firework-footprints-faked.html (accessed July 1, 2011).

FURTHER READING

Berthong, John, *Confucianism: A Short Introduction*, Oneworld, 2000.

Written by a renowned scholar of religious studies at Boston University, this short volume takes the novel approach of following a fictitious Chinese couple of the seventeenth century through a typical day. As they go about their business, they are each confronted with myriad opportunities for correct or incorrect behavior. It offers an experiential introduction to the tenets of Confucianism so influential in Chinese thought.

Fields, Rick, *How the Swans Came to the Lake*, Shambala, 1992.

Weighing in at nearly four hundred pages, this volume is an exhaustive but entertaining history of the development of American Buddhism. Fields traces the story of how Buddhism came to be known in the west, including its influence on the American Transcendentalists, as well as the stories of those immigrant Buddhist communities that did not integrate. The book is an important contribution to the history of religion in America, as well as an entertaining read, illustrated with the stories of many interesting individuals.

Hinton, David, ed., *Classical Chinese Poetry: An Anthology*, Farrar, Straus & Giroux, 2008.

In this collection, Hinton covers all the major periods of classical Chinese poetry, from the oral folk poetry of 1500 BCE to the poets of the Sung Dynasty. Hinton is one of the most respected contemporary translators of both ancient and modern Chinese poetry, and this anthology, complete with introductions to the periods and poets, is an excellent resource for any student.

Smullyan, Raymond M., *The Tao Is Silent*, Harper & Row, 1977.

Smullyan's whimsical and humorous introduction to the cosmology of Taoism does justice to both the ideas presented and the joyous spirit that inspired Li Po in particular. While this book is an overview of the tenets of the Tao, it is also quite funny, and is written with the same kind of irreverent charm for which Li Po was so famous.

Snyder, Gary, *The Gary Snyder Reader*, Counterpoint, 1999.

In this volume, Snyder collects almost fifty years of poems and essays, some of them previously unpublished, in an attempt to expose the layers and experiences of a life in writing. Snyder's graduate work was in Chinese poetry and his lifelong study of Zen Buddhism has deeply influenced his work.

Snyder brings the sensibility of classical Chinese poetry into the American idiom, and this book provides ample opportunity to study the fruits of his labor.

Weinberger, Eliot, and Octavio Paz, *Nineteen Ways of Looking at Wang Wei*, Asphodel Press, 1987.

In this slim volume, Weinberger and Paz examine a short poem by Wang Wei, "Lu Zhai," usually translated as "Deer Park." This poem comprises four lines of five characters each, and the book opens with a short discussion of Chinese grammar and poetics, followed by a transliteration of the poem's characters. The authors follow this with nineteen different translations of the poem into English, French, and Spanish by different translators and poets. Each translation is accompanied by a short essay discussing the choices the translators made, how they chose to define the characters, what syllabic patterns they chose, and which images they used.

SUGGESTED SEARCH TERMS

Li Po

Li Po AND poetry

T'ang Dynasty AND poetry

Taoism AND poetry

Chinese Poetry AND calligraphy

Chinese Poetry AND modernism

Chinese Poetry AND beat poets

David Hinton AND Li Po

Li Po AND The Moon at the Fortified Pass

Witter Bynner AND Li Po

David Hinton AND The Moon at the Fortified Pass

Witter Bynner AND The Moon at the Fortified Pass

Li Bai

Li Bo

The Mother

GWENDOLYN BROOKS

1945

Critically acclaimed Pulitzer Prize-winning poet Gwendolyn Brooks often focused on the experience of poor urban African Americans in her poetry. Known for works that resonate as both deeply personal and culturally and socially conscious, Brooks writes about the tragic emotional aftermath a mother experiences in the years following an abortion in the 1945 poem "The Mother." The language of the work is full of pain, and the images are stark and sorrowful. Throughout the poem, Brooks writes as a mother looking back on moments she will never share with children whose lives were not brought into being. She speaks of the fullness of absence in her life, and of the act of abortion as a sin, a crime, but one for which she takes responsibility. Near the end of the poem, the poet struggles with the concept of life and death, resisting the instinct to label the termination of her pregnancy as a death. Rather, she focuses on the love she still feels for the children who were never born. At various points in the poem, and in particular in its final one-word line, Brooks emphasizes that the mother who is the subject of the poem has had multiple abortions.

"The Mother" was originally published in the collection *A Street in Bronzeville* by Harper & Brothers in 1945. The work later appeared in the collection *Selected Poems*, published by Harper Perennial Modern Classics in 2005.

Gwendolyn Brooks (AP Images)

AUTHOR BIOGRAPHY

Brooks was born on June 7, 1917, in Topeka, Kansas. She grew up in Chicago, Illinois, on the poor South Side. Her father, David Brooks, was the son of a runaway slave. He abandoned medical school to work as a janitor and support his family. Her mother, Keziah Brooks, had been a school teacher before marrying David Brooks. Brooks attended an integrated high school where she was the target of racial animosity and discrimination. She later graduated from Woodrow Wilson Junior College in 1936. Brooks then worked as a maid and as a secretary for a spiritual advisor.

In 1939, Brooks married Henry Lowington Blakely II. The couple had a son in 1940 and a daughter in 1951. The couple divorced in 1969 and reunited in 1973. Henry Blakely died in 1996.

In 1941 and 1942, Brooks studied poetry in a workshop program. Two years later, she won the Midwestern Writers Conference prize, which she won again in 1945. The same year, her first volume of poetry, *A Street in Bronzeville*, was published. The volume garnered several poetry awards, and was followed by Guggenheim fellowships in 1946 and 1947. The work was highly praised and earned Brooks a reputation for poetic excellence. Her second volume of poetry, *Annie Allen*, was published in 1949 and won the Pulitzer Prize for Poetry in 1950. Brooks was the first African American recipient of this award.

During the civil rights movement of the 1950s and 1960s, Brooks's poetry became increasingly infused with a sense of social and racial consciousness. She continued to write prolifically, was influenced by the black solidarity of other poets, and published a number of volumes throughout the 1980s and into the 1990s. Toward the end of her career, Brooks received a Lifetime Achievement Award from the National Endowment for the Arts (1989), a National Book Foundation medal for lifetime achievement (1994), and a National Medal of Arts Award (1995).

Brooks died on December 3, 2000, at her home in Chicago.

POEM TEXT

```
Abortions will not let you forget.
You remember the children you got that you
    did not get,
The damp small pulps with a little or with no
    hair,
The singers and workers that never handled the
    air.
You will never neglect or beat                    5
Them, or silence or buy with a sweet.
You will never wind up the sucking-thumb
Or scuttle off ghosts that come.
You will never leave them, controlling your
    luscious sigh,
Return for a snack of them, with gobbling
    mother-eye.                                  10
I have heard in the voices of the wind the
    voices of my dim
killed children.
I have contracted. I have eased
My dim dears at the breasts they could never
    suck.
I have said, Sweets, if I sinned, if I seized   15
Your luck
And your lives from your unfinished reach,
If I stole your births and your names,
Your straight baby tears and your games,
Your stilted or lovely loves, your tumults,
    your marriages,                              20
```

aches, and your deaths,
If I poisoned the beginnings of your breaths,
Believe that even in my deliberateness I was not
   deliberate.
Though why should I whine,
Whine that the crime was other than mine?—   25
Since anyhow you are dead.
Or rather, or instead,
You were never made.
But that too, I am afraid,
Is faulty: oh, what shall I say, how is the truth
   to be said?   30
You were born, you had body, you died.
It is just that you never giggled or planned or
   cried.

Believe me, I loved you all.
Believe me, I knew you, though faintly, and I
   loved, I loved you
All.   35

MEDIA ADAPTATIONS

- "The Mother" is included on the 2006 *Essential Brooks* audio CD, published by the HarperCollins imprint Caedmon. The CD also contains a number of other poems from *A Street in Bronzeville*, as well as works from Brooks's later collections. Brooks herself reads all of the twenty-seven poems included in the collection.

POEM SUMMARY

The text used for this summary is from *Selected Poems*, Harper & Row, 1963, pp. 4–5. Versions of the poem can be found on the following Web pages: http://www.poets.org/viewmedia.php/prmMID/15829 and http://www.poetryfoundation.org/poem/172081.

Stanza 1

"The Mother" is divided into three stanzas. A stanza is a unit of poetry that divides the lines of verse thematically. It structures the poem in the same way that a paragraph is used to organize a work of prose. In Brooks's first stanza, the narrating persona (a character within the poem who conveys the content of the poem to the reader; this person may or may not be a representation of the poet), speaks rhetorically in the second person, using the word "you" as the subject of the action in this stanza. This unidentified "you" may either be regarded as a person to whom the poem is being addressed by the persona, or as the persona's effort to distance herself from the subject matter. The effect of this use of the second person is that the speaker takes on a dual nature, speaking both as a mother and to a mother. The "you" is a mother who has had several abortions. The focus of this stanza is on memory, but rather than depicting actual memories of the past, the narrating persona describes memories of a fictional past, one that never existed because the aborted children were never born. The persona takes the reader through the children's infancies, describing such intimate, gentle details as the small, damp bodies and the babies' hair. She imagines specific futures for the children and additionally offers more general, abstract images, such as the air the children will never breathe. The persona presents to the mother a variety of experiences to consider, both positive and negative, that are lost to her now. She emphasizes that just as the mother will never buy these children sweets, she will also never neglect or abuse them. She will never curtail her children's thumb-sucking, or protect her children from their fears. In the final two poignant lines of the stanza, the persona describes to the mother the way she will never leave the children, attempting to control a love-choked sigh, and then return to the children to feast on them with her hungry gaze.

Stanza 2

In the second stanza, Brooks shifts the perspective of the poem. Now, rather than addressing the mother as "you," the persona speaks in the first person, and now becomes the subject of the poem, referring to herself as "I" and putting herself exclusively in the role of the mother. This stanza is the longest, and in it the mother reflects on the way she can hear the voices of the children in the wind. In the first stanza, reference to the actual deaths of the children is avoided; the persona speaks rather about the children as her children but also as children that she did not get to have. Now the mother refers specifically to the fact that the children have been killed. She speaks of the sense she has of herself as diminishing, of shrinking into herself as the resulting pain of her actions is acknowledged. For the next nine lines, the mother follows the image of easing a nursing infant from her breast with the acknowledgment of the fact that she has sinned by stealing from the children their lives, names, tears, games, loves, futures, and pain. She additionally asserts that although she ended the lives of the children intentionally, she was not entirely deliberate in her actions. This sentiment offers two avenues of interpretation. It could be read as the mother's suggestion that she did not contemplate at the time of the abortions the fullness of the lives she was terminating, that she did not consider fully the implications of her actions. Alternatively, in saying that she did not act in a deliberate fashion, the mother may be referring to the fact that she had never intended to get pregnant, that she did not deliberately choose a course of action that would lead her to having to abort several pregnancies. The meaning is unclear, and the mother does not pursue this line of thinking any further. In the next several lines, however, the mother chastises herself for whining, for attempting to alleviate her own sense of responsibility. She reiterates once more that the children are dead, but then retreats from this notion, contemplating the idea that rather than being dead, perhaps the children were never fully created. This concept, she goes on to state, is not accurate either. The mother questions how the truth of the matter can be expressed. She acknowledges, on the one hand, how the children had physical bodies, and that they died. On the other hand, the children's lives were ended before they had formed as individuals who could laugh or cry. The mother seems to accept both of these notions as truths, the fact that bodies died, but individual people were not yet formed. Abortion is, the mother seems to be struggling to say, a different kind of death, one that she struggles to put into words and to fully comprehend.

Stanza 3

In the brief final stanza, the mother asks the children to believe that she loved them, and that she knew them in some small ways. She repeats that she loved them, and emphasizes in the final line and word of the poem the fact there were several children whose lives were ended before they were born. The tone of the last stanza, in its simplicity and repetition, is one of a play, or even a prayer, either for understanding, or perhaps for forgiveness.

THEMES

Motherhood

In "The Mother," the persona offers a complex vision of motherhood by imagining what her aborted children's lives would have been like had they lived. She comments further on her role in their demise. Although she attempts to explain her actions briefly, she does not attempt to justify them. Like any mother, the speaker in the poem sighs over her infants, lovingly describing their tiny moist bodies, their nearly hairless heads. Yet, this mother will never get to stroke or nuzzle her children. She wonders about the futures her children might have had, imagines with a sense of powerful sorrow the experiences lost to her children, and lost to herself as a mother. She will not be able to help them stop sucking their thumbs, she will never have the feeling of returning to them after a departure, and drinking in the sight of them. Perhaps with some sense of grim satisfaction, she acknowledges that she will also never neglect or hurt her children.

In the second stanza the speaker's pain, her unimaginable sense of loss, is as tragic as that of any mother who has lost her child in any other fashion. The mother's pain is compounded by the knowledge that she has stolen everything from her children: luck and life, their names, their futures. The mother's sense of confusion regarding her own actions is conveyed when she contrasts the undeniable fact that she deliberately had abortions, with her acknowledgment that, despite these acts, there existed a lack of agency, caution, or intention in her own choices or actions. Her meaning is clouded, yet she seems to be attempting to explain either a shortcoming, a lapse of judgment, an accident, an absence of malice, in what she has done. In this moment, the mother grapples with the fact that she has done something that many mothers would deem unimaginable, acting as an agent in the death of her own children. The speaker turns quickly from this idea, as if it is too painful to continue to contemplate, but the vacuum left by this lack of clarity is at the heart of the poem. The speaker's pain is undeniable and understandable, but what the reader craves—an answer to the question

TOPICS FOR FURTHER STUDY

- In "The Mother," Brooks writes from the perspective of a mother who has had several abortions. At the time the poem was written, abortion was illegal across the United States. Research the more recent history of abortion in America, including the 1973 Supreme Court decision *Roe v. Wade*. What was at issue? What did the courts decide in that case? How are the results applicable and significant today? What challenges to the decision have been made in the twenty-first century? Write a report in which you document this history, using Web sites, such as the Center for Reproductive Rights, which provides an overview of the issues (http://reproductiverights.org/en/document/roe-v-wade-then-and-now), as a guide. Keep in mind that you are writing an objective research paper, one in which you discuss and analyze facts, rather than an argumentative paper, in which you persuade a reader to share your opinions.

- In the 1940s, during the time when Brooks was publishing her early poetry about African American experiences, poets from other parts of the globe explored their own unique experiences. Chilean poet Pablo Neruda, like Brooks, writes of sorrow and death in the poem "Only Death," originally published in the collection *Residence on Earth (1925–1945)*. The poem is available in *The Poetry of Pablo Neruda*, published by Farrar, Straus and Giroux in 2003. Read and analyze Neruda's poem. How does the poet characterize death? What language and imagery does he use to convey the impact of death upon the speaker in the poem? Consider as well the poem's formal structure, its stanzaic divisions, its use of rhythm, sound, and repetition. Write an analysis of the poem in which you discuss these elements and explore Neruda's themes in the poem.

- While African American poets in the 1940s examined the discrimination faced by African Americans during this time period, Japanese Americans were recovering from their horrific experiences of World War II, when Japanese Americans were removed from their homes and placed in internment camps by the U. S. government. *Farewell to Manzanar: A True Story of Japanese American Experience during and after the World War II Internment*, by Jeanne Wakatsuki Houston and James D. Houston, is a memoir aimed at young adults that explores this time period in American history. The work was published in 1973 by Houghton Mifflin and has been reprinted numerous times. With a small book group, read it and discuss the discrimination Japanese Americans faced. How did the family in the book cope with what was happening to them? What was the range of attitudes and emotions of individuals in the camp? Create an online blog in which your group discusses your reactions to and opinions about the book.

- Like Brooks, Robert Hayden is placed in the tradition of African American poetry within the generation of writers that followed the Harlem Renaissance. His work is collected in the 1985 volume published by Liveright, *Collected Poems*, edited by Frederick Glaysher. Read a sampling of Hayden's poetry in order to begin to get a sense of the themes most pertinent to his work. Then, select one or two of his poems and create a visual presentation in which you reproduce the poem and accompany it with artwork that helps express the meaning of the work or works. Consider drawing, collage, or other forms of visual representations of the poetry. Discuss your presentation with the class, describing the way your images sprang from Hayden's language, images, themes, and symbols. Provide a few facts about Hayden's life, including information about when and where he was born, the themes of his poetry, and when he died.

"Why?"—the speaker does not provide. What consequently resonates is the speaker's pain.

Grief

In discussing a mother's post-abortion emotional turmoil, "The Mother" plumbs the depths of a mother's pain and sorrow. The poem opens with the acknowledgement that a mother who has had abortions will never be able to forget. What the speaker in the poem goes on to describe, though, is not the abortion itself, or the events that lead the mother to make the decision, or the agonizing decision-making process itself. Rather, the things a mother cannot forget are the lives that never happened. In describing a mother's relationship with her child, and itemizing all the events in the child's life that would or might have happened, but now never will, the speaker emphasizes her deep sense of loss and emotional suffering. The mother's pain stems from the fact that the children will not have the futures they might have had if they had lived. She itemizes for the reader moments in the children's personal histories that never happened, allowing the reader glimpses into the particulars of the mother's pain. She brings forth small details, such as tears and games, and larger events, marriages, loves, deaths. In the depths of her sorrow, the mother reframes the notion of death.

This section is perhaps the most important indicator of the mother's inability to truly deal with what has happened, to her children, and to herself in the aftermath of the abortions. The mother grapples with the notion that her children were beings with bodies that could die, but that they were not yet formed into the individuals they might have become. Upon creating this way of looking at the deaths of her children, she rejects it as invalid, and then takes it up again. This thought process reveals the psychological dimensions of the way the mother gropes for a means of protecting herself from the emotional trauma that plagues her.

In the poem's final stanza, the speaker expresses the enduring nature of her love, and the reader is left with an understanding that this love will be a source of perpetual pain for the mother. In the repetition of sentiments in this stanza, in the way the mother pleads with her children to believe her and expresses her love three times in this short stanza, the mother's grief takes on desperate notes. In this final stanza of the poem, when the mother asserts how well she loved all of the children she

A woman mourns the loss of her baby. (Tyler Olson / Shutterstock.com)

never had, the reader is made aware of how the mother's pain and sorrow are compounded and intensified by the multiple nature of the abortions that she has had.

STYLE

Rhymed Free Verse Poetry

Free verse poetry is poetry that does not employ regular patterns of meter and rhyme. (Meter is a pattern of unaccented and accented syllables in a line of poetry.) Free verse poetry occasionally incorporates intermittent examples of meter, or rhyme patterns that exist in some stanzas of the poem but do not carry all the way through, or are in other ways interrupted or inconsistent. In "The Mother," Brooks does incorporate the use of some rhyme. However, her use of rhyme, when the poem is examined as a whole, is not consistent or regular. The poet's use of rhyme, while regular in the first stanza, loses its tightly knit pattern as the poem progresses. In the first ten-line stanza, Brooks structures the verse into rhymed couplets (a couplet is a pair of lines), giving these verses a sense of order and control. As the poem grows increasingly emotional in the second stanza, this control dissipates. After the first line of the second stanza, Brooks uses a rhymed quatrain with an *abab* pattern. A quatrain is a series of four lines of verse linked by a rhyming pattern. An *abab* pattern is one in which the endings of the first and third lines of the quatrain rhyme with one another, as do the endings of the second and fourth lines. Just as this pattern is established at the onset of the second stanza, it dissolves. Like the first line of the stanza, the sixth line has no rhyming counterpart. The next nine lines of the stanza feature a series of rhymed couplets interrupted after three pairs of couplets by a single line that is linked back to the second couplet in the series through rhyme. The stanza closes with another rhymed couplet. The final three-line stanza makes use of repeated words, but does not include any rhyme pattern. "The Mother," then, incorporates numerous examples of the structure provided by a rhyme scheme, but it does so in a manner that is at first consistent. As the poem progresses, the rhyme structure resurfaces but is periodically interrupted but single unrhymed lines, while the third stanza abandons any use of rhyme. Brooks's use of this intermittent rhyming structure mirrors the speaker's initial attempts to control her emotions in the first stanza, then mimics waves of grief in the second stanza, as the rhyme pattern shifts, ends, and resumes haltingly. In the final stanza, the effort at control as exemplified by the rhyme pattern disappears completely, demonstrating the way in which the speaker becomes completely immersed in her grief.

Narrating Persona

In "The Mother," Brooks makes use of a persona, a character within the poem, who in this case functions as the subject of the poem. The persona also serves as a first-person narrator, describing her own painful experiences. It is not until the second stanza, however, that the character of the narrating persona begins to fully form. In the first stanza, Brooks makes use of second-person narration. By using the pronoun "you," the narrating persona may either be seen as addressing a secondary audience, or, more likely, referring to herself in the second person. As the poem progresses, and the narrating persona reveals that she has had several abortions, it becomes more apparent that in the first stanza, she was referring to herself and her own personal history. The visceral emotional pain that permeates the poem informs the persona's decision to begin in the second person, as the use of the second person distances the speaker in some ways from the tragedy of her actions.

As the second stanza begins, the persona confesses the truth about her past, revealing that she has heard the voices of her dead children in the wind. The persona then addresses her children directly. The "you" in the poem now shifts in meaning, and no longer serves to exemplify the narrator or an addressed audience, but represents the children whose lives she has terminated. She speaks to them directly, telling them in her first-person speaking voice (using "I") of the things she has taken from them. She discusses the extent to which she feels she has sinned, attempts in some small way to defend her actions, then acknowledges with great grief that the responsibility for these deaths lies with her.

HISTORICAL CONTEXT

Abortion in the 1940s

When Brooks published "The Mother" in 1945, abortion was illegal in all forty-eight states. Women were forced to seek abortions from unlicensed practitioners, often in unsanitary, dangerous conditions. Such abortions often risked the lives of the women upon whom they were performed. Although abortions were often performed by legitimate physicians, albeit illegally, these operations could result in death as well. Prosecutors pursued the convictions of these physicians, but eventually shifted their focus and, according to Leslie J. Reagan in *When Abortion Was a Crime: Women, Medicine, and Law in the United States, 1867–1973*, "worked to shut down the trusted and skilled abortionists, many of them physicians, who had operated clinics for years with little or no police interference." While legal measures were still taken against "inept abortionists who killed their patients," Reagan goes on, this practice was not new, nor was it the "primary focus" of prosecutors. Furthermore, women seeking abortions themselves also became the targets of police

COMPARE & CONTRAST

- **1940s:** African American poetry is characterized by a focus on individual experiences in various settings, such as the South Side of Chicago in Gwendolyn Brooks's poetry. Langston Hughes writes extensively during this portion of his long career as well, composing works infused with elements of African American culture in a mode described as neo-modernist (adhering to the aesthetics of the earlier modernist movement, which focused on establishing innovative modes of expression and rejected traditional poetic structures.)

  Today: Twenty-first-century African American poetry explores a variety of themes, including African American history and cultural traditions, as well as the everyday experiences of modern life. Prominent African American poets include Toi Derricotte, the late Pinkie Gordon Lane, and Sam Cornish. Many of these modern artists pay tribute to other or earlier African American poets through the themes and forms of their works. Cornish, for example, draws on the work of Langston Hughes, while in Derricotte's work, traces of Toni Morrison's influence may be found.

- **1940s:** Abortion is illegal in all forty-eight states in the United States. Skilled physicians of safe, though illegal, abortions are prosecuted alongside doctors whose surgeries have killed their patients. Women seeking abortions or those who have obtained abortions are also sought by authorities and forced to testify against physicians.

  Today: The National Abortion Federation states that about half of all American pregnancies are unintended, and that roughly half of these pregnancies are terminated. Approximately 1.3 million abortions are performed each year. Abortion is made legal as a result of the Supreme Court decision in 1973 in the landmark case known as *Roe v. Wade*.

- **1940s:** Brooks, who lives in Chicago at this time, is inspired by the lives of poor urban African Americans, and writes about their experiences in *A Street in Bronzeville*. In 1940, in the aftermath of the Great Depression of the 1930s, the poverty rate for black families in the United States is approximately 87 percent. About 48 percent of white families live in poverty in 1940.

  Today: The University of Michigan's National Poverty Center reports that in 2009, 14.3 percent of all Americans live in poverty. The rate of poverty among African Americans remains much higher than this national average, with 25.8 percent of African Americans living in poverty.

---

raids on abortionists' offices. Women were publicly humiliated and shamed, "forced to speak of their abortions in the male-dominated spaces of the police station and courtroom," Reagan explains. During the 1940s, in the post-World War II years, women were increasingly expected to bear children. This has been regarded as a backlash against the increased numbers of women in the industrial work force that was necessary during World War II (1939–1945). In examining this trend, Reagan observes that these expectations were largely bestowed on white women, but "women of color also felt the pressure to subordinate themselves to men as wives and mothers." Christopher Cumo, in the 2006 *Historical Dictionary of the 1940s*, describes the way the debate over abortion intensified, with religious groups becoming increasingly vocal on the subject. Cumo cites the arguments of physician Sophia Kleegman, who, Cumo states, "blamed the Catholic Church and Protestant evangelicals for perpetuating a morality of fear

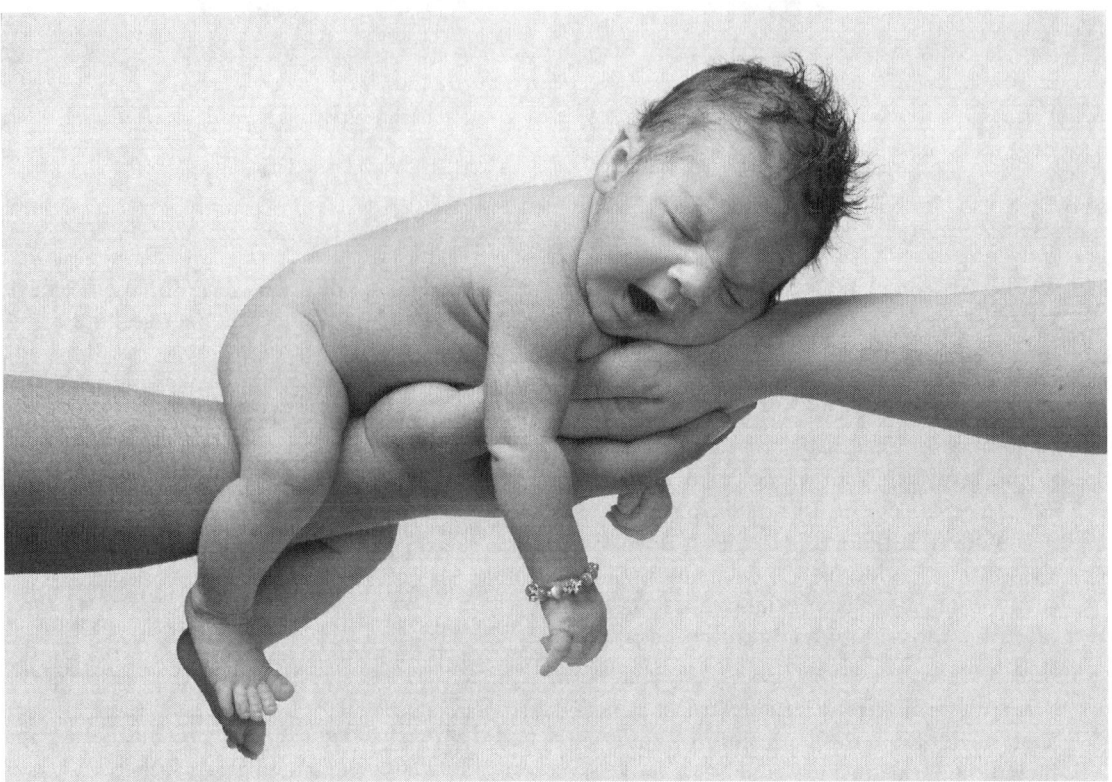

A newborn baby (Nate A. / Shutterstock.com)

and for violating the separation of church and state by codifying dogma into law."

African American Poetry in the 1940s

Brooks began publishing poetry in the aftermath of the Harlem Renaissance, the period in which an enormous upsurge in African American literary and visual artistic creation took place, owing in part to the fact that African Americans had migrated to New York City from the South and settled in Harlem, where they were, to some degree, insulated from the racial discrimination they had previously faced. To this tightly knit community that established itself in the 1920s, artists flocked and flourished, writing of their varied experiences, from life in Harlem, to the violence and discrimination they had endured in the South, to the ways of living experienced by individuals of African descent migrating from other parts of the globe. In the 1940s, a new generation of African American poets emerged. These writers, including Brooks, Robert Hayden, and Melvin Tolson, wrote of individual experiences and did not, unlike the poets of the Harlem Renaissance, coalesce as a group or movement. Brooks, for example, focused on the lives of urban African Americans in Chicago, and combined free verse poetry (poetry in which strict metrical structures and rhyme schemes are not utilized) with metered and rhymed verse, and like Tolson and Hayden, was influenced by the early modernism of other writers. Tolson and Hayden drew on the influences of such modernist writers as T. S. Eliot and Ezra Pound in terms of poetic structure and explored a range of themes often but not exclusively dealing with the African American experience. (Modernism was an early twentieth-century movement in the literary and visual arts in which traditional modes of expression were eschewed in favor of more experimental methods.) Other poets, such as Langston Hughes, had been active in the Harlem Renaissance, but had explored different avenues of expression after the movement faded. Hughes, like Hayden and Tolson, took an increasingly modernist approach in his writing in the 1940s and 1950s. As James Smethurst states in *African-American Poets: 1700s–1940s*, Hughes, along with African American and white writers, such as "Delmore Schwartz, John

Berryman, Robert Lowell, Allen Tate, Randall Jarrell, Gwendolyn Brooks, Melvin Tolson, and Robert Hayden," regarded the modernist work of writers such as Eliot and Pound "as the necessary ground of any truly serious contemporary literature." Smethurst describes this sensibility as neo-Modernism.

CRITICAL OVERVIEW

The 1945 publication of Brooks's first poetry collection, *A Street in Bronzeville*, which contains "The Mother," was followed by her receipt of a National Institute of Arts and Letters grant and an American Academy of Arts and Letters Award in 1946, along with Guggenheim fellowships in 1946 and 1947. Her early career was shaped by such positive critical notice. As Gary Smith points out in a 1983 article for *MELUS*, reviewers of *A Street in Bronzeville* praised Brooks's "versatility and craft as a poet" along with her "stylistic successes." Yet Smith observes that

> not many critics fully understood her achievement in her first book. This difficulty was not only characteristic of critics who examined the formal aspects of prosody in her work, but also of critics who addressed themselves to the social realism in her poetry.

Evaluations of "The Mother" often focus on the emotional power of the poem along with the poem's formal structure. In Farah Jasmine Griffin's analysis of Brooks's work for the *Dictionary of Literary Biography*, Volume 165, *American Poets since World War II, Fourth Series*, she describes the poem as "one of the most poignant" of the first section of *A Street in Bronzeville*. Griffin characterizes the poem as a "dramatic monologue" featuring a first stanza "filled with tightly controlled rhymed couplets, which yield to the emotion-filled longings of the second stanza."

Similarly, D. H. Melhem, in *Gwendolyn Brooks: Poetry and the Heroic Voice*, studies the structure of the poem, noting the way Brooks "employs full rhyme with a touch of slant in this thirty-two-line poem, very irregularly metered." After breaking down the somewhat interrupted nature of the rhyme pattern in the second stanza, Melhem maintains that the poet's use of inconsistent meter "conveys the profound agitation of the speaker" and that Brooks's "tonal control, especially in the first stanza, heightens the tension."

In Brooks's 2000 *New York Times* obituary, Mel Watkins summarizes the success Brooks achieved so early in her career with the publication of *A Street in Bronzeville*. Surveying the trajectory of Brooks's career, Watkins states that

> by the early 1960's Ms. Brooks had reached a high point in her writing career. She was regarded as a grande dame of America's black writers and an honored member of the literary elite, a sought-after teacher and poet who was valued for her sensitive portraits of black women, her precise use of language and the universality of her work.

CRITICISM

Catherine Dominic

Dominic is a novelist and a freelance writer and editor. In the following essay, she studies the speaker's sense of doubt and remorse in Gwendolyn Brooks's poem "The Mother."

In "The Mother," Brooks describes the raw emotional pain endured by a mother who has had several abortions. The language and imagery are heart wrenching, and sorrow pervades the poem. The mother touches on the notions of culpability and regret and offers some glimpse of a sense of justification for her multiple acts of terminating her pregnancies. Some critics have contended that the mother absolves herself of guilt. D. H. Melhem, in *Gwendolyn Brooks: Poetry and the Heroic Voice*, states that the mother "reviews the loss [of her children] judiciously: the children will not be neglected; she will not be burdened." Melhem continues, maintaining that the woman "justifies herself to the aborted children, confessing that her 'crime' was not 'deliberate.' She wanted to shield them from a painful existence." Similarly, Kate Daniels in the 1991 *A Profile of Twentieth-Century American Poetry*, asserts that "the poem is not meant to be a moral condemnation." Melhem quotes Brooks as saying that the mother figure in the poem is "hardly your crowned and praised and 'customary' Mother; but a Mother not unfamiliar, who decides that *she*, rather than her World, will kill her children." Certainly the implication here is what Melhem suggests, that "she wanted to shield [the children] from a painful existence." Nevertheless, one must question whether Brooks intended to imply that the abortions were somehow a preemptive euthanasia (mercy killing) for which the mother felt

WHAT DO I READ NEXT?

- Brooks's collection *In Montgomery: And Other Poems* showcases the poet's later works. The collection was published in 2003 by Third World Press. It offers new and select works from previous volumes and was prepared for publication by Brooks before her death in 2000.

- Brooks published her only novel, *Maud Martha*, in 1953. The work, like her poetry, explores African American life and culture, and the human experience in general, focusing on the mother-daughter relationship as well as race relations. The work is available in a 1993 edition by Third World Press.

- Langston Hughes was a contemporary of Gwendolyn Brooks, and as a critic and peer, he reviewed her work favorably. A large sampling of Hughes's early poetry is available in the 1959 *Selected Poems of Langston Hughes*, published by Knopf.

- In the 1940s, Latin American poets wrote extensively in the surrealist mode. (Surrealism grew out of the modernist experimentalism of the early twentieth century and focused on the exploration of the visions of the unconscious mind. Although the movement thrived in Europe primarily in the 1920s, it was revived as it spread to North America in the 1930s, and by the 1940s had become popular among many Latin American poets). The work of Mexican poet Octavio Paz offers an example of this type of poetry. While his work first appeared in English publication in a 1947 anthology, it is more readily available in the 1987 *The Collected Poems of Octavio Paz: 1957–1987*, published by New Directions.

- *Quiet Storm: Voices of Young Black Poets* is a young-adult poetry collection selected by Lydia Omolola Okutoro, published in 2002 by Jump at the Sun. The work features poetry by well-known African American poets, as well as by new and previously unpublished African American poets.

- *Abortion*, edited by David Haugen, Susan Musser, and Kacy Lovelace, is a part of the young-adult "Opposing Viewpoints" series, published in 2010 by Greenhaven Press. The work presents a variety of viewpoints on this topic using primary source materials such as essays, speeches, and articles.

---

justified. The poem suggests otherwise, that the mother was tormented, if not by remorse and guilt, then at least by a sense of doubt.

In the poem's first stanza, Brooks begins with a simple statement, that abortions do not allow mothers to forget. The abrupt ending to this line forces the reader to pause and consider: if abortions do not permit forgetting, then what is it that is being remembered? In this very first line, Brooks establishes an absence, a loss (of the child's life), as a presence. The void left by a life that did not happen becomes fullness, an entity in its own right that a mother hangs on to. Brooks goes on in the second stanza to explain further. What a mother remembers is the children she had (the babies with whom she became pregnant) but did not have, in the sense that she did not give birth to them, nor did she "have" them in the possessive sense. The images contained in the remaining lines of the stanza depict the children as infants, as adults with careers, as children whose silence is purchased with a sweet treat. In the mother's imagination, they are thumb-sucking children, they are scared of ghosts. Into this realm of positives—the children exist for the mother in a way as real as any memory—Brooks introduces the sense of loss and absence. The children will never breathe air, they will never be harmed by their mother, they will never be bribed with the treat the

"NEVERTHELESS, ONE MUST QUESTION WHETHER BROOKS INTENDED TO IMPLY THAT THE ABORTIONS WERE SOMEHOW A PREEMPTIVE EUTHANASIA (MERCY KILLING) FOR WHICH THE MOTHER FELT JUSTIFIED. THE POEM SUGGESTS OTHERWISE, THAT THE MOTHER WAS TORMENTED, IF NOT BY REMORSE AND GUILT, THEN AT LEAST BY A SENSE OF DOUBT."

mother has imagined, they will never be grateful to her for chasing off the ghosts that have scared them. The mother, in Brooks's depiction, will never be giddy with the sight of her children after some departure or absence. By characterizing the fictional memories of unborn children in this manner, Brooks paints a stark portrait of the mother's pain. It is not a hollow, empty place within her. It is a physical, palpable presence.

The pain the mother carries with her is amplified in the second stanza. Unlike the first stanza, which uses the somewhat distancing voice of the second person, the second stanza is written in the first person. The experiences the mother describes become more personal now that she reveals explicitly to the reader that she is the mother who has had the abortions. Having described the way she has heard her children's voices in the wind, the mother next describes her experience in terms of the constriction she feels. Her word choice suggests the contractions a woman in labor would feel, but the mother is not talking about childbirth when she discusses her sense of contraction. The language suggests a shrinking, a tightening, a hardening. The mother sees herself as diminished, and hard, as if she has had to callous herself against her pain. Despite the enormity of the mother's pain and the way she has hardened herself against it, the mother has not yet revealed a word that reverberates with regret or doubt. As the second stanza progresses, however, Brooks's word choices emphasize the mother's tenuous grasp on any certainty she has that she did the right thing in terminating

her pregnancies. She characterizes her choices as sins, and begins to catalog all she has forcibly taken from her unborn children. She speaks of the act of poisoning the onset of her children's breath, of tainting their lives just as they came into being. The mother then asks that they believe that in her act of termination, she did not act with deliberation. The suggestion here, in the statement about her lack of certainty, is that she hesitated, she paused. She doubted. Sidestepping the notion of blame, the mother does not address the fact that in describing her actions in such a manner, she does not touch on the role of the father or fathers in these pregnancies. She does not inform the reader about the circumstances under which she became pregnant with unwanted children. By stating that she did not act in a deliberate fashion, she suggests that in becoming pregnant she either acted carelessly or was taken advantage of, or, alternatively, that in the moment in which she sought her abortions, her sense of deliberateness, or confidence in her actions, wavered. This eleventh line of the poem is as crucial as it is ambiguous, for in it contains the mysteries of the mother's past and motivations. The line also expresses the certainty of the mother's doubts about her actions.

The remainder of the second stanza reinforces the notion of doubt established in the preceding lines by the discussion of sin and the intimation of a lack of deliberation. In lines twelve through twenty, Brooks develops an increasing sense of emotional confusion in the mother. She questions herself, asking why should she complain or attempt to construe her actions as a crime committed by someone other than herself. The abortions have now been characterized as both sins and crimes, ideas that suggest the mother's implication of herself in both moral and legal wrongdoing. Still, one may act against one's sense of morality without remorse, regret, or doubt. Brooks has, however, already incorporated the mother's sense of doubt into the poem, and she now builds upon it in the next lines, which are devoted to the mother's construing and deconstructing her notions of life and death. She asks why she should cry that the guilt for the transgressions should be ascribed to anyone but her, answering that the children are dead anyway, whether she questions her actions and characterizes them as sins or not. As soon as she declares the children dead, however, the mother rephrases her statement, now depicting their state as unmade rather than terminated. In the next breath, though, the mother admits almost shamefacedly that this view is not accurate either. She bemoans the fact that she does not have the words to state the truth, that she has no way of truly describing the fate of her unborn children. She resolves on a complex notion involving the physical death of a body, stating that the children were born, were physical bodies that died. At the same time, she underscores the fact that these bodies never laughed, made plans, or wept. The implication is that because they never lived life, but rather only existed as bodies with unmade individual natures, they could not die in the traditional sense. This philosophical struggle to define identity and existence implicates the mother in a very real way. She is much freer to absolve herself of what she has characterized as sin and as killing if she establishes the notion that in some ways, the children never existed, not really, as people. This painful struggle calls to mind the question asked often in debates about abortion: When does life begin? For the mother, struggling to come to terms with her pain and her doubt, the answer is complex and mutable. The distinctions the mother makes reveal the extent to which she gropes for a way to protect herself from the psychic trauma that plagues her.

In the poem's final stanza, the speaker expresses the enduring nature of her love, and the reader is left with an understanding that this love will be an eternal source of pain. The mother seems to beg her children for their understanding, pleading with them to know how much she loved all of them. The notions of love and the fact that she is addressing multiple children are both repeated in this stanza. In an examination of Brooks's work in the 1996 *Dictionary of Literary Biography*, Volume 165, *American Poets since World War II, Fourth Series*, Farah Jasmine Griffin studies this last stanza closely. "The final stanza," Griffin asserts, "releases the apology: 'Believe me, I loved you all.'" In her many requests to be believed, the mother asks her children to understand if not her motivation then at least the strength of her love. At the same time, the words, the pleas come across as a humble request for forgiveness, presented by a mother suffocating in her grief for the lives she lost, the lives she took.

Source: Catherine Dominic, Critical Essay on "The Mother," in *Poetry for Students*, Gale, Cengage Learning, 2012.

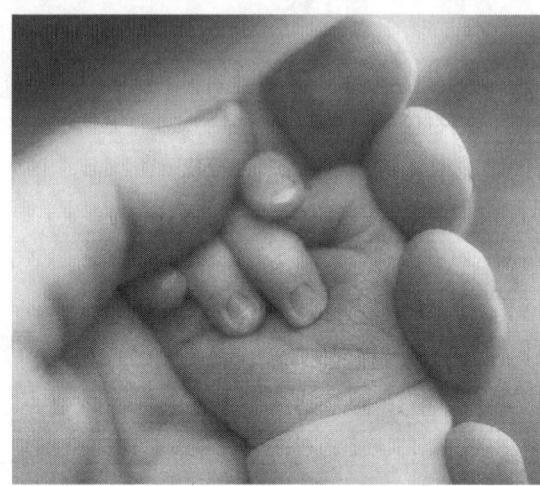

A mother holds her baby's hand. (emin kuliyev / Shutterstock.com)

William H. Hansell

In the following essay, Hansell analyzes what Brooks believes is the appropriate subject matter for an artist—personal experience or relationship to society.

In her first three major poetry anthologies, [*A Street in Bronzeville*, *Annie Allen*, and *The Bean Eaters*], Gwendolyn Brooks portrays "ghetto people" as being largely preoccupied with their personal experience. Busy with their own lives and practical matters, they have little time to reflect on their relationship to the larger society or even to their immediate community. This detachment is presented for the most part as a positive attribute.

In the early works, there are very few poems on the major themes of poems written since the mid-1960s: the nature of blackness and the role of the artist. However, analyses of some poems from the earliest volumes reveal Brooks' ideas about the appropriate subject matter of the artist, and her comments in interviews and elsewhere further substantiate what the analyses suggest.

That immediate and practical needs must take precedence over any "dreams" is the literal meaning of "Kitchenette Building," a poem [included in *A Street in Bronzeville* which] Brooks described as typical of the bulk of her work. Somewhat reminiscent of Eliot's "Preludes," the world described in this poem is squalid, enclosed, almost a trap, and the people in it must devote themselves to the urgencies of their situation. The

> ARTISTS CAN NEVER EXHAUST THE SIGNIFICANCE OF THE IMMEDIATE AND COMMONPLACE, AND ARTISTS WHO IGNORE 'COMMON THINGS' LITERALLY RISK THE LOSS OF CONTACT WITH REALITY."

narrator's speculation on "dreams" gives them a very slim chance of surviving amidst "onion Fumes" and "yesterday's garbage ripening in the hall...." The comic-pathetic overtones of the final description of the narrator rushing to use the bathroom now that "Number Five" is out give a more definite sense of what was implicit in the opening lines: "We are things of dry hours and the involuntary plan, / Grayed in, and gray."

Although "Kitchenette Building" portrays a way of life which ostensibly cannot afford the luxury of art, there are obvious ironies. The poem itself is a product of that environment. Although if circumstances seem to militate against art, *these* circumstances are the subject of this poem. Finally, "Kitchenette Building" illustrates Brooks' commitment to a concept of art which she has never surrendered: the artist must work with the materials most familiar to him, with his own milieu. Not until *Riot*, published in 1970, are ghetto people her primary audience. Before *Riot*, with few exceptions, white, middle-class buyers of books would seem to be the audience to which she directed her poems. Her subject matter, on the other hand, has always derived almost exclusively from an urban black milieu. In 1969, Brooks stated her attitude: "I think it is the task or job or responsibility or pleasure or pride of any writer to respond to her climate. You write about what is in the world." Brooks has also said that art should use familiar materials, because that will enhance its usefulness to the audience. More than the artist or sculptor, the poet should create things that "mean something, will *be* something that a reader may touch." (pp. 261–63)

The importance of imagination in the process of attaining to experiences and insights beyond the physical world is a theme in the four poems [collected in *Annie Allen*] to be discussed next. The characters in the poems are not artists as such; but Brooks surely would not argue that imagination in the individual can enrich life and transcend physical realities if she did not also believe it functioned similarly in the artist. "The Birth in a Narrow Room," for example, accurately described by Stanley Kunitz as "in her most characteristic vein," argues explicitly that the imagination is not confined by seemingly restrictive circumstances. (p. 268)

Part Two of "The Womanhood" is a poem beginning "Life for your child is simple, and is good...." Ostensibly on childhood, the poem also emphasizes the curiosity concerning the commonplace and the sense of adventurousness inborn in those who seek the truth. Trust in himself, aspiration, faith in "undeep and unabiding things," as seen in the child's discovery that he can spill or topple certain objects, are necessities of the spirit, even if sometimes he is injured.... The poem portrays the necessity for some individuals to give their curiosity free range, to trust in themselves, and to believe in the intrinsic value of the concrete world: "undeep and unabiding things." And even in the familiar, the immediate and concrete, there is always a risk, an adventure, and a challenge. Brooks' own curiosity and concern with "undeep and unabiding things" has, of course, been her primary source of poetic materials.

"Maxie Allen" is a poem depicting a generational conflict between a mother and her fanciful daughter, but the poem also stated the power of the imagination to enable an individual to escape the immediate environment. Nonetheless, the young girl in the poem is unable to persuade her mother ("Maxie") that she desires more than material comfort, that vague dreams and aspirations are not satisfied by "lots of jacks and strawberry jam...." (p. 269)

"Memorial to Ed Bland" is an elegy to a man "killed in Germany, March 20, 1945; volunteered for special dangerous mission... wanted to see action...." The poem describes his intense curiosity, even from childhood, and emphasizes his wonderment at things others saw as quite ordinary. Because people saw what he saw but could not fathom what he thought, that is, could not really see into things as he did, they considered him very strange.... Explicitly stated here is the need "people" have to discover some kind of order and regularity in their world, a need that drives many of them to stifle natural curiosity and grow suspicious of the imagination. Because

Brooks became increasingly more concerned with portraying in her poetry the relation of the artist to society, perhaps it is valid to say that an implication in this poem is that unless the artist (Bland, in this poem), with his curiosity and profounder vision, finds some way to convey his truth to people, they will be left only with a very crude and artificial sense of reality.

To sum up, several poems in *Annie Allen* illustrate Brooks' continuing desire to portray her belief that most people's lives would be improved if they allowed their imagination greater scope. They would thus enrich and deepen their awareness of reality.

In *The Bean Eaters* (1960), published eleven years after *Annie Allen*, Brooks continues to portray the immediate environment and ordinary people and events. Her manner and themes are almost identical to those in the two earlier books. But there are leanings or tendencies which will become definite paths in subsequent poems. To focus the better on these tendencies, I shall concentrate on some poems which reveal her concern with the nature and function of art and the artist. "The Artists' and Models' Ball," for example, represents the commonplace as the truly ultimate mystery. The common object resists our perception by being too familiar and obvious and changeable; it refuses to be defined by conventional labels. Here is the entire poem:

> Wonders do not confuse. We call them that
> And close the matter there. But common things
> Surprise us. They accept the names we give
> With calm, and keep them. Easy-breathing them
> We brave our next small business. Well, behind
> Our backs they alter. How were we to know.

Artists can never exhaust the significance of the immediate and commonplace, and artists who ignore "common things" literally risk the loss of contact with reality.

In "The Egg Boiler," Brooks ironically explores the false opposition between the practical and the imaginary. The contrast in the sonnet between the artist concerned with imaginative creations, things cut "out of air," and the man preparing an egg seems intended to dramatize the idea that art must be rooted in the concrete world. The man cooking the egg is a poet of sorts—he cuts his "poetry from wood"—in that he brings passion and love and skill to his task; but his is contemptuous of the "gorgeous Nothingness," the imaginative creations of the artist. In the final line, the man eats his egg and laughs "aloud" at "fools" who have only poetry as the result of their work. But he is not really given the last laugh. The poem itself reveals that art is rooted in the physical world, can portray, in fact, so simple a task as boiling an egg. The artist, therefore, when firmly tied to things, has both the physical world and the imaginative one, both reality and reality transformed into art.

Brooks' portrayal of the positive effects of art forms which respond directly to the needs of the people will begin in earnest in the "New Poems" section of *Selected Poems* (1963). In *The Bean Eaters*, though, she continues in a direction begun in *A Street in Bronzeville*; she continues, that is, to explore the harmful effects of art which is misunderstood and misleading. Reminiscent of "The Sundays of Satin-Legs Smith," "Strong Men Riding Horses: Lester after the Western" portrays a young man's confusion and self-contempt as a result of having seen a film in which strong and courageous men seem such superior beings that Lester can only conclude that he, in contrast, is "pitiful...." (pp. 270–72)

Perhaps none of Brooks' poems so explicitly portrays the human cost of actions motivated by hate as "A Bronzeville Mother Loiters in Mississippi. Meanwhile a Mississippi Mother Burns Bacon," and no other more definitely links behavior and values to the arts and to the myths which shape the individual imagination. "A Bronzeville Mother Loiters in Mississippi" portrays the effect of a murder on the relationship between a husband and wife (the "Mississippi Mother"), both of whom are white. The man has killed a black youth and has been acquitted. All the reader knows at the beginning of the poem, the day after the trial, is that the white woman is deep in fantasy. The recent events make her feel as if she is actually experiencing the action in ballads and fairy tales she read or heard as a child and schoolgirl, in which princesses are rescued from dark villains by adoring knights. We are also told she "never quite / understood" those ballads.

The first scene portrays the white mother fully involved in her own imaginative reconstruction of recent events while she prepares a meal for her family:

> ...the milk-white maid, the "maid mild"
> Of the ballad. Pursued
> By the Dark Villain. Rescued by the fine Prince.
> The Happiness-Ever-After.

She is abruptly brought out of her daydreaming by the smell of burnt bacon. Restored to the everyday world, she becomes literal and matter-of-fact in thinking of the events which triggered her fairy-tale imaginings. She begins to feel that the real-life "villain" was inadequate.... From this thought, she is led into a speculation on what the "Dark Villain" thought and felt when the men confronted him. She thinks of how a child would respond to suddenly brutal men, whom, she imagines, he was accustomed to regarding as standards of proper behavior. Thinking of the "blackish child," especially of his defenselessness and his incomprehension of adult motivation, she reflects momentarily on the essential childishness of all men. Beneath a surface of strength and seeming knowledge and courage, all men are basically children, she thinks, no doubt subconsciously searching for an excuse for her husband's behavior. Further thought about the child, however, suddenly fills her with the ridiculousness of such "combat."

As she begins to remember her own part in the trial, especially the fact that she had helped her husband win acquittal, she is disturbed by the realization that she can no longer remember what the boy did to her. The curious and painful fact forces us to recall the opening line: "From the first it had been like a / Ballad." That is, Brooks implies, the woman's fantasy of herself as the Princess assaulted by a black villain was probably more a factor in her accusation of the boy than anything he actually did. (pp. 273–74)

Her whole concern as she begins to reconsider the lynching with "terrifying clarity" becomes a frantic need to prove worthy of her husband's ferocity:

> It was necessary
> To be more beautiful than ever.
> The beautiful wife.
> For sometimes she fancied he looked at her as though
> Measuring her. As if he considered,
> Had she been worth It?

She begins to imagine what her husband might think of her now and is tormented by the possibility that he may think she wasn't worth "It." The fact that she can only refer to the murder as "It" and can no longer obscure the reality in fantasy, already confirms her repugnance for the actual deed.

She begins to imagine her husband's thoughts:

> Had she been worth the blood, the cramped cries,
> the little stuttering bravado,
> The gradual dulling of those Negro eyes,
> The sudden, overwhelming *little-boyness* in that barn?

These thoughts and her determination never to seem unworthy are interrupted by her husband's appearance for dinner, the trial and publicity very much on his mind. Although he sneers at the Northern press, which had harshly criticized his deed, he appears nervous, self-conscious, especially attentive to his hands. It is clear, however, that his wife feels he is pretending, playing the role of a cold-hearted killer contemptuous of anyone else's opinion.... (pp. 274–75)

When the husband speaks, he is still rationalizing his deed. Ultimately, he says, all blacks should be killed; in the meanwhile smart-alecky blacks must be punished, and the North must be opposed. "Mississippi" must prevail: "Nothing and nothing could stop Mississippi." His speech is interrupted by a squabble between two of his children:

> The Fine Prince leaned across the table and slapped
> The small and smiling criminal.

The wife is suddenly horror-struck and envisions the child covered with blood, blood that went everywhere, touched everything. Even after she has shaken away that sanguine fantasy, she must leave the table and try to conceal the new fear she feels— "The fear, Tying her as with iron." Her husband joins her. The touch of his hands on her shoulder again fills her with horror, and she realizes—or believes—she would be unable to protect herself or the children from him. He could murder them all. The vision of blood oozing everywhere, even "over all of Earth and Mars," returns.

When he embraces her and turns her around to face him, she sees only the red of his lips. Sickness consumes her. Ugly and squalid images of the courtroom return. With a sharpening sense of guilt, she recalls the eyes of the child's mother, "the Decapitated exclamation points in that Other Woman's eyes." Hatred for her husband floods over her as she understands that it was hate, not love, as she had imagined in her dream of knights and princesses, that impelled all his actions and talk. Her maternal sensibilities, aroused by violence against her own child, and her common sense have forced her to an awareness of the actual consequences of her fantasy and of her own share of the guilt. Hating her husband and his action, she must also hate herself. (pp. 275–76)

In portraying in "A Bronzeville Mother Loiters" the close relationship between literature and reality, in particular the fact that literature to some degree can influence behavior and shape reality, Brooks is in a sense developing further a theme in "The Sundays of Satin-Legs Smith." In another sense, by explicitly relating this influence to racial conflicts in this country, Brooks is moving towards the concept of the black artist as political militant. (p. 277)

Source: William H. Hansell, "The Uncommon Commonplace in the Early Poems of Gwendolyn Brooks," in *CLA Journal*, Vol. 30, No. 3, March 1987, pp. 261–77.

Gary Smith

In the following excerpt, Smith examines Brooks's first collection of poetry.

The critical reception of *A Street in Bronzeville* contained, in embryo, many of the central issues in the scholarly debate that continues to engage Brooks's poetry. As in the following quotation from the *New York Times Book Review*, most reviewers were able to recognize Brooks's versatility and craft as a poet:

> If the idiom is colloquial, the language is universal. Brooks commands both the colloquial and more austere rhythms. She can vary manner and tone. In form, she demonstrates a wide range: quatrains, free verse, ballads, and sonnets—all appropriately controlled. The longer line suits her better than the short, but she is not verbose. In some of the sonnets, she uses an abruptness of address that is highly individual.

Yet, while noting her stylistic successes, not many critics fully understood her achievement in her first book. This difficulty was not only characteristic of critics who examined the formal aspects of prosody in her work, but also of critics who addressed themselves to the social realism in her poetry. Moreover, what Brooks gained at the hands of critics who focused on her technique, she lost to critics who chose to emphasize the exotic, Negro features of the book....

The poems in *A Street in Bronzeville* actually served notice that Brooks had learned her craft well enough to combine successfully themes and styles from both the Harlem Renaissance and Modernist poetry. She even achieves some of her more interesting effects in the book by parodying the two traditions. She juggles the pessimism of Modernist poetry with the general optimism of the Harlem Renaissance....

Because of the affinities *A Street in Bronzeville* shares with Modernist poetry and the

> FOR BROOKS, UNLIKE THE RENAISSANCE POETS, THE VICTIMIZATION OF POOR BLACK WOMEN BECOMES NOT SIMPLY A MINOR CHORD BUT A PREDOMINANT THEME OF *A STREET IN BRONZEVILLE*."

Harlem Renaissance, Brooks was initiated not only into the vanguard of American literature, but also into what had been the inner circle of Harlem writers. Two of the Renaissance's leading poets, Claude McKay and Countee Cullen, addressed letters to her to mark the publication of *A Street in Bronzeville*. McKay welcomed her into a dubious but potentially rewarding career:

> I want to congratulate you again on the publication of *A Street in Bronzeville* and welcome you among the band of hard working poets who do have something to say. It is a pretty rough road we have to travel, but I suppose much compensation is derived from the joy of being able to sing. Yours sincerely, Claude McKay. (October 10, 1945.)

Cullen pinpointed her dual place in American literature:

> I have just finished reading *A Street in Bronzeville* and want you to know that I enjoyed it thoroughly. There can be no doubt that you are a poet, a good one, with every indication of becoming a better. I am glad to be able to say 'welcome' to you to that too small group of Negro poets, and to the larger group of American ones. No one can deny you your place there. (August 24, 1945.)

The immediate interest in these letters is how both poets touch upon the nerve ends of the critical debate that surrounded *A Street in Bronzeville*. For McKay, while Brooks has "something to say," she can also "sing"; and for Cullen, she belongs not only to the minority of Negro poets, but also to the majority of American ones. Nonetheless, the critical question for both poets might well have been Brooks's relationship to the Harlem Renaissance. What had she absorbed of the important tenets of the Black aesthetic as expressed during the New Negro Movement? And how had she addressed herself, as a poet, to the literary movement's assertion of the folk and African culture, and its promotion of the arts as the agent to define racial integrity and to fuse racial harmony?

Aside from its historical importance, the Harlem Renaissance—as a literary movement—is rather difficult to define.... Likewise, the general description of the movement as a Harlem Renaissance is often questioned, since most of the major writers, with the notable exceptions of Hughes and Cullen, actually did not live and work in Harlem. Finally, many of the themes and literary conventions defy definition in terms of what was and what was not a New Negro poet. Nonetheless, there was a common ground of purpose and meaning in the works of the individual writers that permits a broad definition of the spirit and intent of the Harlem Renaissance. Indeed, the New Negro poets expressed a deep pride in being Black; they found reasons for this pride in ethnic identity and heritage; and they shared a common faith in the fine arts as a means of defining and reinforcing racial pride. But in the literal expression of these artistic impulses, the poets were either romantics or realists and, quite often within a single poem, both. The realistic impulse, as defined best in the poems of McKay's *Harlem Shadows*, was a sober reflection upon Blacks as second class citizens, segregated from the mainstream of American socioeconomic life, and largely unable to realize the wealth and opportunity that America promised. The romantic impulse, on the other hand, as defined in the poems of Sterling Browns's *Southern Road* (1932), often found these unrealized dreams in the collective strength and will of the folk masses. In comparing the poems in *A Street in Bronzeville* with various poems from the Renaissance, it becomes apparent that Brooks agrees, for the most part, with their prescriptions for the New Negro. Yet the unique contributions she brings to bear upon this tradition are extensive: 1) the biting ironies of intraracial discrimination, 2) the devaluation of love in heterosexual relationships between Blacks, and 3) the primacy of suffering in the lives of poor Black women.

The first clue that *A Street in Bronzeville* was, at the time of its publication, unlike any other book of poems by a Black American is its insistent emphasis on demystifying romantic love between Black men and women. The "*old marrieds*," the first couple encountered on the walking tour of Bronzeville, are nothing like the youthful archetype that the Renaissance poets often portrayed:

> But in the crowding darkness not a word did they say. Though the pretty-coated birds had piped so lightly all the day. And he had seen the lovers in the little side-streets. And she had heard the morning stories clogged with sweets. It was quite a time for loving. It was midnight. It was May. But in the crowding darkness not a word did they say.

In this short, introductory poem, Brooks, in a manner reminiscent of Eliot's alienated *Waste Land* characters, looks not toward a glorified African past or limitless future, but rather at a stifled present. Her old lovers ponder not an image of their racial past or some symbolized possibility of self-renewal, but rather the overwhelming question of what to do in the here-and-now. Moreover, their world, circumscribed by the incantatory line that opens and closes the poem, "But in the crowding darkness not a word did they say," is one that is distinctly at odds with their lives. They move timidly through the crowded darkness of their neighborhood largely ignorant of the season, "May," the lateness of the hour, "midnight," and a particular *raison d'etre*, "a time for loving." Their attention, we infer, centers upon the implicit need to escape any peril that might consume what remains of their lives. The tempered optimism in the poem, as the title indicates, is the fact that they are "old-marrieds": a social designation that suggests the longevity of their lives and the solidity of their marital bond in what is, otherwise, an ephemeral world of change. Indeed, as the prefatory poem in *A Street in Bronzeville*, the "old marrieds," on the whole, debunks one of the prevalent motifs of Harlem Renaissance poetry: its general optimism about the future.

As much as the Harlem Renaissance was noted for its optimism, an important corollary motif was that of ethnic or racial pride. This pride—often thought a reaction to the minstrel stereotypes in the Dunbar tradition—usually focused with romantic idealization upon the Black woman....

In *A Street in Bronzeville*, this romantic impulse for idealizing the Black woman runs headlong into the biting ironies of intraracial discrimination. In poem after poem in *A Street in Bronzeville*, within the well-observed caste lines of skin color, the consequences of dark pigmentation are revealed in drastic terms. One of the more popular of these poems, "The Ballad of Chocolate Mabbie," explores the tragic ordeal of Mabbie, the Black female heroine, who is victimized by her dark skin and her "saucily bold" lover, Willie Boone.... Mabbie's life, of course, is one of unrelieved monotony; her social contacts are limited to those who, like her, are dark skinned, rather than "lemon-hued" or light skinned. But as Brooks makes clear, the larger tragedy of Mabbie's life is the human potential that is squandered:

> Oh, warm is the waiting for joys, my dears! And it cannot be too long. O, pity the little poor chocolate lips
>
> That carry the bubble of song!

But if Mabbie is Brooks's parodic victim of romantic love, her counterpart in "Ballad of Pearl May Lee" realizes a measure of sweet revenge. In outline, Brooks's poem is reminiscent of Cullen's *The Ballad of the Brown Girl* (1927). There are, however, several important differences. The first is the poem's narrative structure: Pearl May Lee is betrayed in her love for a Black man who "couldn't abide dark meat," who subsequently makes love to a white girl and is lynched for his crime of passion, whereas Cullen's "Brown Girl" is betrayed in her love for a white man, Lord Thomas, who violated explicit social taboo by marrying her rather than Fair London, a white girl. Moreover, Cullen's poem, "a ballad retold," is traditional in its approach to the ballad form.... Brooks's ballad, on the other hand, dispenses with the rhetorical invocation of the traditional ballad and begins *in medias res:*

> Then off they took you, off to the jail,
> A hundred hooting after.
> And you should have heard me at my house.
> I cut my lungs with my laughter,
> Laughter, Laughter.
> I cut my lungs with my laughter.

This mocking tone is sustained throughout the poem, even as Sammy, Pearl May Lee's lover, is lynched:

> You paid for your dinner, Sammy boy,
> And you didn't pay with money.
> You paid with your hide and my heart, Sammy boy,
> For your taste of pink and white honey,
> Honey, Honey,
> For your taste of pink and white honey.

Here, one possible motif in the poem is the price that Pearl May Lee pays for her measure of sweet revenge: the diminution of her own capacity to express love and compassion for another—however ill-fated—human being. But the element of realism that Brooks injects into her ballad by showing Pearl May Lee's mocking detachment from her lover's fate is a conscious effort to devalue the romantic idealization of Black love. Furthermore, Pearl May Lee's macabre humor undermines the racial pride and harmony that was an important tenet in the Renaissance prescription for the New Negro. And, lastly, Pearl May Lee's predicament belies the social myth of the Black woman as *objective correlative* of the Renaissance's romanticism....

For Brooks, unlike the Renaissance poets, the victimization of poor Black women becomes not simply a minor chord but a predominant theme of *A Street in Bronzeville*. Few, if any, of her female characters are able to free themselves from the web of poverty and racism that threatens to strangle their lives. The Black heroine in "obituary for a living lady" was "decently wild / As a child," but as a victim of society's hypocritical, puritan standards, she "fell in love with a man who didn't know / That even if she wouldn't let him touch her breasts she / was still worth his hours." In another example of the complex life-choices confronting Brooks's women, the two sisters of "Sadie and Maude" must choose between death-in-life and life-in-death. Maude, who went to college, becomes a "think brown mouse," presumably resigned to spinsterhood, "living all alone / In this old house," while Sadie who "scraped life / With a fine-tooth comb" bears two illegitimate children and dies, leaving as a heritage for her children her "fine-tooth comb." What is noticeable in the lives of these Black women is a mutual identity that is inextricably linked with race and poverty....

Brooks's relationship with the Harlem Renaissance poets, as *A Street in Bronzeville* ably demonstrates, was hardly imitative. As one of the important links with the Black poetic tradition of the 1920s and 1930s, she enlarged the element of realism that was an important part of the Renaissance world-view. Although her poetry is often conditioned by the optimism that was also a legacy of the period, Brooks rejects outright their romantic prescriptions for the lives of Black women. And in this regard, she serves as a vital link with the Black Arts Movement of the 1960s that, while it witnessed the flowering of Black women as poets and social activists as well as the rise of Black feminist aesthetics in the 1970s, brought about a curious revival of romanticism in the Renaissance mode.

However, since the publication of *A Street in Bronzeville*, Brooks has not eschewed the traditional roles and values of Black women in American society; on the contrary, in her subsequent works, *Annie Allen* (1949), *The Bean Eaters* (1960), and *The Mecca* (1968), she has been remarkably consistent in identifying the root cause of intraracial problems within the Black community as white racism and its pervasive socio-economic effects. Furthermore, as one of the chief voices of the Black Arts Movement, she has developed a social vision, in such works as *Riot* (1969), *Family Pictures* (1970), and *Beckonings* (1975), that describes Black women and men as equally integral parts of the struggle for social and economic justice....

Source: Gary Smith, "Gwendolyn Brooks's *A Street in Bronzeville*, the Harlem Renaissance and the Mythologies of Black Women," in *MELUS*, Vol. 10, No. 3, Fall 1983, pp. 33–46.

SOURCES

Beach, Christopher, "From the Harlem Renaissance to the Black Arts Movement," in *The Cambridge Introduction to Twentieth-Century American Poetry*, Cambridge University Press, 2003, pp. 114–36.

Brooks, Gwendolyn, "The Mother," in *Selected Poems*, Harper & Row, 1963, pp. 4–5.

Cumo, Christopher, "Abortion," in *Historical Dictionary of the 1940s*, edited by James Gilbert Ryan and Leonard C. Schlup, M. E. Sharpe, 2006, pp. 3–4.

Daniels, Kate, "The Demise of the 'Delicate Prisons': The Women's Movement in Twentieth-Century American Poetry," in *A Profile of Twentieth-Century American Poetry*, edited by Jack Myers and David Wojahn, Southern Illinois University Press, 1991, pp. 224–53.

Griffin, Farah Jasmine, "Gwendolyn Brooks," in *Dictionary of Literary Biography*, Vol. 165, *American Poets since World War II, Fourth Series*, edited by Joseph Conte, Gale Research, 1996, pp. 81–91.

Melhem, D. H., "*A Street in Bronzeville*," in *Gwendolyn Brooks: Poetry and the Heroic Voice*, University Press of Kentucky, 1987, pp. 16–50.

"Poverty in the United States," in *National Poverty Center*, http://www.npc.umich.edu/poverty/#2 (accessed July 5, 2011).

Reagan, Leslie J., "Raids and Rules," in *When Abortion Was A Crime: Women, Medicine, and Law in the United States, 1867–1973*, University of California Press, 1997, pp. 160–92.

Smethurst, James, "The Adventures of a Social Poet: Langston Hughes from the Popular Front to Black Power," in *African American Poets: 1700s–1940s*, edited by Harold Bloom, Infobase Publishing, 2009, pp. 49–70.

Smith, Gary, "Gwendolyn Brooks's *A Street in Bronzeville*, the Harlem Renaissance and Mythologies of Black Women," in *MELUS*, Vol. 10, No. 3, Fall 1983, pp. 33–46.

Thenstrom, Stephan, and Abigail Thenstrom, "Poverty," in *America in Black and White: One Nation, Indivisible*, Simon & Schuster, 1997, pp. 232–57.

Watkins, Mel, "Gwendolyn Brooks, 83, Passionate Poet, Dies," in *New York Times*, December 5, 2000, http://www.nytimes.com/2000/12/05/books/gwendolyn-brooks-83-passionate-poet-dies.html (accessed July 5, 2011).

"Women Who Have Abortions," in *National Abortion Federation*, http://www.prochoice.org/about_abortion/facts/women_who.html (accessed July 5, 2011).

FURTHER READING

Finney, Nikky, ed., *The Ringing Ear: Black Poets Lean South*, University of Georgia Press, 2007.
> Finney offers a collection of contemporary African American poetry that draws on the South, Southern history and culture, and the Southern African American experience as influences.

Rhynes, Martha E., *Gwendolyn Brooks: Poet from Chicago*, Morgan Reynolds, 2003.
> In this acclaimed young-adult biography, Rhynes offers a survey of Brooks's life and career, and provides some historical context as a framework for understanding Brooks's poetry.

Wicklund, Susan, *This Common Secret: My Journey as an Abortion Doctor*, Public Affairs, 2007.
> Wicklund offers a unique perspective on the abortion debate by discussing her experiences as a physician who has performed abortions as part of her practice. She speaks about her own experience of having an abortion, about the threats against her life and safety made by anti-abortion activists, about the stories of the women she treated, and about abortion and reproductive rights legislation.

Wills, Charles A., *America in the 1940s*, Facts on File, 2006.
> In this resource geared toward a young-adult audience, Wills provides an overview of American history and culture during the 1940s, allowing the student of Brooks's work a cultural and historical perspective on the time period that encompassed Brooks's early career.

SUGGESTED SEARCH TERMS

Gwendolyn Brooks AND African American poetry

Gwendolyn Brooks AND biography

Gwendolyn Brooks AND Chicago

Gwendolyn Brooks AND abortion

Gwendolyn Brooks AND free verse poetry

Gwendolyn Brooks AND activism

Gwendolyn Brooks AND A Street in Bronzeville

Gwendolyn Brooks AND Pulitzer Prize

Gwendolyn Brooks AND Post-Harlem Renaissance

Gwendolyn Brooks AND African American modernism

Night Journey

THEODORE ROETHKE

1941

"Night Journey," written by American poet Theodore Roethke, was published in 1941 in the author's first collection of poems *Open House*. The poem is representative of the early phase of Roethke's career, when he favored traditional poetic forms. "Night Journey," written in short lines, each with three metrical feet and with an irregular rhyme scheme, details the author's journey on a train through the night, apparently as he travels back to his native Michigan. During the journey, he spots bridges, trees, mists, a lake, a mountain pass, and other features of the landscape. It is often that Roethke's poems represent his efforts to pit himself against the void or the abyss. In many respects, his poetry is the cry of a lone voice trying to find meaning and purpose in the face of nothingness. Although that impulse becomes more apparent in his later poems, the image in "Night Journey" of a single voice hurtling through a nighttime landscape suggests Roethke's principal poetic vision.

Roethke's reputation as a poet has grown steadily since the publication of *Open House*, and he is now regarded as one of the major American poets of the twentieth century, valued because his poetry consistently relies on fresh, vivid, and relatively simple language. A later collection, *The Waking Poems, 1933–1953*, won the Pulitzer Prize in 1954. Later still, he won the Bollingen Prize and the Edna St. Vincent Millay Prize, and after his death in 1963, his collection *The Far Field* won the National Book Award for 1965. Roethke combined his career as a poet with that of a college

Theodore Roethke (The Library of Congress)

teacher, and he achieved success despite recurring bouts of mental illness.

He is sometimes associated with the so-called confessional poets, a group that included Sylvia Plath, Robert Lowell, and Anne Sexton. These poets wrote about intensely personal, usually painful feelings and perceptions, and were themselves tormented souls. Although Roethke's poetry is intensely personal, it differs from that of the confessional poets in being more universal in its symbols and images; readers can appreciate it without having to become familiar with the author's biography.

"Night Journey" can be found in *The Collected Poems of Theodore Roethke*, first published in 1966 but available in a more recent edition published by Anchor in 1974.

AUTHOR BIOGRAPHY

Roethke was born on May 25, 1908, in Saginaw, Michigan, to German immigrant parents. His parents made their living with one of the largest greenhouses in western Michigan, and the image of the greenhouse, with its plants, flowers, mosses, weeds, and rocks was one that would dominate his later poetry. In fact, a group of his later poems is informally referred to as the "greenhouse poems." Roethke's domineering father died in 1923, an event that had a profound impact on the poet's frame of mind and his creative impulses.

Roethke attended the University of Michigan from 1925 to 1929, graduating magna cum laude. He originally bowed to his parents' early wish that he become a lawyer, and to that end he enrolled in the Harvard Law School. He withdrew after only one semester and took graduate courses at the University of Michigan and at Harvard. By 1931, the Great Depression was in full swing, and the hard economic times forced him to take a position at Lafayette College in Pennsylvania, where he taught from 1931 to 1935. During a one-year stint teaching at Michigan State College (now University), he suffered the first of several bouts of mental illness (bipolar disorder) and was hospitalized, but he was also able to complete his master's degree at the University of Michigan. He then accepted a teaching post at Pennsylvania State University, where he remained until 1943. Meanwhile, in 1941, he published his first collection of poetry, *Open House*, which contains the poem "Night Journey." In 1943, he accepted another teaching post, this one at Bennington College in Vermont, where he remained until 1947. In 1945, he was hospitalized again for depression. The final fifteen years of his teaching career, beginning in 1947, were spent at the University of Washington in Seattle.

Meanwhile, Roethke's reputation as a poet grew steadily. In 1945, he won a Guggenheim fellowship, allowing him to work on his next book, *The Lost Son and Other Poems* (1948). A second Guggenheim fellowship in 1950 allowed him to complete *Praise to the End!*, published in 1951. In 1953, he published *The Waking*, which won a Pulitzer Prize the following year. His collection *Words for the Wind* received the Bollingen Prize and the National Book Award in 1958, and in 1961, he published a collection of children's poems, *I Am! Says the Lamb*. Throughout these years, he continued to struggle with mental illness and was hospitalized on various occasions. He was a large bear of a man with immense appetites and a tendency to drink heavily, and he had an intense love affair with poet Louise Bogan. He often surprised people with his agility on the tennis court, despite his size, and in fact, he coached tennis at Penn State University.

In 1962, Roethke completed his final collection, *The Far Field*. The book was published after his death on August 1, 1963, from a coronary occlusion (a blockage of blood flow to the heart), suffered while swimming at a friend's pool in Washington. The pool is now the site of a rock garden.

MEDIA ADAPTATIONS

- Readers interested in hearing the voice of Roethke can access *Shorter Poems: Elegy for Jane/My Papa's Waltz*, originally released by Folkways Records in 1962 and available as an MP3 download.

POEM SUMMARY

The text used for this summary is from *Good Poems: American Places*, edited by Garrison Keillor, Penguin, 2011. Versions of the poem can be found on the following Web pages: http://oldpoetry.com/opoem/7676-Theodore-Roethke-Night-Journey and http://famouspoetsandpoems.com/poets/theodore_roethke/poems/16322.

Lines 1–5

The poem begins with an indication that the poet is on a train heading in a westerly direction; most likely, the reader is to infer that Roethke is traveling from his home in the east to his family home in Michigan. He can feel the rocking of the train as he rides in a Pullman, the brand name of railroad sleeping cars for passengers. These cars were named for their developer, George Pullman, who formed the Pullman Palace Car Company and manufactured the cars in the late nineteenth and early twentieth centuries. As the other people in the train sleep, the speaker is awake and looks out into the night landscape.

Lines 6–11

He sees bridges, which he compares to lace made out of iron. Trees appear suddenly, followed by the mists surrounding mountains (possibly the Appalachian Mountains), then a place of bleakness (possibly flat land through Ohio). As the train goes on, he sees a lake (possibly Lake Erie).

Lines 12–15

The poet then comments on how he can feel in his neck the strain of the train as it takes a curve. He notices that the movement of the train awakens his muscles and nerves.

Lines 16–19

The poet then notices a beacon light swinging; it begins in darkness, but then the light blazes and becomes bright. He is perhaps referring to the lights used on railroad tracks to signal to the conductor the direction the train will take at a Y junction, or perhaps he is referring to the light of an oncoming train.

Lines 20–23

The train goes on, thundering through ravines and gullies; although it is nighttime, the poet is able to see the gullies bathed in light, perhaps light from the moon and stars, or perhaps light coming from nearby towns and highways. He goes through a mountain pass, and mist begins to form on the window panes of his train berth. It then begins to rain, and the rain beats down hard on the train windows.

Lines 24–27

He can feel the pounding of the train's wheels on the track bed, as well as the jerking and shoving of the train's pistons. The poem concludes with a simple announcement that the poet has stayed up half the night with the intention of seeing the land that he loves.

THEMES

Travel

"Night Journey," as the title suggests, is about a journey. The poet is traveling back to his home in Michigan by train, although this is an inference not based on anything specific in the poem.

TOPICS FOR FURTHER STUDY

- *Come with Me: Poems for a Journey* is a collection of sixteen young-adult poems by Naomi Shihab Nye, a writer of Palestinian descent. The collection was published by Greenwillow Books in 2000. The poet invites the reader to accompany her on internal journeys but also literal journeys to real and imagined places. After reading the poems in this collection, write a brief essay comparing and contrasting Nye's vision of a journey with Roethke's.

- Imagine that you are asked to provide a multimedia version of "Night Journey" for a publisher. Using the Internet, locate images that you might use to accompany the poem. You might also investigate possibilities for sound effects. Then, using Jing.com, share your multimedia presentation with your classmates.

- Roethke's poetic vision was strongly influenced by the immense greenhouse his parents operated. This greenhouse provided him with images of growth and flowering but also decay and death. Additionally, the glass of the greenhouse inspired him with the image of looking inward to see what is on the inside. Try to imagine a corresponding place or object from your own life, one that might inspire you to write poetry or a short story. If possible, post a picture of the place or object on your social networking site and invite your classmates to comment on the "poetry" of the item you have posted.

- Many creative writers today study at universities, often earning bachelor or master of fine arts degrees. Roethke taught in such programs throughout his career. On the Internet, investigate such a program, perhaps one at a university in your state; alternatively, you could investigate such a program at one of the colleges and universities at which Roethke taught. What kinds of courses are offered? Who is most likely to gain admission to such a program? What kinds of qualifications are needed? Are any of the faculty members in the program you have investigated prominent in the artistic community? Do you believe that it is possible to "teach" poetry (or fiction, or the visual arts) in a university setting? Share your findings and conclusions with your classmates in an oral report.

- Imagine that as Roethke is taking the journey depicted in "Night Journey," he is sitting next to another passenger and commenting on what he sees—and that the other person responds with his or her own observations. Script out the dialogue that might take place and share your script with your classmates, perhaps by recruiting a friend to read the script aloud with you, or record it and post on YouTube.

- Roethke was an avid tennis player. Using the style of "Night Journey," write a poem that depicts not a journey, but a tennis match. As an alternative, write a poem about a journey you have taken; the journey could be one across the country or one just across town. Record what you see, feel, hear, and perhaps even smell during your journey. Post the poem on your social networking site and invite your classmates to comment.

This poem records his observations as he makes the journey. In some respects, the journey is uneventful. The poet rides on the train while other people are sleeping. He views the passing landscape. It is a little unclear how the poet could have seen the passing landscape, given that the journey apparently takes place at night. Perhaps the reader is to infer that there is

A Pullman sleeper car travels through the fog. (Steven Pepple | Shutterstock.com)

just enough light from the moon and stars, or perhaps from nearby cities and highways, to enable him to see the landscape features that he enumerates. In addition to the things he sees, the reader is given a sense of the physical sensations of the journey, including the shaking of the train's wheels and the strain he feels as the train makes a curve.

Landscape

Throughout his poetic career, Roethke was very much attuned to his physical landscape. Many commentators attribute this to his upbringing in Michigan, where his parents operated a large greenhouse. From an early age, Roethke was exposed to the plants, flowers, shrubs, mosses, vines, and other items that might be cultivated and sold at a greenhouse. Thus, as he takes his train journey, he is attuned to the features of the landscape that he passes, including bridges, trees, mountains and mountain passes, mists, ravines, a lake, gullies, and the like. For Roethke, these features of the landscape define the land that, he says, he loves. In this way, the poem bears some similarities to the well-known folk song by Woody Guthrie, "This Land Is Your Land," which was written in 1940, just a year before Roethke wrote "Night Journey" (although the song was not recorded until 1944). This song, too, surveys the American landscape, and it was written in response to the Great Depression and the unequal distribution of wealth in the American population.

Isolation

A theme that runs throughout Roethke's poetry, and in many respects throughout his personal life, is his sense of isolation, of being a lone voice crying out against emptiness, the abyss, and eternity. Many of his poems convey a sense of anguish. The poems try to erode the boundary between the inner and outer life. The natural world becomes an emblem of the self, and traveling through that world is an encounter with the self. The journey, however, is fraught with possibilities. It can lead to transcendence of the self, or it can lead to decay and dissolution, but it is highly characteristic that "Night Journey" involves a lone poetic voice. The other riders on the train are said to be resting. The only consciousness in the poem is that of Roethke himself. He sees the landscape. He feels the straining in his body as the train makes a curve. He feels the pounding of the wheels on the track. His muscles and nerves come awake. In the end, he tells the reader that he is looking at the land he loves. He is isolated, a lone voice, but in this instance his journey enables him to become energized and awakened by the world around him.

STYLE

Meter

Meter refers to the rhythm of a poem, achieved by the pattern of accented and unaccented syllables. "Night Journey" is written in a form called iambic trimeter. The term *iambic* refers to a pattern consisting of a stressed syllable followed by an unstressed syllable. This pair of syllables is called a foot. Other types of metrical feet, however, can consist of three and even four syllables. Also, the *da-DUM* pattern of the iamb is only one possibility; other patterns include *DA-dum*, *da-da-DUM*, and others. Nevertheless, the iamb is the most common metrical foot in English poetry.

The other part of the term trimeter refers to a line with three metrical feet. Many of the lines in "Night Journey" can be scanned (that is, the stressed and unstressed syllables can be marked) according to this pattern: *da-DUM, da-DUM, da-DUM*. Sometimes, the trimeter line is thought of as a half line, with the second half appearing as a separate line. In other words, "Night Journey," consisting of twenty-seven lines, could have been written with, say, thirteen longer lines and the rhythm would be the same. By using short lines made up of iambic trimeters, a relatively uncommon metrical pattern (and his fellow poets remarked that Roethke was a master of the short line), Roethke conveys the sense of the train rapidly hurtling through the night.

The best poets, however, do not allow the metrical pattern to dictate every line and syllable. This pattern can be flexible, with variations throughout the poem. Thus, in the first line of "Night Journey," the first word is stressed rather than unstressed. This word is followed by two unstressed syllables, which in turn are followed by the next stressed syllable. Variations such as this prevent the rhythm of the poem from becoming monotonous and repetitive.

Rhyme

Rhyme refers to the repeated pattern of sounds at the ends of lines. "Night Journey" is a rhymed poem, but Roethke uses a very irregular rhyme scheme, and the word *scheme* seems almost inapplicable. Usually, poets who use rhyme—and not all do—follow a particular pattern. Conventionally, readers can identify the rhyme scheme by using letters to designate repeated sounds. Thus, if two lines end with the words "book" and "cook," those words would be designated as, for example, *A*. Later, if the word "hook" is used, that word would be designated *A* as well. In stanzas of poetry, rhyme schemes will typically take a form such as *ABAB*, or perhaps *ABBA* (assuming a four-line stanza), and this pattern will be repeated in subsequent stanzas, so that the next stanza's scheme is *CDCD* (or *CDDC*). Sometimes poets link stanzas by linking their rhyme schemes, so that two stanzas of a poem might have the scheme *ABAB*, then *BCBC*.

"Night Journey" consists of just a single stanza of twenty-seven lines. Although it uses rhyme, the rhyme scheme does not follow a particular pattern. The result is a rhyme scheme that looks more like an eye-exam chart: *ABBCADEF CDEGHGHICJCKLLKM NCN*. Notice that two of the line endings, designated here as *F* (line 8) and *M* (line 24), do not rhyme with anything. The scheme at some points hints at patterns (*ABBCA*, or *GHGH*), but overall there is no discernible pattern.

The question arises as to why Roethke, during this traditional phase of his early career, would make use of a rhyme "scheme" that is no scheme at all. Each reader might answer the question in a different way, but one possibility is that Roethke was trying to capture a sense of a train rushing through the nighttime landscape. The rhymes link lines, giving the poem a sense of unity, but the nature of the links is constantly changing and shifting, just as the landscape Roethke is writing about constantly shifts and changes as he moves from one locale to another, following a line rather than a pattern that repeats in a circular or repetitive fashion. In this way, the rhymes of the poem are more like assonance, a term generally used to refer to the repetition of vowel sounds within and between lines.

Alliteration

Alliteration is a common feature of poetry. The term refers to repeated consonant sounds, usually at the beginnings of words. Thus, word like "book," "boy," and "butter" would be alliterative. Roethke makes frequent use of alliteration in "Night Journey." Some examples include the repeated *r* sound in line 2 (picked up at the end of line 5), the *f* sound in line 12, the *m* sound in line 8 (picked up again in line 14), and the *b* sound in lines 16, 17, and 20.

As with the poem's rhyme scheme, there is no particular pattern, but alliteration typically does not follow any kind of set pattern. Throughout his career, Roethke was interested in the sounds of words and phrases. Nearly each day he would write in his notebook, and while some of this writing recorded his views on a specific matter at length, much of it consisted of interesting words and phrases, phrases that he regarded as poetic. These phrases, then, frequently formed the raw material of his poems, as though he had gathered a collection of lumber of various widths and lengths and assembled the lumber into a structure. The alliteration in "Night Journey" gives unity to the poem, linking words within lines, then linking those lines to the lines that follow, on and on to again suggest the notion of a train hurtling along, just as the sounds of the poem propel the reader along.

HISTORICAL CONTEXT

The Great Depression

Roethke published his collection *Open House*, which contains the poem "Night Journey," in 1941. He had been working on the collection for ten years. This decade corresponded with the Great Depression in the United States, a depression that extended around the world. Roethke attended college during the 1920s, a decade often referred to as the Roaring Twenties, for it was a time of affluence, growing personal freedom, and optimism about the future. The Roaring Twenties came to an abrupt end in 1929 with the crash of the stock market, when many people's fortunes, large and small, were wiped out. In the years that followed, banks failed, workers lost their jobs (the unemployment rate was as high as 25 percent), veterans of World War I were reduced to selling pencils and apples on the streets, and many people survived on diets of watery soup and rummaged through trash heaps for bits of coal they could use to heat their homes. Throughout the 1930s, the federal government under President Franklin D. Roosevelt tried to alleviate some of the Depression's worst effects but with modest success. The economy rebounded somewhat, only to sink again, and the Depression persisted until the outbreak of World War II.

World War II

The other major historical event that framed the publication of "Night Journey" was the looming war. The smoke of war had already risen above Europe with the German invasion of Poland on September 1, 1939. Throughout the 1930s, war seemed inevitable as the demands of German dictator Adolf Hitler escalated. In 1938, German-speaking Austria succumbed to pressure and united with Germany, an event called the *Anschluss* ("joining"). Weeks later, Hitler demanded autonomy for the Sudetenland, a German-speaking section of Czechoslovakia, and despite diplomatic efforts, Hitler's forces began to occupy Czechoslovakia on October 1, 1938. Hitler then claimed that Poland was persecuting and killing ethnic German Poles. This provided him with a pretense for invading Poland, prompting Great Britain and France to declare war on Germany on September 3, 1939. Full-scale fighting erupted in 1940 with the German invasion of Belgium and the Netherlands.

Meanwhile, tension was mounting in the Pacific. In 1931, Japan invaded Manchuria, and by 1937, Japan was at war with China. In 1940, Japan invaded French Indochina, which caused the United States to stop shipments of machine tools, airplane parts, aviation gasoline, and eventually oil to Japan. Further, Roosevelt ordered a buildup of U.S. military forces in the Philippines to counter Japanese expansion in the Pacific and Southeast Asia. He also ordered that the U.S. fleet be moved from San Diego to Pearl Harbor, Hawaii, where it would be better poised to meet any Japanese threat.

The Japanese regarded these as provocative steps. They concluded that to protect Japan's access to natural resources, principally

COMPARE & CONTRAST

- **1940s:** The United States enters World War II. Japan bombs the U.S. naval base at Pearl Harbor in Hawaii on December 7, 1941, drawing the United States into the war. World War II has been raging in Europe for two years.

  Today: The United States is at war, but the opponent consists of terrorist groups and networks rather than the military forces of nations. American troops continue to fight terrorism in such places as Afghanistan and Iraq.

- **1940s:** The United States comes out of the Great Depression of the 1930s. During the 1930s, unemployment had been high, and many people suffered poverty. The median family income is about $1,500 per year (about $22,800 in 2011 inflation-adjusted dollars).

  Today: The United States is mired in a steep recession that began in 2008. Although many people are unemployed, social safety nets help restrain the level of poverty. The median family income as of 2008 is just over $52,000 per year.

- **1940s:** Mental illness often goes unacknowledged because of the stigma surrounding it. Many people with mental illnesses are hospitalized, sometimes for extended periods, where they undergo such treatments as electroshock therapy, induced seizures, and, in extreme cases, lobotomies.

  Today: There is less stigma associated with mental illness. People with mental illnesses tend to be hospitalized only when the illness is severe, and then as briefly as possible. Treatment options include a vast array of drugs, psychotherapy, psychiatric treatment, and, in some cases, various forms of brain and nerve stimulation using electricity, magnetism, or pulse generators.

- **1940s:** The Pullman rail car company has introduced "roomette" cars with eighteen enclosed private rooms; these cars are used by numerous passenger rail companies.

  Today: The only intercity passenger service is the National Railroad Passenger Corporation, more popularly called Amtrak. Amtrak is a government-owned and government-subsidized corporation.

---

oil and rubber, and to expand its empire in the Pacific, a first strike against the United States was necessary. After careful planning, the Japanese fleet departed Japan in late November 1941 and launched an attack on Pearl Harbor on December 7. Twenty-four hundred Americans were killed, and some twelve hundred were wounded. Numerous ships and planes were destroyed, crippling the American fleet, but fortunately for the United States, its four aircraft carriers stationed at Pearl Harbor were at sea, so the Pearl Harbor attack was not a knockout blow.

The attack stunned the American public. What particularly troubled officials in the Roosevelt administration was that the United States and Japan had been conducting diplomatic talks, presumably to ease tensions. The attack, then, was perceived as a "sneak" attack, and Roosevelt characterized December 7 as a "date which will live in infamy." In response to the attack, the United States declared war on Japan, marking U.S. entry into World War II, a war that would last until Germany and Japan surrendered in 1945.

Although "Night Journey" does not make reference to any of these historical events, they are implicit in the poet's attitude to the landscape and his journey. In 1941, the United States faced grave crises. The economy had been severely depressed for more than a decade, and war clouds were looming on the horizon, yet

The motion of the train keeps the narrator awake through the night. (Seti | Shutterstock.com)

despite these stark realities, Roethke was able to celebrate the land that in the final lines he says he loves.

CRITICAL OVERVIEW

Roethke's reputation grew slowly. His earlier work, including *Open House* (the collection that contained "Night Journey"), was not widely reviewed. Karl Malkoff, in *Theodore Roethke: An Introduction to the Poetry*, notes, however, that *Open House*

> was well received, and its apparent conventionality made possible the near universality of praise never accorded his more controversial later work. Roethke used traditional lyric forms, his content tended to be intellectual rather than sensuous.... Although we can now look back on this work and trace the origins of what were to become Roethke's major themes (e.g., the tension between flesh and spirit, the exploration of the self as a search for identity), there was little indication to someone reading his poems at the time of what was to follow.

It was only beginning in about the 1950s that critics, and particularly other poets, began to regard Roethke as a major American poet, one who was highly admired. Critics began to see him as writing in the tradition of the romantic poets and such American poets as Ralph Waldo Emerson and Walt Whitman.

Two critics summarize the essence of the critical reception of Roethke's poetry. In his essay "Theodore Roethke: A Celebration," Richard A. Blessing makes this generalization in describing the poetry:

> Few, if any, other modern American poets of comparable reputation have absorbed more wholly the concerns of our age into the nerve-ends, nor have more adequately represented in their art the incredible experiences of the age.

Blessing continues by saying:

> If, as I believe, the essential experience of modern life is speed, movement, energy, whirl, a sense of unceasing and often violent motion, Roethke surely took it all into the nerve-endings, into the blood and pulse, into the rhythms of his giant body which became the rhythms of his poetry.

Harry Williams, however, hints at some of the objections to Roethke's poetry in his critical study *"The Edge of What I Have": Theodore Roethke and After:* "It has been demonstrated how some poets revered Roethke's lyricism, his voice of the self proclaiming a drama of the new self, but certain critics have found this preoccupation with the self too narcissistic." Williams refers to another critic, William Pritchard, who in a discussion of the nature of modern lyric poetry, "looks upon Roethke as a representative figure of the 'somnambulistic' poet devoid of irony and changing tone of voice." Blessing then adds that "these 'negative' critics appear to agree on at least two points: Roethke's limited theme that makes him ... merely a personal, self-conscious poet, and his lyric form or lyrical monotone."

CRITICISM

Michael J. O'Neal

O'Neal holds a Ph.D. in English. In the following essay, he examines "Night Journey" as an example of the poetry of simplicity.

One reason that Roethke's poetry has become highly regarded over the years is its simplicity. This is not to say that his poetic vision is simplistic but rather to note that his diction and images are direct, pointed, and conveyed in basic language accessible to a wide range of readers.

English is a unique language in that it is a descendant of different language families. English originated as a Germanic language, meaning that it is closely related to such languages as German, Dutch, and most of the Scandinavian languages. Early in its history, English developed as a separate language on the British Isles among the Germanic tribes that had settled the islands, primarily the Angles and the Saxons. For this reason, much of the basic vocabulary of Anglo-Saxon English is Germanic. Thus, such fundamental words as *mother, father, brother, sister, house, sit,* and thousands of others are what are called cognate words with their German counterparts; that is, they are words that "look" and sound very much the same (for the record, the corresponding German words are *Mutter, Vater, Bruder, Schwester, Haus,* and *Sitzen*; in German, all nouns are capitalized). These are the common words, many of them just a

"RATHER, THE DICTION OF 'NIGHT JOURNEY' REINFORCES THE POEM'S PURPOSE, WHICH IS TO PROPEL THE READER THROUGH A JOURNEY IN SPACE AND RESPOND TO THE JOURNEY ON AN ELEMENTAL, EMOTIONAL LEVEL."

syllable or two, that have been used in day-to-day discourse for centuries; they emerged at a time when there was very little writing, and what writing there was in Europe was done primarily in Latin. It might be worth adding that English swear words tend to be of Germanic origin; few English-speaking people swear in Latin.

English then took a major turn in 1066 with the Norman Invasion. The Normans were a people who occupied Normandy, a region of modern-day France. For reasons not necessary to explain here, William of Normandy, often called William the Conqueror, defeated the Anglo-Saxon nobles, and he and his descendants assumed the throne of England. What was crucial is that he and his followers brought with them the French language, along with French customs and culture. French, however, is a Romance language, not a Germanic one; it is derived from Latin, the language of ancient Rome, which is the root of the word *romance.* In the centuries that followed the Norman Invasion, English therefore became something of a hybrid language, with Romance, Latin-based vocabulary grafted onto the native Germanic, Anglo-Saxon vocabulary. To cite just a single example—and thousands more could be cited—English did not use the German word for "hospital," *Krankenhaus* (or "sick house") but rather adopted the Romance word that gave English *hospital, hospice,* and even *hotel.*

The Anglo-Saxons resented their Norman overlords, but one happy result of the Norman invasion was that thousands of new words were imported into English, particularly after the development of movable type and the printing press in the fifteenth century allowed the publication of hundreds, then thousands of books, many of them requiring a new vocabulary for philosophic, theological, and scientific discourse.

WHAT DO I READ NEXT?

- Several of Roethke's poems are frequently anthologized. Two of the most well known are "My Papa's Waltz" and "The Waking." These poems can be found in *The Collected Poems of Theodore Roethke*, first published in 1966 and are also available in a more recent edition published by Anchor in 1974.
- Readers interested in Roethke's views on creating poetry will find indispensable his book *On Poetry and Craft*, available from Copper Canyon Press in a 2001 edition.
- Roethke had a romantic relationship with award-winning poet Louise Bogan, and the two remained good lifetime friends after the relationship ended. Bogan's poetry bears comparison with Roethke's. Examples include "Last Hill in a Vista" and the "Train Tune." These poems are available in *The Blue Estuary*, the major collection of her poems, published by Farrar, Straus and Giroux in 1968.
- William H. Young and Nancy K. Young are the authors of *The 1930s*, part of the "American Popular Culture through History" series published by Greenwood; this volume was published in 2002. The book, written for young adults, focuses not on major political events but on the arts, activities, culture, and everyday life of America during the 1930s, the decade in which Roethke was writing the poems in *Open House*.
- Readers with more interest in the major political events of the 1930s, when Roethke was writing *Open House*, might start with *America in the 1930s* by Jim Callan, part of Facts on File's "Decades of American History" series for young adults. This volume was published in 2005.
- Arna W. Bontemps was an American poet of Creole heritage. In the same year that Roethke's *Open House* was published (1941), Bontemps, along with Henrietta Bruce Sharon (who provided drawings), published a collection titled *Golden Slippers: An Anthology of Negro Poetry for Young Readers*. The volume was published by Harper & Row. The title might suggest that the poetry is a bit dated, yet many readers continue to find it fresh and relevant.
- Paul Janeczko was a teacher who compiled a number of collections of poetry for young adults. His poems for people taking journeys were collected in *Pocket Poems: Selected Poems for a Journey*, published by Bradbury Press in 1985.

Moreover, the Latinate vocabulary of the Romance languages provided roots for thousands more words. The result is that English probably has more words in its vocabulary than any other language in the world—about a quarter million, perhaps three quarters of a million if distinct meanings of the same word are included. French, in contrast, has about a hundred thousand words. (These are rough estimates, and different estimates are given; the problem is defining precisely what a "word" is. Interestingly, an organization called the Global Language Monitor states that English crossed the one million word threshold at precisely 10:22 a.m. Greenwich Mean Time on June 10, 2009!)

The result for poets and creative writers (and writers in general) is that English provides a rich, democratic, multifaceted vocabulary they can use to modulate tone and style. Some writers prefer the Anglo-Saxon style, relying on basic, elemental words. Other writers prefer a more Latinate vocabulary, relying on newer words derived from Romance-language roots. The distinction became most apparent in the early 1600s through the work of two authors, one known to nearly everyone, the other known only to a few.

The first was Shakespeare, who ransacked not only Anglo-Saxon but also the Romance languages to write with a vocabulary that overflowed with new words such that the vocabulary of his plays and poems includes about thirty thousand distinct words. Many of these coinages are now part of our everyday vocabulary: "accommodation," "dislocate," "obscene," "reliance," "submerged," "demonstrate," "emphasis," and many more.

The other was a cleric named John Bois who played a lead role in a new English translation of the Bible at about the same time. The Authorized Version, usually called the King James Version of the Bible (after English King James I, who authorized the translation), relies on a lean, taut rigorous style, with short sentences and a spare, muscular vocabulary—only about eight thousand distinct words. This became the model for such writers as John Bunyan, Ernest Hemingway, and Robert Frost, and of Theodore Roethke.

Consider "Night Journey." The poem consists of one hundred thirty-six words. Out of that total, a scant twenty-five are more than one syllable, and only one ("suddenness") has three syllables. Among the two-syllable words are such basic words as "into" and "beyond." Many of the other two-syllable words are simply inflected forms of one-syllable words, meaning that the added syllable is the result of a past-tense or plural ending. At least one word, "roadbed," is simply a compound of two basic words. No one, then, is going to excel on a vocabulary test as a result of studying this or any other Roethke poem.

Further, consider the origins of the words in "Night Journey." It is almost impossible for a writer to entirely avoid Latinate or Romance-language words. In this poem, "rhythm" is a Greek word that entered the language through a French word that means "flow." "Piston" comes from Latin/French, as does "ravine." However, the rest of the poem's vocabulary is good old-fashioned Anglo-Saxon/Germanic. "Beacon," for example, comes from the Old English word *beacen*, meaning "sign." (Old English is the term applied to the variety of English spoken and occasionally written from about the mid-fifth century to about 1100 or 1150.) "Bleak" comes from the Old English word *blac*, meaning "pale." "Rattle" retained the meaning of a word in Dutch (another Germanic language), *ratel*. "Blazing" comes from the Old English word *blaese*, meaning "torch." A simple word like "every" is Anglo-Saxon, coming from the Old English *aefre*. Most of the other words in the poem reflect similar Germanic origins. Even the reference to the Pullman railroad car is a happy accident. The surname Pullman derives from an Anglo-Saxon word for "buck" (a male deer or, at the time, horse). It was first used as a nickname for an energetic, frisky young man, but in time it evolved into a surname.

The result is that "Night Journey" is not a poem that appeals to the intellect. It works its magic not through disquisition, commentary, or analysis. The diction of the poem does not convey ideas. The reader does not have to think about the poem. Rather, the diction of "Night Journey" reinforces the poem's purpose, which is to propel the reader through a journey in space and respond to the journey on an elemental, emotional level. The poem presents a succession of images, many of them visual, but some auditory and even kinesthetic, sharing with the reader a sequence of perceptions. This act of perceiving rather than thinking and analyzing was characteristic of Roethke's work. The poet's fundamental poetic vision was an assertion of self in the face of the forever, a kind of cry in the night, or a flicker of consciousness in the face of nothingness. As Roethke makes the journey home, it is indicative that he takes the journey at night. He propels through the darkness, awake and alive, his muscles taut, his nerves firing, as all those around him take their rest. The landscape, the mist, the rain, the pounding of the train's pistons, the shaking of the stone of the roadbed—all awaken the poet to his humanity in the midst of darkness, as though he is undergoing a primitive ritual in the present moment, one that he does not analyze, deconstruct, or recollect. His simple, almost monosyllabic Anglo-Saxon diction allows the reader to share the immediacy of that experience, an experience not filtered through a more complex Latinate vocabulary that is the language of thought and analysis.

Source: Michael J. O'Neal, Critical Essay on "Night Journey," in *Poetry for Students*, Gale, Cengage Learning, 2012.

Raymond Benoit
In the following essay, Roethke lays the foundation for his later work.

Critics agree on the stylistic and psychological breakthrough that distinguishes Roethke's *The Lost Son and Other Poems* (1948), published seven years after his first volume, *Open House*. Two motifs characterize the collection—the world of nature, especially in its minimal forms,

The west was a favorite topic of Theodore Roethke. (Rick Ernst | Shutterstock.com)

and the theme of the lost son of the title poem. These motifs actually first appeared together in a composition Roethke wrote for *Rhetoric* some twenty years earlier as an undergraduate in Carleton Wells's class at the University of Michigan (1925-29). Indeed, the intimacy between nature and father and son in Roethke's boyhood is the warp and woof of the essay: in the past, hiking on Sundays with his father Otto in the Saginaw Valley; in the present, his deprivation of nature by the "inroads of civilization"; and more particularly, his estrangement from nature because of his father's death, abruptly expressed in the last poignantly foreshortened paragraph. The essay, "My Estrangement from Nature," part of the Roethke collection at the University of Washington libraries in Seattle, and here for the first time published in its entirety with gracious permission of Beatrice Roethke Lushington, thus looks forward to the vision and voice of *The Lost Son and Other Poems* in its fundamental emphasis and shape. The poetry too moves from an organic, unconscious unity "alone / In a watery drowse" ("A Field of Light"), through a time of loss and waiting "at the wood's mouth, / By the cave's door" ("The Lost Son"), but then does add significantly beyond the prose a remembered and reawakened bliss when Roethke is again with his father, the "nameless stranger" ("a bird or a tree?") who guides him once more both in the world and beyond the world—"the drops sliding from a lifted oar, / Held up, while the rower breathes, and the small boat drifts quietly shoreward" ("The Shape of the Fire"). The essay may not involve the imaginative leap of the later poetry, but it clearly and feelingly expresses and readies the main material for the alchemy.

MY ESTRANGEMENT FROM NATURE

I doubt if there be any loss so keen as that felt when the influence of nature is taken out of one's life. Even the occasional woodland ramble will become a very large and definite part of a person's physical, mental, and spiritual existence. It is a habit which, to break, causes all the sharp pangs of love. It is well to bear in mind that a high regard for nature is termed "love" by many writers. Cold Emerson really loved nature in his harsh New England way. Ruskin, Wordsworth, and even a suave rhymster [sic] like Dryden, rapturously admired the bounteous "handmaid of God." Among simpler men, the love of nature is formed to an even greater degree. If I ever saw joy of the universe evinced, it was the time I went hiking with a New York elevator man who was emancipated from his cubicle in Manhattan for the first time in years. That old fellow frisked about like a young puppy.

The loss of this thing which has delighted and transported other men has been particularly cruel and poignant to me. I still get glimpses of nature in many forms,—the majestic setting sun, geese flying across the face of the moon, the beguiling wind of spring, a luna butterfly, and those elusive warblers which I can no longer identify. But these momentary flashes are only the more painful because of their briefness. Instead of seeing nature in its grand and entire solitude, I see it interspersed between signboards and hot dog stands as I drive from one town to another. The nature I knew was not primeval, perhaps, but at least it was more or less undisturbed. It consisted of rolling sand hills which supported rabbits and jack pine; occasional idyllic farms which had no barbecue or cider dispensary in front; leisurely and treacherous creeks out of which one could still get pike untainted by the chemical works; and marshy thickets where thrush and oven bird sang. There were miles of country untrod by the devastating type of tourist who has now penetrated to every corner of the land. Right at the edge of town there was a woods which made us a glorius [sic] natural playground. Now men of vision in the Rotary Club have converted it into "Woodland Vista, the Subdivision Beautiful."

If the inroads of civilization have deprived me of nature in many ways, I have also become estranged from her for a far different reason.

Nearly every Sunday my father and I hiked over some part of the valley. He was a strange and ideal companion. Lean and hardy as a hickory sapling, he had the tirelessness of an Indian. His taciturnity and stoicness, too, were Indian-like characteristics. He never rhapsodized over anything as did uncle Charlie (who, moreover, was too fat to be a good woodsman)[.] He merely pointed. Once he fell and painfully twisted his ankle, yet he never bothered to comment about it. Often we would separate for hours without a word concerning where we would meet. Yet we always managed to find each other with little difficulty.

I have gone hundreds of miles hurrying behind his heels and wondering what he was thinking. Occasionally,—a time rare and glorious[—]he would become talkative and reveal himself as the introspective German he was.

Thus, for me, Nature and my father became inseparably intertwined. When I thought of the sand ridges with their pine trees, I thought of him. It always seemed that nature was more gracious and revelatory when he was with me. If other people came along, I was miserable. They always seemed stupid and garrulous. Somehow, it seemed a sort of sacrilege to show an unappreciative stranger a new wood chuck hole.

Now my father is dead. The business of living and trying to learn has confined me to the city. I don't care to hike any more. I always find myself expecting to see his head appear over the edge of the next hill.

Source: Raymond Benoit, "'My Estrangement from Nature': An Undergraduate Theme of Theodore Roethke," in *ANQ*, Vol. 11, No. 1, Winter 1998, pp. 31–33.

Kermit Vanderbilt
In the following excerpt, Vanderbilt delves into the influence of regional America, specifically the Midwest of Roethke's youth and the Pacific Northwest of his last years, on Roethke's poetry.

Since Theodore Roethke's sudden, untimely death in summer of 1963, his work has been the subject of a steadily rising flood of critical assessments. The consensus of most of them is that his career can best be explained as an intense search for identity, wholeness, and grace. He shaped his private meditations into increasingly powerful esthetic forms that are at once original and charged with echoes from his various American and English poet-masters. A further aspect of Roethke's imaginative vision, however, remains to be adequately explored, namely his significant response to a regional America—the Midwest of his youth and, climactically, the Pacific Northwest where he lived his final sixteen years.

I

Roethke arrived in the Northwest in autumn of 1947 to teach poetry at the University of Washington, which remained his academic address until his death. The move from Penn State westward marked the crucial turning point in his career and the beginning of a serious identification with place in America. There were, of course, hints of original identity in Roethke

"AS IT WOULD PREDICTABLY HAVE TO BE FOR THE MERCURIAL ROETHKE, THE FINAL PERIOD IN THE PACIFIC NORTHWEST BECAME AN INTENSE LOVE-HATE AFFAIR WITH THE REGIONAL CULTURE AND GEOGRAPHY."

from the earlier period as he alternatively suppressed, deplored, and finally embraced his Midwest origins. Born in 1908 in Saginaw, Michigan, the son of a strong-willed, Germanic father who operated the local greenhouse, he lived an introverted, troubled childhood that bred lifelong demons of guilt and insecurity. His biographer Allan Seager portrays, and somewhat oversimplifies, Roethke as a self-absorbed youth who scarcely felt a spirit of place in his Upper Midwest:

> There is no memory of Roethke hanging around the old folks listening, like Faulkner, and his old folks were German, anyway. Their stories would have led him back to the Old Country which never interested him. He also ignores all the vivid racy tales of the lumber boom, tales that expressed courage, will, and cunning that might have engaged another man. Unlike Allen Tate or Robert Lowell, he ignores in his poetry the events of his region's history. He must have been aware of the Indians, for he collected a shoebox full of flint arrowheads in his rambles along the riverbanks. But, of course, many boys did that.

Still, the environs of Saginaw and the Upper Midwest were implanted in a young poetic consciousness as a seminal force in the work to come. After graduation from Michigan and a year at Harvard, Roethke taught at Lafayette, returning home in 1935 to teach at Michigan State. In fall semester, he suffered a first mental breakdown. During convalescence, he recorded the following insight about himself in a long medical questionnaire: "Afraid of being localized in space, i.e. a particular place like W. E. Leonard in Madison. Question: What is the *name* of this? Hate some rooms in that sense, a victim of claustrophobia (sp)? Wasn't Dillinger a victim of this? Aren't many of the criminal leader types of this sort [sic]" (The illuminating reference to Dillinger discloses Roethke's self-image of the poet as an outsider in the Midwest community, and recalls the alienation he felt even earlier: in one of his college essays at the University of Michigan, he had discussed "the poet as criminal," the instance being François Villon.)

His first two books of poetry firmly support a one-sided thesis that the maturing Roethke was never a midwestern regionalist, either by sympathetic identity or literary example. The year before *Open House* appeared in 1941, ten of the poems were anthologized in a volume titled *New Michigan Verse*. Hungry for a reputation, Roethke was delighted to be published, but he worried, too, that he might be regarded as a merely regional poet. Yet shortly after, he applied for a Guggenheim grant to write "a series of poems about the America I knew in my middle-western childhood.... poems about people in a particular suburbia." Though he failed to receive the grant, Roethke persisted, and in his successful Guggenheim application three years later, he described two of his three projects as the writing of a distinctively regional verse:

> (1) a dramatic-narrative piece in prose and verse about Michigan and Wisconsin, past and present, which would center around the return of Paul Bunyan as a kind of enlightened and worldly folk-hero.

> (2) a series of lyrics about the Michigan countryside which have symbolical values. I have already begun these. They are not mere description, but have at least two levels of reference.

To William Carlos Williams, who would understand this regional program, Roethke worried over "the Paul Bunyan idea. The more I think about it, the less I like it. But I've got to get some device to organize some of my ideas & feelings about Michigan, etc.—not too solemn or God bless America or Steve Benétish. Maybe it's worth trying, anyway." When *The Lost Son* appeared in 1948, readers would not discover Roethke's early "ideas & feelings about Michigan" to be organized around the Bunyan folk-hero; instead, he had created a primordial myth of the child's Edenic greenhouse world. But the urge to regional description and symbolization, as well as to natural immersion and union, had begun. After 1947 in his adopted Northwest, Roethke increasingly drew from Michigan scenes of his childhood. The Midwest lived in the residue of memory, at times bitter yet also positive and cherished, to sustain the older poet and enrich the strong poems that grace his final, prize-winning years.

II

As it would predictably have to be for the mercurial Roethke, the final period in the Pacific Northwest became an intense love-hate affair with the regional culture and geography. After only a few months there, his life amounted to a sort of physical and spiritual exile. "I tell you, Kenneth," he wrote to Burke, "this far in the provinces you get a little nutty and hysterical: there's the feeling that all life is going on but you're not there." Within the year, he had reverted to the earlier self-characterization of the poet as at best an outlaw celebrity in his tame middle-class community. "As the only serious poet within 1,000 miles of Seattle," he wrote another friend in the East, "I find I have something of the status of a bank robber in Oklahoma or a congressman in the deep south." Throughout his tenure at the University of Washington, he inquired into jobs elsewhere or applied for Fulbrights and other grants that might bring him relief or delivery from the scene at Seattle and the University. This alienation was caused, in part, by what to him was a psychologically depressing climate in the Northwest. The region also affected him physically, exacerbating the arthritis in his knees, the "spurs" in his shoulders, and the bursitis in his tennis elbow (the fiercely competitive poet had been tennis coach both at Lafayette and Penn State).

Yet the Northwest had an immediate, salutary effect on the poet as well. Some eleven years before, a bookless Roethke in Michigan had lamented to Louise Bogan on his twenty-eighth birthday, "No volume out and I can't seem to write anything. You can say what you want, but place does have a lot to do with productivity." By contrast, he exploded with ideas and poems after he arrived in Seattle, as one discovers from the Northwest images and tropes coming alive in the extant notebooks, in their disciplined growth amid the felicitous prunings of the manuscript poems, and in the final harvest of the published work. Through the 1950s, the huge, unlikely poet-teacher had caused an excited flowering of poetry on the Washington campus and in the Seattle community. By the end of the decade he brought home to the Northwest all the major literary prizes in America. He was earning a place among the distinguished regional poets of our literature.

III

The nature of Roethke's regional expression has only begun to be appreciated. His first book of poems in the Northwest appeared in 1951. *Praise to the End!* is a "tensed-up" version of Wordsworth's *Prelude*, according to Roethke, and carries nine new poems which can be read, in one sense, as his completing the "lean-to beginnings" in the previous *Lost Son* collection. Once more he tracks his voyage of the mind's return to the dream logic, Mother Goose rhythms, and purposeful gibberish of childhood, and then back again to the varieties of rebirth after these mythic descents. Oblique and occasionally even direct influences from his early Northwest years can be recognized here and there in the expression and form of these verses.

A stronger promise of the regional poems to come appears in the new verses of his next book, *The Waking: Poems 1933–1953* (1953). "A light Breather," to select one, reveals a joyous dynamism of the spirit, "small" and "tethered" as before but now "unafraid" and "singing." Symptomatic of a new phase, too, are poems like "Elegy for Jane," totally inspired from Northwest experience, and the more ambitious efforts which show the poet escaping from his former prison of the self to engage the circumambient world and the being of other living creatures. Just before the book appeared, he had married Beatrice O'Connell, his student during the year at Bennington a decade before. Seager believes that Roethke's marriage presently led him to a decisive awareness of the Northwest surroundings. As his capacity for feeling reached out to his young Beatrice, "hesitantly, even reluctantly perhaps, he admitted her into those labyrinths within himself where his father still lived, and he began to love her, not in the same way that he loved his father but with a true love nevertheless. And from this time forward, she participated in his growth, encouraged and supported it. Then he could see the mountains, the siskins, the madronas, and begin to use them." Viewed in this regard, segments of the next book, *Words for the Wind* (1958), and especially the "Love Poems," when thoroughly studied for their passionate metaphors of wind and seafoam, light and stones and rippling water as "spirit and nature beat in one breast-bone," reveal the true beginnings of that distinctive Northwest sensibility which fully emerges in Roethke's subsequent poems, gathered in the posthumous *The Far Field* (1964)....

Source: Kermit Vanderbilt, "Theodore Roethke," in *A Literary History of the American West*, Western Literature Association, 1987, pp. 447–55.

SOURCES

"Amtrak," in *Federal Railroad Administration*, U.S. Department of Transportation, http://www.fra.dot.gov/rpd/passenger/30.shtml (accessed June 6, 2011).

Blessing, Richard A., "Theodore Roethke: A Celebration," in *Tulane Studies in English*, Vol. 20, 1972, pp. 169–80.

Horowitz, Daniel, *The Anxieties of Affluence: Critiques of American Consumer Culture, 1939–1979*, University of Massachusetts Press, 2004, p. 262.

"How Many Words Are There in the English Language?," in *Oxford Dictionaries*, http://www.oxforddictionaries.com/page/93 (accessed May 9, 2011).

Kalaidjian, Walter, "Theodore Roethke's Life and Career," in *American National Biography*, edited by John A. Garraty and Mark C. Carnes, Oxford University Press, 1999, http://www.english.illinois.edu/maps/poets/m_r/roethke/bio.htm (accessed May 3, 2011).

Malkoff, Karl, *Theodore Roethke: An Introduction to the Poetry*, Columbia University Press, 1966, pp. 1–17.

McMichael, George, ed., *Anthology of American Literature*, Vol. II, *Realism to the Present*, 2nd ed., Macmillan, 1980, p. 1538.

"Number of Words in the English Language: 1,009,753," in *Global Language Monitor*, May 10, 2011, http://www.languagemonitor.com/no-of-words/ (accessed July 14, 2011).

"Pullman Palace Car Company Collection, 1867–1979," in *Archives Center*, National Museum of American History, http://americanhistory.si.edu/archives/d8181.htm (accessed June 6, 2011).

Roethke, Theodore, "Night Journey," in *Good Poems: American Places*, edited by Garrison Keillor, Penguin, 2011.

"This Land Is Your Land," in *Library of Congress*, http://lcweb2.loc.gov/diglib/ihas/loc.natlib.ihas.200000022/default.html (accessed May 4, 2011).

"USA QuickFacts," in *State and County Quick Facts*, U.S. Census Bureau, http://quickfacts.census.gov/qfd/states/00000.html (accessed May 3, 2011).

Williams, Harry, *"The Edge of What I Have": Theodore Roethke and After*, Bucknell University Press, 1977, pp. 13–36.

FURTHER READING

Jamison, Kay Redfield, *Touched with Fire, Manic-Depressive Illness and the Artistic Temperament*, Free Press, 1996.
 This volume analyzes the mental torment of such composers, artists, and authors as Virginia Woolf, Vincent van Gogh, and George Gordon, Lord Byron. All had either been institutionalized for mental illness or committed suicide. Redfield's analysis links creativity with mental illnesses such as depression and manic-depressive disorder, from which Roethke suffered throughout his adult life.

Llanas, Sheila Griffin, *Modern American Poetry: Echoes and Shadows (Poetry Rocks!)*, Enslow Publishing, 2011.
 This volume, written for young adults, includes clear, accessible discussions of modern American poets. The book's layout includes sprinklings of fun facts about the authors. Readers can find brief overviews of major poets but also more in-depth treatment of poetic styles and techniques that puts Roethke's poetry into the context of modern American poetry.

Seager, Allan, *The Glass House: The Life of Theodore Roethke*, University of Michigan Press, 1991.
 This volume, first published in 1968, is the first full biography of Roethke. Seager was a novelist and short-story writer. The biography, much of it based on interviews with those who knew Roethke, had been authorized in 1965 by Roethke's widow. Interestingly, she did not authorize Seager to quote from Roethke's poems, so the book never does.

Wagoner, David, *Straw for the Fire: From the Notebooks of Theodore Roethke*, Copper Canyon Press, 2006.
 Poet David Wagoner was one of Roethke's students. In this volume, he collects and distills some of the material contained in Roethke's 277 notebooks, everything from jottings and poetic phrases to meditations on love, death, God, teaching, and beauty. Readers can gain insight into the attic of Roethke's mind, as he drew on the material in his notebooks for his poetry.

SUGGESTED SEARCH TERMS

American entry AND World War II

bipolar disorder

confessional poets

Great Depression

greenhouse poems

mental illness AND creativity

meter in poetry

modern American poetry

Theodore Roethke

Theodore Roethke AND Night Journey

Theodore Roethke AND Open House

Theodore Roethke AND confessional poetry

Spring and Fall: To a Young Girl

GERARD MANLEY HOPKINS

1880

"Spring and Fall: To a Young Girl" was written in 1880 by British poet Gerard Manley Hopkins, according to him, as he was walking to a train station. The poem, like many of Hopkins's poems, is a reflection on death and the biblical fall of humankind, addressed to a girl he has named Margaret. That Hopkins would choose such a theme for his poem is not surprising: Hopkins was a Jesuit priest in the Catholic Church, and many of the poems written during the final years of his life reflect his agonizing inner struggles with religious conflict and human suffering.

Hopkins, a nineteenth-century British poet, is in many respects outside the mainstream of Victorian poetry—the great age of such poets as Robert Browning and Alfred Lord Tennyson, who dominated English poetry during the long reign of Queen Victoria. He was a Catholic in largely Protestant England. His poetry is deeply religious, and he did not deal with major social issues or the concerns of the larger community in his poems. His poems were not even published until 1918, long after his death, so he was virtually unknown as a poet during his lifetime. In the eyes of many poets and critics in the period between the two world wars of the twentieth century, he was more of a "modern" poet than a Victorian. Further, his poetic style is highly unusual. He made use of a unique metrical scheme, and the language of his poems could be described as quirky, with unusual word

Gerard Manley Hopkins

forms and lines that rely on multiple meanings of words. His poetic output was slender in comparison with the volumes of verse the major poets produced, so he is generally not regarded as one of the top-tier poets of the Victorian period, although many readers would disagree. His work, though, has been widely admired, and he certainly occupies a position near or at the top of the period's second tier of poets.

Originally published in *Poems* in 1918, "Spring and Fall: To a Young Girl" is widely anthologized. It can be found in *Gerard Manley Hopkins: The Major Works*, published by Oxford University Press in 2009.

AUTHOR BIOGRAPHY

Hopkins was born on July 28, 1844, near London, the oldest of nine children. He attended school at Highgate and then attended Balliol College at Oxford University, where he studied classics from 1863 to 1867. There he was influenced by such major figures as Walter Pater, a prominent critic and essayist; Benjamin Jowett, a renowned classicist; and John Henry Newman, whose highly influential *Apologia pro Vita Sua* (*Defense of One's Life*) explained his very public conversion to Catholicism in 1845. Hopkins grew up in an Anglican family, but he found both the aesthetics and the discipline of Catholicism attractive, so he converted to Catholicism in 1866, a decision that alienated him from his family. He then decided to become a priest and entered the Society of Jesus—the Jesuits—in 1868. What followed were nine years of rigorous training and education (ironically, though, he failed his final theology examination), followed by pastoral work as a parish priest in Sheffield, Oxford, and London (1877–1879), and then three years ministering in the slums of Liverpool, Manchester, and Glasgow. In 1884, he assumed a position as professor of Greek at the newly formed Catholic University College in Dublin, Ireland.

When he became a Jesuit, Hopkins burned all of his early poetry, believing that poetry was inconsistent with the demands of his profession. He rethought this decision and began writing again in 1876 with his major work "The Wreck of the Deutschland," a poem about the death of five nuns in a ship called the *Deutschland* in December 1875. In the years that followed, he wrote several poems that are frequently anthologized, including "God's Grandeur" (1877), "Pied Beauty" (1877), "The Caged Skylark" (1877), "Spring and Fall: To a Young Child" (1880), and "Carrion Comfort" (circa 1885). Some of these poems are exultant, celebrating the glory and grandeur of God and his creation; others reflect the poet's despair.

The final years of his life were uneventful, although he wrestled with depression and religious doubts. He died of typhoid fever on June 8, 1889. His good friend at Oxford, Robert Bridges (who was appointed to the position of Poet Laureate of England in 1913), became his literary executor and arranged for the publication of his poems in 1918.

POEM TEXT

<pre>
Márgarét, áre you gríeving
Over Goldengrove unleaving?
Leáves, líke the things of man, you
With your fresh thoughts care for, can you?
Áh! ás the heart grows older   5
It will come to such sights colder
By and by, nor spare a sigh
</pre>

Though worlds of wanwood leafmeal lie;
And yet you *will* weep and know why.
Now no matter, child, the name: 10
Sórrow's spríngs áre the same.
Nor mouth had, no nor mind, expressed
What heart heard of, ghost guessed:
It ís the blight man was born for,
It is Margaret you mourn for.   15

POEM SUMMARY

The text used for this summary is from *Victorian Poetry and Poetics*, 2nd ed., edited by Walter E. Houghton and G. Robert Stange, Houghton Mifflin, 1968, p. 703. Versions of the poem can be found on the following Web pages: http://www.poets.org/viewmedia.php/prmMID/16074 and http://www.poetryfoundation.org/poem/173665.

Lines 1–2

"Spring and Fall" is a fifteen-line rhymed poem. With the first word, the poet indicates that he is addressing the poem to a young girl named Margaret, although Margaret is not to be taken as a historical person. In lines 1 and 2, he asks the girl whether she is grieving because the leaves are falling from the trees at a place called Goldengrove. This is most likely a reference to a nearby Elizabethan estate house called Golden Grove in Flintshire, England. The house was surrounded by thousands of acres of pastures and woodlands. It is possible, though, that Hopkins had in mind a place called Golden Grove in Wales. This was an estate owned by a seventeenth-century Anglican bishop named Jeremy Taylor, who wrote a daily prayer manual titled *The Golden Grove*.

Lines 3–4

With line 3, the poet then compares the leaves of trees to the worldly things of humankind, and in line 4, he asks whether a young person might care for such worldly things.

Lines 5–9

Beginning with line 5, the poet begins to offer an answer to the question. He notes that a person's heart will age and that it will turn cold at such sights as the falling of the leaves at Goldengrove. As a person such as Margaret ages, she will no longer feel sad about the falling of the leaves, even though a world of wanwood, or pale, bloodless wood, falls leafmeal, or piecemeal, to the ground. In line 9, the poet reveals that Margaret is crying about this state of affairs and wants to know why it happens. Put simply, the girl is witnessing death, signified by the falling of autumn leaves, and wants to know why death happens.

Lines 10–11

The poet, however, does not try to comfort her with soothing words. Instead, he teaches her a theological lesson. In line 10, he states that it does not make any difference what name we give to this inevitable event. The spring of the title turns out to be not a season but rather the source of sorrow, and the fall of the title turns out to be the fall of humankind through original sin as recounted in the biblical book of Genesis.

Lines 12–13

In line 12, the poet says that this truth is one that Margaret cannot verbalize or conceptualize in her mind; language cannot give expression to what the heart knows. Rather, she intuits it in her heart, and her spirit guesses at it.

Lines 14–15

In the poem's final two lines, Hopkins concludes that this fall, which he depends on the reader to recognize as the eating of the forbidden fruit from the Tree of Knowledge of Good and Evil in the Garden of Eden, is a blight. The fall of the leaves at Goldengrove is what people were born for, meaning that people inevitably die. In the final line, he indicates that what Margaret is mourning for is herself. Thus, while the poem at first glance appears to be a poem about nature and the passing of the seasons, it is really about

MEDIA ADAPTATIONS

"Spring and Fall" is included in *The Poetry of Gerard Manley Hopkins*, read by Cyril Cusack. The audio recording was produced by Portable Poetry in 2010. Each of the poems is available as an MP3 download.

the course of every human, who is born with the mark of original sin, the wellspring of sorrow, and eventually dies, like the leaves in autumn. Margaret's name means "pearl," as in the biblical "pearl of great price." This pearl in the New Testament was seen as the immortal soul. If Margaret is to be seen as a soul, then it is natural for her to grieve because of the intuition she has about death.

THEMES

Death
"Spring and Fall" is a poem in large part about death. The situation Hopkins envisions is that a young girl named Margaret sees the falling of the leaves in autumn. She intuits that the falling of the leaves is an indication that things die—that the things of this world are temporary and will ultimately pass away. She is weeping at this realization, but the poet does not try to console her. Instead, he offers her a lesson, telling her that all humankind is born to bear the kind of blight she is lamenting. Ultimately, the poet says, she is mourning herself, for she is part of this inevitable cycle of birth and death, as represented by the seasons.

Original Sin
The other major theme that runs through "Spring and Fall" is that of original sin. According to the Judeo-Christian tradition as recounted in the biblical book of Genesis, God created the first humans, Adam and Eve, and placed them in the Garden of Eden. The garden was a place of innocence and plenty. God's only stipulation was that Adam and Eve not eat from the Tree of Knowledge of Good and Evil, conventionally represented as an apple tree. Satan, the devil, enters the garden and tempts Eve with an apple. She eats of the apple and shares it with Adam. The two have violated God's law, so they are expelled from the Garden of Eden and condemned to a life of struggle and pain. Their actions were the original sin—knowledge of good and evil, along with an effort to rival God in power and knowledge. In Christian theology, God in the person of Jesus Christ had to come to earth to atone for humanity's sins and offer the prospect of salvation in heaven.

"Spring and Fall," then, is not merely a nature poem about the passage of the seasons. Rather, it captures the essence of the fall of man, playing on the dual meanings of the word *fall*. During the autumn, the leaves on trees wither, die, and fall to the ground—an image of death. Spring marks a beginning, but in Hopkins's vision it is the beginning of sorrow. Margaret cannot articulate that she, along with all humans, holds the knowledge of good and evil and thus, like the leaves at Goldengrove, will one day wither and die, all because of original sin.

Seasons
The very title of Hopkins's poem, "Spring and Fall," suggests that the poem is about the passage of the seasons. Historically, creative writers have used the seasons of the year as a metaphor for some fundamental element of the human condition. Spring, for example, is seen as emblematic of new life, growth, fertility, and new beginnings as people emerge from the depths of winter, engage in such activities as planting crops, and enjoy the lengthening days. Summer is a period of growth and warmth, leading to autumn, usually associated with maturity (of crops, for example) and decline. Autumn is followed by winter, with its cold, darkness, and snow, often seen as a kind of image of death. Winter, though, comes to an end, and the cycle of generation, growth, maturity, and decline begins again. This fundamental rhythm of the seasons has influenced human behavior—its patterns of worship, its holidays and celebrations, its labor, its diet—from time immemorial.

Hopkins uses this cycle to advantage in his poem. Margaret is a young girl, one who is in the "spring" of her lifetime, yet she perceives that in autumn, the leaves on the trees die and fall, and she wonders why this happens. Implicit in the dramatic situation of the poem is her questioning of death, of why the physical world is temporary and why things decline and pass away. The poem is not truly a nature poem about the cycle of the seasons; rather, Hopkins uses the metaphors of spring and fall to suggest other, deeper themes, the kind of themes that preoccupied him during much of his later life.

STYLE

Alliteration
Hopkins relies heavily on alliteration, or the repetition of consonant sounds, particularly at the beginnings of words. Prominent examples include

TOPICS FOR FURTHER STUDY

- Conduct online and print research on the Society of Jesus—the Jesuits—in the Catholic Church. When was this order of priests founded? By whom? For what purpose? How do Jesuits differ from ordinary parish priests who do not belong to an order of priests? Why do you think that in former ages, Jesuits came to be regarded by some people as sneaky and duplicitous? How might belonging to the Jesuit order have influenced the nature of Hopkins's poetry? Present your findings in an oral report to your class.

- Conduct online and print research on the places to which Hopkins was assigned after he became a priest. Find images of such places as Liverpool and Manchester—smoky, dirty industrial cities—from the time period. Share these images with your classmates through PowerPoint or SlideShare. Be prepared to speculate how these places might have influenced Hopkins's views and outlook on life.

- Using the Internet or print sources, examine the educational system at Oxford University at the time when Hopkins attended. Why were there separate colleges, such as Hopkins's Balliol College? Did students attend regular classes, or did they meet more frequently with tutors? What types of degrees were awarded, and what subjects did students typically study? What was the social life at Oxford like? Prepare a written report answering some of these questions or any others you think are relevant to your understanding of Hopkins's early life.

- A well-known young-adult novel that deals with religious themes is Judy Blume's 1970 book *Are You There God? It's Me, Margaret*. The novel deals with Margaret's struggle to find religious belief. Imagine that the Margaret of Blume's novel is the same Margaret whom Hopkins is addressing in "Spring and Fall: To a Young Girl." Write a response to the poem from the viewpoint of Blume's Margaret, or conversely, a response to the novel from the viewpoint of Hopkins's Margaret.

- Hopkins's earliest ambition was to be a painter. Locate copies of paintings that were created during the time when he did most of his writing—the late 1870s and the 1880s. Examples might include English painters William Holman Hunt, John Everett Millais, Edward Burne-Jones, or Ford Maddox Brown; French "Impressionist" painters might include Paul Gauguin, Pierre Renoir, Claude Monet, or Paul Cézanne. Assemble a montage of work from these or other painters. Post them on your social-networking site and invite your classmates to comment on similarities they see between Hopkins's poetic subjects or techniques and those of the visual artists.

---

the repeated *g* sound in lines 1 and 2 (and repeated in line 13), the *s* sounds in lines 6 and 7 (picked up again in line 11), the *w* sounds in lines 8 and 9, and the *m* sounds in lines 14 and 15. This use of alliteration helps to unify the poem and give it more of an aural quality. Also, the poem falls roughly into two halves: the first nine lines and the final six lines. Notice that some of the alliterative patterns created in the first half are reused in the second half. Again, this creates a unity between the two halves of the poem. The first half in essence raises a question, while the second half provides a kind of response to the question. By repeating patterns of alliteration, Hopkins more effectively links the two halves of the poem.

Assonance

Closely related to alliteration is assonance, or the repetition of vowel sounds. Assonance is to be distinguished from rhyme, which refers to

A child rejoices in the return of spring. (Yaruta Igor / Shutterstock.com)

Thus, the first line of the poem falls into two halves, the first consisting of the name of the girl, the second half consisting of part of the author's question to her. Each of the halves contains a single stressed syllable. Similarly, the second line contains a stressed syllable in the place name Goldengrove, then a final word that itself contains a single stressed syllable. In commentary on his own poetry, Hopkins emphasized that this use of sprung rhythm—a fixed number of stressed syllables with a variable number of unstressed syllables (which he called slack syllables), all of which can fall into different patterns—gives the poems a musical quality. He stated that sprung rhythm mimicked common speech, that it is the rhythm of music, and that it is the rhythm of nursery rhymes, that most basic form of poetry that is a person's first introduction to rhythmic speech. The meter, then, gives to the poem a kind of elemental, urgent appeal and links it with the spoken language.

the repetition of sounds, including vowels sounds, at the ends of lines. Assonance more properly refers to the echoing of vowel sounds within and between lines. A good example is line 2, with its repetition of the long *o* sound in the first and second words. This *o* sound is picked up again in the rhymes of lines 5 and 6. Lines 7–9 use an "eye" sound in the rhyme, and this sound is echoed in the first words of line 7. Assonance, in combination with alliteration and rhyme, creates a strong sense of unity in the poem. The poem is brief, and the repeated sounds give it a jewel-like quality, as though the words of the poem were all struck from the same precious stone.

Meter

Hopkins is particularly noted for the meter, or rhythm, of his poetry. As an adult, he learned the Welsh language, and that language strongly influenced the rhythm of his poetry in English. He even came up with his own term to describe the rhythm: sprung rhythm. Sprung rhythm is defined by the number of stressed syllables, not the total number of syllables in a line. Drawing on some of the techniques of Old English poetry, he used what are called half lines. In these lines, the number of syllables is not fixed but can vary. What tends not to vary is that each of the half lines has a single heavily stressed syllable.

HISTORICAL CONTEXT

Religion in the Victorian Era

"Spring and Fall" makes no reference to major political, social, or economic events, but in common with all of Hopkins's poetry, it was written in the context of the vigorous religious debates that permeated Victorian society. For centuries, England had been a Protestant nation. King Henry VIII, largely for political purposes, broke with the Church of Rome (the Catholic Church) in the 1530s to form the Anglican Church, also called the Church of England. Later, in the wake of the Protestant Reformation, launched when Martin Luther published his Ninety-five Theses in Wittenberg, Germany, in 1517—a document that challenged some of the practices of the Catholic Church—a large number of Protestant denominations emerged in Europe. Although some countries remained primarily Catholic, including Italy, Spain, and France, Protestantism took root in the more northern countries, including England. For centuries, Protestants and Catholics were at odds with each other, sometimes bitterly so. In England, Catholics could not hold public office, and they were essentially persecuted—or at best discriminated against—until the passage of the Catholic Relief Act of 1829. A place like Oxford University, which Hopkins attended, would

COMPARE & CONTRAST

- **1880s:** The Oxford University Newman Society is established in 1878, with Hopkins as a founding member. As it grows, the society promotes Catholic culture, learning, and faith at the university.

   Today: The Oxford University Newman Society continues to minister to the Catholic community in Oxford and appears in the news for its commentary on controversial events. The society sometimes sponsors solemn High Masses in Latin, keeping alive some of the rituals of traditional Catholicism.

- **1880s:** Cities in the north of England, principally Manchester, Birmingham, Leeds, and others, are major centers of manufacturing during the Industrial Revolution. Many social commentators call attention to the poverty, low wages, lack of job security, and physical dangers of working in the factories of the industrial cities.

   Today: Many of the industrial cities of the north declined after World War II, but today they are undergoing regeneration with new building projects, infrastructure improvements, and development of modern industries.

- **1880s:** Great Britain is the dominant imperial power in the world. During the nineteenth century, Britain adds millions of square miles and hundreds of millions of people to its worldwide empire, which it controls with the world's most powerful navy.

   Today: Great Britain is no longer a major imperial power. It is a major member of the Commonwealth of Nations, which includes fifty-three nations, many of them former British colonies, which cooperate on matters involving trade, human rights, governance, and similar common concerns. Great Britain is a member of several multinational organizations, including the United Nations, NATO, and the European Union.

---

have remained staunchly Anglican, despite efforts to extend civil rights to Catholics.

In discussing English Protestantism, a number of terms are used. One is "Low Church," a term that in general refers to evangelical denominations. These churches had little in the way of hierarchy and formal theology. They were opposed to ritual and the kind of ornamentation usually found in Catholic churches (priestly vestments, incense, statues, music, stained-glass windows, and the like). Because these people dissented from laws enforcing the primacy of Anglicanism, they were often called Dissenters. In contrast were "High Church" Protestants. This was a version of Protestantism that was a little closer to Catholicism. It shared many doctrines with the Catholic Church, and it was not opposed to all ritual and ornamentation. And in fact, it was sometimes referred to as Anglo-Catholicism. A third term that was often used was "Broad Church." This term was applied to "latitudinarians," or those people who gave broad latitude to religious belief and were willing to accept both Low Church and High Church views as legitimate.

The Victorians took these matters seriously. At the same time, they were growing increasingly troubled by some of the revelations of science, particularly in the fields of geology and biology. Although the theory of evolutionary biology was most fully articulated by Charles Darwin in *On the Origin of Species* in 1859, in previous decades numerous geologists were discovering fossil evidence that suggested that the world was much older than people had thought. The upshot was that geology cast into doubt the biblical account of creation—and thus cast into doubt many of the pillars of the Judeo-Christian tradition. In poems, novels, and an avalanche of essays and books, theologians, clerics, and others weighed

A child tries to stop the falling leaves that signal the beginning of winter. (dmitriy Shironosov | Shutterstock.com)

in on these issues. Religion in Victorian England was in a state of turmoil.

It was in this context that the Oxford movement arose. This was an intellectual movement centered at Oxford University. The Oxford movement was also called Tractarianism because of the publication of ninety *Tracts for the Times*, a series of disquisitions on matters of faith and religion written primarily by John Henry Newman, an Anglican minister and a professor at Oxford University. (Catholics might recognize the name of Newman as that given to Catholic "Newman Centers," or Catholic churches affiliated with secular universities throughout the world.) As Newman's religious beliefs evolved, he came to the conclusion that the differences between Anglicanism and Catholicism were insignificant, and in 1845, he underwent a very public and very controversial conversion to Catholicism. For nearly two decades, he endured criticism for this decision, along with attacks on the priesthood and on Catholic doctrine. The criticism prompted him to write *Apologia pro Vita Sua*, or *Defense of One's Life*, first published in 1864. The book became a best seller and continues to be read, although less as a defense of Catholicism and more for its portrait of a profound thinker searching for what he regarded as the truth.

Although all of these events (with the exception of publication of the *Apologia*) had passed by the time Hopkins enrolled at Oxford University, the intellectual ferment that surrounded them remained part of the fabric of Oxford life. Shortly after Hopkins enrolled at Oxford, Newman published his *Apologia*, reanimating the discussion. Later, Hopkins was one of the founding members of the Oxford University Newman Society, established in 1878 and still functioning.

CRITICAL OVERVIEW

When *The Poems of Gerard Manley Hopkins* was published in 1918, the book attracted considerable attention and was widely reviewed because the editor and motive force behind the publication was Robert Bridges, England's Poet Laureate. Because most of the poems in the collection are quite short (the only poem of great length is "The Wreck of the Deutschland"), reviewers had a tendency to comment on the collection as a whole rather than on individual poems. That said, Gerald Roberts, in *Gerard Manley Hopkins: The Critical Heritage*, notes that "Spring and Fall" was "one of the less popular poems."

Interestingly, reviewers tended to praise the poetry while in some ways not knowing what to make of it. It was almost as though they liked the poetry *in spite of* its style, which they found quite foreign. Thus, a contributor to the *Glasgow Herald* writes, "The book is a hard nut to crack." Nevertheless, he continues, "The crudities obscure the intellectual swiftness and the imaginative boldness which are the note of the book." Theodore Maynard, writing in the *New Witness*, was more severe: "I defy anyone to make head or tail of some of Hopkins' poetry." At the same time, in reference to Bridges, he writes: "But the greatest benefit he has conferred upon us is the opening to the world, by the publication of this book, of so rich a legacy of imperishable song." A contributor to the *Saturday Westminster Gazette* expresses a similar ambivalence: Hopkins "was a skilled and daring metrical experimenter, though often betrayed by his own theories into errors of style which seriously interfere with our enjoyment, sometimes even our comprehension, of his poems."

Nevertheless, many reviewers responded to this new poetic voice enthusiastically. Writing in the London *Times Literary Supplement*, Arthur Clutton-Block offers this praise:

> But the verse survives the great test of verse; it is best read aloud; then the very sense becomes clearer and anyone with an ear can hear that the method is not affectation but eagerness to find an expression for the depths of the mind, for things hardly yet consciously thought or felt.

Clutton-Block concludes: "His passion strikes sparks out of the hard, flinty words.... The whole book thrills with spirit." Louise Imogen Guiney, writing in the *Month*, concurs: "Let there be no doubt about the worth of Father Hopkins' literary work. It has winged daring, originality, durable texture, and the priceless excellence of fixing itself in the reader's mind."

CRITICISM

Michael J. O'Neal

O'Neal holds a Ph.D. in English. In the following essay, he examines the position of "Spring and Fall: To a Young Girl," and of Gerard Manley Hopkins in general, in late-nineteenth-century British literature.

Imagine that a reasonably knowledgeable person were to be asked to "name some of the most important writers from the Victorian era—the period running from the 1830s to the turn of the twentieth century, corresponding with the reign of Queen Victoria." Most likely such a person would mention the names of novelists such as Charles Dickens (*A Tale of Two Cities*, *Great Expectations*, and of course *A Christmas Carol*), George Eliot (*Middlemarch*), and probably Thomas Hardy (*The Return of the Native*). Among poets, the first names that would likely come to mind are those of Alfred Lord Tennyson, Matthew Arnold, and Robert Browning, along with Browning's wife, Elizabeth Barrett Browning, best known for "How Do I Love Thee? Let Me Count the Ways." (Interestingly the Victorian era produced little in the way of memorable drama.) However, if in response to this list, someone replied, "But what about Gerard Manley Hopkins?," the response might be something like, "Oh, yes, of course. Hopkins. I always forget about him."

Of course, this imagined conversation is purely speculative, but it is intended to suggest that Hopkins in some indefinable way stands apart from the era in which he wrote. He lived during the Victorian period, yet in some sense he is not thought of as a "Victorian" poet. One reason for this is that as a poet, he had no impact on his age, for with very few exceptions, his poems were not published until 1918, nearly thirty years after his death. By that year, Great Britain had endured four years of the brutality and senseless slaughter of World War I. Over nine hundred thousand men had been killed, and some two million had been wounded. The British Empire was crumbling, and Britannia no longer "ruled the waves" as it had just a generation earlier. In the minds of many postwar Britons, a vast gulf separated them from their Victorian ancestors, whose literature was rapidly coming to be seen as old-fashioned, fusty, and, from the perspective of 1918, written for grandmothers—a former generation that had not seen the things that "modern" Britons had seen.

Another factor that sets Hopkins's poems, including "Spring and Fall," apart from the work of his Victorian contemporaries is his poetic style. The high Victorians tended to be

WHAT DO I READ NEXT?

- A twentieth-century writer who was influenced by the writing of Hopkins was Welsh poet Dylan Thomas. Many readers see strong similarities between the two, and Hopkins's poetry was influenced by his study of the Welsh language. A good example of a Thomas poem that bears comparison with Hopkins is "Here in This Spring" (1936), available in *The Poems of Dylan Thomas, Volume I* (2003).

- Conversely, one of the writers whom Hopkins admired and whose verse influenced his work was the Victorian poet Christina Rossetti. Hopkins likely read such Rossetti poems as "Song" (1848), "A Better Resurrection" (1857), "Have I Not Striven, My God?" (1863). All are available in *Christina Rossetti: The Complete Poems*, edited by Rebecca. W. Crump and Betty S. Flowers and published by Penguin Books in 2001.

- Many of Hopkins's poems have a tone of sadness and despair, but many do not. "Pied Beauty" or "God's Grandeur," both written in 1877, are very different types of poems by Hopkins, ones that are joyous and celebratory. The poems can be found in *Gerard Manley Hopkins: The Major Works*, published by Oxford University Press in 2009.

- The Society of Jesus, or the Jesuits, is an order of Catholic priests of which Hopkins was a member. The order has often been surrounded by an air of secrecy and intrigue, although less so in modern times. Readers interested in the history of the Jesuits might start with *The Cambridge Companion to the Jesuits*, a collection of essays edited by Thomas Worcester and published by Cambridge University Press in 2008.

- *Earth Always Endures: Native American Poems* is a collection of poems for young adults compiled by Neil Philips and published by Viking in 1996. Many of the poems are chants and prayers to the heavens and the gods and provide the reader with insight into another kind of spirituality, that of Native Americans. The book is lavishly illustrated with photographs by Edward S. Curtis.

- If Hopkins were living today, he might appreciate a young-adult novel by Jonathan Safran Foer titled *Extremely Loud and Incredibly Close*, published by Houghton Mifflin in 2005. This novel is about a nine-year-old boy, Oskar Schell, and his kaleidoscopic quest for truth in New York City. The novel was considered a tour de force of narrative technique, for it uses illustrations, odd typographical effects, pages with only a single word or a few words, lists, struck out words, unconventional arrangement of the text on the page, and so forth. In the same way, Hopkins is known for the unique and unconventional style of his poetry.

---

didactic poets. They wrote *about* something, and that "something" tended to be social and religious issues that dominated discussion in the journals and debating societies. The Victorians thought of their time as a transitional age, an age that would bridge older traditions and ways of thinking and a newer, more modern sensibility. The Victorians were "earnest"—a commonly used word at the time—meaning that they took matters seriously. One did not write a sentimental poem just about, say, the flowers of spring or a babbling brook. Such a poem had to have a larger point, a theme, an overarching idea, something that explained to the reader why the flowers or the brook were important in defining the great issues of the age. Historical themes such as the legends surrounding King Arthur and the knights of Camelot were revisited (by Tennyson,

> IN THE FINAL ANALYSIS, IT IS BECAUSE OF HOPKINS'S UNIQUENESS—CALL IT QUIRKINESS, CALL IT ODDITY, CALL IT ECCENTRICITY—THAT HE CONTINUES TO BE READ."

among others) and reinterpreted in ways that shed light on contemporary concerns. Hopkins's poems, including "Spring and Fall," have a very different tone. The poems contain themes, but the themes are conveyed less in the language of the lecture hall and the debating society and more in the language of symbol, deft word play, and concrete images that suggest rather than explain, that hint at meaning rather than insisting on meaning.

By the time Hopkins was writing in the late 1870s and the 1880s, the age of the High Victorians had passed. The "big three"—Tennyson, Browning, and Arnold—were in the twilight of their careers and would pass at about the same time Hopkins did. New poetic sensibilities were taking over. The younger generation of Victorian writers belonged to a movement called the pre-Raphaelites. Among these poets were Dante Gabriel Rossetti, his sister Christina Rossetti, William Morris, and Charles Algernon Swinburne. These poets saw the function of poetry as being more aesthetic than didactic, and for this reason they were associated with a movement often called the aesthetic movement. These terms are always imprecise and overlapping; the poets were "pre-Raphaelites" because many of them were painters as well and they adopted a style like that predating the fifteenth/sixteenth-century Italian painter Raphael.

The aesthetic movement strictly speaking was (and is) associated primarily with decorative arts, such as furniture, wallpaper, textiles, ceramics, and the like, but its meaning was extended to include the aesthetics of creative writing. These writers wrote a type of poetry that was more sensual than that of the earlier High Victorians. They placed more emphasis on human love, passion, beauty, pictorial effects, and, in particular, minute imagery. Much of their work had what has been called a "painterly" effect, as though the rich visual imagery of a painting was captured in a tapestry of poetic words.

It is at this intersection, where the later Victorians forged a path that diverged from that of their elders, that Hopkins does not seem to fit anywhere. One way of looking at it is that if the early High Victorians were like the big-band sound of the 1940s and early 1950s, the late Victorians thought of their poetry more as rock 'n' roll (and frequently their personal lifestyles were equally comparable). Hopkins, however, was a Catholic Jesuit priest. He rejected the bohemian, nonconformist lifestyle and aesthetic outlook of the late Victorians. His principal concern was his relationship with God, so his poetry is infused with a moral vision that was coming to be regarded as slightly outdated. However, his literary style was intensely and remarkably more modern. To continue the analogy, it was as though he adopted the literary style of the rocker but adapted that style to a highly conservative, highly traditional moral outlook to write rock 'n' roll church hymns. (This analogy is not to be taken too literally; the analogy is intended to suggest a kind of parallel in modern times, as one generation of artists, striving for something new and provocative, reacts against the traditions and methods of its predecessors.)

In this way, a reading of "Spring and Fall" is in some ways a disconcerting experience. On the one hand, the poem is about the inevitability of decay and death, as well as about the traditional Christian doctrine of original sin. These are fairly conventional themes. On the other hand, the poem operates not through explanation but through its images. It suggests a highly traditional, orthodox religious viewpoint using many of the techniques of the Aesthetes and thus creating a richly sensual, highly allusive, version of what amounts to a Bible story.

The upshot is that readers still do not know where to "put" Hopkins. Was he a Victorian? In the sense that he wrote during the Victorian era, yes, and he shared with many Victorians a profound interest in a moral, theological vision of the world. Was he a modern poet? According to his friend and literary executor Robert Bridges, England was not ready for Hopkins's poems until nearly three decades after the poet's death. By this time, the so-called imagist

> THE SOURCE OF MARGARET'S GRIEF IS SOMETHING PHENOMENOLOGICALLY OUTSIDE HERSELF—THE CULMINATION OF THE FALL SEASON AND WITH IT THE ONSET OF WINTER MANIFESTED BY THE FALLING LEAVES."

Death comes to us all, even Margaret. (Jeffrey M. Frank / Shutterstock.com)

movement was well under way. Poetry had entered a new age, one that rejected the sentiment and moralizing of the previous century in favor of sharp, precise sensory images. So does that mean that Hopkins was an imagist? Or should he be thought of as a modernist? These kinds of questions can multiply and thus grow ridiculous, for within any literary movement, the best writers continue to stand out as unique despite having affinities with other writers considered part of the movement. In the final analysis, it is because of Hopkins's uniqueness—call it quirkiness, call it oddity, call it eccentricity—that he continues to be read. His slender poetic output continues to foment discussion and interpretation, for his highly elastic, emotionally rendered style allows each generation of readers to project onto the poetry as a way of interpreting the joys and tragedies of human experience.

Source: Michael J. O'Neal, Critical Essay on "Spring and Fall: To a Young Girl," in *Poetry for Students*, Gale, Cengage Learning, 2012.

Jude V. Nixon

In the following excerpt, Nixon contends that Hopkins's desire to be included in Christina Rossetti's anthology influenced his writing of "Spring and Fall."

The now quite familiar argument for the inspiration behind Hopkins' "Spring and Fall: To a Young Child" asserts that lines from the poem describing Margaret's poignant response to the falling leaves may have been derived from George Eliot's *The Mill on the Floss*. As the argument goes, the little girl at the novel's opening, whether Maggie Tulliver or Eliot's authorial persona, becomes Hopkins' Margaret, both of whom lament the all-too-soon demise of the season that in turn analogizes the ephemeralness of things. Hopkins had only recently read *The Mill on the Floss* (1860), and on February 22, 1881, had even solicited John Henry Newman's estimation of Eliot. Heretofore unknown, however, are the subtle echoes, perhaps even direct borrowings, between Hopkins' "Spring and Fall," his "song to the decaying year" ("Now I am minded"), and Christina Rossetti's "Mirrors of Life and Death," with its "long sequence of mourning images." This essay, then, seeks to document the poem's indebtedness to Christina Rossetti and, as well, Hopkins' profound desire to be included in an anthology connected to her.

In comparing these two "Latecomers to the Tractarian Movement," Margaret Johnson finds "many echoes of theme and approach" in Hopkins' "early Oxford poems," a "common theological and aesthetic base," "concordances of subject and metaphor," but each "without knowledge of the other's [lyrics]." But Johnson, and for that matter Rossetti's biographer Jan Marsh, who also acknowledges Rossetti's mentoring of Hopkins, ignore altogether the shaping influence of "Mirrors of Life and Death" on "Spring and Fall." And so too does Jerome Bump, who otherwise demonstrates convincingly that Rossetti, Hopkins' "icon" and "the woman who was to inspire some of his best art in the 1860s," provided him "examples of simple, unified songs" which liberated him from the fetters of pseudo-Keatsian "excesses of his early word-painting." No doubt, says W. H. Gardner, "the poetry of Christina Rossetti exerted a strong influence" on Hopkins' early composition[.] Perhaps more than anything else, Christina Rossetti modeled for Hopkins the poetry of religious faith in which the two—poetry and religion—become interfused and inseparable. That she also remained chaste for the kingdom of heaven's sake might have appealed to him. "Her religion imposed duties so imperative that she could not compromise with them, but, more than that, it made even marriage an impossibility." The two also share the casual openings to poems. "Few poets," says C. M. Bowra, "have her gift of beginning a poem with the most homely and humble words or of using phrases which are consciously trite or commonplace, only to rise to some sudden burst and thereby to show that even in the drabbest conditions there are possibilities of dazzling splendour" (p. 264). In this Hopkins is easily Rossetti's match, with such matter-of-fact, ordinary, and mundane openings that give way to explosive images: "Nothing is so beautiful as Spring" ("Spring"), "On ear and ear two noises too old to end" ("The Sea and the Skylark"), "I remember a house where all were good" ("In the Valley of the Elwy"), "Summer ends now; now, barbarous in beauty, the stooks rise" ("Hurrahing in Harvest"), "Sometimes a lantern moves along the night" ("The Lantern out of Doors"), and "Some candle clear burns somewhere I come by" ("The Candle Indoors").

Considering how much of Hopkins' poetry derived from actual experiences aesthetically appropriated, how much of it is "'autobiographical' fact," it is curious that "Spring and Fall" was "not founded on any real incident," suggesting, perhaps, the poem's mythopoetic origin. Jeffrey B. Loomis observes the poem's ideological affinity to Robert Herrick's ephemeral "Daffodils" and sees Hopkins' young girl modeled in part after Goethe's Margarete: "The childlike epithet may even allude to Goethe's too-innocent heroine Gretchen (Margarethe) in Faust One; of all the Continental writers of his century, Goethe is the only one who receives repeated discussion in Hopkins' letters." Hopkins acknowledged his indebtedness to Rossetti in "A Voice from the World" (1864–65), an answer to "The Convent Threshold" (1862). "I have nearly finished an answer to Miss Rossetti's Convent Threshold, to be called A voice from the world, or something like that," Hopkins told his friend Alexander Baillie in a July 20, 1864 letter, "with which I am at present in the fatal condition of satisfaction." This poetic response, a longer and loosely structured version of "Heaven-Haven," evidently "answered some emotional need," for it shows Hopkins responding with "his own burden of Puseyite guilt" along with the same "powerful sense of sexual transgression [that] haunted Christina's imagination" (Marsh, p. 214). And, in fact, "Rossetti's poetry of religious anguish is arguably as great and terrible as Hopkins's."

Hopkins first met Christina Rossetti through his father's poetry, which was anthologized in *Lyra Eucharistica* and *Lyra Mytica*, collections that also published Rossetti's poems (White, p. 6). Hopkins' earliest reference to Rossetti is in 1864, where she is identified as a contemporary writer of merit. In July 1864, he eventually met her, along with Gabriel, Holman Hunt, Jenny Lind, and the Brownings at a party at the Gurneys. A year later, in his undergraduate essay, "On the Origin of Beauty: A Platonic Dialogue," Hopkins observed a scientific principle at work in the patterns on a girl's dress in the frontpiece to *Goblin Market and Other Poems* (1862). The principle is that all patterns are comprised of either continuous or/and non-continuous lines, what on a subatomic level current theoretical physicists searching for the so-called "Theory of Everything" have called superstrings. Rossetti, like Keats (the patron saint of the Pre-Raphaelite Brotherhood), became for Hopkins the standard by which to estimate poets and poetry. He noted the publication of Rossetti's *The Prince's Progress and Other Poems* (1866) within one month of its release, the appearance of *Commonplace and Other Stories* (1870), and Rossetti's frequent use of assonance. Hopkins mistakenly claimed that Arthur Hughes had illustrated Rossetti's "My heart is like a singing bird," and lamented the fact that she had been displaced ("thrown into the shade") by her brother Gabriel, whom he did not believe her equal (*Further Letters*, p. 119). In fact, Hopkins so desired Rossetti's literary company that he submitted "Barnfloor and Winepress" to Macmillan's, which published Rossetti. He felt that because the magazine embraced Rossetti, whose poetic sensibilities resembled his, it would be receptive to him. Hopkins was especially attracted to Rossetti's "Mirrors of Life and Death," employing it in suggested emendations to Dixon's poems, which have "a medieval colouring like Wm. Morris's and the Rossetti's."

"Mirrors of Life and Death" was printed in the *Athenaeum* on March 17, 1877. In a September 26, 1881 letter to Dixon, Hopkins acknowledged liking especially his "Life and Death" ("this poem has charmed me among the most"), but could not quite understand why "those colours [vermilion, saffron, and white] weave the delight." He noted that Rossetti's "new volume" (*A Pageant and Other Poems*, 1881), which he has not yet seen, has been published, but that he had read "this lovely poem," "Mirrors of Life and Death" (though he mistitled it, calling it "Symbols" instead of "Mirrors") when it was first published in the *Athenaeum*. The same use of colors is employed: "Scarlet and golden and blue." Contextually, the mouse in the poem (which Rossetti kept despite her brother Gabriel's objection to its commonplace character for an elegy) that cares for nuts and acorns cares nothing for "blossoming boughs" or the variegated colors of singing birds, "Scarlet, or golden, or blue" (*Correspondence* 1. 67). A month later, in October 1881, Hopkins returned to "Mirrors of Life and Death," observing that the image in Dixon's *Love's Casuistry* is "sparing" and "beautiful," largely because of its "imaginative reality," especially "the figure of the eagle and the dove," "a noble passage": "Like an eagle, half strength and half grace, Harrying the East and the West" (*Correspondence*). The Rossetti stanza reads:

> As an Eagle, half strength and half grace,
> Most potent to face
> Unwinking the splendour of light;
> Harrying the East and the West,
> Soaring aloft from our sight;
> Yet one day or one night dropped to rest,
> On the low common earth
> Of his birth. (*Complete Poems*, 2:76)

So closely related to Rossetti's language, imagery, and meaning are Hopkins' "Windhover" and "The Caged Skylark," even "God's Grandeur," that one could easily argue an influence. Hopkins, however, does not acknowledge any such indebtedness, nor for that matter any influence "Mirrors of Life and Death" might have had on "Spring and Fall." In a January 24, 1881 letter to Dixon, Hopkins disclosed that "Spring and Fall" was composed in September 1880 while he was "walking from Lydiate," and that a fair copy might be found among Bridges' book of Hopkins' poems (*Correspondence*). Bridges first received the copy on September 5, 1880, although Hopkins was "not well satisfied with it" (*Letters to Bridges*). The poem saw minor changes, from "unleafving" to "unleaving," and from "forests low and leafmeal lie" to "worlds of wanwood leafmeal lie." Bridges suggested the plural "worlds," and might also have suggested the change from "Leaves you with your fresh thoughts can / Feel for like the things of man" to the current "Leaves, like the things of man, you / With your fresh thoughts care for, can you?" In a practice consistent with his composition habits, Hopkins continued to tinker with the poem well up to August 1884.

Hopkins knew Rossetti's poems extremely well, and it is quite possible that she was acquainted with his. In early 1881 Thomas Hall Caine, Dante Gabriel Rossetti's house companion and devotee, was putting together an anthology of poems, *Sonnets of Three Centuries* (1882), "to represent within the limits of a quintessential selection the whole body of native sonnet literature down to our own time." Dixon was invited to contribute, and also submitted for possible inclusion Hopkins' "The Starlight Night" and "The Caged Skylark." On Dixon's suggestion that Hopkins himself submit another sonnet, perhaps one "in ordinary rhythm: or at most a counterpointed one," Hopkins sent Caine three additional poems from which he was to choose one (*Correspondence*). The submissions could have included "Spring and Fall." Caine was impressed, but not Dante Gabriel Rossetti who, because of his influence on Caine, exercised veto power over the selection, and so rejected them, a major disappointment to Hopkins considering how much he read and respected Dante Gabriel Rossetti. Hopkins so wanted to be included that he urged Bridges to convince Caine to accept "Andromeda," a poem well suited to the Pre-Raphaelite archetypal taste. Caine had written, Hopkins told Bridges, apologizing for the rejection and explaining that the anthology intended to "'demonstrate the impossibility of improving upon the acknowledged structure whether as to rhyme-scheme or measure'" (*Letters*). Caine, who wrote as "a she bear robbed of her cubs," had supposedly consulted "a critic of utmost eminence" (p. 128) who supported his decision. I do not wish to enter into this stylistic debate on the sonnet and its conformity to the Hall Caine school, a debate Hopkins had with Dixon over Caine's rejection of the poems (see *Correspondence*). Instead, I merely wish to say, citing W. H. Gardner, that Hopkins' "efforts to redeem the sonnet from a cramping standardization were not appreciated by those who should have been best qualified to judge them" (p. 73). Caine's inability to recognize in Hopkins' poems the subtle nuances of his experimentation with the sonnet form is consistent with the overall early rejection of his verse. "Hopkins' most significant contribution to English verse morphology consisted in a number of variations played upon the traditional Petrarchan or Italian sonnet-form." And "his astute perception of the inherent fitness and beauty of the Petrarchan sonnet led him not to abandon the form but rather to develop its latent possibilities" (Gardner, 1:71–73). This is something the anthology missed.

Publication was clearly on Hopkins' mind, especially appearance in a volume involving Rossetti, even though it meant going against his stated edict not to seek, or at least force, notoriety: "I could wish, I allow, that my pieces could at some time become known but in some spontaneous way so to speak, without my forcing" (*Correspondence*). Hopkins was disappointed in not being included and very hurt, launching, uncharacteristically, a personal attack on Caine. "I do not feel, admiration for him," Hopkins told Bridges. "He may be a competent critic, but the essay on the Supernatural he sent me I think but poorly of. His style is bad. He imitates Matthew Arnold and appears to be his friend [Hopkins wrongly assumed that Arnold was that eminent critic].... But, as I said, I did not wish to quarrel" (*Letters to Bridges*). Later defending his decision to reject Hopkins' poems (in light of public condemnation that Caine "did not know a good sonnet when [he] saw one"), Caine noted that he also rejected some of Bridges' poems, blamed the decision on Gabriel Rossetti's advice, and claimed that Hopkins' poems were "certainly not in 'ordinary rhythm.'"

Caine's "most interesting Sonnet-book" featured "original sonnets from a good many of the newer bards," among them Christina and Dante Gabriel Rossetti, Richard Watson Dixon, Mathilde Blind, Elizabeth Barrett Browning, John Henry Newman, John Keble, Edward Irving, Augusta Webster, Coventry Patmore, and Algernon Swinburne. The collection included forty poets published for the first time, and "a body of sonnets never hitherto published." Caine wanted the volume to represent "a liberal and impartial selection from the sonnets of contemporary writers, of every style and school, to show clearly what is now the character of the sonnet in the present stage of our literature." He intended to argue the legitimacy of the English sonnet as an original, stylistically English and derivative, and distinct from the Italian sonnet form (*Sonnets of Three Centuries*, pp. vii–viii). Rossetti's biographer wondered what her reaction might have been had Hopkins been included in the collection: "So Christina lost the opportunity of seeing sonnets by her own poetic admirer—which may have included God's Grandeur and Spring. Or did she perhaps read them, for the sonnets were at Cheyne Walk during her Lenten visit? Had she been advising Caine, her verdict would surely have been more sympathetic" (Marsh, p. 485).

Hopkins was disappointed by the rejection on scholarly grounds, as well he should have been, because the sonnets of his that Caine possessed clearly complied with the latter's "catholic" expectations. For example, "Spring and Fall," the "little piece" (*Letters*) fits Caine's "little strain" definition of the sonnet, to say nothing of his extended characterization of it as "a short poem limited to the exposition of a single idea, sentiment, or emotion" (*Sonnets*, p. ix). Additionally, Hopkins' obsession with binaries and the two-part structure, employing them even in the sonnet elegy ("The Wreck of the Deutschland"), conforms to the "'sonnet-wave'—twofold in quality as well as movement—[which] embraces flow and ebb of thought or sentiment, and flow and ebb of music" (p. xxii). Finally, "Spring and Fall," with the first thought ending after the eighth line (Margaret's uninformed perspective, now only an intimation of aging and death), which is then answered in the final seven lines (Margaret's ultimate realization of death as something real and real to her—and altogether simulating the rhythms of the ocean), is consistent with Caine's other sense of the sonnet: "For the perfecting of a poem on this pattern the primary necessity, therefore, is, that the thought chosen be such as falls naturally into unequal parts, each essential to each, and the one answering the other." Drawing from Theodore Watts's view of the sonnet as "a wave of melody," Caine said of the poet: "Nor does he fail to find in every impulse animating his muse something that corresponds with the law of movement that governs the sea" (*Sonnets*, p. xxii).

"Spring and Fall" first appeared in August 1893 in Alfred H. Miles's *The Poets and the Poetry of the Century*. There is no indication that Rossetti read the Miles anthology, because her correspondence, sparse on literary details, more often engages domestic concerns—her sister Maria's failing health, which "continues to make us very anxious" (Maria died in November 1876), and her mother's precarious condition (constant nose-bleeds in particular). Rossetti's literary (pre)occupation is often only odd postscripts to her correspondence (*Letters of Christina Rossetti*, p. 93). But we do know that she remained poetically active up to her death in 1894, composing around 1893 her last dirge, "Sleeping at Last." Rossetti's "Mirrors of Life and Death" (1877) and Hopkins' "Spring and Fall" (1880) mirror each other. Both poems are elegies, admitting Rossetti's and Hopkins' obsession with the poetry, if not thoughts, of death, Rossetti more so. Death is the subject of such poems as "After Death," "Dead Before Death," "Sweet Death," "Remember," "Life and Death," "De Profundis," "Song," "Death's Chill Between," "Death-Watches," "Life Out of Death," and "Sleeping at Last." For Rossetti, even "the idea of love turned inexorably to the idea of death," but "a kind of death not closely connected with her usual ideas of an afterworld" (Bowra, p. 256). Hopkins' dirges range from "Spring and Death," "O Death, Death, He is come," "The Wreck of the Deutschland," "The Loss of the Eurydice," "Binsey Poplars," "The Bugler's First Communion," "Felix Randal," "The Leaden Echo and the Golden Echo," "St. Winefred's Well," and "Heraclitean Fire."

In "Spring and Fall," spring symbolizes life, and fall death:

> Margaret, are you grieving
> Over Goldengrove unleaving?
> Leaves, like the things of man, you
> With your fresh thoughts care for, can you?
> Ah! as the heart grows older
> It will come to such sights colder
> By and by, nor spare a sigh
> Though worlds of wanwood leafmeal lie;
> And yet you will weep and know why.
> Now no matter, child, the name:
> Sorrow's springs are the same.
> Nor mouth had, no nor mind, expressed
> What heart heard of, ghost guessed:
> It is the blight man was born for,
> It is Margaret you mourn for.

So fantastical is spring that Margaret's youth is characterized by her mental state, her "fresh thoughts" (aging is only a thing of "the heart"), and she is reminded that the falling leaves, now only the object of her grief and seemingly distant from her, will become in time her own condition: "in the future she will know the reason for a sorrow that is now only a blind grief." As such, the poem is merely an intimation of mortality. The source of Margaret's grief is something phenomenologically outside herself—the culmination of the fall season and with it the onset of winter manifested by the falling leaves. Whether it is her first conscious experience of it is indeterminable. Hopkins clearly perceived the falling leaves as constitutive of human devolution, describing his personal crises to Bridges as the "fallen leaves of my poor life between all the leaves of it" (*Letters to Bridges*). Whereas Margaret in her childlikeness is able only to appreciate the sign, the autumnal speaker apprehends the symbol, something far more deeply interfused. But however preoccupied Margaret is with this natural phenomenon, it remains only a sign to her and retains no symbolic value whatsoever. For while Margaret might well have intuited, however subliminally, the reason for her sorrow, still unnamable ("Now no matter, child, the name"), she appears not to discover in the falling leaves any archetypal signification. The poem thus ends with the inexorableness of death, and Margaret's inevitable demise, a "colder" realization the "older" and more callous heart/speaker discloses to her: "It is the blight man was born for, / It is Margaret you mourn for."

... The surface simplicity of "Spring and Fall" masks a complexity familiar to Hopkins' poetry. The poem possesses the quality of disclosure whereby, as Hopkins once remarked to Bridges, meaning either results effortlessly "as fast as one reads," or, if initially enigmatic, "when once made out to explode" (*Letters to Bridges*). Or rather, like oozed oil crushed, "Spring and Fall" yields the human contraries of seasonal death and rebirth, ignorance and intuition, innocence and experience, childhood and adulthood, joy and sorrow. But the poem's

> "'SPRING AND FALL' IS HOPKINS'S PUREST, MOST COHERENT DARK POEM, FREED FROM THE CONFLICTING VALUES OF THE SELF-DIVIDED CLERIC BY A DISPASSIONATE, ALMOST ENERVATED PESSIMISM."

tour de force is its anatomizing of Margaret's sorrow. Her initial "grieving" over the sign of the season's demise will in time yield to a "weep[-ing]" (when she "know[s] why"), culminating in a "mourn[ing]"—when the sign ("Goldengrove unleaving") capitulates to the symbol ("the blight man was born for"). Not surprisingly, then, Alison Sulloway insists that "Spring and Fall" "deserves further scrutiny because it is a miniature repository of all Hopkins's apocalyptic anxieties." Hopkins recognized in Christina Rossetti a poet who shared similar angst about the face of the deep. It is something of a commonplace that Hopkins owed much to Christina Rossetti. "Mirrors of Life and Death" discloses the subtleties of that indebtedness. In it Hopkins found a masterpiece to admire and do otherwise, the utterance of which is "Spring and Fall."

Source: Jude V. Nixon , "'Goldengrove Unleaving': Hopkins' 'Spring and Fall,' Christina Rossetti's 'Mirrors of Life and Death,' and the Politics of Inclusion," in *Victorian Poetry*, Vol. 43, No. 4, Winter 2005, pp. 473–84.

A. R. Coulthard

In the following excerpt, Coulthard examines the tension between theology and sensuality in Hopkins's verse and contends that Christian piety exerted a constricting influence on his poetry.

Gerard Manley Hopkins struggled throughout his adult life to bring the physical and the spiritual into soul-saving harmony. Even as an Oxford student, he tormented himself with moral disapproval of his sensual inclinations, regretfully noting in his diary, for instance, his inability to conquer his "old habit" of almost daily masturbation (White 120). Hopkins even scrupulously recorded "looking up 'dreadful words' in his lexicon or dictionary, reading 'dangerous things' in the *Saturday Review* and once in *Love's Labour's Lost*, and looking up anatomical drawings in *The Lancet*" (White 114).

Nature was equally voluptuous to Hopkins; he was a tireless walker among its beauties, which he described in lush detail in his notebooks. His sense of self was intimately entwined with natural physicality, as this Whitmanesque characterization attests: "my consciousness and feeling of myself, that taste of myself, ... more distinctive than the smell of walnutleaf or camphour" (qtd. in Houghton and Stange 689).

Yet when this son of the flesh entered the Catholic priesthood against the wishes of his Anglican family, he chose an order so ascetic that part of his novitiate discipline was to wear a chain with "galvanized spikes gripping [the] thigh muscles" for three hours each morning (qtd. in White 182). The reformed aesthete burned his early poems but was careful to keep copies. The strict moralist who ranked seeking literary fame among the vaniest of sins wrote until his death and made sure that his friend Robert Bridges not only had his poems for safekeeping, but also a preface explaining their sprung rhythm metrics.

Poets who leave as few poems as Hopkins did rarely are accorded greatness. What limits his literary achievement, however, is not the brevity of his canon but the fact that he lived his curtailed life as a priest. It is doubtful that Hopkins would have produced a much larger and more varied body of work had he lived longer, especially if he remained in the priesthood, which he showed no signs of abandoning in spite of disenchantment with it. Religion constricted Hopkins's poetry during both its happy and depressed phases. As a devout young priest, he apparently regarded glorifying nature apart from theological dogma in his poems as irreverent. As a disillusioned older cleric, Hopkins lost his enthusiasm for nature and, in the terrible sonnets, took his spiritual crisis as far as it could go short of suicide. When the Christ-haunted poet died at forty-four, he probably had said all he had to say.

Hopkins falls one rung short of greatness not because of small output or narrow range, but because even most of his better poems speak with contrary voices, their superficially tight sonnet form thrown out of kilter by an underlying conflict between Dionysian instincts and self-abnegating moralism. What Hopkins really extols in the nature-devotional poems is nature itself and not the God that made it. What he grieves in the terrible sonnets is not estrangement from God so much as the absence of corporeal pleasure in his religion similar to that which he once felt in nature and self. Apparently without fully understanding the conflict, Hopkins struggled throughout his adult life to bring his adopted self-denying dogma into accord with his instinctive egocentric romanticism. The impossibility of such a union is evident in his poetry. A strained spiritualism which Hopkins probably never internalized taints even the nature lyrics of 1877, the year of his ordination and his most hopeful in the priesthood. The same doctrinaire theology blights most of the later terrible sonnets as well.

Norman White's probing study of Hopkins's life should lay to rest any speculation that Hopkins derived masochistic pleasure from his priestly pain. Numerous excerpts from letters, diaries, and notebooks, such as the 1889 "Nothing to enter but loathing of my life and a barren submission to God's will" (qtd. in White 440), reveal a man whose physical and psychic ills brought him nothing but misery and near-suicidal depression. The mystery of why Hopkins remained a priest can only be explained by his inherent inertia and an unwillingness to admit that he had made a colossal mistake. That celibacy allowed him both to suppress and disguise his homosexuality may have been a secondary motive.

Whatever his private reasons, Hopkins regressed from trying to meld his love of nature with his new profession to a feeling of hopeless entrapment in a way of life he detested. The schizophrenic poetry produced during both stages makes Hopkins a poet of excellent passages more than excellent poems. The early nature-devotional lyrics and the later terrible sonnets, which seem so unlike in tenor and theme, are linked by the fact that in both kinds of poems the best poetry issues from Hopkins's gut and not his cerebral cortex. Whether he was crying out in joy or despair, Hopkins wrote better from his impulsive heart than his theological head.

... "Spring and Fall," written in 1880, is pivotal in Hopkins's psychic journey from the hope of the 1877 nature-devotional lyrics to the despair of the terrible sonnets of the mid-1880s. It is his song of innocence and song of experience rolled into one.

"Spring and Fall" is Hopkins's purest, most coherent dark poem, freed from the conflicting values of the self-divided cleric by a dispassionate, almost enervated pessimism. One has to look very hard, in fact, to find a priest in this poem at all. By 1880, Hopkins's youthful optimism in taking orders had worn off. Not only had church censorship discouraged his creative efforts, but his early years in the priesthood had been neither satisfying nor productive. The hopeful romanticism with which Hopkins had made the biggest decision of his life had quickly come face-to-face with an emotionally debilitating reality.

"Spring and Fall" is a poignant testimony to the loss of youth's naive happiness, more about Hopkins than the child to whom it is ostensibly addressed. Though subtitled "To a Young Child," the poem is really an interior monologue, the somber meditation of its world-weary speaker (or thinker), who, by his own acknowledgement, is "naming" a cause for gloom that Margaret is not yet mature enough to understand:

> Now not matter, child, the name:
> Sorrow's springs are the same.
> Nor mouth had, no nor mind, expressed
> What heart heard of, ghost guessed.

The melancholy adult predicts that the child (and by extension all children of men) is doomed to eventually share his own hopeless condition, for the law of life is a soul-chilling deterioration: "Ah! as the heart grows older / It will come to such sights colder," intones the voice of experience. "Sorrow's springs" don't represent the fall from grace as is sometimes conjectured, but the mere fact of existence. Margaret's only "sin," and the poet's too, is in having lived. Nor are "Sorrow's springs" mere mortality, except in the sense that all things decay, especially the naive optimism of youth, and that the natural result of a life of loss is death. Even at the spring of her young life, Margaret senses in the autumn leaves that decline, more emotional than physical, is "the blight man was born for," but it is Hopkins himself and not Margaret that the poem mourns for. He sees her present unhappy mood as but the precursor of the greater griefs which had already come to him.

"Spring and Fall" was written at a time when Hopkins was first learning to live with a relentless despair. His way of coping with his ontological sorrow in this poem was to universalize it by seeing it even in the instinct of a child, a psychologically dubious supposition. As Hopkins's hope for achievement and contentment waned daily, he recorded his malaise under the guise of an empathetic meditation on a young girl's moment of sadness, crediting her with his own gloomy sentience.

Though the immediate cause of Hopkins's pessimism was his misery in the priesthood, "Spring and Fall" is remarkable for the absence of theology. There is no spiritual consolation for Margaret, or Hopkins, even if "Fall" is read as Biblical and "blight" as sin. Neither is there implication that earthly suffering is the just deserts of fallen humanity. "Spring and Fall" is warped by neither the hopeful religiosity of earlier poems nor the frustrated religiosity of the terrible sonnets. The poem is existential rather than theological in tone and substance, and Hopkins's beloved nature provides no solace, only a visible sign of life's inevitable descent into sadness in its dead and dying leaves.

By 1885, the year Hopkins wrote the terrible (or terrifying or, maybe more properly, terrified) sonnets, his despair had become visceral and virtually constant. He now admitted the cause of his misery, the priesthood in which he no longer could entertain even fleeting hope of happiness. Not only had he given up on the possibility of temporal reward in his profession, but he had begun to doubt eternal compensation as well.

The belief in divine benevolence which had earlier sustained Hopkins, at least on an intellectual level, had all but evaporated. God the protective mother hen had become the uncaring sire who ignores, or devours, his offspring—Hopkins in particular, for these poems rarely generalize. Rather than the universal sorrow of "Spring and Fall," the misery of the terrible sonnets is Hopkins's alone, as if God has singled him out for special abuse. Though Hopkins continued to take his walks despite depression and failing health and to record seasonal changes in his diaries, nature as an uplifter of the spirit disappears along with a caring God from these poems....

Source: A. R. Coulthard, "Gerard Manley Hopkins: Priest vs. Poet," in *Victorian Newsletter*, No. 88, Fall 1995, pp. 35–40.

SOURCES

Clutton-Brock, Arthur, Review of *The Poems of Gerard Manley Hopkins*, in *Gerard Manley Hopkins: The Critical Heritage*, edited by Gerald Roberts, Psychology Press, 1996, pp. 85–86; originally published in *Times Literary Supplement* (London, England), January 9, 1919, p. 19.

Everett, Glenn, "Gerard Manley Hopkins: A Brief Biography," in *The Victorian Web*, http://www.victorianweb.org/authors/hopkins/hopkins12.html (accessed April 26, 2011).

"First World War Casualties," in *History Learning Site*, http://www.historylearningsite.co.uk/FWWcasualties.htm (accessed May 2, 2011).

Guiney, Louise Imogen, "Gerard Hopkins: A Recovered Poet," in *Gerard Manley Hopkins: The Critical Heritage*, edited by Gerald Roberts, Psychology Press, 1996, p. 93; originally published in *Month*, March 1919, p. 205.

Hopkins, Gerard Manley, "Spring and Fall: To a Young Girl," in *Victorian Poetry and Poetics*, 2nd ed., edited by Walter E. Houghton and G. Robert Stange, Houghton Mifflin, 1968, p. 703.

Houghton, Walter E., and G. Robert Stange, eds., *Victorian Poetry and Poetics*, 2nd ed., Houghton Mifflin, 1968, pp. 689–93, 703.

Maynard, Theodore, "The Artist as Hero," in *Gerard Manley Hopkins: The Critical Heritage*, edited by Gerald Roberts, Psychology Press, 1996, pp. 89–90; originally published in *New Witness*, January 24, 1919, p. 260.

Review of *The Poems of Gerard Manley Hopkins*, in *Gerard Manley Hopkins: The Critical Heritage*, edited by Gerald Roberts, Psychology Press, 1996, pp. 83–84; originally published in *Herald* (Glasgow, Scotland), January 2, 1919, p. 3.

Review of *The Poems of Gerard Manley Hopkins*, in *Gerard Manley Hopkins: The Critical Heritage*, edited by Gerald Roberts, Psychology Press, 1996, p. 100; originally published in *Saturday Westminster Gazette*, March 8, 1919, pp. 13–14.

Roberts, Gerald, ed., *Gerard Manley Hopkins: The Critical Heritage*, Psychology Press, 1996, p. 18.

FURTHER READING

Briggs, Asa, *Victorian Cities*, University of California Press, 1993.
    Readers interested in the nature of the Victorian cities to which Hopkins as a priest was assigned might begin with this volume. It traces the development of cities in Victorian England from the dawn to the railway age until the early twentieth century.

Herring, George, *What Was the Oxford Movement?*, Continuum, 2002.

>This volume examines the religious ferment that was centered on Oxford University in the mid-nineteenth century. The Oxford movement, also called Tractarianism, was a revival of so-called High Church religious beliefs that ultimately led many prominent thinkers to convert to Catholicism, just as Hopkins later would.

Hopkins, Gerard Manley, "Author's Preface," in *Toward the Open Field: Poets on the Art of Poetry, 1800–1950*, edited by Melissa Kwasny, Wesleyan University Press, 2004.

>Readers interested in Hopkins's metrical theories can find his own discussion of them in this brief preface, which he wrote in 1883 and which Robert Bridges preserved for inclusion in the 1918 edition of Hopkins's poetry. Hopkins provides a description of sprung rhythm and distinguishes it from what he calls running rhythm. He also demonstrates the connections between his metrical theories and those of the ancient Greeks and Romans, as well as those of earlier English writers.

Mariani, Paul, *Gerard Manley Hopkins: A Life*, Viking, 2008.

>This volume is the most recent book-length biography of Hopkins. It focuses primarily on the poet's inner life. It gives some emphasis to his correspondence with Robert Bridges, his Oxford friend and literary executor after his death.

Melnyk, Julie, *Victorian Religion: Faith and Life in Britain*, Praeger, 2008.

>Melnyk examines the position of religion in Victorian England. She surveys the largest denominations and demonstrates how religious belief was integral to the life of Victorian Britons. She also explores the role religious belief played in literature and art.

SUGGESTED SEARCH TERMS

English Catholicism AND nineteenth century

Gerard Manley Hopkins

Gerard Manley Hopkins AND Spring and Fall: To a Young Girl

Oxford movement

Victorian period

Victorian poetry

Society of Jesus

Jesuits

sprung rhythm

Tractarianism

Gerard Manley Hopkins AND Catholicism

Gerard Manley Hopkins AND Victorian poetry

We Wear the Mask

PAUL LAURENCE DUNBAR

1895

Although Paul Laurence Dunbar also wrote novels, short stories, songs, and plays, he is remembered chiefly as a poet. "We Wear the Mask" was published in 1895 in *Majors and Minors*, his second book of poems, of the six major volumes he would complete in his brief thirty-three years of life. He became famous overnight with this volume because of a favorable review by the white critic William Dean Howells. Dunbar toured the country performing his black dialect poems about slave days, the poems that pleased his audiences. By 1899, he was discouraged that the public was not interested in his other writing in literary English. He had a lyric gift, but the critics dismissed his standard English poems as imitative. The poem "We Wear the Mask" in standard English is now one of his most famous statements about racism in the United States. It explores the pain of having to live according to a racial stereotype.

The son of slaves, Dunbar experienced the continuing legacy of slavery in a time of rampant racism in America. Dunbar's struggle to become the first recognized African American author continued even after his death in 1906. Later critics accused him of catering to whites with his poems depicting slaves on the plantation. Today, he has taken his place as one of the founders of African American literature, and his poems have been memorized by generations of African Americans. Although he felt like a

Paul Laurence Dunbar (The Library of Congress)

failure in his lifetime, he inspired the writers of the Harlem Renaissance in the 1920s.

"We Wear the Mask" can be found in *The Complete Poems of Paul Laurence Dunbar*, published by Dodd, Mead in 1940. It can also be found in *The Collected Poetry of Paul Laurence Dunbar*, edited by Joanne Braxton in a 1993 paperback edition by University Press of Virginia.

AUTHOR BIOGRAPHY

Dunbar was born in Dayton, Ohio, on June 27, 1872, to Joshua Dunbar and Matilda Burton Murphy Dunbar, a widow with two sons by her previous slave marriage. His parents had both been slaves in Kentucky. After emancipation, thousands of freed slaves moved north, and Matilda took her young sons to Dayton and became a laundry woman, until she met and married Joshua. Joshua was an alcoholic, and Matilda obtained a divorce and custody of her sickly son, Paul, of whom she was protective. He went to Dayton Central High School. He was the only black student there, but he was accepted and was an excellent student.

Dunbar began to write seriously at the age of sixteen and published some of his poems locally. His first real encounter with racial discrimination came after high school in 1891. He could only find menial work as an elevator boy. His break came when the Western Association of Writers met in Dayton in 1892. He was invited to give the welcome, which he composed and recited in verse. He made such an impression that he found supporters to help him publish his first collection of poetry, *Oak and Ivy*, in 1892. It contained black dialect poems inspired by the dialect work of James Whitcomb Riley. In 1893, Dunbar went to Chicago to work at the Haitian Pavilion at the Columbian Exposition. There, he met Frederick Douglass, who recognized his talent and employed him.

With the help of patrons, Dunbar published his second volume, *Majors and Minors*, in 1895. It was favorably reviewed by William Dean Howells, a leading white American writer and critic. Dunbar became an overnight celebrity as the first nationally-known black writer in American society. Because of his charm, manners, talent, and musical voice, his readings electrified audiences. In 1896, *Lyrics of a Lowly Life* was published by Dodd, Mead in New York.

In 1897, Dunbar worked as a clerk in the Library of Congress. He married another African American author, Alice Ruth Moore, in 1898, at the height of his fame and productivity. He published his first novel, *The Uncalled*, and his first collection of short stories, *Folks from Dixie*, in that same year. *Lyrics of the Hearthside* was published in 1899.

Dunbar became gravely ill in 1899 with tuberculosis. The Dunbars moved to Denver for his health, where he published his second novel, *The Love of Landry*, and a book of short stories, *The Strength of Gideon*, in 1900. In 1901, *The Fanatics*, his third novel, came out, followed in 1902 by his last novel, *The Sport of the Gods*.

In 1902, Alice and Paul Dunbar separated because of his alcoholism. He spent his last days in Dayton with his mother, still producing until the end: *Lyrics of Love and Laughter* and *In Old Plantation Days* (1903), *The Heart of Happy Hollow* (1904), and *Lyrics of Sunshine and Shadow* (1905). He died of tuberculosis on February 9, 1906, at the age of thirty-three. Many of his poems, essays, and plays were collected and published posthumously.

POEM TEXT

We wear the mask that grins and lies,
It hides our cheeks and shades our eyes,—
This debt we pay to human guile;
With torn and bleeding hearts we smile,
And mouth with myriad subtle-ties.   5

Why should the world be over-wise,
In counting all our tears and sighs?
Nay, let them only see us, while
We wear the mask.

We smile, but, O great Christ, our cries   10
To thee from tortured souls arise.
We sing, but oh the clay is vile
Beneath our feet, and long the mile;
But let the world dream other-wise,
We wear the mask!   15

MEDIA ADAPTATIONS

- *The Paul Laurence Dunbar Collection* is a package of three DVDs and three audiotapes with top African American storytellers reading Dunbar's stories and poems. It was produced by Cerebellum Corporation in 2008 and is available at Barnes & Noble or Amazon.
- *The Poetry of Paul Laurence Dunbar*, narrated by Bobby Norfolk and produced in 2004 by August House, is available as an audio download or audio CD from LearnOutLoud.com.

POEM SUMMARY

The text used for this summary is from *The Complete Poems of Paul Laurence Dunbar*, Dodd, Mead, 1940, p. 71. A version of the poem can be found on the following Web page: www.poemhunter.com/poem/we-wear-the-mask/.

Stanza 1

The poem uses only three rhymes (*a*, *b*, *c*) in three stanzas of an iambic tetrameter lyric, expressing sorrow and anger because the speaker cannot be himself in his society, because of racial prejudice. Stanza one introduces the theme and symbol of the mask.

In the first couplet (*aa*) the speaker includes himself in a group by using the first person plural, we. The group could be African Americans in general, or as some have suggested, African American writers in particular. In either case, they wear a grinning mask that hides their true feelings. This image of the grinning mask evokes an ancient and ritual African mask used for ceremony, hiding the eyes and face of the wearer with an impersonal expression. In that case, the mask carries a divine dignity, something superhuman, mysterious, and perhaps implying a terrible retribution to the enemy in the future.

More to the present point, the image of the mask evokes the constant humiliation blacks endure by having to hide their true feelings in an alien society. The mask suggests the minstrel shows in America where white performers in blackface, or black performers, played stereotypes of plantation darkies, singing and dancing in their happy captivity. Slaves were seen in minstrel shows and newspaper cartoons as stupid and easily manipulated but happy. Even after Emancipation, blacks had to be careful not to call attention to themselves as individuals with opinions or complaints, for fear of violence and persecution. They had to appear complacent and agreeable. The mask is here a symbol of racial prejudice.

The second couplet (*bb*) explains that the inner experience of the group (African Americans) is the exact opposite of their outer appearance. The happy face is forced on them by the malicious social game of compliance they have to play with the people in power. In reality, their hearts are injured by this inhuman repression. The last line of the stanza does not rhyme with the rest of the stanza and is not part of a couplet (*c*) but explains that as they wear the mask of contentment, blacks are also coerced into speaking subtle lies about their agreement with the status quo.

Stanza 2

The beginning couplet returns to the rhyme scheme (*aa*) of the first stanza, thus linking the two together and making a musical repetition. This four-line short middle stanza seems to excuse the persecutors in an ironic and bitter turn, asking why African Americans should expect the world to care or number their wrongs?

The public does not acknowledge the unjust condition of black people or admit complicity with the oppression, perhaps because such sympathy with the black race would call for a great sensitivity it does not seem to possess.

The last two lines answer the question about getting the world's sympathy by declaring, no, it is asking too much to be understood, so it is better that black people should only be seen with the mask on. The third and fourth lines do not rhyme (*bc*), and they are not the same length, thus pulling the reader up short to a sad but inevitable conclusion that there is no remedy. The fourth line has only two feet (a foot is a unit of poetry made of stressed and unstressed syllables) and declares emphatically that blacks in a cruel world have no choice but to wear a mask.

Stanza 3
The last stanza is the longest, with six lines. The first couplet (*aa*) addresses Christ, pleading with cries from the soul for help. Christ alone can see the people suffering beneath their false smiles. The appeal to Christ recalls Negro spirituals affirming faith in God and appealing for heavenly justice for the oppression of believers.

The second couplet (*bb*) declares that even if the black race can sing, the earth is not pleasant to them, and the way is long. The singing of slaves, or a black choir in a church, may be the image invoked here. The line also recalls the message of another of Dunbar's poems, "Sympathy," explaining that a caged bird can sing, but it sings because it is in pain. Dunbar was proud of black music and felt it was more profound than white music, because it had the depth of soul sorrow in it. Like black music, Dunbar's poetry shows a mastery of rhythm and meter. Although he keeps to a pattern (for most of the lines he uses iambic tetrameter—a pattern of four iambs, which are poetic feet containing an unstressed syllable followed by a stressed syllable), he varies the line length and rhyme scheme. The rhythm imitates the power of song, and this comes out when Dunbar's poems are spoken aloud. Nevertheless, the audience should not be fooled, he says, for behind the singing is great suffering. Life seems long to those who must act a part.

The last two lines do not rhyme (*ac*), and again, the last line has only two feet, bringing the reader up short to the repeated conclusion: because the world does not want to hear the truth from them, blacks have to wear a mask. They must live a stereotype instead of being who they are.

THEMES

Racism
"We Wear the Mask" is an open complaint about the racism in America in the 1890s, when racial violence was common. Dunbar describes the basic fear African Americans everywhere lived with, forcing them to hide beneath a social mask so as not to reveal themselves, their feelings, or true opinions. Blacks were persecuted for the slightest reasons, and the poem suggests they have to act a part and stay in their places. The mask grins or pretends to be happy, possibly a reference to the stereotype of the happy and dancing plantation slave. The poet tells the truth, however, about his feelings. The smile is a lie. The poem protests that blacks in America are forced to wear a mask, to hide who they are, in order to survive.

The poem evokes the slavery African Americans endured in America for two and a half centuries. Although Dunbar lived after emancipation, the legacy of slavery continued through various social, legal, and psychological constraints. He was refused white-collar jobs because of his race and forced to work as an elevator boy. Blacks were constrained by Jim Crow laws in the South, denying them their right to vote or to get legal protection. They were economically enslaved by restrictive labor contracts and other unfair laws in the South, and in the North, they were denied jobs and housing. Racial segregation was the norm in American society.

Dunbar never denied his race, and in fact, made many statements on racial injustice. Other poems of his that comment on racism include "The Haunted Oak," "Right's Security," "The Warrior's Prayer," "To the South on Its New Slavery," "Frederick Douglass," and "Ode to Ethiopia." He made overt statements against lynching and racial stereotyping in his journalism. He made a plea for equal rights and assimilation of blacks into mainstream American life.

Deception
Though Dunbar made a breakthrough for his race by being accepted as the first famous

TOPICS FOR FURTHER STUDY

- Compare and contrast two films about racism: *Guess Who's Coming to Dinner* (1967) and *Lady Sings the Blues* (1972). Dunbar, like Billie Holiday, was a gifted artist who succumbed to alcohol and died young. How do both films display the kinds of pressures experienced by African Americans as they try to succeed in white America? Using clips from the films to illustrate Dunbar's ideas, create a reading and commentary on the poem "We Wear the Mask" for *YouTube*.

- Compare Dunbar's "We Wear the Mask" with "Still I Rise" by Maya Angelou. How do the background and lifetime of each poet contribute to the differing messages of the poems? Present the poems and historical backgrounds to a group with visuals, using PowerPoint or Inspiration Presentation Manager, explaining the social progress of African Americans between 1895 and 1978. Do the themes or message of either or both poems still resonate today?

- The Russian Jewish poet Joseph Brodsky (1940–1996) was denounced by the Soviet government, sent to a labor camp, and then thrown out of his country for being a Jew. Read his poem "Moscow Carol," which examines the pain of ostracism. Write a research paper on Brodsky and the effect of Jewish persecution in the Soviet Union on him, referring to this poem and any other of his works that illuminate the topic.

- Using Wikispaces.com create a wiki on "Social Media and Social Justice" displaying evidence from recent world events on the power of social media to address social injustice and violence. On your wiki, display the poem "We Wear the Mask" and pretend you live in Dunbar's day. Foster public opinion against the persecution and illegal lynchings that were countenanced at the time by posting some messages that you and your fellow students construct.

- Using Internet and traditional research, including the Paul Laurence Dunbar Web site at the University of Dayton (http://www.dunbarsite.org/), create an interactive time line of major events that occurred during Dunbar's short lifetime. Include literary, technological, racial (social), political, and economic events with links that explain them. When appropriate, link to writings by Dunbar that reflect these events.

- Compare "We Wear the Mask" with "Tourists" by Sherman Alexie, a poet known for works suitable for young-adult readers. In "Tourists," Alexie turns the tables and imagines the clumsiness of famous white visitors trying to fit into Native American culture. One poem is tragic and the other comic, but what common points do they both make about racism? Have you or your friends ever had similar experiences of not belonging to a group and having to pretend you did? Use Blogspot.com to share thoughts on pretending to fit into an alien culture.

African American poet, he felt he could not express himself fully because he was seen as a dialect writer. The dialect poems seemed to perpetuate black stereotypes, yet these were the ones whites wanted. Critic William Dean Howells declared Dunbar's true voice was heard when he sounded like a Southern field worker. This was true black speech, he implied, whereas if Dunbar tried to speak like white poets, he was speaking in imitation of his betters. This was galling for Dunbar and made him feel he could not be himself as a poet or a man. His success was thus not based on who he was, but who whites thought he was.

psychological, that the black man must endure in a foreign culture that treats him as an inferior outcast. The poem gives the feeling of having no place to go. There is no help on earth, so one must cry out to God to remedy this injustice.

STYLE

Personal Lyric

Lyric poetry is an ancient genre, popular from classical times through the present, in almost every culture. A lyric was originally a song sung to an accompanying lyre or stringed instrument. A lyric poem is short and musical rather than narrative or dramatic and expresses emotions or thoughts. A personal lyric represents the subjective experience of one speaker. Dunbar was influenced by the lyric poetry of Tennyson, Keats, Shelley, Longfellow, and Poe. Famous lyric poems include Tennyson's "Now the Crimson Petal Sleeps" and Edgar Allan Poe's "To Helen."

The fact that lyrics are dominant in Dunbar's poetry is illustrated by the fact that several of his volumes have the word lyric in the title: *Lyrics of Lowly Life*, *Lyrics of the Hearthside*, *Lyrics of Love and Laughter*, and *Lyrics of Sunshine and Shadow*. The lyric was flexible enough to accommodate both Dunbar's poems in literary English (called majors) and his dialect poems (minors) in the volume *Majors and Minors* (1896).

Protest Poem

"We Wear the Mask" is basically a racial protest poem. Dunbar often used iambic tetrameter, as in this poem, for serious subjects. He was inspired by two of his favorite American poets, John Greenleaf Whittier and Henry Wadsworth Longfellow, who wrote abolitionist poems before the Civil War. It was not necessary for him to depend on white models, however, for the history of African American oral traditions shows an emphasis on protest.

The enslaved Africans kept their spirits up with encoded messages in their songs and spirituals. Such familiar religious hymns as "Get on Board Little Children" were a way to talk about freedom and slavery in Biblical terms or to warn about an impending escape attempt. The song "Oh Freedom" is another that was sung at secret meetings on the plantations. It became an anthem

An African American man in contemplation (Blacqbook | Shutterstock.com)

Dunbar was a brilliant and creative artist, but he struggled to overcome the racial stereotype of blacks as slow, lazy, and child-like people. The blacks he portrayed in his dialect poems, singing and dancing on the plantation, were part of the folklore of the past to him, but it was the image that whites wanted to believe about blacks to keep them in a nonthreatening place. Dunbar himself was learned and well-read. He saw himself as middle-class, urbane, and worldly, able to meet other artists from around the world. However, even the most educated black person met a wall of prejudice everywhere and was treated in a demeaning way, as though stupid. Dunbar and other blacks were forced into keeping up the social deception that they were inferior because of their race, although they felt otherwise inside. To announce who they really were could mean trouble and persecution, so African Americans had to hide, lie, or deceive in order to gain acceptance.

Despair

The poet uses several words indicating despair and pain over the situation of having to lie and hide his true self. It is like being in a cage (see his poem, "Sympathy") or being denied one's own life. He describes this sort of false life as a life of torture. One may sing or write poetry, but life is long and hard when one cannot express the truth of the heart. When one is forced to lie out of fear of telling the truth, one loses hope. The despair is so overwhelming that the poet can only call on Christ to hear and alleviate the cries of his race. God is the only hope because the world has no clue about the suffering, both physical and of the civil rights movement. The fact that these protests were coded indicates something important about early African American literature. It was dangerous to express protest too openly. This is the whole point of "We Wear the Mask."

The post-Reconstruction era, when Dunbar was writing, was a time still rife with racial tension. Like fiction writer Charles Waddell Chesnutt (1858–1932), Dunbar learned to write for a double audience, with protest generally muted or told through indirection. In "The Haunted Oak," "We Wear the Mask," and "Sympathy," however, Dunbar's anger at racism is more openly expressed.

His protest poems would be the models for the later protest poems of the Harlem Renaissance in the 1920s and 1930s in such examples as "Incident," and "Saturday's Child" by Countee Cullen. Langston Hughes's "I Too Sing America" asserts that the black voice is part of the American voice.

The protest poems of the 1960s centered around the civil rights movement. For instance, "The Ballad of Birmingham" by Dudley Randall recounted the bombing of children in a church. Because of the later, more aggressive protest poems written by black poets, Dunbar was accused of being an Uncle Tom, accommodating white tastes with black stereotypes in his dialect poems. This is an incorrect assumption, for Dunbar did protest injustice in both his poetry and his prose.

African American Poetry

African American poetry refers to the works of those people who were brought forcibly to this country from Africa and kept in bondage for two and a half centuries. It was forbidden for slaves to learn to read or write, and yet they did both. At first they continued their native oral tradition with songs, spirituals, and sermons. After learning to write, many ex-slaves like Frederick Douglass wrote slave narratives.

Slave poets Lucy Terry, Jupiter Hammon, and Phillis Wheatley had published even before the American Revolution. Phillis Wheatley (1754–1784), a child prodigy and the slave of the Wheatley family, produced polished eighteenth-century verses. She was the first well-known African American author, traveling abroad to promote her work and the work of abolitionists.

During the post-Reconstruction era, from about 1870 until World War I, those black authors who did publish were primarily publishing journalistic prose or fiction or single poems. Dunbar's ambition to be an accepted mainstream poet led him to write in standard European and American poetic forms. When, inspired by James Whitcomb Riley's example to write poetry in regional dialect, he wrote poems in black Southern dialect and became famous for it.

Dunbar preferred poems in literary English, which he felt best expressed who he was, but the dialect poems were the ones his white audience felt expressed the authentic black experience and the ones his publisher wanted. Dunbar's dilemma was a crucial moment in the development of African American poetry. He wrote for two audiences with two different languages. "We Wear the Mask" elucidates the dilemma of being part of two different and opposing cultures.

Dunbar's experiments helped later poets such as Langston Hughes, James Weldon Johnson, Countee Cullen, Claude McKay, and Jean Toomer in the Harlem Renaissance (1920–1940) to integrate these separate modes of expression into an English that could distinctively express the African American voice. It was the revolution of the 1960s that brought African American literature, like other minority literatures, into respectability. With black writers being taken seriously, their work could no longer be denied its place as part of mainstream American literature, and black authors felt free to use whatever language their imaginations could invent.

HISTORICAL CONTEXT

Failure of Reconstruction

Reconstruction is the period after the Civil War from 1865 to 1877 during which the United States tried to restructure American society by abolishing slavery and amending the Constitution (the Thirteenth, Fourteenth, and Fifteenth Amendments) to give civil rights to four million former slaves. While federal troops were stationed in the South, state governments were organized to give blacks the vote and to provide them schools and positions in government. After a disputed presidential election in 1876 that effectively ended Reconstruction, white supremacists in the South reasserted their power and states' rights to enact

COMPARE & CONTRAST

- **1890s:** Paul Laurence Dunbar is hailed as a symbol of racial advancement because he is the first nationally known African American professional writer.

  Today: Barack Obama is hailed as a symbol of racial advancement because he is the first African American president of the United States.

- **1890s:** Racial violence is at an all-time high in the United States because Anglo-Americans feel their racial dominance threatened by the burgeoning African American quest for equality. The end of Reconstruction and the *Plessy v. Ferguson* Supreme Court decision allow the rise of Jim Crow and other segregation laws.

  Today: Although there is still racial tension in the United States, there has been an acknowledged shift towards the United States as a multicultural country with all races participating in professions and public life.

- **1890s:** African American authors have a difficult time getting published or saying what they want with white publishers. As Dunbar noted, the black journals provide African Americans a voice and are part of the struggle for freedom.

  Today: African American authors are Nobel and Pulitzer Prize winners, an accepted part of mainstream American literature, able to publish and speak freely through mainstream publishers or the many presses and journals that exclusively publish black authors' work.

"Jim Crow" laws that led to segregation of the races and deprived blacks of their civil liberties. Peonage, the practice of creditors forcing debtors to work for them, was common in the South and was criticized in Dunbar's poem "To the South on Its New Slavery." Full civil and voting rights for African Americans had to wait almost a century until the civil rights movement in the 1960s. African American historians have called the period from 1877 to the end of World War I the lowest point of race relations in America.

Black Migration to Northern Cities

After the Civil War, the United States changed rapidly from an agrarian economy to industrial capitalism. With emancipation, blacks began migrating from the South to escape poverty and racial violence to the North where there were jobs and more opportunities. The largest migrations happened after Dunbar's death, but he was one of the first to see that racism could be as virulent in the North as in the South, as he depicted in his novel *The Sport of the Gods*.

Racial Discrimination and Racial Violence

The terrorism the Ku Klux Klan and other hate groups visited on blacks in the late nineteenth and early twentieth centuries was largely ignored by both Southern and Northern whites. D. W. Griffith's film *The Birth of a Nation*, released in 1915, clearly casts the Ku Klux Klan as heroes restoring order to the South. W. E. B. DuBois, a black activist whom Dunbar admired, objected to this film as hate propaganda accepted as mainstream history. In the 1890s, when Dunbar began his career, there were hundreds of lynchings in the country. Dunbar was so appalled by this unpunished practice of mob violence that he wrote a poem "The Haunted Oak," and the short story "The Lynching of Jube Benson" in protest. Dunbar was unable to realize his dream of going to Harvard Law School and had to be satisfied with a high school education. He was forced into taking menial jobs and told flatly that newspapers and other businesses did not hire colored people.

Racial Stereotypes: Minstrels and Uncle Remus

Minstrel shows were a form of popular musical and comedy entertainment after the Civil War, lampooning blacks as stupid and superstitious. At first the parts were played by whites in blackface, but later, blacks themselves filled the roles, with stock characters like Jim Crow, Jim Dandy, and Mr. Bones. They sang and danced and spoke in Southern black dialect. Even the most liberal newspapers and magazines of the day spread racist caricatures in articles and cartoons. Popular myths about the good old South were spread in the Uncle Remus stories (1881) by a white journalist, Joel Chandler Harris, who used black folklore and dialect. Because Dunbar also used life on the plantation and black dialect for his dialect poems, he was later criticized for portraying slavery in a comic and acceptable light. Recent critics have shown that the Remus stories were stereotypes, while Dunbar's folk poems transcend such images.

Rise of the Black Middle Class

In spite of tremendous opposition, African Americans found ways to become educated and to succeed, becoming lawyers, doctors, business entrepreneurs, actors, and artists. Dunbar himself is praised as one of the first black professional author in America, able to earn a living by writing and speaking. The strategy for raising blacks to the middle class was hotly debated among black activists. Booker T. Washington (1856–1915) was a slave, but became an educator and leader of the African American community after the Civil War. He pleaded with middle-class whites to let the black race work along separate lines to develop the industrial skills they needed to support themselves economically. He was accused later by W. E. B. Du Bois (1868–1963), a black scholar and political advocate, as being an accommodationist. Although Washington won white support for blacks, he did not push for black college education and equal rights, as DuBois did.

Du Bois's famous statement that a black man lives in double consciousness, having to switch between white and black expectations, is often applied to Dunbar's situation of trying to please both white and black audiences. Du Bois was a founder of the National Association for the Advancement of Colored People (NAACP) and the first black to achieve a doctorate from Harvard; he began the push for civil rights later taken up by Dr. Martin Luther King, Jr.

"We Wear the Mask" was written the year the Supreme Court ruled in Plessy v. Ferguson. *(Jose Gil / Shutterstock.com)*

In spite of Dunbar's early poverty, he grew up in a town that was more integrated than most. Dayton, Ohio, had been the end point of the Underground Railroad and in Dunbar's youth, 10 percent of the population was black. Dunbar graduated from a white high school, where he felt completely accepted and even served as the editor of the school newspaper. He was proud to live a middle-class life with his wife, Alice, in Washington, DC, with other black professionals, a life he describes in his essay "Negro Society in Washington" in the *Saturday Evening Post* in 1901. The black middle class at this point was still segregated from white communities.

CRITICAL OVERVIEW

When Paul Laurence Dunbar published his second collection of poems, *Majors and Minors* (1895), containing "We Wear the Mask," a famous actor, James Herne, sent his copy to the established novelist and critic William Dean Howells, who praised it in *Harper's Weekly* on June 27, 1896. The day was Dunbar's twenty-fourth birthday, and overnight he found himself famous as the first genuine Negro poet of America. Although Howells's attention makes Dunbar famous, the praise does a certain amount of damage, because Howells pronounces Dunbar's standard English poems to be inferior to his dialect pieces. In his lifetime, Dunbar was never able to influence the public to take his standard English poems (such as "We Wear the Mask"), or his prose, very seriously. He established his fame as a performer of his dialect pieces.

Howells's review was slightly revised and reprinted as an introduction to Dunbar's *Lyrics of Lowly Life* in 1896 by the publisher, sealing Dunbar's critical doom. When *Lyrics of the Hearthside* was published in 1899, critics echoed Howells's earlier statements. According to E. W. Metcalf, Jr., in *Paul Laurence Dunbar: A Bibliography*, a contributor to the *Baltimore Herald* in 1899 comments: "Mr. Dunbar's choice of words is happier when he is writing in the musical speech of the Negro." Metcalf also quotes an 1899 *New York Mail and Express* critic who "praises the standard English poems as 'amateur excellence,' but the dialect poems as proving 'his eminence among the dialect writers of America.'" These critics see the standard English poems as imitative.

After Dunbar's death, his widow, Alice Dunbar, tried to correct the idea that the dialect poems represented the poet's voice, asserting that he expressed his true self in the literary poems, but this had little effect at the time. The controversy picked up in the 1920s with the new emphasis on black pride expressed by the Harlem Renaissance, making it appear that Dunbar catered to whites. The first balanced and serious criticism of Dunbar, by Benjamin Brawley in *Paul Laurence Dunbar: Poet of His People*, claims that Dunbar was a genius who was constrained by the racism of his time from speaking as he wanted to but also that he had created a landmark for other black authors with his work.

Nevertheless, the 1940s and 1950s were low points in the appreciation of Dunbar. In *Dunbar Critically Examined*, Victor Lawson declares that Dunbar was an apologist for slavery in his poetry. This charge against Dunbar was gradually erased with the revival of interest at the Centenary Conference on Dunbar in Dayton, Ohio, in 1972. Arna Bontemps, for instance, in "The Relevance of Paul Laurence Dunbar," says the controversy is bogus because Dunbar has become "a household word in the black communities," and all his poems are memorized and loved. Bontemps also noted that the poems "melt our hearts and make us one." Dunbar was also vindicated by Felton O. Best in "Paul Laurence Dunbar's Protest Literature: The Final Years," which concludes that Dunbar was "far more a part of the African American protest tradition than scholars have been led to believe." Felton shows that most of Dunbar's overt racial protest occurs in the stories and prose written between 1898 and 1906, after he achieved fame with his poetry.

CRITICISM

Susan K. Anderson

Andersen holds a Ph.D. in English literature. In the following essay, she discusses why African Americans felt they had to wear a mask of disguise in white America during the 1890s.

Henry Louis Gates, Jr., in his foreword to *In His Own Voice: The Dramatic and Other Uncollected Works of Paul Laurence Dunbar*, concludes that "no poet in the tradition was more crucial in the shaping of a distinct African American poetic diction or voice." Ironically, Paul Dunbar felt he could not express his true voice. "We Wear the Mask" elucidates the pain of his position as a black man trying to dance between black and white cultures. Daniel P. Black, in "Literary Subterfuge: Early African American Writing and the Trope of the Mask," says the mask is "the guiding trope of African American literature" and reads the poem as a "literary manifesto." Disguise is a strategy of survival, and Dunbar's masked fight for equality became a heroic legacy for African American authors and readers.

In *Democracy in America* (1835), Alexis de Tocqueville discusses the racial conflict he saw among the Anglo Americans, the Negroes, and the Indians. This racial conflict, in his analysis, kept America from being the equitable democracy it claimed to be. Native Americans seemed doomed to extinction. The Africans were enslaved, and even when they would eventually be liberated, they would not be accepted by society. De Tocqueville did not see how there could

WHAT DO I READ NEXT?

- *The Absolutely True Diary of a Part-Time Indian* by Sherman Alexie (2007) is a young-adult novel that deals with racism, poverty, and tradition and won the National Book Award. It is a semi-autobiographical story about a young cartoonist who decides to leave the reservation for a white high school.

- *The Paul Laurence Dunbar Reader: A Selection of the Best of Paul Laurence Dunbar's Poetry and Prose, including Writings Never Before Available in Book Form*, edited by Jay Martin and Gossie H. Hudson (1975), offers the reader a feeling for Dunbar's genius in multiple genres. This book began a Dunbar revival by exhibiting his work on racial themes that disproved his Uncle Tom image.

- *The Invisible Man* (1952), by African American writer Ralph Ellison, shows how prejudice makes the individual invisible in society. The book has been called the most important novel on racial stereotyping in America and verifies "We Wear the Mask" with examples of how difficult it has been for blacks to be themselves in a hostile culture.

- Anne Frank's *The Diary of a Young Girl* (1947) is the diary kept by a Dutch Jewish teen in hiding from the Nazis for two years in Amsterdam before she was betrayed in 1944 and sent to her death in a concentration camp. Her diary was found and published by her father after the war and has become world famous for depicting racial persecution.

- Gossie H. Hudson's essay "The Crowded Years: Paul Laurence Dunbar in History," in *A Singer in the Dawn: Reinterpretations of Paul Laurence Dunbar* (1975), offers historical evidence of the racism of Dunbar's time, yet shows that Dunbar did keep his racial integrity, believing that with progress, racial prejudice would die out eventually.

- *The Autobiography of an Ex-Colored Man* (1912), by Dunbar's friend James Weldon Johnson, is the fictional story of a young mulatto living in post-Reconstruction-era America in the late nineteenth and early twentieth centuries. He is forced to choose between embracing his black heritage by becoming a black ragtime musician and "passing" and living as a mediocre white man.

- *We Wear the Mask: African Americans Write American Literature, 1760–1870* (1997), edited by Rafia Zafar, shows the difficult juggling and manipulating African American authors had to endure to create an identity that could embrace both their African heritage and a place in white society. It includes the writing of Phillis Wheatley and Elizabeth Keckley, an ex-slave confidante of a First Lady.

---

ever be racial equality. His grim observation throws light on Paul Laurence Dunbar's struggle to become the first famous African American writer after Reconstruction. He was more than a poet; he became a symbol of what had seemed impossible on the American continent. On his shoulders rested centuries of slavery and racial prejudice. Dunbar paid a price for his fame and for his fragile acceptance by both black and white audiences in the 1890s, the most racially polarized period in American history.

As Cary D. Wintz points out in his introduction to *The Harlem Renaissance*, the artistic breakthroughs of black artists in the 1920s and 1930s were possible because of the work of those nineteenth-century authors such as Frederick Douglass, William Well Brown, James Weldon Johnson, Charles Waddell Chesnutt, and especially Paul Laurence Dunbar. If the Harlem Renaissance was an open statement of racial pride, it had been preceded by decades of difficult experimentation. What would an authentic African

"DISGUISE IS A STRATEGY OF SURVIVAL, AND DUNBAR'S MASKED FIGHT FOR EQUALITY BECAME A HEROIC LEGACY FOR AFRICAN AMERICAN AUTHORS AND READERS."

American literature look like? Would it be a black version of mainstream America, or would it be based on African folk tradition? Dunbar put a foot in both directions, testing the waters. The volume in which "We Wear the Mask" appears, *Majors and Minors,* included poems in literary English in the prevailing style of Tennyson. Dunbar referred to these poems as "Majors" because he felt with them he was on an equal footing with any Anglo-American poet, using the same language and verse form and often the same subject matter. He called his dialect poems that imitated the speech of plantation slaves, "Minors," because to him they were merely colorful folk poems.

William Dean Howells, the white critic who made Dunbar famous, decided the "Minor" poems were the true voice of Dunbar and suggested this would be the future direction of African American writers. Howells proclaimed the standard English poems to be imitative and the dialect poems to be original and fresh. Dunbar was made out to be the Negro Poet Laureate, the black Robert Burns, based on his folk poems. Later black writers, from the Harlem Renaissance in the 1920s to the civil rights movement in the 1960s, rejected the dialect poems and Dunbar for writing them. They seemed to represent the stereotypes that blacks had tried to overcome. The use of dialect was popular in the nineteenth century in the work of Mark Twain and James Whitcomb Riley. Dunbar wrote the dialect poems to preserve historical stories he had heard of old slave days from his parents. He did not think they defined the race or the future of African American writing, nor did he defend slavery in them. Often, the dialect poems indirectly satirize the white masters, such as in "When Malindy Sings." Dunbar complained to his wife, Alice, that he felt his true voice was in the standard English poems. That is where serious statements on race occur, such as in "Sympathy," "The Haunted Oak," and "Ode to Ethiopia."

The writers of the Harlem Renaissance integrated Dunbar's use of both formal English and black dialect to create their masterpieces. Today, critics agree with Dunbar that his authentic voice does occur in his standard English writing, both poetry and prose, but only because his complete work has finally been published and examined. In the decade of his fame, 1896–1906, white publishers mostly wanted his plantation dialect poems because they were popular. He felt he could not truly be heard because white publishers and readers had a preconception of what a black author should write. He had actually experimented with voice, meter, and genre, producing songs, plays, novels, short stories, and poems in several dialects, as well as serious standard-English lyrics.

Above all, he did not want to be seen as an example of race, but as an artist. Howells meant to help Dunbar in his review, revised as the introduction to *Lyrics of a Lowly Life,* saying Dunbar's poetry would tear down the walls of racial prejudice and prove the unity of the human race. His backhanded compliments, however, seem strange to a modern ear; for instance, his insistence on the blackness of Dunbar's skin. Howells felt bound to certify to a white audience that Dunbar was not a mulatto and could write real poetry despite the fact he had not one drop of white blood. This testimony is reminiscent of the trial Phillis Wheatley was forced to undergo before a panel of white judges to certify she was indeed intelligent enough to be the author of her poetry. Such insults show the degree of racial prejudice and misunderstanding at the time.

Wintz talks of the difficulty of black authors getting published, and both Dunbar and Chesnutt were successful because they told plantation stories in dialect, only one step beyond the minstrel shows whites could grasp. Wintz says, "They were far less successful when they challenged these conventions, and especially when they addressed issues of race and racial oppression." Now that all of Dunbar's work is printed, his protest literature stands out more clearly. In recent anthologies, it is mostly the racial statements by Dunbar that are extracted and remembered. He has been exonerated by contemporary critics from being an accommodationist, yet they ask, why did he not write more poems like "We Wear the Mask," "Ode to Ethiopia," and

"Sympathy"? Why does he not sound more like the Harlem Renaissance writers? The answer is in the poem itself, "We Wear the Mask." Dunbar lived in a dangerous time, thirty years earlier than the Harlem Renaissance, when the Civil War memory was so raw, the lynching of blacks was not even punished.

In "Behind the Mask: Paul Laurence Dunbar's Poetry in Literary English," Allan B. Fox calls "We Wear the Mask" an act of "rare courage" showing "the predicament of a man 'of color' in a white society." Joanne Braxton, in her introduction to *The Collected Poetry of Paul Laurence Dunbar*, asserts that in "We Wear the Mask," Dunbar drops the racial mask momentarily to draw the reader "into the inner circle of the black community" to reveal that blacks are not the grinning and dancing primitives most whites wanted to think them. She includes Dunbar's use of irony and humor as part of his literary mask.

In *Paul Laurence Dunbar*, Peter Revell calls "We Wear the Mask" perhaps Dunbar's "finest poem" because it is "a moving cry from the heart of suffering," an "apologia" for all the lies he had to tell to survive. Revell says the poem anticipates the confessions of later black authors who speak from what W. E. B. DuBois called "double-consciousness, this sense of always looking at one's self through the eyes of others, of measuring one's soul by the tape of a world that looks on in amused contempt and pity." DuBois described this experience in *The Soul of Black Folk* (1903), of having two warring identities, as a black and as an American.

This is an early statement on what has now become commonplace for most postcolonial authors who speak with ethnic voices in the language of the former enemy. This double consciousness of identity accounts for Dunbar's "poetry of segregated linguistic domains," as Harryette Mullen calls his two styles in "'When he is least himself': Dunbar and Double Consciousness in African American Poetry." He was African in the dialect poems and a serious American author in literary English, but he did not want to participate in or create a segregated literature. He wanted the freedom to be seen as an artist and move in any direction he imagined.

Dunbar often used his journalism to contradict misconceptions about the black race. In an interview in 1898 with *New York Commercial* called "Negro in Literature," Dunbar says that black poetry will not be essentially different from white poetry. It will not be imitative, but it may sound familiar because "our life is now the same." This is a plea for the kind of integrated society Americans enjoy today. He adds that he hopes no one will make blacks write in only one way, about plantation life in dialect. He also prophetically speaks of the races influencing one another in their artistic pursuits, and this is now an accepted fact. Black and white artists have freely borrowed from one another, making the idea of segregated art—a distinction Howells unthinkingly implies in his review by embracing only the authenticity of black dialect—a ludicrous falsehood.

In "Booker T. Washington," an unpublished article he wrote, Dunbar gives a reason for having to wear a mask in his life and writing. "We have been despised and abused," he says. "We have been misjudged and hated," but from the time blacks became literate and could publish their own words, they gained credibility. The more the black race succeeded, the more they were oppressed: "If we are more hated, it is because we are more formidable." Booker T. Washington, he claimed, was a hero in "the pioneer work of our advancement," and of course, so was Dunbar as a poet and a journalist.

Several critics have seen Dunbar's mask as the metaphor of the trickster. Daniel P. Black says "We Wear the Mask" describes "black writers as 'mask manipulators,' 'double talkers,' and 'word wizards.'" Lillian and Greg Robinson, in "Paul Laurence Dunbar: A Credit to His Race?," give an overview of Dunbar's shifting reputation over the last century. Once reviled as an Uncle Tom trying to be white, today he is often seen as a "trickster" capable of both "transgression and respectability," purposely playing a double game. In *The Trickster*, Harold Bloom says the figure of the trickster is universal and an "archetype of the survivor." The trickster is well known in African folklore and remains in the Americanized version of Brer Rabbit. The trickster is also prevalent in Native American cultures and has been used as a conscious literary stance by Indian poet Sherman Alexie to point out racial injustice.

Whether Dunbar purposely wore a mask as a writer to mislead or whether he felt it forced on him, he did not wear it defensively. James A. Emmanuel, in "Racial Fire in the Poetry of Paul Laurence Dunbar," discusses Dunbar's

Many southern African Americans were sharecroppers at the time the poem was written. (Brian Weed / Shutterstock.com)

racial anger and sees "We Wear the Mask" as admitting to "lying to white people," a theme that prefigures he work of Ralph Ellison's *The Invisible Man.* Saunders Redding speaks of Dunbar's bitterness at not being able to express himself more openly in "Portrait against Background." However, Redding concludes that, despite the obstacles, Dunbar was successful in portraying "the fragility of the human spirit yearning toward the ideal. And that, I submit, is enough."

Source: Susan K. Andersen, Critical Essay on "We Wear the Mask," in *Poetry for Students*, Gale, Cengage Learning, 2012.

Nadia Nurhussein

In the following essay, Nurhussein examines the issues that have led to claims of inauthenticity in Dunbar's poetry, including his emulation of James Whitcomb Riley and his conflict between dialect and literary.

When the Western Association of Writers convened in Paul Laurence Dunbar's hometown of Dayton, Ohio, in 1892, he read a welcome address in verse, which included the following lines:

> So, proud are you who claim the West
> As home land; doubly are you blest
> To live where liberty and health
> Go hand and hand with brains and wealth. (ll.9–12)

Throughout the poem, Dunbar uses the second person in greeting the Midwesterners in the audience, leaving room to question whether he would include himself among them as a "Western" writer, but the poem ends with his offering his own "welcome warm as Western wine, / And free as Western hearts" (ll.23–24). In fact, Dunbar saw his dialect work as belonging, at least in part, to a Midwestern American literary tradition. Moreover, a conspicuously Midwestern tradition of African American art and literature was beginning to develop in the last years of the nineteenth century. Many of the African American poets writing around the turn of the century, including James Edwin Campbell, James David Corrothers, and sibling poets Aaron Belford Thompson, Priscilla Jane Thompson, and Clara Ann Thompson, lived in the Midwest for most or all of their lives. Several of them looked to James Whitcomb Riley, one of the most

> IN EXPLOITING THE INCOMPATIBILITIES AND DISSONANCES BETWEEN WRITTEN AND SPOKEN COMMUNICATION, BETWEEN PERSONAL AND PUBLIC MODES, AND BETWEEN SILENT AND PERFORMATORY READING, DUNBAR UNCOVERED A PECULIAR POETRY READING EXPERIENCE."

famous Midwesterners of the era, as a profound influence upon their work.

After receiving an encouraging letter from Riley following the Western Association of Writers reading, Dunbar and his reputation would come to be associated with the then-established Riley for decades to come. In 1898, enthusiastic rumors were circulating that the two were collaborating on a comic opera. The fantasy pairing made sense: Dunbar and Riley were among the best-selling poets of the 1890s, and their dialect verse shares a nostalgic sentimentality as well as a distinctly Midwestern sensibility. Dunbar's false southernness now seems to us one of the most glaringly inauthentic elements of his poetry, part of a general inauthenticity that readers now find jarring.

Dunbar's inauthenticity can be understood as the consequence of two strategies. The first is his attempt early on to model himself after Riley not only in style, dialect, and theme, but also in performances—performances that, in Dunbar's case, were produced and reinterpreted in the imagined tension between regionalist and African American literature. The second is his attempt to view dialect's perceived orality through the lens of literacy in a way that Riley did not. The centrality of Dunbar's "We Wear the Mask" to his oeuvre has prompted many readers of Dunbar to call upon the mask metaphor in describing his poetics, but the mask may not be the most fitting way to describe Dunbar's experiments with written language. Dunbar's often subtle orthographic experimentation, the means by which he manipulates readers into enacting contradictions and impossibilities, works to refute the possibility of authentic expression in any poetic mode.

In his attempts to view orality through literacy, Dunbar introduces literate modes of communication such as letter writing into what is ordinarily treated as a doubly oral genre—doubly because both dialect and poetry. The epistolary dialect poem written by a fictional character appears to be Dunbar's innovation, signaling a departure from a Rileyesque dialect poetry. This subgenre of dialect poetry, one of Dunbar's most noteworthy experiments, is impossible in theory. The form put pressure on the concept of Dunbar as the genuine article, allowing him to circumvent the authenticity trap of dialect poetry and expanding the dialect poetry genre to include literate navigations of orality.

Despite the fact that the letter is a literate form of communication, the intention behind the language used by Dunbar's dialect letter-writer seems to be to represent his or her own speech phonetically. As a result, the epistolary dialect poem serves as a microcosm of the issues involved in writing dialect poetry. In Dunbar's case, the incompatibility of using a literate form to express speech in a dialect letter invokes the parallel larger-scale incompatibility of using a literate form to express speech in dialect poetry generally. The letter-writer stands in for the poet and makes decisions that mirror the dialect poet's. What Dunbar is doing, in essence, is making the speakers of his epistolary dialect poems into dialect poets themselves. To transcribe speech, these characters would have to be accomplished enough in written English to experiment with it and to recognize where speech departs from writing. Dunbar's choice to represent his character's writing not as illiterate but as simultaneously dialect and highly literate resists the association of dialect-speaking with illiteracy fundamental to so much contemporaneous dialect poetry.

The reading experience Dunbar directs his readers to have, then, is a conflicted one: readers cannot recite the epistolary dialect poem as a dramatic monologue because, simply put, no one can be speaking. Letters, as private communication, are usually written and read silently, in the absence of the addressee and writer respectively. Dunbar's choice of the letter as a model for these poems highlights a tension between a traditional dialect poetry that is performatory and an emerging dialect poetry of silent literacy. His epistolary dialect poem forces its readers to experience an admittedly inauthentic performance, to sense the resistance between the inclination to read dialect aloud and the inclination to read letters silently. In other words, Dunbar effectively makes recitation of these pieces problematic. In so doing, he emphasizes the continuities and tensions between orality and literacy in dialect poetry in general.

Dunbar's reception, in its significant difference from that of Riley (whose characters audiences were willing to treat as inventions), appears to have increased his awareness of the inauthenticity of dialect performance. But even before his emergence on the national stage, Dunbar was pushing his poetry in the direction of inauthenticity. The epistolary dialect poem became for Dunbar a subgenre that would make silent literacy both a crucial and an explicit part of dialect poetry. Although he derived many of his dialect and performance practices from Riley, Dunbar was able to break from him precisely for this reason: because Dunbar's imitations of Riley's dialects were perceived as artificial while his imitations of black southern dialects were praised as authentic, Dunbar turned to making the artifice of the entire endeavor clear, projecting representations of speech onto literate forms in ways that Riley did not, and producing as a result a more complex dialect poetry.

The first stanza of one of Dunbar's uncollected epistolary dialect poems, "Happy! Happy! Happy!," consists of a letter written by a woman (Mandy) to her presumably less educated lover (Julius), ending the relationship. The stanza is followed by five lines that serve as a curious transition in an ambiguous voice, and a third stanza, Julius's response.

"Dear Julius" I've been cogitating,
Long before expatiating,
On the hopeless alterations,
In our mutual relations;
Having mounted in position,
To a loftier condition,
And because I cannot flattah
I must say you are "non grata."

Happy, happy, oh my best of queens,
Makes me feel as mealy as a pot of beans!
Tell you what's the matter
I'm my lady's own "non grata"
An' I'm happy, happy, happy cause I do not know
   what it means.

Dear Mandy I been readin'
With a pleasure most exceedin'
All the pleasant bits of writin'
Dat yo' han' has been inditin'

But you mo' dan fill my measure
Wid de sugar-drip of pleasure,
When you say without a flattah,
I's you' lovin' own "non grata."

Julius's response is written in literary dialect, but Mandy's initial letter is not (with one exception, to which I will return in a moment). Mandy's vocabulary consists of Latinate words ("cogitating," "expatiating," "alterations"), ending finally in an actual Latin phrase ("non grata"). The excessive and often unnecessary commas end-stopping the lines of her stanza contribute to the exaggerated hypotaxis, underscoring the relative scarcity of commas in Julius's stanza. Although it "looks standard," her dialect should not be understood as neutral. The poem mocks the educated woman; she is parodied as a snob. Her dialect, including her pretentious word choice and her awkwardly complex grammar, may be due to her "Having mounted in position / To a loftier condition," making Julius now "non grata" (ll.5–6, 8). In other words, she finds her status new and unfamiliar, and her assumption of this self-important and affected persona, along with its language, fits imperfectly. As much as her language reveals a desperate desire for propriety, her letter writing defies the etiquette rules given in most 19th-century letter-writing guides. Mandy's use of Latinate words in this rejection would be considered an effort to "produce an effect through fine words [that], the manuals warned, should be abandoned for the simple art of expressing true feeling" (Halttunen 119). Take, for example, these instructions from *Miss Leslie's Behavior Book, a Guide and Manual for Ladies*: "The 'wording' of your letter should be as much like conversation as possible, containing (in a condensed form) just what you would be most likely to talk about if you saw your friend," and always avoiding a tone that is "affectedly didactic" (Leslie 166).

Mandy's affected language has dramatic consequences in the poem: we find in the third stanza that Julius apparently misunderstands her letter. He claims that reading her rejection gives him "pleasure." In fact, the word "pleasure" appears twice in the stanza, along with its variant "pleasant," mimicking the triple repetition of "Happy" in the poem's title and in the last line of the second stanza. His letter mirrors Mandy's structurally, especially in its last couplet, but the words ending the lines here are fairly common ones, and three ("readin'," "writin'," and "inditin'") are, not surprisingly, terms related to literacy. If literary dialect is frequently used to give a character the illusion of illiteracy, altering spelling to represent neither a letter-writer's so-called nonstandard speech nor his illiterate writing is what makes this poem substantially different from more conventional dialect poems.

Again, the larger question looming over our readings of this poem is how a person's speech could be reflected in writing a letter, as no letter-writer would write "readin'" unless he or she was purposely diverging from written language. Dunbar forces the poem's representations of speech to challenge the status of standard English. Mandy's letter contains one word in dialect—"flattah" (1.7)—and it is the only word repeated in Julius's stanza aside from its rhyme word ("non grata" 1.8). When we first encounter "flattah," in the context of Mandy's standard English stanza, it is likely to register for most readers as a representation of a form of standard English. We are coaxed into thinking that Mandy speaks it as well as "writes" it. Because of the social difference Mandy introduces as a means of defining her relationship with Julius, readers are led to perceive Mandy's "flattah" as something different from Julius's "flattah." However, our eyes tell us that this is not the case. Dunbar's approach to dialect grows out of his awareness of the prestige dialect as a dialect. Most dialect poetry, in its focus on what are thought of as nonstandard dialects, regards standard dialects as nothing more than the spoken articulation of written language. As such, standard dialects are presumed to be closer to writing. Although Dunbar rarely represents the speech of his standard-English-speaking characters phonetically, as he does here with Mandy's "flattah," his decision to represent Mandy's speech exactly as he represents Julius's (if only for a moment) in effect turns standard English into dialect.

The second stanza seems to be written in Julius's voice, but here the dialect is closer to standard ("I's" in the third stanza is "I'm" in the second). Significantly, "matter" (1.11) is allowed to rhyme with "non grata." Instead of changing the spelling to "mattah," mirroring the phonetic "flattah" in Mandy's and Julius's letters, this stanza allows for nonstandard pronunciation to be represented by standard spellings. A manuscript of the poem shows that, in a working draft, Dunbar toyed with the possibility of writing the line differently—"Tell you what's de mattah"—and the change is a major revision in terms of reading this stanza as transitional. The change to "matter" in the typescript shows that Dunbar intended, through ridding the stanza of most visual markers of dialect, to lead his reader away from the thought that Julius or Mandy would be speaking in this stanza. Moreover, rhyming "matter" with "non grata" urges the reader to pronounce the word without a post-vocalic -r, a pronunciation that could signal any number of English language dialects, some socially privileged and some not. Our perspective shifts. If a reader pronounces "matter" without the "r," he or she will not balk at rhyming the two words. One who does pronounce "matter" with an "r," on the other hand, will become aware of the fact that the poem is treating what is usually, in the United States, the nonstandard pronunciation here as the standard.

Perhaps the strongest evidence of Dunbar's experimentation with dialect perspective is the ambiguity of the last line of this second stanza. If we understand the speaker of this stanza to be Julius, the more plausible choice, the line finally makes no sense: presumably he is happy not because of his ignorance, which is what the line means literally, but because he thinks it is a good thing to be "non grata." The second clause of the line as it appears in the manuscript ("An' I'm happy, happy, happy cause I do' know what it means") makes a coherent reading of Julius's response even more difficult. Reading "do' know" as an elision of "don't know" leaves the poem comic, because Julius is portrayed as a fool. Reading it, on the other hand, as "do know" (with an extraneous apostrophe) may not explain Julius's happiness—unless he was eager to get out of the relationship—but it does mean that Julius is much more knowledgeable than he appears to be. Julius's knowledge of the fact that Mandy's letter is a rejection becomes clear, and this insight, of course, colors our reading of the tone of the final stanza. His letter to Mandy could be sarcastic, or it could be spiteful, but it is no longer foolish. The dialect speaker is not the fool of the poem; instead, it is Mandy, whose pretentiousness is satirized by both Dunbar and Julius.

In exploiting the incompatibilities and dissonances between written and spoken communication, between personal and public modes, and between silent and performatory reading, Dunbar uncovered a peculiar poetry reading experience. The epistolary dialect poem was for Dunbar a productive experiment to test at how many levels of remove he could stand above the poem, to treat dialect not quite as a single mask but as a series of Russian dolls, with Dunbar as dialect poet able to give birth to other dialect poets. It is perhaps in these poems that we sense most perceptibly Dunbar's distance from the surface. Alice Dunbar-Nelson's refutation, in 1914, of Howell's assessment of Dunbar's dialect poetry (she maintained that "it was in the pure English poems that the poet most expressed himself," 124) has persisted as a way of devaluing it and, throughout the twentieth century, readers have faulted Dunbar's dialect poetry for its inauthenticity. Dialect poetry, Henry Louis Gates, Jr., has argued, generally "failed when it tried to cram a live, spoken form into a rigid, written one, oblivious to its internal logic, unaware of its linguistic possibilities, technically inadequate to preserve the poetry as spirit" (190). Consequently, he writes, it "choked and wasted a spirit and produced a mediocre body of trivia" (190). The tension produced by this incompatibility and coercion is precisely what deserves further attention. Dunbar's epistolary dialect poem did not waste an existing form; it developed a new, productive, and strangely complex one.

Source: Nadia Nurhussein, "Paul Laurence Dunbar's Performances and the Epistolary Dialect Poem," in *African American Review*, Vol. 41, No. 2, Summer 2007, pp. 233–38.

Joanne Gabbin

In the following essay, Gabbin probes the idea that Dunbar's unfulfilled personal life was subject matter for his poetry.

>...Then Br'er Adams, a white-haired patriarch, knelt and "took up the cross."—"Anner 'Lizer's Stumblin' Block" (Dunbar, *Best Stories*)

Much of the poetry of Paul Laurence Dunbar reveals the intimate intercessions of a tormented poet, figuratively "taking up the cross." Dunbar's meteoric rise as the most famous black writer in the world at the end of the nineteenth century, his prolific offerings over a short 14-year career (1892–1906), his ambivalence about the branding of his own poetic genius, his precarious stardom in a society that insisted on "separate-but-equal" race relations, and his tragic, unfulfilled personal

" DUNBAR'S PERSONALITY ALLOWS FOR BROAD SWEEPS, FROM CHEERY OPTIMISM TO DEPRESSION."

life represent the subject matter of many intimate intercessions with which the poet wrestled emotionally and spiritually.

Named for the Apostle Paul, the Biblical figure who helped to establish the Christian church, Dunbar took seriously his parents' charge to be a great man who would carry the word to his people. Like Paul, Dunbar suffered as the chosen expounder of his own gospel, the African American literary tradition. Though he experimented with many literary traditions and read extensively the works of Tennyson, Shakespeare, Byron, Shelley, and Poe, among others, he was painfully aware that his own work inspired a debate on the merits of his standard English works as opposed to his more popular dialect pieces that appeared to some too close to the minstrel and plantation traditions. Sterling Brown, in his book *Negro Poetry and Drama* (1937), considered Dunbar a highly gifted man who "took up the Negro peasant as a clown, and made him a likeable person." Brown recognized that Dunbar benefited from a heritage of folk sense that poured out in "flashes of unforced gay humor," "well-turned folk phrases," and "virtuoso rhythms." However, Brown believed that Dunbar was too strongly influenced by the local color poetry of Irwin Russell and the plantation formula of Thomas Nelson Page, and consequently compromised his interpretation of folk life by omitting mention of the hardships that were undoubtedly a part of it. On the other side of the debate, according to Herbert Woodward Martin and Ronald Primeau in the introduction to their book, *In His Own Voice* (2002), "Dunbar wrote about the difficult questions of progress after emancipation, the adjustments of reconstruction, the perils and the promise of migration to Northern cities, the paradoxes of portraying 'Negro' life authentically while a residue of stereotypes remained strong in the society on the whole" (xix). In truth, Dunbar's poetic sensibility led him to subtle uses of irony and veiled allusions to racial dilemmas as he steadily made incursions against the dominant stereotypes of his day.

However, there were other, more personal challenges in Dunbar's life. He wrestled with the thorns of the flesh: chronic health problems that dogged him until his early death, medically-induced alcoholism, self-hatred, latent misogyny, and depression. Though I do not insist that his poems are personal chronicles of his own life, I do, however, advance that Dunbar's poems echo the complex emotional and spiritual sensibility that penned them. In *The Collected Poetry of Paul Laurence Dunbar*, "A Prayer" illustrates his poetic genius coming to terms with a deep sense of something more than this world. The poem also reveals a poet honing an authentic voice, shaped by both romantic and realistic views of life, and mastering a variety of tones, rhythms, and nuances that are at the heart of his genius.

Significantly, Dunbar's poetry gives witness to an intensely religious sensibility that has been shaped in part by the cultural forms, rituals, and beliefs of the black church. Maturing during a period that saw the revival of the so-called Negro spirituals with the work of the Fisk Jubilee Singers, Dunbar heard the eloquent prayers and sermons of near-illiterate church folk barely one generation removed from slavery. As they had firmly accepted the Bible as their spiritual road map, Dunbar created characters in his fiction as well as his poetry who were exhorters of the Word. In the novel *The Uncalled* and such stories as "Old Abe's Conversion," "Anner 'Lizer's Stumblin' Block," and "The Walls of Jericho," we can readily see Dunbar's fascination with folk religion and may be reminded that he seriously considered becoming a minister himself (Brawley xv). In two of his most anthologized poems, "We Wear the Mask" and "Sympathy," Dunbar reveals his reliance on Christian faith as balm for a complex soul often pulled between sin and penance. As Dunbar ingeniously captures the ubiquitous racial patterns of masking, dissimulation, and double consciousness in "We Wear the Mask," we hear:

> We smile, but, O great Christ, our cries
> To thee from tortured souls arise.
> We sing, but oh the clay is vile
> Beneath our feet, and long the mile;
> But let the world dream otherwise,
> We wear the mask! (11.10–15)

Likewise, in "Sympathy" Dunbar grasps the universal cry for freedom, the inevitable theme of African American literature since black poets tried to sing in a strange land. The speaker in the poem metaphorically becomes the caged bird beating its wings against bars that do not give way:

> I know why the caged bird sings, ah me,
> When his wing is bruised and his bosom sore,—
> When he beats his bars and he would be free;
> It is not a carol of joy or glee,
> But a prayer that he sends from his heart's deep core,
> But a plea, that upward to Heaven he flings—
> I know why the caged bird sings! (11.15–21)

In many significant ways Dunbar's poetry is that "prayer that he sends from his heart's deep core." The ritual of praying, a strength of the black church, can act as a frame for discovering four defining patterns in his poetry.

Any authentic prayer in the traditional black church has at least four parts: (1) praise and thanksgiving, (2) confession and sorrow for sins, (3) intercessions or entreaty on behalf of others, and (4) eschatological concerns with death and an afterlife. Black Baptist and Pentecostal churches, especially in the South, maintain a time-honored pattern of praying, often recognizable by such wording as:

> To the God of Abraham, Isaac and Jacob,
> To the Maker of Heaven and Earth,
> Who laid the foundations of the world,
> Thank you for waking me up in my right mind.
> Thank you that my bed was not my winding board.
> Thank you that my sheet was not my shroud.
> Thank you for the articulation of my limbs . . .
> When I've run my last race, sung my last song, prayed my last
> prayer,
> Give me a home in your kingdom
> Where the worried shall cease from troubling
> And the weary shall be at rest. (Trad.)

Many of Dunbar's poems fit neatly into one of these categories. Whether writing about the valor and martyrdom of "The Colored Soldiers" or the dedication and leadership of "Frederick Douglass" or "Robert Gould Shaw" or the beauty and grace of "Alice" or the virtuoso sound "When Malindy Sings," Dunbar produced a significant body of work emanating a racial pride that would not be submerged in a sea of racist stereotypes and plantation tradition nostalgia. In fact, many of his best loved poems, such as "In the Morning," "Little Brown Baby," "The Party," "An Ante-bellum Sermon," "A Negro Love Song," and "When De Co'n Pone's Hot," are more than "jingles in a broken tongue." They encode Dunbar's realization that what some could see only as representations of happy slaves were for him finely drawn portraits of those who survived the devastating institution of slavery with their humanity in tact. In Dunbar's mind, it seems, their triumph of spirit is attributable to the God Force in their lives, as depicted in his poem "God Reigns": "There sways an arm of fearless might—/ 'God reigns and right shall rule'" (11.31–32).

If we look closely at some Dunbar poems that could fall under the rubric "Sorrow for Sin" or confessional poems, it is clear that Dunbar was aware of the mandates of the religion he embraced. That knowledge of sin and transgressions, of which he often made light, convicted him mightily when his own transgressions nipped at his heels, as in "Accountability," "Temptation," and "How Lucy Backslid." He could not shuffle around the alcoholism and philandering that had defiled him. He had to live with the knowledge that his romantic relationship with Alice Ruth Moore, which was to emulate the romance of Elizabeth Barrett and Robert Browning, was forever fractured when he raped her before their wedding vows were pronounced. As much as Dunbar wished to take back that awful act, that sin, no matter his atonement, would haunt him until his death. Dunbar reveals a similar sensibility in "The Pool":

> But, oh I've a wish in my soul, dear love,
> (The wish of a dreamer, it seems,)
> That I might wash free of my sins, dear love,
> In the pool that I see in my dreams. (11.9–12)

Dunbar's personality allows for broad sweeps, from cheery optimism to depression. In such poems as "The Wraith," "Resignation," "She Told Her Beads," "Parted," "Melancholia," and "Conscience and Remorse," Dunbar has his speakers occupy the gray spaces of melancholia and remorse.

However, in the third grouping that I am calling "Intercessions," our gaze turns from the interiority of Dunbar's speakers' confessionals to intercessory meditations. Dunbar came into manhood during one of the gloomiest periods in African American history. In 1883 the US Supreme Court declared the 1875 Civil Rights Act unconstitutional and later legalized Jim Crow segregation in the 1896 *Plessy v. Ferguson* case. While the great warrior Frederick Douglass was still trying to counter resurgent Confederate power by bringing the plight and progress of Black Americans to the world scene at the 1892 Columbia Exposition, Ida B. Wells used her pen to expose horrific accounts of some of the 1,000 lynchings of men, women, and children that occurred between 1882 and 1892. Wells, in a moment of deep despair, wrote in her journal, "If I could, I would take my race in my arms and fly away."

Dunbar, using the greatest weapon that he had, the power of the word, did take his people in his arms. In "To Miss Mary Britton," for example, we hear Dunbar petitioning God to reward this woman for her valiant stand against a separate-coach bill in the early 1890s:

> Give us to lead our cause
> More noble souls like hers,
> The memory of whose deed
> Each feeling bosom stirs;
> Whose fearless voice and strong
> Rose to defend her race,
> Roused Justice from her sleep,
> Drove Prejudice from place. (ll.17–24)

"The Death of the First Born," "The Dedication of Dorothy Hall," and "The Unsung Heroes" are just a few of the poems in which Dunbar's speakers make entreaty for others with a pathos directed at honoring the dead and celebrating life grown out of sacrifice.

Finally, many of his poems deal with eschatological concerns—death and ultimate things. Dunbar's preoccupation with death and dying can be documented by the preponderance of poems in *The Collected Poetry of Paul Laurence Dunbar* that have death as the prominent theme. "Compensation," "Ere Sleep Comes Down to Soothe the Weary Eyes," "After While," "The Right to Die," and "Mortality" are simply a few of the poems that show Dunbar pondering death and what remains after the human slips the mortal coil.

Unfortunately, the many challenges he faced in life made death a welcome friend. Dunbar's struggles with illness from an early age were only equaled by his psychological struggles with race prejudice. The racism that had relegated the shining star of Dayton's Central High School to a job of an elevator operator had also led his famous critic, William Dean Howells, to define Dunbar's literary genius by the absence of miscegenation in his ancestry. Dunbar's own deeply rooted double consciousness pulled him between pride of his racial heritage and disdain for his black skin. As tuberculosis scarred his lungs and his excessive drinking did not cure him but hastened his death, he pined for a love that he had once won and had thrown away. As Eleanor Alexander reports in *Lyrics of Sunshine and Shadow: The Tragic Courtship and Marriage of Paul Laurence Dunbar and Alice Ruth Moore*, Dunbar died without knowing that his estranged wife still loved him.

Despite the tragic circumstances of his life, Dunbar succeeded in demonstrating a poetic genius that had never been seen on this side of the Atlantic. He will be remembered for wresting from the shame of slavery the humanity of those who endured it; he will be remembered for witnessing the faith that had brought so many black people from harm's way to safety. In the poem "When All Is Done," he writes his own epitaph, a reflection of a life grown deep with resolution:

> When all is done, say not my day is o'er,
> And that thro' night I seek a dimmer shore:
> Say rather that my morn has just begun,—
> I greet the dawn and not a setting sun,
> When all is done. (11.13–17)

Source: Joanne Gabbin, "Intimate Intercessions in the Poetry of Paul Laurence Dunbar," in *African American Review*, Vol. 41, No. 2, Summer 2007, pp. 227–31.

SOURCES

Best, Felton O., "Paul Laurence Dunbar's Protest Literature: The Final Years," in *Western Journal of Black Studies*, Vol. 17, No. 1, Spring 1993, p. 54.

Black, Daniel P., "Literary Subterfuge: Early African American Writing and the Trope of the Mask," in *CLA Journal*, Vol. 48, No. 4, 2005, p. 388.

Bloom, Harold, "Introduction," in *The Trickster*, edited by Harold Bloom, Infobase Publishing, 2010, p. xv.

Bontemps, Arna, "The Relevance of Paul Laurence Dunbar," in *A Singer in the Dawn: Reinterpretations of Paul Laurence Dunbar*, edited by Jay Martin, Dodd, Mead, 1975, p. 45.

Brawley, Benjamin, *Paul Laurence Dunbar: Poet of His People*, University of North Carolina Press, Kennikat Press, 1967, pp. 4, 37, 76.

Braxton, Joanne M., "Introduction," in *The Collected Poetry of Paul Laurence Dunbar*, University Press of Virginia, 1993, p. xxii.

de Tocqueville, Alexis, "Chapter XVIII: The Present and Probable Future Condition of the Three Races That Inhabit the Territory of the United States," in *Democracy in America*, Vol. 1, Alfred A. Knopf, 1960, pp. 331–434.

DuBois, W. E. B., *The Souls of Black Folk*, CreateSpace, 2010.

Dunbar, Paul Laurence, "Booker T. Washington," in *In His Own Voice: The Dramatic and Other Uncollected Works of Paul Laurence Dunbar*, edited by Herbert Woodward Martin and Ronald Primeau, Ohio University Press, 2002, pp. 208–209.

———, "Negro in Literature," in *In His Own Voice: The Dramatic and Other Uncollected Works of Paul Laurence Dunbar*, edited by Herbert Woodward Martin and Ronald Primeau, Ohio University Press, 2002, p. 206; originally published in *New York Commercial*, 1898.

———, "We Wear the Mask," in *The Complete Poems of Paul Laurence Dunbar*, Dodd, Mead, 1940, p. 71.

Emmanuel, James, "Racial Fire in the Poetry of Paul Laurence Dunbar," in *A Singer in the Dawn: Reinterpretations of Paul Laurence Dunbar*, edited by Jay Martin, Dodd, Mead, 1975, p. 88.

Fox, Allan B., "Behind the Mask: Paul Laurence Dunbar's Poetry in Literary English," in *Texas Quarterly*, Vol. 14, No. 2, 1971, p. 18.

Gates, Henry Louis, Jr., "Foreword," in *In His Own Voice: The Dramatic and Other Uncollected Works of Paul Laurence Dunbar*, edited by Herbert Woodward Martin and Ronald Primeau, Ohio University Press, 2002, p. xii.

Howells, William Dean, "Introduction to *Lyrics of Lowly Life*," in *The Complete Poems of Paul Laurence Dunbar*, Dodd, Mead, 1940, pp. vii–x.

Lawson, Victor, *Dunbar Critically Examined*, Associated Publishers, 1941, p. 78.

Metcalf, E. W., Jr., *Paul Laurence Dunbar: A Bibliography*, Scarecrow Press, 1975, pp. 131–33.

Mullen, Harryette, "'When He Is Least Himself': Dunbar and Double Consciousness in African American Poetry," in *African American Review*, Vol. 41, No. 2, 2007, p. 278.

Redding, Saunders, "Portrait against Background," in *A Singer in the Dawn: Reinterpretations of Paul Laurence Dunbar*, edited by Jay Martin, Dodd, Mead, 1975, p. 44.

Revell, Peter, *Paul Laurence Dunbar*, Twayne's United States Author Series, No. 298, Twayne Publishers, 1979, pp. 52–53, 71, 90–91, 93, 190.

Robinson, Greg, and Lillian Robinson, "Paul Laurence Dunbar: A Credit to His Race?," in *African American Review*, Vol. 41, No. 2, 2007, p. 215.

Turner, Darwin T., "The Poet and the Myths," in *A Singer in the Dawn: Reinterpretations of Paul Laurence Dunbar*, edited by Jay Martin, Dodd, Mead, 1975, pp. 59–74.

Wintz, Cary D., "Introduction: A Historical Overview of the Harlem Renaissance," in *The Harlem Renaissance: An Anthology*, edited by Cary D. Wintz, Brandywine Press, 2003, p. 3.

FURTHER READING

Best, Felton O., *Crossing the Color Line: A Biography of Paul Laurence Dunbar, 1872–1906*, Kendall Hunt, 1996.

This biography highlights Dunbar's triumph of crossing the color line to become the nation's first nationally known black author accepted by mainstream America.

DuBois, W. E. B., *The Gift of Black Folk: The Negroes in the Making of America*, Square One, 2009.

This new edition of DuBois's study of the contribution of African Americans to American culture, from their labor to their inventions and music, celebrates the 100th anniversary of the National Association of the Advancement of Colored People, which DuBois founded.

Fanon, Frantz, *Black Skin, White Masks*, Grove Press, 1994.

Fanon was a black French psychiatrist and philosopher who supported Algerian independence. His work is important in post-colonial studies because he explains the psychological effects of colonialism and racial prejudice.

Gates, Henry Louis, Jr., *The Signifying Monkey: A Theory of Afro-American Literary Criticism*, Oxford University Press, 1988.

Harvard professor Gates has written one of the most important theoretical statements on African American literature, including introducing the concept of "signifying," the playful linguistic take-off on colonial language that creates a powerful counter-current of meaning. Language and its subtlety are important in black music and poetry, and their functions are not well understood by critics outside the African American literary tradition.

Gebhard, Caroline, "Inventing a 'Negro Literature': Race, Dialect, and Gender in the Early Work of Paul Laurence Dunbar, James Weldon Johnson, and Alice Dunbar-Nelson," in *Post-Bellum: Pre-Harlem African American Literature and Culture, 1877–1919*, edited by Barbara McCaskill and Caroline Gebhard, New York University Press, 2006, pp. 162–78.

The article discusses the cultural difficulties and issues of black authorship in the transition period from Reconstruction to the Harlem Renaissance, focusing on three of the most important black writers at that time. It includes the challenges of Dunbar's wife, Alice, as a writer.

Hurston, Zora Neale, *Their Eyes Were Watching God*, Harper, 1998.

The story of a black woman's difficult journey to selfhood in the South, this novel has become a classic of the Harlem Renaissance period, although it was not popular at the time and was out of print for thirty years until rediscovered in 1978. Hurston skillfully uses black Southern dialect but for her own feminist purposes, not for portraying stereotypes.

SUGGESTED SEARCH TERMS

Paul Laurence Dunbar

We Wear the Mask

Paul Laurence Dunbar AND We Wear the Mask

Paul Laurence Dunbar AND Majors and Minors

African American poetry

Paul Laurence Dunbar AND African American history

Paul Laurence Dunbar AND dialect

Paul Laurence Dunbar AND Harlem Renaissance

Paul Laurence Dunbar AND Booker T. Washington

Paul Laurence Dunbar AND black journalism

Paul Laurence Dunbar AND civil rights

Paul Laurence Dunbar AND W. D. Howells

Paul Laurence Dunbar AND Dayton, Ohio

Who Understands Me But Me

JIMMY SANTIAGO BACA

1990

Chicano author Jimmy Santiago Baca's prodigious literary career began in a most unlikely place: an American prison. Having dropped out of high school in the ninth grade, Baca remained functionally illiterate throughout his troubled teenage years, but a few chance encounters with the magic of such poets as Pablo Neruda and William Wordsworth led him to forge his own education and become a versifying master of the English language—all while serving time.

"Who Understands Me But Me" appears as the penultimate poem in his 1990 collection *Immigrants in Our Own Land and Selected Early Poems*, which was issued eleven years after the original publication of *Immigrants in Our Own Land*. That volume was published in 1979, the same year that Baca was released from his six-year stay in prison on drug-distribution charges. Presumably written during his time in prison, "Who Understands Me But Me" records with bitter resignation the psychological hardships and emotional wounds suffered by the poet in prison—and then transforms into a Whitmanesque tribute to the ineffable beauty and joy to be found within oneself, whatever the circumstances, if one can only train one's eyes and mind to perceive them.

Jimmy Santiago Baca (AP Images)

AUTHOR BIOGRAPHY

Baca was born on January 2, 1952, in Santa Fe, New Mexico. His mother was Chicana (of Mexican heritage), and his father was Apache. Their circumstances were difficult; they divorced when Baca was two. He was eventually left with his grandparents, as his mother escaped to California and his father struggled with alcoholism. Both parents met with tragic deaths. When Baca's grandfather died, the seven-year-old Baca, along with his older brother Mieyo, was deposited in an orphanage in Albuquerque. Remaining there for years, Baca ended up serving time in detention centers and dropping out of high school in the ninth grade, to assimilate into street life in the urban barrios. He wandered through the Southeast for a couple of years and then ended up in Arizona, where at age twenty he was arrested on a drug charge on flimsy evidence. A drug dealer plea-bargained and testified against Baca, and in 1973, he was given a prison sentence that would ultimately be extended to over six years.

While he was held in county jail, the abuse of an old drunk by detectives inspired Baca to exact what little vengeance he could by stealing an attendant's textbook—in which words he could barely read moved him so profoundly that he was left repeating the British author's name, Wordsworth, as he fell asleep. Before long, he wrote down his first hesitant words, and, as he remarks in his memoir *Working in the Dark: Reflections of a Poet of the Barrio* (1992), "From that moment, a hunger for poetry possessed me."

An unfavorable reclassification interview resulted in Baca being transferred to the maximum-security prison in Florence, Arizona, a dehumanizing experience. There, a charitable pen pal named Harry sent him bilingual reading material that allowed him to master grammar, and he began using his writing ability to barter with other convicts. In time, he earned his general equivalency diploma, devoured works by such poetic masters as Federico Garcia Lorca, Walt Whitman, and Denise Levertov, and developed his own style. His first publication came with his submission of poems to *Mother Jones*, followed by his chapbook *Jimmy Santiago Baca* (1978). His major collection *Immigrants in Our Own Land* (1979), published the same year as his release from prison, earned admiring reviews and established Baca as an up-and-coming poetic voice.

Baca's ensuing works solidified his literary status. After publishing three more verse collections through the mid-1980s, he finished the landmark semi-autobiographical poetic narrative *Martin and Meditations on the South Valley* in 1987. This epic treatment of the journey of an orphaned Chicano from town to town and eventually back home won the American Book Award. Baca next wrote *Black Mesa Poems* (1989), another critically praised collection. "Who Understands Me But Me" appears in *Immigrants in Our Own Land and Selected Early Poems* (1990).

Baca's publications since then have included autobiography, a play, a screenplay, short stories, and a novel, as well as additional verse collections. He has taught at the University of California, Berkeley, and Yale University, as well as in prisons throughout America and has made a home for himself on a small farm at Black Mesa, New Mexico.

POEM TEXT

> They turn the water off, so I live without water,
> they build walls higher, so I live without
>   treetops,
> they paint the windows black, so I live without
>   sunshine,
> they lock my cage, so I live without going
>   anywhere,
> they take each last tear I have, I live without
>   tears,   5
> they take my heart and rip it open, I live with-
>   out heart,
> they take my life and crush it, so I live without a
>   future,
> they say I am beastly and fiendish, so I have no
>   friends,

they stop up each hope, so I have no passage
   out of hell,
they give me pain, so I live with pain,
they give me hate, so I live with my hate,
they have changed me, and I am not the same
   man,
they give me no shower, so I live with my smell,
they separate me from my brothers, so I live
   without brothers,
who understands me when I say this is
   beautiful?
who understands me when I say I have found
   other freedoms?
I cannot fly or make something appear in
   my hand,
I cannot make the heavens open or the earth
   tremble,
I can live with myself, and I am amazed at
   myself, my love,
my beauty,
I am taken by my failures, astounded by my
   fears,
I am stubborn and childish,
in the midst of this wreckage of life they
   incurred,
I practice being myself,
and I have found parts of myself never
   dreamed of by me,
they were goaded out from under rocks in my
   heart
when the walls were built higher,
when the water was turned off and the windows
   painted black.
I followed these signs
like an old tracker and followed the tracks
   deep into myself,
followed the blood-spotted path,
deeper into dangerous regions, and found so
   many parts of myself,
who taught me water is not everything,
and gave me new eyes to see through walls,
and when they spoke, sunlight came
   out of their mouths,
and I was laughing at me with them,
we laughed like children and made pacts to
   always be loyal,
who understands me when I say this is beautiful?

POEM SUMMARY

The text used for this summary is from *Immigrants in Our Own Land and Selected Early Poems*, New Directions, 1990, p. 84. Versions of the poem can be found on the following Web pages: http://www.poemhunter.com/poem/who-understands-me-but-me/ and http://www.thubtenchodron.org/PrisonDharma/who_understands_me_but_me-Jimmy.pdf.

Lines 1–16

The first line of "Who Understands Me But Me" begins with a third-person plural pronoun signifying some group able to wield power over the first-person narrator, who, when deprived of water by these persons, must go without. Since water is the human body's most essential sustenance, the reader may at once assume that this group is in a position to oppress the poet to any desired extent. Lines 2–4 continue in the pattern of presenting a restriction imposed by the other persons followed by the helpless response of the poet. He evidently has no means of passing beyond the high walls that obscure the trees. Likewise, if placed in a room with blackened windows, he cannot go elsewhere and must forgo sunshine. Line 4 leaves little doubt that, being trapped in a cage, the poet is a prisoner.

In lines 5–9, the poet focuses on the emotional repercussions of his imprisonment and of the treatment he experiences in prison. He has cried until there are no tears left to cry. With his heart torn open, he has learned to live without feeling. Without any sense of control over his own life, he can no longer imagine a positive future for himself. The captors furthermore instill the poet with the notion that he is evil, making the mutual respect of ordinary friendship impossible. Echoing line 7, line 9 asserts that the captors effectively strangle his hopes, leaving him stuck mentally as well as physically in the hell of the prison.

Lines 10–12 succinctly sum up the relationship between the captors and the poet. They inflict pain, which he must suffer; they treat him with hatred, making him hateful. And in enduring the circumstances inflicted upon him, the poet has evolved into a different person—a hurting, angered man. This state is reflected not only in his psyche but also in his body, which, unwashed, retains his body's odor. Socially, prevented from associating with those he considers brothers, he goes without the love and care of brotherhood.

The closing lines of the first stanza take a somewhat surprising turn. Though every line thus far has presented a stricture or deprivation or punishment inflicted by the captors, the poet asks in line 15 whether anyone can understand that he has found something—perhaps his life, whatever the circumstances—to be beautiful. This beauty may stem from or relate to the alternative freedoms that the poet has happened upon despite his physical imprisonment.

Lines 17–38

The first line of the second stanza signals a departure from the patterned structure of the first stanza, as for the first time the poet appears as the line's primary subject—as if indicating the poet's achievement of a new degree of agency in his life. In lines 17 and 18, the poet acknowledges his mortal limitations—he is not a superhero, a magician, or a god—with the self-evident truth of these statements contributing to a sense that he has attained a degree of psychic equilibrium. That is, in recognizing that he simply lacks the power to alter his circumstances, he can better reconcile himself to those circumstances. Lines 19–20 indicate that a key component of the poet's peace of mind is acceptance of who he is, despite the condemnation inherent in his circumstances, and all that is positive about himself. In accepting himself, he can admit to and face his failures as well as his fears, and he can enjoy a childlike pleasure in simply asserting his will. In lines 23–24, the poet sums up that though his life has been wrecked by his captors—who, after dominating the first stanza, do not appear until the seventh line of the second stanza—he still has a self to claim, something he does consciously through practice.

This practiced self-consciousness has led the poet to discover new parts of himself, parts previously concealed behind obstacles in his heart. The third-person plural pronoun opening line 26 refers to these parts, not the captors, and in fact the captors do not appear again in the poem. The deprivations of lines 27–28—identical to those of the poem's first three lines—are related in passive construction, such that the subjects responsible for the actions, the captors, are eliminated. This suggests that the poet has learned to focus not on those who spark anger in him but rather on the essence of his own existence. Line 28 ends in a period, the only one in the poem, marking a significant break in the line of thought. This could be read as suggesting that the poet is imposing closure on his thoughts about his deprivations; he will not dwell on them but is decidedly moving on.

In line 29, the poet goes beyond describing aspects of himself to depict himself in action, if metaphorically. His following leads and clues to reach his inner self is emphasized through the repetition of that verb three times in lines 29–31. Lines 30–31 evoke a hunter or man of the wilderness—particularly a Native American one (even if the poet's heritage is unknown) of purer times—and suggest the acquired skill and determination needed for the inner tracking to be successful. Psychic risks, if not physical ones, are associated with the poet's efforts, as if unlocking memories or truths might threaten his emotional equilibrium.

The parts of the poet's self are given subjective agency in line 33. These inner facets of the poet taught him to be at peace even with the deprivation of his most basic need, to drink water. They taught him to somehow, as if in a mystic way, see through or beyond the walls surrounding him. These inner facets are personified enough to be able to speak and laugh, in lines 35 and 36, bringing rays of sunshine and companion laughter to the poet himself. He has become allied with—no longer antagonized by—his inner selves, and in accord with their pact of loyalty, the poet will not allow any one side of himself to sabotage his peace of mind. The poem's final line, repeating line 15, brackets the latter half of the poem with this question that the reader may by now imagine an answer to: perhaps, on the one hand, anyone who has read this poem can gain a surface understanding of the beauty that the poet has discovered; but on the other hand, the beauty of one's knowledge of oneself is something that can never be wholly understood by anyone else.

THEMES

Oppression

The first stanza of Baca's poem provides a vivid depiction of the manifold ways an individual can be oppressed and emotionally tortured by a group wielding vindictive control over him. Although the circumstances of imprisonment are not addressed in this poem, the reader is likely, whether through familiarity with the preceding poems in the collection or with the highly regarded author, to be aware that the poet himself indeed spent a stretch of time in a maximum-security American prison. Still, while the poem is autobiographical in inspiration, the lack of personal or historical details lends the sense of a universal prison experience. The omission of any reason for imprisonment, for example, allows the immediate circumstances to take precedence: the captors are denying the captive his humanity. Because he is a captive, the poet

TOPICS FOR FURTHER STUDY

- Read the title poem of Baca's 1979 and 1990 collections, "Immigrants in Our Own Land." In an essay, analyze the poem, in particular discussing the relevance of Baca's metaphorical depiction of jail as a country to which people "immigrate." What does this metaphor reveal about the functioning of American jails, racial attitudes, and life in America for the impoverished? Then compare and contrast this poem with "Who Understands Me But Me," considering the structure, tone, message, and emotional effects of each poem.

- Think of a time in your life when you were overwhelmed by negative emotions but eventually recovered your sense of well-being. Write a poem whose structure resembles that of "Who Understands Me But Me," with the first stanza detailing the nature of your negative state—focusing on whatever aspects of that state you choose, whether the physical circumstances, the person(s) responsible, the emotional hardships, and the second stanza relating your recovery.

- Use PowerPoint or video-editing software to create a multimedia presentation that matches each line of "Who Understands Me But Me" with a photograph, piece of artwork, or graphic—obtained online or from scanned print resources—that represents or offers an interesting juxtaposition with that line. Give the presentation to your class, with each line read as the associated picture is shown.

- In Angela de Hoyos's verse collection *Arise, Chicano! and Other Poems*, which is appropriate for young adults, find a poem that details a person's psychic or cultural awakening. In an essay, compare and contrast this poem with "Who Understands Me But Me," considering the style, tone, narrative voice, circumstances, and authorial perspective in each poem.

- Write a research paper on the state of modern American zoos or on one zoo in particular. Address such concerns as how the zoo obtains its animals, whether and how animals are reintroduced into the wild, how healthy the animals' environments appear to be, the cost-effectiveness of the zoo, and so forth. If feasible, consult the zoo's Web site and contact an official by e-mail to ask outstanding questions.

---

has no choice but to cope with whatever denials and deprivations are inflicted upon him. (As it happens, Baca's imprisonment was unjust; had he believed he deserved his captivity, he might not have felt the same need to relate his experience through verse.)

The repeated use of the third-person plural *they* achieves several effects. Since no individual guards or wardens or other characters are ever identified, this other group retains a disembodied quality. A faceless, bodiless mass, the group presents no ears to hear or heed the prisoner's complaints, accomplishes its many actions without hands, as if supernatural or mechanical, and lacks the ordinary individual's capacity for genuine sympathy or compassionate consideration. Like a tyrannical corporation or government, this group is able to act as it deems beneficial to its own interests with utter disregard for the humanity of those victimized.

The first stanza, especially through the emotionally charged lines 5–11, gives the impression that this oppression is intentional—that the captors believe that the captive deserves such harsh treatment. Their rationale, of course, is questionable. As Baca has indicated in interviews and as this poem suggests, the prison system seems designed not to teach prisoners self-worth, so that they might not commit further crimes for moral reasons, but rather to make prisoners feel worthless—so worthless that they might forgo future crime simply to avoid being treated so poorly ever again.

Baca makes clear in this poem that such rudimentary oppression, such denial of essential human physical and emotional needs, serves only to heighten the prisoner's rage and antagonism toward the system that has imprisoned him. Such rage does not dissipate on its own but builds up, and the enraged prisoner is unlikely to find the equilibrium necessary to abide by society's laws and demands upon release. Rather, he may feel that he must seek vengeance against the system precisely in order to achieve psychic equilibrium. This result is quite the opposite of what the jailers and their institution should hope for. In detailing the numbing, dehumanizing effects of oppression within prison, Baca makes a fierce argument against the rationale behind that oppression.

Suffering

Throughout the first stanza, paired with each declaration of injustice inflicted upon the prisoner is a statement of the deprivation or punishment thus experienced. The first nine lines, as well as line 14, all identify something that the poet must do without. Baca dwells on few material deprivations, highlighting instead aspects of daily life that those not imprisoned can take for granted: being able to see trees, feel sunshine, walk around at will. Those who live in northern climes, with their dark winters, or rainy regions can attest to the fact that denial of sunshine can have substantial effects on people's moods and emotional balance; such effects would surely be compounded for one whose exposure to sunshine is severely limited and always dictated by schedule. In turn, the sight of a chaotic assemblage of green leaves wavering in the breeze can have a palliative effect on the compulsively churning modern human mind; but this, too, is denied the prisoner.

Beyond such minor sufferings loom far profounder ones—the poet figuratively speaks of having his heart ripped open—and the product of all the inhumane treatment is a prisoner who is gutted of emotional stability and feels less than human. For many, the experience of such intense suffering leads only to anguish, to more suffering—for some, tragically, to suicide. For others, suffering can prove to be a transformative experience; instead of being broken, the will rises to seek to nullify or transcend the suffering, even if it cannot be eliminated entirely.

The experience of extreme solitude, instead of leaving one consumed with thoughts of the lost benefits of companionship, can inspire one to instead converse inwardly with oneself—as Baca eventually does—and find psychic equilibrium despite the deprivations being endured. Some might contend that the greatest depths of self-knowledge can only be reached through suffering; in Buddhist thought, suffering is deemed one of the most essential aspects of life. In this poem, Baca progresses through the suffering of the first stanza to reach a meditative plane in the second.

Self-Realization

After the first stanza, detailing the oppression endured by the prisoner, Baca's poem culminates in the second stanza with a series of assertions about the poet's new self-knowledge, renewed self-love, and achievement of self-reliance. The poet says little about the actual process through which these achievements were made, such as whether it entailed extensive reading, religious devotion, or other morale-boosting factors. In fact, the poet gives the impression that this process was almost entirely internal: the persona he establishes in the first stanza, denied virtually everything, has only himself to draw upon to resolve his anguish.

Turning inward, he finds that different parts himself—perhaps such as the boy nourished by his grandparents, a son of the proud Apache, or the youth who proved himself in a job, or the young man who learned how to love—have things to offer this angry man isolated in a prison cell. Calling forth and listening to the various parts of himself, the poet learns how to retain control of his own emotions regardless of the external circumstances—to see beauty where there seems to be none, to feel love where none is given.

The end of the poem is a series of breakthroughs: the walls no longer limit his vision; sunlight reaches him even when the sun is obscured; and even in confinement he can manifest happiness—he can laugh at himself, with the genuine, immediate mirth of a child. With the final word, thoughts of the expansive, infinite beauty of life, discovered by the poet in the

The narrator envisions beauty in the form of happy children. (Anatoliy Samara | Shutterstock.com)

course of his self-realization, may resonate in the reader's mind.

STYLE

Dichotomy

Structurally, "Who Understands Me But Me" is notable for the vivid dichotomy between the first and second stanzas, with the first following a fairly rigid pattern, the second following no pattern at all. The oppressive sense of the opening pattern is no less striking for being self-evident; indeed, the poem derives its power in part from the droning, hammering nature of the catalog of cruelties inflicted by the captors and from the flat, toneless declarations of what the poet must do without. As the lines proceed, the reader, along with the poet, feels all the most beautiful and agreeable aspects of life being stripped away, leaving the captive with literally nothing—nothing to offer comfort, no one to lean on for support, and in sum, no reasons even to be grateful to be alive. This pattern persists through enough lines, with only commas to interrupt the flow, that the reader likely loses count of the hardships, as if caught in an unending stream of punishment and insult. Finally, as the stanza ends with lines 15–16, the poet offers relief, in the form of two questions revealing that he has somehow discovered beauty and freedom despite his circumstances.

As soon as the second stanza opens, the reader realizes the pattern has been not just interrupted but fully broken. Almost startlingly, the poet begins to respond here not with ebullient assertions of his individuality or manhood but with recognition of his limitations. That is, he is not compelled to lash out, to respond to the captors' emotional violence with retributive violence of his own, but rather he seems to have discovered how to dissipate the tensions he is forced to absorb. When this captive deprived of everything is able to speak in lines 19–20 of his sense of awe at his own love and his own beauty, the reader understands that he has not merely escaped the painful pattern of the first stanza but has veritably erased it: he has banished from his mind the negative formulations of what his captors have done to him and what he consequently lacks.

The poet's selective attention on himself, on his persisting emotions and inner beauty, allows him to convert his captivity to a new kind of freedom: though the actions of his body and his external reality remain restricted by his captors, the actions of his mind and his internal reality, he has discovered, can always be his to determine. Accordingly, the second stanza features no pattern at all; the captive has, in an apt if clichéd phrase, freed his mind. Many readers will be familiar with that point of profound relief, reached at the end of a dark period of depression or grief over a loss or lost connection, when the self, sometimes unbidden, at last reverses its polarity and determines to move on—to forget what has caused sorrow and shift focus toward what yet brings joy. It is this paramount shift in focus, this sentimental revolution, that Baca captures with the structural dichotomy in this poem.

Captivity Literature

The tradition of poetry written in captivity is one of the most powerful in all of world literature. This is not to say that imprisoned poets have specifically read and drawn on each other's work; rather, the verse produced by imprisoned poets tends to be similar in such respects as point of view and mode of reflection but utterly different in accord with each poet's precise circumstances. One historical figure admired for his prison poetry is Ho Chi Minh, who came to be revered by nationalist/Communist factions in mid-twentieth-century Vietnam. Famous works of nonpoetic literature written during or based on time in prison include Henry David Thoreau's moral tract "On Civil Disobedience," Martin Luther King, Jr.'s politically seminal "Letter from Birmingham Jail," and Ivan Denisovich's Soviet gulag exposé *One Day in the Life of Ivan Denisovich*. When interviewed for *Callaloo*, Baca noted the interesting fact that many of the most renowned world poets have spent time in prison—usually over populist political beliefs, with some being regarded as national heroes—while most of the canonical American poets have never been anywhere near prison. In this respect, Baca—who not only began writing poetry in prison but also first learned how to read there—is an especially unique author. While his early collections focus on his perspective from prison, his works produced since, from verse to memoir to fiction, expand to address many other aspects of life as he perceives it.

HISTORICAL CONTEXT

Baca's earliest poetry fits into an exceptionally limited historical context: the inside of an Arizona prison in the 1970s. While other imprisoned poets have been emblematic of flammable political situations in their home nations, Baca's circumstances are representative rather of the common plight of minor criminals in the United States, where incarceration rates dwarf those of most other Western nations. When Baca was sentenced in 1973, judges generally had a degree of freedom in determining the appropriate length of a criminal's stay in prison, with consideration for factors like marital status, employment, and the nature of the crime. Parole boards would periodically review sentences and adjust them according to the convict's progress. Unjust convictions would nonetheless occur.

Baca confirms in his autobiographical prose his innocence of the crime of which he was found guilty: possession of an illicit substance with intent to sell. Circumstances had conspired against him: a drug bust was staged while he was coincidentally present, and it devolved into a firefight in which a federal agent was seriously wounded; unarmed and fearing for his life, Baca escaped. The next day's newspaper erroneously reported that he was a drug kingpin who had tried to murder the agent. The man actually dealing drugs on the occasion had given the police a false story incriminating Baca.

Baca turned himself in and was subjected to protracted beatings and abuse by the police and federal agents. His lax court-appointed attorney, as related by Baca in his autobiography, *A Place to Stand: The Making of a Poet*, preemptively conceded that his case was political: "You picked the wrong time to get busted.... It's election time, and you're the judge's ride to a second term." The attorney continued, "With all the play you got in the papers, you're going to be made an example, put behind bars, so voters'll feel safer from criminals like you." The attorney proclaimed that he would only suffer a longer sentence in pleading innocent, so Baca relented and filed a plea bargain of guilty.

Through the 1970s, intense media coverage of cases like Baca's helped stoke nationwide concern about rising crime rates. Also of concern was the potential unfairness of case-by-case sentencing. Accordingly, congressional lawmakers

COMPARE & CONTRAST

- **1970s:** Hispanics constitute some 16 percent of Arizona's population, with the state's total population growing by 50 percent over the decade thanks to the warm climate and influxes of retirees, middle-class whites, and Hispanic immigrants.

  Today: With high immigration rates through the end of the twentieth century, Hispanics account for 30 percent of Arizona's population by 2008, numbering nearly two million out of about 6.5 million who reside in the state.

- **1970s:** Arizona's prison population doubles over the course of the decade, from 1,672 to 3,482. In 1979, the budget of the state's Department of Corrections is $41.4 million.

  Today: Having increased by half since 2000, the number of inmates in Arizona's prisons surpasses 40,000 by 2010—a more than tenfold increase since the late 1970s. The budget of the Department of Corrections has increased twenty-fold, to $949 million in 2010.

- **1970s:** Although a Supreme Court decision briefly nullifies existing death penalties in states, Arizona reenacts a death-penalty statute in 1973. Still, no executions are carried out in Arizona through the end of the decade.

  Today: Since Arizona's first modern-day execution in 1992, some twenty-five death-row convicts have been executed. Meanwhile, between 1970 and 2002, just over one hundred Arizona prisoners scheduled for execution are ultimately found innocent of the crime in question.

---

pushed for federal sentencing guidelines, which would be instated by the 1980s. Arizona prefigured these guidelines in 1978 by adopting a criminal code prescribing minimum and maximum sentences for many felonies. Specifically targeted were crimes involving drug possession or trafficking, driving under the influence, or weapons. The state delineated added penalties for those breaking the law while on probation and other repeat offenders—regardless of whether or not the offenses in question were violent. (Baca, freed in 1979 as a rising published poet, never needed to concern himself with the implications of the 1978 code.) Policy analysts recognize Arizona as having long been a U.S. leader in incarceration rates and the aggressive punishment of criminals. Subsequent amendments to the 1978 code have reclassified some crimes as more severe, extending sentences accordingly; instituted a three-strikes provision, mandating prison time after a third conviction for an aggravated offense; and require that a full 85 percent of a sentence be served before a convict becomes eligible for parole.

In the present day, liberal advocates argue that mandated prison sentences for lesser offenses, separating convicts from their families and support networks, can turn minor offenders into career criminals. In many cases, other rehabilitation options, like fines, supervised work opportunities, substance-abuse treatment, or house arrest, offer more promising chances of bringing about a convict's reform. Politicians have been reluctant to favor these options for fear of appearing too soft on crime. Following the financial meltdown and recession of the late 2000s, however, Arizona, like many states, is facing budgetary shortfalls, and lawmakers are acknowledging that strict sentencing statutes have been found to cost states more than do other rehabilitation alternatives. Funds redirected from Arizona's prison budgets, then, could go toward education, health care, and social support programs.

Baca wrote poetry while incarcerated. (bhathaway / Shutterstock.com)

CRITICAL OVERVIEW

Reviews of Baca's first major collection, *Immigrants in Our Own Land* (1979), were highly favorable. While "Who Understands Me But Me" appears instead in the supplemented 1990 collection *Immigrants in Our Own Land and Selected Early Poems*, it is representative of the 1979 collection in style and context. In the *American Book Review*, Ron Arias remarks,

> Baca reminds me of a jazz musician searching for a melody, and when he finds it he takes it wherever it may lead him. Whether or not the melody or train of images works as a unified piece with a clear theme is of secondary importance to the journey itself, a journey of discovery unbound by prison walls and fences.

Arias concludes that Baca "can be a tight-lined, expansive, gentle, quickpaced or unrushed, quite sober or quite funny. He is a freshly aggressive poet of many abilities, and he tries them all. His is a gifted, young vision."

In the *Northwest Review*, John Addiego finds Baca's early collection valuable "because it addresses a constituency in desperate need of articulate voices... and because Baca's uneven, unschooled style achieves some exceptionally exciting moments in these poems." Addiego declares that Baca's "self explorations are... heartbreakingly honest" and praises the "visual power" of his Whitmanesque "singing."

In the *Dictionary of Literary Biography*, A. Gabriel Meléndez observes that the 1979 collection, reflective of Baca's recent poetic awakening, is "more strongly conditioned by visceral and passionate impulses than by poetry as formalistic craft or incidental pastime." Continuing, Meléndez affirms, "The sense of urgency that emanates from Baca's struggle to release a passionate and desperate cry for recognition, above all else, lends a deeply moving and enduring quality to the collection."

Marion Taylor's comments on the early collection for the *Kliatt Young Adult Paperback Book Guide* seem to precisely characterize "Who Understands Me But Me":

> By defining the prison experience as primarily one of learning how to endure, the mastery of which can be a genuinely liberating experience, the poet suggests not only that poetry can be restorative, but also that human life if given a chance is resilient.

The critic adds, "What these poems discover is a center of freedom and humaneness beyond the bleak realities; they are in their way a hymn and a celebration of the human spirit in extreme situations." Taylor concludes that Baca "has a fine, superb, lyrical gift and a firm command of the resources of the language," and his book is one "determined to bear witness to the truths of the human heart in adversity and it does it with wisdom, courage, beauty and above all, hope."

CRITICISM

Michael Allen Holmes

Holmes is a writer and editor. In the following essay, he identifies Baca's connection with nature in "Who Understands Me But Me" as a fundamental aspect of his sense of self.

Jimmy Santiago Baca gives an account of prison life that progress from chilling to heartwarming in his poem "Who Understands Me But Me." The first stanza focuses on the unkindly actions of the captors and the hardships suffered by the poet, most of which, after the first few lines, are emotional concerns. The second stanza presents what might be called the poet's rebirth, as he transforms himself from a man consumed by anger into one overflowing with love.

Imagery is relatively sparse in this poem, which befits the loosely visualized setting of the cold, bare insides of a prison. Were he a romantic poet, he might have portrayed his emotional upheaval with lavish metaphors conjuring, say, the inside of a freezing, isolated rabbit's den in winter or a tiger pacing its meager yard in a zoo. Baca mentions his cage and notes his beastliness in the first stanza, but he does not flesh out the comparison, instead employing a stark mode of discourse—marked by concise declarations and few adjectives—that reflects the ascetic circumstances imposed on him. After the nature imagery of the first three lines, the natural world is effectively sealed out of the poem until midway through the second stanza. There, images of nature are central in the depiction of the poet's rediscovery of self. Overall, the positioning of the nature imagery suggests that the poet's connection with nature is a fundamental aspect of his sense of self.

Baca's autobiographical prose and interviews hint at the importance of his connection with nature. The natural world did not seem to

THE SPIRITUAL AND PHYSICAL NOURISHMENT OF TRUE SUNSHINE IS NOT SO EASY TO REPLACE, BUT, AS IF FURTHER EMPLOYING MYSTIC POWERS OF VISUALIZATION, THE POET MANAGES TO DRAW LIGHT AND WARMTH FROM HIS INNER SELVES—PERSONIFIED, NOW, AS COMPANIONS WITH WHOM HE CAN LAUGH."

play a large role in his earliest years, because his childhood was dominated by his parents' unstable domestic circumstances. However, as he notes in *A Place to Stand: The Making of a Poet*, he did experience peaceful periods in his grandparents' pueblo, where life was yet more connected with nature. An uncle took Baca and his brother to tend to the animals on his ranch, collect wood in the mountains, and hunt for deer. Baca and a friend often "spent the whole day roaming the village. We crossed fields, played in trees, tracked coyotes, built mud forts in ditch banks, and watched giant frogs crush our dirt village."

When a neighbor was in need, men of the community would gather together to build a house using clapboard and adobe, a clay made from the earth and molded by hand. In his memoir *Working in the Dark: Reflections of a Poet of the Barrio*, Baca tells of these men, "Work of the hands, with the earth, was to them holy work, good for the spirit, that allowed a man to feel his life lived on earth was shared with others." Simply waking and walking through the village brought Baca great pleasure:

> There is much good to say about leaving your house at dawn . . . and breathing in the cold air, walking down a familiar path . . . noticing the changes in the fields around you, and feeling the rising sun on your cheeks and brow.

Through his preadolescent years in an orphanage and his teen years spent often in detention centers, Baca's life became centered around the streets. At this time, his connections with others in his social circles were more important than the sights of treetops, but he does note a significant moment experienced through

WHAT DO I READ NEXT?

- Baca's verse narrative *Martin and Meditations on the South Valley* (1987), delving into the culture of impoverished Chicanos in America, is considered one of his most original and rewarding works.

- The Mexican American author Gary Soto, who was raised in working-class circumstances in California, edited one of Baca's early chapbooks. Soto's verse collection *The Tale of Sunlight* (1978) was nominated for the Pulitzer Prize.

- Like Baca's *Martin and Meditations on the South Valley*, Soto's memoir *Living Up the Street* (1985) won the American Book Award, given by the Before Columbus Foundation for excellence in multicultural writing.

- Another reputable Chicano author is Luis J. Rodriguez, who progressed from gang life in Los Angeles to publishing verse collections beginning with *Poems across the Pavement* (1989).

- A fictional portrayal of life for Mexican American immigrants in urban Los Angeles, with episodes leading to gang violence, is provided in Tony Johnston's novel *Any Small Goodness* (2001), which is appropriate for young adults.

- Baca's life story resembles that of the black Nation of Islam leader Malcolm X, who progressed from early distance from his parents to criminal street life to prison to self-discovery. *The Autobiography of Malcolm X* (1965), written with Alex Haley, is considered essential reading for students of American history.

- One critic compared Baca's voice with that of the Beat poet Allen Ginsberg, whose "Howl," found in *Howl and Other Poems* (1956), expresses the too-long repressed indignity and primal vivacity of the subjugated masses of minorities of all kinds—especially sexual and ideological—in America.

- Baca's verse reminds many readers of the revolutionary free-verse poet Walt Whitman, whose *Leaves of Grass* (1855) is his quintessential celebration of the beauty of the world and of the self.

- Baca has mentioned the Nobel Prize–winning Chilean poet Pablo Neruda as a particularly significant influence. Neruda's work, which ranges from love poetry to surrealism to political rhetoric, is sampled in *Selected Poems* (1997), translated by Stephen Mitchell.

---

nature in his autobiography *A Place to Stand: The Making of a Poet*. Just before the arrest that ultimately left him serving a minimum five-year sentence, when an all-points bulletin for his capture had been issued by the Federal Bureau of Investigation, he took the time to drive from Albuquerque out to the Sandia Mountains (in a car he stole for the purpose) to clear his head. In his book he remarks, "The sky was cold and brilliant and the air pungent with pines and chilled granite. I needed to be out here. This was as close as I'd ever come to believing in God." In other words, this moment out in the vast open wilderness was an acutely spiritual one. After a while, feeling that his options had run out, he was moved further: "I wanted to take off across the snow and lose myself in the forest, moving over boulders and through trees, my path illuminated by the moonlight." However, he was ill prepared for such an undertaking, and he elected to turn himself in.

"Who Understands Me But Me" opens with lines that prioritize a connection with nature. Had Baca fled to the stream-laced mountains, only serious drought—or perhaps God—could have turned off the water, but there in prison, the captors can seize the totalitarian privilege of denying him what every living creature needs. If unable to see trees, the captive is unable to gain from a sympathetic relationship with them. Gazing at a tree's branches swaying in the wind, one may feel a dissipation of tension as one's own body allows the breeze to soften the muscles and stance. Gazing at a tall tree's trunk, one may feel a sense of proud rootedness, of intimate connection to the earth. Baca learned such a sense especially from his Apache grandfather, as he explains in a *Callaloo* interview:

> When we'd go to the fields to work, my grandfather would always tell me how beautiful it was for a man to be gentle with mother earth, how she was our mother and how when we handled the plants we were handling a young woman.

Baca asserted that "we all need to re-educate our children to the indigenous values that we hold as a people," values that allow boys to embrace a degree of femininity and grow into men when "they begin to nourish themselves, taking their sustenance from mother earth and all the things that they see about them." In the poem, being restricted to a room with windows painted black to deny the sunshine is a final environmental insult suffered by the captive. These several deprivations thus establish the setting for the emotional anguish to follow. This anguish might not have reached such extreme depths had the prisoner's connection with nature not been severed. The last twelve lines of the first stanza are utterly devoid of setting—except for the single reference to prison as an inferno—heightening the reader's sense of the poet's isolation.

The poet returns to natural imagery midway through the second stanza, in line 26. In an interview with John Crawford and Annie O. Eysturoy in *This Is about Vision: Interviews with Southwestern Writers*, Baca affirms the foundational role nature plays in the workings of his mind:

> My self is a recipient of the Mestizo culture, and that culture is so much embedded in the earth, and the earth is so much embedded in the subconscious, that you can't pull them apart; we are part of the earth, it is part of us.

Thus, delving into his subconscious is inherently analogous to a journey through nature. Signifying the poet's enduring separation from the life-filled wilderness, rocks are the first natural element to appear here. The obstructions of the first few lines are then mentioned again, but curiously, Baca phrases them in ways that omit the natural elements; he describes the obstructions but not the trees or the sunshine. This perhaps reflects the poet's meditative acceptance of his present state; rather than endlessly yearning for treetops and sunshine that are beyond his reach, he is forced to rediscover his connection with nature inside himself.

He goes on to speak of tracking inner parts of himself, following them deeper and deeper into his psyche. The metaphor of tracking an animal—one whose dripping blood signifies the emotional wounds the prisoner has suffered—recalls Baca's days tracking wild animals with his friend in his grandparents' village. The value of the experience is magnified when the most dangerous regions are reached. As the risk becomes greater—perhaps such as owing to nightfall, lurking predators, or poisonous snakes and scorpions in real life; to raw emotional landscapes, buried pain, or feelings of failure in the poet's psyche—the tracker must rise to the occasion, tap every reserve, and become his ideal self to ensure his survival. These images suggest that the internal journey undertaken by the poet is something of a vision quest, one through he which he may find his spirit animal—perhaps the very animal he has been tracking.

In lines 33–35, the critical natural deprivations of the first three lines are finally overcome. There is little the poet can do to counter the absence of water, which he needs not just spiritually but physically as well; he can only be at peace with its absence until it is at last supplied, an event over which he may not have any control. In speaking of seeing through walls, the poet may be alluding to a newfound ability to visualize with such intensity that the mere imagined sight of treetops—and of distant mountain peaks, rushing rivers, the expansive desert, the open blue sky—can manifest joy in his heart. The spiritual and physical nourishment of true sunshine is not so easy to replace, but, as if further employing mystic powers of visualization, the poet manages to draw light and warmth from his inner selves—personified, now, as companions with whom he can laugh. The poet's imaginative reestablishment of a connection with nature serves to define his emotional resurgence, which amounts to a sort of rebirth or enlightenment.

Baca has indeed spoken of experiencing a rebirth while in prison, in a *Callaloo* interview with John Keene, but he identified language as the critical factor:

> A remarkable thing occurred to me when I came upon language, and I really began to provoke language to decreate me and then to give birth to me again.... When you approach language in this being-reborn sense, you approach language in the way that the Hopis approach language, which is that language is a very real living being.

Language, that is, if used well, can elucidate and even contain who one is as a person. Baca evokes the tracking imagery of "Who Understands Me But Me" when he continues: "Now, when language begins to work itself on you and make certain demands of you, it begins to ask you to risk yourself and walk along its edge." Words and the ideas they represent, then, are what allowed Baca to journey deep within himself like a seasoned tracker, draw on the reserves of nature he had stored as words and images in his mind, and achieve the freedom to roam the endless terrains of his inner self and reconnect with the beauty of the natural world— to feel unstoppable sunshine flood through him, through everything.

Source: Michael Allen Holmes, Critical Essay on "Who Understands Me But Me," in *Poetry for Students*, Gale, Cengage Learning, 2012.

John Addiego
In the following excerpt, Addiego reviews Immigrants in Our Own Land, *praising Baca's style and comparing him favorable to Walt Whitman.*

[Jimmy Santiago Baca's] *Immigrants in Our Own Land* is a howl, a growling wail, a "trip through the mind jail" (as Raul Salinas' poem by that title described the agonizing process of remembering from inside the confines of oppression 15 years ago). This is the jail for real: most of Baca's poetry was written while he was in prison, and I think it's valuable for two reasons: because it addresses a constituency in desperate need of articulate voices (a 1979 study [for Ricardo Chavira's "West Coast Story," *Nuestro*, May, 1980] showed a rising death rate of over 250 Latino gang members per year in the Los Angeles area alone), and because Baca's uneven, unschooled style achieves some exceptionally exciting moments in these poems.

Concerned with his Chicano heritage (the book's title is a reference to the recent acquisition of that part of northern Mexico, or Aztlan, by the U.S., and the creation of a second-class citizenry supposedly protected by the unrecognized Treaty of Hidalgo) and wrestling with imprisonment and poverty, Baca's howl has a slight flavor of Ginsberg, and much more of Ginsberg's spiritual mentor, Whitman. His self-explorations are at times so heartbreakingly honest that the reader cannot help but be disturbed. At other times his singing and cataloguing have such visual power that the reader is taken back to Whitman's spear of grass (with the succinct impression that, in our times, the police are likely to arrest for vagrancy somebody lying on the grass):

> Ah, how lovely, how happy I am just to be me.
> I raise my pink gums like a wild chimpanzee, tilt my head back
> chortling white-toothed, at this amazing zoo and its visitors,
> pockets filled with popcorn, and crunching candy apples.

and later, in the same poem,

> I see it all; the glare of chrome and glaze of windows, the suspense and ambition of young boys playing baseball in parks, and sidewalks splattered with the night's blood, and the policeman sleeping with his wife and farting in the bathroom, and then after, so groomed and polished, passing shops along the street, hello he says to one, hello to another. I sleep in the grass thinking of this, and can be arrested for sleeping on the grass, and I laugh looking at the sky, filling the sky with my laughter.

Source: John Addiego, "A Review of *Immigrants in Our Own Land*," in *Northwest Review*, Vol. 21, No. 1, 1983, pp. 154–55.

Marion Taylor
In the following review, Taylor comments on the lyricism of Baca's poetry, calling it "astonishingly beautiful."

Immigrants in Our Own Land is a very disturbing book of poems because it's so astonishingly beautiful, one does not expect such to come from the pen of a man serving a long prison sentence, as is the case with this poet. These poems go against the current trend of so-called "prison poetry." While these poems do not neglect the bleak realities of prison life what is absent entirely is the strident voice and the ascerbic vision. What these poems discover is a center of freedom and humaneness beyond the bleak realities; they are in their way a hymn and a celebration of the human spirit in extreme situations.

In a world which offers virtually no concrete means of rebuilding a broken life, these poems propose just such a means. By defining the prison experience as primarily one of learning how to endure, the mastery of which can be a genuinely liberating experience, the poet suggests not only that poetry can be restorative, but also that human life if given a chance is resilient.

In "It Started" Baca describes his first encounter with the state-funded poetry workshop and the timid, suspicious first days that finally gave way to communication and friendship. He writes:

> ... But you didn't treat me like a wild ape
> or an elephant. You treated me like Jimmy.
> And who was Jimmy?
> A mass of molten fury in this furnace of steel,
> and yet, my thoughts became ladles, sifting carefully
> through my life, the pain and endurance,
> to the essence of my being...

But beyond the human qualities abundantly present, the real strength of these poems derive from the fact that Baca writes so well. He has a fine, superb, lyrical gift and a firm command of the resources of language. There are no rough edges and the poems move forward with utmost economy. This is a book determined to bear witness to the truths of the human heart in adversity and it does it with wisdom, courage, beauty and above all, hope.

Source: Marion Taylor, "A Review of *Immigrants in Our Own Land*," in *Kliatt Young Adult Paperback Book Guide*, Vol. 14, Spring 1980, p. 20.

SOURCES

Addiego, John, Review of *Immigrants in Our Own Land*, in *Northwest Review*, Vol. 21, No. 1, 1983, pp. 154–55.

Aladama, Frederick Luis, "An Interview with Jimmy Santiago Baca," in *MELUS*, Vol. 30, No. 3, Fall 2005, pp. 113–27.

Arias, Ron, Review of *Immigrants in Our Own Land*, in *American Book Review*, Vol. 4, No. 2, January/February 1982, pp. 11–12.

"Arizona Should End Death Penalty," in *Death Penalty Information Center*, July 28, 2002, http://www.deathpenaltyinfo.org/node/531 (accessed May 23, 2011).

Baca, Jimmy Santiago, *A Place to Stand: The Making of a Poet*, Grove Press, 2001, pp. 17, 87–88, 92.

———, "Who Understands Me But Me," in *Immigrants in Our Own Land and Selected Early Poems*, New Directions, 1990, p. 84.

———, *Working in the Dark: Reflections of a Poet of the Barrio*, Red Crane Books, 1992, pp. 6, 33.

Crawford, John, and Annie O. Eysturoy, "Jimmy Santiago Baca," in *This Is about Vision: Interviews with Southwestern Writers*, edited by William Balassi, et al., University of New Mexico Press, 1990, pp. 183–93.

"Demographic Profile of Hispanics in Arizona, 2008," in *Pew Hispanic Center*, http://pewhispanic.org/states/?stateid=AZ (accessed May 23, 2011).

Kasindorf, Martin, and Patrick McMahon, "Arizona's Hispanic Population Grew by 88 Percent," in *USA Today*, March 27, 2001, http://www.usatoday.com/news/nation/census/az.htm (accessed May 23, 2011).

Keene, John, "'Poetry Is What We Speak to Each Other': An Interview with Jimmy Santiago Baca," in *Callaloo*, Vol. 17, No. 1, Winter 1994, pp. 33–51.

Lopez, Tiffany Ana, "Critical Witnessing in Latina/o and African American Prison Narratives," in *Prose and Cons: Essays on Prison Literature in the United States*, edited by D. Quentin Miller, McFarland, 2005, pp. 62–69.

Meléndez, A. Gabriel, "Jimmy Santiago Baca," in *Dictionary of Literary Biography*, Vol. 122, *Chicano Writers, Second Series*, edited by Francisco A. Lomeli and Carl R. Shirley, Gale Research, 1992, pp. 21–29.

"State by State Database—Arizona," in *Death Penalty Information Center*, http://www.deathpenaltyinfo.org/state_by_state (accessed May 23, 2011).

Taylor, Marion, Review of *Immigrants in Our Own Land*, in *Kliatt Young Adult Paperback Book Guide*, Vol. 14, Spring 1980, p. 20.

Zemansky, Rebekah, "A Push from the Right: More Conservatives Joining Fight to Change Sentencing Guidelines," in *AZ Capitol Times*, May 20, 2011, http://azcapitoltimes.com/news/2011/05/20/a-push-from-the-right-more-conservatives-joining-fight-to-change-sentencing-guidelines/ (accessed May 23, 2011).

FURTHER READING

Burton-Rose, Daniel, ed., *The Celling of America: An Inside Look at the U.S. Prison Industry*, Common Courage Press, 1998.
    This volume provides a collection of accessible essays examining all aspects of modern American incarceration.

Englar, Mary, *The Apache: Nomadic Hunters of the Southwest*, Capstone Press, 2003.
    This brief volume aimed at younger readers offers an introduction to Apache culture and

daily life in Oklahoma, New Mexico, and Arizona, with full-color photographs.

Forché, Carolyn, ed., *Against Forgetting: Twentieth-Century Poetry of Witness*, W. W. Norton, 1993.
> This anthology was compiled to amplify the voices of poets speaking on behalf of minorities and oppressed peoples victimized by war throughout the world.

Griswold del Castillo, Richard, and Richard A. Garcia, *Cesar Chavez: A Triumph of Spirit*, University of Oklahoma Press, 1997.
> Cesar Chavez was the leading figure of a prolonged movement for Latino farmworkers' rights centered in the American Southwest in the mid-twentieth century. This volume celebrates Chavez's accomplishments.

SUGGESTED SEARCH TERMS

Jimmy Santiago Baca AND Who Understands Me But Me

Jimmy Santiago Baca AND Immigrants in Our Own Land

Jimmy Santiago Baca AND Chicano OR Mexican American AND literature

Jimmy Santiago Baca AND online interviews

Jimmy Santiago Baca AND film biography

prison AND poetry OR literature

prison AND rebirth OR awakening OR enlightenment

Arizona AND Department of Corrections

Apache AND Arizona OR New Mexico

Glossary of Literary Terms

A

Abstract: Used as a noun, the term refers to a short summary or outline of a longer work. As an adjective applied to writing or literary works, abstract refers to words or phrases that name things not knowable through the five senses.

Accent: The emphasis or stress placed on a syllable in poetry. Traditional poetry commonly uses patterns of accented and unaccented syllables (known as feet) that create distinct rhythms. Much modern poetry uses less formal arrangements that create a sense of freedom and spontaneity.

Aestheticism: A literary and artistic movement of the nineteenth century. Followers of the movement believed that art should not be mixed with social, political, or moral teaching. The statement "art for art's sake" is a good summary of aestheticism. The movement had its roots in France, but it gained widespread importance in England in the last half of the nineteenth century, where it helped change the Victorian practice of including moral lessons in literature.

Affective Fallacy: An error in judging the merits or faults of a work of literature. The "error" results from stressing the importance of the work's effect upon the reader—that is, how it makes a reader "feel" emotionally, what it does as a literary work—instead of stressing its inner qualities as a created object, or what it "is."

Age of Johnson: The period in English literature between 1750 and 1798, named after the most prominent literary figure of the age, Samuel Johnson. Works written during this time are noted for their emphasis on "sensibility," or emotional quality. These works formed a transition between the rational works of the Age of Reason, or Neoclassical period, and the emphasis on individual feelings and responses of the Romantic period.

Age of Reason: See *Neoclassicism*

Age of Sensibility: See *Age of Johnson*

Agrarians: A group of Southern American writers of the 1930s and 1940s who fostered an economic and cultural program for the South based on agriculture, in opposition to the industrial society of the North. The term can refer to any group that promotes the value of farm life and agricultural society.

Alexandrine Meter: See *Meter*

Allegory: A narrative technique in which characters representing things or abstract ideas are used to convey a message or teach a lesson. Allegory is typically used to teach moral, ethical, or religious lessons but is sometimes used for satiric or political purposes.

Alliteration: A poetic device where the first consonant sounds or any vowel sounds in words or syllables are repeated.

Allusion: A reference to a familiar literary or historical person or event, used to make an idea more easily understood.

Amerind Literature: The writing and oral traditions of Native Americans. Native American literature was originally passed on by word of mouth, so it consisted largely of stories and events that were easily memorized. Amerind prose is often rhythmic like poetry because it was recited to the beat of a ceremonial drum.

Analogy: A comparison of two things made to explain something unfamiliar through its similarities to something familiar, or to prove one point based on the acceptedness of another. Similes and metaphors are types of analogies.

Anapest: See *Foot*

Angry Young Men: A group of British writers of the 1950s whose work expressed bitterness and disillusionment with society. Common to their work is an anti-hero who rebels against a corrupt social order and strives for personal integrity.

Anthropomorphism: The presentation of animals or objects in human shape or with human characteristics. The term is derived from the Greek word for "human form."

Antimasque: See *Masque*

Antithesis: The antithesis of something is its direct opposite. In literature, the use of antithesis as a figure of speech results in two statements that show a contrast through the balancing of two opposite ideas. Technically, it is the second portion of the statement that is defined as the "antithesis"; the first portion is the "thesis."

Apocrypha: Writings tentatively attributed to an author but not proven or universally accepted to be their works. The term was originally applied to certain books of the Bible that were not considered inspired and so were not included in the "sacred canon."

Apollonian and Dionysian: The two impulses believed to guide authors of dramatic tragedy. The Apollonian impulse is named after Apollo, the Greek god of light and beauty and the symbol of intellectual order. The Dionysian impulse is named after Dionysus, the Greek god of wine and the symbol of the unrestrained forces of nature. The Apollonian impulse is to create a rational, harmonious world, while the Dionysian is to express the irrational forces of personality.

Apostrophe: A statement, question, or request addressed to an inanimate object or concept or to a nonexistent or absent person.

Archetype: The word archetype is commonly used to describe an original pattern or model from which all other things of the same kind are made. This term was introduced to literary criticism from the psychology of Carl Jung. It expresses Jung's theory that behind every person's "unconscious," or repressed memories of the past, lies the "collective unconscious" of the human race: memories of the countless typical experiences of our ancestors. These memories are said to prompt illogical associations that trigger powerful emotions in the reader. Often, the emotional process is primitive, even primordial. Archetypes are the literary images that grow out of the "collective unconscious." They appear in literature as incidents and plots that repeat basic patterns of life. They may also appear as stereotyped characters.

Argument: The argument of a work is the author's subject matter or principal idea.

Art for Art's Sake: See *Aestheticism*

Assonance: The repetition of similar vowel sounds in poetry.

Audience: The people for whom a piece of literature is written. Authors usually write with a certain audience in mind, for example, children, members of a religious or ethnic group, or colleagues in a professional field. The term "audience" also applies to the people who gather to see or hear any performance, including plays, poetry readings, speeches, and concerts.

Automatic Writing: Writing carried out without a preconceived plan in an effort to capture every random thought. Authors who engage in automatic writing typically do not revise their work, preferring instead to preserve the revealed truth and beauty of spontaneous expression.

Avant-garde: A French term meaning "vanguard." It is used in literary criticism to describe new writing that rejects traditional approaches to literature in favor of innovations in style or content.

B

Ballad: A short poem that tells a simple story and has a repeated refrain. Ballads were originally intended to be sung. Early ballads, known as folk ballads, were passed down through generations, so their authors are often unknown. Later ballads composed by known authors are called literary ballads.

Baroque: A term used in literary criticism to describe literature that is complex or ornate in style or diction. Baroque works typically express tension, anxiety, and violent emotion. The term "Baroque Age" designates a period in Western European literature beginning in the late sixteenth century and ending about one hundred years later. Works of this period often mirror the qualities of works more generally associated with the label "baroque" and sometimes feature elaborate conceits.

Baroque Age: See *Baroque*

Baroque Period: See *Baroque*

Beat Generation: See *Beat Movement*

Beat Movement: A period featuring a group of American poets and novelists of the 1950s and 1960s—including Jack Kerouac, Allen Ginsberg, Gregory Corso, William S. Burroughs, and Lawrence Ferlinghetti—who rejected established social and literary values. Using such techniques as stream of consciousness writing and jazz-influenced free verse and focusing on unusual or abnormal states of mind—generated by religious ecstasy or the use of drugs—the Beat writers aimed to create works that were unconventional in both form and subject matter.

Beat Poets: See *Beat Movement*

Beats, The: See *Beat Movement*

Belles-lettres: A French term meaning "fine letters" or "beautiful writing." It is often used as a synonym for literature, typically referring to imaginative and artistic rather than scientific or expository writing. Current usage sometimes restricts the meaning to light or humorous writing and appreciative essays about literature.

Black Aesthetic Movement: A period of artistic and literary development among African Americans in the 1960s and early 1970s. This was the first major African-American artistic movement since the Harlem Renaissance and was closely paralleled by the civil rights and black power movements. The black aesthetic writers attempted to produce works of art that would be meaningful to the black masses. Key figures in black aesthetics included one of its founders, poet and playwright Amiri Baraka, formerly known as LeRoi Jones; poet and essayist Haki R. Madhubuti, formerly Don L. Lee; poet and playwright Sonia Sanchez; and dramatist Ed Bullins.

Black Arts Movement: See *Black Aesthetic Movement*

Black Comedy: See *Black Humor*

Black Humor: Writing that places grotesque elements side by side with humorous ones in an attempt to shock the reader, forcing him or her to laugh at the horrifying reality of a disordered world.

Black Mountain School: Black Mountain College and three of its instructors—Robert Creeley, Robert Duncan, and Charles Olson—were all influential in projective verse, so poets working in projective verse are now referred as members of the Black Mountain school.

Blank Verse: Loosely, any unrhymed poetry, but more generally, unrhymed iambic pentameter verse (composed of lines of five two-syllable feet with the first syllable accented, the second unaccented). Blank verse has been used by poets since the Renaissance for its flexibility and its graceful, dignified tone.

Bloomsbury Group: A group of English writers, artists, and intellectuals who held informal artistic and philosophical discussions in Bloomsbury, a district of London, from around 1907 to the early 1930s. The Bloomsbury Group held no uniform philosophical beliefs but did commonly express an aversion to moral prudery and a desire for greater social tolerance.

Bon Mot: A French term meaning "good word." A *bon mot* is a witty remark or clever observation.

Breath Verse: See *Projective Verse*

Burlesque: Any literary work that uses exaggeration to make its subject appear ridiculous, either by treating a trivial subject with profound seriousness or by treating a dignified subject frivolously. The word "burlesque" may also be used as an adjective, as in "burlesque show," to mean "striptease act."

C

Cadence: The natural rhythm of language caused by the alternation of accented and unaccented syllables. Much modern poetry—notably free verse—deliberately manipulates cadence to create complex rhythmic effects.

Caesura: A pause in a line of poetry, usually occurring near the middle. It typically corresponds to a break in the natural rhythm or sense of the line but is sometimes shifted to create special meanings or rhythmic effects.

Canzone: A short Italian or Provencal lyric poem, commonly about love and often set to music. The *canzone* has no set form but typically contains five or six stanzas made up of seven to twenty lines of eleven syllables each. A shorter, five- to ten-line "envoy," or concluding stanza, completes the poem.

Carpe Diem: A Latin term meaning "seize the day." This is a traditional theme of poetry, especially lyrics. A *carpe diem* poem advises the reader or the person it addresses to live for today and enjoy the pleasures of the moment.

Catharsis: The release or purging of unwanted emotions—specifically fear and pity—brought about by exposure to art. The term was first used by the Greek philosopher Aristotle in his *Poetics* to refer to the desired effect of tragedy on spectators.

Celtic Renaissance: A period of Irish literary and cultural history at the end of the nineteenth century. Followers of the movement aimed to create a romantic vision of Celtic myth and legend. The most significant works of the Celtic Renaissance typically present a dreamy, unreal world, usually in reaction against the reality of contemporary problems.

Celtic Twilight: See *Celtic Renaissance*

Character: Broadly speaking, a person in a literary work. The actions of characters are what constitute the plot of a story, novel, or poem. There are numerous types of characters, ranging from simple, stereotypical figures to intricate, multifaceted ones. In the techniques of anthropomorphism and personification, animals—and even places or things—can assume aspects of character. "Characterization" is the process by which an author creates vivid, believable characters in a work of art. This may be done in a variety of ways, including (1) direct description of the character by the narrator; (2) the direct presentation of the speech, thoughts, or actions of the character; and (3) the responses of other characters to the character. The term "character" also refers to a form originated by the ancient Greek writer Theophrastus that later became popular in the seventeenth and eighteenth centuries. It is a short essay or sketch of a person who prominently displays a specific attribute or quality, such as miserliness or ambition.

Characterization: See *Character*

Classical: In its strictest definition in literary criticism, classicism refers to works of ancient Greek or Roman literature. The term may also be used to describe a literary work of recognized importance (a "classic") from any time period or literature that exhibits the traits of classicism.

Classicism: A term used in literary criticism to describe critical doctrines that have their roots in ancient Greek and Roman literature, philosophy, and art. Works associated with classicism typically exhibit restraint on the part of the author, unity of design and purpose, clarity, simplicity, logical organization, and respect for tradition.

Colloquialism: A word, phrase, or form of pronunciation that is acceptable in casual conversation but not in formal, written communication. It is considered more acceptable than slang.

Complaint: A lyric poem, popular in the Renaissance, in which the speaker expresses sorrow about his or her condition. Typically, the speaker's sadness is caused by an unresponsive lover, but some complaints cite other sources of unhappiness, such as poverty or fate.

Conceit: A clever and fanciful metaphor, usually expressed through elaborate and extended comparison, that presents a striking parallel between two seemingly dissimilar things—for example, elaborately comparing a beautiful woman to an object like a garden or the sun. The conceit was a popular device throughout the Elizabethan Age and Baroque Age and was the principal technique of the seventeenth-century English metaphysical poets. This usage of the word conceit is unrelated to the best-known definition of conceit as an arrogant attitude or behavior.

Concrete: Concrete is the opposite of abstract, and refers to a thing that actually exists or a description that allows the reader to experience an object or concept with the senses.

Concrete Poetry: Poetry in which visual elements play a large part in the poetic effect. Punctuation marks, letters, or words are arranged on a page to form a visual design: a cross, for example, or a bumblebee.

Confessional Poetry: A form of poetry in which the poet reveals very personal, intimate, sometimes shocking information about himself or herself.

Connotation: The impression that a word gives beyond its defined meaning. Connotations may be universally understood or may be significant only to a certain group.

Consonance: Consonance occurs in poetry when words appearing at the ends of two or more verses have similar final consonant sounds but have final vowel sounds that differ, as with "stuff" and "off."

Convention: Any widely accepted literary device, style, or form.

Corrido: A Mexican ballad.

Couplet: Two lines of poetry with the same rhyme and meter, often expressing a complete and self-contained thought.

Criticism: The systematic study and evaluation of literary works, usually based on a specific method or set of principles. An important part of literary studies since ancient times, the practice of criticism has given rise to numerous theories, methods, and "schools," sometimes producing conflicting, even contradictory, interpretations of literature in general as well as of individual works. Even such basic issues as what constitutes a poem or a novel have been the subject of much criticism over the centuries.

D

Dactyl: See *Foot*

Dadaism: A protest movement in art and literature founded by Tristan Tzara in 1916. Followers of the movement expressed their outrage at the destruction brought about by World War I by revolting against numerous forms of social convention. The Dadaists presented works marked by calculated madness and flamboyant nonsense. They stressed total freedom of expression, commonly through primitive displays of emotion and illogical, often senseless, poetry. The movement ended shortly after the war, when it was replaced by surrealism.

Decadent: See *Decadents*

Decadents: The followers of a nineteenth-century literary movement that had its beginnings in French aestheticism. Decadent literature displays a fascination with perverse and morbid states; a search for novelty and sensation—the "new thrill"; a preoccupation with mysticism; and a belief in the senselessness of human existence. The movement is closely associated with the doctrine Art for Art's Sake. The term "decadence" is sometimes used to denote a decline in the quality of art or literature following a period of greatness.

Deconstruction: A method of literary criticism developed by Jacques Derrida and characterized by multiple conflicting interpretations of a given work. Deconstructionists consider the impact of the language of a work and suggest that the true meaning of the work is not necessarily the meaning that the author intended.

Deduction: The process of reaching a conclusion through reasoning from general premises to a specific premise.

Denotation: The definition of a word, apart from the impressions or feelings it creates in the reader.

Diction: The selection and arrangement of words in a literary work. Either or both may vary depending on the desired effect. There are four general types of diction: "formal," used in scholarly or lofty writing; "informal," used in relaxed but educated conversation; "colloquial," used in everyday speech; and "slang," containing newly coined words and other terms not accepted in formal usage.

Didactic: A term used to describe works of literature that aim to teach some moral, religious, political, or practical lesson. Although didactic elements are often found in artistically pleasing works, the term "didactic" usually refers to literature in which the message is more important than the form. The term may also be used to criticize a work that the critic finds "overly didactic," that is, heavy-handed in its delivery of a lesson.

Dimeter: See *Meter*

Dionysian: See *Apollonian and Dionysian*

Discordia concours: A Latin phrase meaning "discord in harmony." The term was coined by the eighteenth-century English writer Samuel Johnson to describe "a combination of dissimilar images or discovery of occult resemblances in things apparently unlike." Johnson created the expression by reversing a phrase by the Latin poet Horace.

Dissonance: A combination of harsh or jarring sounds, especially in poetry. Although such combinations may be accidental, poets sometimes intentionally make them to achieve particular effects. Dissonance is also sometimes used to refer to close but not identical rhymes. When this is the case, the word functions as a synonym for consonance.

Double Entendre: A corruption of a French phrase meaning "double meaning." The term is used to indicate a word or phrase that is deliberately ambiguous, especially when one of the meanings is risque or improper.

Draft: Any preliminary version of a written work. An author may write dozens of drafts which are revised to form the final work, or he or she may write only one, with few or no revisions.

Dramatic Monologue: See *Monologue*

Dramatic Poetry: Any lyric work that employs elements of drama such as dialogue, conflict, or characterization, but excluding works that are intended for stage presentation.

Dream Allegory: See *Dream Vision*

Dream Vision: A literary convention, chiefly of the Middle Ages. In a dream vision a story is presented as a literal dream of the narrator. This device was commonly used to teach moral and religious lessons.

E

Eclogue: In classical literature, a poem featuring rural themes and structured as a dialogue among shepherds. Eclogues often took specific poetic forms, such as elegies or love poems. Some were written as the soliloquy of a shepherd. In later centuries, "eclogue" came to refer to any poem that was in the pastoral tradition or that had a dialogue or monologue structure.

Edwardian: Describes cultural conventions identified with the period of the reign of Edward VII of England (1901-1910). Writers of the Edwardian Age typically displayed a strong reaction against the propriety and conservatism of the Victorian Age. Their work often exhibits distrust of authority in religion, politics, and art and expresses strong doubts about the soundness of conventional values.

Edwardian Age: See *Edwardian*

Electra Complex: A daughter's amorous obsession with her father.

Elegy: A lyric poem that laments the death of a person or the eventual death of all people. In a conventional elegy, set in a classical world, the poet and subject are spoken of as shepherds. In modern criticism, the word elegy is often used to refer to a poem that is melancholy or mournfully contemplative.

Elizabethan Age: A period of great economic growth, religious controversy, and nationalism closely associated with the reign of Elizabeth I of England (1558-1603). The Elizabethan Age is considered a part of the general renaissance—that is, the flowering of arts and literature—that took place in Europe during the fourteenth through sixteenth centuries. The era is considered the golden age of English literature. The most important dramas in English and a great deal of lyric poetry were produced during this period, and modern English criticism began around this time.

Empathy: A sense of shared experience, including emotional and physical feelings, with someone or something other than oneself. Empathy is often used to describe the response of a reader to a literary character.

English Sonnet: See *Sonnet*

Enjambment: The running over of the sense and structure of a line of verse or a couplet into the following verse or couplet.

Enlightenment, The: An eighteenth-century philosophical movement. It began in France but had a wide impact throughout Europe and America. Thinkers of the Enlightenment valued reason and believed that both the individual and society could achieve a state of perfection. Corresponding to this essentially humanist vision was a resistance to religious authority.

Epic: A long narrative poem about the adventures of a hero of great historic or legendary importance. The setting is vast and the action is often given cosmic significance through the intervention of supernatural forces such as gods, angels, or demons. Epics are typically written in a classical style of grand simplicity with elaborate metaphors and allusions that enhance the symbolic importance of a hero's adventures.

Epic Simile: See *Homeric Simile*

Epigram: A saying that makes the speaker's point quickly and concisely.

Epilogue: A concluding statement or section of a literary work. In dramas, particularly those of the seventeenth and eighteenth centuries, the epilogue is a closing speech, often in verse, delivered by an actor at the end of a play and spoken directly to the audience.

Epiphany: A sudden revelation of truth inspired by a seemingly trivial incident.

Epitaph: An inscription on a tomb or tombstone, or a verse written on the occasion of a person's death. Epitaphs may be serious or humorous.

Epithalamion: A song or poem written to honor and commemorate a marriage ceremony.

Epithalamium: See *Epithalamion*

Epithet: A word or phrase, often disparaging or abusive, that expresses a character trait of someone or something.

Erziehungsroman: See *Bildungsroman*

Essay: A prose composition with a focused subject of discussion. The term was coined by Michel de Montaigne to describe his 1580 collection of brief, informal reflections on himself and on various topics relating to human nature. An essay can also be a long, systematic discourse.

Existentialism: A predominantly twentieth-century philosophy concerned with the nature and perception of human existence. There are two major strains of existentialist thought: atheistic and Christian. Followers of atheistic existentialism believe that the individual is alone in a godless universe and that the basic human condition is one of suffering and loneliness. Nevertheless, because there are no fixed values, individuals can create their own characters—indeed, they can shape themselves—through the exercise of free will. The atheistic strain culminates in and is popularly associated with the works of Jean-Paul Sartre. The Christian existentialists, on the other hand, believe that only in God may people find freedom from life's anguish. The two strains hold certain beliefs in common: that existence cannot be fully understood or described through empirical effort; that anguish is a universal element of life; that individuals must bear responsibility for their actions; and that there is no common standard of behavior or perception for religious and ethical matters.

Expatriates: See *Expatriatism*

Expatriatism: The practice of leaving one's country to live for an extended period in another country.

Exposition: Writing intended to explain the nature of an idea, thing, or theme. Expository writing is often combined with description, narration, or argument. In dramatic writing, the exposition is the introductory material which presents the characters, setting, and tone of the play.

Expressionism: An indistinct literary term, originally used to describe an early twentieth-century school of German painting. The term applies to almost any mode of unconventional, highly subjective writing that distorts reality in some way.

Extended Monologue: See *Monologue*

F

Feet: See *Foot*

Feminine Rhyme: See *Rhyme*

Fiction: Any story that is the product of imagination rather than a documentation of fact. Characters and events in such narratives may be based in real life but their ultimate form and configuration is a creation of the author.

Figurative Language: A technique in writing in which the author temporarily interrupts the order, construction, or meaning of the writing for a particular effect. This interruption takes the form of one or more figures of speech such as hyperbole, irony, or simile. Figurative language is the opposite of literal language, in which every word is truthful, accurate, and free of exaggeration or embellishment.

Figures of Speech: Writing that differs from customary conventions for construction, meaning, order, or significance for the purpose of a special meaning or effect. There are two major types of figures of speech: rhetorical figures, which do not make changes in the meaning of the words, and tropes, which do.

Fin de siecle: A French term meaning "end of the century." The term is used to denote the last decade of the nineteenth century, a transition period when writers and other artists abandoned old conventions and looked for new techniques and objectives.

First Person: See *Point of View*

Folk Ballad: See *Ballad*

Folklore: Traditions and myths preserved in a culture or group of people. Typically, these are passed on by word of mouth in various forms—such as legends, songs, and proverbs—or preserved in customs and ceremonies. This term was first used by W. J. Thoms in 1846.

Folktale: A story originating in oral tradition. Folktales fall into a variety of categories, including legends, ghost stories, fairy tales, fables, and anecdotes based on historical figures and events.

Foot: The smallest unit of rhythm in a line of poetry. In English-language poetry, a foot is typically one accented syllable combined with one or two unaccented syllables.

Form: The pattern or construction of a work which identifies its genre and distinguishes it from other genres.

Formalism: In literary criticism, the belief that literature should follow prescribed rules of construction, such as those that govern the sonnet form.

Fourteener Meter: See *Meter*

Free Verse: Poetry that lacks regular metrical and rhyme patterns but that tries to capture the cadences of everyday speech. The form allows a poet to exploit a variety of rhythmical effects within a single poem.

Futurism: A flamboyant literary and artistic movement that developed in France, Italy, and Russia from 1908 through the 1920s. Futurist theater and poetry abandoned traditional literary forms. In their place, followers of the movement attempted to achieve total freedom of expression through bizarre imagery and deformed or newly invented words. The Futurists were self-consciously modern artists who attempted to incorporate the appearances and sounds of modern life into their work.

G

Genre: A category of literary work. In critical theory, genre may refer to both the content of a given work—tragedy, comedy, pastoral—and to its form, such as poetry, novel, or drama.

Genteel Tradition: A term coined by critic George Santayana to describe the literary practice of certain late nineteenth-century American writers, especially New Englanders. Followers of the Genteel Tradition emphasized conventionality in social, religious, moral, and literary standards.

Georgian Age: See *Georgian Poets*

Georgian Period: See *Georgian Poets*

Georgian Poets: A loose grouping of English poets during the years 1912-1922. The Georgians reacted against certain literary schools and practices, especially Victorian wordiness, turn-of-the-century aestheticism, and contemporary urban realism. In their place, the Georgians embraced the nineteenth-century poetic practices of William Wordsworth and the other Lake Poets.

Georgic: A poem about farming and the farmer's way of life, named from Virgil's *Georgics*.

Gilded Age: A period in American history during the 1870s characterized by political corruption and materialism. A number of important novels of social and political criticism were written during this time.

Gothic: See *Gothicism*

Gothicism: In literary criticism, works characterized by a taste for the medieval or morbidly attractive. A gothic novel prominently features elements of horror, the supernatural, gloom, and violence: clanking chains, terror, charnel houses, ghosts, medieval castles, and mysteriously slamming doors. The term "gothic novel" is also applied to novels that lack elements of the traditional Gothic setting but that create a similar atmosphere of terror or dread.

Graveyard School: A group of eighteenth-century English poets who wrote long, picturesque meditations on death. Their works were designed to cause the reader to ponder immortality.

Great Chain of Being: The belief that all things and creatures in nature are organized in a hierarchy from inanimate objects at the bottom to God at the top. This system of belief was popular in the seventeenth and eighteenth centuries.

Grotesque: In literary criticism, the subject matter of a work or a style of expression characterized by exaggeration, deformity, freakishness, and disorder. The grotesque often includes an element of comic absurdity.

H

Haiku: The shortest form of Japanese poetry, constructed in three lines of five, seven, and five syllables respectively. The message of a *haiku* poem usually centers on some aspect of spirituality and provokes an emotional response in the reader.

Half Rhyme: See *Consonance*

Harlem Renaissance: The Harlem Renaissance of the 1920s is generally considered the first significant movement of black writers and artists in the United States. During this period, new and established black writers published more fiction and poetry than ever before, the first influential black literary journals were established, and black authors and artists received their first widespread recognition and serious critical appraisal. Among the major writers associated with this period are Claude McKay, Jean Toomer, Countee Cullen, Langston Hughes, Arna Bontemps, Nella Larsen, and Zora Neale Hurston.

Hellenism: Imitation of ancient Greek thought or styles. Also, an approach to life that focuses on the growth and development of the intellect. "Hellenism" is sometimes used to refer to the belief that reason can be applied to examine all human experience.

Heptameter: See *Meter*

Hero/Heroine: The principal sympathetic character (male or female) in a literary work. Heroes and heroines typically exhibit admirable traits: idealism, courage, and integrity, for example.

Heroic Couplet: A rhyming couplet written in iambic pentameter (a verse with five iambic feet).

Heroic Line: The meter and length of a line of verse in epic or heroic poetry. This varies by language and time period.

Heroine: See *Hero/Heroine*

Hexameter: See *Meter*

Historical Criticism: The study of a work based on its impact on the world of the time period in which it was written.

Hokku: See *Haiku*

Holocaust: See *Holocaust Literature*

Holocaust Literature: Literature influenced by or written about the Holocaust of World War II. Such literature includes true stories of survival in concentration camps, escape, and life after the war, as well as fictional works and poetry.

Homeric Simile: An elaborate, detailed comparison written as a simile many lines in length.

Horatian Satire: See *Satire*

Humanism: A philosophy that places faith in the dignity of humankind and rejects the medieval perception of the individual as a weak, fallen creature. "Humanists" typically believe in the perfectibility of human nature and view reason and education as the means to that end.

Humors: Mentions of the humors refer to the ancient Greek theory that a person's health and personality were determined by the balance of four basic fluids in the body: blood, phlegm, yellow bile, and black bile. A dominance of any fluid would cause extremes in behavior. An excess of blood created a sanguine person who was joyful, aggressive, and passionate; a phlegmatic person was shy, fearful, and sluggish; too much yellow bile led to a choleric temperament characterized by impatience, anger, bitterness, and stubbornness; and excessive black bile created melancholy, a state of laziness, gluttony, and lack of motivation.

Humours: See *Humors*

Hyperbole: In literary criticism, deliberate exaggeration used to achieve an effect.

I

Iamb: See *Foot*

Idiom: A word construction or verbal expression closely associated with a given language.

Image: A concrete representation of an object or sensory experience. Typically, such a representation helps evoke the feelings associated with the object or experience itself. Images are either "literal" or "figurative." Literal images are especially concrete and involve little or no extension of the obvious meaning of the words used to express them. Figurative images do not follow the literal meaning of the words exactly. Images in literature are usually visual, but the term "image" can also refer to the representation of any sensory experience.

Imagery: The array of images in a literary work. Also, figurative language.

Imagism: An English and American poetry movement that flourished between 1908 and 1917. The Imagists used precise, clearly presented images in their works. They also used common, everyday speech and aimed for conciseness, concrete imagery, and the creation of new rhythms.

In medias res: A Latin term meaning "in the middle of things." It refers to the technique of beginning a story at its midpoint and then using various flashback devices to reveal previous action.

Induction: The process of reaching a conclusion by reasoning from specific premises to form a general premise. Also, an introductory portion of a work of literature, especially a play.

Intentional Fallacy: The belief that judgments of a literary work based solely on an author's stated or implied intentions are false and misleading. Critics who believe in the concept of the intentional fallacy typically argue that the work itself is sufficient matter for interpretation, even though they may concede that an author's statement of purpose can be useful.

Interior Monologue: A narrative technique in which characters' thoughts are revealed in a way that appears to be uncontrolled by the author. The interior monologue typically aims to reveal the inner self of a character. It portrays emotional experiences as they occur at both a conscious and unconscious level. Images are often used to represent sensations or emotions.

Internal Rhyme: Rhyme that occurs within a single line of verse.

Irish Literary Renaissance: A late nineteenth- and early twentieth-century movement in Irish literature. Members of the movement aimed to reduce the influence of British culture in Ireland and create an Irish national literature.

Irony: In literary criticism, the effect of language in which the intended meaning is the opposite of what is stated.

Italian Sonnet: See *Sonnet*

J

Jacobean Age: The period of the reign of James I of England (1603-1625). The early literature of this period reflected the worldview of the Elizabethan Age, but a darker, more cynical attitude steadily grew in the art and literature of the Jacobean Age. This was an important time for English drama and poetry.

Jargon: Language that is used or understood only by a select group of people. Jargon may refer to terminology used in a certain profession, such as computer jargon, or it may refer to any nonsensical language that is not understood by most people.

Journalism: Writing intended for publication in a newspaper or magazine, or for broadcast on a radio or television program featuring news, sports, entertainment, or other timely material.

K

Knickerbocker Group: A somewhat indistinct group of New York writers of the first half of the nineteenth century. Members of the group were linked only by location and a common theme: New York life.

Kunstlerroman: See *Bildungsroman*

L

Lais: See *Lay*

Lake Poets: See *Lake School*

Lake School: These poets all lived in the Lake District of England at the turn of the nineteenth century. As a group, they followed no single "school" of thought or literary practice, although their works were uniformly disparaged by the *Edinburgh Review*.

Lay: A song or simple narrative poem. The form originated in medieval France. Early French *lais* were often based on the Celtic legends and other tales sung by Breton minstrels—thus the name of the "Breton lay." In fourteenth-century England, the term "lay" was used to describe short narratives written in imitation of the Breton lays.

Leitmotiv: See *Motif*

Literal Language: An author uses literal language when he or she writes without exaggerating or embellishing the subject matter and without any tools of figurative language.

Literary Ballad: See *Ballad*

Literature: Literature is broadly defined as any written or spoken material, but the term most often refers to creative works.

Lost Generation: A term first used by Gertrude Stein to describe the post-World War I generation of American writers: men and women haunted by a sense of betrayal and emptiness brought about by the destructiveness of the war.

Lyric Poetry: A poem expressing the subjective feelings and personal emotions of the poet. Such poetry is melodic, since it was originally accompanied by a lyre in recitals. Most Western poetry in the twentieth century may be classified as lyrical.

M

Mannerism: Exaggerated, artificial adherence to a literary manner or style. Also, a popular style of the visual arts of late sixteenth-century Europe that was marked by elongation of the human form and by intentional spatial distortion. Literary works that are self-consciously high-toned and artistic are often said to be "mannered."

Masculine Rhyme: See *Rhyme*

Measure: The foot, verse, or time sequence used in a literary work, especially a poem. Measure is often used somewhat incorrectly as a synonym for meter.

Metaphor: A figure of speech that expresses an idea through the image of another object. Metaphors suggest the essence of the first object by identifying it with certain qualities of the second object.

Metaphysical Conceit: See *Conceit*

Metaphysical Poetry: The body of poetry produced by a group of seventeenth-century English writers called the "Metaphysical Poets." The group includes John Donne and Andrew Marvell. The Metaphysical Poets made use of everyday speech, intellectual analysis, and unique imagery. They aimed to portray the ordinary conflicts and contradictions of life. Their poems often took the form of an argument, and many of them emphasize physical and religious love as well as the fleeting nature of life. Elaborate conceits are typical in metaphysical poetry.

Metaphysical Poets: See *Metaphysical Poetry*

Meter: In literary criticism, the repetition of sound patterns that creates a rhythm in poetry. The patterns are based on the number of syllables and the presence and absence of accents. The unit of rhythm in a line is called a foot. Types of meter are classified according to the number of feet in a line. These are the standard English lines: Monometer, one foot; Dimeter, two feet; Trimeter, three feet; Tetrameter, four feet; Pentameter, five feet; Hexameter, six feet (also called the Alexandrine); Heptameter, seven feet (also called the "Fourteener" when the feet are iambic).

Modernism: Modern literary practices. Also, the principles of a literary school that lasted from roughly the beginning of the twentieth century until the end of World War II. Modernism is defined by its rejection of the literary conventions of the nineteenth century and by its opposition to conventional morality, taste, traditions, and economic values.

Monologue: A composition, written or oral, by a single individual. More specifically, a speech given by a single individual in a drama or other public entertainment. It has no set length, although it is usually several or more lines long.

Monometer: See *Meter*

Mood: The prevailing emotions of a work or of the author in his or her creation of the work. The mood of a work is not always what might be expected based on its subject matter.

Motif: A theme, character type, image, metaphor, or other verbal element that recurs throughout a single work of literature or occurs in a number of different works over a period of time.

Motiv: See *Motif*

Muckrakers: An early twentieth-century group of American writers. Typically, their works exposed the wrongdoings of big business and government in the United States.

Muses: Nine Greek mythological goddesses, the daughters of Zeus and Mnemosyne (Memory). Each muse patronized a specific area of the liberal arts and sciences. Calliope presided over epic poetry, Clio over history, Erato over love poetry, Euterpe over music or lyric poetry, Melpomene over tragedy, Polyhymnia over hymns to the gods, Terpsichore over dance, Thalia over comedy, and Urania over astronomy. Poets and writers traditionally made appeals to the Muses for inspiration in their work.

Myth: An anonymous tale emerging from the traditional beliefs of a culture or social unit. Myths use supernatural explanations for natural phenomena. They may also explain cosmic issues like creation and death. Collections of myths, known as mythologies, are common to all cultures and nations, but the best-known myths belong to the Norse, Roman, and Greek mythologies.

N

Narration: The telling of a series of events, real or invented. A narration may be either a simple narrative, in which the events are recounted chronologically, or a narrative with a plot, in which the account is given in a style reflecting the author's artistic concept of the story. Narration is sometimes used as a synonym for "storyline."

Narrative: A verse or prose accounting of an event or sequence of events, real or invented. The term is also used as an adjective in the sense "method of narration." For example, in literary criticism, the expression "narrative technique" usually refers to the way the author structures and presents his or her story.

Narrative Poetry: A nondramatic poem in which the author tells a story. Such poems may be of any length or level of complexity.

Narrator: The teller of a story. The narrator may be the author or a character in the story through whom the author speaks.

Naturalism: A literary movement of the late nineteenth and early twentieth centuries. The movement's major theorist, French novelist Emile Zola, envisioned a type of fiction that would examine human life with the objectivity of scientific inquiry. The Naturalists typically viewed human beings as either the products of "biological determinism," ruled by hereditary instincts and engaged in an endless struggle for survival, or as the products of "socioeconomic determinism," ruled by social and economic forces beyond their control. In their works, the Naturalists generally ignored the highest levels of society and focused on degradation: poverty, alcoholism, prostitution, insanity, and disease.

Negritude: A literary movement based on the concept of a shared cultural bond on the part of black Africans, wherever they may be in the world. It traces its origins to the former French colonies of Africa and the Caribbean. Negritude poets, novelists, and essayists generally stress four points in their writings: One, black alienation from traditional African culture can lead to feelings of inferiority. Two, European colonialism and Western education should be resisted. Three, black Africans should seek to affirm and define their own identity. Four, African culture can and should be reclaimed. Many Negritude writers also claim that blacks can make unique contributions to the world, based on a heightened appreciation of nature, rhythm, and human emotions—aspects of life they say are not so highly valued in the materialistic and rationalistic West.

Negro Renaissance: See *Harlem Renaissance*

Neoclassical Period: See *Neoclassicism*

Neoclassicism: In literary criticism, this term refers to the revival of the attitudes and styles of expression of classical literature. It is generally used to describe a period in European history beginning in the late seventeenth century and lasting until about 1800. In its purest form, Neoclassicism marked a return to order, proportion, restraint, logic, accuracy, and decorum. In England, where Neoclassicism perhaps was most popular, it reflected the influence of seventeenth- century French writers, especially dramatists. Neoclassical writers typically reacted against the intensity and enthusiasm of the Renaissance period. They wrote works that appealed to the intellect, using elevated language and classical literary forms such as satire and the ode. Neoclassical works were often governed by the classical goal of instruction.

Neoclassicists: See *Neoclassicism*

New Criticism: A movement in literary criticism, dating from the late 1920s, that stressed close textual analysis in the interpretation of works of literature. The New Critics saw little merit in historical and biographical analysis. Rather, they aimed to examine the text alone, free from the question of how external events—biographical or otherwise—may have helped shape it.

New Journalism: A type of writing in which the journalist presents factual information in a form usually used in fiction. New journalism emphasizes description, narration, and character development to bring readers closer to the human element of the story, and is often used in personality profiles and in-depth feature articles. It is not compatible with "straight" or "hard" newswriting, which is generally composed in a brief, fact-based style.

New Journalists: See *New Journalism*

New Negro Movement: See *Harlem Renaissance*

Noble Savage: The idea that primitive man is noble and good but becomes evil and corrupted as he becomes civilized. The concept of the noble savage originated in the Renaissance period but is more closely identified with such later writers as Jean-Jacques Rousseau and Aphra Behn.

O

Objective Correlative: An outward set of objects, a situation, or a chain of events corresponding to an inward experience and evoking this experience in the reader. The term frequently appears in modern criticism in discussions of authors' intended effects on the emotional responses of readers.

Objectivity: A quality in writing characterized by the absence of the author's opinion or feeling about the subject matter. Objectivity is an important factor in criticism.

Occasional Verse: poetry written on the occasion of a significant historical or personal event. *Vers de societe* is sometimes called occasional verse although it is of a less serious nature.

Octave: A poem or stanza composed of eight lines. The term octave most often represents the first eight lines of a Petrarchan sonnet.

Ode: Name given to an extended lyric poem characterized by exalted emotion and dignified style. An ode usually concerns a single, serious theme. Most odes, but not all, are addressed to an object or individual. Odes are distinguished from other lyric poetic forms by their complex rhythmic and stanzaic patterns.

Oedipus Complex: A son's amorous obsession with his mother. The phrase is derived from the story of the ancient Theban hero Oedipus, who unknowingly killed his father and married his mother.

Omniscience: See *Point of View*

Onomatopoeia: The use of words whose sounds express or suggest their meaning. In its simplest sense, onomatopoeia may be represented by words that mimic the sounds they denote such as "hiss" or "meow." At a more subtle level, the pattern and rhythm of sounds and rhymes of a line or poem may be onomatopoeic.

Oral Tradition: See *Oral Transmission*

Oral Transmission: A process by which songs, ballads, folklore, and other material are transmitted by word of mouth. The tradition of oral transmission predates the written record systems of literate society. Oral transmission preserves material sometimes over generations, although often with variations. Memory plays a large part in the recitation and preservation of orally transmitted material.

Ottava Rima: An eight-line stanza of poetry composed in iambic pentameter (a five-foot line in which each foot consists of an unaccented syllable followed by an accented syllable), following the abababcc rhyme scheme.

Oxymoron: A phrase combining two contradictory terms. Oxymorons may be intentional or unintentional.

P

Pantheism: The idea that all things are both a manifestation or revelation of God and a part of God at the same time. Pantheism was a common attitude in the early societies of Egypt, India, and Greece—the term derives from the Greek *pan* meaning "all" and *theos* meaning "deity." It later became a significant part of the Christian faith.

Parable: A story intended to teach a moral lesson or answer an ethical question.

Paradox: A statement that appears illogical or contradictory at first, but may actually point to an underlying truth.

Parallelism: A method of comparison of two ideas in which each is developed in the same grammatical structure.

Parnassianism: A mid nineteenth-century movement in French literature. Followers of the movement stressed adherence to well-defined artistic forms as a reaction against the often chaotic expression of the artist's ego that dominated the work of the Romantics. The Parnassians also rejected the moral, ethical, and social themes exhibited in the works of French Romantics such as Victor Hugo. The aesthetic doctrines of the Parnassians strongly influenced the later symbolist and decadent movements.

Parody: In literary criticism, this term refers to an imitation of a serious literary work or the signature style of a particular author in a ridiculous manner. A typical parody adopts the style of the original and applies it to an inappropriate subject for humorous effect. Parody is a form of satire and could be considered the literary equivalent of a caricature or cartoon.

Pastoral: A term derived from the Latin word "pastor," meaning shepherd. A pastoral is a literary composition on a rural theme. The conventions of the pastoral were originated by the third-century Greek poet Theocritus, who wrote about the experiences, love affairs, and pastimes of Sicilian shepherds. In a pastoral, characters and language of a courtly nature are often placed in a simple setting. The term pastoral is also used to classify dramas, elegies, and lyrics that exhibit the use of country settings and shepherd characters.

Pathetic Fallacy: A term coined by English critic John Ruskin to identify writing that falsely endows nonhuman things with human intentions and feelings, such as "angry clouds" and "sad trees."

Pen Name: See *Pseudonym*

Pentameter: See *Meter*

Persona: A Latin term meaning "mask." *Personae* are the characters in a fictional work of literature. The *persona* generally functions as a mask through which the author tells a story in a voice other than his or her own. A *persona* is usually either a character in a story who acts as a narrator or an "implied author," a voice created by the author to act as the narrator for himself or herself.

Personae: See *Persona*

Personal Point of View: See *Point of View*

Personification: A figure of speech that gives human qualities to abstract ideas, animals, and inanimate objects.

Petrarchan Sonnet: See *Sonnet*

Phenomenology: A method of literary criticism based on the belief that things have no existence outside of human consciousness or awareness. Proponents of this theory believe that art is a process that takes place in the mind of the observer as he or she contemplates an object rather than a quality of the object itself.

Plagiarism: Claiming another person's written material as one's own. Plagiarism can take the form of direct, word-for-word copying or the theft of the substance or idea of the work.

Platonic Criticism: A form of criticism that stresses an artistic work's usefulness as an agent of social engineering rather than any quality or value of the work itself.

Platonism: The embracing of the doctrines of the philosopher Plato, popular among the poets of the Renaissance and the Romantic period. Platonism is more flexible than Aristotelian Criticism and places more emphasis on the supernatural and unknown aspects of life.

Plot: In literary criticism, this term refers to the pattern of events in a narrative or drama. In its simplest sense, the plot guides the author in composing the work and helps the reader follow the work. Typically, plots exhibit causality and unity and have a beginning, a middle, and an end. Sometimes, however, a plot may consist of a series of disconnected events, in which case it is known as an "episodic plot."

Poem: In its broadest sense, a composition utilizing rhyme, meter, concrete detail, and expressive language to create a literary experience with emotional and aesthetic appeal.

Poet: An author who writes poetry or verse. The term is also used to refer to an artist or writer who has an exceptional gift for expression, imagination, and energy in the making of art in any form.

Poete maudit: A term derived from Paul Verlaine's *Les poetes maudits* (*The Accursed Poets*), a collection of essays on the French symbolist writers Stephane Mallarme, Arthur Rimbaud, and Tristan Corbiere. In the sense intended by Verlaine, the poet is "accursed" for choosing to explore extremes of human experience outside of middle-class society.

Poetic Fallacy: See *Pathetic Fallacy*

Poetic Justice: An outcome in a literary work, not necessarily a poem, in which the good are rewarded and the evil are punished, especially in ways that particularly fit their virtues or crimes.

Poetic License: Distortions of fact and literary convention made by a writer—not always a poet—for the sake of the effect gained. Poetic license is closely related to the concept of "artistic freedom."

Poetics: This term has two closely related meanings. It denotes (1) an aesthetic theory in literary criticism about the essence of poetry or (2) rules prescribing the proper methods, content, style, or diction of poetry. The term poetics may also refer to theories about literature in general, not just poetry.

Poetry: In its broadest sense, writing that aims to present ideas and evoke an emotional experience in the reader through the use of meter, imagery, connotative and concrete words, and a carefully constructed structure based on rhythmic patterns. Poetry typically relies on words and expressions that have several layers of meaning. It also makes use of the effects of regular rhythm on the ear and may make a strong appeal to the senses through the use of imagery.

Point of View: The narrative perspective from which a literary work is presented to the reader. There are four traditional points of view. The "third person omniscient" gives the reader a "godlike" perspective, unrestricted by time or place, from which to see actions and look into the minds of characters. This allows the author to comment openly on characters and events in the work. The "third person" point of view presents the events of the story from outside of any single character's perception, much like the omniscient point of view, but the reader must understand the action as it takes place and without any special insight into characters' minds or motivations. The "first person" or "personal" point of view relates events as they are perceived by a single character. The main character "tells" the story and may offer opinions about the action and characters which differ from those of the author. Much less common than omniscient, third person, and first person is the "second person" point of view, wherein the author tells the story as if it is happening to the reader.

Polemic: A work in which the author takes a stand on a controversial subject, such as abortion or religion. Such works are often extremely argumentative or provocative.

Pornography: Writing intended to provoke feelings of lust in the reader. Such works are often condemned by critics and teachers, but those which can be shown to have literary value are viewed less harshly.

Post-Aesthetic Movement: An artistic response made by African Americans to the black aesthetic movement of the 1960s and early '70s. Writers since that time have adopted a somewhat different tone in their work, with less emphasis placed on the disparity between black and white in the United States. In the words of post-aesthetic authors such as Toni Morrison, John Edgar Wideman, and Kristin Hunter, African Americans are portrayed as looking inward for answers to their own questions, rather than always looking to the outside world.

Postmodernism: Writing from the 1960s forward characterized by experimentation and continuing to apply some of the fundamentals of modernism, which included existentialism and alienation. Postmodernists have gone a step further in the rejection of tradition begun with the modernists by also rejecting traditional forms, preferring the anti-novel over the novel and the anti-hero over the hero.

Pre-Raphaelites: A circle of writers and artists in mid nineteenth-century England. Valuing the pre-Renaissance artistic qualities of religious symbolism, lavish pictorialism, and natural sensuousness, the Pre-Raphaelites cultivated a sense of mystery and melancholy that influenced later writers associated with the Symbolist and Decadent movements.

Primitivism: The belief that primitive peoples were nobler and less flawed than civilized peoples because they had not been subjected to the tainting influence of society.

Projective Verse: A form of free verse in which the poet's breathing pattern determines the lines of the poem. Poets who advocate projective verse are against all formal structures in writing, including meter and form.

Prologue: An introductory section of a literary work. It often contains information establishing the situation of the characters or presents information about the setting, time period, or action. In drama, the prologue is spoken by a chorus or by one of the principal characters.

Prose: A literary medium that attempts to mirror the language of everyday speech. It is distinguished from poetry by its use of unmetered, unrhymed language consisting of logically related sentences. Prose is usually grouped

Glossary of Literary Terms

into paragraphs that form a cohesive whole such as an essay or a novel.

Prosopopoeia: See *Personification*

Protagonist: The central character of a story who serves as a focus for its themes and incidents and as the principal rationale for its development. The protagonist is sometimes referred to in discussions of modern literature as the hero or anti-hero.

Proverb: A brief, sage saying that expresses a truth about life in a striking manner.

Pseudonym: A name assumed by a writer, most often intended to prevent his or her identification as the author of a work. Two or more authors may work together under one pseudonym, or an author may use a different name for each genre he or she publishes in. Some publishing companies maintain "house pseudonyms," under which any number of authors may write installations in a series. Some authors also choose a pseudonym over their real names the way an actor may use a stage name.

Pun: A play on words that have similar sounds but different meanings.

Pure Poetry: poetry written without instructional intent or moral purpose that aims only to please a reader by its imagery or musical flow. The term pure poetry is used as the antonym of the term "didacticism."

Q

Quatrain: A four-line stanza of a poem or an entire poem consisting of four lines.

R

Realism: A nineteenth-century European literary movement that sought to portray familiar characters, situations, and settings in a realistic manner. This was done primarily by using an objective narrative point of view and through the buildup of accurate detail. The standard for success of any realistic work depends on how faithfully it transfers common experience into fictional forms. The realistic method may be altered or extended, as in stream of consciousness writing, to record highly subjective experience.

Refrain: A phrase repeated at intervals throughout a poem. A refrain may appear at the end of each stanza or at less regular intervals. It may be altered slightly at each appearance.

Renaissance: The period in European history that marked the end of the Middle Ages. It began in Italy in the late fourteenth century. In broad terms, it is usually seen as spanning the fourteenth, fifteenth, and sixteenth centuries, although it did not reach Great Britain, for example, until the 1480s or so. The Renaissance saw an awakening in almost every sphere of human activity, especially science, philosophy, and the arts. The period is best defined by the emergence of a general philosophy that emphasized the importance of the intellect, the individual, and world affairs. It contrasts strongly with the medieval worldview, characterized by the dominant concerns of faith, the social collective, and spiritual salvation.

Repartee: Conversation featuring snappy retorts and witticisms.

Restoration: See *Restoration Age*

Restoration Age: A period in English literature beginning with the crowning of Charles II in 1660 and running to about 1700. The era, which was characterized by a reaction against Puritanism, was the first great age of the comedy of manners. The finest literature of the era is typically witty and urbane, and often lewd.

Rhetoric: In literary criticism, this term denotes the art of ethical persuasion. In its strictest sense, rhetoric adheres to various principles developed since classical times for arranging facts and ideas in a clear, persuasive, appealing manner. The term is also used to refer to effective prose in general and theories of or methods for composing effective prose.

Rhetorical Question: A question intended to provoke thought, but not an expressed answer, in the reader. It is most commonly used in oratory and other persuasive genres.

Rhyme: When used as a noun in literary criticism, this term generally refers to a poem in which words sound identical or very similar and appear in parallel positions in two or more lines. Rhymes are classified into different types according to where they fall in a line or stanza or according to the degree of similarity they exhibit in their spellings and sounds. Some major types of rhyme are "masculine" rhyme, "feminine" rhyme, and "triple" rhyme. In a masculine rhyme, the rhyming sound falls in a single accented syllable, as with "heat" and "eat." Feminine rhyme is a rhyme of two syllables, one stressed and one unstressed, as with "merry" and "tarry." Triple rhyme matches the sound of the accented syllable and the two unaccented syllables that follow: "narrative" and "declarative."

Rhyme Royal: A stanza of seven lines composed in iambic pentameter and rhymed *ababbcc*. The name is said to be a tribute to King James I of Scotland, who made much use of the form in his poetry.

Rhyme Scheme: See *Rhyme*

Rhythm: A regular pattern of sound, time intervals, or events occurring in writing, most often and most discernably in poetry. Regular, reliable rhythm is known to be soothing to humans, while interrupted, unpredictable, or rapidly changing rhythm is disturbing. These effects are known to authors, who use them to produce a desired reaction in the reader.

Rococo: A style of European architecture that flourished in the eighteenth century, especially in France. The most notable features of *rococo* are its extensive use of ornamentation and its themes of lightness, gaiety, and intimacy. In literary criticism, the term is often used disparagingly to refer to a decadent or over-ornamental style.

Romance: A broad term, usually denoting a narrative with exotic, exaggerated, often idealized characters, scenes, and themes.

Romantic Age: See *Romanticism*

Romanticism: This term has two widely accepted meanings. In historical criticism, it refers to a European intellectual and artistic movement of the late eighteenth and early nineteenth centuries that sought greater freedom of personal expression than that allowed by the strict rules of literary form and logic of the eighteenth-century neoclassicists. The Romantics preferred emotional and imaginative expression to rational analysis. They considered the individual to be at the center of all experience and so placed him or her at the center of their art. The Romantics believed that the creative imagination reveals nobler truths—unique feelings and attitudes—than those that could be discovered by logic or by scientific examination. Both the natural world and the state of childhood were important sources for revelations of "eternal truths." "Romanticism" is also used as a general term to refer to a type of sensibility found in all periods of literary history and usually considered to be in opposition to the principles of classicism. In this sense, Romanticism signifies any work or philosophy in which the exotic or dreamlike figure strongly, or that is devoted to individualistic expression, self-analysis, or a pursuit of a higher realm of knowledge than can be discovered by human reason.

Romantics: See *Romanticism*

Russian Symbolism: A Russian poetic movement, derived from French symbolism, that flourished between 1894 and 1910. While some Russian Symbolists continued in the French tradition, stressing aestheticism and the importance of suggestion above didactic intent, others saw their craft as a form of mystical worship, and themselves as mediators between the supernatural and the mundane.

S

Satire: A work that uses ridicule, humor, and wit to criticize and provoke change in human nature and institutions. There are two major types of satire: "formal" or "direct" satire speaks directly to the reader or to a character in the work; "indirect" satire relies upon the ridiculous behavior of its characters to make its point. Formal satire is further divided into two manners: the "Horatian," which ridicules gently, and the "Juvenalian," which derides its subjects harshly and bitterly.

Scansion: The analysis or "scanning" of a poem to determine its meter and often its rhyme scheme. The most common system of scansion uses accents (slanted lines drawn above syllables) to show stressed syllables, breves (curved lines drawn above syllables) to show unstressed syllables, and vertical lines to separate each foot.

Second Person: See *Point of View*

Semiotics: The study of how literary forms and conventions affect the meaning of language.

Sestet: Any six-line poem or stanza.

Setting: The time, place, and culture in which the action of a narrative takes place. The elements of setting may include geographic location, characters' physical and mental environments, prevailing cultural attitudes, or the historical time in which the action takes place.

Shakespearean Sonnet: See *Sonnet*

Signifying Monkey: A popular trickster figure in black folklore, with hundreds of tales about this character documented since the 19th century.

Simile: A comparison, usually using "like" or "as," of two essentially dissimilar things, as in "coffee as cold as ice" or "He sounded like a broken record."

Slang: A type of informal verbal communication that is generally unacceptable for formal writing. Slang words and phrases are often colorful exaggerations used to emphasize the speaker's point; they may also be shortened versions of an often-used word or phrase.

Slant Rhyme: See *Consonance*

Slave Narrative: Autobiographical accounts of American slave life as told by escaped slaves. These works first appeared during the abolition movement of the 1830s through the 1850s.

Social Realism: See *Socialist Realism*

Socialist Realism: The Socialist Realism school of literary theory was proposed by Maxim Gorky and established as a dogma by the first Soviet Congress of Writers. It demanded adherence to a communist worldview in works of literature. Its doctrines required an objective viewpoint comprehensible to the working classes and themes of social struggle featuring strong proletarian heroes.

Soliloquy: A monologue in a drama used to give the audience information and to develop the speaker's character. It is typically a projection of the speaker's innermost thoughts. Usually delivered while the speaker is alone on stage, a soliloquy is intended to present an illusion of unspoken reflection.

Sonnet: A fourteen-line poem, usually composed in iambic pentameter, employing one of several rhyme schemes. There are three major types of sonnets, upon which all other variations of the form are based: the "Petrarchan" or "Italian" sonnet, the "Shakespearean" or "English" sonnet, and the "Spenserian" sonnet. A Petrarchan sonnet consists of an octave rhymed *abbaabba* and a "sestet" rhymed either *cdecde, cdccdc,* or *cdedce.* The octave poses a question or problem, relates a narrative, or puts forth a proposition; the sestet presents a solution to the problem, comments upon the narrative, or applies the proposition put forth in the octave. The Shakespearean sonnet is divided into three quatrains and a couplet rhymed *abab cdcd efef gg.* The couplet provides an epigrammatic comment on the narrative or problem put forth in the quatrains. The Spenserian sonnet uses three quatrains and a couplet like the Shakespearean, but links their three rhyme schemes in this way: *abab bcbc cdcd ee.* The Spenserian sonnet develops its theme in two parts like the Petrarchan, its final six lines resolving a problem, analyzing a narrative, or applying a proposition put forth in its first eight lines.

Spenserian Sonnet: See *Sonnet*

Spenserian Stanza: A nine-line stanza having eight verses in iambic pentameter, its ninth verse in iambic hexameter, and the rhyme scheme ababbcbcc.

Spondee: In poetry meter, a foot consisting of two long or stressed syllables occurring together. This form is quite rare in English verse, and is usually composed of two monosyllabic words.

Sprung Rhythm: Versification using a specific number of accented syllables per line but disregarding the number of unaccented syllables that fall in each line, producing an irregular rhythm in the poem.

Stanza: A subdivision of a poem consisting of lines grouped together, often in recurring patterns of rhyme, line length, and meter. Stanzas may also serve as units of thought in a poem much like paragraphs in prose.

Stereotype: A stereotype was originally the name for a duplication made during the printing process; this led to its modern definition as a person or thing that is (or is assumed to be) the same as all others of its type.

Stream of Consciousness: A narrative technique for rendering the inward experience of a character. This technique is designed to give the impression of an ever-changing series of thoughts, emotions, images, and memories in the spontaneous and seemingly illogical order that they occur in life.

Structuralism: A twentieth-century movement in literary criticism that examines how literary texts arrive at their meanings, rather than the meanings themselves. There are two major types of structuralist analysis: one examines the way patterns of linguistic structures unify a specific text and emphasize certain elements of that text, and the other interprets the way literary forms and conventions affect the meaning of language itself.

Structure: The form taken by a piece of literature. The structure may be made obvious for ease of understanding, as in nonfiction works, or may obscured for artistic purposes, as in some poetry or seemingly "unstructured" prose.

Sturm und Drang: A German term meaning "storm and stress." It refers to a German literary movement of the 1770s and 1780s that reacted against the order and rationalism of the enlightenment, focusing instead on the intense experience of extraordinary individuals.

Style: A writer's distinctive manner of arranging words to suit his or her ideas and purpose in writing. The unique imprint of the author's personality upon his or her writing, style is the product of an author's way of arranging ideas and his or her use of diction, different sentence structures, rhythm, figures of speech, rhetorical principles, and other elements of composition.

Subject: The person, event, or theme at the center of a work of literature. A work may have one or more subjects of each type, with shorter works tending to have fewer and longer works tending to have more.

Subjectivity: Writing that expresses the author's personal feelings about his subject, and which may or may not include factual information about the subject.

Surrealism: A term introduced to criticism by Guillaume Apollinaire and later adopted by Andre Breton. It refers to a French literary and artistic movement founded in the 1920s. The Surrealists sought to express unconscious thoughts and feelings in their works. The best-known technique used for achieving this aim was automatic writing—transcriptions of spontaneous outpourings from the unconscious. The Surrealists proposed to unify the contrary levels of conscious and unconscious, dream and reality, objectivity and subjectivity into a new level of "super-realism."

Suspense: A literary device in which the author maintains the audience's attention through the buildup of events, the outcome of which will soon be revealed.

Syllogism: A method of presenting a logical argument. In its most basic form, the syllogism consists of a major premise, a minor premise, and a conclusion.

Symbol: Something that suggests or stands for something else without losing its original identity. In literature, symbols combine their literal meaning with the suggestion of an abstract concept. Literary symbols are of two types: those that carry complex associations of meaning no matter what their contexts, and those that derive their suggestive meaning from their functions in specific literary works.

Symbolism: This term has two widely accepted meanings. In historical criticism, it denotes an early modernist literary movement initiated in France during the nineteenth century that reacted against the prevailing standards of realism. Writers in this movement aimed to evoke, indirectly and symbolically, an order of being beyond the material world of the five senses. Poetic expression of personal emotion figured strongly in the movement, typically by means of a private set of symbols uniquely identifiable with the individual poet. The principal aim of the Symbolists was to express in words the highly complex feelings that grew out of everyday contact with the world. In a broader sense, the term "symbolism" refers to the use of one object to represent another.

Symbolist: See *Symbolism*

Symbolist Movement: See *Symbolism*

Sympathetic Fallacy: See *Affective Fallacy*

T

Tanka: A form of Japanese poetry similar to *haiku*. A *tanka* is five lines long, with the lines containing five, seven, five, seven, and seven syllables respectively.

Terza Rima: A three-line stanza form in poetry in which the rhymes are made on the last word of each line in the following manner: the first and third lines of the first stanza, then the second line of the first stanza and the first and third lines of the second stanza, and so on with the middle line of any stanza rhyming with the first and third lines of the following stanza.

Tetrameter: See *Meter*

Textual Criticism: A branch of literary criticism that seeks to establish the authoritative text of a literary work. Textual critics typically compare all known manuscripts or printings of a single work in order to assess the meanings of differences and revisions. This procedure allows them to arrive at a definitive version that (supposedly) corresponds to the author's original intention.

Theme: The main point of a work of literature. The term is used interchangeably with thesis.

Thesis: A thesis is both an essay and the point argued in the essay. Thesis novels and thesis plays share the quality of containing a thesis which is supported through the action of the story.

Third Person: See *Point of View*

Tone: The author's attitude toward his or her audience may be deduced from the tone of the work. A formal tone may create distance or convey politeness, while an informal tone may encourage a friendly, intimate, or intrusive feeling in the reader. The author's attitude toward his or her subject matter may also be deduced from the tone of the words he or she uses in discussing it.

Tragedy: A drama in prose or poetry about a noble, courageous hero of excellent character who, because of some tragic character flaw or *hamartia*, brings ruin upon him- or herself. Tragedy treats its subjects in a dignified and serious manner, using poetic language to help evoke pity and fear and bring about catharsis, a purging of these emotions. The tragic form was practiced extensively by the ancient Greeks. In the Middle Ages, when classical works were virtually unknown, tragedy came to denote any works about the fall of persons from exalted to low conditions due to any reason: fate, vice, weakness, etc. According to the classical definition of tragedy, such works present the "pathetic"—that which evokes pity—rather than the tragic. The classical form of tragedy was revived in the sixteenth century; it flourished especially on the Elizabethan stage. In modern times, dramatists have attempted to adapt the form to the needs of modern society by drawing their heroes from the ranks of ordinary men and women and defining the nobility of these heroes in terms of spirit rather than exalted social standing.

Tragic Flaw: In a tragedy, the quality within the hero or heroine which leads to his or her downfall.

Transcendentalism: An American philosophical and religious movement, based in New England from around 1835 until the Civil War. Transcendentalism was a form of American romanticism that had its roots abroad in the works of Thomas Carlyle, Samuel Coleridge, and Johann Wolfgang von Goethe. The Transcendentalists stressed the importance of intuition and subjective experience in communication with God. They rejected religious dogma and texts in favor of mysticism and scientific naturalism. They pursued truths that lie beyond the "colorless" realms perceived by reason and the senses and were active social reformers in public education, women's rights, and the abolition of slavery.

Trickster: A character or figure common in Native American and African literature who uses his ingenuity to defeat enemies and escape difficult situations. Tricksters are most often animals, such as the spider, hare, or coyote, although they may take the form of humans as well.

Trimeter: See *Meter*

Triple Rhyme: See *Rhyme*

Trochee: See *Foot*

U

Understatement: See *Irony*

Unities: Strict rules of dramatic structure, formulated by Italian and French critics of the Renaissance and based loosely on the principles of drama discussed by Aristotle in his *Poetics*. Foremost among these rules were the three unities of action, time, and place that compelled a dramatist to: (1) construct a single plot with a beginning, middle, and end that details the causal relationships of action and character; (2) restrict the action to the events of a single day; and (3) limit the scene to a single place or city. The unities were observed faithfully by continental European writers until the Romantic Age, but they were never regularly observed in English drama. Modern dramatists are typically more concerned with a unity of impression or emotional effect than with any of the classical unities.

Urban Realism: A branch of realist writing that attempts to accurately reflect the often harsh facts of modern urban existence.

Utopia: A fictional perfect place, such as "paradise" or "heaven."

Utopian: See *Utopia*

Utopianism: See *Utopia*

V

Verisimilitude: Literally, the appearance of truth. In literary criticism, the term refers to aspects of a work of literature that seem true to the reader.

Vers de societe: See *Occasional Verse*

Vers libre: See *Free Verse*

Verse: A line of metered language, a line of a poem, or any work written in verse.

Versification: The writing of verse. Versification may also refer to the meter, rhyme, and other mechanical components of a poem.

Victorian: Refers broadly to the reign of Queen Victoria of England (1837-1901) and to anything with qualities typical of that era. For example, the qualities of smug narrowmindedness, bourgeois materialism, faith in social progress, and priggish morality are often considered Victorian. This stereotype is contradicted by such dramatic intellectual developments as the theories of Charles Darwin, Karl Marx, and Sigmund Freud (which stirred strong debates in England) and the critical attitudes of serious Victorian writers like Charles Dickens and George Eliot. In literature, the Victorian Period was the great age of the English novel, and the latter part of the era saw the rise of movements such as decadence and symbolism.

Victorian Age: See *Victorian*

Victorian Period: See *Victorian*

W

Weltanschauung: A German term referring to a person's worldview or philosophy.

Weltschmerz: A German term meaning "world pain." It describes a sense of anguish about the nature of existence, usually associated with a melancholy, pessimistic attitude.

Z

Zarzuela: A type of Spanish operetta.

Zeitgeist: A German term meaning "spirit of the time." It refers to the moral and intellectual trends of a given era.

Cumulative Author/Title Index

A
A Pièd (McElroy): V3
Accounting (Alegría): V21
Ackerman, Diane
    On Location in the Loire Valley: V19
Acosta, Teresa Palomo
    My Mother Pieced Quilts: V12
Acquainted with the Night (Frost): V35
Addonizio, Kim
    Knowledge: V25
Address to the Angels (Kumin): V18
After Apple Picking (Frost): V32
The Afterlife (Collins): V18
An African Elegy (Duncan): V13
After Raphael (Brock-Broido): V26
Ah, Are You Digging on My Grave? (Hardy): V4
Ai
    Reunions with a Ghost: V16
Aiken, Conrad
    The Room: V24
Air for Mercury (Hillman): V20
Akhmatova, Anna
    Everything is Plundered: V32
    I Am Not One of Those Who Left the Land: V36
    Midnight Verses: V18
    Requiem: V27
Alabama Centennial (Madgett): V10
The Alchemy of Day (Hébert): V20
Alegría, Claribel
    Accounting: V21
Alexander, Elizabeth
    The Toni Morrison Dreams: V22

Alexie, Sherman
    The Powwow at the End of the World: V39
All (Dao): V38
All I Was Doing Was Breathing (Mirabai): V24
All It Takes (Phillips): V23
All Shall Be Restored (Ryan): V36
Allegory (Bang): V23
Alvarez, Julia
    Exile: V39
Always (Apollinaire): V24
America, America (Youssef): V29
American Poetry (Simpson): V7
Amichai, Yehuda
    Not like a Cypress: V24
    Seven Laments for the War-Dead: V39
Ammons, A. R.
    The City Limits: V19
Anasazi (Snyder): V9
An Ancient Gesture (Millay): V31
And What If I Spoke of Despair (Bass): V19
Angelou, Maya
    Harlem Hopscotch: V2
    On the Pulse of Morning: V3
    Still I Rise: V38
    Woman Work: V33
Angle of Geese (Momaday): V2
Annabel Lee (Poe): V9
Anniversary (Harjo): V15
Anonymous
    Barbara Allan: V7
    Go Down, Moses: V11
    Lord Randal: V6
    The Seafarer: V8

    Sir Patrick Spens: V4
    Swing Low Sweet Chariot: V1
Anorexic (Boland): V12
Another Feeling (Stone): V40
Another Night in the Ruins (Kinnell): V26
Answers to Letters (Tranströmer): V21
An Anthem (Sanchez): V26
Anthem for Doomed Youth (Owen): V37
Any Human to Another (Cullen): V3
anyone lived in a pretty how town (cummings): V30
Apollinaire, Guillaume
    Always: V24
Apple sauce for Eve (Piercy): V22
Archaic Torso of Apollo (Rilke): V27
Arnold, Matthew
    Dover Beach: V2
Ars Poetica (MacLeish): V5
The Arsenal at Springfield (Longfellow): V17
The Art of the Novel (Sajé): V23
Art Thou the Thing I Wanted (Fulton): V25
An Arundel Tomb (Larkin): V12
Arvio, Sarah
    Memory: V21
As I Walked Out One Evening (Auden): V4
Ashbery, John
    Paradoxes and Oxymorons: V11
    Self-Portrait in a Convex Mirror: V28
Astonishment (Szymborska): V15

At the Bomb Testing Site (Stafford): V8
At the Cancer Clinic (Kooser): V24
An Attempt at Jealousy (Tsvetaeva): V29
Atwood, Margaret
   Mushrooms: V37
   Siren Song: V7
Auden, W. H.
   As I Walked Out One Evening: V4
   Funeral Blues: V10
   Musée des Beaux Arts: V1
   September 1, 1939: V27
   The Unknown Citizen: V3
Aurora Leigh (Browning): V23
Auto Wreck (Shapiro): V3
Autobiographia Literaria (O'Hara): V34
Autumn Begins in Martins Ferry, Ohio (Wright): V8

B

Babii Yar (Yevtushenko): V29
Baca, Jimmy Santiago
   Who Understands Me But Me: V40
Baggott, Julianna
   What the Poets Could Have Been: V26
Ballad of Birmingham (Randall): V5
Ballad of Orange and Grape (Rukeyser): V10
Bang, Mary Jo
   Allegory: V23
Baraka, Amiri
   In Memory of Radio: V9
Barbara Allan (Anonymous): V7
Barbarese, J. T.
   Walk Your Body Down: V26
Barbie Doll (Piercy): V9
Barot, Rick
   Bonnard's Garden: V25
Barrett, Elizabeth
   Sonnet 43: V2
The Base Stealer (Francis): V12
Bashō, Matsuo
   Falling Upon Earth: V2
   The Moon Glows the Same: V7
   Temple Bells Die Out: V18
Bass, Ellen
   And What If I Spoke of Despair: V19
Baudelaire, Charles
   Hymn to Beauty: V21
   Invitation to the Voyage: V38
The Bean Eaters (Brooks): V2
Because I Could Not Stop for Death (Dickinson): V2
Bedtime Story (MacBeth): V8
Behn, Robin
   Ten Years after Your Deliberate Drowning: V21

Bell, Marvin
   View: V25
La Belle Dame sans Merci (Keats): V17
The Bells (Poe): V3
Beowulf (Wilbur): V11
Berry, Wendell
   The Peace of Wild Things: V30
Berryman, John
   Dream Song 29: V27
Beware: Do Not Read This Poem (Reed): V6
Beware of Ruins (Hope): V8
Bialosky, Jill
   Seven Seeds: V19
Bidart, Frank
   Curse: V26
Bidwell Ghost (Erdrich): V14
Biele, Joelle
   Rapture: V21
Birch Canoe (Revard): V5
Birches (Frost): V13
Birdfoot's Grampa (Bruchac): V36
Birney, Earle
   Vancouver Lights: V8
A Birthday (Rossetti): V10
Bishop, Elizabeth
   Brazil, January 1, 1502: V6
   Filling Station: V12
   The Fish: V31
   The Man-Moth: V27
The Black Heralds (Vallejo): V26
A Black Man Talks of Reaping (Bontemps): V32
The Black Snake (Oliver): V31
Black Zodiac (Wright): V10
Blackberry Eating (Kinnell): V35
Blackberrying (Plath): V15
Blake, William
   The Fly: V34
   The Lamb: V12
   London: V40
   A Poison Tree: V24
   The Tyger: V2
A Blessing (Wright): V7
"Blighters" (Sassoon): V28
Blood Oranges (Mueller): V13
The Blue Rim of Memory (Levertov): V17
Blumenthal, Michael
   Inventors: V7
Bly, Robert
   Come with Me: V6
   Driving to Town Late to Mail a Letter: V17
Bogan, Louise
   Song for the Last Act: V39
   Words for Departure: V21
Boland, Eavan
   Anorexic: V12
   Domestic Violence: V39
   It's a Woman's World: V22
   Outside History: V31

Bonnard's Garden (Barot): V25
Bontemps, Arna
   A Black Man Talks of Reaping: V32
Borges and I (Borges): V27
Borges, Jorge Luis
   Borges and I: V27
The Boy (Hacker): V19
Bradstreet, Anne
   To My Dear and Loving Husband: V6
   Upon the Burning of Our House, July 10th, 1666: V33
Brazil, January 1, 1502 (Bishop): V6
The Bridegroom (Pushkin): V34
Bright Star! Would I Were Steadfast as Thou Art (Keats): V9
Brock-Broido, Lucie
   After Raphael: V26
Brodsky, Joseph
   Odysseus to Telemachus: V35
The Bronze Horseman (Pushkin): V28
Brontë, Emily
   Old Stoic: V33
Brooke, Rupert
   The Soldier: V7
Brooks, Gwendolyn
   The Bean Eaters: V2
   The Explorer: V32
   The Mother: V40
   The Sonnet-Ballad: V1
   Strong Men, Riding Horses: V4
   We Real Cool: V6
Brouwer, Joel
   Last Request: V14
Brown, Fleda
   The Women Who Loved Elvis All Their Lives: V28
Browning, Elizabeth Barrett
   Aurora Leigh: V23
   Sonnet 43: V2
   Sonnet XXIX: V16
Browning, Robert
   My Last Duchess: V1
   Porphyria's Lover: V15
Bruchac, Joseph
   Birdfoot's Grampa: V36
Bryant, William Cullen
   Thanatopsis: V30
Bukowski, Charles
   The Tragedy of the Leaves: V28
Burns, Robert
   A Red, Red Rose: V8
Business (Cruz): V16
The Bustle in a House (Dickinson): V10
But Perhaps God Needs the Longing (Sachs): V20
Butcher Shop (Simic): V7
Byrne, Elena Karina
   In Particular: V20

Byron, Lord
  Childe Harold's Pilgrimage: V35
  The Destruction of Sennacherib: V1
  She Walks in Beauty: V14
  When We Two Parted: V29

C

Camouflaging the Chimera (Komunyakaa): V37
The Canterbury Tales (Chaucer): V14
Cargoes (Masefield): V5
Carroll, Lewis
  Jabberwocky: V11
  The Walrus and the Carpenter: V30
Carruth, Hayden
  I, I, I: V26
Carson, Anne
  New Rule: V18
Carson, Ciaran
  The War Correspondent: V26
Carver, Raymond
  The Cobweb: V17
Casey at the Bat (Thayer): V5
Castillo, Ana
  While I Was Gone a War Began: V21
Cavafy, C. P.
  Ithaka: V19
Cavalry Crossing a Ford (Whitman): V13
Celan, Paul
  Late and Deep: V21
The Centaur (Swenson): V30
Cervantes, Lorna Dee
  Freeway 280: V30
The Chambered Nautilus (Holmes): V24
Chang, Diana
  Most Satisfied by Snow: V37
The Charge of the Light Brigade (Tennyson): V1
Chaucer, Geoffrey
  The Canterbury Tales: V14
Chicago (Sandburg): V3
Ch'ien, T'ao
  I Built My Hut beside a Traveled Road: V36
Childe Harold's Pilgrimage (Byron): V35
Childhood (Rilke): V19
Chin, Marilyn
  How I Got That Name: V28
Chocolates (Simpson): V11
Chorale (Young): V25
Christ Climbed Down (Ferlinghetti): V28
The Cinnamon Peeler (Ondaatje): V19

Cisneros, Sandra
  Once Again I Prove the Theory of Relativity: V19
The City Limits (Ammons): V19
Civilian and Soldier (Soyinka): V40
Clampitt, Amy
  Iola, Kansas: V27
  Syrinx: V39
Classic Ballroom Dances (Simic): V33
Clifton, Lucille
  Climbing: V14
  homage to my hips: V29
  Miss Rosie: V1
Climbing (Clifton): V14
The Cobweb (Carver): V17
Coleridge, Samuel Taylor
  Frost at Midnight: V39
  Kubla Khan: V5
  The Rime of the Ancient Mariner: V4
Colibrí (Espada): V16
Collins, Billy
  The Afterlife: V18
Come with Me (Bly): V6
The Constellation Orion (Kooser): V8
Concord Hymn (Emerson): V4
The Conquerors (McGinley): V13
Conscientious Objector (Millay): V34
The Continuous Life (Strand): V18
Conversation with a Stone (Szymborska): V27
Cool Tombs (Sandburg): V6
Cooper, Jane
  Rent: V25
Corrina's Going A-Maying (Herrick): V39
The Cossacks (Pastan): V25
The Country Without a Post Office (Shahid Ali): V18
Courage (Sexton): V14
The Courage That My Mother Had (Millay): V3
Crane, Stephen
  War Is Kind: V9
The Creation (Johnson): V1
Creeley, Robert
  Fading Light: V21
The Cremation of Sam McGee (Service): V10
The Crime Was in Granada (Machado): V23
Cruz, Victor Hernandez
  Business: V16
Cullen, Countee
  Any Human to Another: V3
cummings, e. e.
  anyone lived in a pretty how town: V30
  i was sitting in mcsorley's: V13
  in Just: V40
  l(a: V1

  maggie and milly and molly and may: V12
  old age sticks: V3
  since feeling is first: V34
  somewhere i have never travelled,gladly beyond: V19
Curse (Bidart): V26
The Czar's Last Christmas Letter. A Barn in the Urals (Dubie): V12

D

Daddy (Plath): V28
Dao, Bei
  All: V38
The Darkling Thrush (Hardy): V18
Darwin in 1881 (Schnackenberg): V13
Daughter-Mother-Maya-Seeta (Vazirani): V25
Dawe, Bruce
  Drifters: V10
Daylights (Warren): V13
The Dead (Mitchell): V35
Dear Reader (Tate): V10
The Death of the Ball Turret Gunner (Jarrell): V2
The Death of the Hired Man (Frost): V4
Defining the Grateful Gesture (Sapia): V40
Death Sentences (Lazić): V22
A Description of the Morning (Swift): V37
Deep Woods (Nemerov): V14
de la Mare, Walter
  The Listeners: V39
Dennis, Carl
  The God Who Loves You: V20
The Destruction of Sennacherib (Byron): V1
Dickey, James
  The Heaven of Animals: V6
  The Hospital Window: V11
Dickinson, Emily
  Because I Could Not Stop for Death: V2
  The Bustle in a House: V10
  "Hope" Is the Thing with Feathers: V3
  I Died for Beauty: V28
  I felt a Funeral, in my Brain: V13
  I Heard a Fly Buzz—When I Died—: V5
  I'm Nobody! Who Are You?: V35
  Much Madness Is Divinest Sense: V16
  My Life Closed Twice Before Its Close: V8
  A Narrow Fellow in the Grass: V11
  The Soul Selects Her Own Society: V1

Success Is Counted Sweetest: V32
There's a Certain Slant of Light: V6
This Is My Letter to the World: V4
Digging (Heaney): V5
Divakaruni, Chitra Banerjee
   My Mother Combs My Hair: V34
Diving into the Wreck (Rich): V29
Dobyns, Stephen
   It's like This: V23
Domestic Violence (Boland): V39
Do Not Go Gentle into that Good Night (Thomas): V1
Donne, John
   Holy Sonnet 10: V2
   Song: V35
   A Valediction: Forbidding Mourning: V11
Doty, Mark
   The Wings: V28
Dove, Rita
   Geometry: V15
   Grape Sherbet: V37
   This Life: V1
Dover Beach (Arnold): V2
Dream Song 29 (Berryman): V27
Dream Variations (Hughes): V15
Drifters (Dawe): V10
A Drink of Water (Heaney): V8
Drinking Alone Beneath the Moon (Po): V20
Driving to Town Late to Mail a Letter (Bly): V17
Drought Year (Wright): V8
The Drunken Boat (Rimbaud): V28
Dubie, Norman
   The Czar's Last Christmas Letter. A Barn in the Urals: V12
Du Bois, W. E. B.
   The Song of the Smoke: V13
Duffy, Carol Ann
   Originally: V25
Dugan, Alan
   How We Heard the Name: V10
Dulce et Decorum Est (Owen): V10
Dunbar, Paul Laurence
   Sympathy: V33
   We Wear the Mask: V40
Duncan, Robert
   An African Elegy: V13
Dunn, Stephen
   The Reverse Side: V21
Duration (Paz): V18

E

The Eagle (Tennyson): V11
Early in the Morning (Lee): V17
Easter 1916 (Yeats): V5
Eating Poetry (Strand): V9
Ego-Tripping (Giovanni): V28
Elegy for My Father, Who is Not Dead (Hudgins): V14
Elegy Written in a Country Churchyard (Gray): V9
An Elementary School Classroom in a Slum (Spender): V23
Elena (Mora): V33
Eliot, T. S.
   The Hollow Men: V33
   Journey of the Magi: V7
   The Love Song of J. Alfred Prufrock: V1
   The Waste Land: V20
Emerson, Claudia
   My Grandmother's Plot in the Family Cemetery: V27
Emerson, Ralph Waldo
   Concord Hymn: V4
   The Rhodora: V17
   The Snow-Storm: V34
Erdrich, Louise
   Bidwell Ghost: V14
Espada, Martín
   Colibrí: V16
   We Live by What We See at Night: V13
Ethics (Pastan): V8
Evans, Mari
   When In Rome: V36
Everything is Plundered (Akhmatova): V32
The Exhibit (Mueller): V9
Exile (Alvarez): V39
The Explorer (Brooks): V32

F

Fable for When There's No Way Out (Dao): V38
Facing It (Komunyakaa): V5
Fading Light (Creeley): V21
Falling Upon Earth (Bashō): V2
A Far Cry from Africa (Walcott): V6
A Farewell to English (Hartnett): V10
Farrokhzaad, Faroogh
   A Rebirth: V21
Fear (Mistral): V37
Fenton, James
   The Milkfish Gatherers: V11
Ferlinghetti, Lawrence
   Christ Climbed Down: V28
Fern Hill (Thomas): V3
Fiddler Crab (Jacobsen): V23
Fifteen (Stafford): V2
Filling Station (Bishop): V12
Finch, Anne
   A Nocturnal Reverie: V30
Fire and Ice (Frost): V7
The Fish (Bishop): V31
The Fish (Moore): V14
Flounder (Trethewey): V39
The Fly (Blake): V34
Follower (Heaney): V30
For a New Citizen of These United States (Lee): V15
For An Assyrian Frieze (Viereck): V9
For Jean Vincent D'abbadie, Baron St.-Castin (Nowlan): V12
For Jennifer, 6, on the Teton (Hugo): V17
For the Sake of Strangers (Laux): V24
For the Union Dead (Lowell): V7
For the White poets who would be Indian (Rose): V13
For the Young Who Want To (Piercy): V40
The Force That Through the Green Fuse Drives the Flower (Thomas): V8
Forché, Carolyn
   The Garden Shukkei-en: V18
The Forest (Stewart): V22
400-Meter Freestyle (Kumin): V38
Four Mountain Wolves (Silko): V9
Fragment 16 (Sappho): V38
Fragment 2 (Sappho): V31
Francis, Robert
   The Base Stealer: V12
Fraser, Kathleen
   Poem in Which My Legs Are Accepted: V29
Freeway 280 (Cervantes): V30
From the Rising of the Sun (Milosz): V29
Frost at Midnight (Coleridge): V39
Frost, Robert
   Acquainted with the Night: V35
   After Apple Picking: V32
   Birches: V13
   The Death of the Hired Man: V4
   Fire and Ice: V7
   Mending Wall: V5
   Nothing Gold Can Stay: V3
   Out, Out—: V10
   The Road Not Taken: V2
   Stopping by Woods on a Snowy Evening: V1
   The Wood-Pile: V6
Fu, Tu
   Jade Flower Palace: V32
Fully Empowered (Neruda): V33
Fulton, Alice
   Art Thou the Thing I Wanted: V25
Funeral Blues (Auden): V10

G

Gacela of the Dark Death (García Lorca): V20
Gallagher, Tess
   I Stop Writing the Poem: V16

García Lorca, Federico
   Gacela of the Dark Death: V20
   The Guitar: V38
   Lament for Ignacio Sánchez Mejías: V31
The Garden Shukkei-en (Forché): V18
Geometry (Dove): V15
Ghazal (Spires): V21
Ghost of a Chance (Rich): V39
The Gift (Lee): V37
Ginsberg, Allen
   Howl: V29
   A Supermarket in California: V5
Gioia, Dana
   The Litany: V24
Giovanni, Nikki
   Ego-Tripping: V28
   Knoxville, Tennessee: V17
   Winter: V35
Glück, Louise
   The Gold Lily: V5
   The Mystery: V15
Go Down, Moses (Anonymous): V11
Goblin Market (Rossetti): V27
The God Who Loves You (Dennis): V20
The Gold Lily (Glück): V5
Good Night, Willie Lee, I'll See You in the Morning (Walker): V30
Goodison, Lorna
   The River Mumma Wants Out: V25
A Grafted Tongue (Montague): V12
Graham, Jorie
   The Hiding Place: V10
   Mind: V17
Grandmother (Mort): V34
Grape Sherbet (Dove): V37
Gray, Thomas
   Elegy Written in a Country Churchyard: V9
The Greatest Grandeur (Rogers): V18
Gregg, Linda
   A Thirst Against: V20
Grennan, Eamon
   Station: V21
Grudnow (Pastan): V32
The Guitar (Lorca): V38
Gunn, Thom
   The Missing: V9

H

H.D.
   Helen: V6
   Sea Rose: V28
Hacker, Marilyn
   The Boy: V19
Hahn, Kimiko
   Pine: V23
Hall, Donald
   Names of Horses: V8

HaNagid, Shmuel
   Two Eclipses: V33
Hanging Fire (Lorde): V32
Hardy, Thomas
   Ah, Are You Digging on My Grave?: V4
   The Darkling Thrush: V18
   The Man He Killed: V3
Harjo, Joy
   Anniversary: V15
   Remember: V32
Harlem (Hughes): V1
Harlem Hopscotch (Angelou): V2
Hartnett, Michael
   A Farewell to English: V10
Hashimoto, Sharon
   What I Would Ask My Husband's Dead Father: V22
Hass, Robert
   The World as Will and Representation: V37
Having a Coke with You (O'Hara): V12
Having it Out with Melancholy (Kenyon): V17
Hawk Roosting (Hughes): V4
Hawthorne (Lowell): V36
Hayden, Robert
   Runagate Runagate: V31
   Those Winter Sundays: V1
Heaney, Seamus
   Digging: V5
   A Drink of Water: V8
   Follower: V30
   Midnight: V2
   The Singer's House: V17
Heart's Needle (Snodgrass): V29
The Heaven of Animals (Dickey): V6
Hébert, Anne
   The Alchemy of Day: V20
Hecht, Anthony
   "More Light! More Light!": V6
The Heights of Macchu Picchu (Neruda): V28
Heine, Heinrich
   The Lorelei: V37
Hejinian, Lyn
   Yet we insist that life is full of happy chance: V27
Helen (H.D.): V6
Herbert, George
   Virtue: V25
Herbert, Zbigniew
   Why The Classics: V22
Herrick, Robert
   Corrina's Going A-Maying: V39
   The Night Piece: To Julia: V29
   To the Virgins, to Make Much of Time: V13
The Hiding Place (Graham): V10
High Windows (Larkin): V3
The Highwayman (Noyes): V4

Hikmet, Nazim
   Letter to My Wife: V38
Hillman, Brenda
   Air for Mercury: V20
The Hippopotamus (Nash): V31
Hirsch, Edward
   Omen: V22
Hirshfield, Jane
   Three Times My Life Has Opened: V16
His Speed and Strength (Ostriker): V19
Hoagland, Tony
   Social Life: V19
The Hollow Men (Eliot): V33
Holmes, Oliver Wendell
   The Chambered Nautilus: V24
   Old Ironsides: V9
Holy Sonnet 10 (Donne): V2
homage to my hips (Clifton): V29
Hongo, Garrett
   The Legend: V25
   What For: V33
Hope, A. D.
   Beware of Ruins: V8
Hope Is a Tattered Flag (Sandburg): V12
"Hope" Is the Thing with Feathers (Dickinson): V3
Hopkins, Gerard Manley
   Pied Beauty: V26
   Spring and Fall: To a Young Girl: V40
The Horizons of Rooms (Merwin): V15
The Horses (Hughes): V32
The Hospital Window (Dickey): V11
Housman, A. E.
   Loveliest of Trees, the Cherry Now: V40
   To an Athlete Dying Young: V7
   When I Was One-and-Twenty: V4
How I Got That Name (Chin): V28
How We Heard the Name (Dugan): V10
Howe, Marie
   What Belongs to Us: V15
Howl (Ginsberg): V29
Hudgins, Andrew
   Elegy for My Father, Who is Not Dead: V14
Hugh Selwyn Mauberley (Pound): V16
Hughes, Langston
   Dream Variations: V15
   I, Too: V30
   Harlem: V1
   Mother to Son: V3
   The Negro Speaks of Rivers: V10
   Theme for English B: V6
   The Weary Blues: V38

Hughes, Ted
   Hawk Roosting: V4
   The Horses: V32
   Perfect Light: V19
Hugo, Richard
   For Jennifer, 6, on the Teton: V17
Hum (Lauterbach): V25
Hunger in New York City (Ortiz): V4
Huong, Ho Xuan
   Spring-Watching Pavilion: V18
Hurt Hawks (Jeffers): V3
Huswifery (Taylor): V31
Hymn to Aphrodite (Sappho): V20
Hymn to Beauty (Baudelaire): V21
An Hymn to the Evening (Wheatley): V36

I

I Am Learning to Abandon the World (Pastan): V40
I Am Not One of Those Who Left the Land (Akhmatova): V36
I Built My Hut beside a Traveled Road (Ch'ien): V36
I Died for Beauty (Dickinson): V28
I felt a Funeral, in my Brain (Dickinson): V13
I Go Back to May 1937 (Olds): V17
I Hear America Singing (Whitman): V3
I Heard a Fly Buzz—When I Died— (Dickinson): V5
I, I, I (Carruth): V26
I Stop Writing the Poem (Gallagher): V16
I, Too (Hughes): V30
I Wandered Lonely as a Cloud (Wordsworth): V33
i was sitting in mcsorley's (cummings): V13
The Idea of Ancestry (Knight): V36
The Idea of Order at Key West (Stevens): V13
If (Kipling): V22
I'm Nobody! Who Are You? (Dickinson): V35
In a Station of the Metro (Pound): V2
In Flanders Fields (McCrae): V5
in Just (cummings): V40
In Memory of Radio (Baraka): V9
In Music (Milosz): V35
In Particular (Byrne): V20
In Response to Executive Order 9066: All Americans of Japanese Descent Must Report to Relocation Centers (Okita): V32
In the Land of Shinar (Levertov): V7
In the Suburbs (Simpson): V14
Incident in a Rose Garden (Justice): V14
Inventors (Blumentha): V7
Invitation to the Voyage (Baudelaire): V38
Iola, Kansas (Clampitt): V27
An Irish Airman Foresees His Death (Yeats): V1
Island of the Three Marias (Ríos): V11
Ithaka (Cavafy): V19
It's a Woman's World (Boland): V22
It's like This (Dobyns): V23

J

Jabberwocky (Carroll): V11
Jacobsen, Josephine
   Fiddler Crab: V23
Jade Flower Palace (Fu): V32
Jarrell, Randall
   The Death of the Ball Turret Gunner: V2
   Losses: V31
Jazz Fantasia (Sandburg): V33
Jeffers, Robinson
   Hurt Hawks: V3
   Shine Perishing Republic: V4
Johnson, James Weldon
   The Creation: V1
Jonson, Ben
   On My First Son: V33
   Song: To Celia: V23
The Journey (Oliver): V40
Journey of the Magi (Eliot): V7
Justice, Donald
   Incident in a Rose Garden: V14

K

Keats, John
   La Belle Dame sans Merci : V17
   Bright Star! Would I Were Steadfast as Thou Art: V9
   Ode on a Grecian Urn : V1
   Ode to a Nightingale: V3
   On the Grasshopper and the Cricket: V32
   To Autumn: V36
   When I Have Fears that I May Cease to Be: V2
Kelly, Brigit Pegeen
   The Satyr's Heart: V22
Kenyon, Jane
   Having it Out with Melancholy: V17
   Let Evening Come: V39
   "Trouble with Math in a One-Room Country School": V9
Kilroy: (Viereck): V14
Kim, Sue (Suji) Kwock
   Monologue for an Onion: V24
Kindness (Nye): V24
King James Bible
   Psalm 8: V9
   Psalm 23: V4
Kinnell, Galway
   Another Night in the Ruins: V26
   Blackberry Eating: V35
   Saint Francis and the Sow: V9
Kipling, Rudyard
   If: V22
Kizer, Carolyn
   To an Unknown Poet: V18
Knight, Etheridge
   The Idea of Ancestry: V36
Knowledge (Addonizio): V25
Knoxville, Tennessee (Giovanni): V17
Koch, Kenneth
   Paradiso: V20
Komunyakaa, Yusef
   Camouflaging the Chimera: V37
   Facing It: V5
   Ode to a Drum: V20
   Slam, Dunk, & Hook: V30
Kooser, Ted
   At the Cancer Clinic: V24
   The Constellation Orion: V8
Kubla Khan (Coleridge): V5
Kumin, Maxine
   Address to the Angels: V18
   400-Meter Freestyle: V38
Kunitz, Stanley
   The War Against the Trees: V11
Kyger, Joanne
   September: V23

L

l(a (cummings): V1
The Lady of Shalott (Tennyson): V15
Lake (Warren): V23
The Lake Isle of Innisfree (Yeats): V15
The Lamb (Blake): V12
Lament for Ignacio Sánchez Mejías (Lorca): V31
Lament for the Dorsets (Purdy): V5
Landscape with Tractor (Taylor): V10
Lanier, Sidney
   Song of the Chattahoochee: V14
Larkin, Philip
   An Arundel Tomb: V12
   High Windows: V3
   Toads: V4
The Last Question (Parker): V18
Last Request (Brouwer): V14
Late and Deep (Celan): V21
The Latin Deli: An Ars Poetica (Ortiz Cofer): V37
Lauterbach, Ann
   Hum: V25
Laux, Dorianne
   For the Sake of Strangers: V24
Lawrence, D. H.
   Piano: V6

Layton, Irving
   A Tall Man Executes a Jig: V12
Lazarus, Emma
   The New Colossus: V37
Lazić, Radmila
   Death Sentences: V22
Leda and the Swan (Yeats): V13
Lee, Li-Young
   Early in the Morning: V17
   For a New Citizen of These United States: V15
   The Gift: V37
   The Weight of Sweetness: V11
Legal Alien (Mora): V40
The Legend (Hongo): V25
Lepidopterology (Svenbro): V23
Let Evening Come (Kenyon): V39
Letter to My Wife (Hikmet): V38
Levertov, Denise
   The Blue Rim of Memory: V17
   In the Land of Shinar: V7
   A Tree Telling of Orpheus: V31
Leviathan (Merwin): V5
Levine, Philip
   Starlight: V8
Lim, Shirley Geok-lin
   Pantoun for Chinese Women: V29
Lineage (Walker): V31
The Listeners (de la Mare): V39
The Litany (Gioia): V24
London (Blake): V40
Longfellow, Henry Wadsworth
   The Arsenal at Springfield: V17
   Paul Revere's Ride: V2
   A Psalm of Life: V7
   The Tide Rises, the Tide Falls: V39
   The Wreck of the Hesperus: V31
Lord Randal (Anonymous): V6
Lorde, Audre
   Hanging Fire: V32
   What My Child Learns of the Sea: V16
The Lorelei (Heine): V37
Losses (Jarrell): V31
Lost in Translation (Merrill): V23
Lost Sister (Song): V5
The Lotus Flowers (Voigt): V33
Love Calls Us to the Things of This World (Wilbur): V29
The Love Song of J. Alfred Prufrock (Eliot): V1
Lovelace, Richard
   To Althea, From Prison: V34
   To Lucasta, Going to the Wars: V32
Loveliest of Trees, the Cherry Now (Housman): V40
Lowell, Amy
   The Taxi: V30

Lowell, Robert
   Hawthorne: V36
   For the Union Dead: V7
   The Quaker Graveyard in Nantucket: V6
Loy, Mina
   Moreover, the Moon: V20
Lucinda Matlock (Masters): V37

M
MacBeth, George
   Bedtime Story: V8
Machado, Antonio
   The Crime Was in Granada: V23
MacLeish, Archibald
   Ars Poetica: V5
Madgett, Naomi Long
   Alabama Centennial: V10
maggie and milly and molly and may (cummings): V12
Malroux, Claire
   Morning Walk: V21
The Man He Killed (Hardy): V3
The Man-Moth (Bishop): V27
Marlowe, Christopher
   The Passionate Shepherd to His Love: V22
Marriage (Moore): V38
A Martian Sends a Postcard Home (Raine): V7
Marvell, Andrew
   To His Coy Mistress: V5
Masefield, John
   Cargoes: V5
Mastectomy (Ostriker): V26
Masters, Edgar Lee
   Lucinda Matlock: V37
Maternity (Swir): V21
Matsuo Bashō
   Falling Upon Earth: V2
   The Moon Glows the Same: V7
   Temple Bells Die Out: V18
Maxwell, Glyn
   The Nerve: V23
McCrae, John
   In Flanders Fields: V5
McElroy, Colleen
   A Piéd: V3
McGinley, Phyllis
   The Conquerors: V13
   Reactionary Essay on Applied Science: V9
McHugh, Heather
   Three To's and an Oi: V24
McKay, Claude
   The Tropics in New York: V4
Meeting the British (Muldoon): V7
Memoir (Van Duyn): V20
Memory (Arvio): V21
Mending Wall (Frost): V5
Merlin Enthralled (Wilbur): V16

Merriam, Eve
   Onomatopoeia: V6
   Two People I Want to Be Like: V37
Merrill, James
   Lost in Translation: V23
Merwin, W. S.
   The Horizons of Rooms: V15
   Leviathan: V5
Metamorphoses (Ovid): V22
Midnight (Heaney): V2
Midnight Verses (Akhmatova): V18
Midsummer, Tobago (Walcott): V34
The Milkfish Gatherers (Fenton): V11
Millay, Edna St. Vincent
   An Ancient Gesture: V31
   Conscientious Objector: V34
   The Courage That My Mother Had: V3
   Wild Swans: V17
Milosz, Czeslaw
   From the Rising of the Sun: V29
   In Music: V35
   Song of a Citizen: V16
Milton, John
   [On His Blindness] Sonnet 16: V3
   On His Having Arrived at the Age of Twenty-Three: V17
   When I Consider (Sonnet XIX): V37
Mind (Graham): V17
Miniver Cheevy (Robinson): V35
Mirabai
   All I Was Doing Was Breathing: V24
Miracles (Whitman): V39
Mirror (Plath): V1
Miss Rosie (Clifton): V1
The Missing (Gunn): V9
Mistral, Gabriela
   Fear: V37
Mitchell, Susan
   The Dead: V35
Momaday, N. Scott
   Angle of Geese: V2
   A Simile: V37
   To a Child Running With Outstretched Arms in Canyon de Chelly: V11
Monologue for an Onion (Kim): V24
Montague, John
   A Grafted Tongue: V12
Montale, Eugenio
   On the Threshold: V22
The Moon at the Fortified Pass (Po): V40
The Moon Glows the Same (Bashō): V7
Moon Rondeau (Sandburg): V36
Moore, Marianne
   The Fish: V14
   Marriage: V38
   Poetry: V17

Mora, Pat
  Elena: V33
  Legal Alien: V40
  Uncoiling: V35
"More Light! More Light!" (Hecht): V6
Moreover, the Moon (Loy): V20
Morning Walk (Malroux): V21
Mort, Valzhyna
  Grandmother: V34
Most Satisfied by Snow (Chang): V37
The Mother (Brooks): V40
Mother to Son (Hughes): V3
Much Madness Is Divinest Sense (Dickinson): V16
Muldoon, Paul
  Meeting the British: V7
  Pineapples and Pomegranates: V22
Mueller, Lisel
  Blood Oranges: V13
  The Exhibit: V9
Musée des Beaux Arts (Auden): V1
Mushrooms (Atwood): V37
Mushrooms (Plath): V33
Music Lessons (Oliver): V8
Muske-Dukes, Carol
  Our Side: V24
My Father's Song (Ortiz): V16
My Grandmother's Plot in the Family Cemetery (Emerson): V27
My Last Duchess (Browning): V1
My Life Closed Twice Before Its Close (Dickinson): V8
My Mother Combs My Hair (Divakaruni): V34
My Mother Pieced Quilts (Acosta): V12
My Papa's Waltz (Roethke): V3
The Mystery (Glück): V15

N

Names of Horses (Hall): V8
A Narrow Fellow in the Grass (Dickinson): V11
Nash, Ogden
  The Hippopotamus: V31
Native Guard (Trethewey): V29
The Negro Speaks of Rivers (Hughes): V10
Nemerov, Howard
  Deep Woods: V14
  The Phoenix: V10
Neruda, Pablo
  Fully Empowered: V33
  The Heights of Macchu Picchu: V28
  Sonnet LXXXIX: V35
  Tonight I Can Write: V11
The Nerve (Maxwell): V23
The New Colossus (Lazarus): V37

New Rule (Carson): V18
Night Journey (Roethke): V40
The Night Piece: To Julia (Herrick): V29
A Nocturnal Reverie (Finch): V30
A Noiseless Patient Spider (Whitman): V31
Not like a Cypress (Amichai): V24
Not Waving but Drowning (Smith): V3
Nothing Gold Can Stay (Frost): V3
Nowlan, Alden
  For Jean Vincent D'abbadie, Baron St.-Castin: V12
Noyes, Alfred
  The Highwayman: V4
Nye, Naomi Shihab
  Kindness: V24
  Shoulders: V33
The Nymph's Reply to the Shepherd (Raleigh): V14

O

O Captain! My Captain! (Whitman): V2
Ode on a Grecian Urn (Keats): V1
Ode to a Drum (Komunyakaa): V20
Ode to a Nightingale (Keats): V3
Ode to the West Wind (Shelley): V2
Odysseus to Telemachus (Brodsky): V35
Of Modern Poetry (Stevens): V35
O'Hara, Frank
  Autobiographia Literaria: V34
  Having a Coke with You: V12
  Poem (Lana Turner Has Collapsed): V38
  Why I Am Not a Painter: V8
Okita, Dwight
  In Response to Executive Order 9066: All Americans of Japanese Descent Must Report to Relocation Centers: V32
old age sticks (cummings): V3
Old Ironsides (Holmes): V9
Olds, Sharon
  I Go Back to May 1937: V17
Old Stoic (Brontë): V33
Oliver, Mary
  The Black Snake: V31
  The Journey: V40
  Music Lessons: V8
  Wild Geese: V15
Omen (Hirsch): V22
On Being Brought from Africa to America (Wheatley): V29
On Freedom's Ground (Wilbur): V12
[On His Blindness] Sonnet 16 (Milton): V3
On His Having Arrived at the Age of Twenty-Three (Milton): V17

On Location in the Loire Valley (Ackerman): V19
On My First Son (Jonson): V33
On the Grasshopper and the Cricket (Keats): V32
On the Pulse of Morning (Angelou): V3
On the Threshold (Montale): V22
Once Again I Prove the Theory of Relativity (Cisneros): V19
Ondaatje, Michael
  The Cinnamon Peeler: V19
  To a Sad Daughter: V8
One Is One (Ponsot): V24
One of the Smallest (Stern): V26
Onomatopoeia (Merriam): V6
Oranges (Soto): V30
Ordinary Words (Stone): V19
Originally (Duffy): V25
Ortiz, Simon
  Hunger in New York City: V4
  My Father's Song: V16
Ortiz Cofer, Judith
  The Latin Deli: An Ars Poetica: V37
Ostriker, Alicia
  His Speed and Strength: V19
  Mastectomy: V26
Our Side (Muske-Dukes): V24
Out, Out— (Frost): V10
Outside History (Boland): V31
Overture to a Dance of Locomotives (Williams): V11
Ovid, (Naso, Publius Ovidius)
  Metamorphoses: V22
Owen, Wilfred
  Anthem for Doomed Youth: V37
  Dulce et Decorum Est: V10
Oysters (Sexton): V4
Ozymandias (Shelley): V27

P

Pak Tu-Jin
  River of August: V35
Pantoun for Chinese Women (Lim): V29
Paradiso (Koch): V20
Paradoxes and Oxymorons (Ashbery): V11
Parker, Dorothy
  The Last Question: V18
The Passionate Shepherd to His Love (Marlowe): V22
Pastan, Linda
  The Cossacks: V25
  Ethics: V8
  Grudnow: V32
  I Am Learning to Abandon the World: V40
Paul Revere's Ride (Longfellow): V2
Pavese, Cesare
  Two Poems for T.: V20

Paz, Octavio
    Duration: V18
    Sunstone: V30
    Two Bodies: V38
The Peace of Wild Things (Berry): V30
Perfect Light (Hughes): V19
Phillips, Carl
    All It Takes: V23
The Phoenix (Nemerov): V10
Piano (Lawrence): V6
Pied Beauty (Hopkins): V26
Piercy, Marge
    Apple sauce for Eve: V22
    Barbie Doll: V9
    To Be of Use: V32
    For the Young Who Want To: V40
Pine (Hahn): V23
Pineapples and Pomegranates (Muldoon): V22
Pinsky, Robert
    Song of Reasons: V18
Plath, Sylvia
    Blackberrying: V15
    Daddy: V28
    Mirror: V1
    Mushrooms: V33
A Psalm of Life (Longfellow): V7
Po, Li
    Drinking Alone Beneath the Moon: V20
    The Moon at the Fortified Pass: V40
Poe, Edgar Allan
    Annabel Lee: V9
    The Bells: V3
    The Raven: V1
Poem in Which My Legs Are Accepted (Fraser): V29
Poem (Lana Turner Has Collapsed) (O'Hara): V38
Poetry (Moore): V17
A Poison Tree (Blake): V24
Ponsot, Marie
    One Is One: V24
Pope, Alexander
    The Rape of the Lock: V12
Porphyria's Lover (Browning): V15
Portrait of a Couple at Century's End (Santos): V24
Possibilities (Szymborska): V34
Pound, Ezra
    Hugh Selwyn Mauberley: V16
    In a Station of the Metro: V2
    The River-Merchant's Wife: A Letter: V8
The Powwow at the End of the World (Alexie): V39
Practice (Voigt): V23
Prayer to the Masks (Senghor): V36
Pride (Ravikovitch): V38
Proem (Tennyson): V19

Psalm 8 (King James Bible): V9
Psalm 23 (King James Bible): V4
Purdy, Al
    Lament for the Dorsets: V5
    Wilderness Gothic: V12
Pushkin, Alexander
    The Bridegroom: V34
    The Bronze Horseman: V28

Q

The Quaker Graveyard in Nantucket (Lowell): V6
Queen-Ann's-Lace (Williams): V6

R

Raine, Craig
    A Martian Sends a Postcard Home: V7
Raleigh, Walter, Sir
    The Nymph's Reply to the Shepherd: V14
Ramanujan, A. K.
    Waterfalls in a Bank: V27
Randall, Dudley
    Ballad of Birmingham: V5
The Rape of the Lock (Pope): V12
Rapture (Biele): V21
The Raven (Poe): V1
Ravikovitch, Dahlia
    Pride: V38
Reactionary Essay on Applied Science (McGinley): V9
A Rebirth (Farrokhzaad): V21
A Red, Red Rose (Burns): V8
The Red Wheelbarrow (Williams): V1
Reed, Ishmael
    Beware: Do Not Read This Poem: V6
Remember (Harjo): V32
Remember (Rossetti): V14
Rent (Cooper): V25
Requiem (Akhmatova): V27
Reunions with a Ghost (Ai): V16
Revard, Carter
    Birch Canoe: V5
The Reverse Side (Dunn): V21
The Rhodora (Emerson): V17
Rich, Adrienne
    Diving into the Wreck: V29
    Ghost of a Chance: V39
    Rusted Legacy: V15
Richard Cory (Robinson): V4
Rilke, Rainer Maria
    Archaic Torso of Apollo: V27
    Childhood: V19
Rimbaud, Arthur
    The Drunken Boat: V28
The Rime of the Ancient Mariner (Coleridge): V4
Ríos, Alberto
    Island of the Three Marias: V11

River of August (Pak): V35
The River-Merchant's Wife: A Letter (Pound): V8
The River Mumma Wants Out (Goodison): V25
The Road Not Taken (Frost): V2
Robinson, E. A.
    Miniver Cheevy: V35
    Richard Cory: V4
Roethke, Theodore
    My Papa's Waltz: V3
    Night Journey: V40
    The Waking: V34
Rogers, Pattiann
    The Greatest Grandeur: V18
The Room (Aiken): V24
Rose, Wendy
    For the White poets who would be Indian: V13
Rossetti, Christina
    A Birthday: V10
    Goblin Market: V27
    Remember: V14
    Up-Hill: V34
Ruefle, Mary
    Sentimental Education: V26
Rukeyser, Muriel
    Ballad of Orange and Grape: V10
    St. Roach: V29
Runagate Runagate (Hayden): V31
Russian Letter (Yau): V26
Rusted Legacy (Rich): V15
Ryan, Kay
    All Shall Be Restored: V36

S

Sachs, Nelly
    But Perhaps God Needs the Longing: V20
Sailing to Byzantium (Yeats): V2
Saint Francis and the Sow (Kinnell): V9
Sajé, Natasha
    The Art of the Novel: V23
Salter, Mary Jo
    Trompe l'Oeil: V22
Sanchez, Sonia
    An Anthem: V26
Sandburg, Carl
    Chicago: V3
    Cool Tombs: V6
    Hope Is a Tattered Flag: V12
    Jazz Fantasia: V33
    Moon Rondeau: V36
Santos, Sherod
    Portrait of a Couple at Century's End: V24
Sapia, Yvonne
    Defining the Grateful Gesture: V40

Cumulative Author/Title Index

Sappho
  Fragment 16: V38
  Fragment 2: V31
  Hymn to Aphrodite: V20
Sassoon, Siegfried
  "Blighters": V28
A Satirical Elegy on the Death of a Late Famous General (Swift): V27
The Satyr's Heart (Kelly): V22
Schnackenberg, Gjertrud
  Darwin in 1881: V13
  Supernatural Love: V25
Sea Canes (Walcott): V39
Sea Rose (H.D.): V28
The Seafarer (Anonymous): V8
The Second Coming (Yeats): V7
Seeing You (Valentine): V24
Self in 1958 (Sexton): V36
Self-Portrait (Zagajewski): V25
Self-Portrait in a Convex Mirror (Ashbery): V28
Senghor, Léopold Sédar
  Prayer to the Masks: V36
Sentimental Education (Ruefle): V26
September (Kyger): V23
September 1, 1939 (Auden): V27
Service, Robert W.
  The Cremation of Sam McGee: V10
Seven Ages of Man (Shakespeare): V35
Seven Laments for the War-Dead (Amichai): V39
Seven Seeds (Bialosky): V19
Sexton, Anne
  Courage: V14
  Oysters: V4
  Self in 1958: V36
  Young: V30
Shahid Ali, Agha
  The Country Without a Post Office: V18
Shakespeare, William
  Seven Ages of Man: V35
  Sonnet 18: V2
  Sonnet 19: V9
  Sonnet 29: V8
  Sonnet 30: V4
  Sonnet 55: V5
  Sonnet 116: V3
  Sonnet 130: V1
Shapiro, Karl
  Auto Wreck: V3
She Walks in Beauty (Byron): V14
Shelley, Percy Bysshe
  Ode to the West Wind: V2
  Ozymandias: V27
  Song to the Men of England: V36
  To a Sky-Lark: V32
Shine, Perishing Republic (Jeffers): V4

Shoulders (Nye): V33
Sidney, Philip
  Ye Goatherd Gods: V30
Silko, Leslie Marmon
  Four Mountain Wolves: V9
  Story from Bear Country: V16
Simic, Charles
  Butcher Shop: V7
  Classic Ballroom Dances: V33
  Prodigy: V36
A Simile (Momaday): V37
Simpson, Louis
  American Poetry: V7
  Chocolates: V11
  In the Suburbs: V14
since feeling is first (cummings): V34
The Singer's House (Heaney): V17
Sir Patrick Spens (Anonymous): V4
Siren Song (Atwood): V7
60 (Tagore): V18
Slam, Dunk, & Hook (Komunyakaa): V30
Small Town with One Road (Soto): V7
Smart and Final Iris (Tate): V15
Smith, Stevie
  Not Waving but Drowning: V3
Snodgrass, W. D.
  Heart's Needle: V29
Snow-Bound (Whittier): V36
The Snow-Storm (Emerson): V34
Snyder, Gary
  Anasazi: V9
  True Night: V19
Social Life (Hoagland): V19
The Soldier (Brooke): V7
Solzhenitsyn, Alexander
  A Storm in the Mountains: V38
Some People Like Poetry (Szymborska): V31
somewhere i have never travelled,gladly beyond (cummings): V19
Song (Donne): V35
Song, Cathy
  Lost Sister: V5
Song for the Last Act (Bogan): V39
Song of a Citizen (Milosz): V16
Song of Reasons (Pinsky): V18
Song of the Chattahoochee (Lanier): V14
The Song of the Smoke (Du Bois): V13
Song: To Celia (Jonson): V23
Song to the Men of England (Shelley): V36
Sonnet 16 [On His Blindness] (Milton): V3
Sonnet 18 (Shakespeare): V2
Sonnet 19 (Shakespeare): V9
Sonnet 29 (Shakespeare): V8
Sonnet 30 (Shakespeare): V4

Sonnet XXIX (Browning): V16
Sonnet 43 (Browning): V2
Sonnet 55 (Shakespeare): V5
Sonnet 75 (Spenser): V32
Sonnet LXXXIX (Neruda): V35
Sonnet 116 (Shakespeare): V3
Sonnet 130 (Shakespeare): V1
The Sonnet-Ballad (Brooks): V1
Soto, Gary
  Oranges: V30
  Small Town with One Road: V7
The Soul Selects Her Own Society (Dickinson): V1
Southbound on the Freeway (Swenson): V16
Soyinka, Wole
  Civilian and Soldier: V40
  Telephone Conversation: V27
Spender, Stephen
  An Elementary School Classroom in a Slum: V23
  What I Expected: V36
Spenser, Edmund
  Sonnet 75: V32
Spires, Elizabeth
  Ghazal: V21
Spring and Fall: To a Young Girl (Hopkins): V40
Spring-Watching Pavilion (Huong): V18
St. Roach (Rukeyser): V29
Stafford, William
  At the Bomb Testing Site: V8
  Fifteen: V2
  Ways to Live: V16
Stanza LXXXIII (Stein): V38
Starlight (Levine): V8
Station (Grennan): V21
Stein, Gertrude
  Stanza LXXXIII: V38
Stern, Gerald
  One of the Smallest: V26
Stevens, Wallace
  The Idea of Order at Key West: V13
  Of Modern Poetry: V35
  Sunday Morning: V16
Stewart, Susan
  The Forest: V22
Still I Rise (Angelou): V38
The Stolen Child (Yeats): V34
Stone, Ruth
  Another Feeling: V40
  Ordinary Words: V19
Stopping by Woods on a Snowy Evening (Frost): V1
Storm Ending (Toomer): V31
A Storm in the Mountains (Solzhenitsyn): V38
Story from Bear Country (Silko): V16
Strand, Mark
  The Continuous Life: V18
  Eating Poetry: V9

Strong Men, Riding Horses (Brooks): V4
Success Is Counted Sweetest (Dickinson): V32
Sunday Morning (Stevens): V16
Sunstone (Paz): V30
A Supermarket in California (Ginsberg): V5
Supernatural Love (Schnackenberg): V25
Svenbro, Jesper
   Lepidopterology: V23
Swenson, May
   The Centaur: V30
   Fable for When There's No Way Out: V38
   Southbound on the Freeway: V16
Swift, Jonathan
   A Description of the Morning: V37
   A Satirical Elegy on the Death of a Late Famous General: V27
Swing Low Sweet Chariot (Anonymous): V1
Swir, Anna
   Maternity: V21
Sympathy (Dunbar): V33
Syrinx (Clampitt): V39
Szymborska, Wisława
   Astonishment: V15
   Conversation with a Stone: V27
   Possibilities: V34
   Some People Like Poetry: V31

T

Tagore, Rabindranath
   60: V18
A Tall Man Executes a Jig (Layton): V12
Tate, James
   Dear Reader: V10
   Smart and Final Iris: V15
The Taxi (Lowell): V30
Taylor, Edward
   Huswifery: V31
Taylor, Henry
   Landscape with Tractor: V10
Tears, Idle Tears (Tennyson): V4
Teasdale, Sara
   There Will Come Soft Rains: V14
Telephone Conversation (Soyinka): V27
Temple Bells Die Out (Bashō): V18
Ten Years after Your Deliberate Drowning (Behn): V21
Tennyson, Alfred, Lord
   The Charge of the Light Brigade: V1
   The Eagle: V11
   The Lady of Shalott: V15
   Proem: V19
   Tears, Idle Tears: V4
   Ulysses: V2

Thanatopsis (Bryant): V30
Thayer, Ernest Lawrence
   Casey at the Bat: V5
Theme for English B (Hughes): V6
There's a Certain Slant of Light (Dickinson): V6
There Will Come Soft Rains (Teasdale): V14
A Thirst Against (Gregg): V20
This Is Just to Say (Williams): V34
This Life (Dove): V1
Thomas, Dylan
   Do Not Go Gentle into that Good Night: V1
   Fern Hill: V3
   The Force That Through the Green Fuse Drives the Flower: V8
Those Winter Sundays (Hayden): V1
Thoughts of Hanoi (Vinh): V39
Three Times My Life Has Opened (Hirshfield): V16
Three To's and an Oi (McHugh): V24
The Tide Rises, the Tide Falls (Longfellow): V39
Tintern Abbey (Wordsworth): V2
To a Child Running With Outstretched Arms in Canyon de Chelly (Momaday): V11
To a Sad Daughter (Ondaatje): V8
To a Sky-Lark (Shelley): V32
To Althea, From Prison (Lovelace): V34
To an Athlete Dying Young (Housman): V7
To an Unknown Poet (Kizer): V18
To Autumn (Keats): V36
To Be of Use (Piercy): V32
To His Coy Mistress (Marvell): V5
To His Excellency General Washington (Wheatley): V13
To Lucasta, Going to the Wars (Lovelace): V32
To My Dear and Loving Husband (Bradstreet): V6
To the Virgins, to Make Much of Time (Herrick): V13
Toads (Larkin): V4
Tonight I Can Write (Neruda): V11
The Toni Morrison Dreams (Alexander): V22
Toomer, Jean
   Storm Ending: V31
The Tragedy of the Leaves (Bukowski): V28
Tranströmer, Tomas
   Answers to Letters: V21
A Tree Telling of Orpheus (Levertov): V31
Trethewey, Natasha
   Flounder: V39
   Native Guard: V29
Trompe l'Oeil (Salter): V22

The Tropics in New York (McKay): V4
True Night (Snyder): V19
Tsvetaeva, Marina
   An Attempt at Jealousy: V29
Two Bodies (Paz): V38
Two Eclipses (HaNagid): V33
Two Poems for T. (Pavese): V20
Two People I Want to Be Like (Merriam): V37
The Tyger (Blake): V2

U

Ulysses (Tennyson): V2
Uncoiling (Mora): V35
Ungaretti, Giuseppe
   Variations on Nothing: V20
The Unknown Citizen (Auden): V3
Up-Hill (Rossetti): V34
Upon the Burning of Our House, July 10th, 1666 (Bradstreet): V33

V

A Valediction: Forbidding Mourning (Donne): V11
Valentine, Jean
   Seeing You: V24
Vallejo, César
   The Black Heralds: V26
Van Duyn, Mona
   Memoir: V20
Vancouver Lights (Birney): V8
Variations on Nothing (Ungaretti): V20
Vazirani, Reetika
   Daughter-Mother-Maya-Seeta: V25
Viereck, Peter
   For An Assyrian Frieze: V9
   Kilroy: V14
View (Bell): V25
Vinh, Nguyen Thi
   Thoughts of Hanoi: V39
Virtue (Herbert): V25
Voigt, Ellen Bryant
   The Lotus Flowers: V33
   Practice: V23

W

Walcott, Derek
   A Far Cry from Africa: V6
   Midsummer, Tobago: V34
   Sea Canes: V39
Waldner, Liz
   Witness: V26
Walker, Alice
   Good Night, Willie Lee, I'll See You in the Morning: V30
   Women: V34
Walker, Margaret
   Lineage: V31

Walk Your Body Down (Barbarese): V26
The Walrus and the Carpenter (Carroll): V30
The Waking (Roethke): V34
The War Against the Trees (Kunitz): V11
The War Correspondent (Carson): V26
War Is Kind (Crane): V9
Warren, Rosanna
   Daylights: V13
   Lake: V23
The Waste Land (Eliot): V20
Waterfalls in a Bank (Ramanujan): V27
Ways to Live (Stafford): V16
We Live by What We See at Night (Espada): V13
We Real Cool (Brooks): V6
We Wear the Mask (Dunbar): V40
The Weary Blues (Hughes): V38
The Weight of Sweetness (Lee): V11
What Belongs to Us (Howe): V15
What For (Hongo): V33
What I Expected (Spender): V36
What I Would Ask My Husband's Dead Father (Hashimoto): V22
What My Child Learns of the Sea (Lorde): V16
What the Poets Could Have Been (Baggott): V26
Wheatley, Phillis
   An Hymn to the Evening: V36
   On Being Brought from Africa to America: V29
   To His Excellency General Washington: V13
When I Consider (Sonnet XIX) (Milton): V37
When I Have Fears That I May Cease to Be (Keats): V2
When I Heard the Learn'd Astronomer (Whitman): V22
When In Rome (Evans): V36
When I Was One-and-Twenty (Housman): V4
When We Two Parted (Byron): V29
While I Was Gone a War Began (Castillo): V21

Whitman, Walt
   Cavalry Crossing a Ford: V13
   I Hear America Singing: V3
   Miracles: V39
   A Noiseless Patient Spider: V31
   O Captain! My Captain!: V2
   When I Heard the Learn'd Astronomer: V22
Whittier, John Greenleaf
   Snow-Bound: V36
Who Understands Me But Me (Baca): V40
Whoso List to Hunt (Wyatt): V25
Why I Am Not a Painter (O'Hara): V8
Why The Classics (Herbert): V22
Wilbur, Richard
   Beowulf: V11
   Love Calls Us to the Things of This World: V29
   Merlin Enthralled: V16
   On Freedom's Ground: V12
Wild Geese (Oliver): V15
Wild Swans (Millay): V17
Wilderness Gothic (Purdy): V12
Williams, William Carlos
   Overture to a Dance of Locomotives: V11
   Queen-Ann's-Lace: V6
   The Red Wheelbarrow: V1
   This Is Just to Say: V34
The Wings (Doty): V28
Winter (Giovanni): V35
Witness (Waldner): V26
Woman Work (Angelou): V33
Women (Walker): V34
The Women Who Loved Elvis All Their Lives (Brown): V28
The Wood-Pile (Frost): V6
Words Are the Diminution of All Things (Wright): V35
Words for Departure (Bogan): V21
Wordsworth, William
   I Wandered Lonely as a Cloud: V33
   Lines Composed a Few Miles above Tintern Abbey: V2
   The World Is Too Much with Us: V38
The World as Will and Representation (Hass): V37

The World Is Too Much with Us (Wordsworth): V38
The Wreck of the Hesperus (Longfellow): V31
Wright, Charles
   Black Zodiac: V10
   Words Are the Diminution of All Things: V35
Wright, James
   A Blessing: V7
   Autumn Begins in Martins Ferry, Ohio: V8
Wright, Judith
   Drought Year: V8
Wyatt, Thomas
   Whoso List to Hunt: V25

Y

Yau, John
   Russian Letter: V26
Yeats, William Butler
   Easter 1916: V5
   An Irish Airman Foresees His Death: V1
   The Lake Isle of Innisfree: V15
   Leda and the Swan: V13
   Sailing to Byzantium: V2
   The Second Coming: V7
   The Stolen Child: V34
Ye Goatherd Gods (Sidney): V30
Yet we insist that life is full of happy chance (Hejinian): V27
Yevtushenko, Yevgeny
   Babii Yar: V29
Young (Sexton): V30
Young, Kevin
   Chorale: V25
Youssef, Saadi
   America, America: V29

Z

Zagajewski, Adam
   Self-Portrait: V25

Cumulative Nationality/Ethnicity Index

Acoma Pueblo
Ortiz, Simon
   Hunger in New York City: V4
   My Father's Song: V16

African American
Ai
   Reunions with a Ghost: V16
Angelou, Maya
   Harlem Hopscotch: V2
   On the Pulse of Morning: V3
   Still I Rise: V38
   Woman Work: V33
Baraka, Amiri
   In Memory of Radio: V9
Bontemps, Arna
   A Black Man Talks of Reaping: V32
Brooks, Gwendolyn
   The Bean Eaters: V2
   The Explorer: V32
   The Mother: V40
   The Sonnet-Ballad: V1
   Strong Men, Riding Horses: V4
   We Real Cool: V6
Clifton, Lucille
   Climbing: V14
   homage to my hips: V29
   Miss Rosie: V1
Cullen, Countee
   Any Human to Another: V3
Dove, Rita
   Geometry: V15
   Grape Sherbet: V37
   This Life: V1
Dunbar, Paul Laurence
   Sympathy: V33
   We Wear the Mask: V40
Evans, Mari
   When In Rome: V36
Giovanni, Nikki
   Ego-Tripping: V28
   Knoxville, Tennessee: V17
   Winter: V35
Hayden, Robert
   Runagate Runagate: V31
   Those Winter Sundays: V1
Hughes, Langston
   Dream Variations: V15
   Harlem: V1
   I, Too: V30
   Mother to Son: V3
   The Negro Speaks of Rivers: V10
   Theme for English B: V6
   The Weary Blues: V38
Johnson, James Weldon
   The Creation: V1
Knight, Etheridge
   The Idea of Ancestry: V36
Komunyakaa, Yusef
   Camouflaging the Chimera: V37
   Facing It: V5
   Ode to a Drum: V20
   Slam, Dunk, & Hook: V30
Lorde, Audre
   Hanging Fire: V32
   What My Child Learns of the Sea: V16
Madgett, Naomi Long
   Alabama Centennial: V10
McElroy, Colleen
   A Pièd: V3
Phillips, Carl
   All It Takes: V23
Randall, Dudley
   Ballad of Birmingham: V5
Reed, Ishmael
   Beware: Do Not Read This Poem: V6
Sanchez, Sonia
   An Anthem: V26
Toomer, Jean
   Storm Ending: V31
Trethewey, Natasha
   Flounder: V39
   Native Guard: V29
Walker, Alice
   Good Night, Willie Lee, I'll See You in the Morning: V30
   Women: V34
Walker, Margaret
   Lineage: V31
Wheatley, Phillis
   An Hymn to the Evening: V36
   On Being Brought from Africa to America: V29
   To His Excellency General Washington: V13

American
Ackerman, Diane
   On Location in the Loire Valley: V19
Acosta, Teresa Palomo
   My Mother Pieced Quilts: V12
Addonizio, Kim
   Knowledge: V25
Ai
   Reunions with a Ghost: V16

Aiken, Conrad
: *The Room:* V24
Alegría, Claribel
: *Accounting:* V21
Alexander, Elizabeth
: *The Toni Morrison Dreams:* V22
Alexie, Sherman
: *The Powwow at the End of the World:* V39
Alvarez, Julia
: *Exile:* V39
Ammons, A. R.
: *The City Limits:* V19
Angelou, Maya
: *Harlem Hopscotch:* V2
: *On the Pulse of Morning:* V3
: *Still I Rise:* V38
: *Woman Work:* V33
Ashbery, John
: *Paradoxes and Oxymorons:* V11
: *Self-Portrait in a Convex Mirror:* V28
Arvio, Sarah
: *Memory:* V21
Auden, W. H.
: *As I Walked Out One Evening:* V4
: *Funeral Blues:* V10
: *Musée des Beaux Arts:* V1
: *September 1, 1939:* V27
: *The Unknown Citizen:* V3
Baca, Jimmy Santiago
: *Who Understands Me But Me:* V40
Baggott, Julianna
: *What the Poets Could Have Been:* V26
Bang, Mary Jo
: *Allegory:* V23
Barbarese, J. T.
: *Walk Your Body Down:* V26
Barot, Rick
: *Bonnard's Garden:* V25
Bass, Ellen
: *And What If I Spoke of Despair:* V19
Behn, Robin
: *Ten Years after Your Deliberate Drowning:* V21
Bell, Marvin
: *View:* V25
Berry, Wendell
: *The Peace of Wild Things:* V30
Berryman, John
: *Dream Song 29:* V27
Bialosky, Jill
: *Seven Seeds:* V19
Bidart, Frank
: *Curse:* V26
Biele, Joelle
: *Rapture:* V21

Bishop, Elizabeth
: *Brazil, January 1, 1502:* V6
: *Filling Station:* V12
: *The Fish:* V31
: *The Man-Moth:* V27
Blumenthal, Michael
: *Inventors:* V7
Bly, Robert
: *Come with Me:* V6
: *Driving to Town Late to Mail a Letter:* V17
Bogan, Louise
: *Song for the Last Act:* V39
: *Words for Departure:* V21
Bontemps, Arna
: *A Black Man Talks of Reaping:* V32
Bradstreet, Anne
: *To My Dear and Loving Husband:* V6
: *Upon the Burning of Our House, July 10th, 1666:* V33
Brock-Broido, Lucie
: *After Raphael:* V26
Brodsky, Joseph
: *Odysseus to Telemachus:* V35
Brooks, Gwendolyn
: *The Bean Eaters:* V2
: *The Explorer:* V32
: *The Mother:* V40
: *The Sonnet-Ballad:* V1
: *Strong Men, Riding Horses:* V4
: *We Real Cool:* V6
Brouwer, Joel
: *Last Request:* V14
Bruchac, Joseph
: *Birdfoot's Grampa:* V36
Bryant, William Cullen
: *Thanatopsis:* V30
Bukowski, Charles
: *The Tragedy of the Leaves:* V28
Byrne, Elena Karina
: *In Particular:* V20
Carruth, Hayden
: *I, I, I:* V26
Carver, Raymond
: *The Cobweb:* V17
Castillo, Ana
: *While I Was Gone a War Began:* V21
Cervantes, Lorna Dee
: *Freeway 280:* V30
Chang, Diana
: *Most Satisfied by Snow:* V37
Chin, Marilyn
: *How I Got That Name:* V28
Cisneros, Sandra
: *Once Again I Prove the Theory of Relativity:* V19
Clampitt, Amy
: *Iola, Kansas:* V27
: *Syrinx:* V39

Clifton, Lucille
: *Climbing:* V14
: *homage to my hips:* V29
: *Miss Rosie:* V1
Collins, Billy
: *The Afterlife:* V18
Cooper, Jane
: *Rent:* V25
Crane, Stephen
: *War Is Kind:* V9
Creeley, Robert
: *Fading Light:* V21
Cruz, Victor Hernandez
: *Business:* V16
Cullen, Countee
: *Any Human to Another:* V3
cummings, e. e.
: *anyone lived in a pretty how town:* V30
: *in Just:* V40
: *i was sitting in mcsorley's:* V13
: *l(a:* V1
: *maggie and milly and molly and may:* V12
: *old age sticks:* V3
: *since feeling is first:* V34
: *somewhere i have never travelled,gladly beyond:* V19
Dennis, Carl
: *The God Who Loves You:* V20
Dickey, James
: *The Heaven of Animals:* V6
: *The Hospital Window:* V11
Dickinson, Emily
: *Because I Could Not Stop for Death:* V2
: *The Bustle in a House:* V10
: *"Hope" Is the Thing with Feathers:* V3
: *I Died for Beauty:* V28
: *I felt a Funeral, in my Brain:* V13
: *I Heard a Fly Buzz—When I Died—:* V5
: *I'm Nobody! Who Are You?:* V35
: *Much Madness Is Divinest Sense:* V16
: *My Life Closed Twice Before Its Close:* V8
: *A Narrow Fellow in the Grass:* V11
: *The Soul Selects Her Own Society:* V1
: *Success Is Counted Sweetest:* V32
: *There's a Certain Slant of Light:* V6
: *This Is My Letter to the World:* V4
Divakaruni, Chitra Banerjee
: *My Mother Combs My Hair:* V34
Dobyns, Stephen
: *It's like This:* V23
Dove, Rita
: *Geometry:* V15
: *Grape Sherbet:* V37
: *This Life:* V1

Dubie, Norman
    The Czar's Last Christmas Letter.
    A Barn in the Urals: V12
Du Bois, W. E. B.
    The Song of the Smoke: V13
Dugan, Alan
    How We Heard the Name: V10
Dunbar, Paul Laurence
    Sympathy: V33
    We Wear the Mask: V40
Duncan, Robert
    An African Elegy: V13
Dunn, Stephen
    The Reverse Side: V21
Eliot, T. S.
    The Hollow Men: V33
    Journey of the Magi: V7
    The Love Song of J. Alfred
        Prufrock: V1
Emerson, Claudia
    My Grandmother's Plot in the
        Family Cemetery: V27
Emerson, Ralph Waldo
    Concord Hymn: V4
    The Rhodora: V17
    The Snow-Storm: V34
Erdrich, Louise
    Bidwell Ghost: V14
Espada, Martín
    Colibrí: V16
    We Live by What We See at Night:
        V13
Evans, Mari
    When In Rome: V36
Ferlinghetti, Lawrence
    Christ Climbed Down: V28
Forché, Carolyn
    The Garden Shukkei-En: V18
Francis, Robert
    The Base Stealer: V12
Fraser, Kathleen
    Poem in Which My Legs Are
        Accepted: V29
Frost, Robert
    Acquainted with the Night: V35
    After Apple Picking: V32
    Birches: V13
    The Death of the Hired Man:
        V4
    Fire and Ice: V7
    Mending Wall: V5
    Nothing Gold Can Stay: V3
    Out, Out—: V10
    The Road Not Taken: V2
    Stopping by Woods on a Snowy
        Evening: V1
    The Wood-Pile: V6
Fulton, Alice
    Art Thou the Thing I Wanted:
        V25
Gallagher, Tess
    I Stop Writing the Poem: V16

Ginsberg, Allen
    Howl: V29
    A Supermarket in California: V5
Gioia, Dana
    The Litany: V24
Giovanni, Nikki
    Ego-Tripping: V28
    Knoxville, Tennessee: V17
    Winter: V35
Glück, Louise
    The Gold Lily: V5
    The Mystery: V15
Graham, Jorie
    The Hiding Place: V10
    Mind: V17
Gregg, Linda
    A Thirst Against: V20
Gunn, Thom
    The Missing: V9
H.D.
    Helen: V6
    Sea Rose: V28
Hacker, Marilyn
    The Boy: V19
Hahn, Kimiko
    Pine: V23
Hall, Donald
    Names of Horses: V8
Harjo, Joy
    Anniversary: V15
    Remember: V32
Hashimoto, Sharon
    What I Would Ask My Husband's
        Dead Father: V22
Hass, Robert
    The World as Will and
        Representation: V37
Hayden, Robert
    Runagate Runagate: V31
    Those Winter Sundays: V1
Hecht, Anthony
    "More Light! More Light!": V6
Hejinian, Lyn
    Yet we insist that life is full of
        happy chance: V27
Hillman, Brenda
    Air for Mercury: V20
Hirsch, Edward
    Omen: V22
Hirshfield, Jane
    Three Times My Life Has Opened:
        V16
Hoagland, Tony
    Social Life: V19
Holmes, Oliver Wendell
    The Chambered Nautilus: V24
    Old Ironsides: V9
Hongo, Garrett
    The Legend: V25
    What For: V33
Howe, Marie
    What Belongs to Us: V15

Hudgins, Andrew
    Elegy for My Father, Who is Not
        Dead: V14
Hughes, Langston
    Dream Variations: V15
    Harlem: V1
    I, Too: V30
    Mother to Son: V3
    The Negro Speaks of Rivers: V10
    Theme for English B: V6
    The Weary Blues: V38
Hugo, Richard
    For Jennifer, 6, on the Teton: V17
Jarrell, Randall
    The Death of the Ball Turret
        Gunner: V2
    Losses: V31
Jeffers, Robinson
    Hurt Hawks: V3
    Shine, Perishing Republic: V4
Johnson, James Weldon
    The Creation: V1
Justice, Donald
    Incident in a Rose Garden: V14
Kelly, Brigit Pegeen
    The Satyr's Heart: V22
Kenyon, Jane
    Having it Out with Melancholy:
        V17
    Let Evening Come: V39
    "Trouble with Math in a
        One-Room Country School":
        V9
Kim, Sue (Suji) Kwock
    Monologue for an Onion: V24
Kinnell, Galway
    Another Night in the Ruins: V26
    Blackberry Eating: V35
    Saint Francis and the Sow: V9
Kizer, Carolyn
    To An Unknown Poet: V18
Knight, Etheridge
    The Idea of Ancestry: V36
Koch, Kenneth
    Paradiso: V20
Komunyakaa, Yusef
    Camouflaging the Chimera: V37
    Facing It: V5
    Ode to a Drum: V20
    Slam, Dunk, & Hook: V30
Kooser, Ted
    At the Cancer Clinic: V24
    The Constellation Orion: V8
Kumin, Maxine
    Address to the Angels: V18
    400-Meter Freestyle: V38
Kunitz, Stanley
    The War Against the Trees: V11
Kyger, Joanne
    September: V23
Lanier, Sidney
    Song of the Chattahoochee: V14

Lauterbach, Ann
   Hum: V25
Laux, Dorianne
   For the Sake of Strangers: V24
Lazarus, Emma
   The New Colossus: V37
Lee, Li-Young
   Early in the Morning: V17
   For a New Citizen of These United States: V15
   The Gift: V37
   The Weight of Sweetness: V11
Levertov, Denise
   The Blue Rim of Memory: V17
   In the Land of Shinar: V7
   A Tree Telling of Orpheus: V31
Levine, Philip
   Starlight: V8
Lim, Shirley Geok-lin
   Pantoun for Chinese Women: V29
Longfellow, Henry Wadsworth
   The Arsenal at Springfield: V17
   Paul Revere's Ride: V2
   A Psalm of Life: V7
   The Tide Rises, the Tide Falls: V39
   The Wreck of the Hesperus: V31
Lorde, Audre
   Hanging Fire: V32
   What My Child Learns of the Sea: V16
Lowell, Amy
   The Taxi: V30
Lowell, Robert
   Hawthorne: V36
   For the Union Dead: V7
   The Quaker Graveyard in Nantucket: V6
Loy, Mina
   Moreover, the Moon: V20
MacLeish, Archibald
   Ars Poetica: V5
Madgett, Naomi Long
   Alabama Centennial: V10
Masters, Edgar Lee
   Lucinda Matlock: V37
McElroy, Colleen
   A Pièd: V3
McGinley, Phyllis
   The Conquerors: V13
   Reactionary Essay on Applied Science: V9
McHugh, Heather
   Three To's and an Oi: V24
McKay, Claude
   The Tropics in New York: V4
Merriam, Eve
   Onomatopoeia: V6
   Two People I Want to Be Like: V37
Merrill, James
   Lost in Translation: V23

Merwin, W. S.
   The Horizons of Rooms: V15
   Leviathan: V5
Millay, Edna St. Vincent
   An Ancient Gesture: V31
   Conscientious Objector: V34
   The Courage that My Mother Had: V3
   Wild Swans: V17
Mitchell, Susan
   The Dead: V35
Momaday, N. Scott
   Angle of Geese: V2
   A Simile: V37
   To a Child Running With Outstretched Arms in Canyon de Chelly: V11
Montague, John
   A Grafted Tongue: V12
Moore, Marianne
   The Fish: V14
   Marriage: V38
   Poetry: V17
Mora, Pat
   Elena: V33
   Legal Alien: V40
   Uncoiling: V35
Mueller, Lisel
   The Exhibit: V9
Muske-Dukes, Carol
   Our Side: V24
Nash, Ogden
   The Hippopotamus: V31
Nemerov, Howard
   Deep Woods: V14
   The Phoenix: V10
Nye, Naomi Shihab
   Kindness: V24
   Shoulders: V33
O'Hara, Frank
   Autobiographia Literaria: V34
   Having a Coke with You: V12
   Poem (Lana Turner Has Collapsed): V38
   Why I Am Not a Painter: V8
Olds, Sharon
   I Go Back to May 1937: V17
Oliver, Mary
   The Black Snake: V31
   The Journey: V40
   Music Lessons: V8
   Wild Geese: V15
Ortiz, Simon
   Hunger in New York City: V4
   My Father's Song: V16
Ortiz Cofer, Judith
   The Latin Deli: An Ars Poetica: V37
Ostriker, Alicia
   His Speed and Strength: V19
   Mastectomy: V26

Okita, Dwight
   In Response to Executive Order 9066: All Americans of Japanese Descent Must Report to Relocation Centers: V32
Parker, Dorothy
   The Last Question: V18
Pastan, Linda
   The Cossacks: V25
   Ethics: V8
   Grudnow: V32
   I Am Learning to Abandon the World: V40
Phillips, Carl
   All It Takes: V23
Piercy, Marge
   Apple sauce for Eve: V22
   Barbie Doll: V9
   For the Young Who Want to: V40
   To Be of Use: V32
Pinsky, Robert
   Song of Reasons: V18
Plath, Sylvia
   Blackberrying: V15
   Daddy: V28
   Mirror: V1
   Mushrooms: V33
Poe, Edgar Allan
   Annabel Lee: V9
   The Bells: V3
   The Raven: V1
Ponsot, Marie
   One Is One: V24
Pound, Ezra
   Hugh Selwyn Mauberley: V16
   In a Station of the Metro: V2
   The River-Merchant's Wife: A Letter: V8
Randall, Dudley
   Ballad of Birmingham: V5
Reed, Ishmael
   Beware: Do Not Read This Poem: V6
Revard, Carter
   Birch Canoe: V5
Rich, Adrienne
   Diving into the Wreck: V29
   Ghost of a Chance: V39
   Rusted Legacy: V15
Ríos, Alberto
   Island of the Three Marias: V11
Robinson, E. A.
   Miniver Cheevy: V35
   Richard Cory: V4
Roethke, Theodore
   My Papa's Waltz: V3
   Night Journey: V40
   The Waking: V34
Rogers, Pattiann
   The Greatest Grandeur: V18

Rose, Wendy
   For the White poets who would be Indian: V13
Ruefle, Mary
   Sentimental Education: V26
Rukeyser, Muriel
   Ballad of Orange and Grape: V10
Ryan, Kay
   All Shall Be Restored: V36
   St. Roach: V29
Salter, Mary Jo
   Trompe l'Oeil: V22
Sanchez, Sonia
   An Anthem: V26
Sandburg, Carl
   Chicago: V3
   Cool Tombs: V6
   Jazz Fantasia: V33
   Moon Rondeau: V36
   Hope Is a Tattered Flag: V12
Santos, Sherod
   Portrait of a Couple at Century's End: V24
Sapia, Yvonne
   Defining the Grateful Gesture: V40
Schnackenberg, Gjertrud
   Darwin in 1881: V13
   Supernatural Love: V25
Sexton, Anne
   Courage: V14
   Oysters: V4
   Self in 1958: V36
   Young: V30
Shapiro, Karl
   Auto Wreck: V3
Silko, Leslie Marmon
   Four Mountain Wolves: V9
   Story from Bear Country: V16
Simic, Charles
   Butcher Shop: V7
   Classic Ballroom Dances: V33
   Prodigy: V36
Simpson, Louis
   American Poetry: V7
   Chocolates: V11
   In the Suburbs: V14
Snodgrass, W. D.
   Heart's Needle: V29
Snyder, Gary
   Anasazi: V9
   True Night: V19
Song, Cathy
   Lost Sister: V5
Soto, Gary
   Oranges: V30
   Small Town with One Road: V7
Spires, Elizabeth
   Ghazal: V21
Stafford, William
   At the Bomb Testing Site: V8
   Fifteen: V2
   Ways to Live: V16
Stein, Gertrude
   Stanza LXXXIII: V38
Stern, Gerald
   One of the Smallest: V26
Stevens, Wallace
   The Idea of Order at Key West: V13
   Of Modern Poetry: V35
   Sunday Morning: V16
Stewart, Susan
   The Forest: V22
Stone, Ruth
   Another Feeling: V40
   Ordinary Words: V19
Strand, Mark
   The Continuous Life: V18
Swenson, May
   The Centaur: V30
   Fable for When There's No Way Oot: V38
   Southbound on the Freeway: V16
Tate, James
   Dear Reader: V10
   Smart and Final Iris: V15
Taylor, Edward
   Huswifery: V31
Taylor, Henry
   Landscape with Tractor: V10
Teasdale, Sara
   There Will Come Soft Rains: V14
Thayer, Ernest Lawrence
   Casey at the Bat: V5
Toomer, Jean
   Storm Ending: V31
Trethewey, Natasha
   Flounder: V39
   Native Guard: V29
Valentine, Jean
   Seeing You: V24
Van Duyn, Mona
   Memoir: V20
Vazirani, Reetika
   Daughter-Mother-Maya-Seeta: V25
Viereck, Peter
   For An Assyrian Frieze: V9
   Kilroy: V14
Voigt, Ellen Bryant
   The Lotus Flowers: V33
   Practice: V23
Waldner, Liz
   Witness: V26
Walker, Alice
   Good Night, Willie Lee, I'll See You in the Morning: V30
   Women: V34
Walker, Margaret
   Lineage: V31
Warren, Rosanna
   Daylights: V13
   Lake: V23
Wheatley, Phillis
   An Hymn to the Evening: V36
   On Being Brought from Africa to America: V29
   To His Excellency General Washington: V13
Whitman, Walt
   Cavalry Crossing a Ford: V13
   I Hear America Singing: V3
   Miracles: V39
   A Noiseless Patient Spider: V31
   O Captain! My Captain!: V2
   When I Heard the Learn'd Astronomer: V22
Whittier, John Greenleaf
   Snow-Bound: V36
Wilbur, Richard
   Beowulf: V11
   Love Calls Us to the Things of This World: V29
   Merlin Enthralled: V16
   On Freedom's Ground: V12
Williams, William Carlos
   Overture to a Dance of Locomotives: V11
   Queen-Ann's-Lace: V6
   The Red Wheelbarrow: V1
   This Is Just to Say: V34
Wright, Charles
   Black Zodiac: V10
   Words Are the Diminution of All Things: V35
Wright, James
   A Blessing: V7
   Autumn Begins in Martins Ferry, Ohio: V8
Yau, John
   Russian Letter: V26
Young, Kevin
   Chorale: V25

Argentinian

Borges, Jorge Luis
   Borges and I: V27

Arab American

Nye, Naomi Shihab
   Kindness: V24
   Shoulders: V33

Asian American

Chang, Diana
   Most Satisfied by Snow: V37
Chin, Marilyn
   How I Got That Name: V28
Hahn, Kimiko
   Pine: V23

Hashimoto, Sharon
   What I Would Ask My Husband's Dead Father: V22
Hongo, Garrett
   The Legend: V25
   What For: V33
Kim, Sue (Suji) Kwok
   Monologue for an Onion: V24
Lim, Shirley Geok-lin
   Pantoun for Chinese Women: V29
Okita, Dwight
   In Response to Executive Order 9066: All Americans of Japanese Descent Must Report to Relocation Centers: V32
Yau, John
   Russian Letter: V26

Australian
Dawe, Bruce
   Drifters: V10
Hope, A. D.
   Beware of Ruins: V8
Wright, Judith
   Drought Year: V8

Belarusian
Mort, Valzhyna
   Grandmother: V34

Canadian
Atwood, Margaret
   Mushrooms: V37
   Siren Song: V7
Birney, Earle
   Vancouver Lights: V8
Carson, Anne
   New Rule: V18
Hébert, Anne
   The Alchemy of Day: V20
Jacobsen, Josephine
   Fiddler Crab: V23
Layton, Irving
   A Tall Man Executes a Jig: V12
McCrae, John
   In Flanders Fields: V5
Nowlan, Alden
   For Jean Vincent D'abbadie, Baron St.-Castin: V12
Ondaatje, Michael
   The Cinnamon Peeler: V19
   To a Sad Daughter: V8
Purdy, Al
   Lament for the Dorsets: V5
   Wilderness Gothic: V12
Service, Robert W.
   The Cremation of Sam McGee: V10
Strand, Mark
   Eating Poetry: V9

Chilean
Mistral, Gabriela
   Fear: V37
Neruda, Pablo
   Fully Empowered: V33
   The Heights of Macchu Picchu: V28
   Sonnet LXXXIX: V35
   Tonight I Can Write: V11

Chinese
Ch'ien, T'ao
   I Built My Hut beside a Traveled Road: V36
Chin, Marilyn
   How I Got That Name: V28
Dao, Bei
   All: V38
Fu, Tu
   Jade Flower Palace: V32
Po, Li
   Drinking Alone Beneath the Moon: V20
   The Moon at the Fortified Pass: V40

Egyptian
Cavafy, C. P.
   Ithaka: V19

English
Alleyn, Ellen
   A Birthday: V10
Arnold, Matthew
   Dover Beach: V2
Auden, W. H.
   As I Walked Out One Evening: V4
   Funeral Blues: V10
   Musée des Beaux Arts: V1
   September 1, 1939: V27
   The Unknown Citizen: V3
Blake, William
   The Fly: V34
   The Lamb: V12
   London: V40
   A Poison Tree: V24
   The Tyger: V2
Bradstreet, Anne
   To My Dear and Loving Husband: V6
   Upon the Burning of Our House, July 10th, 1666: V33
Brontë, Emily
   Old Stoic: V33
Brooke, Rupert
   The Soldier: V7
Browning, Elizabeth Barrett
   Aurora Leigh: V23
   Sonnet XXIX: V16
   Sonnet 43: V2
Browning, Robert
   My Last Duchess: V1
   Porphyria's Lover: V15
Byron, Lord
   Childe Harold's Pilgrimage: V35
   The Destruction of Sennacherib: V1
   She Walks in Beauty: V14
   When We Two Parted: V29
Carroll, Lewis
   Jabberwocky: V11
   The Walrus and the Carpenter: V30
Chaucer, Geoffrey
   The Canterbury Tales: V14
Coleridge, Samuel Taylor
   Frost at Midnight: V39
   Kubla Khan: V5
   The Rime of the Ancient Mariner: V4
de la Mare, Walter
   The Listeners: V39
Donne, John
   Holy Sonnet 10: V2
   Song: V35
   A Valediction: Forbidding Mourning: V11
   The Waste Land: V20
Eliot, T. S.
   The Hollow Men: V33
   Journey of the Magi: V7
   The Love Song of J. Alfred Prufrock: V1
Fenton, James
   The Milkfish Gatherers: V11
Finch, Anne
   A Nocturnal Reverie: V30
Gray, Thomas
   Elegy Written in a Country Churchyard: V9
Gunn, Thom
   The Missing: V9
Hardy, Thomas
   Ah, Are You Digging on My Grave?: V4
   The Darkling Thrush: V18
   The Man He Killed: V3
Herbert, George
   Virtue: V25
Herrick, Robert
   Corrina's Going A-Maying: V39
   The Night Piece: To Julia: V29
   To the Virgins, to Make Much of Time: V13
Hopkins, Gerard Manley
   Pied Beauty: V26
   Spring and Fall: To a Young Girl: V40
Housman, A. E.
   To an Athlete Dying Young: V7
   When I Was One-and-Twenty: V4

Hughes, Ted
   Hawk Roosting: V4
   The Horses: V32
   Loveliest of Trees, the Cherry Now: V40
   Perfect Light: V19
Jonson, Ben
   On My First Son: V33
   Song: To Celia: V23
Keats, John
   La Belle Dame sans Merci: V17
   Bright Star! Would I Were Steadfast as Thou Art: V9
   Ode on a Grecian Urn: V1
   Ode to a Nightingale: V3
   On the Grasshopper and the Cricket: V32
   To Autumn: V36
   When I Have Fears that I May Cease to Be: V2
Kipling, Rudyard
   If: V22
Larkin, Philip
   An Arundel Tomb: V12
   High Windows: V3
   Toads: V4
Lawrence, D. H.
   Piano: V6
Levertov, Denise
   The Blue Rim of Memory: V17
   In the Land of Shinar: V7
   A Tree Telling of Orpheus: V31
Lovelace, Richard
   To Althea, From Prison: V34
   To Lucasta, Going to the Wars: V32
Loy, Mina
   Moreover, the Moon: V20
Marlowe, Christopher
   The Passionate Shepherd to His Love: V22
Marvell, Andrew
   To His Coy Mistress: V5
Masefield, John
   Cargoes: V5
Maxwell, Glyn
   The Nerve: V23
Milton, John
   [On His Blindness] Sonnet 16: V3
   On His Having Arrived at the Age of Twenty-Three: V17
   When I Consider (Sonnet XIX): V37
Noyes, Alfred
   The Highwayman: V4
Owen, Wilfred
   Anthem for Doomed Youth: V37
   Dulce et Decorum Est: V10
Pope, Alexander
   The Rape of the Lock: V12
Raine, Craig
   A Martian Sends a Postcard Home: V7
Raleigh, Walter, Sir
   The Nymph's Reply to the Shepherd: V14
Rossetti, Christina
   A Birthday: V10
   Goblin Market: V27
   Remember: V14
   Up-Hill: V34
Sassoon, Siegfried
   "Blighters": V28
Service, Robert W.
   The Cremation of Sam McGee: V10
Shakespeare, William
   Seven Ages of Man: V35
   Sonnet 18: V2
   Sonnet 19: V9
   Sonnet 29: V8
   Sonnet 30: V4
   Sonnet 55: V5
   Sonnet 116: V3
   Sonnet 130: V1
Shelley, Percy Bysshe
   Ode to the West Wind: V2
   Ozymandias: V27
   Song to the Men of England: V36
   To a Sky-Lark: V32
Sidney, Philip
   Ye Goatherd Gods: V30
   Ozymandias: V27
Smith, Stevie
   Not Waving but Drowning: V3
Spender, Stephen
   An Elementary School Classroom in a Slum: V23
   What I Expected: V36
Spenser, Edmund
   Sonnet 75: V32
Swift, Jonathan
   A Description of the Morning: V37
   A Satirical Elegy on the Death of a Late Famous General: V27
Taylor, Edward
   Huswifery: V31
Taylor, Henry
   Landscape with Tractor: V10
Tennyson, Alfred, Lord
   The Charge of the Light Brigade: V1
   The Eagle: V11
   The Lady of Shalott: V15
   Proem: V19
   Tears, Idle Tears: V4
   Ulysses: V2
Williams, William Carlos
   Overture to a Dance of Locomotives: V11
   Queen-Ann's-Lace: V6
   The Red Wheelbarrow: V1
   This Is Just to Say: V34
Wordsworth, William
   I Wandered Lonely as a Cloud: V33
   Lines Composed a Few Miles above Tintern Abbey: V2
   The World Is Too Much with Us: V38
Wyatt, Thomas
   Whoso List to Hunt: V25

French

Apollinaire, Guillaume
   Always: V24
Baudelaire, Charles
   Hymn to Beauty: V21
   Invitation to the Voyage: V38
Malroux, Claire
   Morning Walk: V21
Rimbaud, Arthur
   The Drunken Boat: V28

German

Amichai, Yehuda
   Not like a Cypress: V24
   Seven Laments for the War-Dead: V39
Blumenthal, Michael
   Inventors: V7
Erdrich, Louise
   Bidwell Ghost: V14
Heine, Heinrich
   The Lorelei: V37
Mueller, Lisel
   Blood Oranges: V13
   The Exhibit: V9
Rilke, Rainer Maria
   Archaic Torso of Apollo: V27
   Childhood: V19
Roethke, Theodore
   My Papa's Waltz: V3
   Night Journey: V40
   The Waking: V34
Sachs, Nelly
   But Perhaps God Needs the Longing: V20
Sajé, Natasha
   The Art of the Novel: V23

Ghanaian

Du Bois, W. E. B.
   The Song of the Smoke: V13

Greek

Cavafy, C. P.
   Ithaka: V19
Sappho
   Fragment 16: V38
   Fragment 2: V31
   Hymn to Aphrodite: V20

Hispanic American

Alvarez, Julia
  Exile: V39
Baca, Jimmy Santiago
  Who Understands Me But Me: V40
Castillo, Ana
  While I Was Gone a War Began: V21
Cervantes, Lorna Dee
  Freeway 280: V30
Cruz, Victor Hernandez
  Business: V16
Espada, Martín
  Colibrí: V16
Mora, Pat
  Elena: V33
  Legal Alien: V40
  Uncoiling: V35
Ortiz Cofer, Judith
  The Latin Deli: An Ars Poetica: V37
Sapia, Yvonne
  Defining the Grateful Gesture: V40
Walcott, Derek
  Sea Canes: V39
Williams, William Carlos
  Overture to a Dance of Locomotives: V11
  Queen-Ann's-Lace: V6
  The Red Wheelbarrow: V1
  This Is Just to Say: V34

Indian

Divakaruni, Chitra Banerjee
  My Mother Combs My Hair: V34
Mirabai
  All I Was Doing Was Breathing: V24
Ramanujan, A. K.
  Waterfalls in a Bank: V27
Shahid Ali, Agha
  Country Without a Post Office: V18
Tagore, Rabindranath
  60: V18
Vazirani, Reetika
  Daughter-Mother-Maya-Seeta: V25

Indonesian

Lee, Li-Young
  Early in the Morning: V17
  For a New Citizen of These United States: V15
  The Gift: V37
  The Weight of Sweetness: V11

Iranian

Farrokhzaad, Faroogh
  A Rebirth: V21

Iraqi

Youssef, Saadi
  America, America: V29

Irish

Boland, Eavan
  Anorexic: V12
  Domestic Violence: V39
  It's a Woman's World: V22
  Outside History: V31
Carson, Ciaran
  The War Correspondent: V26
Grennan, Eamon
  Station: V21
Hartnett, Michael
  A Farewell to English: V10
Heaney, Seamus
  Digging: V5
  A Drink of Water: V8
  Follower: V30
  Midnight: V2
  The Singer's House: V17
Muldoon, Paul
  Meeting the British: V7
  Pineapples and Pomegranates: V22
Swift, Jonathan
  A Description of the Morning: V37
  A Satirical Elegy on the Death of a Late Famous General: V27
Yeats, William Butler
  Easter 1916: V5
  An Irish Airman Foresees His Death: V1
  The Lake Isle of Innisfree: V15
  Leda and the Swan: V13
  Sailing to Byzantium: V2
  The Second Coming: V7
  The Stolen Child: V34

Israeli

Amichai, Yehuda
  Not like a Cypress: V24
  Seven Laments for the War-Dead: V39
Ravikovitch, Dahlia
  Pride: V38

Italian

Apollinaire, Guillaume
  Always: V24
Montale, Eugenio
  On the Threshold: V22
Pavese, Cesare
  Two Poems for T.: V20
Ungaretti, Giuseppe
  Variations on Nothing: V20

Jamaican

Goodison, Lorna
  The River Mumma Wants Out: V25
McKay, Claude
  The Tropics in New York: V4
Simpson, Louis
  In the Suburbs: V14

Japanese

Ai
  Reunions with a Ghost: V16
Bashō, Matsuo
  Falling Upon Earth: V2
  The Moon Glows the Same: V7
  Temple Bells Die Out: V18

Jewish

Amichai, Yehuda
  Not like a Cypress: V24
  Seven Laments for the War-Dead: V39
Bell, Marvin
  View: V25
Blumenthal, Michael
  Inventors: V7
Brodsky, Joseph
  Odysseus to Telemachus: V35
Espada, Martín
  Colibrí: V16
  We Live by What We See at Night: V13
HaNagid, Shmuel
  Two Eclipses: V33
Heine, Heinrich
  The Lorelei: V37
Hirsch, Edward
  Omen: V22
Pastan, Linda
  The Cossacks: V25
  Ethics: V8
  Grudnow: V32
  I Am Learning to Abandon the World: V40
Piercy, Marge
  Apple sauce for Eve: V22
  Barbie Doll: V9
  For the Young Who Want to: V40
  To Be of Use: V32
Ravikovitch, Dahlia
  Pride: V38
Sachs, Nelly
  But Perhaps God Needs the Longing: V20
Shapiro, Karl
  Auto Wreck: V3
Stern, Gerald
  One of the Smallest: V26

Jewish American
Lazarus, Emma
  The New Colossus: V37

Kiowa
Momaday, N. Scott
  Angle of Geese: V2
  A Simile: V37
  To a Child Running With Outstretched Arms in Canyon de Chelly: V11

Korean
Pak Tu-Jin
  River of August: V35

Lithuanian
Milosz, Czeslaw
  From the Rising of the Sun: V29
  In Music: V35
  Song of a Citizen: V16

Malaysian
Lim, Shirley Geok-lin
  Pantoun for Chinese Women: V29

Mexican
Paz, Octavio
  Duration: V18
  Sunstone: V30
  Two Bodies: V38
Soto, Gary
  Oranges: V30
  Small Town with One Road: V7

Native American
Ai
  Reunions with a Ghost: V16
Alexie, Sherman
  The Powwow at the End of the World: V39
Baca, Jimmy Santiago
  Who Understands Me But Me: V40
Bruchac, Joseph
  Birdfoot's Grampa: V36
Erdrich, Louise
  Bidwell Ghost: V14
Harjo, Joy
  Anniversary: V15
  Remember: V32
Momaday, N. Scott
  Angle of Geese: V2
  A Simile: V37
  To a Child Running With Outstretched Arms in Canyon de Chelly: V11
Ortiz, Simon
  Hunger in New York City: V4
  My Father's Song: V16

Revard, Carter
  Birch Canoe: V5
Rose, Wendy
  For the White poets who would be Indian: V13
Silko, Leslie Marmon
  Four Mountain Wolves: V9
  Story from Bear Country: V16

Nigerian
Soyinka, Wole
  Civilian and Soldier: V40
  Telephone Conversation: V27

Osage
Revard, Carter
  Birch Canoe: V5

Peruvian
Vallejo, César
  The Black Heralds: V26

Philippine
Barot, Rick
  Bonnard's Garden: V25

Polish
Herbert, Zbigniew
  Why The Classics: V22
Milosz, Czeslaw
  From the Rising of the Sun: V29
  In Music: V35
  Song of a Citizen: V16
Swir, Anna
  Maternity: V21
Szymborska, Wisława
  Astonishment: V15
  Conversation with a Stone: V27
  Possibilities: V34
  Some People Like Poetry: V31
Zagajewski, Adam
  Self-Portrait: V25

Roman
Ovid (Naso, Publius Ovidius)
  Metamorphoses: V22

Romanian
Celan, Paul
  Late and Deep: V21

Russian
Akhmatova, Anna
  Everything is Plundered: V32
  I Am Not One of Those Who Left the Land: V36
  Midnight Verses: V18
  Requiem: V27

Brodsky, Joseph
  Odysseus to Telemachus: V35
Merriam, Eve
  Onomatopoeia: V6
  Two People I Want to Be Like: V37
Pushkin, Alexander
  The Bridegroom: V34
  The Bronze Horseman: V28
Shapiro, Karl
  Auto Wreck: V3
Solzhenitsyn, Alexander
  A Storm in the Mountains: V38
Tsvetaeva, Marina
  An Attempt at Jealousy: V29
Yevtushenko, Yevgeny
  Babii Yar: V29

St. Lucian
Walcott, Derek
  A Far Cry from Africa: V6
  Midsummer, Tobago: V34

Scottish
Burns, Robert
  A Red, Red Rose: V8
Duffy, Carol Ann
  Originally: V25
MacBeth, George
  Bedtime Story: V8

Senegalese
Senghor, Léopold Sédar
  Prayer to the Masks: V36
Wheatley, Phillis
  An Hymn to the Evening: V36
  On Being Brought from Africa to America: V29
  To His Excellency General Washington: V13

Serbian
Lazić, Radmila
  Death Sentences: V22

Spanish
García Lorca, Federico
  Gacela of the Dark Death: V20
  The Guitar: V38
  Lament for Ignacio Sánchez Mejías: V31
HaNagid, Shmuel
  Two Eclipses: V33
Machado, Antonio
  The Crime Was in Granada: V23
Williams, William Carlos
  The Red Wheelbarrow: V1

Sri Lankan
Ondaatje, Michael
 The Cinnamon Peeler: V19
 To a Sad Daughter: V8

Swedish
Sandburg, Carl
 Chicago: V3
 Cool Tombs: V6
 Jazz Fantasia: V33
 Moon Rondeau: V36
 Hope Is a Tattered Flag: V12
Svenbro, Jesper
 Lepidopterology: V23

Tranströmer, Tomas
 Answers to Letters: V21

Turkish
Hikmet, Nazim
 Letter to My Wife: V38

Vietnamese
Huong, Ho Xuan
 Spring-Watching Pavilion: V18
Thomas, Dylan
 Do Not Go Gentle into that Good Night: V1

 Fern Hill: V3
 The Force That Through the Green Fuse Drives the Flower: V8
Vinh, Nguyen Thi
 Thoughts of Hanoi: V39

Yugoslavian
Lazić, Radmila
 Death Sentences: V22
Simic, Charles
 Butcher Shop: V7
 Classic Ballroom Dances: V33
 Prodigy: V36

Subject/Theme Index

Numerical

1920s (Decade)
   in Just: 95–96
1940s (Decade)
   The Mother: 202–204
1970s (Decade)
   For the Young Who Want To: 55–57
1980s (Decade)
   Legal Alien: 129–130
   For the Young Who Want To: 55–57

A

Abortion
   The Mother: 196–199, 201–208
Acceptance
   The Moon at the Fortified Pass: 184, 188, 192
   Who Understands Me But Me: 279
Activism
   For the Young Who Want To: 59, 60
African American culture
   The Mother: 212–215
   We Wear the Mask: 256
African American literature
   The Mother: 204–205
   We Wear the Mask: 260, 263–271
African history
   Civilian and Soldier: 23–25, 28–32
Afterlife
   Civilian and Soldier: 21
Alienation
   Legal Alien: 127, 128–129, 132–135

Alliteration
   Night Journey: 223
   Spring and Fall: To a Young Girl: 237–238
Allusions
   I Am Learning to Abandon the World: 75
   in Just: 92, 99
   Loveliest of Trees, the Cherry Now: 158, 164, 175
Ambiguity
   The Mother: 207
American culture
   Legal Alien: 128, 129
Anger
   For the Young Who Want To: 48, 59, 63
Anguish
   Who Understands Me But Me: 281, 288
Animals
   Another Feeling: 4, 5–6, 13
Antithesis. *See* Contrast
Art and society
   The Mother: 208–212
   For the Young Who Want To: 48–52
Assimilation
   Defining the Grateful Gesture: 33
Assonance
   Spring and Fall: To a Young Girl: 238–239
Atheism
   I Am Learning to Abandon the World: 80–81
Authority
   London: 153–155

Autobiographical fiction
   I Am Learning to Abandon the World: 86–87
   Who Understands Me But Me: 283

B

Beauty
   in Just: 105
   Loveliest of Trees, the Cherry Now: 158, 160, 161, 163, 166–167
   The Moon at the Fortified Pass: 180, 191
   Who Understands Me But Me: 276, 278, 279, 281–283, 285, 289, 290
Bible
   Defining the Grateful Gesture: 41–43
Birth
   in Just: 98
British history
   London: 142, 147–150
   Spring and Fall: To a Young Girl: 239–241
Buddhism
   The Moon at the Fortified Pass: 181–183, 187

C

Captive-captor relationships
   Who Understands Me But Me: 278, 280
Change
   Civilian and Soldier: 31
   in Just: 93–94, 97–100
   Loveliest of Trees, the Cherry Now: 173

Subject/Theme Index

Chaos
   The Journey: 109
Childhood
   I Am Learning to Abandon the World: 84–87
   in Just: 89, 91
   London: 152
   Spring and Fall: To a Young Girl: 249
Chinese culture
   The Moon at the Fortified Pass: 181–182, 187
Chinese history
   The Moon at the Fortified Pass: 185, 187–188
Choice
   I Am Learning to Abandon the World: 80
Christianity
   Spring and Fall: To a Young Girl: 237
   We Wear the Mask: 272
Civil rights
   Legal Alien: 130–131
Classicism
   Loveliest of Trees, the Cherry Now: 165–167
Coming of age
   in Just: 94
Communion
   Defining the Grateful Gesture: 46
Compassion
   Another Feeling: 4
Confession
   Another Feeling: 13
Confessional poetry
   Legal Alien: 129
Confidence
   The Journey: 112
Confinement
   London: 153–156
   We Wear the Mask: 272
Confucianism
   The Moon at the Fortified Pass: 189
Confusion
   Civilian and Soldier: 20–21
   The Mother: 199, 207
Consciousness
   Another Feeling: 13
   Night Journey: 222, 228
Contempt. *See* Disdain
Contradiction
   Civilian and Soldier: 22, 26–28
Contrast
   Civilian and Soldier: 26–28
   Defining the Grateful Gesture: 41–44
   I Am Learning to Abandon the World: 71, 72
   Legal Alien: 129
   Spring and Fall: To a Young Girl: 249
   Who Understands Me But Me: 282
Control (Psychology)
   London: 156
Courage
   Who Understands Me But Me: 285, 290
Creativity
   For the Young Who Want To: 50
Cruelty
   Who Understands Me But Me: 282
Cubism
   in Just: 94
Cultural conflict
   Legal Alien: 127–129, 132, 134
Cultural criticism
   For the Young Who Want To: 60
Cultural identity
   Legal Alien: 124, 126, 127–128, 132–135, 137, 138–140

D

Death
   Another Feeling: 1–2, 13, 16
   Civilian and Soldier: 19, 20, 22, 23, 26–28
   I Am Learning to Abandon the World: 70–74, 78–81
   London: 147, 154, 156
   Loveliest of Trees, the Cherry Now: 158, 160, 161–163
   The Mother: 199, 201, 207, 208
   Spring and Fall: To a Young Girl: 234, 236, 237, 244, 248, 249, 251–252
Decay
   Spring and Fall: To a Young Girl: 244, 251
Deception
   We Wear the Mask: 257–259, 263
Dedication
   For the Young Who Want To: 48
Deformity
   Another Feeling: 4
Derision. *See* Disdain
Despair
   Civilian and Soldier: 30
   Spring and Fall: To a Young Girl: 251
   We Wear the Mask: 259
Destruction
   Civilian and Soldier: 18, 20–21
   London: 153, 156
Determination
   The Journey: 112
Dichotomy. *See* Contrast
Disability
   Another Feeling: 4
Discomfort
   Legal Alien: 126–127, 134
Discrimination
   Legal Alien: 127, 130–131
   The Mother: 213–214
   For the Young Who Want To: 59
Disdain
   For the Young Who Want To: 60
Disillusionment
   in Just: 94
Distance
   Another Feeling: 3
Domesticity
   I Am Learning to Abandon the World: 70
Doubt
   The Mother: 207
Duty
   For the Young Who Want To: 61

E

Economics
   London: 150
Education
   For the Young Who Want To: 53–54
Emotions
   Another Feeling: 7
   The Journey: 115, 120
   Legal Alien: 124–126, 134–135
   Loveliest of Trees, the Cherry Now: 175
   The Moon at the Fortified Pass: 193–194
   The Mother: 196, 205
   Night Journey: 228
   Who Understands Me But Me: 283
Empathy
   Another Feeling: 4–5, 9, 13, 15
Emptiness
   Night Journey: 221
Endurance
   Who Understands Me But Me: 290
Enjambment
   Another Feeling: 8
Environmentalism
   The Journey: 116–117
Escape
   The Journey: 111
   London: 154
Ethics
   Another Feeling: 5–7
Ethnic identity
   Legal Alien: 124, 126, 127–128, 132–135, 137, 138–140
   We Wear the Mask: 266, 272, 273
Existentialism
   Spring and Fall: To a Young Girl: 251–252
Exploitation
   London: 152–153

F

Fall of man
  Spring and Fall: To a Young Girl: 234, 236, 237
Fate
  I Am Learning to Abandon the World: 70
  The Moon at the Fortified Pass: 181, 183–184, 191–192
Fear
  Another Feeling: 4, 13
  Civilian and Soldier: 19, 21
  London: 155
Fear of death
  Another Feeling: 5, 6, 13
Female-male relations
  For the Young Who Want To: 62
Feminism
  I Am Learning to Abandon the World: 75–77
  The Journey: 112, 115–116
  For the Young Who Want To: 56–58, 60
Foreshadowing
  Another Feeling: 3
Forgiveness
  The Mother: 208
Free verse
  Another Feeling: 8
  Defining the Grateful Gesture: 37–38
  The Journey: 109–111, 114
  in Just: 89, 91, 94
  Legal Alien: 125, 129
  The Mother: 201–202
  For the Young Who Want To: 48, 54, 55–56
Free will
  Defining the Grateful Gesture: 45
Freedom
  Who Understands Me But Me: 278, 282, 283, 285, 289, 290
Frustration
  Legal Alien: 134
Futility
  Loveliest of Trees, the Cherry Now: 161

G

Ghosts
  Civilian and Soldier: 19–20
Gratitude
  Defining the Grateful Gesture: 33–37, 43, 45
Great Depression
  Night Journey: 223
Greed
  London: 154
Greek mythology
  in Just: 92, 99

Grief
  Another Feeling: 1, 12, 16
  The Mother: 201, 208
  Spring and Fall: To a Young Girl: 249, 251
Guilt
  Defining the Grateful Gesture: 34, 45, 46
  The Mother: 207

H

Harlem Renaissance
  The Mother: 204, 212–215
  We Wear the Mask: 265
Heaven
  The Moon at the Fortified Pass: 181, 191
Heritage
  Legal Alien: 126, 138–140
Hispanic American culture
  Defining the Grateful Gesture: 35, 39, 43
  Legal Alien: 124, 128, 129, 132–135, 138–140
Hispanic American history
  Legal Alien: 130–131
Hispanic American literature
  Legal Alien: 129, 137
Homosexuality
  Loveliest of Trees, the Cherry Now: 167–170
Hope
  Civilian and Soldier: 20, 30
  Legal Alien: 135
  Who Understands Me But Me: 285, 290
Hopelessness
  London: 147
Human condition
  The Journey: 109
  Legal Alien: 135
Human nature
  London: 152
Human rights
  Civilian and Soldier: 28
Human spirit
  Who Understands Me But Me: 285, 289
Humanity
  in Just: 93
Humiliation
  We Wear the Mask: 256
Humility
  Defining the Grateful Gesture: 46

I

Identity
  Civilian and Soldier: 32
  I Am Learning to Abandon the World: 72

Ignorance
  Spring and Fall: To a Young Girl: 249
Imagery
  For the Young Who Want To: 48
Imagery (Literature)
  Civilian and Soldier: 22–23, 26
  I Am Learning to Abandon the World: 72, 73–74
  The Journey: 119–120
  London: 147
  Loveliest of Trees, the Cherry Now: 161–162, 172–173
  The Moon at the Fortified Pass: 180–181
  The Mother: 205, 206
  Night Journey: 228
  Spring and Fall: To a Young Girl: 244
  Who Understands Me But Me: 286
  For the Young Who Want To: 54–55, 65–68
Imagination
  The Mother: 209, 210
  Who Understands Me But Me: 288
Imagism
  I Am Learning to Abandon the World: 74–75
Immigrant life
  Defining the Grateful Gesture: 33, 35–37
Immortality
  The Moon at the Fortified Pass: 180
Imprisonment
  Who Understands Me But Me: 276, 278, 279–281, 283–286
Individual *vs.* society
  The Moon at the Fortified Pass: 180–181, 190–192
Individualism
  The Journey: 115
Industrialization
  London: 148–149
Injustice
  London: 142, 146, 150, 151, 153
  We Wear the Mask: 259
Innocence
  in Just: 92–93, 98
  London: 152–153
  Loveliest of Trees, the Cherry Now: 175, 176
  Spring and Fall: To a Young Girl: 249
Intellect
  Loveliest of Trees, the Cherry Now: 175
Intuition
  The Journey: 115
  Spring and Fall: To a Young Girl: 236, 237, 249

Subject/Theme Index

Irony
    Another Feeling: 3, 13
    The Journey: 120
    The Mother: 210, 213–214
    We Wear the Mask: 266, 271
    For the Young Who Want To: 50, 54–55, 59
Isolation
    I Am Learning to Abandon the World: 84
    Legal Alien: 128–129, 132–135
    Night Journey: 221–222
    Who Understands Me But Me: 288

J

Journey. *See* Travel
Joy
    in Just: 89, 92, 98
    London: 152
    Spring and Fall: To a Young Girl: 249
    Who Understands Me But Me: 276
Justification
    The Mother: 205–206

L

Landscape
    Night Journey: 221
Language and languages
    Another Feeling: 15
    Civilian and Soldier: 26, 27
    Defining the Grateful Gesture: 38, 43
    I Am Learning to Abandon the World: 74
    The Journey: 111, 115–117, 120
    in Just: 91, 101, 102–107
    Legal Alien: 124, 125–126, 133–138
    Loveliest of Trees, the Cherry Now: 176
    The Moon at the Fortified Pass: 184–185
    The Mother: 205, 207
    Night Journey: 217, 226–228
    We Wear the Mask: 265, 266
    Who Understands Me But Me: 289, 290
    For the Young Who Want To: 48, 54–55, 58, 59, 68
Life and death
    Civilian and Soldier: 26
    I Am Learning to Abandon the World: 72
    The Mother: 196, 207
Life (Philosophy)
    Civilian and Soldier: 20, 21, 23, 26–27
    I Am Learning to Abandon the World: 71
Light and darkness
    The Journey: 111
Local color
    We Wear the Mask: 271
Loneliness
    Another Feeling: 1
    I Am Learning to Abandon the World: 84
    Legal Alien: 128–129, 134
Longing
    The Moon at the Fortified Pass: 192, 193
Loss
    Another Feeling: 16
    The Mother: 206–207
Lost Generation
    in Just: 94–95
Love
    I Am Learning to Abandon the World: 72
    The Mother: 199, 201, 208
Lyric poetry
    The Journey: 121–122
    We Wear the Mask: 259

M

Manipulation
    The Journey: 109, 111, 119
Marriage
    London: 146, 147
    London: 144 144
Meaning of life
    Loveliest of Trees, the Cherry Now: 164
    The Moon at the Fortified Pass: 191
    Night Journey: 217
Melancholy
    The Moon at the Fortified Pass: 192
Memorialization
    Another Feeling: 13
    Defining the Grateful Gesture: 43
Memory
    Another Feeling: 7, 10–13
    Civilian and Soldier: 28–32
    I Am Learning to Abandon the World: 84–87
    in Just: 91
Metaphors
    Another Feeling: 13
    Defining the Grateful Gesture: 38
    I Am Learning to Abandon the World: 72, 75
    The Journey: 109, 110, 112, 115–116, 119–120
    in Just: 101, 105
    Loveliest of Trees, the Cherry Now: 175
    We Wear the Mask: 266, 272
    Who Understands Me But Me: 279
    For the Young Who Want To: 66
Middle class
    We Wear the Mask: 262
Midwestern United States
    Night Journey: 231
Misery
    London: 144, 145–146, 155
Misfortune
    Another Feeling: 3
Modern life
    The Journey: 109
Modernism (Literature)
    The Mother: 212–215
    Spring and Fall: To a Young Girl: 242–245
Morality
    Spring and Fall: To a Young Girl: 244
Mortality
    Loveliest of Trees, the Cherry Now: 161, 175
Mother-child relationships
    Defining the Grateful Gesture: 37
    The Mother: 198–199, 201
Motherhood
    The Mother: 198, 199–201
Motifs
    For the Young Who Want To: 66–67
Motivation
    Civilian and Soldier: 20, 21
Mourning. *See* Grief
Music
    I Am Learning to Abandon the World: 72
    The Moon at the Fortified Pass: 178
Mystery
    The Moon at the Fortified Pass: 191

N

Narrators
    Another Feeling: 7–8
    The Mother: 202
Nature
    I Am Learning to Abandon the World: 70, 73–74
    The Journey: 109, 112, 116, 118, 120–121
    in Just: 93, 99
    Loveliest of Trees, the Cherry Now: 158, 160, 161, 163–164, 170–174
    The Moon at the Fortified Pass: 178, 189–192
    Night Journey: 228–230
    Spring and Fall: To a Young Girl: 251
    Who Understands Me But Me: 286, 287–288

Nigerian Civil War, 1967-1970
  Civilian and Soldier: 18, 24–25
Nothingness
  Night Journey: 217, 228

O

Opposites
  Civilian and Soldier: 26–28
  I Am Learning to Abandon the World: 72
Oppression (Politics)
  London: 150, 153
  We Wear the Mask: 257
  Who Understands Me But Me: 278
Original sin
  Spring and Fall: To a Young Girl: 237, 244
Outsiders
  Legal Alien: 128
Oxymorons. *See* Contradiction

P

Pain
  Legal Alien: 125, 134, 135
  London: 156
  The Mother: 199, 201, 205, 207, 208
  For the Young Who Want To: 59–60
Parables
  Defining the Grateful Gesture: 41, 43
Paradoxes
  For the Young Who Want To: 65
Passion
  The Moon at the Fortified Pass: 193
Passivity
  The Moon at the Fortified Pass: 191
Pathos
  The Moon at the Fortified Pass: 181
Personal responsibility
  For the Young Who Want To: 59–61
Personification
  The Journey: 110
Philosophy
  I Am Learning to Abandon the World: 78–81
  Loveliest of Trees, the Cherry Now: 175
Point of view (Literature)
  Loveliest of Trees, the Cherry Now: 176
Politics
  Civilian and Soldier: 20
  I Am Learning to Abandon the World: 83
Poverty
  Defining the Grateful Gesture: 35–37, 41

Power (Philosophy)
  I Am Learning to Abandon the World: 71
  London: 153–154
  The Moon at the Fortified Pass: 181, 191
Prejudice
  We Wear the Mask: 256, 259
Prostitution
  London: 144 144
Protest
  We Wear the Mask: 259–260
Psychoanalysis
  The Journey: 118
Punishment
  Who Understands Me But Me: 282

R

Racial violence
  We Wear the Mask: 261
Racism
  We Wear the Mask: 254, 256, 257, 259, 261–262, 273
Rage
  Who Understands Me But Me: 281
Realism
  The Mother: 212
Reality
  Civilian and Soldier: 23
  The Mother: 211–212
Rebirth
  Spring and Fall: To a Young Girl: 249
  Who Understands Me But Me: 288–289
Reform
  Civilian and Soldier: 32
Regret
  Another Feeling: 7
  The Mother: 205–206
Rejection
  Legal Alien: 132
Religion
  Defining the Grateful Gesture: 41–46
  I Am Learning to Abandon the World: 80–81
  London: 144–147, 150, 153
  Spring and Fall: To a Young Girl: 234, 239–241, 251
  We Wear the Mask: 272
Relinquishment
  I Am Learning to Abandon the World: 71–72, 80
Remorse
  Another Feeling: 4, 6
  The Mother: 208
Repetition
  London: 147, 154
  Loveliest of Trees, the Cherry Now: 164–165
  The Mother: 201

Repression
  London: 145, 146
Resentment
  Defining the Grateful Gesture: 45
Resignation
  Who Understands Me But Me: 276
Resilience
  Who Understands Me But Me: 285, 290
Resolve. *See* Determination
Responsibility
  The Mother: 196, 199
Resurrection
  Civilian and Soldier: 20
Revelation
  I Am Learning to Abandon the World: 72
Reverence
  Defining the Grateful Gesture: 34, 45
Rhythm
  in Just: 91, 105–106
  London: 147
  Night Journey: 222
  Spring and Fall: To a Young Girl: 239, 248
Rituals
  Defining the Grateful Gesture: 44, 46
Roman Catholicism
  Defining the Grateful Gesture: 43–46
  Spring and Fall: To a Young Girl: 234, 239–241
Romanticism
  The Journey: 115, 118–120

S

Sadness
  Defining the Grateful Gesture: 44
  Spring and Fall: To a Young Girl: 252
Sarcasm
  For the Young Who Want To: 58, 60
Seasons
  Loveliest of Trees, the Cherry Now: 173
  Spring and Fall: To a Young Girl: 237, 249
Secularism
  I Am Learning to Abandon the World: 70, 78, 80
Self consciousness
  Who Understands Me But Me: 279
Self control
  The Journey: 112
Self determination
  Who Understands Me But Me: 283
Self examination (Psychology)
  Another Feeling: 9
Self identity
  Legal Alien: 127

Self knowledge
- Who Understands Me But Me: 281

Self love
- Who Understands Me But Me: 281, 282

Self preservation
- The Journey: 109, 111–112, 114, 115, 119, 120

Self realization
- Loveliest of Trees, the Cherry Now: 167
- Who Understands Me But Me: 281–282
- For the Young Who Want To: 64

Self worth
- For the Young Who Want To: 59, 60

Sentimentality
- Loveliest of Trees, the Cherry Now: 158, 163

Setting (Literature)
- The Journey: 111
- in Just: 91, 99
- Loveliest of Trees, the Cherry Now: 170–174

Sexuality
- I Am Learning to Abandon the World: 72, 75
- in Just: 92, 99
- London: 144, 146

Shame
- Defining the Grateful Gesture: 44–46

Silence
- Civilian and Soldier: 20

Simplicity
- The Journey: 117
- Loveliest of Trees, the Cherry Now: 167
- Night Journey: 217, 226–228

Sin
- Defining the Grateful Gesture: 43–46
- The Mother: 196, 207

Slavery
- We Wear the Mask: 254, 257, 274

Social change
- in Just: 98

Social criticism
- The Moon at the Fortified Pass: 192

Social protest
- London: 142, 144–145, 150, 153

Solitude
- Who Understands Me But Me: 281

Sorrow
- The Mother: 205
- Spring and Fall: To a Young Girl: 236–237, 249–252

Spirituality
- Defining the Grateful Gesture: 44
- London: 152
- The Moon at the Fortified Pass: 191
- Spring and Fall: To a Young Girl: 250, 251

Stereotypes (Psychology)
- We Wear the Mask: 254, 256, 257, 259, 262, 265, 271, 272
- For the Young Who Want To: 60

Stoicism
- I Am Learning to Abandon the World: 78–80

Strength
- The Journey: 112

Struggle
- I Am Learning to Abandon the World: 72
- The Moon at the Fortified Pass: 192
- The Mother: 208

Success
- For the Young Who Want To: 50, 51, 59–60

Suffering
- I Am Learning to Abandon the World: 78
- London: 142, 144, 146, 150, 153
- We Wear the Mask: 265
- Who Understands Me But Me: 281

Survival
- We Wear the Mask: 265

Symbolism
- Another Feeling: 15
- Civilian and Soldier: 20, 29–32
- I Am Learning to Abandon the World: 71
- The Journey: 111, 112, 120
- in Just: 97–100, 104
- Legal Alien: 126
- London: 147
- Loveliest of Trees, the Cherry Now: 160, 161, 170
- The Moon at the Fortified Pass: 178, 181–183
- Spring and Fall: To a Young Girl: 249, 250
- We Wear the Mask: 256

Sympathy
- Another Feeling: 6
- We Wear the Mask: 257

T

Taoism
- The Moon at the Fortified Pass: 180, 181, 183–184, 187, 189–192

Technology
- in Just: 98

Tension
- Defining the Grateful Gesture: 33
- The Mother: 205

Terror
- Another Feeling: 4, 13
- The Journey: 110

Time
- in Just: 97–100

Tone
- Defining the Grateful Gesture: 38–39
- in Just: 99–100
- Loveliest of Trees, the Cherry Now: 175
- For the Young Who Want To: 50

Tragedy (Calamities)
- The Mother: 196, 199

Transcendence
- The Moon at the Fortified Pass: 181

Transformation
- Who Understands Me But Me: 281, 286
- For the Young Who Want To: 62, 64

Translation
- The Moon at the Fortified Pass: 184–185, 189

Travel
- The Journey: 110
- Night Journey: 217, 219–221

Trickery
- We Wear the Mask: 266

Truth
- in Just: 105
- The Mother: 199, 208

U

Uncertainty
- Civilian and Soldier: 21–22

Understanding
- Another Feeling: 4
- Civilian and Soldier: 21–22, 32

United States history
- We Wear the Mask: 260–261

Unity
- I Am Learning to Abandon the World: 71

V

Victimization
- Civilian and Soldier: 21–22

Victorian culture
- Loveliest of Trees, the Cherry Now: 167–170
- Spring and Fall: To a Young Girl: 239–241

Victorian period literature, 1832-1901
- Loveliest of Trees, the Cherry Now: 165–167
- Spring and Fall: To a Young Girl: 242–245

Violence
  Civilian and Soldier: 18, 20, 26
Vulnerability
  For the Young Who Want To: 63

W
Wars
  Civilian and Soldier: 18, 20–22, 26–28
  London: 144, 145–146, 149
  The Moon at the Fortified Pass: 181, 182, 191–192
Wealth
  Defining the Grateful Gesture: 41–42
Western United States
  Night Journey: 232
Wisdom
  Defining the Grateful Gesture: 33
  The Journey: 121
  Who Understands Me But Me: 285, 290
Women's rights
  For the Young Who Want To: 56–57
Wonder
  in Just: 91
Work
  For the Young Who Want To: 49, 50, 60, 61
World War II, 1939-1945
  Night Journey: 223–225

Y
Yin and *yang*
  The Moon at the Fortified Pass: 181–182, 184, 191
Yoruba culture
  Civilian and Soldier: 27–28
Youth
  Loveliest of Trees, the Cherry Now: 158

Cumulative Index of First Lines

A

A brackish reach of shoal off Madaket,— (The Quaker Graveyard in Nantucket) V6:158

"A cold coming we had of it (Journey of the Magi) V7:110

A few minutes ago, I stepped onto the deck (The Cobweb) V17:50

A gentle spring evening arrives (Spring-Watching Pavilion) V18:198

A line in long array where they wind betwixt green islands, (Cavalry Crossing a Ford) V13:50

A narrow Fellow in the grass (A Narrow Fellow in the Grass) V11:127

A noiseless patient spider, (A Noiseless Patient Spider) V31:190–91

A pine box for me. I mean it. (Last Request) V14: 231

A poem should be palpable and mute (Ars Poetica) V5:2

A stone from the depths that has witnessed the seas drying up (Song of a Citizen) V16:125

A tourist came in from Orbitville, (Southbound on the Freeway) V16:158

A wind is ruffling the tawny pelt (A Far Cry from Africa) V6:60

a woman precedes me up the long rope, (Climbing) V14:113

Abortions will not let you forget. (The Mother) V40:197

About me the night moonless wimples the mountains (Vancouver Lights) V8:245

About suffering they were never wrong (Musée des Beaux Arts) V1:148

According to our mother, (Defining the Grateful Gesture) V40:34

Across Roblin Lake, two shores away, (Wilderness Gothic) V12:241

After the double party (Air for Mercury) V20:2–3

After the party ends another party begins (Social Life) V19:251

After you finish your work (Ballad of Orange and Grape) V10:17

Again I've returned to this country (The Country Without a Post Office) V18:64

"Ah, are you digging on my grave (Ah, Are You Digging on My Grave?) V4:2

All Greece hates (Helen) V6:92

All is fate (All) V38:17

All my existence is a dark sign a dark (A Rebirth) V21:193–194

All night long the hockey pictures (To a Sad Daughter) V8:230

All over Genoa (Trompe l'Oeil) V22:216

All the world's a stage, And all the men and women merely players (Seven Ages of Man) V35:213

All winter your brute shoulders strained against collars, padding (Names of Horses) V8:141

Also Ulysses once—that other war. (Kilroy) V14:213

Always (Always) V24:15

Among the blossoms, a single jar of wine. (Drinking Alone Beneath the Moon) V20:59–60

Anasazi (Anasazi) V9:2

"And do we remember our living lives?" (Memory) V21:156

And God stepped out on space (The Creation) V1:19

And what if I spoke of despair—who doesn't (And What If I Spoke of Despair) V19:2

Animal bones and some mossy tent rings (Lament for the Dorsets) V5:190

Announced by all the trumpets of the sky, (The Snow-Storm) V34:195

Any force— (All It Takes) V23:15

April is the cruellest month, breeding (The Waste Land) V20:248–252

As I perceive (The Gold Lily) V5:127

As I walked out one evening (As I Walked Out One Evening) V4:15

As I was going down impassive Rivers, (The Drunken Boat) V28:83

As in an illuminated page, whose busy edges (Bonnard's Garden) V25:33

Cumulative Index of First Lines

As virtuous men pass mildly away (A Valediction: Forbidding Mourning) V11:201
As you set out for Ithaka (Ithaka) V19:114
At five in the afternoon. (Lament for Ignacio Sánchez Mejías) V31:128–30
At night the dead come down to the river to drink (The Dead) V35:69
At noon in the desert a panting lizard (At the Bomb Testing Site) V8:2
At six I lived for spells: (What For) V33:266
Ay, tear her tattered ensign down! (Old Ironsides) V9:172

B

Back then, before we came (On Freedom's Ground) V12:186
Bananas ripe and green, and ginger-root (The Tropics in New York) V4:255
Be happy if the wind inside the orchard (On the Threshold) V22:128
Because I could not stop for Death— (Because I Could Not Stop for Death) V2:27
Before the indifferent beak could let her drop? (Leda and the Swan) V13:182
Before you know what kindness really is (Kindness) V24:84–85
Below long pine winds, a stream twists. (Jade Flower Palace) V32:145
Bent double, like old beggars under slacks, (Dulce et Decorum Est) V10:109
Between my finger and my thumb (Digging) V5:70
Beware of ruins: they have a treacherous charm (Beware of Ruins) V8:43
Bi-lingual, Bi-cultural, (Legal Alien) V40:125
Bright star! would I were steadfast as thou art— (Bright Star! Would I Were Steadfast as Thou Art) V9:44
But perhaps God needs the longing, wherever else should it dwell, (But Perhaps God Needs the Longing) V20:41
By the rude bridge that arched the flood (Concord Hymn) V4:30
By way of a vanished bridge we cross this river (The Garden Shukkei-en) V18:107

C

Cassandra's kind of crying was (Three To's and an Oi) V24:264
Celestial choir! enthron'd in realms of light, (To His Excellency General Washington) V13:212
Come with me into those things that have felt his despair for so long— (Come with Me) V6:31
Complacencies of the peignoir, and late (Sunday Morning) V16:189
Composed in the Tower, before his execution ("More Light! More Light!") V6:119

D

Darkened by time, the masters, like our memories, mix (Black Zodiac) V10:46
Dear Sirs: (In Response to Executive Order 9066: All Americans of Japanese Descent Must Report to Relocation Centers) V32:129
Death, be not proud, though some have called thee (Holy Sonnet 10) V2:103
Devouring Time, blunt thou the lion's paws (Sonnet 19) V9:210
Disoriented, the newly dead try to turn back, (Our Side) V24:177
Do not go gentle into that good night (Do Not Go Gentle into that Good Night) V1:51
Do not weep, maiden, for war is kind (War Is Kind) V9:252
Does the road wind up-hill all the way? (Up-Hill) V34:279
Don Arturo says: (Business) V16:2
Drink to me only with thine eyes, (Song: To Celia) V23:270–271
(Dumb, (A Grafted Tongue) V12:92

E

Each day the shadow swings (In the Land of Shinar) V7:83
Each morning the man rises from bed because the invisible (It's like This) V23:138–139
Each night she waits by the road (Bidwell Ghost) V14:2
Even rocks crack, I tell you, (Pride) V38:177
Even when you know what people are capable of, (Knowledge) V25:113
Everything has been plundered, betrayed, sold out, (Everything Is Plundered) V32:113

F

Face of the skies (Moreover, the Moon) V20:153
Falling upon earth (Falling Upon Earth) V2:64
Farewell, thou child of my right hand, and joy; (On My First Son) V33:166
Far far from gusty waves these children's faces. (An Elementary School Classroom in a Slum) V23:88–89
Fast breaks. Lay ups. With Mercury's (Slam, Dunk, & Hook) V30:176–177
First, the self. Then, the observing self. (I, I, I) V26:97
Five years have past; five summers, with the length (Tintern Abbey) V2:249
Flesh is heretic. (Anorexic) V12:2
For a long time the butterfly held a prominent place in psychology (Lepidopterology) V23:171–172
For Jews, the Cossacks are always coming. (The Cossacks) V25:70
For three years, out of key with his time, (Hugh Selwyn Mauberley) V16:26
Forgive me for thinking I saw (For a New Citizen of These United States) V15:55
Frogs burrow the mud (Winter) V35:297
From my mother's sleep I fell into the State (The Death of the Ball Turret Gunner) V2:41
From the air to the air, like an empty net, (The Heights of Macchu Picchu) V28:137

G

Gardener: Sir, I encountered Death (Incident in a Rose Garden) V14:190
Gather ye Rose-buds while ye may, (To the Virgins, to Make Much of Time) V13:226
Gazelle, I killed you (Ode to a Drum) V20:172–173
Get up, get up for shame, the Blooming Morne (Corinna's Going A-Maying) V39:2
Glory be to God for dappled things— (Pied Beauty) V26:161
Go, and catch a falling star, (Song) V35:237
Go down, Moses (Go Down, Moses) V11:42

God save America, (America, America) V29:2
Grandmothers who wring the necks (Classic Ballroom Dances) V33:3
Gray mist wolf (Four Mountain Wolves) V9:131
Grown too big for his skin, (Fable for When There's No Way Out) V38:42

H

"Had he and I but met (The Man He Killed) V3:167
Had we but world enough, and time (To His Coy Mistress) V5:276
Hail to thee, blithe Spirit! (To a Sky-Lark) V32:251
Half a league, half a league (The Charge of the Light Brigade) V1:2
Having a Coke with You (Having a Coke with You) V12:105
He clasps the crag with crooked hands (The Eagle) V11:30
He was found by the Bureau of Statistics to be (The Unknown Citizen) V3:302
He was seen, surrounded by rifles, (The Crime Was in Granada) V23:55–56
Hear the sledges with the bells— (The Bells) V3:46
Heart, you bully, you punk, I'm wrecked, I'm shocked (One Is One) V24:158
Her body is not so white as (Queen-Ann's-Lace) V6:179
Her eyes the glow-worm lend thee; (The Night Piece: To Julia) V29:206
Her eyes were coins of porter and her West (A Farewell to English) V10:126
Here, above, (The Man-Moth) V27:135
Here, she said, *put this on your head.* (Flounder) V39:58
Here they are. The soft eyes open (The Heaven of Animals) V6:75
His Grace! impossible! what dead! (A Satirical Elegy on the Death of a Late Famous General) V27:216
His speed and strength, which is the strength of ten (His Speed and Strength) V19:96
Hog Butcher for the World (Chicago) V3:61
Hold fast to dreams (Dream Variations) V15:42
Hope is a tattered flag and a dream out of time. (Hope is a Tattered Flag) V12:120
"Hope" is the thing with feathers— ("Hope" Is the Thing with Feathers) V3:123
How do I love thee? Let me count the ways (Sonnet 43) V2:236
How is your life with the other one, (An Attempt at Jealousy) V29:23
How shall we adorn (Angle of Geese) V2:2
How soon hath Time, the subtle thief of youth, (On His Having Arrived at the Age of Twenty-Three) V17:159
How would it be if you took yourself off (Landscape with Tractor) V10:182
Hunger crawls into you (Hunger in New York City) V4:79

I

I am fourteen (Hanging Fire) V32:93
I am not a painter, I am a poet (Why I Am Not a Painter) V8:258
I am not with those who abandoned their land (I Am Not One of Those Who Left the Land) V36:91
I am silver and exact. I have no preconceptions (Mirror) V1:116
I am the Smoke King (The Song of the Smoke) V13:196
I am trying to pry open your casket (Dear Reader) V10:85
I became a creature of light (The Mystery) V15:137
I Built My Hut beside a Traveled Road (I Built My Hut beside a Traveled Road) V36:119
I cannot love the Brothers Wright (Reactionary Essay on Applied Science) V9:199
I caught a tremendous fish (The Fish) V31:44
I died for Beauty—but was scarce (I Died for Beauty) V28:174
I don't mean to make you cry. (Monologue for an Onion) V24:120–121
I don't want my daughter (Fear) V37:71
I do not know what it means that (The Lorelei) V37:145
I felt a Funeral, in my Brain, (I felt a Funeral in my Brain) V13:137
I gave birth to life. (Maternity) V21:142–143
I have been one acquainted with the night. (Acquainted with the Night) V35:3
I have eaten (This Is Just to Say) V34:240
I have just come down from my father (The Hospital Window) V11:58
I have met them at close of day (Easter 1916) V5:91
I have sown beside all waters in my day. (A Black Man Talks of Reaping) V32:20
I haven't the heart to say (To an Unknown Poet) V18:221
I hear America singing, the varied carols I hear (I Hear America Singing) V3:152
I heard a Fly buzz—when I died— (I Heard a Fly Buzz— When I Died—) V5:140
I know that I shall meet my fate (An Irish Airman Foresees His Death) V1:76
I know what the caged bird feels, alas! (Sympathy) V33:203
I leant upon a coppice gate (The Darkling Thrush) V18:74
I lie down on my side in the moist grass (Omen) v22:107
I looked in my heart while the wild swans went over. (Wild Swans) V17:221
I love to go out in late September (Blackberry Eating) V35:23
I met a traveller from an antique land (Ozymandias) V27:173
I prove a theorem and the house expands: (Geometry) V15:68
I saw that a star had broken its rope (Witness) V26:285
I see them standing at the formal gates of their colleges, (I go Back to May 1937) V17:112
I shall die, but that is all that I shall do for Death. (Conscientious Objector) V34:46
I shook your hand before I went. (Mastectomy) V26:122
I sit in one of the dives (September 1, 1939) V27:234
I sit in the top of the wood, my eyes closed (Hawk Roosting) V4:55
I thought, as I wiped my eyes on the corner of my apron: (An Ancient Gesture) V31:3
I thought wearing an evergreen dress (Pine) V23:223–224
I, too, sing America. (I, Too) V30:99
I wandered lonely as a cloud (I Wandered Lonely as a Cloud) V33:71

Cumulative Index of First Lines

I was angry with my friend; (A Poison Tree) V24:195–196
I was born in the congo (Ego-Tripping) V28:112
I was born too late and I am much too old, (Death Sentences) V22:23
I was born under the mudbank (Seeing You) V24:244–245
I was sitting in mcsorley's. outside it was New York and beautifully snowing. (i was sitting in mcsorley's) V13:151
I WENT to the dances at Chandlerville, (Lucinda Matlock) V37:171
I will arise and go now, and go to Innisfree, (The Lake Isle of Innisfree) V15:121
If all the world and love were young, (The Nymph's Reply to the Shepard) V14:241
If ever two were one, then surely we (To My Dear and Loving Husband) V6:228
If every time their minds drifted, (What the Poets Could Have Been) V26:261
If I should die, think only this of me (The Soldier) V7:218
If you can keep your head when all about you (If) V22:54–55
If you want my apartment, sleep in it (Rent) V25:164
I'm delighted to see you (The Constellation Orion) V8:53
I'm Nobody! Who are you? (I'm Nobody! Who Are You?) V35:83
"Imagine being the first to say: *surveillance*," (Inventors) V7:97
Impatient for home, (Portrait of a Couple at Century's End) V24:214–215
In 1790 a woman could die by falling (The Art of the Novel) V23:29
In 1936, a child (Blood Oranges) V13:34
In a while they rose and went out aimlessly riding, (Merlin Enthralled) V16:72
In China (Lost Sister) V5:216
In ethics class so many years ago (Ethics) V8:88
In Flanders fields the poppies blow (In Flanders Fields) V5:155
In India in their lives they happen (Ways to Live) V16:228
In May, when sea-winds pierced our solitudes, (The Rhodora) V17:191

In such a night, when every louder wind (A Nocturnal Reverie) V30:119–120
In the bottom drawer of my desk . . . (Answers to Letters) V21:30–31
In the evening (Another Night in the Ruins) V26:12
In the groves of Africa from their natural wonder (An African Elegy) V13:3
In the Shreve High football stadium (Autumn Begins in Martins Ferry, Ohio) V8:17
In the sixty-eight years (Accounting) V21:2–3
In Xanadu did Kubla Khan (Kubla Khan) V5:172
Ink runs from the corners of my mouth (Eating Poetry) V9:60
Is it the boy in me who's looking out (The Boy) V19:14
'Is there anybody there?' said the Traveller, (The Listeners) V39:135
It is a cold and snowy night. The main street is deserted. (Driving to Town Late to Mail a Letter) V17:63
It is an ancient Mariner (The Rime of the Ancient Mariner) V4:127
It is in the small things we see it. (Courage) V14:125
It is said, the past (Russian Letter) V26:181
It little profits that an idle king (Ulysses) V2:278
It looked extremely rocky for the Mudville nine that day (Casey at the Bat) V5:57
It must be troubling for the god who loves you (The God Who Loves You) V20:88
It seems vainglorious and proud (The Conquerors) V13:67
It starts with a low rumbling, white static, (Rapture) V21:181
It was in and about the Martinmas time (Barbara Allan) V7:10
It was many and many a year ago (Annabel Lee) V9:14
It was not dying: everybody died. (Losses) V31:167–68
It was the schooner Hesperus, (The Wreck of the Hesperus) V31:317
Its quick soft silver bell beating, beating (Auto Wreck) V3:31
I've got the children to tend (Woman Work) V33:289
I've known rivers; (The Negro Speaks of Rivers) V10:197

J

Januaries, Nature greets our eyes (Brazil, January 1, 1502) V6:15
Just off the highway to Rochester, Minnesota (A Blessing) V7:24
just once (For the White poets who would be Indian) V13:112

L

l(a (l(a) V1:85
Las casitas near the gray cannery, (Freeway 280) V30:62
Leave Crete and come to me now, to that holy temple, (Fragment 2) V31:63
Legs! (Poem in Which My Legs Are Accepted) V29:262
Let me not to the marriage of true minds (Sonnet 116) V3:288
Let the light of late afternoon (Let Evening Come) V39:116
Let us console you. (Allegory) V23:2–3
Listen, my children, and you shall hear (Paul Revere's Ride) V2:178
Little Fly, (The Fly) V34:70
Little Lamb, who made thee? (The Lamb) V12:134
Long long ago when the world was a wild place (Bedtime Story) V8:32
Lovliest of trees, the cherry now (Loveliest of Trees, the Cherry Now) V40:159

M

Made of the first gray light (One of the Smallest) V26:141
maggie and milly and molly and may (maggie & milly & molly & may) V12:149
Márgarét, áre you grieving (Spring and Fall: To a Young Girl) V40:235
Mary sat musing on the lamp-flame at the table (The Death of the Hired Man) V4:42
May breath for a dead moment cease as jerking your (Curse) V26:75
Men with picked voices chant the names (Overture to a Dance of Locomotives) V11:143
Miniver Cheevy, child of scorn, (Miniver Cheevy) V35:126
Morning and evening (Goblin Market) V27:92
"Mother dear, may I go downtown (Ballad of Birmingham) V5:17

Much Madness is divinest Sense— (Much Madness is Divinest Sense) V16:86
My black face fades (Facing It) V5:109
My dear Telemachus, (Odysseus to Telemachus) V35:146
My father stands in the warm evening (Starlight) V8:213
My friend, are you sleeping? (Two Eclipses) V33:220
my grandmother (Grandmother) V34:95
My grandmothers were strong. (Lineage) V31:145–46
My heart aches, and a drowsy numbness pains (Ode to a Nightingale) V3:228
My heart is like a singing bird (A Birthday) V10:33
My life closed twice before its close— (My Life Closed Twice Before Its Close) V8:127
My long two-pointed ladder's sticking through a tree (After Apple Picking) V32:3
My mistress' eyes are nothing like the sun (Sonnet 130) V1:247
My one and only! (Letter to My Wife) V38:114
My uncle in East Germany (The Exhibit) V9:107

N

Nature's first green is gold (Nothing Gold Can Stay) V3:203
No easy thing to bear, the weight of sweetness (The Weight of Sweetness) V11:230
No monument stands over Babii Yar. (Babii Yar) V29:38
Nobody heard him, the dead man (Not Waving but Drowning) V3:216
Not like a cypress, (Not like a Cypress) V24:135
Not like the brazen giant of Greek fame, (The New Colossus) V37:238
Not marble nor the gilded monuments (Sonnet 55) V5:246
Not the memorized phone numbers. (What Belongs to Us) V15:196
Now as I was young and easy under the apple boughs (Fern Hill) V3:92
Now as I watch the progress of the plague (The Missing) V9:158
Now hardly here and there a Hackney-Coach (A Description of the Morning) V37:48
Now I rest my head on the satyr's carved chest, (The Satyr's Heart) V22:187
Now one might catch it see it (Fading Light) V21:49

O

O Captain! my Captain, our fearful trip is done (O Captain! My Captain!) V2:146
O Lord our Lord, how excellent is thy name in all the earth! who hast set thy glory above the heavens (Psalm 8) V9:182
O my Luve's like a red, red rose (A Red, Red Rose) V8:152
O what can ail thee, knight-at-arms, (La Belle Dame sans Merci) V17:18
"O where ha' you been, Lord Randal, my son? (Lord Randal) V6:105
O wild West Wind, thou breath of Autumn's being (Ode to the West Wind) V2:163
Oh, but it is dirty! (Filling Station) V12:57
old age sticks (old age sticks) V3:246
On a shore washed by desolate waves, *he* stood, (The Bronze Horseman) V28:27
On either side the river lie (The Lady of Shalott) V15:95
On the seashore of endless worlds children meet. The infinite (60) V18:3
Once some people were visiting Chekhov (Chocolates) V11:17
Once upon a midnight dreary, while I pondered, weak and weary (The Raven) V1:200
Once you saw a drove of young pigs (Another Feeling) V40:3
One day I'll lift the telephone (Elegy for My Father, Who Is Not Dead) V14:154
One day I wrote her name upon the strand, (Sonnet 75) V32:215
One foot down, then hop! It's hot (Harlem Hopscotch) V2:93
one shoe on the roadway presents (A Piéd) V3:16
Our vision is our voice (An Anthem) V26:34
Out of the hills of Habersham, (Song of the Chattahoochee) V14:283
Out walking in the frozen swamp one gray day (The Wood-Pile) V6:251
Oysters we ate (Oysters) V4:91

P

Pentagon code (Smart and Final Iris) V15:183
Poised between going on and back, pulled (The Base Stealer) V12:30

Q

Quinquireme of Nineveh from distant Ophir (Cargoes) V5:44
Quite difficult, belief. (Chorale) V25:51

R

Recognition in the body (In Particular) V20:125
Red men embraced my body's whiteness (Birch Canoe) V5:31
Remember me when I am gone away (Remember) V14:255
Remember the sky you were born under, (Remember) V32:185
Riches I hold in light esteem, (Old Stoic) V33:143

S

Season of mists and mellow fruitfulness, (To Autumn) V36:295–296
Shall I compare thee to a Summer's day? (Sonnet 18) V2:222
She came every morning to draw water (A Drink of Water) V8:66
She reads, of course, what he's doing, shaking Nixon's hand, (The Women Who Loved Elvis All Their Lives) V28:273
She sang beyond the genius of the sea. (The Idea of Order at Key West) V13:164
She walks in beauty, like the night (She Walks in Beauty) V14:268
She was my grandfather's second wife. Coming late (My Grandmother's Plot in the Family Cemetery) V27:154
Side by side, their faces blurred, (An Arundel Tomb) V12:17
since feeling is first (since feeling is first) V34:172
Since the professional wars— (Midnight) V2:130
Since then, I work at night. (Ten Years after Your Deliberate Drowning) V21:240
S'io credesse che mia risposta fosse (The Love Song of J. Alfred Prufrock) V1:97
Sky black (Duration) V18:93

Cumulative Index of First Lines

Sleepless as Prospero back in his bedroom (Darwin in 1881) V13:83
so much depends (The Red Wheelbarrow) V1:219
So the man spread his blanket on the field (A Tall Man Executes a Jig) V12:228
So the sky wounded you, jagged at the heart, (Daylights) V13:101
Softly, in the dark, a woman is singing to me (Piano) V6:145
Some say a host of cavalry, others of infantry, (Fragment 16) V38:62
Some say it's in the reptilian dance (The Greatest Grandeur) V18:119
Some say the world will end in fire (Fire and Ice) V7:57
Something there is that doesn't love a wall (Mending Wall) V5:231
Sometimes walking late at night (Butcher Shop) V7:43
Sometimes, a lion with a prophet's beard (For An Assyrian Frieze) V9:120
Sometimes, in the middle of the lesson (Music Lessons) V8:117
somewhere i have never travelled,gladly beyond (somewhere i have never travelled,gladly beyond) V19:265
South of the bridge on Seventeenth (Fifteen) V2:78
Stop all the clocks, cut off the telephone, (Funeral Blues) V10:139
Strong Men, riding horses. In the West (Strong Men, Riding Horses) V4:209
Such places are too still for history, (Deep Woods) V14:138
Sundays too my father got up early (Those Winter Sundays) V1:300
Sweet day, so cool, so calm, so bright, (Virtue) V25:263
Swing low sweet chariot (Swing Low Sweet Chariot) V1:283

T

Taped to the wall of my cell are 47 pictures: 47 black (The Idea of Ancestry) V36:138
Take heart, monsieur, four-fifths of this province (For Jean Vincent D'abbadie, Baron St. Castin) V12:78
Take sheds and stalls from Billingsgate, (The War Correspondent) V26:235
Talent is what they say (For the Young Who Want To) V40:49
Tears, idle tears, I know not what they mean (Tears, Idle Tears) V4:220
Tell me not, in mournful numbers (A Psalm of Life) V7:165
Tell me not, Sweet, I am unkind, (To Lucasta, Going to the Wars) V32:291
Temple bells die out. (Temple Bells Die Out) V18:210
That is no country for old men. The young (Sailing to Byzantium) V2:207
That negligible bit of sand which slides (Variations on Nothing) V20:234
That time of drought the embered air (Drought Year) V8:78
That's my last Duchess painted on the wall (My Last Duchess) V1:165
The apparition of these faces in the crowd (In a Station of the Metro) V2:116
The Assyrian came down like the wolf on the fold (The Destruction of Sennacherib) V1:38
The bored child at the auction (The Wings) V28:242
The brief secrets are still here, (Words Are the Diminution of All Things) V35:316
The bright moon lifts from the Mountain of (The Moon at the Fortified Pass) V40:180
The broken pillar of the wing jags from the clotted shoulder (Hurt Hawks) V3:138
The bud (Saint Francis and the Sow) V9:222
The Bustle in a House (The Bustle in a House) V10:62
The buzz saw snarled and rattled in the yard (Out, Out—) V10:212
The couple on the left of me (Walk Your Body Down) V26:219
The courage that my mother had (The Courage that My Mother Had) V3:79
The Curfew tolls the knell of parting day (Elegy Written in a Country Churchyard) V9:73
The day? Memorial. (Grape Sherbet) V37:109
The fiddler crab fiddles, glides and dithers, (Fiddler Crab) V23:111–112
The force that through the green fuse drives the flower (The Force That Through the Green Fuse Drives the Flower) V8:101
The Frost performs its secret ministry, (Frost at Midnight) V39:75
The grains shall be collected (All Shall Be Restored) V36:2
The grasses are light brown (September) V23:258–259
The green lamp flares on the table (This Life) V1:293
THE GUN full swing the swimmer catapults (400-Meter Freestyle) V38:2
The house is crammed: tier beyond tier they grin ("Blighters") V28:3
The ills I sorrow at (Any Human to Another) V3:2
The instructor said (Theme for English B) V6:194
The king sits in Dumferling toune (Sir Patrick Spens) V4:177
The land was overmuch like scenery (Beowulf) V11:2
The last time I saw it was 1968. (The Hiding Place) V10:152
The Lord is my shepherd; I shall not want (Psalm 23) V4:103
The man who sold his lawn to standard oil (The War Against the Trees) V11:215
The moon glows the same (The Moon Glows the Same) V7:152
The old man (Birdfoot's Grampa) V36:21
The old South Boston Aquarium stands (For the Union Dead) V7:67
The others bent their heads and started in ("Trouble with Math in a One-Room Country School") V9:238
The pale nuns of St. Joseph are here (Island of Three Marias) V11:79
The Phoenix comes of flame and dust (The Phoenix) V10:226
The plants of the lake (Two Poems for T.) V20:218
The poetry of earth is never dead: (On the Grasshopper and the Cricket) V32:161
The rain set early in to-night: (Porphyria's Lover) V15:151
The river brought down (How We Heard the Name) V10:167
The room is full (My Mother Combs My Hair) V34:132
The rusty spigot (Onomatopoeia) V6:133

The sea is calm tonight (Dover Beach) V2:52
The sea sounds insincere (The Milkfish Gatherers) V11:111
The slow overture of rain, (Mind) V17:145
The Soul selects her own Society— (The Soul Selects Her Own Society) V1:259
The summer that I was ten— (The Centaur) V30:20
The sun that brief December day (Snow-Bound) V36:248–254
"The sun was shining on the sea, (The Walrus and the Carpenter) V30:258–259
The surface of the pond was mostly green— (The Lotus Flowers) V33:107
The tide rises, the tide falls, (The Tide Rises, the Tide Falls) V39:280
The time you won your town race (To an Athlete Dying Young) V7:230
The way sorrow enters the bone (The Blue Rim of Memory) V17:38
The whiskey on your breath (My Papa's Waltz) V3:191
The white ocean in which birds swim (Morning Walk) V21:167
The wind was a torrent of darkness among the gusty trees (The Highwayman) V4:66
The windows were open and the morning air was, by the smell of lilac and some darker flowering shrub, filled with the brown and chirping trills of birds. (Yet we insist that life is full of happy chance) V27:291
The world is too much with us, late and soon, (The World Is Too Much with Us) V38:300
There are blows in life, so hard ... I just don't know! (The Black Heralds) V26:47
There are strange things done in the midnight sun (The Cremation of Sam McGee) V10:75
There have been rooms for such a short time (The Horizons of Rooms) V15:79
There is a hunger for order, (A Thirst Against) V20:205
There is a pleasure in the pathless woods (Childe Harold's Pilgrimage, Canto IV, stanzas 178–184) V35:46
There is no way not to be excited (Paradiso) V20:190–191
There is the one song everyone (Siren Song) V7:196

There will come soft rains and the smell of the ground, (There Will Come Soft Rains) V14:301
There you are, in all your innocence, (Perfect Light) V19:187
There's a Certain Slant of Light (There's a Certain Slant of Light) V6:211
There's no way out. (In the Suburbs) V14:201
These open years, the river (For Jennifer, 6, on the Teton) V17:86
These unprepossessing sunsets (Art Thou the Thing I Wanted) V25:2–3
They eat beans mostly, this old yellow pair (The Bean Eaters) V2:16
They said, "Wait." Well, I waited. (Alabama Centennial) V10:2
They say a child with two mouths is no good. (Pantoun for Chinese Women) V29:241
They turn the water off, so I live without water, (Who Understands Me But Me) V40:277
they were just meant as covers (My Mother Pieced Quilts) V12:169
This girlchild was: born as usual (Barbie Doll) V9:33
This is a litany of lost things, (The Litany) V24:101–102
This is my letter to the World (This Is My Letter to the World) V4:233
This is the Arsenal. From floor to ceiling, (The Arsenal at Springfield) V17:2
This is the black sea-brute bulling through wave-wrack (Leviathan) V5:203
This is the ship of pearl, which, poets feign, (The Chambered Nautilus) V24:52–53
This poem is concerned with language on a very plain level (Paradoxes and Oxymorons) V11:162
This tale is true, and mine. It tells (The Seafarer) V8:177
Thou still unravish'd bride of quietness (Ode on a Grecian Urn) V1:179
Three days Natasha'd been astray, (The Bridegroom) V34:26
Three times my life has opened. (Three Times My Life Has Opened) V16:213
Time in school drags along with so much worry, (Childhood) V19:29

to fold the clothes. No matter who lives (I Stop Writing the Poem) V16:58
To him who in the love of Nature holds (Thanatopsis) V30:232–233
To replay errors (Daughter-Mother-Maya-Seeta) V25:83
To weep unbidden, to wake (Practice) V23:240
Toni Morrison despises (The Toni Morrison Dreams) V22:202–203
Tonight I can write the saddest lines (Tonight I Can Write) V11:187
tonite, *thriller* was (Beware: Do Not Read This Poem) V6:3
Truth be told, I do not want to forget (Native Guard) V29:183
Turning and turning in the widening gyre (The Second Coming) V7:179
'Twas brillig, and the slithy toves (Jabberwocky) V11:91
'Twas mercy brought me from my pagan land, (On Being Brought from Africa to America) V29:223
Two bodies face to face (Two Bodies) V38:251
Two roads diverged in a yellow wood (The Road Not Taken) V2:195
Tyger! Tyger! burning bright (The Tyger) V2:263

W

wade (The Fish) V14:171
Wailing of a flute, a little drum (In Music) V35:105
Wanting to say things, (My Father's Song) V16:102
We are saying goodbye (Station) V21:226–227
We came from our own country in a red room (Originally) V25:146–147
We cannot know his legendary head (Archaic Torso of Apollo) V27:3
We could be here. This is the valley (Small Town with One Road) V7:207
We met the British in the dead of winter (Meeting the British) V7:138
We real cool. We (We Real Cool) V6:242
We tied branches to our helmets. (Camouflaging the Chimera) V37:21

We wear the mask that grins and lies, (We Wear the Mask) V40:256
Well, son, I'll tell you (Mother to Son) V3:178
What dire offense from amorous causes springs, (The Rape of the Lock) V12:202
What happens to a dream deferred? (Harlem) V1:63
What I expected was (What I expected) V36:313–314
What of the neighborhood homes awash (The Continuous Life) V18:51
What passing-bells for these who die as cattle? (Anthem for Doomed Youth) V37:3
What thoughts I have of you tonight, Walt Whitman, for I walked down the sidestreets under the trees with a headache self-conscious looking at the full moon (A Supermarket in California) V5:261
Whatever it is, it must have (American Poetry) V7:2
When Abraham Lincoln was shoveled into the tombs, he forgot the copperheads, and the assassin . . . in the dust, in the cool tombs (Cool Tombs) V6:45
When despair for the world grows in me (The Peace of Wild Things) V30:159
When he spoke of where he came from, (Grudnow) V32:73
When I consider how my light is spent ([On His Blindness] Sonnet 16) V3:262
When I consider how my light is spent (When I Consider (Sonnet XIX) V37:302
When I die, I want your hands on my eyes: (Sonnet LXXXIX) V35:259
When I go away from you (The Taxi) V30:211–212

When I have fears that I may cease to be (When I Have Fears that I May Cease to Be) V2:295
When I heard the learn'd astronomer, (When I Heard the Learn'd Astronomer) V22:244
When I see a couple of kids (High Windows) V3:108
When I see birches bend to left and right (Birches) V13:14
When I was a child (Autobiographia Literaria) V34:2
When I was born, you waited (Having it Out with Melancholy) V17:98
When I was one-and-twenty (When I Was One-and-Twenty) V4:268
When I watch you (Miss Rosie) V1:133
When Love with confinéd wings (To Althea, From Prison) V34:254
When the mountains of Puerto Rico (We Live by What We See at Night) V13:240
When the world was created wasn't it like this? (Anniversary) V15:2
When they said *Carrickfergus* I could hear (The Singer's House) V17:205
When we two parted (When We Two Parted) V29:297
When you consider the radiance, that it does not withhold (The City Limits) V19:78
When you look through the window in Sag Harbor and see (View) V25:246–247
When, in disgrace with Fortune and men's eyes (Sonnet 29) V8:198
Whenever Richard Cory went down town (Richard Cory) V4:116
Where dips the rocky highland (The Stolen Child) V34:216
While I was gone a war began. (While I Was Gone a War Began) V21:253–254

While my hair was still cut straight across my forehead (The River-Merchant's Wife: A Letter) V8:164
While the long grain is softening (Early in the Morning) V17:75
While this America settles in the mould of its vulgarity, heavily thickening to empire (Shine, Perishing Republic) V4:161
While you are preparing for sleep, brushing your teeth, (The Afterlife) V18:39
Who has ever stopped to think of the divinity of Lamont Cranston? (In Memory of Radio) V9:144
Whose woods these are I think I know (Stopping by Woods on a Snowy Evening) V1:272
Whoso list to hunt: I know where is an hind. (Whoso List to Hunt) V25:286
Why should I let the toad *work* (Toads) V4:244
With thorns, she scratches (Uncoiling) V35:277

Y

You are small and intense (To a Child Running With Out-stretched Arms in Canyon de Chelly) V11:173
You can't hear? Everything here is changing. (The River Mumma Wants Out) V25:191
You do not have to be good. (Wild Geese) V15:207
You should lie down now and remember the forest, (The Forest) V22:36–37
You stood thigh-deep in water and green light glanced (Lake) V23:158
You were never told, Mother, how old Illya was drunk (The Czar's Last Christmas Letter) V12:44

Cumulative Index of Last Lines

A

... a capital T in the endless mass of the text. (Answers to Letters) V21:30–31

a fleck of foam. (Accounting) V21:2–3

A heart that will one day beat you to death. (Monologue for an Onion) V24:120–121

A heart whose love is innocent! (She Walks in Beauty) V14:268

a man then suddenly stops running (Island of Three Marias) V11:80

A perfect evening! (Temple Bells Die Out) V18:210

a space in the lives of their friends (Beware: Do Not Read This Poem) V6:3

A sudden blow: the great wings beating still (Leda and the Swan) V13:181

A terrible beauty is born (Easter 1916) V5:91

About him, and lies down to pleasant dreams. (Thanatopsis) V30:232–233

About my big, new, automatically defrosting refrigerator with the built-in electric eye (Reactionary Essay on Applied Science) V9:199

about the tall mounds of termites. (Song of a Citizen) V16:126

Across the expedient and wicked stones (Auto Wreck) V3:31

affirming its brilliant and dizzying love. (Lepidopterology) V23:171

Ah, dear father, graybeard, lonely old courage-teacher, what America did you have when Charon quit poling his ferry and you got out on a smoking bank and stood watching the boat disappear on the black waters of Lethe? (A Supermarket in California) V5:261

All. (The Mother) V40:198

All deaths have a lingering echo (All) V38:17

All losses are restored and sorrows end (Sonnet 30) V4:192

Amen. Amen (The Creation) V1:20

Anasazi (Anasazi) V9:3

and a vase of wild flowers. (The War Correspondent) V26:239

and all beyond saving by children (Ethics) V8:88

and all the richer for it. (Mind) V17:146

And all we need of hell (My Life Closed Twice Before Its Close) V8:127

And, being heard, doesn't vanish in the dark. (Variations on Nothing) V20:234

and changed, back to the class ("Trouble with Math in a One-Room Country School") V9:238

and chant him a blessing, a sutra. (What For) V33:267

And covered up—our names— (I Died for Beauty) V28:174

And dances with the daffodils. (I Wandered Lonely as a Cloud) V33:71

And death i think is no parenthesis (since feeling is first) V34:172

And Death shall be no more: Death, thou shalt die (Holy Sonnet 10) V2:103

and destruction. (Allegory) V23:2–3

And drunk the milk of Paradise (Kubla Khan) V5:172

And each slow dusk a drawing-down of blinds. (Anthem for Doomed Youth) V37:3

and fear lit by the breadth of such calmly turns to praise. (The City Limits) V19:78

And Finished knowing—then— (I Felt a Funeral in My Brain) V13:137

And gallop terribly against each other's bodies (Autumn Begins in Martins Ferry, Ohio) V8:17

And gathering swallows twitter in the skies. (To Autumn) V36:295–296

and go back. (For the White poets who would be Indian) V13:112

And handled with a Chain— (Much Madness is Divinest Sense) V16:86

And has not begun to grow a manly smile. (Deep Woods) V14:139

Cumulative Index of Last Lines

And his own Word (The Phoenix) V10:226
And I am Nicholas. (The Czar's Last Christmas Letter) V12:45
And I let the fish go. (The Fish) V31:44
And I was unaware. (The Darkling Thrush) V18:74
And in the suburbs Can't sat down and cried. (Kilroy) V14:213
And it's been years. (Anniversary) V15:3
and joy may come, and make its test of us. (One Is One) V24:158
And kept on drinking. (Miniver Cheevy) V35:127
And laid my hand upon thy mane—as I do here. (Childe Harold's Pilgrimage, Canto IV, stanzas 178–184) V35:47
and leaving essence to the inner eye. (Memory) V21:156
And life for me ain't been no crystal stair (Mother to Son) V3:179
And like a thunderbolt he falls (The Eagle) V11:30
And makes me end where I begun (A Valediction: Forbidding Mourning) V11:202
And 'midst the stars inscribe Belinda's name. (The Rape of the Lock) V12:209
And miles to go before I sleep (Stopping by Woods on a Snowy Evening) V1:272
and my father saying things. (My Father's Song) V16:102
And no birds sing. (La Belle Dame sans Merci) V17:18
And not waving but drowning (Not Waving but Drowning) V3:216
And oh, 'tis true, 'tis true (When I Was One-and-Twenty) V4:268
And reach for your scalping knife. (For Jean Vincent D'abbadie, Baron St.-Castin) V12:78
and retreating, always retreating, behind it (Brazil, January 1, 1502) V6:16
And School-Boys lag with Satchels in their Hands. (A Description of the Morning) V37:49
And settled upon his eyes in a black soot ("More Light! More Light!") V6:120
And shuts his eyes. (Darwin in 1881) V13: 84
and so cold (This Is Just to Say) V34:241
And so live ever—or else swoon to death (Bright Star! Would I Were Steadfast as Thou Art) V9:44

and strange and loud was the dingoes' cry (Drought Year) V8:78
and stride out. (Courage) V14:126
and sweat and fat and greed. (Anorexic) V12:3
And that has made all the difference (The Road Not Taken) V2:195
And the deep river ran on (As I Walked Out One Evening) V4:16
And the midnight message of Paul Revere (Paul Revere's Ride) V2:180
And the mome raths outgrabe (Jabberwocky) V11:91
And the Salvation Army singing God loves us.... (Hope is a Tattered Flag) V12:120
And therewith ends my story. (The Bridegroom) V34:28
and these the last verses that I write for her (Tonight I Can Write) V11:187
And the tide rises, the tide falls, (The Tide Rises, the Tide Falls) V39:280
and thickly wooded country; the moon. (The Art of the Novel) V23:29
And those roads in South Dakota that feel around in the darkness . . . (Come with Me) V6:31
and to know she will stay in the field till you die? (Landscape with Tractor) V10:183
and two blankets embroidered with smallpox (Meeting the British) V7:138
and waving, shouting, *Welcome back*. (Elegy for My Father, Who Is Not Dead) V14:154
And—which is more—you'll be a Man, my son! (If) V22:54–55
and whose skin is made dusky by stars. (September) V23:258–259
And wild for to hold, though I seem tame.' (Whoso List to Hunt) V25:286
And would suffice (Fire and Ice) V7:57
And yet God has not said a word! (Porphyria's Lover) V15:151
and you spread un the thin halo of night mist. (Ways to Live) V16:229
and your dreams, my Telemachus, are blameless. (Odysseus to Telemachus) V35:147
And Zero at the Bone— (A Narrow Fellow in the Grass) V11:127

(answer with a tower of birds) (Duration) V18:93
Around us already perhaps future moons, suns and stars blaze in a fiery wreath. (But Perhaps God Needs the Longing) V20:41
aspired to become lighter than air (Blood Oranges) V13:34
As any She belied with false compare (Sonnet 130) V1:248
As ever in my great Task-Master's eye. (On His Having Arrived at the Age of Twenty-Three) V17:160
As far as Cho-fu-Sa (The River-Merchant's Wife: A Letter) V8:165
as it has disappeared. (The Wings) V28:244
As the contagion of those molten eyes (For An Assyrian Frieze) V9:120
As they lean over the beans in their rented back room that is full of beads and receipts and dolls and clothes, tobacco crumbs, vases and fringes (The Bean Eaters) V2:16
as we crossed the field, I told her. (The Centaur) V30:20
As what he loves may never like too much. (On My First Son) V33:166
at home in the fish's fallen heaven (Birch Canoe) V5:31
away, pedaling hard, rocket and pilot. (His Speed and Strength) V19:96

B

Back to the play of constant give and change (The Missing) V9:158
Beautiful & dangerous. (Slam, Dunk, & Hook) V30:176–177
Before it was quite unsheathed from reality (Hurt Hawks) V3:138
before we're even able to name them. (Station) V21:226–227
behind us and all our shining ambivalent love airborne there before us. (Our Side) V24:177
Bi-laterally. (Legal Alien) V40:125
Black like me. (Dream Variations) V15:42
Bless me (Hunger in New York City) V4:79
bombs scandalizing the sanctity of night. (While I Was Gone a War Began) V21:253–254
But, baby, where are you?" (Ballad of Birmingham) V5:17

But be (Ars Poetica) V5:3
But for centuries we have longed for it. (Everything Is Plundered) V32:34
but it works every time (Siren Song) V7:196
but the truth is, it is, lost to us now. (The Forest) V22:36–37
But there is no joy in Mudville—mighty Casey has "Struck Out." (Casey at the Bat) V5:58
But we hold our course, and the wind is with us. (On Freedom's Ground) V12:187
by a beeswax candle pooling beside their dinnerware. (Portrait of a Couple at Century's End) V24:214–215
by good fortune (The Horizons of Rooms) V15:80

C

Calls through the valleys of Hall. (Song of the Chattahoochee) V14:284
chickens (The Red Wheelbarrow) V1:219
clear water dashes (Onomatopoeia) V6:133
Columbia. (Kindness) V24:84–85
Come, my *Corinna*, come, let's goe aMaying. (Corinna's Going A-Maying) V39:6
come to life and burn? (Bidwell Ghost) V14:2
comfortless, so let evening come. (Let Evening Come) V39:116
Comin' for to carry me home (Swing Low Sweet Chariot) V1:284
cool as from underground springs and pure enough to drink. (The Man-Moth) V27:135
crossed the water. (All It Takes) V23:15

D

Dare frame thy fearful symmetry? (The Tyger) V2:263
"Dead," was all he answered (The Death of the Hired Man) V4:44
deep in the deepest one, tributaries burn. (For Jennifer, 6, on the Teton) V17:86
Delicate, delicate, delicate, delicate—now! (The Base Stealer) V12:30
Die soon (We Real Cool) V6:242
Do what you are going to do, I will tell about it. (I go Back to May 1937) V17:113
down from the sky (Russian Letter) V26:181
Down in the flood of remembrance, I weep like a child for the past (Piano) V6:145
Downward to darkness, on extended wings. (Sunday Morning) V16:190
drinking all night in the kitchen. (The Dead) V35:69
Driving around, I will waste more time. (Driving to Town Late to Mail a Letter) V17:63
dry wells that fill so easily now (The Exhibit) V9:107
dust rises in many myriads of grains. (Not like a Cypress) V24:135
dusty as miners, into the restored volumes. (Bonnard's Garden) V25:33

E

endless worlds is the great meeting of children. (60) V18:3
Enjoy such liberty. (To Althea, From Prison) V34:255
Eternal, unchanging creator of earth. Amen (The Seafarer) V8:178
Eternity of your arms around my neck. (Death Sentences) V22:23
even as it vanishes—were not our life. (The Litany) V24:101–102
ever finds anything more of immortality. (Jade Flower Palace) V32:145
every branch traced with the ghost writing of snow. (The Afterlife) V18:39

F

fall upon us, the dwellers in shadow (In the Land of Shinar) V7:84
Fallen cold and dead (O Captain! My Captain!) V2:147
False, ere I come, to two, or three. (Song) V35:237
father. (Grape Sherbet) V37:110
filled, never. (The Greatest Grandeur) V18:119
Firewood, iron-ware, and cheap tin trays (Cargoes) V5:44
Fled is that music:—Do I wake or sleep? (Ode to a Nightingale) V3:229
For I'm sick at the heart, and I fain wad lie down." (Lord Randal) V6:105
For nothing now can ever come to any good. (Funeral Blues) V10:139
For the coming winter (Winter) V35:297
For the love of God they buried his cold corpse. (The Bronze Horseman) V28:31
For the world's more full of weeping than he can understand. (The Stolen Child) V34:217
forget me as fast as you can. (Last Request) V14:231
4:25:9 (400—Meter Freestyle) V38:3
from one kiss (A Rebirth) V21:193–194

G

garish for a while and burned. (One of the Smallest) V26:142
going where? Where? (Childhood) V19:29
guilty about possessing appetite. (Defining the Grateful Gesture) V40:34

H

Had anything been wrong, we should certainly have heard (The Unknown Citizen) V3:303
Had somewhere to get to and sailed calmly on (Mus,e des Beaux Arts) V1:148
half eaten by the moon. (Dear Reader) V10:85
hand over hungry hand. (Climbing) V14:113
Happen on a red tongue (Small Town with One Road) V7:207
hard as mine with another man? (An Attempt at Jealousy) V29:24
Has no more need of, and I have (The Courage that My Mother Had) V3:80
Has set me softly down beside you. The Poem is you (Paradoxes and Oxymorons) V11:162
Hath melted like snow in the glance of the Lord! (The Destruction of Sennacherib) V1:39
He rose the morrow morn (The Rime of the Ancient Mariner) V4:132
He says again, "Good fences make good neighbors." (Mending Wall) V5:232
He writes down something that he crosses out. (The Boy) V19:14
here; passion will save you. (Air for Mercury) V20:2–3
History theirs whose languages is the sun. (An Elementary School Classroom in a Slum) V23:88–89

Cumulative Index of Last Lines

How at my sheet goes the same crooked worm (The Force That Through the Green Fuse Drives the Flower) V8:101
How can I turn from Africa and live? (A Far Cry from Africa) V6:61
How sad then is even the marvelous! (An Africian Elegy) V13:4

I

I am a true Russian! (Babii Yar) V29:38
I am black. (The Song of the Smoke) V13:197
I am going to keep things like this (Hawk Roosting) V4:55
I am not brave at all (Strong Men, Riding Horses) V4:209
I could not see to see— (I Heard a Fly Buzz—When I Died—) V5:140
I cremated Sam McGee (The Cremation of Sam McGee) V10:76
I didn't want to put them down. (And What If I Spoke of Despair) V19:2
I have been one acquainted with the night. (Acquainted with the Night) V35:3
I have just come down from my father (The Hospital Window) V11:58
I hear it in the deep heart's core. (The Lake Isle of Innisfree) V15:121
I know why the caged bird sings! (Sympathy) V33:203
I lift my lamp beside the golden door!" (The New Colossus) V37:239
I never writ, nor no man ever loved (Sonnet 116) V3:288
I rest in the grace of the world, and am free. (The Peace of Wild Things) V30:159
I romp with joy in the bookish dark (Eating Poetry) V9:61
I see Mike's painting, called SARDINES (Why I Am Not a Painter) V8:259
I shall but love thee better after death (Sonnet 43) V2:236
I should be glad of another death (Journey of the Magi) V7:110
I stand up (Miss Rosie) V1:133
I stood there, fifteen (Fifteen) V2:78
I take it you are he? (Incident in a Rose Garden) V14:191
I, too, am America. (I, Too) V30:99

I turned aside and bowed my head and wept (The Tropics in New York) V4:255
I would like to tell, but lack the words. (I Built My Hut beside a Traveled Road) V36:119
If Winter comes, can Spring be far behind? (Ode to the West Wind) V2:163
I'll be gone from here. (The Cobweb) V17:51
I'll dig with it (Digging) V5:71
Imagine! (Autobiographia Literaria) V34:2
In a convulsive misery (The Milkfish Gatherers) V11:112
In an empty sky (Two Bodies) V38:251
In balance with this life, this death (An Irish Airman Foresees His Death) V1:76
in earth's gasp, ocean's yawn. (Lake) V23:158
In Flanders fields (In Flanders Fields) V5:155
In ghostlier demarcations, keener sounds. (The Idea of Order at Key West) V13:164
In hearts at peace, under an English heaven (The Soldier) V7:218
In her tomb by the side of the sea (Annabel Lee) V9:14
in the family of things. (Wild Geese) V15:208
in the grit gray light of day. (Daylights) V13:102
In the rear-view mirrors of the passing cars (The War Against the Trees) V11:216
In these Chicago avenues. (A Thirst Against) V20:205
in this bastion of culture. (To an Unknown Poet) V18:221
in your unsteady, opening hand. (What the Poets Could Have Been) V26:262
iness (l(a) V1:85
Into blossom (A Blessing) V7:24
Is Come, my love is come to me. (A Birthday) V10:34
is love—that's all. (Two Poems for T.) V20:218
is safe is what you said. (Practice) V23:240
is going too fast; your hands sweat. (Another Feeling) V40:3
is still warm (Lament for the Dorsets) V5:191
It asked a crumb—of Me ("Hope" Is the Thing with Feathers) V3:123

It had no mirrors. I no longer needed mirrors. (I, I, I) V26:97
It is Margaret you mourn for. (Spring and Fall: To a Young Girl) V40:236
It is our god. (Fiddler Crab) V23:111–112
it is the bell to awaken God that we've heard ringing. (The Garden Shukkei-en) V18:107
it over my face and mouth. (An Anthem) V26:34
It rains as I write this. Mad heart, be brave. (The Country Without a Post Office) V18:64
It takes life to love life. (Lucinda Matlock) V37:172
It was your resting place." (Ah, Are You Digging on My Grave?) V4:2
it's always ourselves we find in the sea (maggie & milly & molly & may) V12:150
its bright, unequivocal eye. (Having it Out with Melancholy) V17:99
It's the fall through wind lifting white leaves. (Rapture) V21:181
its youth. The sea grows old in it. (The Fish) V14:172

J

Judge tenderly—of Me (This Is My Letter to the World) V4:233
Just imagine it (Inventors) V7:97

K

kisses you (Grandmother) V34:95

L

Laughing the stormy, husky, brawling laughter of Youth, half-naked, sweating, proud to be Hog Butcher, Tool Maker, Stacker of Wheat, Player with Railroads and Freight Handler to the Nation (Chicago) V3:61
Learn to labor and to wait (A Psalm of Life) V7:165
Leashed in my throat (Midnight) V2:131
Leaving thine outgrown shell by life's un-resting sea (The Chambered Nautilus) V24:52–53
Let my people go (Go Down, Moses) V11:43
Let the water come. (America, America) V29:4

life, our life and its forgetting. (For a New Citizen of These United States) V15:55
Life to Victory (Always) V24:15
like a bird in the sky … (Ego-Tripping) V28:113
like a shadow or a friend. *Colombia.* (Kindness) V24:84–85
like it better than being loved. (For the Young Who Want To) V40:50
Like Stone— (The Soul Selects Her Own Society) V1:259
Little Lamb, God bless thee. (The Lamb) V12:135
Look'd up in perfect silence at the stars. (When I Heard the Learn'd Astronomer) V22:244
love (The Toni Morrison Dreams) V22:202–203
Loved I not Honour more. (To Lucasta, Going to the Wars) V32:291
Luck was rid of its clover. (Yet we insist that life is full of happy chance) V27:292

M

'Make a wish, Tom, make a wish.' (Drifters) V10: 98
make it seem to change (The Moon Glows the Same) V7:152
May be refined, and join the angelic train. (On Being Brought from Africa to America) V29:223
may your mercy be near. (Two Eclipses) V33:221
midnight-oiled in the metric laws? (A Farewell to English) V10:126
Monkey business (Business) V16:2
More dear, both for themselves and for thy sake! (Tintern Abbey) V2:250
More simple and more full of pride. (I Am Not One of Those Who Left the Land) V36:91
must always think good thoughts. (Letter to My Wife) V38:115
My foe outstretchd beneath the tree. (A Poison Tree) V24:195–196
My love shall in my verse ever live young (Sonnet 19) V9:211
My soul has grown deep like the rivers. (The Negro Speaks of Rivers) V10:198
My soul I'll pour into thee. (The Night Piece: To Julia) V29:206

N

never to waken in that world again (Starlight) V8:213
newness comes into the world (Daughter-Mother-Maya-Seeta) V25:83
Nirvana is here, nine times out of ten. (Spring-Watching Pavilion) V18:198
No, she's brushing a boy's hair (Facing It) V5:110
no—tell them *no*— (The Hiding Place) V10:153
Noble six hundred! (The Charge of the Light Brigade) V1:3
nobody,not even the rain,has such small hands (somewhere i have never travelled,gladly beyond) V19:265
Nor swim under the terrible eyes of prison ships. (The Drunken Boat) V28:84
Not a roof but a field of stars. (Rent) V25:164
not be seeing you, for you have no insurance. (The River Mumma Wants Out) V25:191
Not even the blisters. Look. (What Belongs to Us) V15:196
Not of itself, but thee. (Song: To Celia) V23:270–271
Not to mention people. (Pride) V38:177
Nothing, and is nowhere, and is endless (High Windows) V3:108
Nothing gold can stay (Nothing Gold Can Stay) V3:203
Now! (Alabama Centennial) V10:2
nursing the tough skin of figs (This Life) V1:293

O

O Death in Life, the days that are no more! (Tears, Idle Tears) V4:220
O Lord our Lord, how excellent is thy name in all the earth! (Psalm 8) V9:182
O Roger, Mackerel, Riley, Ned, Nellie, Chester, Lady Ghost (Names of Horses) V8:142
o, walk your body down, don't let it go it alone. (Walk Your Body Down) V26:219
Of all our joys, this must be the deepest. (Drinking Alone Beneath the Moon) V20:59–60
of blackberry-eating in late September. (Blackberry Eating) V35:24
of blood and ignorance. (Art Thou the Thing I Wanted) V25:2–3
of gentleness (To a Sad Daughter) V8:231
of love's austere and lonely offices? (Those Winter Sundays) V1:300
of peaches (The Weight of Sweetness) V11:230
Of the camellia (Falling Upon Earth) V2:64
Of the Creator. And he waits for the world to begin (Leviathan) V5:204
of our festivities (Fragment 2) V31:63
Of what is past, or passing, or to come (Sailing to Byzantium) V2:207
Of which the chronicles make no mention. (In Music) V35:105
Oh that was the garden of abundance, seeing you. (Seeing You) V24:244–245
Old Ryan, not yours (The Constellation Orion) V8:53
On rainy Monday nights of an eternal November. (Classic Ballroom Dances) V33:3
On the dark distant flurry (Angle of Geese) V2:2
on the frosty autumn air. (The Cossacks) V25:70
On the look of Death— (There's a Certain Slant of Light) V6:212
On the reef of Norman's Woe! (The Wreck of the Hesperus) V31:317
On your head like a crown (Any Human to Another) V3:2
One could do worse that be a swinger of birches. (Birches) V13:15
"Only the Lonely," trying his best to sound like Elvis. (The Women Who Loved Elvis All Their Lives) V28:274
or a loose seed. (Freeway 280) V30:62
Or does it explode? (Harlem) V1:63
Or hear old Triton blow his wreathed horn. (The World Is Too Much with Us) V38:301
Or help to half-a-crown." (The Man He Killed) V3:167
Or if I die. (The Fly) V34:70
Or just some human sleep. (After Apple Picking) V32:3
or last time, we look. (In Particular) V20:125
or last time, we look. (In Particular) V20:125
Or might not have lain dormant forever. (Mastectomy) V26:123

Cumulative Index of Last Lines

or nothing (Queen-Ann's-Lace) V6:179
Or pleasures, seldom reached, again pursued. (A Nocturnal Reverie) V30:119–120
Or the dazzling crystal. (What I Expected) V36:313–314
or the one red leaf the snow releases in March. (ThreeTimes My Life Has Opened) V16:213
   ORANGE forever. (Ballad of Orange and Grape) V10:18
our every corpuscle become an elf. (Moreover, the Moon) V20:153
Our love shall live, and later life renew." (Sonnet 75) V32:215
outside. (it was New York and beautifully, snowing . . . (i was sitting in mcsorley's) V13:152
owing old (old age sticks) V3:246

P

patient in mind remembers the time. (Fading Light) V21:49
Penelope, who really cried. (An Ancient Gesture) V31:3
Perhaps he will fall. (Wilderness Gothic) V12:242
Petals on a wet, black bough (In a Station of the Metro) V2:116
Plaiting a dark red love-knot into her long black hair (The Highwayman) V4:68
Powerless, I drown. (Maternity) V21:142–143
Práise him. (Pied Beauty) V26:161
Pro patria mori. (Dulce et Decorum Est) V10:110

Q

Quietly shining to the quiet Moon. (Frost at Midnight) V39:75

R

Rage, rage against the dying of the light (Do Not Go Gentle into that Good Night) V1:51
Raise it again, man. We still believe what we hear. (The Singer's House) V17:206
Remember. (Remember) V32:185
Remember the Giver fading off the lip (A Drink of Water) V8:66
Ride me. (Witness) V26:285
rise & walk away like a panther. (Ode to a Drum) V20:172–173
Rises toward her day after day, like a terrible fish (Mirror) V1:116

S

Sans teeth, sans eyes, sans taste, sans everything. (Seven Ages of Man) V35:213
Shall be lifted—nevermore! (The Raven) V1:202
shall be lost. (All Shall Be Restored) V36:2
Shall you be overcome. (Conscientious Objector) V34:46
Shantih shantih shantih (The Waste Land) V20:248–252
share my shivering bed. (Chorale) V25:51
she'd miss me. (In Response to Executive Order 9066: All Americans of Japanese Descent Must Report to Relocation Centers) V32:129
Show an affirming flame. (September 1, 1939) V27:235
Shuddering with rain, coming down around me. (Omen) V22:107
Simply melted into the perfect light. (Perfect Light) V19:187
Singing of him what they could understand (Beowulf) V11:3
Singing with open mouths their strong melodious songs (I Hear America Singing) V3:152
Sister, one of those who never married. (My Grandmother's Plot in the Family Cemetery) V27:155
Sleep, fly, rest: even the sea dies! (Lament for Ignacio Sánchez Mejías) V31:128–30
slides by on grease (For the Union Dead) V7:67
Slouches towards Bethlehem to be born? (The Second Coming) V7:179
so like the smaller stars we rowed among. (The Lotus Flowers) V33:108
So long lives this, and this gives life to thee (Sonnet 18) V2:222
So prick my skin. (Pine) V23:223–224
so that everything can learn the reason for my song. (Sonnet LXXXIX) V35:260
Somebody loves us all. (Filling Station) V12:57
Speak through my words and my blood. (The Heights of Macchu Picchu) V28:141
spill darker kissmarks on that dark. (Ten Years after Your Deliberate Drowning) V21:240

Stand still, yet we will make him run (To His Coy Mistress) V5:277
startled into eternity (Four Mountain Wolves) V9:132
Still clinging to your shirt (My Papa's Waltz) V3:192
Stood up, coiled above his head, transforming all. (A Tall Man Executes a Jig) V12:229
strangers ask. *Originally?* And I hesitate. (Originally) V25:146–147
Surely goodness and mercy shall follow me all the days of my life: and I will dwell in the house of the Lord for ever (Psalm 23) V4:103
switch sides with every jump. (Flounder) V39:59
syllables of an old order. (A Grafted Tongue) V12:93

T

Take any streetful of people buying clothes and groceries, cheering a hero or throwing confetti and blowing tin horns . . . tell me if the lovers are losers . . . tell me if any get more than the lovers . . . in the dust . . . in the cool tombs (Cool Tombs) V6:46
Than from everything else life promised that you could do? (Paradiso) V20:190–191
Than that you should remember and be sad. (Remember) V14:255
that does not see you. You must change your life. (Archaic Torso of Apollo) V27:3
that might have been sweet in Grudnow. (Grudnow) V32:74
That then I scorn to change my state with Kings (Sonnet 29) V8:198
that there is more to know, that one day you will know it. (Knowledge) V25:113
That when we live no more, we may live ever (To My Dear and Loving Husband) V6:228
That's the word. (Black Zodiac) V10:47
The benediction of the air. (Snow-Bound) V36:248–254
the bigger it gets. (Smart and Final Iris) V15:183
The bosom of his Father and his God (Elegy Written in a Country Churchyard) V9:74
the bow toward torrents of *veyz mir*. (Three To's and an Oi) V24:264

Cumulative Index of Last Lines

The crime was in Granada, his Granada. (The Crime Was in Granada) V23:55–56
The dance is sure (Overture to a Dance of Locomotives) V11:143
The eyes turn topaz. (Hugh Selwyn Mauberley) V16:30
the flames? (Another Night in the Ruins) V26:13
The frolic architecture of the snow. (The Snow-Storm) V34:196
The garland briefer than a girl's (To an Athlete Dying Young) V7:230
The Grasshopper's among some grassy hills. (On the Grasshopper and the Cricket) V32:161
The guidon flags flutter gayly in the wind. (Cavalry Crossing a Ford) V13:50
The hands gripped hard on the desert (At the Bomb Testing Site) V8:3
The holy melodies of love arise. (The Arsenal at Springfield) V17:3
the knife at the throat, the death in the metronome (Music Lessons) V8:117
"The Lady of Shalott." (The Lady of Shalott) V15:97
The lightning and the gale! (Old Ironsides) V9:172
The lone and level sands stretch far away. (Ozymandias) V27:173
the long, perfect loveliness of sow (Saint Francis and the Sow) V9:222
The Lord survives the rainbow of His will (The Quaker Graveyard in Nantucket) V6:159
The man I was when I was part of it (Beware of Ruins) V8:43
the quilts sing on (My Mother Pieced Quilts) V12:169
The red rose and the brier (Barbara Allan) V7:11
The self-same Power that brought me there brought you. (The Rhodora) V17:191
The shaft we raise to them and thee (Concord Hymn) V4:30
the skin of another, what I have made is a curse. (Curse) V26:75
The sky became a still and woven blue. (Merlin Enthralled) V16:73
The song of the Lorelei. (The Lorelei) V37:146
The spirit of this place (To a Child Running With Outstretched Arms in Canyon de Chelly) V11:173
The town again, trailing your legs and crying! (Wild Swans) V17:221
the unremitting space of your rebellion (Lost Sister) V5:217
The woman won (Oysters) V4:91
The world should listen then—as I am listening now. (To a Sky-Lark) V32:252
their dinnerware. (Portrait of a Couple at Century's End) V24:214–215
their guts or their brains? (Southbound on the Freeway) V16:158
Then chiefly lives. (Virtue) V25:263
There are blows in life, so hard … I just don't know! (The Black Heralds) V26:47
There is the trap that catches noblest spirits, that caught— they say— God, when he walked on earth (Shine, Perishing Republic) V4:162
there was light (Vancouver Lights) V8:246
"They also serve who only stand and wait." ([On His Blindness] Sonnet 16) V3:262
"They also serve who only stand and wait." (When I Consider (Sonnet XIX)) V37:302
They are going to some point true and unproven. (Geometry) V15:68
They have not sown, and feed on bitter fruit. (A Black Man Talks of Reaping) V32:21
They rise, they walk again (The Heaven of Animals) V6:76
They say a child with two mouths is no good. (Pantoun for Chinese Women) V29:242
They think I lost. I think I won (Harlem Hopscotch) V2:93
They'd eaten every one." (The Walrus and the Carpenter) V30:258–259
This is my page for English B (Theme for English B) V6:194
This Love (In Memory of Radio) V9:145
Tho' it were ten thousand mile! (A Red, Red Rose) V8:152
Though I sang in my chains like the sea (Fern Hill) V3:92
Till human voices wake us, and we drown (The Love Song of J. Alfred Prufrock) V1:99
Till Love and Fame to nothingness do sink (When I Have Fears that I May Cease to Be) V2:295
Till the gossamer thread you fling catch somewhere, O my soul. (A Noiseless Patient Spider) V31:190–91
To an admiring Bog! (I'm Nobody! Who Are You?) V35:83
To be a queen! (Fear) V37:71
To every woman a happy ending (Barbie Doll) V9:33
to float in the space between. (The Idea of Ancestry) V36:138
to glow at midnight. (The Blue Rim of Memory) V17:39
to its owner or what horror has befallen the other shoe (A Pièd) V3:16
To live with thee and be thy love. (The Nymph's Reply to the Shepherd) V14:241
To mock the riddled corpses round Bapaume. ("Blighters") V28:3
To see the cherry hung with snow. (Loveliest of Trees, the Cherry Now) V40:160
"To strengthen whilst one stands." (Goblin Market) V27:96
To strive, to seek, to find, and not to yield (Ulysses) V2:279
To the moaning and the groaning of the bells (The Bells) V3:47
To the temple, singing. (In the Suburbs) V14:201
To wound myself upon the sharp edges of the night? (The Taxi) V30:211–212
too. (Birdfoot's Grampa) V36:21
torn from a wedding brocade. (My Mother Combs My Hair) V34:133
Turned to that dirt from whence he sprung. (A Satirical Elegy on the Death of a Late Famous General) V27:216

U

Undeniable selves, into your days, and beyond. (The Continuous Life) V18:51
under each man's eyelid. (Camouflaging the Chimera) V37:21
unexpectedly. (Fragment 16) V38:62
until at last I lift you up and wrap you within me. (It's like This) V23:138–139
Until Eternity. (The Bustle in a House) V10:62

unusual conservation (Chocolates) V11:17
Uttering cries that are almost human (American Poetry) V7:2

W

War is kind (War Is Kind) V9:253
watching to see how it's done. (I Stop Writing the Poem) V16:58
water. (Poem in Which My Legs Are Accepted) V29:262
We are satisfied, if you are; but why did I die? (Losses) V31:167–68
we tread upon, forgetting. Truth be told. (Native Guard) V29:185
We wear the mask! (We Wear the Mask) V40:256
Went home and put a bullet through his head (Richard Cory) V4:117
Were not the one dead, turned to their affairs. (Out, Out—) V10:213
Were toward Eternity— (Because I Could Not Stop for Death) V2:27
What will survive of us is love. (An Arundel Tomb) V12:18
When I died they washed me out of the turret with a hose (The Death of the Ball Turret Gunner) V2:41
When locked up, bear down. (Fable for When There's No Way Out) V38:43
When the plunging hoofs were gone. (The Listeners) V39:136
when they untie them in the evening. (Early in the Morning) V17:75
when you are at a party. (Social Life) V19:251
When you have both (Toads) V4:244
Where deep in the night I hear a voice (Butcher Shop) V7:43
Where ignorant armies clash by night (Dover Beach) V2:52
Which Claus of Innsbruck cast in bronze for me! (My Last Duchess) V1:166
Which for all you know is the life you've chosen. (The God Who Loves You) V20:88
which is not going to go wasted on me which is why I'm telling you about it (Having a Coke with You) V12:106
which only looks like an *l*, and is silent. (Trompe l'Oeil) V22:216
whirring into her raw skin like stars (Uncoiling) V35:277
white ash amid funereal cypresses (Helen) V6:92
Who are you and what is your purpose? (The Mystery) V15:138
Who toss and sigh and cannot rest. (The Moon at the Fortified Pass) V40:180
who understands me when I say this is beautiful? (Who Understands Me But Me) V40:278
Why am I not as they? (Lineage) V31:145–46
Wi' the Scots lords at his feit (Sir Patrick Spens) V4:177
Will always be ready to bless the day (Morning Walk) V21:167
will be easy, my rancor less bitter . . . (On the Threshold) V22:128
"Will hear of as a god." (How we Heard the Name) V10:167
Wind, like the dodo's (Bedtime Story) V8:33
windowpanes. (View) V25:246–247
With courage to endure! (Old Stoic) V33:144
With gold unfading, WASHINGTON! be thine. (To His Excellency General Washington) V13:213
with my eyes closed. (We Live by What We See at Night) V13:240
With silence and tears. (When We Two Parted) V29:297
with the door closed. (Hanging Fire) V32:93
With the slow smokeless burning of decay (The Wood-Pile) V6:252
With what they had to go on. (The Conquerors) V13:67
Without cease or doubt sew the sweet sad earth. (The Satyr's Heart) V22:187
Would scarcely know that we were gone. (There Will Come Soft Rains) V14:301
Wrapped in a larger. (Words are the Diminution of All Things) V35:316

Y

Ye know on earth, and all ye need to know (Ode on a Grecian Urn) V1:180
Yea, beds for all who come. (Up-Hill) V34:280
You live in this, and dwell in lovers' eyes (Sonnet 55) V5:246
You may for ever tarry. (To the Virgins, to Make Much of Time) V13:226
you who raised me? (The Gold Lily) V5:127
You're all that I can call my own. (Woman Work) V33:289
you'll have understood by then what these Ithakas mean. (Ithaka) V19:114

MADISON COUNTY
CANTON PUBLIC LIBRARY SYSTEM
Canton, MS 39046

5/17/18